Auschwitz, the Allies and Censorship of the Holocaust

What was the extent of Allied knowledge regarding the mass murder of Jews at Auschwitz during the Second World War? The question is one that continues to prompt heated historical debate, and Michael Fleming's important new book offers a definitive account of just how much the Allies knew. By tracking Polish and other reports about Auschwitz from their source, and surveying how knowledge was gathered, controlled and distributed to different audiences, the book examines the extent to which information about the camp was passed on to the British and American authorities, and how the dissemination of this knowledge was limited by propaganda and information agencies in the West. In a fascinating new study, the author reveals that the Allies had extensive knowledge of the mass killing of Jews at Auschwitz much earlier than was previously thought, but the publicizing of this information was actively discouraged in Britain and the US.

MICHAEL FLEMING is a Professor of History at the Polish University Abroad, London.

Auschwitz, the Allies and Censorship of the Holocaust

Michael Fleming

CAMBRIDGE
UNIVERSITY PRESS

University Printing House, Cambridge CB2 8BS, United Kingdom

One Liberty Plaza, 20th Floor, New York, NY 10006, USA

477 Williamstown Road, Port Melbourne, VIC 3207, Australia

314-321, 3rd Floor, Plot 3, Splendor Forum, Jasola District Centre, New Delhi - 110025, India

79 Anson Road, #06-04/06, Singapore 079906

Cambridge University Press is part of the University of Cambridge.

It furthers the University's mission by disseminating knowledge in the pursuit of education, learning and research at the highest international levels of excellence.

www.cambridge.org
Information on this title: www.cambridge.org/9781107633667

© Michael Fleming 2014

This publication is in copyright. Subject to statutory exception and to the provisions of relevant collective licensing agreements, no reproduction of any part may take place without the written permission of Cambridge University Press.

First published 2014
First paperback edition 2021

A catalogue record for this publication is available from the British Library

Library of Congress Cataloging in Publication data
Fleming, Michael, author.
Auschwitz, the allies and censorship of the Holocaust / Michael Fleming.
    p.   cm.
ISBN 978-1-107-06279-5 (Hardback)
1. World War, 1939–1945–Atrocities.   2. Auschwitz (Concentration camp)–
Censorship.   3. Holocaust, Jewish (1939–1945)–Censorship.
4. Genocide–Censorship–Great Britain.   5. Genocide–Censorship–United
States.   6. Genocide–Moral and ethical aspects–Great Britain.
7. Genocide–Moral and ethical aspects–United States.   8. World War,
1939–1945–Jews.   I. Title.
D804.7.M67F54 2014
940.53'18–dc23   2013040358

ISBN 978-1-107-06279-5 Hardback
ISBN 978-1-107-63366-7 Paperback

Cambridge University Press has no responsibility for the persistence or accuracy of URLs for external or third-party internet websites referred to in this publication, and does not guarantee that any content on such websites is, or will remain, accurate or appropriate.

Contents

Acknowledgements		*page* vi
List of abbreviations		viii
1	Introduction	1
2	Censorship, self-censorship and the discursive environment	32
3	The Polish Government in Exile in London	78
4	Intelligence about Auschwitz: November 1940–February 1943	128
5	British suppression of news of Auschwitz: March 1943–June/July 1944	167
6	Reassessing the significance of the Vrba–Wetzler report	219
7	Conclusion	258
	Appendix I: *Information about Auschwitz to reach the West, November 1942–June 1944*	282
	Appendix II: *Archives and historians*	304
	Notes	308
	Bibliography	381
	Index	397

Acknowledgements

While writing this book I have benefited enormously from the advice, criticism and assistance of a great number of people. First and foremost I would like to thank Anna Taborska. In the 2000s Anna worked on two landmark BBC series dealing with Auschwitz and the Second World War respectively as an assistant producer and researcher responsible for Polish-language research. Anna generously shared her insights and provided ongoing criticism as the book took shape. I am also especially grateful to colleagues and friends who read various drafts of the book. Special thanks are due to Colin Clarke, Adrian Kelly, Antony Polonsky, Halina Taborska and Marian Turski, whose comments and criticisms have been extremely helpful.

During the course of the research process, I benefited from the assistance of various scholars, who forwarded me documents, clarified points which they made in their own books or papers, or took time out of their schedules to discuss various issues I felt were important. I would like to thank Katarzyna Person, Laurel Leff, Barbara Rogers, Adam Puławski, Dariusz Stola, Adam Cyra, Wojciech Rappak, Jan Láníček, Janusz Gmitruk and Richard Breitman. I would especially like to thank Marek Kornat for inviting me to present work in progress at the regular modern history seminar held at the Institute of History, Polish Academy of Sciences (Warsaw) in October 2012. I thank the seminar participants for their questions, comments and criticisms (see Chapter 4).

I also would like to thank the staff at various archives who responded to my repeated queries and extended me a great deal of assistance. I am very grateful to Irena Czernichowska at the Hoover Institute at Stanford; to Els Boonen at the BBC Written Archives Centre; to Heide Pirwitz-Bujnowska and Zofia Żarek at the Polish Underground Movement Study Trust, London; to Jadwiga Kowalska at the Polish Institute and Sikorski Museum, London; to Elżbieta Pagór and Elżbieta Urban at the Polish Library, London; and to Tomasz Jabłoński at the New Documents Archive (AAN) in Warsaw. I am also grateful to Celeste Gold, and to Marta Krzemińska, who translated an important Hebrew-language document for me.

Acknowledgements   vii

The final part of the research for this book was funded by a grant from the Jagiellonian University Polish Research Centre in London Project which facilitated a two-month stay in Warsaw, gathering and checking material at the New Documents Archive and at the Institute for National Remembrance. I would like to thank the Jagiellonian University for its support.

I thank the BBC Written Archives Centre for permission to cite BBC material in this book. Finally, I would also like to thank Michael Watson, Amanda George, Vania Cunha and John Gaunt at Cambridge University Press.

There is no doubt that the book has been much improved by the help and criticisms I have received from colleagues. However, I am solely responsible for the shortcomings of the text and any errors.

Abbreviations

AALC	Archive of Adam and Lidia Ciołkosz (PUMST, London)
AAN	New Documents Archive – Archiwum Akt Nowych (Warsaw)
AJA	American Jewish Archives (Cincinnati)
AK	Home Army – Armia Krajowa
AKD	The Home Army in Documents – *Armia Krajowa w Dokumentach*
AZHRL	Archive of the Historical Institute of the Peasant Movement – Archiwum Zakładu Historii Ruchu Ludowego (Warsaw)
BBC	British Broadcasting Corporation
BBC WAC	British Broadcasting Corporation Written Archives Centre (Caversham)
BOAC	British Overseas Airways Corporation
CAB	Cabinet Office
CAC	Churchill Archive Centre (Cambridge)
CZA	Central Zionist Archives (Jerusalem)
DRW	Division of Reports Washington
FO	Foreign Office
FRUS	Foreign Relations of the United States
HIA	Hoover Institute Archives (Stanford, California)
HL	Hartley Library (Southampton)
IPN	Institute of National Remembrance – Instytut Pamięci Narodowej (Warsaw)
ISR	Inter-services Research Bureau
JIC	Joint Intelligence Committee
JRL	John Rylands Library (Manchester)
JTA	Jewish Telegraphic Agency
MP	Member of Parliament
MSW	Ministry of the Interior – Ministerstwo Spraw Wewnętrznych

MSZ	Ministry of Foreign Affairs – Ministerstwo Spraw Zagranicznych
NA	National Archives (London)
NKVD	People's Commissariat for the Interior – Narodnyi Kommissariat Vnutrennikh D'el
ONR	National Radical Camp – Obóz Narodowo-Radykalny
PAT	Polish Telegraphic Agency – Polska Agencja Telegraficzna
PFR	*Polish Fortnightly Review*
PIASA	Polish Institute of Arts and Sciences of America (New York)
PIS	Polish Social Information Bureau – Polskie Biuro Informacji Społecznej
PISM	Polish Institute and Sikorski Museum (London)
POSK	Polish Social and Cultural Association – Polski Ośrodek Społeczno-Kulturalny
POW	Prisoner of War
PPR	Polish Workers' Party – Polska Partia Robotnicza
PPS	Polish Socialist Party – Polska Partia Socjalistyczna
PUMST	Polish Underground Movement (1939–1945) Study Trust (London)
PWE	Political Warfare Executive
RAF	Royal Air Force
SIS	Secret Intelligence Service
SOE	Special Operations Executive
SS	Defence Corps/Protection Squadron – Schutzstaffel
SS-WVHA	SS Central Economic and Administrative Office – SS-Wirtschafts-Verwaltungshauptamt
TAP	Secret Polish Army – Tajna Armia Polska
UN	United Nations
US NA	United States National Archives (Washington, DC)
USSR	Union of Soviet Socialist Republics
WJC	World Jewish Congress
WL	Wiener Library (London)
WO	War Office
WRN	Freedom, Equality and Independence – Wolność-Równość-Niepodległość (Polish Socialist Party – Polska Partia Socjalistyczna)
YVA	Yad Vashem Archives (Jerusalem)
ZWZ	Union for Armed Struggle – Związek Walki Zbojnej
ŻOB	Jewish Fighting Organization – Żydowska Organizacja Bojowa

1 Introduction

At the beginning of the 1980s two books were published that have shaped both scholarly and popular understandings of the Holocaust ever since. Walter Laqueur's *The Terrible Secret: Suppression of the Truth about Hitler's 'Final Solution'* in 1980 was followed by Martin Gilbert's *Auschwitz and the Allies* in 1981. Laqueur demonstrated that 'news of the "final solution" had been received in 1942 all over Europe', and sought to explain why this information was 'frequently misunderstood' (Laqueur 1998: 197). The reasons advanced by Laqueur have proven invaluable, as scholars have attempted to understand contemporary responses to the Holocaust. Gilbert's text covered similar ground to Laqueur, and there is a frequent overlap of source material and similar understandings of this material.

Gilbert's study focused specifically on Allied knowledge of Auschwitz, and claimed that '[i]t was not until the summer of 1944 that the Allies knew that Jews were being deported to Auschwitz from throughout Europe, and were being murdered there' (Gilbert 2001b: viii). Gilbert situates his study within the wider context of Nazi racial policy, and Allied knowledge of, and responses to, this policy, providing arguments that continue to exert influence on how the history of knowledge of the camp is understood. The plausibility of his contention that the fact that Auschwitz also functioned as a death camp for Jews was unknown in the West until the summer of 1944 is echoed within scholarly discourse on contemporary Western knowledge of the Holocaust in general. The characteristics of this discourse, popularized by Laqueur, have been examined by Kalb (2003: 7) in his discussion of journalism and the Holocaust. Kalb argued that publicising news of the Holocaust was constrained by the following issues:

1. The Nazis attempted to conceal their actions.
2. The Allies were intent on winning the war (consideration of the destruction of Europe's Jews was a 'side' issue).
3. Anti-Semitism in the West undermined efforts to publicize Nazi atrocities against Jews and respond supportively.

2   Introduction

4. The crime was so enormous that it was 'unbelievable'.
5. The story of the Holocaust was an inside story (both in that it was 'inside' information, and in that news of the Holocaust was published inside newspapers, rather than in prominent front-page positions). Kalb (2003: 9) suggested that for journalists with inside knowledge 'it feels uncomfortable leading the parade – much more comfortable simply covering it objectively'.

Laqueur (1998: 201–2) also drew attention to the fact that 'neither the United States Government, nor Britain, nor Stalin showed any pronounced interest in the fate of the Jews', and argued that 'even after it had been accepted in London and Washington that the information about mass slaughter was correct, the British and US governments showed much concern that it should not be given too much publicity'.

Since Gilbert wrote in 1981, subsequent scholars such as Bauer (1997),[1] Conway (1997), Van Pelt (2002), Linn (2004) and Medoff (2011) have endorsed Gilbert's argument that the West first knew of Auschwitz in June 1944 with the dissemination of a report on the camp transmitted by two Jewish escapees, Rudolf Vrba and Alfred Wetzler; a further report from two later Jewish escapees, Czesław Mordowicz and Arnošt Rosin; and a report written in December 1943 and January 1944 by a Polish escapee, Jerzy Tabeau.[2] Linn (2004: 4) writes, 'The Vrba/Wetzler report is the first document about the Auschwitz death camp to reach the free world and to be accepted as credible. Its authenticity broke the barrier of scepticism and apathy that had existed up to that point.' In noting a 'barrier of scepticism', Linn must be referring to information about the camp that did reach the West, but was not fully appreciated. Gilbert (2001) records that the Allies received information about Auschwitz as a death camp for Jews from 1942, but argues that, at the time, the patchwork of data did not create a general understanding of what was happening at the camp. Gilbert (2001: 340–1) concedes, however, that 'even with the hindsight available in June 1944' the references to Auschwitz-Birkenau 'do add up to a definite and detailed picture', and explains the failure of the Allies to recognize the truth about the camp as being due to failures 'of imagination, of response, of Intelligence, of piecing together and evaluating what was known, of co-ordination, of initiative, and even at times of sympathy'.

Gilbert's main argument that the Allies remained unaware of the function of Auschwitz is based on the claim that just seven significant pieces of information had reached the West prior to the Vrba–Wetzler report of June 1944, none of which, 'for different reasons, made any impact' (Gilbert 2001: 340).[3] They are:

Introduction 3

1. A report from a lady from Sosnowiec, 25 November 1942.[4]
2. A report composed in London by a Polish courier, 18 April 1943.
3. A report in *The Times*, 26 May 1943 (does not mention Auschwitz – but Kraków, 'where all trace of them [deported Jews] has been lost').
4. A report in *The Times*, 1 June 1943.
5. A letter from Będzin, 17 July 1943.
6. A report from Bratislava, 1 September 1943.
7. A report printed by the Polish Consulate General in Istanbul in a bulletin entitled *Polska pod okupacją niemiecką*, 15 March 1944.

These seven pieces of information are categorically different. The report from the lady from Sosnowiec, the letter from Będzin and the report from a Polish courier, for example, are source data; that is, they are based on eyewitness testimony. Gilbert does not fully elaborate on how this information was distributed. The reports in *The Times*, in *Polska pod okupacją niemiecką* and in the report from Bratislava are distributed data; that is, they draw on information from prior reports, but Gilbert does not discuss these prior reports, or whether those original data were distributed through other channels. Furthermore, Gilbert's argument rests, in part, on the belief that the Nazis attempted to conceal the true function of Auschwitz from 1942 when the mass gassing of Jews began. Such an assumption would help support Gilbert's contention that very little information reached the West.

In fact, Auschwitz, and what was happening there, was well known in the districts surrounding the camp. As Mary Fulbrook (2012: 234) has pointed out, 'the factory of death at Auschwitz was not hidden away from public visibility in the manner of the 'Operation Reinhard' death camps of the east – Bełżec, Treblinka, and Sobibór'. Fulbrook (2012: 230) cites testimony from the Nuremberg trials stating that flames from the camp 'could be seen as far away as the Upper Silesian city of Kattowitz, some thirty kilometres distant', and that there was a 'drifting smell of burning flesh from the area of the camp'. Information about the murder of Jews at Auschwitz was delivered to the Jewish Agency in the autumn of 1942 by the lady from Sosnowiec, as noted by Gilbert. Information about the camp was also delivered to the Polish Underground in Warsaw and forwarded to London during 1942.[5]

Following Gilbert's *Auschwitz and the Allies*, Van Pelt (2002: 145), in his book *The Case for Auschwitz: Evidence from the Irving Trial*, argues that 'in 1943, when the four crematoria came into operation in Birkenau, the name "Birkenau" occasionally surfaced in relation to the Holocaust, but no one connected it with Auschwitz.' Even if its veracity remains highly questionable, such a statement only makes sense if the nature of

4   Introduction

Auschwitz is thought to have remained unknown until the dissemination of the Vrba–Wetzler report in June 1944.[6] Van Pelt continues this line of argument, contending that

[t]here remained a kind of interpretative 'gap' between the few accounts of the camp at Auschwitz as a particularly violent concentration camp meant mainly for Polish resistors, Birkenau as a destination for Jews of unknown geographical location, the Holocaust in general, and the town of Auschwitz as a site of massive industrial activity.

These claims can only be made if one ignores the information forwarded to the Polish Government in Exile by the Polish Underground (or presumes that it stalled with that government), the BBC broadcasts and articles published in Western newspapers on the camp (starting in November 1942), and gives no consideration to the impact of British censorship.

Gilbert's argument that representatives of the US and the UK governments were not informed about the true nature of the camp was also adopted by David Engel in his pioneering two-volume study of the Polish Government in Exile and Jews (1987 and 1993), in which he claimed that the Polish government was in possession of information about Jews at Auschwitz, but chose not to publicise it.[7] In contrast, however, Richard Breitman (1996: 177–9) shows that the Polish Government in Exile *did* pass on information about the camp and Jews during 1943 and 1944. Breitman refers to four pieces of data – a report from the head of the Directorate of Civilian Resistance (Kierownictwo Walki Cywilnej) in Poland from 23 March 1943; a document written in London on 18 April 1943 by a Polish courier, which was passed to Dr Ignacy Schwarzbart of the Polish National Council and of the World Jewish Congress; a report that was handed to the Joint Chiefs of Staff (United States) in June 1943; and a Polish military intelligence report from summer 1943 that was passed to the US Office of Strategic Services – to argue that 'Gilbert's claim that the Allies could not have responded to Auschwitz-Birkenau for the first two years of its existence because of a lack of knowledge will not stand in the light of new evidence' (Breitman 1996: 180).[8] In more recent research on German police and German railway communications intercepted by analysts at Bletchley Park, Breitman has argued that such data could have helped construct a picture of what was happening at the camp (Breitman 1999). He shows that through these intercepts the British were able to calculate the death toll of registered prisoners at the camp on 26 September 1942. Unregistered prisoners – that is, the vast majority of Jews killed – were not reported by radio.[9]

Further evidence of Allied knowledge of the camp was revealed in 1999 by Barbara Rogers, who located, at the British National Archives

Introduction 5

in Kew, the memorandum handed by Jewish representatives to President Roosevelt on 8 December 1942, which mentions the slaughter of Jews at the camp. The document was subsequently forwarded by Rabbi Maurice Perlzweig to the British Embassy in Washington and from there to the British Foreign Office. Rogers also highlighted several other pieces of evidence that support the view that the Allies knew what was happening at Auschwitz well before the arrival of the Vrba–Wetzler report in June 1944.

Despite this research, the narrative that the true function of the camp was unknown in the West until June 1944 remains dominant. Tony Kushner (2005: 196) is especially critical of assertions of Auschwitz's 'elusive nature', and contends that 'Anglo-American knowledge of Auschwitz particularly has been subject to ahistorical and incomplete research, overstating its role in the "Final Solution" at the expense of camps such as Treblinka, Sobibór, Bełżec and Chełmno in 1942 and ignoring what was known about it through Polish and other sources'. In raising these issues, Kushner highlights the urgent need for a more thorough and holistic approach to the question of Allied knowledge of Auschwitz, in the wider context of Nazi extermination policy. A further important issue is the significant mismatch between Polish scholarship on Polish knowledge of the camp, which points to the fact that the mass killing of Jews at the camp was well known in Poland, and the narrative that maintains that such knowledge did not penetrate to the West. This mismatch implies either that the Polish Underground (Home Army – Armia Krajowa, and its civilian counterpart) failed to forward information, or that the Polish Government in Exile failed to pass it on to its Western allies. If this were the case, as maintained most forcibly by David Engel (1987; 1993) in the context of a broader argument about Jews falling outside Poles' 'universe of obligation', it would have profound implications for understandings of Polish–Jewish relations and the debate on the nature of the Polish Government in Exile.

The hegemony of such a discourse narrows the questions that can be asked; frames understandings of the relationship between Poles, Jews and the Polish Government in Exile; and influences the way in which research is actually conducted. For example, if it is accepted that the Polish Government in Exile and/or the Polish Underground tended to conceal data about the annihilation of Jews, then the search for, and interpretation of, documents that may indicate that the Polish government passed on information may not be undertaken at the same intensity. There are some notable exceptions. Adam Puławski (2009), for instance, has completed some painstaking research tracking the flow of information from Poland to the Polish Government in Exile, and

6   Introduction

argued that news about Jews was marginalized in messages sent to London by the Polish Underground.

Dariusz Stola (1997: 10) has noted that the distribution of news about the liquidation of the Warsaw ghetto in the summer of 1942 was restricted by Polish Deputy Defence Minister General Modelski. Such findings, however, need to be historicised. Stola (1997: 2–3) has made several important points on Polish information gathering and distribution (see below), including recognising that data passed through several hands before it was considered for dispatch. He also maintains that any judgement about the restriction of the distribution of news about Jews received via secret channels in London in the summer of 1942 has to be understood in the context of the arrest of Swedes and Poles involved in couriering reports out of Poland via Sweden.[10] As Stola argues, this breach in intelligence security has to be taken into consideration when assessing the decision made in London to restrict news distribution. The security of compromised intelligence cells has to be re-established, and normal practice in such circumstances usually includes limiting information distribution until this has been achieved.

In addition, scholarship on knowledge of the camp, and on the Holocaust more generally, has not fully explored the impact of British and American censorship policy, and how this policy impacted on a key gatekeeper of information – the Polish Government in Exile. The assumption to date has been that the Polish Government in Exile was not constrained by its Western allies in reporting what was happening to Jews in Poland. However, I will show in Chapters 2 and 3 of this study that this assumption is faulty. Both the US and the UK governments were concerned that stories about Jews could provoke anti-Semitism on the one hand, and stimulate demands from civil-society activists for rescue and refuge on the other.[11]

Furthermore, the Polish Government in Exile based in London had to respond to frequent accusations of anti-Semitism from the British press and British parliamentarians, while negotiating the liberal politics of both Britain and the United States, which formally condemned anti-Semitism, though neither country seriously tackled widespread domestic anti-Semitism and anti-alienism.

Any news which the Polish Government in Exile forwarded, or wished to forward and distribute, confronted British and American administrations sensitive to indigenous anti-Semitic sentiment. Consequently, before the claim can be made that the Polish Government in Exile did not forward, or delayed, the forwarding of information about atrocities and the mass killing of Jews to the Allies, it has to be established precisely how information could be received by Poland's British and American

Introduction 7

allies, how it could then be disseminated, and the scope of independence of 'official' Polish publications within a Britain marred by pervasive anti-Semitism and controlled by a 'voluntary' censorship regime. It is also important to assess the kind of information the British and later the Americans actually wanted. In the context of war, the Allies focused on gaining data of military and strategic value.[12] There was, therefore, little demand from the Allies for information about the fate of Poland's and Europe's Jews and, when this sort of information was supplied, it was generally unwanted.[13]

In Chapter 5 I discuss an intelligence report which was extremely widely distributed and formed the basis of a Polish Ministry of Information and Documentation press release in March 1944. Juxtaposing the evidence from the United States and Britain indicates that the specific information it contained about the killing of Jews at Auschwitz was censored, and the British mainstream press reported only a portion of the data that the press release contained. Crucially, it did not publish the main information that the Polish press release sought to publicise: 'It is not possible to estimate the exact figure of people put to death in gas chambers attached to crematoria but it certainly exceeds half a million, mostly Jews, both Polish and from other countries'.[14]

The issue of Polish press freedom is especially important given that it is not only serious scholars such as Gilbert (2001) and Rogers (1999b) who highlight that the official English-language publication of the Polish Government in Exile – the *Polish Fortnightly Review* – does not mention the systematic killing of Jews in Auschwitz; Holocaust deniers do also. For Gilbert (2001), the lack of data in the *Polish Fortnightly Review* is to be explained by the lack of knowledge about the camp, while for Rogers (1999b: 94) the *Polish Fortnightly Review* 'is a useful source in establishing what was known by the British government regarding Auschwitz-Birkenau'. But for Holocaust deniers such as Aynat (1991), this silence is used as evidence for the spurious and, in many jurisdictions, criminal claim that the gas chambers did not exist.

The argument developed in Chapter 3 contends that the *Polish Fortnightly Review*, for which the British government (Ministry of Information) 'vetted and approved the source material to be published before it went on sale to the public in Britain' (Rogers, 1999b: 94), is an unsuitable source for trying to establish either Polish or Western knowledge of the systematic killing of Jews at Auschwitz. Instead, the *Polish Fortnightly Review* and the Polish government's Polish-language daily *Dziennik Polski* (*Polish Daily*) should be read with a deep understanding of British censorship policy, of British concerns about publishing news of atrocities and about Jews and of the Polish government's adherence to

8   Introduction

the British censorship regime. Such an approach historicises these two publications, and helps reveal the political context and the constraints under which they were published. Such readings encourage more sensitive thinking about the Polish Government in Exile's policy towards Jews without relying on explanations based on social distance, Polish anti-Semitism and victim competition alone.

The output of the *Polish Fortnightly Review* and *Dziennik Polski* during the war has been repeatedly discussed by scholars. Analysis of these two papers allows an assessment of the information, including about the Holocaust, presented to the general public in Britain by the Polish government. In addition to the *Polish Fortnightly Review* and *Dziennik Polski*, the Polish government also distributed news from Poland through the Polish Telegraphic Agency (PAT). PAT reported on the Holocaust and occasionally on Auschwitz. The news disseminated by PAT was guided, in the main, towards other news agencies (i.e. the press) rather than the general public. Analysis of the existing PAT bulletins released in London and through the Polish Information Center in New York allows a fuller assessment of the kind of data that the Polish government released into various public domains. It also reveals that the press on both sides of the Atlantic had access to more information about the Holocaust, and about Auschwitz, than was printed in newspapers. This discrepancy highlights the degree to which specific news of the Holocaust was marginalised or censored in the mainstream press in Britain and in the United States at various points in time.[15]

A further consideration of some importance is the way in which the Polish Government in Exile and its representatives were evaluated and treated by their British allies. It is telling of the climate in Britain in 1941 that Alexander Cadogan, the permanent under-secretary for foreign affairs, was moved to write to other British ministries, advising them that it was

of the highest importance from the point of view of the foreign policy of His Majesty's Government that the status of these Governments [i.e. the various Governments in Exile] should be fully recognised and protected, and their representatives should be treated not merely as the representatives of Foreign Governments, but as Allies.[16]

The prior discussion in the Foreign Office on the treatment of these governments was even more frank, and demanded that 'Allied governments and their representatives must be treated with full consideration as Allies and not simply as "damned foreigners"'.[17]

Appreciating the British and American contexts in which the Polish Government in Exile and its representatives operated is crucial to

Introduction

assessing official Polish responses to information concerning Jews which came from Poland. These contexts cannot, as it is frequently claimed and implied they can, be understood as simply encouraging the Poles to respond to demands for Jewish equality. Nor can Polish revelations about the Jewish tragedy be solely understood as ploys to enhance Polish diplomatic standing in Britain and the US, though both are important considerations. It is vital to take into account the American and British roles in marshalling, choreographing and, indeed, limiting the distribution of information about the destruction of European Jews. I discuss this issue in Chapter 2.

This book, therefore, seeks to fill some major gaps in our understanding of Western knowledge of Auschwitz as a Nazi death camp for Jews, by tracking Polish and other reports about the camp from their source, through intermediaries, to their final dissemination to Western governmental agencies/departments, the pages of newspapers and the airwaves. Most of the reports that Gilbert mentions are far more significant and were distributed more widely, and in different forms, than Gilbert acknowledges. To take one example, the report of a lady from Sosnowiec is the most probable source for an article in the *New York Times* on 25 November 1942, and for the paragraph on the slaughter of Jews at Oświęcim in the memorandum handed to President Roosevelt on 8 December 1942 (see Chapter 4). In addition, a far greater number of reports about the killing of Jews at the camp were available to the public during the war than Gilbert recognises, and these reports featured in the *New York Times*, the *Washington Post*, the *Los Angeles Times*, the *Jewish Chronicle*, the BBC, *Dziennik Polski* and elsewhere. The subscription-only supplement to the *East London Observer* – the *Polish Jewish Observer*, which was first published in February 1942 – provided the most detailed coverage of the plight of Jews in Poland available in Britain. Surprisingly, this newspaper seems to have been overlooked by scholars analysing Western knowledge of the Holocaust and Auschwitz in particular. Since Gilbert and Laqueur wrote, the National Archives in Britain and in the United States have released additional data, and archives in Poland have become more easily accessible, allowing the tracking of some reports from Auschwitz to London and beyond.

In addition, charting the trajectories of specific intelligence reports clarifies and corrects existing knowledge on key documents, and links disconnected Polish- and English-language scholarship. The best example is a report, first cited by Hilberg (1985: 1127), and subsequently referred to by Richard Breitman (1996: 179), which revealed that 468,000 non-registered Jews had been killed at Auschwitz through to September 1942. Drawing on the covering note of Paul Birkland, the

10   Introduction

assistant US military attaché in London, describing the report to his superiors, both Hilberg and Breitman contend that this report was compiled in December 1943 by a Polish intelligence agent, a woman, whom Breitman identifies as Wanda. The date of the report's compilation and the sex of the agent is information which the Poles supplied to the Americans when passing over the document. However, as I show in Chapter 5, it is not true. Polish documents reveal a surprising source, one which the Polish Underground was very keen to conceal. Furthermore, Western scholarship on this report to date has only tracked its distribution to the offices of various US agencies and departments, but in reality it was far more widely distributed. Polish scholarship, in turn, has discussed the source of the document, but has not examined its path to the United States, via Britain.

In the chapters that follow I track, as far as possible, forty-five reports.[18] There is documentary evidence that Western decision makers had the opportunity to become familiar with what was happening at the camp as early as December 1942 and January 1943, and circumstantial evidence that information was handed to the Western Allies earlier, in November 1942. Information about the camp flowed throughout 1943 and into 1944, and there are solid bases for the claim that British and American decision makers were well aware of what was happening at the camp through 1943.

The key argument made in Chapters 4 and 5 is that news of Auschwitz flowed steadily into London from the opening of the camp, and that three phases of information management about the camp can be identified prior to the distribution of the Vrba–Wetzler report (beginning in June 1944). In the first period – from late 1940 to the summer of 1942, knowledge of the camp in the West largely reflected knowledge in Warsaw – it was understood as a harsh concentration camp, primarily for Poles.[19] In the second period, from August 1942 to March 1943, there was a disjuncture between what was known in the West and what was known in Warsaw. News of the mass gassing of Jews had reached London by November 1942, but this information was suppressed by the Polish and, in all probability, the British governments. In the third period running from late March 1943 through to the dissemination of the Vrba–Wetzler report in June–July 1944, the Polish government can be documented as having distributed the reports it received from Poland about the camp. The Western Allies were continuously advised of what was happening at Auschwitz through 1943 and 1944. These reports were suppressed by the British government (and the American government).

The argument that the Polish Government in Exile in London (or the Polish Underground in Poland) withheld information about Auschwitz

Introduction

has been compelling for many scholars because there is relatively little documentation about the camp in files at the British National Archives at Kew, and the extent of the material published in the British and American press has not been appreciated. Chapters 4 and 5 and Appendix I demonstrate that information about the mass murder of Jews at the camp was published on both sides of the Atlantic in 1942, 1943 and 1944.

The most probable reason for there being relatively few documents in the archives at Kew is that they were weeded from FO, PWE and SOE files and redirected to selected officials with a view to postwar war crime trials, rather than the commonly accepted view that such documents do not or did not exist. For example, on 8 October 1942, Victor Cavendish-Bentinck wrote to Alexander Cadogan at the Foreign Office, calling for two officials to be given the task of collecting evidence of atrocities. Though this initially focused on crimes against British nationals, it was later expanded to include nationals of Allied countries. Roger Allen, a trained lawyer and Foreign Office official, together with a Mr Campbell, systematically collated news of atrocities received by the British (Smith 2004: 119). Data on atrocities were directed to these officials. Roger Allen, for example, gave a presentation on atrocities to the Joint Intelligence Committee on 22 December 1942.[20]

In May 1943 the Postal and Telegraph Censorship Office intercepted a letter from Ignacy Schwarzbart (a member of the Polish National Council) to the World Jewish Congress in New York.[21] In Chapter 5 this letter and its origin are discussed in detail. Here it is sufficient to note that this letter contained information about Jews being killed on a mass scale at Auschwitz, and that it noted methods of murder including the use of gas chambers. This letter was very widely circulated in the Foreign Office and in the Political Warfare Executive. The reason for the wide circulation, however, had nothing to do with the news from Auschwitz. Instead, the fact that the letter highlighted general conditions and sentiment in Poland attracted FO and PWE attention. For this reason it is found in FO files at Kew. Similarly, most other documents at the National Archives that mention Auschwitz and the mass killing of Jews at that camp do so in passing – it is not their main focus.

The intercepted letter is very important for two reasons. First, it demonstrates that British officials in the FO, the PWE and elsewhere had been informed of the true nature of Auschwitz (again) in May 1943; second, it helps to explain the dearth of documents at Kew referring to the mass slaughter of Jews at Auschwitz. The Foreign Office cover sheet assigns page 3 of the document (the page discussing Auschwitz) to Roger Allen, the official responsible for collecting reports on atrocities.

12   Introduction

The collection of data about atrocities against Jews, according to this document, was undertaken, but acting on information about German atrocities against Jews, as Chapter 2 will show, was extremely problematic for the Foreign Office.[22]

The relative lack of documents about Auschwitz in FO files is due to the way information about the camp was managed and apprehended by FO, PWE and SOE officials. The evidence from the minutes of the 22 December 1942 JIC meeting and the cover sheet of the intercepted letter discussed above strongly suggest that information about atrocities against Jews at Auschwitz was collected and stored with a view to war crimes trials. It was not understood as providing reasons to provide refuge to Europe's persecuted Jews or to initiate retaliation.

Laqueur (1980: 7) notes that 'all intelligence from Poland was passed to SIS automatically from the Polish Bureau II, except that concerning purely domestic affairs'.[23] Information about the Nazi persecution of Jews was forwarded. In Chapter 5, it is argued that the Polish intelligence reports that focused on atrocities in Poland, titled *aneks*, were routinely passed to the British. Few of these survive in the British Archives, but it is almost certain that these reports were forwarded to Roger Allen at the FO. However, Allen's tranche of documents has not been located. This could be because these documents have been filed poorly at the National Archives, meaning that scholars have been unable to locate or to chance upon them, that they remain under lock and key in either the Foreign Office or the intelligence services (MI5/MI6), or that they have been destroyed.[24]

Consequently, the available Foreign Office documents only provide a limited insight into FO officials' knowledge of the camp during the war. But it is possible to establish broadly who knew what, when and how about the camp through a detailed examination of contemporary newspapers, broadcasts and documents from the Polish government and Polish intelligence.[25]

Knowledge of Auschwitz specifically, and of the Holocaust in general, is complicated not just by the challenges posed by the documentary record. Even today, processing the enormity of the crime is difficult. In the 1940s specific difficulties arose. Referring to contemporary knowledge of the Holocaust, Yehuda Bauer (1978: 18) has contended that the process of knowing about the Holocaust was not straightforward. Receiving information was only the first step. Bauer writes,

The process of knowing usually came in a number of stages; first the information had to be disseminated; then, it had to be believed; then, it had to be internalized, that is, some connection had to be established between the new reality and a possible course of action; finally, there came action, if and when action came.

Introduction

Yet even this description is too simple. Stola (1997: 2) stresses that the dissemination of the information, Bauer's first stage, is in the middle of a larger process of gathering, sifting, evaluating, encrypting, de-encrypting, evaluating, re-evaluating for security reasons (i.e. not to compromise sources) and consideration of newsworthiness prior to publication. Dissemination was also conditioned by the attitude of the British Foreign Office and the British Ministry of Information, as well as the state of British–Polish relations.

The second stage of Bauer's model is also problematic. The issue of believability has been extensively discussed in the Holocaust literature. Often cited is the meeting between the American supreme justice Felix Frankfurter, Jan Karski and the Polish ambassador to the United States, Jan Ciechanowski (1887–1973). Karski had witnessed the Holocaust unfold during 1942, and met with President Roosevelt in July 1943. In August he met with Frankfurter and told him about what was happening to Jews in occupied Poland. Frankfurter responded, 'I am unable to believe what you have told me', in response to which Ciechanowski accused Frankfurter of calling Karski a liar. Frankfurter replied, 'I did not say that he was lying, I said that I could not believe him. There is a difference'. Laurel Leff (2003: 54) understands that Frankfurter did not doubt the veracity of what Karski had told him, but refused 'to accept that reality', whilst a Polish British historian (Ciechanowski 2005: 538) suggests that Frankfurter 'was not inclined to believe the report', and argues that, for many British and American people, 'the unvarnished truth about the scale of German atrocities against Jews was beyond their comprehension'. Leff's view is more nuanced than the more common interpretation that Frankfurter simply did not believe Karski, and declarations of disbelief that are found in the documentary record should not automatically be classed as denials of truthfulness, but should be critically assessed.[26]

Frankfurter's comments came over a year after the first official Allied recognition of the Nazi extermination programme. On 9 July 1942, Brendan Bracken, the British minister of information, held a press conference at the Ministry in which Polish and British speakers spoke about the mass murder of Jews. The following day's press recorded that 700,000 Jews had, at that point, been killed. Later that year, on 17 December 1942, a UN declaration highlighting the Nazis' bestial extermination policy was released in the US, UK and USSR.[27] The press on both sides of the Atlantic reported on the German atrocities. By 1943, then, the broad contours of the Nazi programme were well understood. Death camps at Sobibór, Bełżec and Treblinka had been highlighted in official communiqués. Frankfurter did not doubt the truth spoken by the

14   Introduction

eyewitness Jan Karski, but expressed a sentiment that still resonates today – the mass murder of millions of Jews was absolutely shocking; it was *unbelievable*.

The enormity of the crime speaks to the problematic stage three in Bauer's model – internalization. Evidence from British intelligence suggests that, for those gathering and sifting through the data, internalization was well under way by the summer of 1941 as German Order Police (Ordnungspolizei) radio intercepts were being decoded at Bletchley Park. As I discuss more fully in Chapter 2, the director of Hut 3, who had responsibility for advising British prime minister Winston Churchill on the data derived from these intercepts, proposed to discontinue mentioning the killing of Jews because it was so well understood. For other groups, internalization was no doubt far more problematic, as recognition of the new reality, shock at that reality and powerlessness to stem the slaughter encouraged oscillation between the two senses of unbelievable.[28] For those not privy to intelligence reports, the reticence of Western governments to officially reiterate throughout the war the scale of the Nazi murder of European Jewry inhibited people in the West and continental Europe (i.e. Hungary) from internalizing the news.

The way in which news of the Holocaust was presented played a key role in encouraging the public in Britain and the US to believe or disbelieve the news. The placing of stories about the systematic mass killing and atrocities deep inside newspapers, as Lipstadt (1986) and Leff (2005) demonstrate, had an adverse effect on the public's understanding of the Holocaust as it was taking place. In Britain, the relative dearth of news in the mainstream press and on the BBC's Home Service, the frequent lack of detail in the information that was disseminated, and only rare government confirmation that the stories were true (for example, in July and December 1942) marginalized the material, and arguably encouraged some scepticism towards it.

In Chapter 6, I argue that calls for rescue efforts and the bombing of Auschwitz were intensified after the dissemination of the Vrba–Wetzler report in 1944 because the function of the camp became known to a wider variety of people, not because it became known to important actors for the first time. Officials of the Polish, British and American governments, as well as leading Jewish figures, had known for over a year. The wide distribution of the Vrba–Wetzler report overcame British (and American) control over the dissemination of information about the camp. For those learning the details of the camp, the information was believable, in part because internalization of the truth became possible for more people as the opportunity for action came into view. Discussion of belief/disbelief in this connection is important insofar as it helps to

Introduction 15

explain the action of non-government actors, but it does not explain the action of government officials (in Britain), who were definitely aware of what was happening at Auschwitz from January 1943, and probably knew as early as November 1942.

The story of how and when information about the camp reached the West is not only of historical interest. It raises, as indicated, serious issues about Polish–Jewish relations, the role of the Polish Government in Exile, and Allied responses and responsibilities. It also re-problematizes the debate about the bombing of the camp, and brings to the fore the neglected topic of plans to attack the camp formulated by the Polish intelligence officer and Auschwitz escapee Witold Pilecki, amongst others. Furthermore, the story of knowledge of the camp currently plays a key role in contemporary memory politics in Poland and beyond.

In the conclusion, I discuss how the suspicion that the Polish Government in Exile held back important information about the camp has contributed to the troubled postwar relations between Poles and Jews, and I argue that British wartime censorship, together with the relative lack of critical scholarship on how this censorship framed and frequently determined what exiled governments could say in Britain, has fostered misunderstanding between groups and skewed scholarly understanding of who knew what and when about Auschwitz. In addition, I argue that, due to the porousness of research on some key reports about the camp (i.e. those highlighting the mass murder of Jews), unfounded claims have been made about authorship to suggest that certain resistance cells in the camp played a particularly important role in informing the world about Auschwitz. It is true that establishing precise authorship of many reports is rarely possible, and the appropriate response is to state this clearly. It is also true that specific resistance cells played a variety of roles in transmitting information out of the camp. In very general terms, Witold Pilecki and his group were important until his escape in April 1943, and after this point people associated with Józef Cyrankiewicz assumed increasing significance. There are cases where the evidentiary record on specific intelligence reports does not support the claims made for these cells, and their actual activities have become less important than the ideological purposes which they can be made to serve today.

In Poland, and to a lesser extent in the US, there is a fierce debate over memory of the role of Pilecki and Cyrankiewicz at the camp, which speaks to understandings of Poland's communist past and its postwar anti-communist Underground. A part of this debate considers Polish–Jewish relations, and makes tendentious claims linking Auschwitz, Polish martyrdom and the communist takeover. Pilecki forwarded information about the camp, including about the systematic German killing of Jews,

16   Introduction

and in 1948 was sentenced to death by a Warsaw court for his postwar espionage activities. Under the malign influence of the anti-Semitic myth of *Żydokomuna*, this history is sometimes framed as one in which a good Polish patriot was executed by communists (read Jewish communists).[29] By charting the trajectories of reports used in this way, the attempt to dress malign stereotypes in the imprimatur of historical research can be exposed and the current round of victim competition which informs some 'historical' work can be robustly rejected.

Auschwitz – an overview

Located in Silesia, some fifty kilometres south-west of Kraków, the Polish town of Oświęcim was incorporated into the territory of the Third Reich following the Nazi occupation in 1939, and assumed its German-language name of Auschwitz. At the beginning of the Second World War, the town had an estimated population of 12,000, of whom 5,000 were Jewish. Yisrael Gutman (1994: 7) cites the German historian Martin Broszat for the reason that this town was chosen for the location of a concentration camp being that it lay at the junction of eastern Upper Silesia, the General Government and the Warthegau, and was thus a convenient place for the 'large number of Polish prisoners captured by the security police' to be warehoused.

Prison overcrowding in the Katowice district in late 1939 was becoming an increasing problem for the German police and gendarmerie, with repeated complaints from police functionaries to their superiors. These complaints aligned with the SS medium-term view to establish additional camps to incarcerate large numbers of people prior to military advances into foreign countries. Concentration camps inspector Richard Glücks was ordered to assess several sites, with a view to establishing a new camp on 1 February 1940. The former Polish army barracks at Oświęcim were examined and selected by inspector Arpad Wigand. Glücks wrote to the SS leader (Reichsführer) Heinrich Himmler on 21 February, advising him of Oświęcim's suitability.

Negotiations with the German Army over securing the barracks were concluded in early April, and by the end of that month Himmler had ordered Glücks to establish a quarantine camp for 10,000 prisoners. Glücks, in turn, appointed Rudolf Hoess commandant (Piper 2000: 53–6). In May 1940, 200–300 Jews from the town of Oświęcim were allocated by the German mayor to begin the construction of the camp (Piper 2002: 137).

Auschwitz was, at first, a concentration camp of some severity. Only later did it expand to incorporate a range of functions at various sub-camps,[30] and develop the apparatus of industrial killing – the gas chambers. The first prisoners, thirty German criminals sent from another concentration camp, Sachsenhausen, arrived on 20 May 1940. These criminals were to play a significant role at the camp, as they assumed intermediate positions of control between the SS wardens and the rank-and-file prisoners. Some of these 'kapos' were particularly brutal to subsequent arrivals; a few, such as Otto Küsel and Fritz Biessgen, were supportive (Strzelecka and Setkiewicz 2000: 65). The first transport, of 728 Polish political prisoners, arrived on 14 June 1940 from Tarnów prison, and included a small number of Jews. This date is normally considered the founding of the camp.

During the first months of the camp, prisoners were assigned tasks to build and fence in the camp. The first crematorium to dispose of the bodies of those who succumbed to the harsh regime was installed in July 1940, a task which also involved civilian workers. It was operational to burn corpses on 15 August.

The initial rationale of the camp, to house 10,000 Polish political prisoners prior to their transfer to other camps in Germany, was abandoned in the summer of 1940 and the camp was allocated the role of the central concentration camp for Poland and other European countries.[31] However, resources for building and equipping the camp were not readily available, and Hoess therefore practised what was known as 'organizing' (a camp euphemism for sourcing required items by whatever means) on a large scale. Even barbed wire had to be pilfered, as Rees (2005: 38) notes.

With a view towards camp security and SS financial interests, Himmler ordered an exclusion zone around the camp and decreed that this area should be exploited to the full for farming, animal husbandry and fishing. The population of villages in this area was expelled; Pławy on 8 March 1941; Babice, Broszkowice, Brzezinka, Budy, Harmęże and Rajsko between 7 and 12 April (Strzelecka and Setkiewicz 2000: 73). These villages provided raw materials to build the camp. Rajsko became the seat of the SS and Police Hygiene Institute (Hygienisch-Bakteriologische Untersuchungsstelle der Waffen SS Süd-Ost Auschwitz). The institute was renamed Hygiene Institut SS und Polizei Auschwitz on 2 May 1944. An area around the camp that extended some forty square kilometres was considered by the SS to be a zone of interest and was patrolled by the camp garrison, local Gestapo and police – a fact which later (1943) discouraged a proposed Home Army attack on the camp.

In March 1941, Himmler visited the camp. Up to that point some 10,900 prisoners, mainly Poles, had been held there (Gutman 1994: 16), but extensive expansion followed Himmler's visit. An increase in

18   Introduction

capacity to 30,000 prisoners was ordered, as was the building of a new camp to hold 100,000 prisoners of war, and the allocation of 10,000 prisoners to construct a huge industrial complex at nearby Monowice/Monowitz (Auschwitz III). By the end of 1941, the main camp (Auschwitz I) could accommodate some 18,000 prisoners. Construction at Brzezinka/Birkenau (Auschwitz II – about three kilometres from the main camp) began in October 1941, and parts of that camp, with fences and watchtowers, were complete in 1942.[32] It was at this camp that the mass extermination of Jews took place, beginning in the second quarter of 1942 and continuing through to late 1944.

Construction of Birkenau was undertaken by regular concentration camp inmates and Soviet prisoners of war. Some 12,000 POWs were registered and were housed in Auschwitz I. They were marched each day to Birkenau, but were frequently too exhausted to complete the tasks assigned to them. Within several months almost all of them had died due to the punishing regime. Rees (2005: 82) quotes Auschwitz prisoner Kazimierz Smoleń: 'They were beaten more by the SS and given a harder time'. The first gassing victims at the camp were Soviet prisoners of war in August 1941, followed by the gassing of 250 (mostly Polish) prisoners from the camp hospital and 600 Soviet POWs on 3 September in Block 11 at the main camp (Auschwitz I) (Czech 1992: 84). Soviet prisoners of war arrived at the camp throughout its existence without being registered, and were killed immediately (Piper 2002: 56, 151).

A women's sector was established in the main camp (Auschwitz I) in March 1942, but was moved to Auschwitz II in August. There were also sectors for men at Auschwitz II, and the camp held people from many countries, most of them Jews. In February 1943, a Gypsy family camp was created.

Conditions at the concentration camp contributed to a high mortality rate. Epidemics of various diseases such as typhus and dysentery spread through the camp's weakened prisoner population and were exacerbated by the poor hygiene and overcrowding in the barracks. According to Gutman (1994: 27), the death rate from disease increased dramatically between July 1942 and March 1943, and ranged from 19 to 25 per cent per month. It was only brought under control in May 1943 when the mortality rate dropped to 5.2 per cent in the main camp.

Furthermore, death was induced through labour at Auschwitz, as at other slave-labour camps. The growing demand for labour to satisfy the needs of the German war economy was confronted by the ideological demand to exterminate the Jews. This tension was resolved in favour of ideology. But other prisoner groups saw conditions improve slightly. From October 1942, food packages from outside the camp were

Auschwitz – an overview

accepted, and camp doctors were instructed to improve hygiene. The camp population increased, and by August 1943 there were 74,000 prisoners, increasing to 105,168 in the following August, excluding unregistered prisoners (Piper 1994b: 39).

On 15 May 1943 the SS-WVHA (SS-Wirtschafts-Verwaltungshauptamt – SS-Central Economic and Administrative Office) introduced new regulations to incentivize prisoners to work. These included rewards of tobacco and reductions in punishments and restrictions – such as being allowed to write and receive letters, additional food, money and, for some non-Jews, permission to use the camp's brothel, which was located in Block 24 (Piper 2002: 340).[33] Nevertheless, the mortality rate remained high. This problem was explained by Gerhard Maurer, director of Department D-II in the Economic Administration Head Office, 'as a medical problem *of the prisoners*' rather than the result of 'catastrophic mismanagement governing supply, shelter or sanitation in the [camps], not to mention violence' (Allen 2002: 185, Allen's emphasis).

Auschwitz was but one of a network of concentration camps created by the Nazi state, but its diversity of function and scale mark it out as exceptional within this network. The role it assumed from 1942 through to the end of 1944 as a key location in the Nazi 'Final Solution', for which it is now infamously known, mirrored the operations at the Aktion Reinhard camps. These camps were constructed to exterminate European Jewry, and included the death camps at Bełżec, Sobibór and Treblinka. Killing of Jews on a mass scale also took place at the Majdanek concentration camp.

Murder by gas took place at Chełmno/Kulmhof (fifty kilometres from Łódź) from early December 1941. At first Jews from the surrounding district were loaded into sealed vans and gassed with carbon monoxide. From January 1942 Jews from the Łódź ghetto were taken to be killed at Chełmno.[34] The technology of gassing people advanced with the use of prussic acid (trade name Zyklon B – first used at Auschwitz in the late summer of 1941 on Soviet prisoners (Fulbrook, 2012: 218)). The construction of Bełżec was completed in late February 1942, in mid-April the first gassings at Sobibór took place, and in July Treblinka received its first victims from the Warsaw ghetto. At Auschwitz, the first transports of Jews to be killed immediately arrived from Slovakia in May 1942, though Jews had been gassed at the camp earlier. On 15 February 1942 Jews from the Zagłębie Dąbrowskie region were gassed in the gas chamber in Auschwitz I and from 20 March Jews were murdered in the gas chambers installed in a farmhouse at Birkenau (Bunker Number I) (Fulbrook, 2012: 221; Czech 1992: 144).

20   Introduction

The death camps were the final stage in an incremental programme that began with the ascendancy of Hitler to power in Germany in 1933. Raul Hilberg (1985) summarizes this programme as comprising five distinct operations: definition of victims, disenfranchisement, concentration, exploitation, destruction. Through the 1930s, Nazi racial policy targeted the Jews for hostile treatment, and passed a series of laws limiting their civil freedom, from what work they could do and whom they could liaise with, to confiscation of material wealth and physical incarceration. The German Jewish academic, Victor Klemperer, charts this process in some detail in his diaries.[35] The British Political Warfare Executive (also known as the Political Intelligence Department, discussed in Chapter 2) compiled a document that was circulated amongst its officials on 24 March 1944. The document was entitled 'Special Annex on the persecution of the Jews', and summarized Nazi racial policy, indicating British awareness of the entire process. It began with a quote from Hitler, declaring 'his hatred of Jewry and his mission to destroy it', and listed anti-Jewish policies and laws, including the expulsion of Jews from government offices and liberal professions, and the Nuremberg laws that prohibited relations between Jews and those of 'German or Kindred blood' and forbade Jews employing women below the age of forty-five in their households. It also discussed fines levied on the Jewish community in 1938. The document then stated that 'the German policy of extermination was planned and executed in three stages' during the war: the setting up of ghettos, labour and concentration camps; mass deportation of Jews to these places; and finally their liquidation there.[36]

The Nazi invasion of Poland was followed, in 1940, by the creation of ghettos which concentrated Jews in particular parts of towns and cities, and physically separated them from the gentile population. Overcrowding hindered sanitation, the food supply for the mass of the population was limited, and disease and hunger increased. Hilberg (1985: 1219) estimates the number of Jews who died due to the programme of ghettoization and its concomitant dramatic reduction in living standards at over 800,000. Piper (2006: 7) rightly notes that the German policy of ghettoization and 'planned' hunger and disease sought to destroy Europe's Jews through 'natural causes' and argues that 'the policies of evictions and resettlements should be seen as an integral part of the plan to exterminate the Jews'.

The population of the ghettos was then put to work for the German war economy – the most significant and long-lasting example in this respect was that in Łódź, which was not liquidated until 1944. In Warsaw, around 400,000 Jews were crammed into an area of about 3.4 square kilometres. The ghetto in Warsaw was created in October 1940 and surrounded by high walls. Communication with the 'Aryan' side was difficult, but possible. Jan Karski, a member of the Polish Underground, was able to access the ghetto and, in late 1942 and early 1943, personally informed Polish and British leaders in London of its conditions.

Fulbrook (2012: 352) demonstrates that those policies which disenfranchised, expropriated, ghettoized and instituted slave labour, together with widespread terror and killings, prefaced and arguably made easier the final round-up prior to transport to the death camps. The 'Final Solution' may not have been predicted by those mid-level Nazi administrators engaged in planning the concentration and subjugation of Jews, but Fulbrook (2012: 355) is correct in stating that the road to the gas chambers was one which 'they had in large measure made possible by laying the practical foundations'. These civilian administrators were responsible for implementing Nazi racial policy which had a devastating impact on Jewish communities in occupied Europe. 'Social murder' was an inherent feature of Nazi colonial racism.[37]

However, the process of destruction did not always linearly follow the model. Following the Nazi invasion of the Soviet Union on 22 June 1941, Jews were simply murdered en masse by roving task forces (*Einsatzgruppen*), which were responsible for tens of thousands of killings. At Babi Yar outside Kiev, over 33,000 Jews were shot in two days. The operations of the *Einsatzgruppen* were supplemented by killings carried out by German Order Police, as Christopher Browning (1992) amongst others, has highlighted. Raul Hilberg (1985: 1219) estimates the total number of Jews killed in these open-air operations at over 1.3 million. The murder of Jews in this manner in eastern Poland and the western USSR was known in real time by British intelligence operatives through the intercepts of German police radio communications (the *Einsatzgruppen* communications were more secure). Churchill was informed during the summer of 1941.

In 1942, significant centres of annihilation included Bełżec, Sobibór, Chełmno (Kulmhof), Treblinka and Majdanek. These are the places in which the bulk of Polish Jewry was murdered. Treblinka took most of its victims from Warsaw, mainly during the summer of 1942. Treblinka continued to function as a death camp through to spring 1943. An estimated 750,000 Jews were killed there. Jews from eastern and south-eastern Poland, including cities such as Białystok and Lwów, were murdered at Bełżec (550,000) and Sobibór (200,000). At Chełmno, a minimum of 150,000 Jews from central Poland, including Łódź, were killed, while about 60,000 Jews were also murdered at Majdanek – a mixed concentration and death camp.[38] At Auschwitz, to which Jews from various European countries were sent, it is estimated that 200,000

22   Introduction

people, mainly Jews, perished in 1942 alone (Rees 2005: 179). However, it is important to note that 'direct physical extermination, such as the *Einsatzgruppen* massacres and later the application of more "efficient" gas chambers, did not so much concern total annihilation per se as merely the method, the timeframe and the rate at which it should be executed' (Piper 2006: 7). The German policy of depriving Jews of their liberty, livelihoods and homes, their 'resettlement' and overcrowding in ghettos, have to be seen as a fundamental part of German racial planning, in just the same way as the death camps.[39]

The systematic killing of Jews from outside Poland began at Auschwitz in May 1942 (the deportations from Slovakia), but not on the scale that developed in 1943 or the level witnessed in the spring and summer of 1944 with the arrival of the Hungarian Jews. Approximately one million Jews were killed at the camp, 438,000 from Hungary in the early summer of 1944 (Hilberg 1985: 1219; Piper 1992: 92;[40] Rees 2005: 302). Prior to these deportations, fewer Jews had been killed at Auschwitz than in the open-air slaughters or in the gas chambers at Treblinka and Bełżec, or had perished in the ghettos as a result of privation or disease. Kushner (2005: 196) therefore has a case when he argues that Auschwitz's role in the 'Final Solution' has been overstated.

However, the destruction of Hungarian Jews, which (as I will show in Chapter 5) had been anticipated in March 1944 in the West, made Auschwitz the deadliest of all the camps if judged by the number of its victims. Scholarly debate has been haunted since the late 1970s by the question whether anything could have been done to save these people. The narrative articulated by Gilbert, positing a lack of knowledge about the camp until June 1944, loads the scales towards a negative answer. If the deadly function of the camp was known a year, or more, earlier, then the substance of this particular debate is fundamentally altered. The practical issues of bombing range and accuracy remain, of course, but bombing was not necessarily the only way to stop or slow the rate of the mass murder, as I will highlight in Chapter 6.

The machinery of mass killing continued to function at Auschwitz throughout the summer and early autumn of 1944. On 7 October, the members of the *Sonderkommando* crew of Crematorium IV – Jews forced to burn the corpses of those gassed – revolted, after it became apparent that they were about to be murdered. Some 250 members of the *Sonderkommando* were killed fighting, 200 survivors were shot. Three days later, an allied statement on 10 October 1944 was broadcast on the BBC at 6 p.m. and 9 p.m. following the receipt of Polish intelligence regarding German plans to liquidate the camp. The statement did not stop the slaughter at Brzezinka (Birkenau) and did not mention Jews (Gilbert 2001: 325).

The gassing of Jews at Auschwitz continued until the end of the month. On 2 November 1944 murder through the use of Zyklon B in the gas chambers finally ceased as the Eastern Front approached (Czech 2000: 220). The rate of prisoner evacuation from the camp increased (the transfer of prisoners from Auschwitz had been taking place through the summer), but killings at the camp continued, largely through shooting. Though some prisoners were evacuated from the camp via rail, thousands of others were force-marched to other camps, or simply marched. On these marches prisoners died from hypothermia and exhaustion, others were shot by SS guards for being slow or tired, or for removing snow from their shoes (Strzelecki 2000: 30). Other prisoners were beaten to death. Some 3,000 Auschwitz prisoners perished on the death marches through the Katowice and Opole districts in January 1945 (Strzelecki 2000: 35). The number of those who lost their lives along other death march routes is not known. These death marches mark a final stage of the Nazi programme of murder. Finally, on 27 January 1945, Soviet troops reached the camp and liberated 7,000 prisoners (Czech 2000: 231).

News from occupied Poland

In September 1939 Poland was overrun by the German Army invading from the west and north, and, from 17 September, the Soviet Army from the east. The country was divided, by prior agreement between Germany and the USSR. Many Polish politicians, soldiers and civilians fled, often via Romania, and reached the safety of France that same year. A Government in Exile was set up, first in France and then, following the fall of France in 1940, in London. At the same time, members of the Polish Army and civilians formed a series of resistance groups. One organization, Service for the Victory of Poland (Służba Zwycięstwu Polski) was established by General Michał Karaszewicz-Tokarzewski on 27 September 1939. It was reorganized to form the Union for Armed Struggle (Związek Walki Zbojnej – ZWZ) that General Sikorski, the premier of the Polish Government in Exile, ordered to be created seven weeks later. Kazimierz Sosnkowski headed the military as a whole, and Stefan Rowecki assumed leadership of the ZWZ in the zone of German occupation. This organization became the Home Army (Armia Krajowa – AK) in February 1942 – a non-political military organization. In addition, there existed a series of parallel resistance organizations, often linked to particular political parties or outlooks. Over the course of 1940–2, most of these were subsumed within the military structures of the ZWZ and later the AK, though this process was accompanied by debate.

24   Introduction

Alongside the military organization, civilian structures of an underground state were created, including the position of delegate – essentially a deputy prime minister in occupied Poland. This post was held successively by Cyryl Ratajski, Jan Piekałkiewicz, Jan Stanisław Jankowski and Stefan Korboński. A forum for political discussion, the Political Consultative Committee (Polityczny Komitet Porozumiewawczy) had been formed in 1940, and evolved into the Home Political Representation (Krajowa Reprezentacja Polityczna – KRP) in 1943, and into the Council of National Unity (Rada Jedności Narodowej – RJN) in January 1944.

The civilian underground state did not have day-to-day control over the military wing, but was responsible for its budget. There was close co-operation between the two elements of the underground movement, with some important radio messages and reports being sent by the civilian delegate and the leader of the military wing together. Nevertheless, there was a division of labour in the type of message radioed to London by the civilian and military wings of the Underground. Messages sent by General Stefan Rowecki, commander of the Home Army until he was captured by the Germans in the summer of 1943, focused on military matters – German troop movements or the progress of couriers across Europe, for example. Messages sent by the delegate were generally more broad-ranging and highlighted what was happening to the population in Poland, including to Jews.

Communication with the West was difficult, but over time courier routes and radio communication were set up. It was not until September 1940 that a reliable radio infrastructure was established, which allowed the sending of short messages directly to London. Given the dangerous nature of sending messages (the Germans employed snatch squads to locate and capture radios and radio operators), as well as reception issues, messages were necessarily brief. It is estimated that at various points in the war between 40 and 50 per cent of radio messages sent to London were not received. In addition, messages had to be encrypted and decrypted, which added some delay to the relay of information that was not considered top priority at any given moment.

Couriered reports provided expansive details on the situation in Poland. Like radio messages, not all reports carried by couriers reached London. Between 1 April 1940 and 1 April 1941, some fourteen reports were sent, only seven arrived; between 1 April 1941 and 1 April 1942, thirty-one reports were sent, two fell into enemy hands and seventeen were received in London; between 1 April 1942 and 1 April 1943, thirty-five were sent, four fell to the enemy and eighteen were received in London; and between 1 April 1943 and 1 April 1944, thirty-four were sent and twenty-eight were received.[41]

News from occupied Poland

Radio messages were received by Bureau II of the Polish General Staff Headquarters, based at the Rubens Hotel in Victoria, London. Messages were also received by Bureau VI, the Polish equivalent of the British Special Operations Executive. Headed by Colonel Michał Protasewicz ('Rawa'), Bureau VI enjoyed close contact with SOE personnel, including its leading figures such as Colonel Colin Gubbins and Harold Perkins.[42] From July 1942, its personnel met with representatives from SOE fortnightly, and intelligence was passed on (Bines 2008: 95). Cable communication between SOE and Bureau VI also allowed the transfer of information. Radio messages were also received by the Social Department of the Polish Ministry of the Interior (Adamczyk and Gmitruk 2012: 46).[43]

Following the decryption of information, staff at Bureau II would pass the message to the minister of the interior – in 1942 this was Stanisław Mikołajczyk, who would distribute it to the Polish Cabinet and often to members of the Polish National Council (the wartime parliament). As a matter of routine, Mikołajczyk insisted on the confidentiality of material in order not to compromise sources, unless otherwise authorized (Stola 1997: 1). Information gained in this manner was carefully reviewed prior to public dissemination to ensure that sources were protected. The National Council ultimately had two Jewish members: the Zionist Ignacy Schwarzbart and, later, the Bundist Shmuel Zygielbojm, and both these representatives had access to information sent from Poland and received by Mikołajczyk.[44] Walter Laqueur (1998: 112) notes that Zygielbojm, who 'was not by nature the most trusting of men', had no complaints that any data received by the Polish government from the Polish Underground was being withheld.

Longer reports, which provided details of the situation in the country, were sent via courier, and particularly important ones were carried by multiple couriers via different routes.[45] This applies to a report from March 1943, which highlighted the killing of Jews at Auschwitz, and arrived in London that same month. Courier routes included Warsaw–Gdynia–Stockholm–RAF flight to London, and Warsaw–Zakopane–Budapest–Istanbul–London. Some couriers traversed Central Europe, France and Spain to reach Gibraltar or Lisbon, meaning that the time taken for a report to reach its destination could vary from a few weeks to several months, even a year. To facilitate this information transfer, the Poles operated important intelligence centres in neutral countries such as Sweden (Stockholm) and Turkey (Istanbul). From Stockholm, a weekly RAF flight carried Polish material to London,[46] but there were also intelligence cells within Axis-controlled Europe, as in Budapest.

Until the early summer of 1942 the so-called 'Swedish connection' was of particular importance. A group of Swedish businessmen couriered

26   Introduction

reports out of Poland. The significant Bund report that arrived in London in May 1942 was transported to Stockholm by the Swede Sven Norrman, for instance (Lewandowski 2001), but, in the summer of 1942, Poles and Swedes involved in this operation were arrested by the Germans. The Swedish route was later re-established and was used during 1943, 1944 and 1945.

Information was also obtained from Poland via the 'air bridge' operated by the Special Operations Executive. Supplies and trained men were taken to Poland; information and significant individuals were transported to Britain. This form of communication was particularly hazardous, but played an important role in supplying the Home Army during the war. Planes landed at prearranged, remote locations, where the Home Army had cleared a makeshift runway and set up landing lights. Such operations depended a great deal on the cover of night, and consequently the number of missions was reduced during the summer.

In the summer of 1940, just after Auschwitz accepted its first transport of Polish prisoners from Tarnów prison, the leadership of the ZWZ recognized a need to gain information about the camp. Major Jan Włodarkiewicz of the Secret Polish Army (Tajna Armia Polska – TAP), a military organ with a right-wing ideological orientation, spoke with Stefan Rowecki about getting somebody into the camp to supply intelligence. Włodarkiewicz volunteered his friend Witold Pilecki.[47] Pilecki allowed himself to be arrested on 19 September in 1940 and, by the end of October, gave an oral report to a prisoner about to be released from Auschwitz. The released prisoner, Aleksander Wielkopolski, transmitted it to the Polish Underground in Warsaw. Messages were also taken out by escaped prisoners. For example, Stanisław Gustaw Jaster carried a report from Pilecki when he audaciously escaped from Auschwitz with Kazimierz Piechowski, Józef Lempart and Eugeniusz Bendera in an SS staff car, wearing SS uniforms, in June 1942 (Świebocki 1996: 239).

Information from inside the camp was also transmitted by a secret radio held in the basement of Block 20 in the main camp (Auschwitz I) between the spring and autumn of 1942. Block 20 belonged to the camp hospital, and SS guards tended to avoid it from fear of disease (Garliński 1994: 100).[48] Further conduits for information included the Home Army, the peasant battalions and a group from the Polish Socialist Party. Messages were left in 'letterboxes' (hiding places) by prisoners working outside the camp, to be picked up by members of the Underground later (Świebocki 2000: 150, 273). In March 1941, the Prisoners' Aid Committee (Komitet Pomocy Więźniom) was founded in the town of Oświęcim, but did not achieve its objectives of helping prisoners. It was not until mid-1943, with the creation of the Committee for Aid to Concentration Camp Prisoners (Pomoc Więźniom Obozów Koncentracyjnych) in Kraków, which drew its members primarily from the Socialist and Peasant parties, that organized aid and information transfer proceeded in earnest.

In addition, Auschwitz inmates working outside the camp's wires were able to pass information to the local population living in the area surrounding the Auschwitz complex. German civilian contractors and even SS members were also used to transmit information out of the camp (Świebocki 2000: 271). As I demonstrate in Chapters 4 and 5, some of this information concerned what was happening to the Jews. Much was forwarded to the Home Army leaders and Polish civilian leaders in Warsaw, and from there transmitted or couriered across occupied Europe to the Polish Government in Exile in London. As a result of this intelligence-gathering operation, news of Jews at Auschwitz reached London at an average rate of around two reports a month between November 1942 and June 1944 (see Appendix I). The Polish government routinely passed on the information to its Western allies and the press. But getting the information to the British in London did not guarantee further distribution.[49]

Sources

The source material referred to in this book comes from archives in Britain, Poland, Israel and the United States. In Britain, collections at the National Archives in Kew have long been an important source for Holocaust scholars. Foreign Office documents and Cabinet papers have been repeatedly mined, though there are few references therein to Auschwitz. Other material, including intelligence reports on specific individuals and the documents of the Ministry of Information, have shed light on British censorship policy. However, there are significant gaps in the British records. Some material forwarded to the British by Polish intelligence during the Second World War was destroyed, considered irrelevant or unimportant to the realization of British war aims (Ciechanowski 2005: 540; Breitman 2004: 185). Intelligence material originating from the Polish Bureau II of the General Staff Headquarters and handed over to the British was destroyed after the war (Suchcitz and Ciechanowski 2005: 24–6). During the war the British Secret Intelligence Service routinely destroyed material handed to it by Bureau II after assessment (Maresch 2004: 3). Appendix II explores further the absences in the British archival record.

Elsewhere in London, the Polish Underground Movement (1939–1945) Study Trust and the Polish Institute and Sikorski Museum hold documents

28   Introduction

pertaining to the Polish Underground and the Polish Government in Exile. Here, too, there are substantial gaps in the documentary record. Some reports sent from Poland and received by the Polish General Staff Headquarters in London were destroyed. Following the withdrawal of British and American recognition of the Polish Government in Exile in July 1945, staff of the Polish Bureau II burned a great number of documents from the bureau's archive (at St Paul's School in London), in order to protect operatives in case the archive was seized or passed to the new Polish government in Warsaw (Suchcitz and Ciechanowski 2005: 14). Other records of Polish intelligence operations and the Polish Government in Exile were dispersed. It is widely believed that former service personnel (and now inheritors) may have some documents, and efforts are under way to locate them.

The absence of documents therefore means that the trajectory of some reports from Auschwitz cannot be precisely mapped, but 'echoes' of missing documents can be detected in other archives. For example, a press release from the Polish Government in Exile from 1944 has not been found in files in London, but a copy received by the Polish Information Center in New York is located in the Hoover Institute Archives at Stanford. It is therefore possible to reconstruct some, though by no means all, of the information missing from the collections in London by analysis of relevant documents at archives in Poland and in the United States.

Another key source in London is the British Library's newspaper library at Colindale. An analysis of press reports allows an assessment of what was known to different publics. The major newspapers – *The Times*, the *Daily Telegraph*, the *Manchester Guardian*, the *New York Times* – and publications such as the *Jewish Chronicle*, the *Polish Fortnightly Review* and *Dziennik Polski* have all attracted scholarly attention. To date, however, there has been little effort to demonstrate precisely where published stories came from. By tracking reports from Poland, it is now possible to show how editors repackaged information released by the Polish government and what pieces of information were included and excluded, and to show in some detail the contours of the censorship regime. The newspaper library also holds copies of a very significant newspaper which has generally been ignored by scholars. The *Polish Jewish Observer*, a supplement of the *City and East London Observer*, an east London local paper, published the most detailed account available in Britain of the Holocaust as it unfolded. The source of a significant proportion of its articles was information from the Polish Government in Exile. The paper actually published almost verbatim texts from Polish intelligence reports about Auschwitz throughout 1943 and 1944.

Sources   29

The fact that this paper has been almost entirely ignored by Holocaust scholars is perplexing.

The Polish Library (POSK), London, also holds important Polish newspapers, including copies of *Poland Fights*, which reported on Auschwitz in April 1943, and a few copies of the New York-based Polish Jewish newspaper *Nasza Trybuna*, as well as copies of the *Polish Jewish Observer*. In addition, the Polish Library holds copies of *Polska pod okupacją niemiecką* and *Pologne occupée*, two news bulletins published by the Polish Consulate in Istanbul that reported on the Holocaust, including information about Auschwitz.

The way in which the British Foreign Office sought to narrate the war can be investigated through the directives of the Political Warfare Executive and the minutes of the European Service of the BBC. From 1941, the head of the European Service was the high-flying Foreign Office official Ivone Kirkpatrick. Records of the Political Warfare Executive are located at the National Archives. At the BBC's Written Archives Centre at Caversham, service directives and minutes of the various foreign-language services allow an assessment of how PWE directives were carried through to the microphone. However, not all programme scripts still exist, including those around some key dates. The Polish Service records of news bulletins do not include scripts for the key months of December 1942 and July 1944. Other services' records are likewise incomplete, but some sense of BBC European output can be constructed from PWE directives and the weekly service meetings (where they exist). The Churchill Archive Centre in Cambridge also holds BBC broadcast scripts and broadcast directives. These are located in the papers of Noel Newsome and Douglas Ritchie, the editor and assistant editor of European News at the BBC during the war.

Other important documents are located at the Rylands Library in Manchester, the Hartley Library in Southampton and the Wiener Library in London. The Rylands Library holds the records of the *Manchester Guardian*. This collection includes correspondence between the editor of the paper and Joel Cang, who, during the war, published the *Polish Jewish Observer* – the only newspaper in Britain that frankly reported on what was happening at Auschwitz. The collection also includes some limited correspondence between the editor and the minister of information. The Hartley Library holds records of the World Jewish Congress (British Section) and the papers of its political secretary, Alexander Easterman. Examination of these documents is invaluable to assess how and when leading Jewish figures in Britain were advised of the true function of Auschwitz. Documents at the Wiener Library include correspondence between leading British Jewish

30   Introduction

representatives, the minister of information and the BBC, and analysis of the scope and scale of anti-Semitism in Britain.

Outside Britain, archives in the United States, Israel and Poland hold some very important documents to evaluate knowledge of Auschwitz in the West. In Warsaw, the New Documents Archive (Archiwum Akt Nowych) contains many intelligence reports produced and collected by the Polish Underground, including the earliest reports detailing mass killing of Jews at Auschwitz. The Institute of National Remembrance (Instytut Pamięci Narodowej) holds documents collected by Ignacy Schwarzbart. The Archive of the Historical Institute of the Peasant Movement (Archiwum Zakładu Historii Ruchu Ludowego) holds the papers of Stanisław Kot. These papers include a collection of radio messages sent from Warsaw to London, the minutes of Kot's meeting with Jewish representatives in Angers in 1940 and radio monitoring reports from the Polish Ministry of Information and Documentation. The Auschwitz-Birkenau State Museum holds a great deal of material about the Nazi camp. In this book I have made use of reports sent out of the camp, mainly by inmates, and gathered information about specific prisoners.

The National Library in Warsaw also holds a number of important documents, including some Polish Telegraphic Agency bulletins released by the Polish Information Center in New York during 1943. It also holds some copies of *Nasza Trybuna* and *Our Tribune* that supplement the collection held at the Polish Library in London.

In Israel, Yad Vashem and the Central Zionist Archives hold significant documents relating to the Jewish Agency and the activities of Ignacy Schwarzbart. In the United States, the National Archives in Washington hold important intelligence files enabling the tracking of Polish source material to the United States' Office of Strategic Services (the forerunner of the Central Intelligence Agency), military personnel and elsewhere. The archive of the Jewish Telegraphic Agency in New York (available online) is an important resource holding the news reports published by the Jewish Telegraphic Agency.[50] The American Jewish Archive in Cincinnati holds significant documents relating to the World Jewish Congress, and the Roosevelt Library and Archive contains relevant material on the War Refugee Board. The Hoover Institute Archive is the repository of a great deal of material on the Polish Government in Exile and on the Polish government's information office in New York.

In addition to documents from archives, several collections are invaluable for any engagement with Polish intelligence and the Polish government. The first is the series of volumes published by the Polish Undergound Movement (1939–1945) Study Trust, entitled

Terminology

Armia Krajowa w Dokumentach (The Home Army in Documents). The second important collection of documents is contained in the 1968 special edition of *Zeszyty Oświęcimskie*, published by the Auschwitz-Birkenau State Museum, which reproduces many of the Polish Underground's (both military and civilian) documents on Auschwitz.

Ivone Kirkpatrick's autobiography, as well as the biographies of Brendan Bracken, the British minister of information; Winston Churchill; Lord Beaverbrook; Robert Bruce Lockhart, the director-general of the Political Warfare Executive, amongst others, provide a useful insight into the personalities and the politics of the period, but are also helpful in understanding how information about the camp was distributed and, importantly, contained.

Finally, the secondary literature on Auschwitz and the Polish Government in Exile, which in both English and Polish is substantial, provides a great deal of information on the camp, without which this work would not have been possible.

Terminology

Auschwitz is the German name for Oświęcim. Auschwitz-Birkenau is the standard way to refer to the camp in English-speaking countries and elsewhere. In this book, however, a great deal of reference is made to Polish source material and to contemporary newspaper reports. In these sources the camp is referred to as Oświęcim, with or without the diacritic marks. Polish sources through 1943 and 1944 generally do not distinguish between the two camps (Auschwitz and Birkenau), and simply refer to Oświęcim in its entirety. The camp complex was administered as a single unit. Reference to Auschwitz-Birkenau occasionally occurs in the contemporary source material, and does so more frequently after July 1944. In order to maintain some consistency I refer generally to Oświęcim when the source material does so, and Auschwitz when that name is used. In the general discussion or analysis of the camp I follow standard English-language practice and refer to Auschwitz or Auschwitz-Birkenau, without prejudice. I use the two names, Oświęcim and Auschwitz, again without prejudice, to describe the camp complex. I only refer to Auschwitz I, Birkenau (Auschwitz II), Monowitz (Auschwitz III) and various sub-camps to emphasize the differences between these places.

2 Censorship, self-censorship and the discursive environment

Censorship is routinely conceived as an authority, usually the state, prohibiting the publication and broadcasting of certain information. Britain's chief press censor Rear-Admiral George Pirie Thomson published a book entitled *Blue Pencil Admiral* in 1947, which outlined his activities as censor during the Second World War. A blue pencil was used to cross out text which was not fit for publication. Prohibiting the distribution of information is a strategy to inhibit understandings that sanctioned information may provide. The exclusion of certain data from public circulation is the most explicit and bluntest tool of any particular censorship regime. More subtle and less obvious methods of censorship are more common.

In relation to the Holocaust, Laurel Leff (2005) and Deborah Lipstadt (1986) demonstrate that news of the Nazi programme of genocide was published in American newspapers, but generally tucked away deep inside the papers, without prominence. Leff (2005: 341) records that only forty-four stories out of 24,000 that featured on the front page of the *New York Times* during the war had anything to do with Jews, and just over half of these considered what was happening to Jews in Europe. The way in which information is presented therefore plays a crucial role in facilitating understanding and in influencing how recipients respond to that information. Burying news of genocide deep inside newspapers, as Leff and Lipstadt have argued, inhibited comprehension of what was happening to the Jews of Europe during the Second World War, and encouraged scepticism towards those reports that were published.

A censorship regime therefore includes limitation of the circulation of information and, importantly, the manner in which particular news is routinely framed, where it is placed in the media landscape and when.[1] This raises the question why certain news is routinely framed in a particular way. In what follows, the notion of newsworthiness that underpins the framing decisions of editors and broadcasters is explored. This is followed by an examination of how Jews were perceived in Britain prior to and during the Second World War in order to explain the way in which news about Jews was reported, marginalized and omitted.

The discursive environment

The limitations placed by state authorities on media outlets in their reporting of news is one aspect of a censorship regime. Prior to the involvement of any official censor, however, information must first be considered to be newsworthy by editors and broadcasters.[2] Discrete events rather than continuous processes tend to be privileged. It is often the case that a story that may be considered newsworthy is often judged by editors in the context of real and perceived important vested interests. The 2011 phone-hacking scandal in the United Kingdom, where journalists from the now defunct newspaper the *News of the World* hacked into the telephones of public figures, politicians and possibly a murdered schoolgirl, amongst others, was certainly a newsworthy story that had been bubbling subterraneously in the world of current-affairs journalism for a considerable time. It only received the publicity it deserved after persistent investigation by the liberal newspaper *The Guardian*, which did not agree with the Metropolitan Police's initial view that there was no substantial issue to warrant attention. In this case, media outlets that were not part of the wider corporation which owned the *News of the World* made a very newsworthy story front-page news. The story became a significant political and media scandal.

Stereotypes, and the way in which media outlets judge their readers' or audiences' social and political sympathies, also influence what information becomes news. In Britain, a missing photogenic white girl or woman from a stable middle-class nuclear family is more likely to attract media attention than someone who does not share those characteristics. This hierarchy is so common both in Britain and in the US that it has acquired a name – 'missing white girl syndrome'. As the feminist scholar Sarah Stillman (2007: 491) has noted, this hierarchy positions some women 'as deserving of our collective resources, while making the marginalisation and victimisation of other groups of women, such as low-income women of colour, seem natural'.

The hierarchy of those deserving/not deserving of our concern is not fixed. Communities of concern stretch from the streets we live on to include those residing in distant lands, but with whom we share a range of commonalities, which may include beliefs, background, way of life and language, amongst other features. These transnational communities are increasingly recognized as agents of social change and political importance. In contrast, some people living beside us, whom we may pass regularly whilst going about our daily business, such as the homeless, the poor or recent immigrants, may not be viewed as equally valuable to us. So while transnational communities may expand the geographic horizon of our 'universe of obligation', there are also some significant groups who may be physically close, and may even share our citizenship status, but are not incorporated within our 'universe of obligation'. The issue of justifying these inclusions and exclusions is therefore an important element in how we narrate our personal stories, define ourselves and legitimate our actions, though much of this processing occurs without too much self-reflection. Indeed, these mental boundaries that position people and groups within a hierarchy of concern and obligation often become 'common-sense', unquestioned and indeed unquestionable. As such they form a crucial part of the discursive environment in which statements can be made without contestation about one group, but may provoke widespread outrage or incredulity if levelled at another group.

Stereotypes about particular groups and members of such groups often inhibit inter-group communication, and what communication there is may be marred by distortions and misunderstandings due to initial unquestioned assumptions. In addition, groups are differentially affected by what the sociologist Pierre Bourdieu terms 'symbolic violence'. This 'is not a logic of "communicative interaction" where some make propaganda aimed at others ... It is much more powerful and insidious than that: being born in a social world, we accept a whole range of postulates, axioms, which go without saying and require no inculcating' (Bourdieu and Wacquant 2004: 273).

The content of a particular national identity can thus be seen as axiomatic. As such, a cartography of inclusion and exclusion is written into the dominant idea of a specific nation, and indicates which groups can be accommodated within a particular national community without disturbing the unstated definitional assumptions and how those who do not conform to the accepted norm are conceived and treated. Often, these unsaid principles emerge in debates about immigration policy as issues of integration, assimilation and, over the last couple of decades, multicultural citizenship. In the case of Britain, Tariq Modood (2007) has forcefully argued that an 'out-of-date national story, for example, alienates new communities, who want to be written into the narrative backwards as well as forward', and has contended that multiculturalism 'is incomplete and one-sided without a continual remaking of national identity'. Modood's argument is important, as he identifies white reticence as a stumbling block in creating a more inclusive community in Britain. The old stories of empire, which excluded, marginalized and hierarchically ordered the histories of those differentially incorporated within the empire, are a barrier to developing communities of concern and obligation, of creating a new 'we' in an increasingly culturally diverse Britain.

The discursive environment 35

Current concerns about multicultural citizenship and about extending the varied immigrant communities full respect through the promotion of an inclusive narrative is in marked contrast to 1930s and 1940s Britain. Through the first half of the twentieth century and beyond, assimilation to what were conceived to be British norms was expected. Groups outside these norms were required to minimize their differences if they wished to be seen as British. As Tony Kushner (2004: 263) has noted, 'Assimilation was still seen as the solution to the so-called "Jewish Question" in liberal thinking'. In this view, the reason for the persistence of anti-Semitism in the modern world 'was because Jews insisted on retaining their difference, or rather went beyond a religious identity that was perceived as being compatible with national belonging' (Kushner, 2004: 263). Consequently, as Geoffrey Alderman (1995: 129) points out, Jews had to 'conform to what they felt were Gentile expectations of acceptable Jewish behaviour' if they were to be welcomed into British society. Concretely, this demanded narrowing the expression of Jewish identity, which in practice often meant limiting it to controlled religious elements that did not unduly disturb wider British sensibilities. It also supposed Jewish participation in, and endorsement of, dominant expressions of British identity, themselves inflected by Protestant Christianity. Nevertheless, this was frequently not enough, as any form of Jewish identity remained outside the accepted notion of Britishness to some in Britain.

Jews were not the only minority group coerced by the culture of the majority to assimilate to dominant norms and reject aspects of the wider sense of what, in their case, being Jewish was or could be. Other groups (such as Roman Catholics) faced similar pressures, but during the 1930s and the first half of the 1940s, the discursive regime which coerced Jews played an important role in limiting actions to highlight the anti-Semitic events in Europe and in justifying the limitation of news about Jews.[3] Discourses about Jews strongly affected what could be said about Jews, and when and how it could be said, what policies government officials considered appropriate in relation to Jews, and how Jews themselves could react and attempt to sustain agency in an environment marked by persistent and frequently malign views about them. David Cesarani (1989: 7) rightly argues that 'the state, society and culture in Britain operated a discourse about Jews that was exclusive and oppressive, that eventuated in and legitimated discrimination'.

The trajectory to such a state of affairs was set by a notion of assimilation which offered inclusion into the wider society so long as social and cultural differences were minimized, though the majority often retained the right to view minorities' adherence to hegemonic norms as simulation. The wave of Jewish immigration in the late nineteenth and early twentieth centuries from parts of Poland incorporated into the tsarist empire and elsewhere in Eastern Europe excited a great deal of debate, and provoked the passing of the 1905 Aliens Act, which, under the cover of limiting the flow of economic migrants, aimed to stem Jewish immigration. Liberal arguments about extending formal equality to immigrants and rejecting anti-Semitism were articulated at the same time as entrance to the country was limited. But the balance between dashing the hopes of many Eastern European Jews to settle in Britain, while at the same time challenging expressions of anti-Semitism, was uneasy, and anti-Semitic statements and actions by the wider population, often fomented by the proto-fascist British Brothers League, were not infrequent.

William Evans Gordon, the Conservative Member of Parliament for Stepney between 1900 and 1907, won his seat arguing against Jewish immigration, but maintained that 'the moment we allow this agitation [anti-immigration] to be used as a cloak for religious passion or racial animosity we put ourselves in the wrong'.[4] Yet Gordon sometimes came very close to the boundary between anti-immigration and anti-Semitism, especially when he positioned recent immigrants as a threat to the wider British community. On 29 January 1902, Gordon claimed in Parliament that '[n]ot a day passes but English families are ruthlessly turned out to make room for foreign invaders'. According to Gordon, landlords raised rents, which forced English families to seek accommodation elsewhere. Immigrants moved into these properties in numbers (reducing per capita housing costs) and overcrowding was the result. Gordon rhetorically asked,

Does any sane man believe that these immigrants are objected to on account of their religion? They are objected to not because they are Jew or Gentile, but purely on social and economic grounds. The Jewish people who are already here are as much interested in restriction as any other part of the community.[5]

By arguing that the solution to the problem was stemming immigration, rather than, for example, tightening housing control, Gordon positioned foreigners as problematic. These foreigners – 'the inexhaustible army of the houseless poor from Russia, Poland, Roumania, and the whole of Eastern Europe' – were seen not only as a threat to those English families forced to leave the East End by rising rents, but as an element that could provoke anti-Semitism in the country. British Jews, Gordon reasoned, had a key task in inhibiting their co-religionists from coming to Britain:

The discursive environment 37

As the numbers coming from abroad increase, so their chances in life diminish. Employment, house accommodation, the means of earning a living grow less and less. And though the charity and benevolence of the Hebrew community is as boundless as their wealth, that too has its limits which must soon be reached. It is that very charity, indeed, which among other things attracts so many of their co-religionists here, and I do not doubt but that those who dispense it regard the future with grave misgiving. We look with confidence for the support of the leaders of Jewish opinion in this matter; indeed, in many instances, we have it already. They know better than anyone else the evil and dangers which the influx, if continued much longer, will entail. If they range themselves against the natural and rising feeling of the people on this subject, then, indeed, there is a grave risk of an anti-Semitic colour being imparted to this controversy. We appeal to their English citizenship, to their patriotism, and Imperial spirit to help us in dealing with what they I am sure will admit is a situation of extreme gravity.[6]

Gordon's invocation of British Jews' citizenship and patriotism against non-British Jews clearly indicates the boundaries of acceptable Jewish conduct. Empathy and support for co-religionists could, according to Gordon, only be stretched so far. The demands of citizenship trumped all other pulls of loyalty and obligation, and British Jews were expected to act in a particular way. Refusal to conform to these expectations would bring into question Jews' Britishness and cause the possible unleashing of British anti-Semitic sentiment. Such statements clearly indicate how the leaders of British Jewry were pressured to adopt a particular position towards Eastern European Jews.

Parts of the labour movement, as Cohen (2003: 83) has documented, also exhibited hostility towards Jewish immigration. In 1895 the Trades Union Congress compiled a series of demands to be assented to by those running for Parliament in the forthcoming general election. Most demands focused on making sure potential representatives were committed to securing improvements in the work and life conditions of the working class. However, the final demand was to limit Jewish immigration. Calls to restrict immigration frequently coincided with more generally defined anti-Jewish rhetoric, which adversely impacted on Jews in Britain, whose status was both implicitly and explicitly queried. Debates about Jewish immigration within sections of the labour movement also allowed anti-Semitic sentiment to be expressed and malign stereotypes to be propagated.

The concerns about immigration articulated at the turn of the century were given a new expression in the 1930s by Oswald Mosley's British Union of Fascists, which sought to tap into British anti-immigrant and anti-Semitic sentiment. In his 1936 publication 'Fascism: 100 questions asked and answered', Mosley articulated the standard anti-Semitic trope of the period arguing that

38 Censorship, self-censorship and the discursive environment

Jews must put the interests of Britain before those of Jewry, or be deported from Britain. This is not a principle of racial or religious persecution. Any well-governed nation must insist that its citizens owe allegiance to the nation, and not to co-racialists and co-religionists resident outside its borders or organized as a state within the State. The Jews, as a whole, have chosen to organize themselves as a nation within the Nation and to set their interests before those of Great Britain. They must, like everyone else, put 'Britain First' or leave Britain. (Mosley 1936: 35)

One of the most striking elements of Mosley's argument is its proximity to Gordon's demand thirty years earlier that British Jews demonstrate loyalty to Britain by behaving in a particular way. This perspective was widespread, and helps to account for the British Union of Fascists' appeal – from its founding in 1932 to the withdrawal of the support it enjoyed from the Rothermere press (*Daily Mail*) in 1934.

The BBC was well placed to highlight where fascist precepts led, through its news coverage of Germany. However, during the 1930s the BBC was particularly sensitive to Foreign Office policy relating to Germany – a policy which sought to maintain stability in Europe.[7] As the Nazi policy against Jews intensified, so news about Jews on the BBC was limited. Between 1933 and 1938 there was not a single programme dedicated to German actions against Jews (Milland 1998b: 12). When Jews were mentioned, they were presented as a political minority and 'there was a tendency to seek to rationalise Nazi anti-Semitism by seeking to comprehend it by reference to Jewish behaviour' (Milland 1998b: 13). The general policy of minimizing news of the persecution of Jews was well established before the outbreak of the war in September 1939, and British anti-Semitism allowed Foreign Office policy on Jews to remain without serious challenge.

British anti-Semitism also helps to explain how Jews were presented, marginalized and ignored in the British media as the Nazi onslaught against Jews in occupied Europe intensified in the early 1940s, and Cohen's (2003: 80) claim that Britain was 'profoundly antisemitic' requires only minor qualification. British anti-Semitism co-existed with the British political class's conception of Britain as a liberal and just society. *Explicit* public expressions of anti-Semitism were generally, though not always, confined to the fringes of political discourse. For example, although anti-Jewish sentiment helped frame the debate on immigration during the first years of the twentieth century, the 1905 Aliens Act described those who were to be denied access to Britain without explicit reference to the main group of potential migrants to be excluded from Britain by the legislation – poor Eastern European Jews.

The discursive environment 39

The 1905 Aliens Act sought to prevent the entry to Britain of those without the means to 'decently support' themselves or their dependants, 'lunatics' and those who might become a charge on the public purse, those sentenced to a crime (not political) in a country with which the United Kingdom had an extradition agreement, and those subjected to an expulsion order.[8] The Act would allow admission to Britain to those seeking entrance 'solely to avoid persecution or punishment on religious or political grounds'. The right of immigration was offered to 'asylum seekers', but not to economic migrants, and the Act also provided the legal basis for the expulsion of unwanted immigrants and the prosecution of those transporting migrants to Britain (shipping personnel).

The legislation focused on the contingent economic characteristics of immigrants. In this way, the mass of poor Eastern European Jews (and others) who sought a new life in Britain could be denied entry on economic rather than religious or racial grounds, while those fleeing religious or political oppression could be accommodated. However, proving religious or political oppression to the British authorities could be difficult. The series of pogroms in the Russian Empire between 1903 and 1906, following on from the pogroms of 1881–4, was a factor in the migration of Eastern European Jews westward, but the frequently murderous violence against Jews in the Pale of Settlement was not understood as a legitimate basis to allow poor Eastern European Jews to enter Britain. The focus of the asylum clause in the 1905 Aliens Act was narrow, and provided the British with a legal basis to prevent those who could not prove active persecution to the satisfaction of British officials from entering Britain.

The Act bestowed on the Home Secretary a great deal of leeway to interpret who exactly should be allowed entry. This important power was maintained in the 1914 Aliens Restriction Act, which required foreigners to report to the police and provided the grounds for their deportation. This Act, assented to during the First World War, was followed by the 1919 Aliens Act, and subsequent Alien Orders tightened restrictions on foreigners in Britain.

The 1919 Act was accompanied by anti-alien sentiment in the country, exacerbated by a deteriorating economic situation and rising unemployment. The summer of 1919 witnessed race riots in a number of British port cities, including Liverpool and Cardiff.[9] Under this Act, those identified as aliens were subject to a number of restraints in Britain, while non-aliens were exempted. This included special penalties for actions that were 'likely to cause sedition or disaffection amongst any of His Majesty's Forces ... Allies ... or civilian population', and for promoting 'industrial unrest in any industry in which he has not been

40   Censorship, self-censorship and the discursive environment

bona fide engaged for at least two years immediately preceding in the United Kingdom'.[10] Arguably, this second point was informed by stereotypes of some immigrant groups having left-wing political sympathies. Through the period from 1919 to 1938, the Home Secretary maintained a largely discretionary regime as to who exactly could come and live in Britain. In 1938 visa restrictions were imposed on people (most often Jews) from Germany and Austria, but, as Louise London (2000) has shown, the Home Office remained reluctant to spell out policy precisely. This lack of clarity preserved the ability of the Home Secretary and the government as a whole to be as restrictive or as generous in regard to immigration control as they chose. In March of that year, the House of Commons rejected the motion of Josiah Wedgwood MP that called for the wholesale admission of refugees by 210 votes to 142.[11] On 23 March, the British press was united in its approval of the decision to restrict immigration. The populist *Daily Express* clearly explained the issue to its readers:

there is a powerful agitation here to admit all Jewish refugees without question or discrimination. It would be unwise to overload the basket like that. It would stir up the elements here that fatten on anti-Semitic propaganda. They would point to the fresh tide of foreigners, almost all belonging to the extreme Left. They would ask: What if Poland, Hungary, Rumania also expel their Jewish citizens? Must we admit them too? Because we DON'T want anti-Jewish uproar we DO need to show common sense in not admitting all applicants. (cited in Sherman 1973: 94)

The *Daily Express* article highlighted two axioms that framed thinking about Jewish immigrants in Britain. First, the increase in the number of Jews would stimulate anti-Semitism; and second, Jews were on the extreme left of the political spectrum. Both these ascribed characteristics were viewed unfavourably in 1938, and increasingly so during the war years when national unity and continuous industrial production were highly sought-after.

British immigration policy and the social sentiment that it both reflected and, indeed, contributed to in the period from 1905 to 1938 had, at best, an unsettling effect on recent and even more established immigrant communities. It highlighted the liberal homogenizing drift of state policy more generally, outlined the contours of legitimate Britishness, and thereby framed hierarchies of belonging. Immigrants' incorporation within the notion of Britishness was marked by significant ambivalences – ambivalences that also affected those who did not conform to the Protestant Christian norm. In these circumstances, established British Jewish communities were attuned to the way in which the wider society's perceptions of recent Jewish immigrants could be

The discursive environment 41

overdetermined to also include British Jews. The pressure to subscribe to these expectations of appropriate Jewish behaviour was therefore malign in a number of different ways. It limited the practical options that British Jewry had in relation to co-religionists abroad, coerced British Jews to act in particular ways in response to policy initiatives of the government, and restricted the expression of British Jewishness to forms that did not challenge *idées fixes* about the notion of Britishness. In practical terms, during the war especially, this encouraged Jews to focus on anti-Semitism and attempts to limit it. Bolchover (1993: 145) argues, '[f]ear of anti-semitism dogged the community and anti-semitic stereotypes were internalised'. During the war representatives of British Jewry met with the minister of information on several occasions. These meetings were taken up with the question of anti-Semitism in Britain and ways to inhibit it.[12] Anti-Semitism conceived as either religious or racial discrimination was certainly an issue which was condemned across the mainstream political spectrum and had no place within the liberal imagination of what constituted Britishness, though there was no recognition that the homogenizing pressures placed on Jews and others were unfair, discriminatory and harmful.

One way to combat anti-Semitism, according to Gordon's 1902 argument, was to limit immigration. But, as highlighted above, the implicit argument that Jews brought anti-Semitism with them was not challenged. The general acceptance of Gordon's contention across a broad spectrum of respectable British opinion further limited British Jewry's options. They were assigned, as Gordon made clear, a key role in inhibiting Jewish immigration, but also in policing recent Jewish immigrants.[13] The behaviour of recent immigrants was a concern for the wider Jewish community in the United Kingdom, and Bolchover (1993: 145) notes that '[m]uch effort was expanded [by the community during the war] on apologetics and disciplining Jewish behaviour, particularly in trade'. For example, *The Times* found space on 23 May 1942, at the top centre of page 2, for an article entitled 'Jews in the black market', reporting on the condemnation by Dr Joseph Hertz (the chief rabbi) of dishonest practices and greed in business. The chief rabbi – speaking at the synagogue in affluent St John's Wood – argued that 'Jewish participation in this and other offences has given rise to a grave defamation of Judaism and the Jewish name'.[14] The report highlighted to gentile readers that Jewish leaders were acting against what were seen as antisocial practices, but the article could also be read by some readers as indicating that there was some truth to the malign stereotype of Jewish avarice. Given the limited number of articles in *The Times* that mentioned Jews at all during the war years, this piece gives an insight into how Jews

42   Censorship, self-censorship and the discursive environment

were perceived. The chief rabbi's speech was also highlighted in that week's *Jewish Chronicle* and in the *East London Observer* – a paper with a significant working-class Jewish readership – on 29 May 1942.[15] It is unlikely that many of those that the chief rabbi addressed in St John's Wood were engaged in black-market activity. This was, in general, a British middle-class congregation, and hence his speech can be understood as encouraging British Jews to exert influence over more recent Jewish immigrants who resided in the East End of London. The *East London Observer* subsequently published several articles on black-market activities.

In relation to immigration, Samuel Hoare, the British Home Secretary between 1937 and 1939, considered that Jewish leaders in Britain were

> averse from allowing very large numbers of Jews to enter this country or from allowing the entry of Jews whom they had not themselves approved, since they were afraid of an anti-Jewish agitation in this country. For the same reason they were unwilling to give definite figures as to the number of Jews admitted, since they were afraid that any number published would be attacked from both sides as being too big or too little. (cited in Bolchover 1993: 49)[16]

Hoare's view was undoubtedly correct, and it reflected the general position of the British government and the views of mainstream politicians. Its significance lies in the fact that the leadership of British Jewry sought to mirror and domesticate for themselves the dominant view about Jewish immigration to the country. Although British Jewry contributed to the discourse about Jewish immigration, they did so from a position not of their making or choosing.

British anti-alienism, both explicit and inhering within the dominant discourses about Britishness, together with the fear of anti-Semitism, was fundamental in framing the way British Jews responded to the Nazi onslaught against Jews in Europe. Throughout the war, the number and intensity of British Jewry's interventions on behalf of co-religionists suffering in continental Europe were limited, while the investigation, mapping and analysis of British anti-Semitism were tasks pursued with some vigour. During the 1930s and 1940s, Jews in Britain had no single dominant voice which could speak on behalf of the whole community. The government's worries about anti-Semitism provided ideological support to British Jewry's focus on, and response to, anti-Semitism in Britain. Combating anti-Semitism was an issue to which Jews of various political orientations could devote energy.[17]

This anxiety about anti-Semitism during the war was well founded. Leslie Hore-Belisha, the Secretary of State for War from May 1937 to January 1940, was Jewish. As minister, he initiated a series of reforms to the armed services, but alienated some senior soldiers. Anti-Semitism in

The discursive environment 43

the War Office and elsewhere in the British government played a role in his removal from office in January 1940, as Josiah Wedgwood noted in the House of Commons on 16 January 1940.[18] Anti-Semitism was also recorded amongst the wider British population. The Ministry of Information assessed public opinion in the country through its Home Intelligence Reports. The 17 December 1942 report recorded that 'the "wholesale murder of Jews in Poland" is said to have caused "extreme horror"' and that it was 'hoped something may be done to save the children'. There was no comment on whether adults should also be saved. Anti-Semitism 'aggravated by reports of "regulation dodging"' and the prosecutions for 'black market offences' were mentioned.[19] A week later, the report which assessed opinion during the period of maximum publicity around the UN declaration of 17 December 1942 and the debates in Parliament in which the slaughter of European Jewry was highlighted noted 'widespread indignation, anger and disgust' over the revelations of Nazi atrocities and the Nazi policy of exterminating the Jews, but also anti-Jewish sentiment, with one regional report suggesting that 'the atrocity propaganda has given rise to talk of Jews and black-markets after a period when it seemed to have decreased'.[20]

The tendency to rationalize harms inflicted on others, or, more bluntly, to blame the victims for the actions taken against them, was not an unusual response and not limited to attempts to understand Nazi policy against Jews.[21] A 1941 planning document from the Ministry of Information indicated that the tendency to blame the victim was well recognized by British propagandists.[22] The Home Intelligence Report of 31 December 1942 found 'no evidence that the popularity of Jews in this country has increased', noting the view that 'Abroad – greatest sympathy; in England – general feeling that they badly want controlling'.[23] The following report from the first week of January 1943 indicated that the publicity given to German anti-Jewish atrocities made people 'more conscious of the Jews they do not like here'.[24] The Tube disaster of 3 March 1943 at Bethnal Green, in which 173 people lost their lives, was blamed on panicking Jews, according to the Home Intelligence Report from that week.[25]

After the Bermuda conference of April 1943, which was a response to the UN declaration of December 1942, the British War Cabinet on 10 May 1943 discussed 'signs of increasing anti-Semitic feeling in this country', and noted that 'from this point of view, it would be preferable in public sentiments to avoid implying that refugees were necessarily Jewish and refer to refugees by nationality rather than by race'. It was further agreed to manage the forthcoming parliamentary debate on the conference, since there was a 'risk that a disproportionate number of the speeches might be by Members holding extreme views in favour of

44   Censorship, self-censorship and the discursive environment

the free admission of refugees to this country', by inviting the Whips to arrange for some Members, 'who would put a more balanced point of view', to intervene in the debate.[26]

In addition, following the receipt of a letter and a report dated 18 May 1943 which highlighted the killing of Jews at Treblinka and Auschwitz, sent by Józef Zarański of the Polish Embassy in London (who wrote on behalf of the Polish ambassador, Edward Raczyński), the Foreign Office was concerned that some Members of Parliament who had received the same information on the extermination of the Jews might raise the issue in the House of Commons.[27] It was proposed that the reply to any such question should acknowledge the fresh evidence from the Polish government and that 'all such information can only stir us to renewed determination to beat down the Hitlerite system and inflict just punishment on those responsible for the crimes'.[28] This was the standard Foreign Office line: winning the war would end the Nazi atrocities.

In mid-1944, after a great deal of information about the slaughter of European Jewry was known in Britain, the Ministry of Information's Home Intelligence Report of 2 June 1944 wearily reported criticism levelled against Jews following 'familiar lines'. These were black-market activities – Jews being blamed for the rise in the price of houses and whisky; for running poultry 'rackets'; for dealing in cash and thus evading income tax; for evading national service; for obtaining goods in short supply. Jews were also criticized for evacuating to safe areas, for their ability to run cars, for using taxis for pleasure, for shopping and for gambling offices. In the North East, Jews were identified as fomenting industrial unrest, and the role played by Jewish communists in coal strikes was stressed – though the report notes that this was not 'confined to Jews'.[29]

Anti-Semitic attitudes in Britain, as noted in these intelligence reports, were depicted as fairly widespread, and British politicians sought not to aggravate negative sentiment through a strategy of minimizing Jewish stories in the press and limiting the number of Jews in Britain, despite the evident Jewish need for sanctuary in the face of the Nazi extermination programme.[30] Even after victory in Europe in May 1945, Home Secretary Herbert Morrison argued that Jewish refugees in Britain should be removed, because 'if the Jews were allowed to remain here they might be an explosive element in the country, especially if the economic situation deteriorated'.[31] He remained 'seriously alarmed regarding the possibility of anti-Semitism in this country'.[32] As Bloxham and Kushner (2005: 194) have argued, 'between 1939 and 1950, the idea that Jews bring anti-Semitism with them was taken to its logical extreme, becoming in itself ingrained into bureaucratic mentality and practice'.

The discursive environment 45

The government's general policy line to minimize news about Jews was not seriously challenged by British Jewry. And even debates in Parliament about Jews in Europe, or campaigns to highlight the annihilation of the Jews of Europe, were not driven in the main by Jewish MPs. Josiah Wedgwood, who moved from the House of Commons to the House of Lords in 1942, often complained that it was he, a non-Jew, who spoke up for the Jews while Jewish members did not (Harris 2004: 303, Bolchover 1993: 109).[33] Bolchover (1993: 29) notes that British Jews were 'eager to avoid giving the impression of any sort of Jewish political interest as represented by Jewish MPs or others in public life', and 'Jewish leaders were even anxious that the efforts of non-Jews on their behalf, unfettered by the restraints felt by Anglo-Jewry, might compromise the community's position as loyal British citizens' (Bolchover 1993: 109). This position arguably handicapped efforts to discuss the fate of Jews in Europe as the war unfolded. Nevertheless, Jewish MPs did act and were heavily involved in disseminating news of the unfolding Holocaust.

British Jews were extremely concerned by what was happening to Jews in Europe, often to friends or relatives, but the view that a Jewish intervention would be counter-productive in an environment perceived as anti-alien and anti-Semitic was not uncommon. BBC records note that a delegation from the Board of Deputies, led by the chairman, Professor Selig Brodetsky, met with BBC officials in April 1942. The delegation offered the BBC advice, contending that '"any direct campaign against anti-Semitism" would do more harm than good' and advocating an indirect method that highlighted the 'creditable achievement of Jews'.[34] Gabriel Milland (1998b: 34) speculates that the position of the Board of Deputies 'may have been based on their contacts in the Ministry of Information, where doctrine now stated that "exhortative" propaganda had little effect'.

This perspective was shared throughout the British political and media classes. Oliver Locker-Lampson, a Conservative MP who had campaigned for Jews fleeing Nazi persecution to be given British citizenship during the 1930s, met with Sir Richard Maconachie, the controller of the BBC's Home Service, on 7 June 1943 to highlight the importance of counteracting anti-Semitism in Britain. Maconachie responded by arguing, in line with the dominant thinking at the time, that 'a pro-Jewish broadcast ... would be only likely to make matters worse, since the anti-semites would demand a right to reply, which would be difficult to refuse'. Maconachie referred to the views expressed by the delegation led by Professor Brodetsky a year earlier to further justify the BBC's position.[35]

It is worth noting that, across the Atlantic, Arthur Sulzberger, the American Jewish proprietor of the *New York Times*, rationalized the

46 Censorship, self-censorship and the discursive environment

relative lack of focus on Jews in his newspaper in much the same way. In rejecting calls to publish letters attacking anti-Semitism, Sulzberger in 1936 argued that his paper had to show 'both sides of the argument' and therefore would not publish anti-anti-Semitism letters since it wished to avoid giving publicity 'to those who might urge the extension of anti-Semitism' (cited in Leff 2005: 32). Sulzberger remained true to this perspective throughout the war years, which had a profound effect on how news of the Holocaust was disseminated in the United States. The *New York Times* did nonetheless publish a story on what was happening to the Jews in Europe, on average, every other day (Leff 2003: 51), but rarely gave any of these stories prominence. They were routinely tucked deep inside the paper. Leff (2003: 51) records that the paper published 1,147 stories on the Jews of Europe during the war, 203 in 1940, 197 in 1941, 149 in 1942, 184 in 1943 and 210 in 1944. This is in marked contrast to the volume of stories in the British press, where the total output of the quality press (*The Times*, the *Daily Telegraph* and the *Manchester Guardian*) and a large portion of the popular press (*Daily Mirror* and *Daily Express*) did not eclipse the *New York Times* figure.

The pressures of cultural homogenization present in the United Kingdom, which so powerfully shaped British Jewry's response to Jewish immigration during the first decades of the twentieth century and influenced its reactions to the Holocaust, operated in a similar fashion in the United States, though there were also significant differences. Arthur Sulzberger confronted the difficulties of presenting news about Jews whilst affirming the precepts of assimilatory liberalism on a regular basis. He vigorously defended the view that Jews were simply a religious group and strongly argued against Zionistic conceptions of Jews as a people. Repeatedly, he universalized the situation of Jews, even when the experience of Jews was not shared by other groups. For instance, the *New York Times* through the 1930s insisted that the refugee crisis emanating from Germany was not a Jewish problem. Leff (2005: 33) highlights an editorial from 22 July 1939, in which it was explained that the problem

posed by the German refugees constitutes a test of civilization itself ... It has nothing to do with race or creed. It is not a Jewish refugee problem or a Gentile problem. It does not belong to Europe or to America. It is the problem of mankind.

On the one hand, universalizing an experience which disproportionately affected one group – a group which was often viewed with considerable suspicion and even contempt – facilitated the publication of news about a desperate situation and encouraged an American audience, marked by varying degrees of anti-Semitism, to engage with the news from

Germany, but, on the other, it distorted that news and hindered a holistic understanding of what was happening in Germany and, later, in the occupied countries. As Leff (2005) documents, Sulzberger's understanding of his American Jewish identity, and his awareness of how others conceived of him and his newspaper, had a significant impact on the editorial line taken in the *New York Times*, a line which failed to highlight the systematic Nazi assault on Jewish communities in Europe. This is significant because other American newspapers took their cue from the *New York Times*. In short, despite its influence, relative power and high proportion of Jewish readers, the *New York Times* did not challenge the discursive environment that limited expression of Jewishness under the rubric of assimilation, and marginalized Jewish experiences.

As in the UK, American conceptions of Jews and their appropriate place in society played an important role in adjudging what could be reported, how it would be reported and when. The *New York Times* was exceptional in the American press, in the sense that it did in fact report news about European Jewry, though the way it was presented hindered comprehension of what was happening. Other papers, with smaller international operations, tended not to report news concerning European Jews. In such circumstances, formal censorship was rarely required. Voluntary and, in the case of Arthur Sulzberger, principled self-censorship could be relied on to frame the Jewish experience in occupied Europe in ways which did not provoke latent anti-Semitism or challenge the justice of the liberal assimilatory model of integration. News about the annihilation of Jews was relegated to the inside pages, without prominence, where it could, and often did, escape notice.

In the context of war, however, the British government did not merely rely on self-censorship of the sort outlined above. It also took measures to ensure media outlets understood what was permissible, and actively limited the flow of information.

Reporting news about Jews in Britain

The dissemination of news in Britain about Jews was constrained by British government censorship and propaganda policy. Even before the war started, officials in the planning section of the Ministry of Information advised on 10 August 1939 that 'no special propaganda addressed to Jews is necessary outside Palestine'.[36] This policy of addressing Jews as *only* nationals of the state in which they resided could not adequately accommodate the changing reality as Nazi racial planning unfolded following the invasion of Poland. It did, however, follow the liberal principle that Jews were (or should be) assimilated within the

48   Censorship, self-censorship and the discursive environment

nation-state in which they resided. Any other expression of Jewishness was deemed illegitimate and, in relation to Zionist ambitions amongst European Jews, capable of creating unwanted problems in Palestine.[37]

The promotion of the view that Jewish audiences in Europe should only be addressed as citizens of the states in which they lived increased the likelihood that issues which heavily impacted on Jews specifically would be marginalized or narrated as part of a wider experience affecting all nationals. What was considered 'benign neglect' (practised because of British political concerns) of the specific Jewish experience of Nazi rule was nothing of the sort, and encouraged (though such encouragement was often not required) Allied governments (including the Polish Government in Exile) to narrate the war primarily in terms of the suffering of nationals (Poles, Czechs and so on). The specific Jewish experience was frequently obfuscated in the press on both sides of the Atlantic.

In addition, as the war progressed, various key figures in the British government, including officials at the Foreign Office, expressed scepticism about many atrocity stories, and considered that some of them constituted propaganda, especially if they originated from Polish and Jewish sources (most news of the Holocaust came from these sources), that would provoke sentiments negative for the war effort. The final claim was particularly serious. The media were censored, in the final analysis, by Defence Regulations, reinstituted through the Emergency Powers (Defence) Act of 24 August 1939. The so called D-notice system, developed during the First World War, had operated on a voluntary basis, but had given the Home Secretary sweeping powers. Defence Regulation 3 'provided that no person should obtain, record, publish or have any document containing information which "would or might be directly or indirectly useful to any enemy"' (Hinsley and Simkins 1990: 24), and Defence Regulation 39B allowed the Home Secretary to prevent or limit publication that 'would or might be prejudicial to the defence of the realm or the official prosecution of the war' (Hinsley and Simkins 1990: 24).

These powers were posited as a last resort should the modified voluntary censorship regime not be adequate. Though the conceived object of these powers was primarily to prevent militarily useful information being passed on purpose or by accident to the enemy, the Home Secretary had a great deal of discretion in defining what information could be useful for the enemy. His opinion, therefore, carried a great deal of weight, and, given that Herbert Morrison remained through the war years gravely concerned about British anti-Semitism, the press marginalization of stories about Jews had the imprimatur of sanction from the top of the British government.

The Ministry of Information and the Political Warfare Executive

The Ministry of Information had responsibility for censorship and operated a robust policy, especially after Winston Churchill's good friend Brendan Bracken took on the brief in 1941.[38] Churchill had insisted that Bracken take the post, and gave him 'all the backing he required' (Lysaght 1979: 190). Operating out of Senate House in the University of London, censors from the War Office, Admiralty, Air Ministry, Foreign Office and Home Security, acting under the auspices of the Ministry of Information, outlined what could and could not be published, and what required official clearance (Taylor 1999: 161; Hinsley and Simkins 1990: 24). Bracken's was an important appointment and re-energized the ministry after two years of administrative drift. His ability to establish the Ministry of Information as an influential body in the war effort was down, in part, to his personal association with Churchill, as this gave him extra leverage to make sure material that was newsworthy was released from various British ministries. Bracken was a member, along with Professor Frederick Lindemann (Lord Cherwell), the intelligence officer Desmond Morton and, at times, Lord Beaverbrook (William Maxwell Aitken), of Churchill's kitchen cabinet. Bracken even kept an office in Downing Street and 'saw Churchill too often for there to be much written correspondence between them' (Stenton, 2000: 30). Crocket (1990: 12) quotes Beaverbrook: 'the PM, Brendan and I used to meet every evening; we settled most things'. Bracken was therefore very well placed within the British government to shape the Ministry of Information into a significant institution.

Bracken's approach to controlling the media was liberal, but patrician. Earlier in his career he had worked for the well-connected Conservative MP Oliver Locker-Lampson on the monthly *Empire Review* and, in 1928, had bought a 50 per cent stake in *The Economist*, prior to becoming the Conservative MP for North Paddington in 1929 – a seat he held until the Labour landslide of 1945. Through the 1930s he was a loyal supporter of Churchill, and remained connected with both newspaper proprietors and politicians. According to Crockett (1990: 13), Bracken

genuinely believed in press freedom and saw an autonomous, powerful Ministry of Information as a guarantee of that freedom. The press rallied to his side, recognising that at last they had a Minister who would fight vigorously for the release of more news from the Service Departments and the Foreign Office.

However, press freedom during war, for Bracken, went hand in hand with 'responsibility'. The quid pro quo for the release of information

50   Censorship, self-censorship and the discursive environment

from the various ministries was newspapers' adherence to the government's general policy on the war effort.

For newspapers, the arrival of Bracken augured a greater degree of government accessibility and the release of news stories allowing the media to play a key role in narrating the war. The minister was able to exercise control over the press in a number of different ways. First and foremost, Bracken practised 'voluntary' censorship by liaising with newspaper proprietors: the owners of the *Daily Telegraph* and the *Daily Sketch*, Lord Camrose and Lord Kemsley respectively, 'were generally ready to insist that their editors did not embarrass the government' (Lysaght 1979: 199). Bracken maintained good terms with the editor of *The Times*, R.M. Barrington-Ward, and made concerted efforts to improve relations with the owner of the *Daily Mail*, Lord Rothermere, since that paper proved, at times, unreliable from the government's point of view.

There were a couple of papers with which Bracken had continuing problems: the *Daily Mirror* and the *Sunday Pictorial*, whose managing editor, Cecil King, considered the *Mirror* to be the 'only opposition in wartime' (Lysaght 1979: 200), and *The Observer*, which was owned by Lord Astor. Bracken had good relations with the editor of *The Observer*, J.L. Garvin, and supported him in a disagreement with the owner. When Garvin was subsequently sacked, Bracken's influence over the paper was diminished. Bracken maintained cordial relations with William Percival Crozier, the editor of the *Manchester Guardian*.[39] The final part of the press landscape was dominated by Lord Beaverbrook's papers, the *Daily Express* and *Sunday Express* and London's *Evening Standard*. These titles generally reflected Beaverbrook's views through their editors, and were not silent in challenging some government policies or embarrassing ministers. For example, in July 1944, the *Evening Standard* noted that Bracken's father had been denied a gun licence forty years previously on account of his (Irish) Nationalist sympathies. Bracken attempted to suppress the story (Taylor 1972: 551).

The *Jewish Chronicle*, the principal weekly publication aimed at British Jewry, faced both editorial and publication challenges. Given its restricted readership and the disciplining effect of British liberalism, together with the widespread concerns about anti-Semitism, the paper seemed only occasionally to have had special advice from the Ministry of Information. But from September 1939, like all British newspapers, *The Chronicle* faced limitations on the number of pages permitted due to newsprint shortages. The distribution of paper was administered by the Paper Control Office. By July 1940 the consumption of newsprint in Britain shrank by 60 per cent (Cesarani 1994: 167). This increased pressure for space in newspapers and forced editors rigorously to

The Ministry of Information and the Political Warfare Executive   51

prioritize their news objectives in the context of British censorship policy. By March 1941, the situation had become tougher as newspapers were allotted a set ration of newsprint. Newspapers were shorter and print frequently became smaller, as editors sought to deal with the contraction of space. Pressure to reject stories that were not deemed essential increased. Casual sales of the *Jewish Chronicle* ceased in November 1941 and the editors called on subscribers to distribute the paper. One effect of the cessation of casual sales was to severely limit the possibility of non-subscribers coming across the news published in the paper.

The *Jewish Chronicle* carried stories of the Holocaust as it unfolded, and, like other papers in Britain – *The Times*, the *Telegraph*, the *Manchester Guardian* etc. – there was a tendency to marginalize the stories about atrocities.[40] David Cesarani (1994: 173) observes, 'Reports of massacres and killings were accepted as routine occurrences and were carried deep inside the paper, rarely meriting editorial comment'. Similarities with the wider British, and indeed the émigré Polish, press extended to how the *Jewish Chronicle* reported atrocities against Jews, and German actions against other groups. There was a distinct lack of balance in editorial commentary. David Cesarani (1994: 175) highlights that the murder of one-third of Bessarabian Jewry was reported in early November 1941 without comment, while the Nazi taking of 100 French hostages a few weeks later, in early December, merited an editorial piece. Cesarani (1994: 175) explains this editorial line as being the result of the immense difficulty in 'sifting rumour and contradictory fragments of information' and the 'intense pressure not to appear solely concerned with the plight of Jews'.

In other newspapers, where the fate of Jews was not so keenly felt, 'Jewish' stories were more deeply buried, shortened or not reported. Even in the *Jewish Chronicle*, which carried some reports from Europe about the Nazi actions against Jews, voluntary self-censorship, as illustrated in the frequent lack of editorial comment about these actions, was supplemented by the omission of important information about the Nazi atrocities. For example, an article on Oświęcim from March 1944 (discussed in Chapter 5), based on a press release from the Polish Government in Exile, did not reveal the full extent of the systematic killing at the camp. Whether this lack of detail in this important report was the result of Ministry of Information 'advice' or due to decisions made by the *Jewish Chronicle*'s editors cannot be conclusively established.

More formally, Brendan Bracken's influence over the press through his regular contact with owners and editors was supplemented by the government's power over the production of newspapers through its control of the paper supply, and by the promise or the withholding of

52   Censorship, self-censorship and the discursive environment

government advertisements – an important source of newspaper income. In short, in Britain, the Ministry of Information provided media editors with advice through private communications, meaning that specific legal measures were not required. The position was spelled out in a memorandum, agreed to by the Foreign Secretary (Anthony Eden), the Home Secretary (Herbert Morrison) and the minister of information (Brendan Bracken) on 12 November 1941, which recorded that the 'news department of the Foreign Office [which had an office in the Ministry of Information and liaised with it] advises the press both on the accuracy of its material and on the advisability of publishing it. Most papers are co-operative, and this procedure is effective over a large field'.[41]

The 'voluntary' scheme's attractions were also articulated:

The indiscretions of a controlled press are much more embarrassing than those of a free press. A Government which has any control over the material published can be alleged by foreign Powers to be responsible for everything which appears in the press, and however wise and vigilant the censors may be, some of the material passed will, nevertheless, offend some foreign susceptibilities. When the resultant complaint is made the Foreign Office will no longer have the answer that the press is free ... The influence of a controlled press is far less than that of a press renowned for its freedom.[42]

In addition, the British government, and the Ministry of Information in particular, had one further tool to ensure the press published the right material. In March 1941, the director of the News Division of the Ministry of Information, Jock Brebner, wrote to the head of Press and Censorship at the same ministry, Cyril Radcliffe, arguing that 'experience has shown that in war time more news becomes public through the medium of official announcements than in peacetime'.[43] The government, therefore, was in a privileged position to set the tone and content of the news as official announcements assumed greater significance. This point is especially important in relation to news of the Holocaust, and highlights the crucial role played by official announcements, declarations and conferences in disseminating information on the Nazi programme of extermination.

This 'voluntary' regime of censorship was enhanced by more rigorous measures. The ministry vetted all information coming into and leaving Britain via the news wires. Prior to the First World War, Britain's worldwide cable network had been rerouted by the Post Office so that all commercial cables met at a single point – the London headquarters of the Press Association. The Press Association provided overseas news to the British press. Reuters, located in the same building, handled news heading overseas (Taylor 1999: 161). Knightley (2001: 2650) notes, 'Every press, commercial or private message leaving Britain, whether

The Ministry of Information and the Political Warfare Executive   53

by mail, cable, wireless, or telephone, was censored'. Censorship of news occurred prior to its distribution to Fleet Street, the BBC and the foreign and provincial press (Taylor 1999: 161). Therefore, overseas news received on the news wires by media outlets did not require further censorship. However, uncensored information reached the Polish Government in Exile via encrypted radio messages and via couriers sent by the Polish Underground during the war. This information was generally communicated to British officials in the Foreign Office and the Political Warfare Executive, and these two offices offered advice regarding what information could be disseminated, and they played a significant role in framing news from Polish (and Jewish) sources.[44]

In addition to the printed press, the Ministry of Information had a strong interest in the broadcasts of the BBC. Bracken made the 'clear-sighted distinction ... between the overseas and home services of the BBC' (Lysaght 1979: 202): overseas broadcasts were the voice of Britain at war and therefore required sustained government input, while the Home Service was censored in the same way as newspapers – that is, it operated under the same 'voluntary' regime as newspapers. Bracken did not deem it necessary to have legislation passed to increase government control over the BBC. In this way, Bracken sought to maintain control over the BBC's overseas broadcasts, but to sustain its 'renowned' independence (which would maintain its standing and influence overseas), which in turn would allow the British government and the Foreign Office to deflect criticism from the government to the BBC.

In August 1941, the Political Warfare Executive (PWE) was established on the advice of a ministerial committee composed of Brendan Bracken, Anthony Eden and Hugh Dalton. In theory, the PWE was under the control of the Ministry of Information for administration, the Foreign Office for policy and the Ministry of Economic Warfare for liaison with irregular special operations. In practice, as Robert Bruce Lockhart, an under-secretary of the Foreign Office and the director-general of the PWE, noted, 'it was impossible to separate policy from administration' (Young 1980: 20).[45] Prime Minister Churchill approved the organization on 21 August, and the PWE was handed the brief to co-ordinate British propaganda to enemy and enemy-occupied countries.[46] The organization sought to conceal its activities from public and, indeed, parliamentary attention. Robert Bruce Lockhart, in his role as chairman of the PWE's executive committee, provided general briefings to a parliamentary committee headed by Commander Stephen King-Hall, but close parliamentary supervision was avoided. In a letter dated 30 April 1942, Anthony Eden rejected King-Hall's proposal for formal liaison between the parliamentary sub-committee and the PWE on the grounds that

54 Censorship, self-censorship and the discursive environment

many PWE activities were secret. Eden then stated that he wished to keep all of PWE's activities secret as he did not want British 'propaganda policy to be the subject of open debate'. Eden reasoned that 'once it becomes the subject of debate it ceases to be propaganda and simply provides the enemy with ammunition for counter-propaganda'.[47]

The PWE's tasks included framing how the war was to be narrated. For example, the PWE issued weekly directives to the BBC's European Service on what news to highlight and the angle to take. These directives were secret during the war, and the PWE worked to ensure that the media echoed British policy; the BBC was a key tool in this endeavour. The PWE also issued policy guidelines to Radio Świt (a British-controlled station broadcasting from the UK, but disguised so it seemed as though it broadcast from Poland), to ensure that the Allied (read British) war news policy was consistent across the airwaves. One of Świt's main objectives was to 'stimulate resistance to the invader on the part of all classes of the population', though it was recognized that the audience was mainly composed of organized listening posts.[48]

The PWE provided a forum for regular meetings between the Foreign Secretary (Anthony Eden), the minister of economic warfare who had responsibility for SOE (Hugh Dalton, later Roundell Palmer (Lord Selborne)) and the minister of information (Brendan Bracken), with a Foreign Office official (Robert Bruce Lockhart) acting as chairman. The PWE drew staff from the Foreign Office and the Ministry of Information. Importantly, it had a base at Bush House, the BBC's key broadcasting centre in central London, as well as at Woburn Abbey outside London.[49] In a letter to Churchill dated 6 June 1944, Bracken outlined the organization:

The British Political Warfare Executive is, through its Director-General, under my administrative control and I am responsible to Parliament for its activities. Its output conforms with the Foreign policy of the Government and it accordingly refers to the Foreign Secretary all proposals involving questions of policy.[50]

The close co-ordination between the PWE, the Foreign Office and the Ministry of Information, including personnel secondments, helped to ensure that British propaganda was effectively communicated to different audiences, at home, in enemy countries and in occupied countries alike.

In addition, Ivone Kirkpatrick, the head of the Central Department at the Foreign Office – who after the war would become under-secretary of state at the Foreign Office, and was considered prior to the war to be 'one of [then Foreign Secretary] Lord Halifax's best men' (Briggs 1995: 304) – took up a position at the Ministry of Information on 8 April 1940 to encourage close co-operation between the BBC and the Ministry of

The Ministry of Information and the Political Warfare Executive   55

Information. His primary task was to ensure that the news editors of the BBC Overseas Services were fully cognizant of the foreign political problems of the day, and, most importantly, the Foreign Office's policy line (Kirkpatrick 1959: 151).

In February 1941 he became foreign adviser to the BBC (Taylor 1999: 170; Kirkpatrick 1959: 154), ensuring that British foreign-policy object-ives were well understood. Kirkpatrick's influence was substantially enhanced in October 1941 when he was appointed controller for the BBC's European Service.[51] As Allan Powell, chairman of the BBC's Governors, noted to Bracken on 18 September 1941, Kirkpatrick's 'time will largely be taken up by his daily association with PWE [Political Warfare Executive] and by the supervision of the carrying of their policy into effect right up to the microphone' (Briggs 1995: 310). Stenton (2000: 25) notes that 'Kirkpatrick's job was to impose instructions [from the PWE] on the BBC from within'. During the early part of his tenure at the BBC, Kirkpatrick echoed Bracken's sentiments:

the European Division will derive its policy instruction through its Controller, from the Government's new Political Warfare Executive which, as announced by the Prime Minister, is responsible to the Minister of Information and the Minister of Economic Warfare. This institution will be translated into broadcasting terms by the Director of Propaganda [at the BBC, Noel Newsome] and conveyed to the staff in his directives and by other means. (cited in Briggs 1995: 313)

In practice, the issued directives were not universally obeyed and, for some officials at the PWE, Kirkpatrick was to become 'more BBC than the BBC' in his defence of the BBC's independence (Briggs 1995: 383). Kirkpatrick (1959: 156) himself recognized the delicacy of touch that his position demanded:

too many people in the Ministry of Information and in other Government departments tried to influence and guide the B.B.C. in their day-to-day handling of affairs. Since the interests of Government departments or even sections of the Ministry of Information were apt to conflict, guidance from different official sources was often contradictory.

As the key person linking the BBC, the Ministry of Information, the PWE and the Foreign Office, Kirkpatrick's judgement was very significant, though important policy questions were discussed with colleagues in the Foreign Office and the Foreign Office line was generally followed.[52]

Kirkpatrick made two key appointments to deal with the day-to-day running of the European Service: Noel Newsome as head of the editorial side, and Douglas Ritchie as his deputy, who 'were responsible until the end of the war for every word spoken at the Bush House microphones' (Kirkpatrick 1959: 159).

56   Censorship, self-censorship and the discursive environment

Furthermore, in relation to the BBC's Polish Service, the Polish Service's editor, Gregory MacDonald, 'had a substantial share in the preparation of PWE directives' (Briggs 1995: 381). The role of these people and others helped preserve for the BBC some scope for manoeuvre and editorial independence. Nevertheless, Bracken was able to advise the prime minister in June 1944 that he was 'entirely satisfied that the output of the European Service of the BBC is being effectively controlled by His Majesty's Government through the agency of this Political Warfare Executive'.[53]

Harris (2004) notes that there emerged differences in the reporting of the war between the Home Service – delivered in English for the British audience – and the European Service – delivered in a wide range of European languages for audiences in continental Europe. In January 1943, for example, the European Service ran reports on deportations of Poles from the Lublin/Zamość region of Poland.[54] To the consternation of the Polish minister of the interior, the Home Service refused 'point blank a request from the European Service to use this material' in Home Service broadcasts.[55]

The variation between the two services reflected the different goals that the European Service sought to achieve in relation to the various audiences in enemy and occupied Europe; the work of liaison officials from governments in exile attempting to influence how the war was narrated back to their home countries; and, importantly, the way the British sought to narrate the war for domestic audiences. As Kirkpatrick (1959: 161) records, 'Our most difficult task was to satisfy the demands of the Allied Governments in Exile'. These differences had a significant impact on dissemination of news of what was happening to the Jews, and consequently on the knowledge acquired by various groups on the destruction of Europe's Jews. Listeners in occupied countries tuning in to the European Service could be better informed, at least on this issue, than British listeners tuning in to the Home Service.[56]

As we have seen, key decision makers at the BBC were attuned to the policy line of the Foreign Office, were familiar with its key figures and maintained good contacts with them. Indeed, Kirkpatrick was not alone in being seconded to the BBC from the Foreign Office during the war. His Foreign Office colleague, Frank Savery – the Foreign Office's counsellor to the Polish Embassy in London – also had an advisory role with the BBC's Polish Service, officially as an East European language supervisor, but he was also a key liaison officer between the British and Polish governments on the issue of BBC broadcasting to Poland (and elsewhere). Throughout the war, Savery attended editorial meetings at Bush House with Gregory MacDonald, Count Jan Baliński-Jundziłł

The Ministry of Information and the Political Warfare Executive   57

(the Polish Government in Exile's liaison officer), and a representative of the Political Warfare Executive (Briggs 1995: 423). These meetings helped set the policy for exactly how news scripts for overseas broadcasts were vetted prior to broadcast, and there can be little doubt that Foreign Office officials were well aware of the contents of the BBC's European Service's broadcasts – including its German and Polish services. These editorial meetings contributed to the micro-decisions of what specifically should be broadcast and influenced the directives to the news teams regarding how the news should be framed.

In addition, these meetings should be understood as a mid-level managerial forum where different stakeholders could articulate their views and make their complaints. For example, the Polish representative, Count Baliński, repeatedly complained through 1942 and 1943 that information supplied by the Polish Government in Exile was not being broadcast and that texts were being cut. The minutes of the forty-eighth meeting of the Polish Service's editorial staff (22 January 1943) record that Ivone Kirkpatrick advised Baliński 'that the Censors were not under BBC control, but were responsible to the FO [Foreign Office] and suggested that any further difficulty should be referred directly to him' (Kirkpatrick).[57]

In March 1943, Baliński again brought attention to British censorship, highlighting that neither a story about the deportation of people from fifty-seven villages in the Lublin district nor an account of the killing of fifty Germans during the battle for the Warsaw ghetto had been used. At the fifty-sixth meeting (19 March 1943), Baliński was assured that the first story would be used, and that enquiries would be made regarding the second story (which meant that approval from Kirkpatrick would be sought). At the following meeting, Baliński was advised that the ghetto material would also be used. These minutes indicate that the dissemination of material handed over to the British by the Polish Government in Exile was tightly controlled, and highlight British sensitivity towards material that related to or discussed Jews.

Foreign Office officials recognized the significance of the broadcasts to Poland. The British ambassador to the Polish Government in Exile, Howard Kennard, wrote to the British Foreign Secretary, Anthony Eden, on 17 February 1941, summarizing the importance of BBC broadcasts to Poland:

The news received by this channel circulated in the German occupation with remarkable speed. An informant recently arrived in this country described how, on receipt through the BBC bulletin of an important announcement of the British PM, he was sent by his political leaders to a neighbouring town in the General Government to convey the news.

58   Censorship, self-censorship and the discursive environment

Kennard noted that the main disseminators of news were Jews, commenting that, 'as Poles have a touching belief that thanks to their international connections the Jews are always well informed, stories heard from Jews often receive more credence than they deserve'.[58]

Although the number of radio sets in Poland declined steeply from 869,000 in 1938 to 405,000 in 1946 due to confiscation and destruction (Briggs 1995: 167), news broadcast from the UK on the BBC, or Radio Świt, was widely circulated orally and through the underground press, and played an important role in sustaining morale as well as providing information about the war effort. The Foreign Office and British intelligence community monitored the influence of the BBC in Poland through the war, in part by taking soundings from Polish couriers who arrived in Britain.[59] For example, Jan Nowak-Jeziorański, who was considered an A-grade informant (highly reliable), highlighted in his debriefing with British intelligence in December 1943 the importance of the BBC for the Poles.[60] In January 1944, Nowak-Jeziorański discussed the BBC's reception in Poland with BBC officials from the European Service.[61] Jan Karski also provided information on the reception of the BBC in Poland to British officials in late 1942 or early 1943.[62]

The European Service of the BBC also received letters from listeners in Europe throughout the war, and recent arrivals were interviewed (Kirkpatrick 1959: 159). In addition, the impact of broadcasting was assessed at the British media monitoring station in Stockholm. Reports from Stockholm helped the European Service to adjust its broadcasts to increase its influence on the various audiences in Europe.

The importance of the BBC was emphasized in 1942 by Brendan Bracken in a speech to the House of Commons on 8 April. The BBC broadcast the story on its European Service that evening, stating that 140 news bulletins were broadcast every day, that there were 1.5 million listeners in Germany, and that these broadcasts supplied 500 clandestine papers with their text. Bracken described the European Service as the voice of 'Free Europe'.[63] However, the voice of 'Free Europe' was frequently hesitant in directly referring to Jews, a hesitancy that reflected government policy.

In London, the Ministry of Information, in line with the concerns of the British Cabinet, and the Home Secretary in particular, sought to limit material that mentioned Jews. In a planning document entitled 'Combating the apathetic outlook of "What have I got to lose even if Germany wins"' from 25 July 1941, material about the war that could be publicized was described:

The Ministry of Information and the Political Warfare Executive   59

It should not be too extreme. Sheer 'horror' stuff such as the concentration camp torture stories like Jan Valtin's 'Out of the Night' repel the normal mind. In self-defence people prefer to think that the victims were specially marked men – and probably a pretty bad lot anyway. A certain amount of horror is needed but it must be used very sparingly and must deal always with treatment of indisputably innocent people. Not with violent political opponents. And not with Jews.[64]

The BBC followed this policy. On 26 September 1942, in an internal memo on broadcasting news of Nazi atrocities in allied countries, Sir Richard Maconachie cautioned that 'in the case of [atrocities committed against] Jewish children it would be better not to refer to their race'.[65] There was, however, no need for a strongly articulated policy to spell out that stories about Jews should be limited or framed in a particular way, and even in the case of the BBC (one of the organizations whose records are accessible) the evidence of such a policy, while present, reads as restatements of well-understood and established guidelines.

The marginalization of stories about atrocities against Jews was also sanctioned by a more universal BBC policy that was repeatedly articulated throughout the war. An internal BBC document, first circulated in 1940, entitled 'Presentation of News: Giving flesh to the bones – Description, interpretation, and comment', suggested that if news 'was not a hundred per cent "hard"' then the decision whether to use the information should be made on the basis of answers to the following questions:

1. Is it a useful contribution to the bulletin, to the impression we are using our bulletin to create?
2. Is it likely to be true and its use therefore in keeping with our integrity?
3. Will it be accepted as true by the listener?[66]

The document then pointed out that, 'Truth being often stranger than fiction, plenty of true reports have to be rejected on the grounds of incredibility.' The Nazi programme of genocide against Europe's Jews posed a serious problem for the British broadcaster. Without Foreign Office approval and confirmation, the news was not 'hard'. 'News' was appraised in relation to the three questions above, and given the scale of the slaughter and the use of gas chambers, information about the Holocaust was liable to be rejected.

A second policy statement, distributed to the BBC's European sub-editors on 12 February 1940, stated that 'all news and views, in addition to stimulating interest, must, however unobtrusively, serve the one real and fundamental propagandist aim of helping us to win the war as rapidly

60   Censorship, self-censorship and the discursive environment

as possible'.[67] News of mass murder was therefore problematic, but it could be put to propaganda use occasionally. A policy document from early 1942, entitled 'Propaganda to Europe', argued that atrocity stories could be used to exploit the fear and guilt emotions of the enemy or enemy populations.[68] Lindley Fraser's broadcasts on the German Service followed this policy and made several references to the Nazi mass murder of Jews during the war.[69] Broadcasting news of the Holocaust to the domestic audience was a different matter. The issues of believability, British anti-Semitism and maintaining BBC credibility all played a role in restricting the dissemination of information about atrocities against Jews to listeners in Britain.

Broadcast policy determined by the Political Warfare Executive limited the dissemination of news about the Holocaust on Radio Świt, which broadcast to Poland. An undated document (but most probably from late 1942 or early 1943) produced by the PWE's Research Unit provided broadcasting guidelines to the station's operators and reiterated the station's principal aims. These were:

to attack the enemies' morale in Poland ... to sustain the morale of the Polish people and to prepare for their active and effective intervention in the hostilities when the time arises ... to contribute to the formation of a strong and vigorous unified Poland after the cessation of hostilities.[70]

In relation to 'atrocity propaganda' the guidelines advised that 'in general this form of propaganda is more appropriate to countries which have not experienced German occupation'. It also instructed operators 'not [to] weaken verisimilitude by informing the Poles of things they see daily'. The 'Jewish Question' was also specifically highlighted. The guidelines stated: 'Express sympathy for the suffering of the Jews and indignation at their treatment. The Germans will be required to compensate them after the war. Avoid controversial issues.'[71] These guidelines were discussed with the Poles, and consultation with senior Polish politicians was frequent, but it was not an equal relationship, despite the British proclaiming their willingness to defer to the Poles on purely internal Polish matters.[72] The definition of what constituted 'purely internal matters' ultimately rested with the British. Issues relating to Poland's minority populations, including Jews, remained under British control since they had a significant bearing on the British foreign-policy position. For example, minorities east of the Soviet 1939 line of occupation highlighted the question of Poland's postwar borders; Poland's Jews brought up the issues of refugee policy, rescue and retaliation. And while extending expressions of sympathy towards Jews and stating that the Germans would have to compensate them at the end of the war were

The Ministry of Information and the Political Warfare Executive   61

approved by the PWE, highlighting the mechanisms and scale of the Holocaust remained 'controversial'.

Harold Osborne of the PWE was responsible for reading and approving all work prior to dissemination; Ernest Thurtle (a junior government minister from the Labour Party) liaised between the Research Unit and Polish sources of information.[73] The Polish government could express its views, but it was expected to adhere to the general broadcasting principles. News of atrocities against Jews was seen as 'controversial' by British officials, and broadcasting news about atrocities to Poland was judged to be unnecessary. The result was that news of the unfolding Holocaust, as far as can be established, rarely featured on Radio Świt. Radio Świt, though employing Poles, was, as Laqueur (1998: 116) notes, 'a British station'.[74]

Documents contained in Stanisław Mikołajczyk's files on Radio Świt at the Hoover Institute Archive suggest that its broadcasts were not too dissimilar from the BBC's European Service in relation to Jews and atrocities.[75] Since Świt and the European Service received guidance and instructions from the same office (PWE), this should not be surprising. General policy for the BBC's European Service dovetailed with more specific policies that marginalized stories about the Nazi atrocities against Jews.

On 27 April 1943, Sir Richard Maconachie, at that point the BBC's Home Service Controller, noted in a confidential memorandum that '[t]he Director-General after discussion with the Chairman considers the present time is not opportune for dealing with the Jewish problem in our programmes' (Harris 2004: 300).[76] At this point the Warsaw ghetto uprising was in progress.[77] This assertion closely mirrored the government's line. The government expected the BBC to function as a key propaganda tool and, on the issue of news about Jews broadcast to domestic audiences, the BBC was fairly reliable. In 1941 Brendan Bracken advised the House of Commons that the BBC governors 'have always recognised that in wartime it is necessary and right that the Government should control the policy of the BBC in matters affecting the war effort, the publication of news, and the conduct of propaganda' (Briggs 1995: 308, Harris 2004: 315). The outline of the BBC policy in relation to the Jews, given by Director-General Robert Foot on 18 November 1943, and agreed to by the BBC's board, could easily have been delivered by a representative of the government:

We should not promote ourselves or accept any propaganda in the way of talks, discussion, or features, with the object of trying to correct the undoubted anti-Semitic feeling which is held very largely throughout the country; but that we should confine ourselves to reporting in the news bulletins, the facts, as they are

62 Censorship, self-censorship and the discursive environment

reported, from time to time, of Jewish persecutions, as well as any notable achievements by Jews ... After full consideration we are convinced that in the interests of Jews themselves, this is the right policy to adopt at the present time, and any other policy would tend to increase rather than decrease the anti-Jewish feeling in this country. (Harris 2004: 300)[78]

For the BBC, 'facts' referred to stories confirmed (and therefore approved) by the Foreign Office. The same was true for Radio Świt. The Foreign Office was well aware that confirming stories could have foreign-policy implications. The UN declaration of 17 December 1942 and the debates in Parliament that focused on the systematic Nazi killing of Jews led to political pressure for a more relaxed immigration policy. The issue of Jewish refugees was discussed by the War Cabinet Committee on the Reception and Accommodation of Jewish Refugees – a committee that included Home Secretary Herbert Morrison, Foreign Secretary Anthony Eden and the Secretary of State for the Colonies, Oliver Stanley.

Home Secretary Morrison sought to limit the number of foreign Jewish refugees allowed into Britain, arguing that 'there is considerable anti-Semitism under the surface in this country. If there were any substantial increase in the number of Jewish refugees or if these refugees did not leave this country after the war, we should be in for serious trouble'.[79] The April 1943 Bermuda conference was judged a success precisely because it dampened calls for the Allies to provide refuge to those suffering Nazi persecution and did not commit the UK to relax border controls. As David Cesarani (1994: 180) argues, 'The Bermuda Conference on refugees, called into being by Britain and America in response to the public outcry in December 1942, was essentially a public relations exercise'. The British and American governments could be seen as doing something in response to news released in November and December 1942 by various concerned publics in the West and by the various exiled governments. However, it was clear to Ignacy Schwarzbart in July 1943 that the 'results of the Bermuda Conference were very negligible'.[80]

Importantly, the experience of highlighting the annihilation of Jews in December 1942 encouraged Foreign Office officials to take an even more conservative approach to news about Jews through 1943 and 1944. Jeremy Harris (2004: 316) persuasively argues that 'the joint declaration [i.e. the UN declaration] by the Allies attacking Germany's treatment of the Jews seemed to produce a counter-reaction both in the Foreign Office and the BBC, as the issue became more sensitive', and quotes the Foreign Office response to MP David Robertson's call for the BBC to broadcast for thirty days the details of 'the punishment that awaits all

The Ministry of Information and the Political Warfare Executive   63

those who are guilty of atrocities against Jews': 'We cannot afford to give this question such prominence that it would overshadow or exclude other themes which it is important for our propaganda to put across at this stage of the war.' In the context of ongoing genocide, such a response, though highlighting the need to publicize a broad spectrum of measures in the fight against Nazism, is indicative of the Foreign Office's desire to limit information about the fate of Jews, after the publicity devoted to it in mid-December 1942. Elsewhere, the reports in the *Jewish Chronicle*, which through December 1942 drew attention to the 'Most terrible massacre of all time' (11 December 1942), were not continued at the same intensity through 1943. Cesarani (1994: 179) argues that 'in the course of 1943, the sense of urgency tailed off'. This allowed the Foreign Office policy to remain without serious challenge.

The pressure for the December UN declaration had been mounting since the previous June, when information from a report from the Jewish labour organization in Poland, the Bund, was broadcast by the BBC on 2 June 1942. The Polish premier, General Władysław Sikorski, mentioned the killing of 'tens of thousands of Jews' in a 9 June broadcast on the BBC's Polish Service. This was followed on 9 July by a conference in London on German atrocities in Poland, chaired by Brendan Bracken, who, temporarily suspending general British policy guidelines on reporting news of Jews, drew on the Bund report and highlighted that 700,000 Jews had been killed in Poland. That evening Cardinal Hinsley, the Roman Catholic archbishop of Westminster, broadcast on the BBC's Home Service that 'the Nazis have massacred 700,000 Jews since the outbreak of war' (Bracken 1942: 55). Consequently, 'In the middle of 1942 the Press began to be filled with story after story telling of the actual slaughter of Jews' (Sharf 1964: 91). However, the news published and broadcast in June and July 1942 was exceptional. Both before and after June–July, the volume of news about Poland's Jews was markedly lower.

Rogers (1999a: 9) questions why Bracken chose to suspend his ministry's policy guidelines at this point, and not all branches of the government welcomed the development. The main reason is probably Bracken's (and Churchill's) view that such news demanded dissemination and that suppression was not a workable option, given the mounting pressure from the Polish Government in Exile and Jewish representatives on the Polish National Council, and the possibility of 'spinning' the information to German audiences as part of propaganda strategy (see Chapter 3).[81] In these circumstances, Noel Newsome's general directive to the BBC European Service on 26 June 1942 required the following angle to be taken:

64   Censorship, self-censorship and the discursive environment

The Jewish massacre story is now out and should be run big ... For occupied countries, don't treat the Jews as a race apart but as fellow-citizens of Europe standing solid with the rest of us against the Nazis. The Jew is indeed the enemy of the Nazis just like the rest of us. His special suffering entitles him to special honour.[82]

Newsome put these sentiments into practice himself. He was responsible for a series of talks on the European Service which were broadcast under the title of *Man in the Street*. The talk of 26 June focused on the massacre of Jews in occupied Poland and was particularly direct. Newsome highlighted the use of 'mobile lethal chambers' and described Hitler as the 'Satanic apostle of Death'.[83] The broadcasts on the BBC's European Service (especially its Polish Service) and the minutes of the meetings of the Polish Service's editorial team indicate that the dissemination of news of what was happening to Jews in Poland was closely managed.[84]

By September 1942 the 'voluntary' code of censorship had been reasserted, as Maconachie's 26 September internal memo readily illustrates, but the Polish Government in Exile pressed for further action in its dealings with the British through November and early December 1942, resulting in the declaration on 17 December.[85] Following the Bermuda conference of April 1943, the views of the Home Office and the Foreign Office on the presentation of news about Jews were fully re-established. In addition to Home Office concerns about anti-Semitism in Britain, the Foreign Office worried about the situation in the Middle East. According to Frank Roberts, an official in the Central Department (Germany Desk), the Foreign Office had to be careful not 'to give the Arabs the impression that we had suddenly turned over into a pro-Jewish, pro-Zionist organisation' (Milne 1995). Early 1943 saw a drop in media reports about Jews.

The dissemination of news about the Holocaust by the BBC followed the British government's informal tightening and loosening of policy on reporting the Nazi actions against Jews. As we have seen, late June and early July 1942 saw a relaxing of restrictions in the run-up to, and in the immediate aftermath of, the press conference held at the British Ministry of Information (Senate House) on 9 July; policy then was tightened until late November and December 1942. However, as we will discuss in Chapter 3, the period between July and November 1942 also coincided with a diminution in the amount of news about Jewish persecution being distributed by the Polish Government in Exile.

Through the first half of 1943 further discussion of the extermination of Jews was not encouraged, but it was not until after the Bermuda conference (19–29 April 1943) and the subsequent debate in the House of Commons (5 May 1943) that the effective tightening of policy was

The Ministry of Information and the Political Warfare Executive   65

achieved.[86] Policy was very cautiously loosened in March 1944, following the German takeover of Hungary, and reluctantly loosened in late June 1944 in the wake of the distribution of the Vrba–Wetzler report.

But the lulls and peaks in reporting the Holocaust also reflected that '[n]ews is event-, not process-oriented: bombing raids, invasions, and naval battles are the stuff of news, not delayed, often hearsay accounts of the wheels of the murder machine grinding relentlessly on' (Novick 1999: 23).[87] Government press conferences, debates in Parliament, UN declarations, pronouncements of senior politicians, are all newsworthy events. Both of the reporting peaks of 1942 occurred in relation to state-sanctioned and state-choreographed news releases. The peak of July 1944 was less controlled, as news about Hungarian Jews came from many sources, and their fate had been widely anticipated.

On 24 March 1944 President Roosevelt issued a warning to the Nazis about the mass killing of Jews. He stated,

In one of the blackest crimes of all history – begun by the Nazis in the days of peace and multiplied by them a hundred times in time of war – the wholesale systematic murder of the Jews of Europe goes on unabated every hour. As a result of the events of the last few days hundreds of thousands of Jews, who while living under persecution have at least found a haven from death in Hungary and the Balkans, are now threatened with annihilation as Hitler's forces descend more heavily upon these lands. That these innocent people, who have already survived a decade of Hitler's fury, should perish on the very eve of triumph over the barbarism which their persecution symbolizes, would be a major tragedy.

It is therefore fitting that we should again proclaim our determination that none who participate in these acts of savagery shall go unpunished. (cited in Dale Jones, 2004: 106)

That same day the PWE printed an aide-mémoire for its staff which gave a fair description of the Holocaust up to that point, including the killing of Jews by gas at Oświęcim.[88] Between the peaks in coverage, information on the Holocaust was broadcast and printed, but usually tucked deep in the inside pages of newspapers or reported on the airwaves at non-peak times. A perceptive and motivated reader/listener could learn a great deal about the Holocaust as it unfolded, but the less inquisitive would remain ignorant of much, especially during the reporting lulls.

The July 1942 peak in reporting highlighted the scale (at that point) of the Nazi programme of extermination. In December 1942 further slaughter was revealed, and the Allied response was extensively discussed both in print and on radio. These two periods open and close a specific narrative arc about the Nazi genocidal programme and the Allied reactions to it. The subsequent Bermuda conference and its aftermath functioned as an afterword to the main story. Further news of the extermination of the Jews

66   Censorship, self-censorship and the discursive environment

was deemed unnecessary and counterproductive (from the point of view of the war effort, of inhibiting anti-Semitism and of inhibiting a refugee crisis), and Foreign Office officials argued that the salvation of the Jews rested on the defeat of Nazi Germany. Old news could be repeated or repackaged. For example, the account of Jan Karski (the famous Polish courier) of Bełżec (in reality Izbica) was 'secured' by Arthur Koestler for a BBC News Talk on the European Service on 2 July 1943.[89] It was broadcast in all languages at the request of Noel Newsome, seven months after Karski had delivered his information.[90]

The precedence of the Foreign Office views was important in restricting the broadcasting and publishing of news of the unfolding Holocaust. In early 1943, Lord Selborne wanted the Polish courier, Jan Karski, to 'inform as many people as possible' about what he saw in occupied Poland. Unlike the Foreign Office and PWE officials, he thought stories of German atrocities were good propaganda (Wood and Jankowski 1994: 172). Derek Tangye, a MI5 agent, arranged a meeting for Karski with Freddie Kuh, head of the American Associated Press Bureau in London (Tangye 1990: 88). During the first half of 1943 Karski met many journalists, publishers and writers, including Victor Gollancz and Arthur Koestler. However, PWE and Ministry of Information censorship, together with the acquiescence of newspaper editors, controlled the flow of news of Nazi actions against Jews to the general public. Koestler's broadcast based on Karski's testimony reiterated information that had been circulating in Britain and the US since the previous December, and can be understood as an attempt to respond to demands to highlight what was happening to Jews without revealing more recent news that could stimulate demands for more robust actions such as retaliation or the provision of sanctuary in Britain for refugees.

On 5 December 1943, the Home Service broadcast a news talk at 1 p.m., entitled 'Report of atrocities against Jews', which charted the scale of the atrocities since the UN declaration the previous December. The presenter, Frederick Allen, informed listeners, 'By the end of March it is estimated that one million – yes, one million – Jews had been executed or had died in Polish [sic] camps'.[91] Such talks and news reports were relatively rare on the Home Service, and tended to under-report the actual scale of the slaughter. Estimates from Polish and Jewish sources were higher. Elsewhere, atrocity fatigue set in. Dina Porat (1990: 41) records that in Palestine 'the extermination ceased to command special attention once the details had become familiar' and notes that a month of mourning in late 1942 'proved to be too great a burden on the public'.

British intelligence and the Foreign Office

The transformation of Auschwitz from a concentration camp of particular severity to include a death camp occurred, in earnest, in May 1942.[92] It was not publicized during 1942 by the Polish Government in Exile and others as a centre where the extermination of Jews was taking place, and was not accommodated within the two choreographed reporting peaks of June–July 1942 and December 1942. Consequently, any reports about Jews being systematically killed at the camp could not be easily integrated into the established narrative arc that reached its conclusion with the UN declaration in December 1942. News of *another* death camp in this sense added nothing and was therefore redundant in the context of British and US policy.

British intelligence operatives had faced a similar issue a year earlier, in September 1941, in relation to the mass slaughter of Jews carried out by the German Order Police. Nigel de Grey, later the deputy director of the Government Code and Cipher School at Bletchley Park, but at that point the head of research at Hut 3, read deciphered German Order Police communications. He reported to Churchill on 12 September: 'The fact that the police are killing all Jews that fall into their hands should now be sufficiently well appreciated. It is therefore not proposed to continue reporting these butcheries specially unless so requested' by the prime minister (cited in Smith 2004: 116). Smith (2004: 116) argues that the word 'specially' suggests that the reports on what was happening to the Jews were commissioned by Churchill himself.[93] The practice of British intelligence of not reporting on the massacres of Jews in autumn 1941 was followed in 1943 by the British Foreign Office, the PWE and the Ministry of Information, though for different reasons.

For British intelligence, the killing of Jews by the Nazis was recognized as standard practice and was not seen as enhancing an intelligence picture of Nazi activities in the East that would help the war effort. The Foreign Office, the PWE and the Ministry of Information handling of information about the Holocaust related to how the war was to be narrated to various constituencies. The dissemination of news about Auschwitz therefore faced a series of censorship issues. In addition to British and American concerns about reporting news of atrocities and Jews, any effort to reveal that Auschwitz included a death camp for Jews was confronted by the fact that such information (that the Nazis were systematically exterminating Jews) did not add anything new, other than another location.

Auschwitz, according to Cesarani (1994: 181) 'was never clearly perceived as the nodal point of the exterminating programme'. This is

68   Censorship, self-censorship and the discursive environment

certainly true for the British general public, partially because the information about the camp that reached the West was not fully appreciated due to the way in which the news of the unfolding Holocaust was choreographed in 1942. This, inadvertently, entrenched a narrative about the functions of various camps, including Auschwitz itself, and, given the general censorship line that discouraged specifically 'Jewish' stories and the preference to incorporate Jews as part of the respective nations in which they resided, disseminating news of the post-May 1942 functions of the camp was extremely challenging. These handicaps help, in part, to explain why news of the killing of Jews at Auschwitz that was disseminated through 1943 and 1944 failed to make an impact, and partially account for why Auschwitz as a site of non-Jewish Polish suffering continued to frame popular understandings of the camp through to late 1944.

It was only in mid-1944, with the tide of war turned decisively against the Germans, and the fate of Hungarian Jewry in the balance, that the opportunity to supplement the action–reaction narrative with a third movement – rescue, aimed at saving Jews (rather than just winning the war) – came into view as a real possibility and was articulated by a variety of officials and community leaders with some vigour, evidently energized by the establishment of the War Refugee Board by President Roosevelt in January 1944. It was in this new discursive context that news of Auschwitz as a death camp could be disseminated and make some impact on both policy-making constituencies and community groups. Nevertheless, the control of information remained very important, and a key way to regulate the dissemination of data, and influence how published material was understood, was for important information gatekeepers (the Foreign Office, Ministry of Information, PWE) to withhold distribution approval or acknowledgement.

During 1943, the Foreign Office itself, as well as other branches of government, expressed scepticism of some reports received from both Poles and Jews, detailing atrocities in Nazi-occupied Europe, and in Poland in particular. Scepticism was certainly aligned with wider policy objectives, and it is probable that this response to news of atrocities through 1943 and 1944 was a strategy to marginalize those stories and to legitimate inaction, rather than, as has often been assumed, an honest reaction to 'unbelievable' news. Victor Cavendish-Bentinck, head of the Joint Intelligence Committee (who had access to German Order Police and railway intercepts, which indicated the mass movement and killing of Jews), commented on reports of atrocities against Poles in August 1943, arguing that 'we weaken our case against the Germans by publicly giving credence to atrocity stories for which we have no evidence'. He was of the view that it was 'incorrect to describe Polish information regarding

British intelligence and the Foreign Office

German atrocities as "trustworthy". The Poles, and to a far greater extent the Jews, tend to exaggerate German atrocities in order to stoke us up. They seem to have succeeded'.[94]

Cavendish-Bentinck was writing in the context of increased pressure from the Polish Government in Exile on the British government to issue a formal statement on German atrocities in Poland, especially during the meeting between Churchill and Roosevelt at the Quebec conference.[95] On 5 August 1943 the Polish prime minister and minister for foreign affairs handed to Clement Attlee (deputy prime minister and leader of the Labour Party) an aide-mémoire detailing German atrocities against Poles in Poland, which called both for the punishment of the German criminals and efforts to limit the Germans' outrages.[96] This was passed to Owen O'Malley at the Foreign Office on 20 August. The aide-mémoire was, in the main, fairly restrained in its tone and provided a dated chronology of various atrocities starting on 24 December 1942 through to 28 July 1943. The entry for 17 July 1943 became the focus of the Foreign Office summary of the aide-mémoire, and it is on this summary that Cavendish-Bentinck commented. The summary stated,

Some children are killed on the spot, others are separated from their parents and either sent to Germany to be brought up as Germans or sold to German settlers or despatched with the women and old men to concentration camps, where they are now being systematically put to death in gas chambers.[97]

Cavendish-Bentinck's remarks have been the subject of much debate, due to the importance attached to them during the David Irving libel trial. Van Pelt (2002: 127) highlights the fact that Cavendish-Bentinck was referring to alleged atrocities against gentile Poles, not Jews, in the Zamość region, many of whom were sent to Auschwitz as well as to Majdanek.[98] The scepticism of Cavendish-Bentinck and others in the Foreign Office on the issue of gas chambers related specifically to the details in the Polish aide-mémoire, and not to gas chambers in general, in the context of a proposed British government statement on German atrocities in Poland. Foreign Office officials were concerned that the evidence, in this case – essentially being the entry for 17 July 1943 in the aide-mémoire – was thin, and sought to remove the reference to gas chambers from the statement of His Majesty's Government after it had been released. For instance, Roger Allen at the Foreign Office (Dominions and Intelligence Department) noted on 27 August,

I have never really understood the advantage of the gas chamber over the simpler machine gun, or the equally simple starvation method. These stories may or may not be true, but in any event I submit we are putting out a statement on evidence which is far from conclusive, and which we have no means of assessing.[99]

70 Censorship, self-censorship and the discursive environment

The Foreign Office was aware, as the memos of late August 1943 indicate, that giving official credence to reports of the use of gas chambers to kill the peasants of the Zamość and Lublin regions would have implications for policy as well as for British government credibility.[100] The deportations and atrocities in the Zamość area had been highlighted by Stanisław Mikołajczyk (at that point Polish minister of the interior, and leader of the Peasant Party) in a BBC Polish News Talk on 29 December 1942. Mikołajczyk reported, 'Peasants who show special qualities of leadership are sent off separately to Oświęcim', and argued that the Nazi plan had three stages: 'The first stage was the merciless destruction of the intelligentsia and of political, spiritual, scientific and social leaders. Next came the extermination of the Jews. And now they have begun a mass-extermination of the Polish peasants.'[101] This three-stage conceptualization of German policy in Poland was echoed in the PWE's central directive of 6 January 1943.[102] The directive noted 'the employment of Poland as a slaughter-house for Jews from other parts of Europe' and argued that the third stage of persecution – 'the extermination of the Polish people themselves in various carefully chosen districts' had 'only just begun'. The persecution of Poles allowed the PWE to narrate the persecution of Jews as part of a common pattern – in line with the established propaganda policy.[103] Mikołajczyk, at this point, was clearly concerned that the German anti-Jewish programme had been extended to non-Jewish Poles. In the Zamość and Lublin areas, German violence against Polish peasants had intensified, but those Poles who were sent to Auschwitz were not automatically dispatched to the gas chambers, though most did perish due to the camp's harsh regime.[104] The ethnic cleansing of these regions was only halted with the advance of the Eastern Front in 1943, and the resistance of those to be evicted – many of whom took to the forests and joined underground resistance cells.

Cavendish-Bentinck's claim that there was 'no evidence' to support the Polish assertions suggests that evidence the British had received from either Jewish or Polish sources was often questioned when it did not conform to British policy concerns; intelligence from the same sources on military operations was more readily accepted and often highly rated.[105] Given that the Polish Government in Exile had been campaigning for over seven months on behalf of the Polish population of the Zamość region without much return in the way of concrete action by the British government, Cavendish-Bentinck's comments also indicate the difficulties faced by the Poles in effectively communicating atrocity intelligence they had to the British. Communicating news about Jews faced additional difficulties, especially during the 'lull' periods of news reporting (that is, outside the periods of British-sanctioned choreographed news events).

Thus British responses to atrocity stories in general, and to news of the slaughter of Jews in particular, were aligned with efforts to narrate the war as a British fight against tyranny in order to sustain the British people's morale and commitment to the war effort. Focus on the Jewish tragedy, it was thought, could undermine British unity and increase anti-Semitism in Britain. There was also the conscious desire to avoid the excesses of First World War propaganda, in part because it was felt that some information would be believed neither at home, leading to mistrust in information propagated by the state, nor abroad, thereby alienating allies and potential allies in enemy countries.

It is therefore likely that the British reluctance to respond to, or even note, many of the reports about atrocities against Jews affected how the Poles engaged with their erstwhile ally. For example, the Polish courier Jan Karski met British foreign minister Anthony Eden on 4 February 1943.[106] Karski provided an account of the fate of the Jews in Poland, which resulted in Eden reporting to the War Cabinet only that 'the entire population of Warsaw, including the remnants of the Jews, is united in their hatred for, and resistance to, the Germans'. Everything else Karski had said, according to his colleague Jan Nowak-Jeziorański, was expunged from the record.[107] Nowak-Jeziorański argued in 2001 that

the UK and US officialdom for a long time preferred to pretend that they were not aware of the scale of the Holocaust. That is why in all the internal reports based on the testimony of Jan Karski, and a year later based on my account, the information provided by us on the genocide of the Jews was removed.[108]

The example set at the top of the Foreign Office was mimicked by the Foreign Office's staff.[109] Since Jews were the prime victims of Nazi atrocities, the policy to downplay them disproportionately impacted on how Nazi policy against Jews was presented and understood.

However, the British censorship policy was not monolithic. As we have seen, the national press, the BBC and the official publications of Allied governments were subject to advice from the Ministry of Information, the Political Warfare Executive and the Foreign Office. Influential and prestigious publications like the *Jewish Chronicle* also came under this 'voluntary' regime. News of German atrocities against Jews from these outlets was limited and generally marginalized. In contrast, a local paper in east London, the *City and East London Observer*, from February 1942, carried a weekly subscription-only supplement entitled the *Polish Jewish Observer* which largely escaped the censorship regime.[110]

This supplement published detailed stories about what was happening to Jews in occupied Poland, including at Auschwitz. This was possible because the *City and East London Observer* had no real standing and had

72 Censorship, self-censorship and the discursive environment

very restricted circulation amongst parts of the East End Jewish working class; the subscription distribution for the supplement, which aimed specifically to publish news about Jews in Poland, further restricted its readership. The subscription list for the *Polish Jewish Observer* has not been located, and it is probable that it no longer exists. This prevents a detailed mapping of the newspaper's circulation.[111] However, there is some evidence that British intelligence monitored the paper as several stories that were published on 24 March 1944 relating to Stanisław Kot (at that point, the Polish minister of information) were collected and filed by the intelligence service.[112] Two weeks later (7 April 1944) the *Polish Jewish Observer* published a front-page story on the mass murder of Jews at Auschwitz.

The *Polish Jewish Observer*'s self-censorship in reporting what was happening to Jews in Poland was considerably less marked than that of papers which attracted Ministry of Information attention, and which had wider concerns, including the *Jewish Chronicle* (the voice of British Jewry) and *Dziennik Polski* (an official organ of an allied government).[113] Arguably, stories in the *Polish Jewish Observer* could be more easily dismissed than those appearing in more prestigious, trusted – and hence controlled – publications, including the *Jewish Chronicle*, the rest of the national press and the BBC.

The freedom of the *Polish Jewish Observer* to publish about Jews and about atrocities strongly indicates that the censorship regime in Britain was hierarchically ordered. Marginal press outlets with very restricted circulation were significantly less controlled than more prestigious, more widely circulated publications. This becomes increasingly apparent when it is noted that the publisher of the *Polish Jewish Observer* was Joel Cang, who, during the 1930s, had been the Warsaw correspondent for the *Manchester Guardian* and also worked for the *Jewish Chronicle*. After the war Cang briefly returned to Poland to provide stories for these two papers (and *The Times*). He later became an editor on the *Jewish Chronicle*'s foreign-affairs desk. Through the war Cang maintained good contacts with these two papers.[114] It is therefore almost certain that, through Cang, as well as through Jewish representatives on the Polish National Council, both the *Manchester Guardian* and the *Jewish Chronicle* had access to the same information about Auschwitz that reached Britain and was published in the *Polish Jewish Observer* throughout the war.[115] It is also probable that Cang advised journalist colleagues in Britain of stories published in the *Polish Jewish Observer*.[116]

There was no clear boundary between formal 'advice' given by the Ministry of Information and editors' self-censorship in the name of 'responsibility' or the British war effort, but the latter phenomenon was extremely powerful. The *East London Observer* (not the subscription-only supplement) itself did not publish more than a couple of stories on the Holocaust or events in Poland through the war, and its pro-USSR editorial line contrasted with the tone of the *Polish Jewish Observer*. In short, the two papers were very different, with little evidence of any cross-over or synergy in reporting the war. Even the stories of global significance, such as a September 1943 article highlighting that over half a million Jews had been killed at Oświęcim, were not picked up by the *East London Observer*, meaning that only subscribers to the *Polish Jewish Observer* were informed of this news.

Information about German atrocities against Jews remained restricted and controlled in Britain despite one outlet publishing detailed information that had been distributed by the Polish government. It is in this context that the comments made by the Home Secretary, Herbert Morrison, at the Hackney Rotary Club on Tuesday 13 May 1943, praising the free press, should be placed. Morrison argued that 'taking our press as a whole, it has played the game by the nation's cause ... A free press has been a great asset to the nation in time of war'.[117] Morrison's notion of a free press thus referred to a press that was aware of its 'responsibilities' during the national crisis of war, and moderated its behaviour accordingly.

UK–US censorship liaison

Censorship came under the purview of the Ministry of Information in May 1940. In December 1940, the British established their Censorship Western Area Office in New York. Co-operation with the Americans was fairly close, and 'there was an informal arrangement by which they [the US authorities] would receive any interesting information derived from British censorship operations in the western hemisphere' (Hinsley and Simkins 1990: 144). In fact, the sharing of material intercepted by British Postal Censorship was somewhat more formalized. The 1943 Postal Censorship Allocation List – the instruction manual that advised censors where to forward particular pieces of intercepted information – provided details of the sort of intercepted material to be forwarded on to various British government departments and agencies. It also included twenty pages of instructions of the kind of material to be passed to the Americans through the Division of Reports, Washington (DRW) – the office established to co-ordinate British–American postal censorship and the channel through which material was handed to the Americans.[118]

The allocation list notes that 'by mutual agreement, information derived from intercepted communications is interchanged between

74   Censorship, self-censorship and the discursive environment

British and US Censorships'.[119] Intercepted material passed to the Americans was subsequently distributed to various US government departments. Significantly, in May 1943, Ignacy Schwarzbart's post, which included Jerzy Salski's account of the mass murder of Jews at Auschwitz, was intercepted and forwarded by Postal Censorship to the DRW and then onwards to American Censorship.[120]

This kind of close co-operation and exchange of intercepted post was regulated in 1941, following the US's entry into the war, by an agreement between the UK, the US and Canada, which aimed to effect as much co-operation as was possible.[121] Transatlantic mail, for instance, passed through censorship posts at Bermuda and Trinidad, and the British shared techniques for searching diplomatic bags with the Americans (Breitman and Goda 2005: 14). The War Office also liaised with US authorities on the issue of censorship, and in October 1941 there was an exchange of protocols used to classify the level of secrecy accorded to documents.[122] In this manner, much information crossing the Atlantic was controlled.[123]

In the US itself, there was widespread recognition of the need for censorship during the war. At the end of December 1941, Stephen Early, press secretary to President Roosevelt, commented that it is an 'amazing fact to me to see the press and radio asking for rather than standing solidly against such a thing as censorship' (cited in Sweeney 2001: 3). Media institutions were keen that censorship be universal within the state, so that no particular organization had an unfair competitive advantage.

Byron Price, the executive editor at the Associated Press, was brought in by Roosevelt to head up the Office of Censorship when it was founded on 19 December 1941. It was endowed with wide-ranging powers to censor communications coming into and going out of the United States. In March 1942, the US Attorney General Francis Biddle expressed his view that Price could control the 900 commercial radio stations in the country (Sweeney 2001: 7). Like the Ministry of Information in Britain, the Office of Censorship adopted a voluntary censorship regime within the borders of the country and a mandatory regime for material crossing the country's borders. This voluntary regime was framed by a set of guidelines published on 15 January 1942, which 'regulated' print publications and broadcasts within the US.

The movement of personnel – from the privately owned media sector to state organizations – reflected the different media landscape in the US compared with Britain (in Britain, as discussed above, the movement was in the opposite direction – from the state to the BBC). In the United States, there was no organization analogous to the BBC in scope or influence, or with comparable links to the state apparatus. Nevertheless, in both countries the free press was brought under censorship. And in both countries, the legal power that underpinned the voluntary regime was occasionally invoked. In the US, Fr Charles Coughlin's anti-Semitic magazine *Social Justice* was sanctioned, while in Britain the pro-USSR (and frequently anti-Polish) *Daily Worker* was banned for a period in 1941 and 1942.

Co-operation between the British Ministry of Information and the US Office of Censorship was enhanced by Byron Price sending a representative, John Knight, to London. The British chief press censor, Admiral George Pirie Thomson, recalled in his 1947 book that 'British and US censorships were working together in London in closest harmony' (Thomson 1947: 174). The US model of censorship relied very heavily on self-censorship, and Byron Price worked to ensure that the voluntary system functioned effectively by building trusting relations with the media community. In relation to the stories from Europe about Jews, the tone of reporting was strongly influenced by the newspaper of record, the *New York Times*, and its proprietor, Arthur Sulzberger.

Another important institution that heavily impacted on the narration of the war in the US was established in June 1942 by the US government. The Office of War Information had the remit to better control the content and form of information relating to the war (in a broad sense) which was published, broadcast and distributed in the United States. Headed by the journalist, author and broadcaster Elmer Davis, it was also tasked with communicating the government's policy, and ensuring information not of benefit to the enemy was disseminated.[124]

The BBC's director of European Broadcasts, Noel Newsome, visited the United States in September 1942, and was advised of the mission and internal procedures of the Office of War Information (OWI). Newsome spoke with senior OWI officials in New York; among them were the news section radio control chief and the director of overseas outposts. Newsome also visited the OWI headquarters in Washington, DC.[125] By October 1942, the Office of War Information had established close links with Britain's Political Warfare Executive. At 12 noon every Wednesday, the PWE's central directive was available for the Office of War Information,[126] and the close relationship between these offices allowed the story of the war to be co-ordinated on both sides of the Atlantic.[127]

Like its British counterparts – the Ministry of Information and the Political Warfare Executive – the Office of War Information was sensitive to American public opinion regarding Jews, and 'occasionally intervened especially to ensure that the plight of the Jews did not overshadow that of

76   Censorship, self-censorship and the discursive environment

any group and that Jews did not figure prominently in denunciations of Nazi brutality' (Milland 2001: 1078). As in Britain, American censors were concerned that the mention of Jews could inflame anti-Semitism.

Wyman (2007: 9) notes that '[i]n the spring of 1942, sociologist David Riesman described anti-Semitism in the US as "slightly below the boiling point"'. That same year the Office of War Information sought to censor a small New York magazine, *She*, which published a survey which revealed anti-Jewish attitudes in 75 per cent of those women surveyed. Towards the end of the war pollster 'Elmo Roper warned, "anti-Semitism has spread all over the nation and is particularly virulent in urban centres"' (Sweeney 2001: 94). On 14 January 1944, the *Jewish Chronicle* in London published a front-page story entitled 'More Jew baiting in USA', which described anti-Jewish slogans being written on doors and windows over the Halloween period in Hartford, Connecticut. It quoted a report from the *Hartford Times* to the effect that '[t]he extent of the area in which the epithets were placed on doors and windows suggests that this was not children's work, but a demonstration of bigotry or worse by adults'. The *Jewish Chronicle* carried further stories on anti-Semitism in the US over the subsequent months.[128]

Further similarities with the British practice of censorship existed in the American 'voluntary' approach. As noted, the American newspaper of record, the *New York Times*, needed no official persuading to marginalize stories coming from Europe depicting the atrocities inflicted on Jews. Deborah Lipstadt (1986) has extensively documented this phenomenon across American media, noting that atrocity stories were frequently seen as 'propaganda' or 'greatly exaggerated' and, even as late as December 1944, that Americans did not believe in the 'existence of gas chambers and death camps' despite the widespread publicity given to the Vrba–Wetzler report, the Mordowicz–Rosin report and Jerzy Tabeau's report (*A Report of a Polish Major*) in a publication of the Executive Office of the US War Refugee Board entitled *German Extermination Camps: Auschwitz and Birkenau*, published in November 1944 (Lipstadt 1986: 241, 242).

In a context characterized by varying degrees of antipathy towards Jews and recent immigrants, and where the Nazis could make political capital out of Allied aid to Jews, Lipstadt (1986: 272) indicates that Allied policy makers considered that

the most efficacious thing for the Allies to do was to try to ignore the tragedy and make sure those whose responsibility it was to disseminate information did the same. And the press, having convinced itself that there was nothing that could be done and having inured itself to the moral considerations of what was happening, followed suit.

The anti-Jewish discursive environment on both sides of the Atlantic proved a significant barrier to the dissemination of news about the fate of Jews in Europe. In both cases, close active censorship was rarely required, since *idées fixes* about Jews, about how society perceived Jews and would react to news about Jews, and about the impact that such a reaction could have on the war effort inhibited challenge to the prejudicial discursive environment. Nevertheless, active censorship played an important role in regulating news about Jews, especially in the dissemination of information in English in and from Britain, as the policy practised by the Ministry of Information (outlined above) indicates. Milland's (2001: 1077) observation that in Britain a 'web of informal links between the state and this industry [media] ensured that newspapers were prepared to follow the state's preferred line' can be extended, without too much qualification, to the United States. In both cases 'voluntary' self-censorship was significant in judging what, in fact, was news. It is into this Anglo-American context that information gathered by the Polish Government in Exile and others regarding the destruction of European Jews was presented.

3 The Polish Government in Exile in London

The Polish Government in Exile arrived in London in 1940 after the fall of France.[1] Attitudes towards this government in Britain were not altogether welcoming. For many, especially those on the political Left, the Polish Government in Exile had not sufficiently distanced itself from the pre-war reactionary Sanacja regime, a regime that exhibited considerable hostility towards Poland's minority communities, including its 3.3 million Jews. Although the premier, Władysław Sikorski, had publicly rejected the policies of the Sanacja, being a member of the Front Morges, an anti-regime alliance of centrist parties in the 1930s, and had spent the later part of that decade as an instructor at the École supérieure de guerre in France, the government failed to allay the suspicions of many in Britain that it continued to pursue exclusionary right-wing politics. Part of the problem was that it did include people sympathetic towards the pre-war Polish government, including in its armed forces. On the civilian side, the political parties from both the Left and the Right were represented in the Cabinet of the Polish Government in Exile, including those from the Right who endorsed ethno-nationalist visions of Poland's future. Despite these voices within the government, key leaders sought, with varying degrees of energy, to formulate more inclusive processes and policy (Michlic 2006: 145).

This desire for greater inclusiveness was expressed in the creation of the National Council (Rada Narodowa), the government's parliament, in December 1939, on which two Jewish representatives sat. Ignacy Schwarzbart represented Zionist organizations and Shmuel Zygielbojm represented the principal Jewish socialist party, the Bund (from February 1942).[2] Attempts were also made to co-opt a member of the Ukrainian minority onto the council, but this was unsuccessful, because of the potential Ukrainian representatives' unwillingness to endorse the demand that the pre-war Polish borders be re-established after the war. Since this was a main war aim of the Polish Government in Exile, no compromise could be reached (Stola 1995: 45).

The Polish Government in Exile in London 79

Despite outward signs of plurality, consensus within the National Council was only maintained with difficulty and amid continuing tensions. Within the government, anti-Semitic members aligned with National Democracy – the integral nationalists who fostered anti-minority sentiment in pre-war Poland – had some influence. Politicians such as Marian Seyda and Tadeusz Bielecki did not jettison their anti-Jewish perspectives on arrival in Western Europe. For instance, Seyda, who was a minister without portfolio, adopted a pragmatic approach. At a meeting of the National Council which took place on 9 January 1940 in Angers, France, Seyda declared that 'the use of anti-Semitism is an undesirable strategy at the present time', but only eight months later, in London, he contributed to the first issue of *Jestem Polakiem* (I am a Pole), a paper published by former members of the far right National Radical Camp (Obóz Narodowo Radykalny) (Wróbel 2003: 513), which profoundly disturbed Polish Jews in Britain, as well as sections of the Polish Government in Exile.

Seyda defended his position by arguing that he had made a patriotic statement and criticized the Polish Jewish journalist Jerzy Szapiro for bringing ethno-nationalist statements in *Jestem Polakiem* to the attention of the British press (Michlic 2006: 146). Szapiro was the former bureau chief for the *New York Times* in Warsaw who had managed to reach Paris following the German invasion of Poland (Leff 2005: 78).[3] *Jestem Polakiem* was a continual source of concern for the leadership of the Polish Government in Exile (including Sikorski) as it damaged the reputation of the government.

The government's official publication – *Dziennik Polski* – was in general tightly controlled, but a review of *Alarm* – a volume of Antoni Słonimski's poetry – written by a former Kraków art historian, Karol Estreicher, slipped through the editorial process and featured on page three of the 17 August 1940 edition of the paper. The review questioned Polish Jews' status as Poles and had the potential to inflame tensions between the Polish government and important constituencies in Britain.[4] Estreicher worked in London as Sikorski's secretary and ran a team of people recording Polish cultural losses during the war. The article in *Dziennik Polski* was written in a personal capacity, but due to Estreicher's position within the Government in Exile he was heavily criticized by Jan Stańczyk during the 26 and 28 August 1940 sitting of the Polish Council of Ministers.[5] Fortunately for the Polish Government in Exile, this article did not attract a great deal of attention outside Polish circles, and Wróbel's (2003: 528) assertion that '[n]ot a single anti-Semitic article appeared in *Dziennik Polski* during the entire war' requires only very minor qualification. However, the view expressed by Estreicher was not

80   The Polish Government in Exile in London

uncommon, and integral nationalists, such as Tadeusz Bielecki, Adam Doboszyński and others, repeatedly expressed it orally and in the Polish émigré press not directly controlled by the government.

A further source of anxiety for the Polish leadership was anti-Semitism in the Polish armed forces. There is no sound way to assess how the level of anti-Semitic sentiment in the Polish forces evacuated to Britain in 1940 compared with that found in the British military but it certainly was fairly common, and attracted the attention of some members of the British parliament. The MP Denis Noel Pritt, described by George Orwell as 'perhaps the most effective pro-Soviet publicist' in Britain, who had been expelled from the Labour Party for defending the Soviet invasion of Finland, repeatedly lobbied the Foreign Office on the issue of anti-Semitism in the Polish forces based first in France and later in Britain.[6] It is quite possible that Pritt was concerned about the discrimination and hostility faced by Polish Jewish service personnel, but there are strong grounds to suspect that Pritt's interventions were politically inspired.

The Soviet justification for its invasion and occupation of eastern Poland partially rested on the notion that it was liberating national minorities oppressed by the Sanacja regime, and it created false statistics describing the occupied zone as being more heavily populated by minorities than revised 1931 census figures would suggest. On 22 October 1939, the Soviet government held elections for regional assemblies. These assemblies subsequently requested that parts of eastern Poland be incorporated into the Belarusian or the Ukrainian Soviet Socialist Republic respectively. At the same time thousands of Polish citizens (including Jews) were deported to the depths of the USSR through 1940.[7] The Soviet attitude to the Polish Government in Exile was hostile, and it sought to depict the Polish government as a reactionary clique. Given that Pritt was extremely sensitive to Soviet policy, it is highly likely that Pritt's concern for the welfare of the Jewish members of Poland's armed forces was not unconnected with his propagation of Soviet policy.

The result of Pritt's initial letter to Richard Austen (Rab) Butler, the Foreign Office minister, was a Foreign Office investigation led by Roger Makins of the Central Department. Makins concluded that 'it seems quite on the cards that anti-Semitism is in fact quite rife in the Polish Army, but in this particular case [an anti-Semitic speech by a Polish Army captain] some allowance must be made for the mess-room exuberance of a Polish officer'.[8] This conclusion confirmed the phenomenon, but downplayed it because the British did not wish to embarrass their Polish ally and because the anti-Semitism detected was not particularly extraordinary in the context of pervasive British anti-Semitism. Butler wrote to Pritt on 27 July 1940, pointing out that 'there had undoubtedly

The Polish Government in Exile in London 81

been a certain amount of anti-Semitic feeling in the Army. No reports have so far reached us of any active persecution'. Butler referred Pritt to the official Polish government position, which had been articulated repeatedly through late 1939 and the first half of 1940. As early as 6 October 1939, Sikorski had endorsed the equal political and civil rights of Polish Jews. This was followed on 3 November 1940, and then again on 23 February 1942, by resolutions which proclaimed the government's commitment to pluralist principles based on the equality of Polish citizens regardless of race or religion.

Pritt remained unsatisfied and, on 5 August 1940, General Sikorski tried to end decisively the scandal, declaring that any soldier who took up arms for Poland was a Pole regardless of race or religion, and that the military authorities would take active care that these orders were observed. This declaration did temper the adverse publicity, but it did not extinguish anti-Semitism in the Army or the hostility of sections of the British parliament and press. Through August 1940, a series of British MPs launched attacks on the Polish Government in Exile. The communist pro-Soviet MP William Gallacher denounced the 'anti-Soviet and anti-Semitic propaganda' in the Polish press as 'Fascist', and on 27 August the Labour MP Josiah Wedgwood drew a parallel between Polish and German feeling towards Jews (Wróbel 2003: 513). The unremitting hostility of the pro-Soviet *Daily Worker* was also a perennial source of concern for the Polish Government in Exile.

These British parliamentarians who expressed greater or lesser degrees of sympathy with the Soviet Union were not alone in their hostility to the Polish Government in Exile. The conservative and liberal press frequently mocked and caricatured the government, for example through cartoons.[9] Stenton (2000: 282) contends that 'Beaverbrook's *Evening Standard* was alert for expressions of objectionable Polish opinion from the moment the Poles came to Britain' and argues that Poland was conceived as a 'backwater cursed with a haughty elite'. The response of the Government in Exile was to attempt to isolate the most damaging émigré publications and to work together with the British government to force their closure. After the Polish government adopted a policy that 'only one Polish political paper should be published' (Wróbel 2003: 513–14), *Jestem Polakiem* was condemned as a 'violation of national discipline' and closed in May 1941. Other papers had their publication suspended, such as *Wiadomości Polskie* (the Polish News), which insisted that there could be no compromise on restoring the 1939 borders and opposed the Polish government's policy on Polish–Soviet relations.[10] *Dziennik Polski* emerged as the single political paper, but given that it 'was run by representatives of the various allied governing parties, it was

82   The Polish Government in Exile in London

inconsistent and lacked a clear ideological profile', according to its Polish critics (Wróbel 2003: 514). *Dziennik Polski*'s reporting of the Holocaust was marked by the political tensions within the Government in Exile, but it was also influenced by pressures placed on it by the British.[11]

In drawing attention to anti-Semitism in the Polish Army and press, critics of the Polish Government in Exile identified a key flaw and – in the Anglo-American context – political weakness of that government. The cultural and social inheritance of the Second Republic carried by the Poles abroad was not something that could be overcome easily, and declarations by government officials and political leaders opposing anti-Semitism could easily be dismissed as exercises in bad faith and hypocrisy, or explained as being strategically expedient by critics such as Pritt, Gallacher and Wedgwood. In the eyes of many, though not all, of those Poles evacuated to Britain, and in Poland itself, the Jews were often perceived as a community apart.

The radical ethno-nationalism of the National Democrats, together with the less tolerant sentiment that had been hardening across the political spectrum during the second half of the 1930s, positioned Jews outside many Poles' 'universe of obligation', though the social distance between particular Polish and Jewish groups and individuals varied. Legislation passed in Poland on 31 March 1938 deprived some people – eighty-eight percent of them Jewish – of Polish citizenship (Michlic 2006: 148). For Polish Jews, therefore, restoring citizenship was a key issue. On 28 November 1941, this discriminatory legislation was overturned, but only because the more right-wing elements of the National Democrats had withdrawn from the Polish Government in Exile following the signing of the Sikorski–Maisky agreement of 30 July 1941.[12] Though it did not secure any guarantees on the Polish borders (hence the withdrawals from the Polish Government in Exile), this agreement paved the way for a Polish Army under General Władysław Anders to operate within the umbrella of Allied efforts against Germany, and it also enabled Polish citizens deported to the USSR in 1940 to leave the USSR via Persia alongside Anders's soldiers.

On 1 September 1941, in the context of a weakened political Right within the Polish Government in Exile, the twenty-seventh edition of the government's official English-language publication, the *Polish Fortnightly Review*, was entirely devoted to a discussion of the legal position of Jews in Poland. The *Review* highlighted the arrival of Jews in Poland from states that were hostile towards them in the Middle Ages and their situation in the lands ruled by the different partitioning powers in the nineteenth century, and listed the equal rights Jews enjoyed in independent Poland. The *Review* argued that in interwar Poland the high

The Polish Government in Exile in London

proportion of Jews in the population and Jewish significance in certain business sectors 'provided a jumping-off ground for anti-semitic tendencies in certain spheres of Polish society',[13] and noted the influence, within small sections of society, of anti-Semitism emanating from Germany. The *Review* concluded that Polish Jews enjoyed full rights in every respect as a matter of law.

It then proceeded to outline the Nazi anti-Jewish regulations, before discussing the policy of the Government in Exile. Here it highlighted the government's declaration on the equality of national minorities from 18 December 1939; Sikorski's 5 August 1940 declaration; Minister Jan Stańczyk's 3 November 1940 statement proclaiming equality in a liberated Poland irrespective of race, creed or origin; Sikorski's trip to the US in April 1941 where he stated that all Polish citizens 'and therefore the Jews also would be bound by a single principle: equal rights, equal duties';[14] and the resolution of the National Council of 10 June 1941, which reiterated Sikorski's statement in the US.[15] It also emphasized that the Polish government 'regards all cultivation of an anti-Semitic policy as harmful'.[16]

This edition was a firm response to allegations in Britain that the government was anti-Semitic, or that it pursued anti-Semitic policies. As an exercise in public relations it achieved some temporary success, but the government and its armed forces were haunted by accusations of anti-Semitism throughout the war. In relation to the Army, as we have seen, there was truth to a sizable proportion of these accusations. But in addition, just as the Polish government's Jewish policy was sometimes pitched to gain favour with various Jewish constituencies and to improve the government's image with its Western allies, those like Pritt who were opposed to the government or hostile to the Poles in London used accusations of anti-Semitism instrumentally.[17]

The presence of some anti-Semites in the government and within the Polish press corps made it easy for harmful generalizations, and for the view that the Polish government was particularly hostile to Jews, to gain wide currency. The 1 September 1941 edition of the *Polish Fortnightly Review* was therefore the government's attempt to appeal to public opinion by demonstrating that its policies were firmly in accordance with those of liberal Britain and the US. For this reason, the Polish government defined Polish Jews as part of the Polish nation.

As we saw in Chapter 2, British censorship policy insisted that Jews be treated as part of the nation in which they resided/held citizenship prior to the outbreak of war, and Polish Jews' official access to the British government was mediated through the Polish Government in Exile, which is often depicted by scholars as being pragmatic/instrumentalist

84   The Polish Government in Exile in London

in its resolutions on Jews. According to this view, the government's Western context is explicitly or implicitly seen as having a role in mitigating the anti-Jewish policies or views of its members (Engel 1987, 1993), and this perspective certainly has an evidentiary base. Mikołajczyk, minister of the interior until 1943 and then prime minister after Sikorski's death, refused to distance his Peasant Party from its 1935 position, which endorsed and encouraged Jewish emigration from Poland, in a February 1941 meeting with Ignacy Schwarzbart. Michlic (2006: 152) argues that this 'shows both the strength of the pre-1939 ideological heritage of the peasant movement and its instrumental use of the concept of a civic Poland in the wartime period'.

However, the Polish Government in Exile's oscillation on the civic/ethnic concept of Poland was not just the result of Western governments pulling the Poles to the civic side, while heritage and recent history pulled it towards ethnic homogeneity. The matrix of forces was more complex. From the very beginning of the war in 1939, the British sought to sustain their relations with the Soviet Union by accepting the Soviet occupation of eastern Poland insofar as it followed ethnographic and cultural lines. The British Foreign Office official, Frank Savery, suggested in his January 1940 meeting with Polish Foreign Ministry official Tadeusz Kunicki that population transfer could be a policy to create a more nationally homogeneous Polish state.

The Foreign Office commissioned the Foreign Research and Press Service, based at Balliol College, Oxford University, to investigate population transfer on a case-by-case basis in May 1940. The context in which this endorsement of national homogeneity took place was the widespread contention, shared on both sides of the Atlantic, that minorities had destabilized the European state system, especially in the 1930s. Increasing national homogeneity in the postwar period was on the West's political agenda during the war. And although the international focus was on the future of German minorities in Europe, the notion that national heterogeneity within a state was a weakness inevitably became more generalized. In relation to Poland specifically, Frank Savery, in an important memorandum from January 1940 which was widely distributed within the Foreign Office, noted that the interwar 'attempt to create a Polish State containing within its borders large alien, i.e. non-Polish, elements, amounting in all to about 30 per cent of the total population, has not proved a success'.[18]

The British did, however, wish Jews to remain in their countries of citizenship/origin, and refused to recognize Jews as a national group throughout the war. Any movement of Jews had serious implications for the Mandate in Palestine, in particular. The ideal situation would

The Polish Jewish full assimilation to the dominant culture in a way that followed the British model, a model which, as we saw in Chapter 2, was in essence anti-Semitic. William Denis Allen of the Foreign Office clearly stated British policy towards Jews in August 1942: 'Jews must be treated as nationals of existing states and not as having any separate Jewish nationality apart from the nationality shown in their passports'.[19] The fundamental difference in the British position and the position of sections of the Polish Government in Exile was one of process rather than principle. Increased homogeneity in Poland was widely called for, but, in the case of Jews, the British wished to see assimilation mainly for British strategic reasons, while some Poles wished to see emigration.

The Polish Government in Exile was also advised of a collapse in tolerance in Poland towards national minorities, including Jews, as the war progressed. In February 1940, Jan Karski wrote a report which included information on Polish reactions to the Nazi onslaught on Polish Jewry, in which he noted considerable hostility to Jews. The population, according to Karski, was split between those who were strongly critical of the Nazis' actions, and those who saw the Nazis as solving Poland's 'Jewish problem'. David Engel (1987: 64) demonstrates that Polish officials, realizing how damaging the report was, censored it so that the depth of anti-Jewish sentiment would not become known to Poland's British and French allies, and thus undermine their cause. It is likely that Karski himself revised the report (Engel 1983: 3).

The dual nature of all reports received by the Polish government in London needs to be noted. On the one hand, reports transmitted the news from Poland as understood by their respective authors. They were objective in the sense that they relayed this information as faithfully as possible. On the other hand, the reports actually sent could colour debate and political decisions made in London. They had the capacity to strengthen one faction vis-à-vis another (for example, National Democrats versus the left-leaning parties, with the Peasant Party empowered by its ability to cast its votes to swing decisions either way). As well as providing 'facts', they constituted political interventions to narrate the war in a particular way. For example, news of pervasive anti-Semitism in Poland from sources sympathetic to National Democracy could be seen as attempts to remove the mention of Jews from the political agenda. That is, if anti-Semitism was seen to be high in Poland, National Democrats could argue in the National Council and Cabinet for their vision of a future ethnically homogeneous Poland. Highlighting the plight of the Jews, from this perspective, was unnecessary. Since no scientific opinion surveys were possible during the war, data from various reports indicating widespread anti-Semitism constituted the best

86   The Polish Government in Exile in London

information available on social sentiment towards Jews, but should be treated with some caution.[20]

Several reasons for the decline in tolerance can be posited. First, the occupying Germans published anti-Semitic propaganda, which impacted on sections of Polish society. The German civilian administrator (*Landrat*) of Będzin, Udo Klausa, for example, on 11 September 1942 noted the importance of sustaining anti-Semitism amongst Poles in order to strengthen the racial hierarchy between different groups and to prevent solidarity between Poles and Jews developing (Fulbrook 2012: 273). Second, parts of society attempted to rationalize German anti-Jewish policy by examining the conduct of Jews. Blaming victims for the harms inflicted upon them was not limited to Poles. In Britain, a similar process of rationalization occurred in the Foreign Office, in the media and amongst the wider British population.

Third, German policy in Poland to execute those who aided Jews, and the provision of incentives to turn Jews over to the German authorities, further distanced some sections of the Polish public from Jews. These threats and incentives worked to discipline the Polish population, hardened in-group boundaries in some Polish milieux and further excluded Polish Jewish citizens from the notion of Polishness. Fourth, the failure of the Catholic Church to speak clearly against the persecution of Jews, together with traditional Catholic anti-Judaism, allowed antagonism towards Jews to deepen amongst some parts of Polish society.

Eleven months after Karski's report, the British were advised of anti-Jewish sentiment in Poland by Stanisław Kot, minister of the interior between 1940 and 1941 in the Polish Government in Exile, who had been charged by Prime Minister Sikorski to run subversive and underground civil activities in Poland.[21] In January 1941, Kot received a report from Prince Janusz Radziwiłł, a Polish aristocrat and leading figure in the nationalist and anti-Semitic Conservative Party during the 1930s, who remained in occupied Poland.[22] Kot secretly passed the information on to the Foreign Office's Frank Savery on 9 January 1941. Radziwiłł argued that the resolution of 3 November 1940, broadcast by Jan Stańczyk, in which he declared that 'the Jews ... as Polish citizens shall be equal with the Polish community in duties and in rights in liberated Poland', made a very poor impression in Poland.[23]

Radziwiłł stated:

Anti-Semitism still continues to exist among all spheres of the population: it has only taken another form. Polish opinion does not approve the violence applied to the Jews, but on the other side it must be emphatically declared that public opinion would not permit the return of the Jews to the positions and influence which they had before the war. The Jews have lost their dominating position

The Polish Government in Exile in London   87

especially in the economic world – in the wholesale trade and in industry – and Polish society will not admit that they should re-obtain the strongholds they have lost. Our Government (i.e. General Sikorski's Government in London) does not realise sufficiently this state of feeling. This can be seen for instance from the last broadcast of Minister Stanczyk, which contains a promise that in liberated Poland, the Jews will have equal rights with Poles. This speech made a disastrous impression in Poland even amongst the workmen belonging to the Polish Socialist Party. Anti-Semitic feelings have been strengthened by the attitude of the Jews, who, for instance, maintain that it is the fault of the Poles who unnecessarily provoked the war that they, i.e. the Jews, are now suffering so severely. When the war is happily over, the Jewish question will not cease to be a question of extreme actuality in Poland. This fact must be recognised by the Poles in London.[24]

Kot's motive in passing this information on to Savery was probably to advise the British of some of the tensions that the Polish Government in Exile was trying to deal with. There is also the possibility that he wanted to provide justification for his assertion, in conversations with representatives of British Jewry in France held in spring 1940, that the majority (two-thirds) of Jews would have to leave Poland after the war (Michlic 2006: 148; Stola 1995: 73), a position for which Kot was later criticized.[25] But the British were not averse to using Kot's statements for their own purposes. In 1940 Rabbi Maurice Perlzweig (a founder of the World Jewish Congress, and the first chairman of its British section) was invited by Rabbi Stephen Wise, president of the American Jewish Congress, to give a series of talks across the US.[26] Before he commenced his lecture tour, Perlzweig was thoroughly briefed by the British Ministry of Information. The British aim was to gain American Jewish support for the British (and Allied) cause prior to the US entry into the war. According to Nicholas Cull (1995: 55), Perlzweig's frank discussion of British appeasement of Arab insurgents and 'the anti-Semitism of the Polish vice-premier in exile Kott [sic], who spoke of resettling all Polish Jews in Southern Russia at war's end . . . established his credibility'. The mission was a success, as the Washington Convention of the American Jewish Congress gave a guarded endorsement of the Allies.

Like the Polish Government in Exile, the British (even within the FO) considered American Jewry an influential constituency in the United States.[27] The FO commentary on Radziwiłł's letter clearly sets out British thinking on this issue at the beginning of 1941. I.Z. Mackenzie contended that it was 'natural enough . . . that Poles surrounded by complaining Jews do not appreciate the importance of Jewish opinion to the Allied cause – and the value of M. Stanczyk's speech as a reply to complaints of anti-Semitism'.[28] Despite the fact that Kot's views on the desirability of resettling Jews had been earlier highlighted by an informal

88   The Polish Government in Exile in London

Ministry of Information publicist (Perlzweig), the British, especially Foreign Office officials, were keen for the Poles to adopt inclusive policies towards Polish Jews both for the short-term objective of managing (especially American) Jewish opinion prior to the US entry into the war, and for the longer-term objective of inhibiting migration out of Poland.

The Polish Government in Exile therefore played an important role in the Allied propaganda pitch to American Jewry. But intense ethno-nationalist pressures were exerted both in the form of information about sentiment in Poland and within the government's Cabinet itself. They were exacerbated by unchallenged stories of Jews welcoming the Soviet occupation of eastern Poland. Leading figures in the Polish Government in Exile, and in the British Foreign Office and War Office, accepted as fact that the behaviour of Jews in Soviet-occupied Poland fell below that expected of Polish citizens. In May 1940, during the Pritt controversy over anti-Semitism in the Polish Army, a War Office official (the signature is illegible) wrote to Roger Makins at the Foreign Office stating that '[t]he Jews' behaviour in Poland during the Russian advance must clearly have caused a feeling of animosity in Army circles which I think is justified'.[29] British officialdom's acceptance of how Polish Jews behaved during the Soviet occupation remained unaltered through the war. In July 1944, for example, Frank Savery wrote a report that discussed Polish–Jewish relations prior to and during the war. He highlighted 'over-population' and economic competition as factors in damaging Polish–Jewish relations in the pre-war period. Savery considered that due to the 'vast diminution of the Jewish population in Poland, the Jewish problem has ceased to be insoluble', but cautioned that attempts by Jews to 're-establish the old monopoly [in trade] will be vigorously resisted'. Savery then called on his Foreign Office colleagues

to remember that in 1939 very numerous elements of the Jewish proletariat in the east did in fact cooperate at once and very enthusiastically with the Soviet authorities; there is no doubt that in many cases Jews denounced to the Soviet authorities Polish officers who were concealed or disguised – officers who may have subsequently lost their lives at Katyn.[30]

Regardless of the questionable veracity of some of these claims, the fact that both British and Polish officials and leaders accepted them had an influence on Polish–Jewish relations specifically, and on how Polish Jews were apprehended more broadly.[31] General Anders, commander of the Polish II Corps, was certainly not the only Allied leader or official to view anti-Jewish sentiment in the Army as having been provoked by Jewish pro-Soviet activities in eastern Poland in 1939–41, and to call for the suppression of anti-Semitism not on principle, but on the grounds of

The Polish Government in Exile in London   89

political expediency, given the presumed strength of Jews' political influence in the US and the UK.[32] Senior Polish and British figures were generally agreed on how best to engage with Jewish audiences, but understandings formed about both Western and Polish Jewry, which informed policy, were, at least in part, informed by anti-Semitic stereotypes (Jewish influence in the West, Jewish proclivity for communism in Poland).

Following the US entry into the war in December 1941, the British were less concerned about gaining American Jewish favour. The situation for the Polish Government in Exile was somewhat different, for they continued to see both British and American Jewish opinion as important, and this divergence in perception fostered some tensions between the Poles and the British. Throughout 1942, the British were concerned about the activities of Zionists and what they saw as 'a campaign for the recognition of a distinct Jewish nationality'. Frank Roberts of the Foreign Office articulated the British position in a letter to Godfrey Lias at the Ministry of Information, dated 21 August 1942. Roberts argued that the issue of securing recognition for Jewish nationality was 'part of the propaganda for a Jewish sovereign state in Palestine and it also no doubt aims at securing separate Jewish representation at any Peace Settlement (the campaign for a Jewish Army ... has this in view)'. This 'Zionist' frame could accommodate disparate demands by Jewish representatives, of varying political hues, to have their voices heard, and Roberts maintained that

[r]ecent symptoms of the campaign [for the recognition of Jewish nationality] have been attempts by the Jewish Agency for Palestine to adhere to the United Nations Declaration, by various British Jewish bodies to obtain specific recognition of the sufferings of Jews in the Allied Declaration of 13th January on war crimes, and by religious Jews to secure representation in the councils of the Polish and Czechoslovak Governments in London.[33]

Roberts clearly indicated that the Foreign Office not only resisted various Jewish attempts to have a specific Jewish perspective heard at international fora, but also opposed the highlighting of Jewish suffering and looked askance at the possibility of Jewish religious representation on the councils of Allied governments. In addition, the Foreign Office expected Allied governments in London to follow the British line, and Roberts critically evaluated the fact that 'several of our allies are susceptible to pressure. General Sikorski in particular has in the past given us reason to suspect that he was not averse from embarrassing His Majesty's Government if he could at the same time appease influential Zionists'.[34] The Government in Exile's policy in relation to Jews had to contend with the

90   The Polish Government in Exile in London

British general policy not to highlight specific Jewish suffering, but it also faced similar pressures from within government itself (from the political Right) and from some Poles abroad and at home.

The Polish government sought to balance its perceived strategic interests by responding to the demands of non-Polish Jewry, its obligations to Polish Jewish citizens, the rising ethno-nationalist sentiment in Poland and its own Polish Cabinet, and the perspectives of its British and American allies. The solutions to these complex and contradictory demands were marked by considerable ambiguities.

The first policy plank was to continue to argue, mainly in private with British officials and politicians, for increased homogeneity in postwar Poland. Sikorski, for example, met with Foreign Secretary Anthony Eden on 19 January 1942, and advised him that it was impossible for a future Poland to have over 3 million Jews.[35] In December 1942, sufficiently emboldened by the growing Allied consensus on increasing the national homogeneity of postwar European states, through population transfers if necessary, Sikorski sent a memorandum to Allied governments endorsing the transfer of German minority communities.[36] Though referring specifically to Germans, the Polish Government in Exile's memorandum indicated that one of its policy goals was to create a more homogeneous postwar nation-state, and this had implications for all minorities. Frank Savery's point, that the high proportion of interwar Poland's population belonging to a national minority constituted a problem, was shared more or less across the Polish political spectrum. Those on the nationalist Right saw minorities as a problem in essence. Those at the Centre and some on the Left saw the proportion of minorities in the total population as the problem; reducing the proportion to manageable levels would solve the minority issue.

This was the point Stanisław Kot had tried to make with representatives of British Jewry in 1940. Those who remained could be integrated and assimilated. Thus the argument about minorities within the Polish Government in Exile was not only an articulation of ethno-nationalist perspectives (National Democrats), but flawed attempts at overcoming the perceived weaknesses of the Second Republic (Sikorski, Kot, Polish Peasant Party). These attempts were flawed because they did not challenge ethno-centric precepts which divided good ethnic Poles from problematic non-ethnic Poles, or problematize the contingent nature of these categories. They did, however, constitute a response to news from Poland of the decline in tolerance towards minorities, which was being received throughout the war. The Poles were not alone in thinking that increased homogeneity was desirable and indeed necessary. The Americans and the British did also, as part of their planning to create a postwar

The Polish Government in Exile in London

Europe freed from the perennial threat of war and irredentist tensions that accompanied the rise of nationalism on the Continent in the 1930s.

The second policy plank was to petition the American and British governments to make formal statements condemning Nazi atrocities against Jews, but the Polish government also turned to other institutions to act. On 3 January 1943 the president, Władysław Raczkiewicz, following receipt of information about the Nazi anti-Jewish programme from the courier Jan Karski, sent a telegram to Pope Pius XII. Making reference to German anti-Jewish actions, including the programme of extermination, Raczkiewicz appealed to the Pope to condemn the German terror.[37]

The third plank was to conform, without too much resistance, to British demands and censorship policy to downplay the stories about Jews. Raczkiewicz's letter to the Pope can therefore be seen as the final act of the choreographed focus on the German crimes against Jews that peaked with the 17 December UN declaration.[38]

The first plank – increasing national homogeneity – is usually emphasized by scholars and commentators, and the importance of the second plank often underestimated. In a context in which news was managed and choreographed, and official government announcements assumed particular importance, the Polish government's lobbying efforts were very significant, achieving success in July and December 1942. These efforts indicate that, while Polish Jews may have been outside many gentile Poles' 'universe of obligation', the Polish government did in fact attempt, with varying commitment, to highlight the plight of Polish Jewry.

The fact that no further Allied declarations mentioning Jews were made until Roosevelt issued a warning to Germany in March 1944, following pressure from the War Refugee Board, reflects the tightening of British and American control over news about Jews and the declining status of Poland within the Grand Alliance.[39] In this context, it is important to recognize that information about the situation of Jews in Poland was shared with allies and the press in Britain. The *Polish Jewish Observer*, the subscription-only supplement of the *East London Observer*, routinely published articles derived from the Polish Underground's radio messages and couriered reports through 1943 and 1944, and perhaps from early 1942.[40] The British mainstream press chose not to publish material handed to it and did not reprint material from the *Polish Jewish Observer*. These editorial decisions were beyond the control of the Polish government. The marginalization of 'Jewish' stories generally reflects British, not Polish, policy.

The significance of the third plank, however, is rarely recognized. As early as February 1941, a letter to Prime Minister Churchill from, in all

92   The Polish Government in Exile in London

likelihood, Lord Hood of the Ministry of Information (the letter is unsigned), advised that 'we should be in a position to satisfy ourselves that the propaganda policy of the Allied Governments is, in fact, in accordance with the approved policy of the Cabinet'. The letter added that he was in consultation with the Foreign Office on 'how best to secure control both of broadcast and official announcements issued by the Allied Governments so as to ensure that they are unobjectionable both from propaganda and security standpoints'.[41] These objectives were largely achieved through the work of the Political Warfare Executive and the Ministry of Information after Brendan Bracken became minister. Control over Allied governments' official releases was maintained by the press censor of the British Ministry of Information. The revised edition of defence notices of 1942, for example, outlined censorship procedures and information subject to censorship, and stated, 'Material obtained from or issued by Allied Governments in the United Kingdom should not be regarded as free from Censorship objection unless issued officially through the Ministry of Information or another British Government Department.'[42] This policy was reiterated on 10 May 1943. C. Powell wrote on behalf of Rear-Admiral George Pirie Thomson, the chief press censor, to Roger Eckersley at the BBC, noting that the censor discriminated between press releases made by British ministries and those made by Allied governments. He pointed out that he 'could see no objection to the news staff using last minute and unstamped [i.e. by the censor] items which have been officially released by a Government department in this country. We must make it clear, however, that it does not apply to items officially released by Allied Government Authorities'. Powell added that the censor did not 'allow publication of a lot of matter which you yourselves [the BBC] put out on your Foreign Language Propaganda Services [i.e. the European Service]'.[43]

The scope of British control over the media therefore placed a premium on the Polish government's ability to influence its British ally. British control impacted on the official Polish press and on the circulation of government press releases and announcements, and limited both how the Poles reported information from Poland and what they could publicly report. British censorship policy therefore played a crucial disciplining function in the type of news that could reasonably be expected to be released to the public through mainstream media and official Allied government publications.[44]

Many scholars (e.g., Engel 1987, 1993; Michlic 2006) have argued that the Polish government often marginalized news of the Holocaust and frequently narrated stories of atrocities against Jews as part of a wider story of atrocities committed by the Germans in Poland. Engel suggests that this was done largely because the Poles were concerned that the Jewish tragedy might overshadow that of the ethnic Poles. But this contention, if made with reference to the Polish press, government press releases, speeches and announcements, has to acknowledge the influence that the British censorship regime had on Allied governments in London. For example, Stefan Korboński, the head of the Directorate of Civilian Resistance (Kierownictwo Walki Cywilnej), recorded in his postwar book on the Polish underground state that the reports he sent to London on the deportations of Jews from Warsaw to death camps were ignored. Korboński stated that he finally received information from the Polish government (it is not clear from whom exactly) explaining that '[n]ot all your telegrams are fit for publication'.[45] Stories of atrocities against Jews fell foul of the 'voluntary' censorship regime operated by the British, and this has to be taken into account when assessing the Polish press.

British (and American) limited receptivity to news of the extermination of the Jews meant that the Holocaust, for the most part, could only be narrated in the mainstream press as part of a wider tragedy. Clearly, such a discursive framework was aligned with the sentiment of part of the exile government's Cabinet. Many Poles were sensitive to 'excessive' coverage of the fate of Jews, and, had more prominence been given in official publications to the Jewish plight, this might have provoked a legitimacy crisis within the Polish government.[46] The British censorship policy eased some of this tension. This explains, in part, the government's acceptance of the censorship regime but, as noted above, Sikorski was seen by British Foreign Office officials as liable to contravene this regime at times.[47] It is therefore incorrect to argue that news of atrocities committed against Jews was frequently marginalized in Polish official publications and announcements due to the actions of the Polish government alone.

The marginality of news about Jews in the official Polish government press indicates more about Polish adherence to British censorship policy than about the Polish government's attitude to Polish Jews. As noted, much Polish intelligence on the situation of Jews in occupied Poland that was received in Britain was published in English, in London, in the *Polish Jewish Observer* – the one newspaper that escaped British censorship on account of its limited distribution. It is possible to argue that the publishing of news of the Jewish plight in an obscure, subscription-only newspaper dissipated anger against the British censorship regime. The Ministry of Information could argue (in bad faith) that the British government did not control what editors of mainstream papers published, and that the 'free' press itself had elected not to publish stories about Jews and atrocities. The publication of details in the *Polish Jewish*

94   The Polish Government in Exile in London

Observer provided Ministry of Information officials with evidence that news was not suppressed and moderated demands for further publicity since detailed news of the Holocaust was available (though often some months late) in Britain, but in a publication without influence or a significant readership.

Despite the fairly firm restrictions placed on the Polish government, it did have some room for manoeuvre in the context of British censorship, which was not always fully exploited. For example, Polish minister of information Stanisław Stroński rejected a call in November 1942 to appeal to ethnic Poles to aid their Jewish co-citizens, contending that it was 'superfluous to exhort the [Polish] community, for it is precisely the homeland which passes on the information and protests against the oppression of the Jews, and an exhortation would be grist for the German mill'.[48] Stroński was concerned that such an exhortation would make a negative impact in Poland, given the general decline in toleration towards minorities detailed in several reports that reached the government. But even had Stroński responded positively to the request, it cannot automatically be assumed that the British would have enabled such a specific broadcast to be made.

Both formally and informally, the Polish government passed on information to the British Foreign Office, including reports about Auschwitz, as is shown in Chapters 4 and 5. Stanisław Kot, a minister in the Polish government, maintained close relations with Frank Savery, and repeatedly passed him intelligence on conditions in Poland, including those endured by Polish Jews. In August 1941, for instance, Savery forwarded Anthony Eden information from Kot about the 'famine conditions prevailing among the poorer classes in the Warsaw ghetto'; news that 'Warsaw Rabbis have granted dispensations from sundry ritual obligation, including even the celebration of the Sabbath'; and the concerns of Polish observers who 'clearly fear that the Jewish proletariat is becoming more and more communistically inclined and will probably be a foyer of communist activity when the German regime collapses in Poland'.[49] In a subsequent letter to Frank Roberts at the Foreign Office, Savery adjudged the soundness of the first point made to Eden superior to that of the subsequent two points, and advised Roberts that '[s]hould any use be made for propaganda purposes of [the material] the fact that it comes from Polish Government sources should be carefully concealed'.[50] This pattern of information transfer was repeated, with the source of data frequently concealed – especially if passed or leaked without the considered approval of the Polish government.[51]

Engel (1987: 200) argues that '[n]o matter how dubious the regime's behaviour in handling the news of the deportations from Warsaw, the

The Polish Government in Exile in London   95

Poles in London were still the first to convey effectively to the governments of the West even some appreciation of the Jewish situation', and Laqueur (1998: 117) suggests that after July 1942 the Polish Government in Exile 'began to provide figures [in relation to the number of Jews killed by the Nazis] that were too low', maintaining that this constituted a change in 'information policy'.[52] Engel is right to draw attention to the way the Polish government handled news from the Warsaw ghetto in the late spring and summer of 1942, but due weight has to be given to the difficulties in presenting this information to the British. Similarly, Laqueur's contention highlights that at times and in some fora lower numbers were publicly provided.[53] There were a number of reasons for this.

First, the Polish government was concerned about reports being believable (or, more precisely, acceptable) to various audiences. This demanded that reports submitted to the British adhered to British policy and sensitivities.[54] According to Polish foreign minister Edward Raczyński, 'we had to be absolutely precise and very cautious not to meet with the criticism that we exaggerated' (Breitman 1999: 12). Stola (1997: 8) suggests that Raczyński's 'opinions were influenced by the attitudes of his British colleagues in the Foreign Office', and in such circumstances 'caution' rather than 'precision' triumphed. For this most important audience, numbers were – had to be – reduced.[55]

Second, British censorship policy tightened in the summer of 1942, in the sense that news about Jews was marginalized once more; and third, the Poles were concerned about intelligence security following the liquidation of the 'Swedish connection'. Greater caution was exercised over the release of information and its particular content. On 27 July 1942, following the arrest of Poles and Swedes involved in gathering and transporting intelligence to Sweden, the Polish deputy defence minister General Izydor Modelski demanded an enhancement of censorship in an order to the head of military censorship. He argued,

It is absolutely unacceptable to disclose any news which was obtained by correspondence or [brought by] secret couriers, from the country and about the country ... One may allow only publication of information which has already been presented by the press or radio of the enemy or neutral countries. In each case such news should have a reference to its source ... In case of doubt, please stop publication. Do not make public without the consent of the Sixth Department of the Supreme Commander's Staff.[56]

These factors make *singular* focus on the influential narrative of victim competition somewhat less compelling. The release of specific information in the West about German actions against Jews by the Polish government was influenced by the British context and security concerns.

96   The Polish Government in Exile in London

More often than not, the result was to emphasize Polish suffering in relation to Jewish suffering, but this outcome should not be seen solely as a consequence of Polish government policy.

Recognizing that the British inhibited Allied governments based in London from highlighting the fate of Jews, as indicated by Roberts's letter to Lias in August 1942, helps, in part, to explain Sikorski's failure to mention at the St James's Palace Conference in London in January 1942 the particular horrors faced by Polish Jews. This conference, chaired by Sikorski, directly discussed German atrocities. Sikorski and the Polish Government in Exile were also constrained by ethno-nationalist sentiment within the Cabinet, and in Polish public opinion. The exile government was therefore inhibited from speaking immediately and clearly about the Jewish plight by reports from Poland that recorded declining tolerance towards Jews amongst the Polish population, by the fear that a Polish quisling could emerge and, importantly, by the British.[57]

In his role as chairman of the Inter-Allied Conference on War Crimes, Sikorski replied on 9 May to a 1 May 1942 letter from the British Section of the World Jewish Congress that called for a specific declaration that mentioned German actions against Jews. On 16 May, Sikorski, using some of the same formulations used in the letter to the WJC, replied to the British Board of Deputies' Joint Foreign Committee, which had earlier (18 February) made the same request as the WJC for a declaration. In his letters to Jewish representatives, Sikorski argued that specific mention of Jews would indicate tacit recognition of race theory.[58] A letter from Michał Potulicki of the Polish Ministry of Foreign Affairs to Godfrey Lias of the British Ministry of Information indicates that Sikorski's replies were agreed to by 'other Governments concerned'.[59] These replies were heartily approved by the British, as they followed their policy.[60]

In relation to Sikorski's May 1942 letters to Jewish representatives, David Engel (1987: 178) argued that 'the Polish government simply wished to avoid calling special attention to the German massacre of the Jewish population of Poland'. This assertion is too strong, though Engel is right to note that the Polish government did not highlight the massacres of Poland's Jewish citizens. Sikorski wrote to Jewish representatives in his capacity as chairman of an Allied organization on behalf of the Allies. Allies were consulted, and Foreign Office documents referring to the Jewish requests for a declaration repeatedly stressed that the British government did not recognize a Jewish nationality.[61] Sikorski's replies therefore demonstrate the Polish government's adherence to the British-led policy line of not highlighting German actions against Jews, rather than any specifically Polish policy of marginalizing news about Jews. The British policy line was also reflected by the complete lack of any BBC broadcast on Jews being routinely murdered by the Nazis during the first five months of 1942 (Milland 1998b: 34).

Foreign Office officials applauded Sikorski's responses to Jewish representatives. One official stated that 'General Sikorski has behaved all right in this particular case' and Frank Roberts noted that 'General Sikorski behaved correctly'.[62] In the first five months of 1942 it was not politic for the Polish Government in Exile in the British context to highlight the torment that Jews suffered at the hands of the Germans in mainstream fora, despite the growing body of evidence of their mass-scale slaughter. This, of course, does not exculpate the Polish government's failure to attempt to bring to public attention the Nazi programme against Poland's Jewish population.

The Bund report: May–July 1942

In May 1942 a report from the underground Jewish Socialist Party, the Bund, which had been carried by Sven Norrman to Stockholm, arrived in London.[63] Shmuel Zygielbojm lobbied hard for the information to be disseminated and, on 2 June, the news was carried on the BBC European Service. On 6 June the Government in Exile prepared a note to the Allies, calling for the suppression of war crimes and the punishment of war criminals to be made key war objectives. Sikorski responded to the Bund report, and in the context of British censorship policy and British Foreign Office sensitivities about talking about Jews, his BBC broadcast on 9 June 1942 to Poland was both symbolically and politically significant.

Hitherto, his speech has been judged fairly harshly. Engel (1987: 180) argued that the small proportion of Sikorski's broadcast (5 per cent) that referred to Jews, the failure to mention the gas vans at Chełmno and Sikorski's description of 'tens of thousands' of Jews as having perished, rather than the 700,000 stated in the Bund report, constituted an attempt to minimize the Jewish tragedy. It is true that the report had been received with initial scepticism by members of the Polish Government in Exile, and Stanisław Mikołajczyk, then minister of the interior, sought to incorporate the report as part of a general story of suffering in Poland (which he later did). But even Zygielbojm, at first, 'found it difficult to absorb the news' (Blatman 2004: 300). Dariusz Stola (1997: 8) quotes Adam Pragier, a leader of the Polish Socialist Party in London: 'The Bund should have written that [the Germans] killed 7,000 people. Then we could provide the news to the British, with a slight chance they would believe us'. Jan Nowak-Jeziorański, a Polish courier highly rated by British intelligence, records that Ignacy Schwarzbart pleaded with him not to quote to the British the large number of Jews killed by the

Germans on the grounds that they would simply not be believed.[64] The reduced numbers in Sikorski's speech can, therefore, be more accurately described as an attempt to disseminate news of German actions against Jews within a broadcasting context controlled, in the final analysis, by the Political Warfare Executive. The omission of any reference to gas vans and the limited amount of attention devoted to Jewish matters in the broadcast all conformed with British policy.

Like all material broadcast by the BBC, Sikorski's speech was vetted, and any deviation from the agreed script could have resulted in the switch censor halting the broadcast. The lowering of the numbers did have the adverse effect of inhibiting a full appreciation of the scale of the German killings, but it is not clear whether an accurate citation of the Bund report would have allowed such an appreciation either, given Bauer's (1978) account of the process of knowing.

Nevertheless, Sikorski was frank in presenting Nazi policy against Jews. He stated that '[t]he Jewish population in Poland is doomed to annihilation in accordance with the maxim: "Slaughter all the Jews regardless of how the war will end"' (Bolchover 1993: 8).[65] The Polish prime minister had identified the Nazi genocidal intentions, something that the British and American governments were extremely reluctant to do, even in the autumn of 1942, and Sikorski had stretched British censorship policy to the limit.[66]

Together with the efforts of Zygielbojm, who met journalists in London to advise them of the news from Poland, Sikorski increased the pressure on the British government to make a formal denunciation of German atrocities. Zygielbojm did not want the information to appear in the Jewish press first, and managed to place the news with the *Daily Telegraph*.[67] His success reflects a loosening of British censorship policy, almost certainly at the behest of Brendan Bracken. This loosening may be due to the British, and Churchill in particular, becoming aware of German railway radio intercepts which would have confirmed the reports from Poland, and a desire to respond to the concerted pressure of an ally. It is unlikely that Foreign Office officials encouraged the temporary suspension of censorship policy in relation to Jews, and although the precise decision-making process on this issue is not revealed in the existing documentary record, the circumstantial evidence points to Bracken (with the support of Churchill) overcoming resistance in the PWE and the FO (and the Home Office).[68] For example, there were no references to Jews in the PWE weekly directive to the BBC's Polish Service for the period 27 June–3 July 1942, which was approved by Robert Bruce Lockhart on 26 June, or during the subsequent weeks.

The dissemination of news of the mass killing of Jews depended on British receptivity to this news and willingness to act on it. Although the PWE's directives to the Polish Service did not mention Jews during late June, there was a distinct change in the tone and substance of the general directives (written by Noel Newsome, who was ultimately accountable to Ivone Kirkpatrick) to the BBC's European Service in the second third of June 1942. This was reflected clearly in the difference in tone and content in the minutes of the BBC Polish Service weekly meetings.

The meeting of 19 June 1942 discussed persecution in Poland without focusing on Jews. Frank Savery suggested 'that attention might be drawn, subject to the approval of the Polish authorities, to the fact that the women of Poland had been particularly hard hit in the new wave of persecution', and Noel Newsome noted that the continual use of women and children in this way was a constant theme across the European Service. This was because women and children were perceived to be 'innocents', in contrast to other possible victim categories. The meeting also discussed British attitudes to persecution in Poland, and it was agreed 'that the best way of keeping the public fully informed would be a periodical résumé of atrocities as a result of the considered policy of the Germans in Poland'.[69]

During the following week, the policy changed, and the 24 June BBC general directive called for full prominence to be given to reports of 'brutal German excesses against Jews in Lwow, Jaslo and other towns of the Lublin and Lodz departments'; to the 60,000 Jews executed in Vilna; and the concentration of Jews in the Lublin district, where they were 'shot in great numbers, starved, and allowed to perish of diseases'.[70] The evidence of atrocities against Jews was released, and the directive also declared that '[t]here will be retribution for Jewish victims'. It seems that during this period Noel Newsome at the BBC was able to exercise some independence, most probably because the Ministry of Information (Bracken), PWE and FO were not in complete agreement on how to deal with the information derived from the Bund report.

The release of news about Jews in June and July 1942 indicates that, at least during those months, the Poles (inclusive of Polish Jews such as Zygielbojm) could exploit differences of opinion within the British government. After July 1942, this became more difficult as any differences in policy between the key ministries (Ministry of Information, Foreign Office) on the issue of Jews were far fewer, and the Foreign Office took the important decisions.[71]

The next day (25 June) the *Daily Telegraph* ran the Bund story on page 5, with the headline 'Germans murder 700,000 Jews in Poland'. The article also reported on the mobile gas chamber vans at Chełmno.

100   The Polish Government in Exile in London

The editor/proprietor of the *Telegraph* deemed that other stories – Churchill attending the Pacific War Council, 'Congo Rubber for the Allies', and the new bishop of Winchester, all page 1 stories – were more important than the report detailing the annihilation of Polish Jewry.

On 26 June Noel Newsome's general directive, referring to the *Telegraph*'s 'scoop', highlighted that the news about the killing of Jews was out, and called for it to be widely broadcast, in the context of wider persecution.[72] At the 26 June 11 a.m. BBC meeting to discuss the Polish Service broadcast, Director of European Broadcasts Noel Newsome noted that the persecution story 'was being developed in all services and that the topic had been included in the Weekly Directive for the German Service in particular'.

It was agreed that Zygielbojm 'should broadcast in German on the massacre of Jews in Poland', with a Hebrew introduction; also that the chief rabbi would broadcast in English and a Polish rabbi would broadcast to Poland; and finally, a Catholic churchman would broadcast to German Catholics.[73] The British were clearly gearing up for a serious propaganda operation, which aimed to inform German audiences of the scale of the atrocities committed by the German occupation authorities in Poland, and such a shift in British propaganda policy required approval at a very high level.

On the German Service on 27 June, Lindley Fraser reported that the official estimate for the number of Jews killed in Poland was 700,000, and bluntly stated that they had 'been starved, gassed, shot or beaten to death by the German occupying authorities'.[74] On 30 June, the BBC general directive declared that '[t]he massacre of the Jews is still very much in the news' – a reference to a page 5 article in the *Daily Telegraph* entitled 'More than 1,000,000 Jews killed in Europe', a page 2 article in *The Times* entitled 'Massacre of Jews – over 1,000,000 dead since the war began', and articles in other national and regional newspapers that were published the same day.[75] The directive also indicated how the news should be presented: 'pick on some ghastly but not numerically astronomical incident as the headline and bring in the total casualties incidentally. Big figures blunt sensibility'. The directive also called for the expression '"Hitler chamber" for lethal chambers' to be popularized. This instruction was generally ignored and not reissued, suggesting that the author of the directive (Noel Newsome) exceeded his remit.[76]

The BBC's Home Service was circumspect in its reporting of the news. On 29 June, in its 6 p.m., 9 p.m. and midnight bulletins, it reported on a conference held by the British Section of the World Jewish Congress in London which had highlighted the information from the Bund report. The Home Service gave no prominence to the news of massacres.

The Bund report: May–July 1942

Similarly, news about the annihilation of Jews in Poland, published in the British press, followed, in the main, orchestrated events. Both the stories in *The Times* and the *Daily Telegraph* on 30 June 1942 did not publish on the Bund report or on information supplied directly by Zygielbojm, but on the WJC conference the previous day.[77] The fact that this conference was reported at all is significant in the British context. *The Times* article noted Labour MP Sydney Silverman's speech, in which he declared that a million Jews had lost their lives by being shot or as a result of poor living conditions, and a speech by Ignacy Schwarzbart calling for retaliation.[78]

Despite this publicity James Middleton, the Labour Party secretary, wrote to Dr Schneier Levenberg of Poale Zion (who in turn forwarded Middleton's letter to Schwarzbart) advising that he had 'been very struck with the fact that this ghastly story of Jewish persecution has not received wider reference in the press throughout the country. There seems to have been a bad slip-up in the publicity that this story deserves'.[79] It was not until 9 and 10 July that the massacre story returned to *The Times*. On 9 July, the paper reported on page 2 the broadcast on the BBC's European (German) Service of Cardinal Hinsley, the head of the Catholic Church in England, in which he called on Christian Germans to 'resist these black deeds of shame' – a reference to the massacre of 700,000 Jews in Poland by the Nazis, to which he had previously drawn attention. The German Service of the BBC also broadcast a talk by Richard Crossman on its Women's Programme, which highlighted the 700,000 Jews murdered in Poland.[80]

The Home Service's 9 p.m. news bulletin – which attracted the largest audiences of the BBC's news broadcasts – transmitted Bracken's take on the Bund report.[81] This report included the first reference to gas chambers on the Home Service. Milland (1998b: 51) notes that 'the Home Service was only going to report news of the Final Solution when official bodies chose to give it their stamp of approval'. This is true if 'official bodies' are taken to refer to the Ministry of Information, PWE and Foreign Office. On 10 July, on page 3, *The Times* reported on the press conference at the British Ministry of Information, which high-lighted the atrocities committed against Jews in occupied Poland, in an article entitled 'German record in Poland – torture and murder – British pledge of retribution'.

The Polish press also reported the news about the mass killing of Jews. The news on the inside pages of *The Times* and the *Daily Telegraph* on 30 June made the front page of *Dziennik Polski*. A week earlier it had reported on typhus and hunger in the Warsaw ghetto. *Dziennik Polski* on 10 July devoted a considerable amount of space to reporting on the 9 July conference at the Ministry of Information. On page 1 of *Dziennik Polski*,

102 The Polish Government in Exile in London

the main story highlighted Mikołajczyk's statement at the conference, in which he said that the 'number of Polish citizens who have been shot or murdered in other ways ... amounts to over 400,000'. However, on page 2, the full story about the annihilation of Jews was published, but in the form of Jews speaking about the Jewish plight. Clearly, this was an editorial decision, as news from the conference could have been presented in a variety of ways, including strong emphasis on Bracken's speech. As it was, Zygielbojm was noted as reporting that 700,000 Jews had been murdered, and Schwarzbart as noting that Jews were being concentrated by Hitler in Poland.

The 1 and 15 July editions of the *Polish Fortnightly Review* reported on the Nazi mass killing of Jews, but in this publication the news was narrated as part of a wider programme of atrocities committed in Poland. The front page on 1 July carried the headline 'Documents from Poland – German attempts to murder a nation'. On pages 4 and 5, under the title 'Destruction of the Jewish population', five paragraphs discussed the extermination of Jews and constituted the fifth of nine stories focusing on Nazi atrocities and policy in Poland. It was squeezed between a report on the extermination of Polish intellectuals and the killing of the 'ten martyrs of Pruszków' – a report on the German execution of ten Poles in response to Polish sabotage of German farms.

In the 15 July edition, the *Review*'s front page was dedicated to news of public executions. Page 4 reported on the 9 July press conference at the British Ministry of Information, leading with Bracken's speech and followed by Mikołajczyk's, while page 7 contained Zygielbojm's and Schwarzbart's speeches. This edition also framed the annihilation of the Jews as part of a wider pattern of atrocities committed in Poland. The Bund's information was presented in similar ways in the two official publications of the Polish government, though in *Dziennik* the Jewish plight was more clearly highlighted.

The effort to publicize news of German atrocities was not limited to the press and the BBC. The Polish Ministry of Information, in co-operation with Bracken, published a booklet entitled *Bestiality ... Unknown in Any Previous Record of History*, which printed the speeches made at the 9 July conference at Senate House, and other documents from Poland. In form, structure and content, this booklet closely followed the 15 July edition of the *Polish Fortnightly Review*. The Jewish plight was narrated as part of a larger programme of German atrocities in Poland. Nevertheless, in the sections which focused on the Jews, it displayed a distinct lack of co-ordination between contributors, reflecting their particular agendas.

The data on the number of Jews killed by the Nazis varied according to contributor despite the single ultimate source – the Bund report, which

The Bund report: May–July 1942

stated that 700,000 Jews had been annihilated. Bracken, Zygielbojm and Polish information minister, Stanisław Stroński, all declared that 700,000 Jews from Poland had been killed. Mikołajczyk cited a figure of '400,000 Polish citizens (Poles and Jews)' (Bracken 1942: 44). The booklet also published a map of concentration camps that incarcerated Poles – and here 'Poles' seems to include Jews as it featured Bełżec and Treblinka. The map located Oświęcim, which was extensively discussed in the text, though Jews at the camp were not specifically highlighted.

The news of the German mass killing of Jews highlighted at the 9 July conference reverberated for the following couple of weeks, and the BBC's European Service broadcast British responses. Churchill's message, on 22 July, of retribution for those persecuting Jews was followed on 23 July by the Labour Party's and Trades Union Congress's denunciation of the persecution of the Jews. In the United States, there was a mass meeting at Madison Square Gardens on 21 July organized by the American Jewish Congress, the Jewish Labor Committee and B'nai B'rith to which Winston Churchill and Franklin Roosevelt sent statements condemning atrocities.[82] On 23 July, the chaplain of the House of Representatives read a special prayer for the Jewish victims of Nazi rule to open a session of the House (Laqueur 1980: 12).

However, by late July less news and less detail about what was happening to Jews in Eastern Europe was broadcast or printed. On 26 July news of Jews being deported to the east was broadcast, and on 11 August a broadcast noted Romanian Jews being sent to occupied Russia. The final significant attempts to focus attention on what was happening to Jews in Europe included Zygielbojm's pamphlet *Stop Them Now!*, which was published by Liberty Press in London in September, with an introduction by the MP Josiah Wedgwood, and a protest rally against Nazi atrocities in Poland and Czechoslovakia organized by the Labour Party that took place at Caxton Hall, London, on 2 September.[83] Zygielbojm spoke and referred once more to the 700,000 Jews murdered in Poland. The British Home Secretary also delivered a speech in which he declared that 'no decent people can fail to have been shocked and appalled by the successive revelations of shameless and conscienceless savagery that have come out of Europe in these latter days' (Dobbs et al., 1942: 11).[84] The newspaper-reading public, however, were not informed that Nazi atrocities against Jews had been highlighted by Zygielbojm. The British press, reporting on the rally the following day, did not mention Jews.[85]

Six days later, in the House of Commons, Churchill mentioned the Nazi deportations of Jews from France in a long speech on the war situation, describing these Nazi actions as the 'most bestial, the most

104   The Polish Government in Exile in London

squalid and the most senseless of all their offences', but did not draw attention to what was happening in occupied Poland.[86]

The Ministry of Information's Home Intelligence Reports do not record the impact in Britain of the news about German atrocities against Jews released in June–July.[87] Unlike later in the year, in December 1942, Ministry of Information officials did not seem to have been prepared to monitor the impact of the 9 July conference on public opinion. This may reflect the fact that the decision to sanction the release of information was taken relatively late and without a great deal of discussion or co-ordination with those monitoring public opinion, or that the utility of the Home Intelligence Reports to support policy positions was not, at that point, recognized.[88]

The Home Intelligence Report for the period 21 July to 28 July simply listed anti-Semitism as one of several constant topics being cited in reports from the north-east region (Leeds) and from the London region. The following week's Home Intelligence (Number 96) Report listed anti-Semitism again as a constant topic. The 98th Home Intelligence Report covering the period 11–17 August provided fuller details, noting 'a slight increase in anti-Jewish feeling' due to allegations that Jews avoided military service, took part in black-market activities and had access to petrol to run their cars.[89] The references to anti-Semitism in July 1942 were cursory, reminding readers of the report of the continual significance of the prejudice. The more extensive discussion of anti-Semitism in August can be read, in the context of news about the Holocaust and British sensitivities about Jews, as an invitation to cease publicizing information regarding the German atrocities against Jews. The Holocaust was returned to the margins of wartime news.

The UN declaration: November–December 1942

During the summer of 1942 the Nazi genocide of Europe's Jews continued, in the death camps at Chełmno, Treblinka, Sobibór and Bełżec, and at mixed camps such as Majdanek and Auschwitz. The Jews of Warsaw were crowded onto freight trains and sent to the camp at Treblinka, where they were gassed. Reports of these horrendous crimes in the press in the West were few, but, following the 9 July conference, there had been no indication that Nazi policy towards Jews had changed either. So while the general population in Britain and in the US could, and often did, choose to disbelieve much of the information released which highlighted the Nazi slaughter of European Jewry, decision makers on both sides of the Atlantic were aware of the trajectory of Nazi Jewish policy.

The UN declaration: November–December 1942

The reduction in the flow of information from the Government in Exile about the genocide ensured that there was no running commentary on the killing process. Instead, periodic indicative summaries of atrocities committed against Jews appeared, in accordance with general British policy. But even such reports required significant effort – from Zygielbojm and Schwarzbart in particular. Thus the relative absence of news about the Holocaust during the summer of 1942 reflects both reduced receptivity to such news within Britain (tighter 'voluntary' censorship), and reduced distribution of such news by the Polish Government in Exile, not merely the latter, as is often assumed. For example, following the July conference, the British Ministry of Information could undertake a number of actions: it could call on the Polish government to supply information about what was happening to Jews, it could continue to publicize information already in hand, or it could inhibit the dissemination of such information.

It is the latter option that seems to have been pursued. During late summer and early autumn 1942 there were virtually no broadcasts on German actions against Jews on the BBC's Home Service.[90] The most significant was Lord Vansittart's talk on 1 September 1942 in which he declared that 'hundreds of thousands of Polish Jews have already perished'. For this broadcast, the Polish minister of foreign affairs, Edward Raczyński, sent Vansittart a congratulatory letter applauding his reference to the 'German Question' (Raczyński 1962: 121).[91] But during the summer of 1942 an important telegram that would help return the Holocaust to the news agenda in the West was making slow progress through the British Foreign Office and American State Department.

The Riegner telegram was critically important in breaking the relative silence of news about Jews, which lasted from mid-July 1942 through the summer and early autumn. This telegram was based on information passed by the German industrialist Eduard Schulte, a director of a mining company with headquarters in Breslau (Wrocław), to a business friend, Isidor Koppelmann, in late July 1942. Koppelmann in turn advised the press secretary of the Swiss Federation of Jewish Communities, Benjamin Sagalowitz. Recognizing the significance of the information, Sagalowitz called Gerhart Riegner, the representative of the World Jewish Congress in Geneva. Schulte was deemed by Koppelmann to be a reliable source, and his information outlined the extermination policy of the German state, allowing Riegner to make sense of a series of other reports which had reached him, including those describing the concentration and deportation of Jews from Western Europe.

On 8 August 1942 Riegner went to the American Consulate in Geneva and spoke with Howard Elting, the vice consul. Riegner requested that a

106   The Polish Government in Exile in London

telegram be sent through official channels to Rabbi Stephen Wise, and for American intelligence to check the information. Riegner also went to the British Consulate and requested the same telegram be sent to Sydney Silverman – MP and member of the British Section of the World Jewish Congress.[92] This telegram requested that New York (that is, Stephen Wise) be informed, suggesting that Riegner had doubts whether the State Department would pass on the information.[93] Riegner's telegram read:

Received alarming report stating that, in the Fuhrer's Headquarters, a plan has been discussed, and is under consideration, according to which all Jews in countries occupied or controlled by Germany numbering $3\frac{1}{2}$ to 4 millions should, after deportation and concentration in the East, be at one blow exterminated, in order to resolve, once and for all the Jewish question in Europe. Action is reported to be planned for the autumn. Ways of execution are still being discussed including the use of prussic acid. We transmit this information with all the necessary reservation, as exactitude cannot be confirmed by us. Our informant is reported to have close connexions with the highest German authorities, and his reports are generally reliable. Please inform and consult New York.[94]

The message to London was received by the Foreign Office on 10 August, and for seven days the information was not passed on. Officials were wary of the report. On 15 August Frank Roberts advised colleagues that the Foreign Office could not hold up the telegram for much longer, and 'feared that [the report] could have embarrassing consequences' (Laqueur 1998: 79). It was eventually forwarded on to Silverman. In his covering note to Silverman, Richard Law, Anthony Eden's deputy, advised that '[w]e have no information bearing on or confirming this story'.[95] At the Foreign Office, Silverman was seen by Sir Brograve Beauchamp, the parliamentary private secretary to the parliamentary under-secretary of state (and Conservative MP for Walthamstow East, 1931–45) and Colonel Charles Ponsonby, the parliamentary private secretary to Eden. Silverman requested the provision of facilities to telephone Stephen Wise in the United States. This was refused on the ground that the Germans listened in to such conversations.[96] This may have been true, but hard-wire telephone cables from Britain to the United States would have had to be physically tapped into.

Silverman was also advised to consider whether action by Jewish institutions might 'annoy the Germans and make any action they were proposing to take even more unpleasant than it might otherwise have been' (Laqueur 1998: 80). In short, Silverman was strongly discouraged from acting on the cable, although he was able to telegraph Wise through the War Office. Wise received the telegram on 28 August and managed to contact Secretary of State Sumner Welles on 2 September. Wise agreed

The UN declaration: November–December 1942 107

not to publicize the information in the telegram until confirmation could be given. In late September, in a letter to Silverman, Alexander Easterman (political secretary of the WJC in London) quoted a note received from Maurice Perlzweig, in which Perlzweig described the initial response of WJC leaders in the United States to Riegner's telegram. Perlzweig wrote that the telegram

> had what I can only describe as a shattering effect. Nobody here is disposed to doubt that the information is at least substantially correct. It is desperately difficult to know what to do. We thought at first of publication, but then it occurred to us that when the news seeps through to Europe it will have a demoralizing effect on those who are marked as hopeless victims. We decided to seek the best advice possible and Wise, who telephoned immediately to Washington, has made certain that it shall be brought to the notice of the very highest quarters. We shall act, if act we can, as soon as the advice and aid we seek become available.[97]

Jewish leaders in the US were well aware of the problems in disseminating information about the extermination of Jews in an American social context marked by pervasive anti-Semitism. For these leaders, the wish to secure US government advice (i.e. permission) to disseminate the news illustrates how the fairly hostile discursive landscape in the US restricted Jews' scope for action. Even with the information from Riegner, information which senior WJC officials did not doubt, they were hesitant. Jewish leaders clearly recognized that securing a minimally receptive environment for the news depended on the US government confirming the news. However, empowering the state to be the arbiter of whether information could be released increased the state's power over the flow of information, and augmented the voluntary censorship regime.

Perlzweig's argument that the news would have a demoralizing effect on 'hopeless victims' implied that, for potential victims, ignorance was a better state than full knowledge of the Nazi extermination policy that would soon engulf them. Though British officials would echo this sentiment repeatedly through 1943 and 1944, largely to protect perceived British interests, it is moot. Perlzweig and his colleagues were probably trying to rationalize, at least in part, the delay in disseminating the news. For example, Perlzweig and Irving Miller's cable to Easterman of 1 October 1942 does not read as though senior WJC personnel were seeking to lead on the dissemination of news about the Nazi extermination policy; they wrote, 'Problem receiving consideration of highest authorities whose guidance imperative'.[98]

The strategy of working with the US government did have merit as government confirmation of the information received by Riegner offered a greater chance of it being accepted by civil society and the general

108   The Polish Government in Exile in London

public.[99] On 9 October, Easterman received a further telegram, this time from Wise, Goldmann and Perlzweig, which advised that the US State Department 'chief' (Sumner Welles) urged 'postponement [of] publicity until [the] right effect [was] producible [in the] entire American press'.[100] Confirming the veracity of the Riegner telegram was not the only issue that delayed its dissemination during the autumn of 1942. Information from Riegner's telegram was circulated among Allied governments in London, and further information reached Washington from the American Legation in Bern. On 22 October, Riegner and Richard Lichtheim, the Geneva representative of the Jewish Agency, handed over further documents that provided evidence of the Nazi extermination programme to the US representative in Bern, Leland Harrison.

The significance of Riegner's telegram rested on both the substance of the telegram – that is, the information it divulged to its readers – and the role played by the addressee. Rabbi Stephen Wise was the most prominent American Jewish leader and had access to senior officials at the State Department. By lobbying and liaising with the Secretary of State directly, Wise overcame the State Department's resistance to the dissemination of the news and opened a channel through which information about Nazi anti-Jewish atrocities could reach decision makers. The State Department was thereby placed in a situation to which it had to respond. On 24 November Wise was able to publicly reveal that Sumner Welles had authenticated the information received from Riegner. The authority of the State Department was thereby attached to the claims made in the Riegner telegram and subsequent reports. This altered the discursive landscape in which news of the extermination of Europe's Jews was situated.

Across the Atlantic, the Polish Government in Exile began from October 1942 to publish an increasing number of articles about the slaughter of Jews in *Dziennik Polski*. On 28 September 1942 General Rowecki sent Stanisław Mikołajczyk a message that framed the German terror against Poles as being similar to that endured by Jews.[101] On 15 October, Mikołajczyk responded with, in all probability, an awareness of the Riegner telegram, requesting that Rowecki send information about the persecution of Jews as quickly as possible.[102] Prime Minister Sikorski briefly mentioned Jews in a speech delivered at the Albert Hall on 29 October.[103] At the same event, the chief rabbi, Dr Hertz, also spoke, though his presence at the Albert Hall and the fact that he addressed the audience was all but ignored by the British media.[104] Dr Hertz was direct in his criticism of the reporting of the unfolding Holocaust, pointing to the malign impact of the British censorship regime. He stated that

The UN declaration: November–December 1942

the plain man rarely saw down in black and white any attention-compelling information on these massacres. Such indifference encouraged the gorillas of Berlin to go on perfecting their technique of extermination. The British public could not show its undying hatred of all bestiality, if so much of that bestiality was carelessly screened from public knowledge. (cited in Bolchover 1993: 98)

It was not until late November that the Polish government committed itself fully to publicizing the plight of the Jews. This shift in policy, like the Polish response to the Bund report, has often been understood as an exercise in political expediency. For example, the Representation of Polish Jewry (Reprezentacja Żydostwa Polskiego), an independent organization based in Palestine representing activists from the major Jewish parties of pre-war Poland except for the Bund and the Revisionists which sought to gain equal rights for Jews in a liberated Poland, wrote to the Polish Consulate in Tel Aviv, headed by Henryk Rosmarin, on 6 November 1942. The Reprezentacja requested that the Polish government provide official confirmation that the population of the Warsaw ghetto had fallen from half a million people to 100,000. Rosmarin sent the request on 10 November and the Polish foreign minister replied on 23 November stating that this could not be confirmed, though efforts to obtain the information were being made.[105]

Engel (1987: 197) notes that the Polish foreign minister could have confirmed the fall in the population of the ghetto in Warsaw and argues that the arrival of Jews from Poland in Palestine who provided eyewitness testimony to what was happening in Poland meant that the Polish 'government could no longer continue to draw the curtain over its own knowledge'. In fact, the following day, 24 November 1942, the Polish government released a memorandum recording that only 40,000 ration cards had been printed for Jews in Warsaw in October.[106] This was reported on page 10 of the *New York Times* on 25 November. Earlier, on 16 November, Ignacy Schwarzbart (Polish National Council) had been advised by the Polish government that there were 140,000 Jews in Warsaw. Schwarzbart sent this information to the Jewish Agency, the British Section of the WJC, the Board of Deputies' Foreign Affairs Committee and the Council of Polish Jews in Great Britain.[107] Raczyński's response to the Reprezentacja reflects the Polish government's subscription to the Allied propaganda and censorship policy rather than any specifically Polish policy of concealing information. Advising a member of the Polish National Council of the situation in Warsaw could not be criticized, whereas forwarding data to a non-governmental organization could be.

The dissemination of information from the returnees to Palestine was significant, but the availability of information from Palestine was not the

110   The Polish Government in Exile in London

determining factor in altering the Polish policy position. Rather, the confirmation of the Riegner telegram and the press conference by Rabbi Wise (on 24 November 1942) in the United States signalled to the Polish government that information that it possessed about German actions against Jews now had the possibility of being received by its allies. The pressure applied by Jewish and socialist representatives in the Polish National Council, and by the Reprezentacja, was important, but the Polish government's upsurge in activity on behalf of Poland's Jewish citizens reflects the change in the discursive landscape following Welles's confirmation of the information in the Riegner telegram. The Polish government adhered to Allied censorship policy and in November and December 1942 was able to exploit the window of opportunity to press for further action that the confirmation of the Riegner telegram had opened. In addition, by late November security concerns following the liquidation of the 'Swedish connection' had also been overcome.

The circulation of the Riegner telegram stimulated a wave of lobbying on both sides of the Atlantic, which increased pressure on officials in both the State Department and the Foreign Office to respond. Despite this, notes of caution were sounded. Penkower (2002: 173) quotes the Jewish Agency's political department director Bernard Joseph's argument that '[i]f we announce that millions of Jews have been slaughtered by the Nazis, we will justifiably be asked where the millions of Jews are for whom we need to provide a home in Eretz Israel after the war ends'.[108] The news of the mass killing of Europe's Jews was a story which was carefully weighed by organizations and governments within the Allied camp for its medium- and long-term policy implications.

Members of the Polish National Council, however, pressed the exile government to adopt a proactive policy in response to the mass killing of Polish Jewish citizens. At the session of the National Council on 27 November, the Polish government issued a call for the Allies to condemn the German extermination policy. Earlier, on 25 November 1942, the exile government forwarded a summary of a report on the destruction of Polish Jewry that was possibly carried by the Polish courier and eyewitness Jan Karski to Alexander Easterman of the British Section of the World Jewish Congress, who, along with the Labour MP Sydney Silverman, met British Foreign Secretary Anthony Eden's deputy, Richard Law, on 26 November. Silverman called for a four-power declaration (Britain, the USSR, the US and China). Law advised colleagues in the Foreign Office that 'unless some kind of gesture' was made Silverman and his friends 'will cause a lot of trouble'.[109]

The Polish government lobbied the Western Allies for a formal declaration to be made. It was the Polish government, rather than, as

The UN declaration: November–December 1942   111

is commonly assumed, the British government, which initiated the process that resulted in the UN declaration of 17 December 1942. FO official Frank Roberts reminded his colleagues that 'the origin of the declaration was Polish rather than British but it is true that we had to do most of the work connected with it'.[110] The Polish Government in Exile did not make political capital out of this fact, which suggests that its policy was somewhat less instrumental than is often claimed.[111] The efforts of Jewish representatives were also important. The lobbying by Polish officials and Jewish representatives in November and December 1942 calling for a UN declaration also serves to illustrate the information dissemination strategy of the Polish government towards the Holocaust that was sustained through the rest of the war. Information was passed directly to the Allies. It was also passed, often indirectly, to representatives of various Jewish organizations.[112] This approach allowed both the Polish government and the Jewish organizations to petition the Western Allies.[113]

In the final week of November 1942, a series of articles appeared in the British press on the mass slaughter of Jews, most of which came from Polish sources. On 24 November, on page 3, the *Daily Telegraph* declared, 'European Jewry is being exterminated: mass butchery by Gestapo'; on 25 November, on page 2, the paper reported, 'Mass murder of Polish Jews – Himmler orders "extermination"'. This article mentioned the death camps of Treblinka, Bełżec and Sobibór. Two days later, on 27 November, the *Jewish Chronicle* published a front-page article entitled 'Destruction of Polish Jewry: mass murder by Nazis, 250,000 dead in 6 months', which drew on information received from the Polish Government in Exile. This story repeated much of the information earlier reported in the *Daily Telegraph*, and the exile government played a key role in the dissemination of this news.

The role played by the Ministry of Information in approving the publication of 'Jewish' stories is not known for certain. However, given the informal nature of the 'voluntary' censorship regime it is possible that the publication of such stories was initially agreed to by Bracken in private conversation with newspaper editors and proprietors, and that the State Department's confirmation of the veracity of the Riegner telegram signalled to the British press that news from Poland about Jews could now be published. On 26 November, in a front-page story entitled 'Liquidation of the Warsaw ghetto', *Dziennik Polski* published in Polish the same information handed over to the *Daily Telegraph* for its 25 November article. On 30 November, the front page of *Dziennik Polski* carried the headline 'Country, Government, National Council against the mass murder of Jews in Poland'.

112   The Polish Government in Exile in London

The 1 December 1942 edition of the *Polish Fortnightly Review* was devoted in its entirety to news of the Jews in Poland. The front-page headline, 'Extermination of the Polish Jewry – what happened in the Warsaw ghetto', introduced an extensive analysis of Nazi ghetto policy and practice in Warsaw. Page 2 had a subtitle, 'Mass murder under the guise of deportation'; page 4 featured an 'Extraordinary report from the Jew extermination camp at Bełżec'; page 7 published the declaration of the Polish government and the resolution of the Polish National Council which highlighted the German crimes and the Polish protest against these crimes.

Ignacy Schwarzbart maintained pressure on the Polish government to continue to publicize news of the German atrocities. At the session of the Polish National Council of 25 November 1942, Schwarzbart had alleged that Sikorski's brief reference to Jews in his 29 October speech at the Albert Hall had been removed from the BBC broadcast to Poland. This allegation was printed in the bulletin of the Jewish Telegraphic Agency on 27 November.[114] The Polish minister of information, Stanisław Stroński, contacted Ivone Kirkpatrick at the BBC, who provided documentary proof that the speech, inclusive of the reference to Jews, had in fact been broadcast several times.

Dziennik Polski published a story detailing the entire affair about the BBC broadcast on 3 December.[115] It is possible that Schwarzbart's allegation was made to highlight the inadequacy of that brief reference, to demonstrate to the Polish government his seriousness in ensuring that the government pursued all options to highlight the fate of Poland's Jews with vigour, and to ensure that the British were also aware of his concerns, and to encourage them to act.[116] A week later, *Dziennik* reported on its front page that a third of Polish Jews had already perished during the German occupation.[117]

During early December 1942, the public was being prepared for an official British government announcement on the Nazi mass killing of Jews through the media attention devoted to the issue.[118] On 2 December the Soviet ambassador to London expressed interest in a joint declaration (Laqueur 1998: 225). The 8 December PWE directive sent to the British ambassador in Washington informed him that 'in view of increased violence of German persecution of Jews a statement representing the views of HMG, the United States and Soviet Governments is under consideration and may be published at an early date'.[119] The following day the PWE directive reiterated that a statement was forthcoming, noting that the Polish government had provided the evidence and called for the fullest facts to be disseminated even if the statement was postponed. The PWE directive for 9 December went on to declare,

The UN declaration: November–December 1942

'Anti-semitism was a potent weapon of Nazi political warfare. The time has now come to use it against them'. The general directive to the BBC European Service for 10 December called for bulletins to broadcast news on '[i]nside the Festung Europa with particular reference to the massacre of the Jews'.[120] That same day, Polish foreign minister Edward Raczyński addressed a note to British Foreign Secretary Anthony Eden and the governments of the United Nations, detailing the mass slaughter of the Jews. This data was later described by Foreign Office officials as 'a good summary of existing information from Polish sources',[121] indicating that Polish intelligence on the annihilation of Jews had already been assessed.

The British press continued to highlight the news from Poland. On 2 December, the *Daily Telegraph* had a page 5 story reporting on Sydney Silverman's statement that the Nazis had killed two million Jews; on 4 December the paper reported the Polish foreign minister's meeting with Anthony Eden, in which Raczyński outlined the Polish government's position. Raczyński demanded reprisals, the dissemination of the information of the extermination of the Jews and an Allied conference to send a stern warning to Germany. These demands had originally been made at the meeting of the Polish National Council the previous week. *The Times* on 4 December featured a prominent article on page 3, entitled 'Nazi war on Jews – deliberate plan for extermination', drawing on reports from Berlin and Poland. On 7 December an equally prominent article appeared on page 3, entitled 'Terror against Jews – European pogrom – US and Soviet in London talks', which highlighted efforts to co-ordinate an Allied response to 'mass murder'. On 10 December another page 3 article in the *Daily Telegraph* noted a meeting of MPs, chaired by Sydney Silverman, which discussed the atrocities committed against Jews, and on 11 December page 5 featured a headline, '1,000,000 Polish Jews killed', recording that the Polish foreign minister had circulated a diplomatic note on this issue.

In contrast, the BBC's Home Service failed to report most of the information that was circulating in the British press, largely under pressure from the Foreign Office. On 2 December 1942 in a memorandum to colleagues at the Foreign Office, Wedgwood Harrison noted that Mr Cummings, the BBC's liaison officer between the Home Service and the Foreign Office, had been advised to 'soft pedal' the story about the extermination of the Jews prior to any Foreign Office decision on the issue.[122] Cummings in turn issued a circular to key figures in the European Service, stating that 'they [the FO] ask us if possible to hold up any news issued from Jewish quarters until the FO are able to say what has been agreed; or, at all events, to treat such news with great discretion'.[123]

114   The Polish Government in Exile in London

Milland (1998b: 67) suggests that the FO wanted to make sure that the UN declaration made an impact, but by inhibiting the BBC, which remained a trusted source of information for the British population, from broadcasting the news, the reception of reports in newspapers was affected. The lack of timely BBC confirmation adversely impacted on the British comprehension of what was happening to Jews in Europe. Contra Milland, it is likely that the Foreign Office was trying to manage the news agenda and *limit* the impact of news about the mass murder of Jews.[124] For this reason, Harrison had advised Cummings that the Foreign Office did not want to give the impression that they 'were deliberately trying to kill the story', as the FO recognized that this was not possible given the wide circulation the news had received following the authentication of the claims made in the Riegner telegram.[125]

Foreign Office officials were well aware of the likely result of confirming the news from Poland. Frank Roberts was very concerned about possible parliamentary questions that might be provoked by the UN declaration. Roberts advised colleagues in the Foreign Office in an internal memo on 16 December 1942 that

although we do not want to provoke it ourselves, it is possible that Members may ask what practical steps are being taken by H.M.G. to assist the emigration of Jews from occupied Europe. It may be difficult to satisfy M.P.s on this point as the position is (a) that the Home Office will not permit any large scale increase of immigration into this country even if the Jews could get here; (b) that the Colonial Empire can hardly be expected to absorb more refugees than have already been poured into it although a little is being done in regard to Palestine; (c) neutral countries in Europe can hardly be expected to help much.[126]

The FO strategy of 'soft pedalling' the news of atrocities prior to 17 December did enable officials to co-ordinate an Allied response to the horrific news in December 1942. It also allowed the Foreign Office to pre-empt, to a degree, calls for refuge. So while the FO sought to limit the demands that the news of atrocities against Jews could provoke in Britain, others, including Polish Jews, continued to press for action.

On 4 December the *Jewish Chronicle* reported on the atrocities. The special session of the Polish National Council, in which Zygielbojm called for reprisals, for a leaflet drop over Germany and for an Allied Conference, was highlighted. A week later, the paper noted that a delegation of Jewish leaders had met with President Roosevelt on 8 December at the White House and advised him of the atrocities. The delegation handed Roosevelt a memorandum with details of the Nazi extermination programme.[127] The front page of the paper carried the headline 'Two million Jews slaughtered'.

The UN declaration: November–December 1942   115

The PWE sent a central directive on 15 December 1942 to the British ambassador in Washington (who forwarded it to the US Office of War Information), which outlined British policy in relation to the publicization of news of the extermination of Jews:

Although the news within the last few days has lent itself to emphasis on the Jewish question, our line is to treat Jewish persecution factually and as part of a deliberate plan of extermination which includes other minorities. We suggest that the American contribution to this would be statements by European minority leaders on the Jewish question as part of a common pattern.[128]

The House of Lords discussed atrocities in Poland that same day. Though the focus was on Polish citizens, Jews were mentioned and Lord Selborne noted that 'the Jewish citizens of Poland have suffered particularly severely'.[129]

In contrast to the restrained tone of the BBC news bulletins in late November and early December 1942, Noel Newsome used his *Man in the Street* talk of 15 December 1942 to draw attention to what was happening to Europe's Jews. Entitled 'A stigma for generations', the talk was broadcast on the BBC's European Service and referred to Hitler's policy to 'exterminate every Jew in Europe'. Newsome argued that '[t]he Jews in Europe are faced with extermination. The Germans are faced with a shame and disgrace which will not be wiped out for generations.' Although noting the Nazi extermination policy, Newsome focused on the disgrace that Nazi actions brought on Germany.[130]

Zygielbojm attempted to keep the pressure on the British. On 15 December, he sent a telegram to Churchill calling on the prime minister to find ways to save those few Polish Jews who had survived the Nazi slaughter. A reply was ultimately sent at the end of December stating that the government was 'investigating all practical means of bringing relief to the victims of the German terror'.[131] The same telegram was also sent to President Roosevelt and released by the Polish Telegraphic Agency.[132]

On 16 December, the PWE central directive, referring to the UN declaration that was to be released the following day, called for the broadcast news to highlight 'the deliberate plan of Jewish extermination' as the 'one war aim that Hitler still hopes to achieve in the few months remaining to him', to emphasize that the Germans and their vassals would be judged by their 'attitude to Hitler's plan' and to send a message of encouragement to the Jews.[133]

The following day, 17 December 1942, saw the release of the UN declaration in the US, the USSR and Britain. In the House of Commons, Anthony Eden declared,

116 The Polish Government in Exile in London

The attention of the Governments of Belgium, Czechoslovakia, Greece, Luxemburg, the Netherlands, Norway, Poland, the United States of America, the United Kingdom of Great Britain and Northern Ireland, the Union of Soviet Socialist Republics and Yugoslavia, and of the French National Committee has been drawn to numerous reports from Europe that the German authorities, not content with denying to persons of Jewish race in all the territories over which their barbarous rule has been extended the most elementary human rights, are now carrying into effect Hitler's oft repeated intention to exterminate the Jewish people in Europe. From all the occupied countries Jews are being transported, in conditions of appalling horror and brutality, to Eastern Europe. In Poland, which has been made the principal Nazi slaughterhouse, the ghettoes established by the German invaders are being systematically emptied of all Jews except a few highly skilled workers required for war industries. None of those taken away are ever heard of again. The able-bodied are slowly worked to death in labour camps. The infirm are left to die of exposure and starvation or are deliberately massacred in mass executions. The number of victims of these bloody cruelties is reckoned in many hundreds of thousands of entirely innocent men, women and children.

The above-mentioned Governments and the French National Committee condemn in the strongest possible terms this bestial policy of cold-blooded extermination. They declare that such events can only strengthen the resolve of all freedom-loving peoples to overthrow the barbarous Hitlerite tyranny. They re-affirm their solemn resolution to ensure that those responsible for these crimes shall not escape retribution, and to press on with the necessary practical measures to this end.[134]

Members of Parliament stood in silence in support of the UN protest against the Nazi crimes. The UN declaration was also read in the House of Lords by the Lord Chancellor, Viscount Simon.

Noel Newsome's general directive for the BBC's European Service on 17 December read:

The issue today of the joint declaration about the massacre of the Jews simultaneously in London, Moscow and Washington is a story of historic importance. It is also of enormous value for political warfare. The scene in the House of Commons today when all members stood in silence in tribute to the murdered Jews gives this story solemnity and picturesque interest which entitles us on all counts to make this great international protest our lead story for the day. I think it would create a tremendous impression in Europe if we led all our bulletins for the next few hours with this story.[135]

That same day the *Daily Telegraph* ran a story on page 3 entitled 'Jewish atrocities', which described events in Poland and gave readers notice of the UN declaration. On 18 December, news of the UN declaration reached the front page, and further information on MPs pledging retribution featured on page 3. Both *Dziennik Polski* and the *Jewish Chronicle* devoted their front pages to the story. The general directive for the BBC's European Service for 18 December called for the Allied statement to

The UN declaration: November–December 1942

remain one of the main stories for the day, and for the presentation of 'the extermination of the Jews simply as a personal policy dictated by Hitler'. A piece on the Warsaw ghetto by Frank Savery was highlighted as containing good copy.[136] The BBC's Home Service did not report at all on the Holocaust on 18 December 1942, and, as Milland (1998b: 100) notes, 'news of the Final Solution was left to trail off in a matter of days after the issuing of the [UN] Declaration'.

Four days later, the *Daily Telegraph* reported calls for action by the Board of Deputies, and the contention of Eleanor Rathbone MP that neutral countries should accept refugees.[137] The immediate response to the UN declaration in Britain was to increase pressure on the British government to act, and to provide sanctuary at home and abroad for the Jews targeted by the Nazi regime. Immediately after Eden had delivered the declaration at the House of Commons, the Independent Labour MP for Glasgow Shettleston, John McGovern, asked whether those who escaped occupied territories would be given sanctuary. Eden's response was very measured:

Certainly we should like to do all we possibly can. There are, obviously, certain security formalities which have to be considered. It would clearly be the desire of the United Nations to do everything they could to provide wherever possible an asylum for these people, but the House will understand that there are immense geographical and other difficulties in the matter.[138]

The British and US governments sought to manage public outcry and demands that sanctuary for refugees be provided by promising a conference on the issue. This took place in Bermuda in April 1943. The BBC reported the opening of the conference on 19 April, broadcasting on the Home Service that the aim was 'to find out how best to deal with the problem of helping victims of the Axis'. The fact that the main victims were Jews was not highlighted.[139]

Since the outcome of the conference committed neither government to any serious action, and helped to defuse demands to aid Europe's Jews, it was adjudged a success by the Foreign Office. The Bermuda conference also allowed the Foreign Office to argue that it was doing everything possible and to give the impression that it was constrained by its American ally. Ignacy Schwarzbart in July 1943 contended that 'the political centre of gravity of the problem lies in Washington', suggesting that the British government was encountering 'some difficulties from the US Government without whose collaboration they cannot obviously in the present circumstances undertake any steps'.[140] Schwarzbart was not entirely correct; neither the British nor the Americans were keen to divert resources to aid Europe's Jews.

118   The Polish Government in Exile in London

The internationalization of the issue (the situation of Jews in Nazi-controlled Europe), through the UN declaration of December 1942 and through the conference at Bermuda, changed the geographic scale at which those seeking to aid Jews suffering under Nazi tyranny had to operate. Increasingly, political representatives from Poland and civil-society activitists had to make judgements about how the relationship between the Allies worked, and about the policy positions taken by the various governments, in order to petition the right people at the right time. In Britain, the National Committee for the Rescue from Nazi Terror was established in March 1943 to challenge the British government's failure to alter its policy in relation to Jews in Nazi-controlled Europe after the UN declaration. This committee was headed by the MP Eleanor Rathbone and included many public figures, including the publisher Victor Gollancz; the archbishop of York; the chief rabbi; and the chairman of the Board of Deputies, Professor Selig Brodetsky, amongst others.

On 19 May 1943 refugee policy was discussed in the House of Commons, but there was no change in British policy.[141] By the summer of 1943 Foreign Office obduracy had worn down members of the National Committee, and demands that British policy include a commitment to rescue and provide refuge to Europe's Jews were increasingly muted. Instead, attention was turned to combating and averting anti-Semitism in Britain. Rathbone was dismissed as an 'impatient idealist' by the Foreign Office (Cohen 2001: 93), and the National Committee for the Rescue from Nazi Terror was unable to pressure the British government to alter its policy position in favour of Europe's Jews. In some part, this was due to members of the committee accepting, like Schwarzbart, that the stumbling block was in Washington, DC, not London. Even if this was true, the National Committee was unable to respond effectively and act at the transnational scale. The failure of efforts to change British policy during the spring and summer of 1943 demonstrates how the Foreign Office was able to use the internationalization of the issue (rescue/refuge for Europe's Jews) to explain inaction. The implied complexity of the American–British relationship proved to be a barrier to civil-society pressure to effect policy change.

Schwarzbart continued to demand that policies to assist Europe's Jews be put in place by the Allies, and paid increasing attention to the attitude of the United States government. At the end of July 1943, he called on Mikołajczyk to petition the American government to help Europe's Jews. That same month Jan Karski spoke with American officials and intelligence figures about the situation in Poland and discussed Nazi policy against Jews. On 28 July, Karski met with President Roosevelt. Informing and lobbying US officials was necessary given the significance of the

The UN declaration: November–December 1942

United States in the war effort, but arguably it also had the unintended consequence of relieving pressure on the Foreign Office, and the British more generally, to respond to calls to aid Europe's Jews.

Not until the final stages of the war did either the British or the United States government make significant statements on the persecution of the Jews again. Both Britain and the US recognized that formal declarations had domestic consequences which could impact on policy, on how the war was being narrated and even on war objectives. Neither government wanted Nazi Germany to send the Jews of occupied Europe to the West. The British ambassador to the United States, Viscount Halifax, referring to an earlier memo on Jewish refugees, wrote late in the war (7 April 1944) to Anthony Eden, clearly revealing the British concern about refugees that was constant through the war: 'I should not suppose the risk of Hitler unloading millions of Jews on us is very serious'.[142] Both the British and the Americans, after the December 1942 declaration, shared the fear that sustained and energetic measures to offer sanctuary to the persecuted Jews of Europe might actually be successful.[143]

Following the UN declaration, the Polish government complained that the publicity in Britain given to the declaration and to further stories of massacres in Poland was inadequate. William Denis Allen of the German Department at the Foreign Office was inclined to concede this point in an internal memo on 26 January 1943. He explained this to colleagues by pointing to

limitations imposed by considerations of space in the newspapers and of time in radio broadcasts, and of the fact that from the point of view of news value saturation point is soon reached and the constant repetition of horror stories is apt to produce mere boredom rather than active sympathy.[144]

These considerations were not conceived as challenges to be overcome in order to keep public attention on the annihilation of Europe's Jews, but as reasons to close the story down.

Allen then highlighted the key issue:

From the point of view of policy there is also a real danger that an active publicity campaign might, as happened in the case of the Jewish Declaration, stir up an active demand that something shall be done. This might be unfortunate and embarrassing, since in actual fact there is little we can do to help the Poles short of winning the war.[145]

From this memo and subsequent commentary, it is clear that FO officials viewed their role in the UN declaration, at least in part, as performing a favour for the Polish government. Allen noted, for example, that the Polish Government, as the 'prime movers behind the joint declaration of the 17th December', obtained 'especial publicity for the sufferings of

120   The Polish Government in Exile in London

the Jews in Poland, which was the only country mentioned in the declaration itself', and recorded the help extended to the Polish government, including the British Ministry of Information printing the government's circular, speeches on the BBC and, revealingly, the broadcast of the declaration in Britain.

In a commentary on Allen's memo, Frank Roberts drew attention to the Polish government's request to broadcast a warning in Lithuanian to discourage Lithuanians who collaborated with the Germans from persisting in their actions, highlighting that such a broadcast had implications for Anglo-Soviet relations. Both these officials expressed exasperation with the Polish government, Allen due to its focus on the need for retaliation (which the British were disinclined to sanction), and Roberts, on the fact that 'the Poles completely ignore all that has been done in the past', and on delays on the Polish side in drafting messages. Roberts's condescending final point – that '[w]e [Foreign Office] and PWE are, however, doing our best to help the Poles along' – highlights the unequal and patronizing relationship between the British and the Poles, something that was to be clearly exposed in May 1943.[146]

Geopolitics and controlling the Polish press

Through 1943, relations between the Polish government and the British became increasingly strained as Polish efforts to publicize atrocities against Polish citizens, and to broadcast messages to the different national groups within the 1939 borders of Poland, were thwarted. The British, for their part, were keen not to antagonize the Soviet Union. The USSR was doing most of the actual fighting against the Germans, and British sensitivity to the concerns of the USSR had been a continuous strand of policy since 1939.[147]

During the first half of 1941 the Polish government planned to publish a book that outlined conditions in Poland under German and Soviet occupation. By late spring a copy in French was given very limited circulation. The British, however, expressed negative views on the desirability of the section on the Soviet occupation being published in English in Britain. And by late June, with the German invasion of the Soviet Union, the geopolitical situation changed radically. Frank Savery impressed on the Polish foreign minister, August Zaleski, that there was no advantage 'in choosing this moment to expose Moscow's crimes', especially when they, the Poles, were seeking the release of Polish prisoners held in the Soviet Union.[148] Only the section dealing with the German occupation was published. The Foreign Office liaised with the State Department to inhibit publication of the Soviet section in the

US, and the Polish government, with a view to improving Polish–Soviet relations, was receptive to British and American pressure. An opportune time to highlight the conditions endured under the Soviet occupation did not arise again, which made it difficult for the British and American public to understand Polish hostility to the USSR later in the war.[149]

In a similar fashion, the Foreign Office urged that a publication entitled *The Story of Wilno* be withdrawn, curtailed the Polish government's ambitions to broadcast to Polish Ukrainian citizens in Ukrainian, and had reservations about a special broadcast on the BBC's Home Service to mark Polish Independence Day, so as not to antagonize the Soviet Union.[150] The Polish liaison officer to the BBC, Count Baliński, handed a memorandum to Frank Roberts of the Foreign Office on 20 June 1942 in which he drew attention to the censorship of broadcasts on the BBC's Polish Service. He highlighted that a special broadcast on Wilno was cancelled and noted that the region around the city had seen an upsurge in Nazi persecutions, including the shooting of 400 Poles for the killing of two Germans and the 'wholesale massacre of Jews'. Baliński argued that it was imperative that this information be broadcast.[151]

Later that year, the Foreign Office micro-managed a warning broadcast over the BBC to Lithuanians collaborating with the Germans, and, at the urging of several officials, including the senior Foreign Office official, Orme Sargent, the text was revised. The draft version submitted by the Polish government on 26 October 1942 noted that the 'police force and Lithuanian Schutzmannschaften have been wilfully persecuting and maltreating the non-Lithuanian inhabitants of the so-called Generalbezirk Litauen – Poles as well as White Ruthenians and Jews'. Here, the main victim groups are White Ruthenians and Jews, whilst Poles are an additional group of victims. Sargent called for the removal of the mention of 'White Russians' (i.e. White Ruthenians – Belarusians) and the rephrasing of the final part of the sentence to read 'Poles and Jews'. One victim group is ignored so as not to disturb the USSR (the mention of White Ruthenians would raise the question of the Polish eastern border), and the other groups are given equal weight.[152] The Soviet Embassy in London was advised of the warning to Lithuanians prior to broadcast through the BBC.

In early 1943, the exile government wished to broadcast to Poland a special message marking Orthodox Christmas on 6 January, which would appeal to Ukrainians and White Ruthenians (Belarusians). The broadcast was cancelled at the behest of the British, in order not to antagonize the USSR by indirectly affirming Poland's 1939 borders. The Polish minister of information wrote a measured letter of complaint to the British Foreign Secretary, in which he highlighted the Polish

122   The Polish Government in Exile in London

government's awareness of British sensitivity to the USSR, the Polish desire not to embarrass the British government, and Polish insistence that it should be able to address Polish citizens within Poland's 1939 borders, stressing that it 'was inadmissible that the Russian question should be artificially introduced into the internal affairs of Poland'.[153] Stroński pointedly remarked that

[i]n former times, the Polish Government was often reproached with not taking sufficient heed in Poland of nationalities and denominations other than the Polish majority, and now it is being prevented from acknowledging their existence and expressing its good will towards them.[154]

In extensive Foreign Office commentary on this issue, Frank Roberts noted that all attempts by the Poles to broadcast to Ukrainians in Ukrainian had been rejected. He stated that the Polish government had pointed out that this group was recognized as a nationality in pre-war Poland. Roberts also reminded colleagues that the British had not, officially, recognized any change in Poland's borders. For the Poles, therefore, addressing Ukrainian Polish citizens in Ukrainian was a reasonable demand. For the British, equally, it posed potential problems with the USSR. Foreign Office officials, aware of the strength of feeling on the Polish side, were prepared to accommodate the Polish request for a broadcast on Orthodox New Year. But this was seen as a special case. Ivone Kirkpatrick expressed the view that the Poles 'must be allowed to have a fling sometimes and be given discretion to decide how often they should enjoy the luxury of a fling. My own experience leads me to think that the Poles overestimate their own discretion in the matter'.[155]

At the same time Polish Government policy, informed by the resolution of the National Council of 27 November 1942, sought reprisals for atrocities committed in Poland by Germans. The British were unconvinced by such a policy, a view which dismayed the Poles, but which they reluctantly accepted. In a letter to General Sikorski dated 13 January 1943, Churchill cited the distance to Poland, the weather and the fact that the American Air Force was not equipped with aircraft that could bomb targets in Poland as reasons for refusing Polish demands for reprisals.[156] Churchill attempted to soften the news by assuring the Polish government that, in reports on bombing raids on Germany, the contribution of Polish airmen would be mentioned. Clearly, Churchill's intention was not to patronize Britain's ally, but reducing the Polish demand for reprisals to a promise that due credit would be given to efforts of Polish airmen risked misinterpretation.

Later, in January 1943, the Polish government was of the view that even threats of reprisals and messages of encouragement were being

Geopolitics and controlling the Polish press 123

censored by the BBC – a reference to Clement Attlee's speech in the House of Commons on 19 January which was cut for broadcast. In Parliament Attlee spoke of the suffering of the Jews, stated that the 'German authorities have pursued a deliberate policy of reducing the Polish people to slavery ... [Allied] power to strike back at the oppressors [was] increasing ... [and] recent raids on Berlin [demonstrated the Allied] ability to deal heavy blows at the very heart of the enemy's strength'.[157] In a letter to Ivone Kirkpatrick, Ambassador Raczyński angrily argued,

Publicity happens to be the only way by which you can help our suffering people in their most cruel ordeal. It is needed not in order to give Polish emigrants abroad a vain satisfaction but for a very real purpose, and I cannot understand what policy the BBC is pursuing by grudging us this support.[158]

Later that month Prime Minister Sikorski and Ambassador Raczyński met Foreign Secretary Eden. They raised the issue of censorship, highlighted the integrity of the Polish frontiers and the right of the Polish government to use Ukrainian to address Ukrainian Polish citizens. Eden noted Soviet sensitivities.[159] In February, William Strang at the Foreign Office summarized British policy towards the Polish frontiers in an internal communication, noting that the FO 'discourage[s] ... any reference by Poles to their Eastern frontier'.[160] This policy, through the PWE, as examined in Chapter 2, was then carried out at the BBC. The output report (which assessed the impact of broadcasting) on the Polish Service for 19–25 February notes the angry response from the Polish National Council to the BBC refusal to broadcast on the issue of the eastern frontier.[161]

The difficulties of early 1943 were soon eclipsed by the full-blown crisis that followed the German revelation of the Katyń graves in April. Soviet documents released under the Gorbachev and Yeltsin governments demonstrate that the decision to massacre over 22,000 Polish officers (including several hundred Jews) was taken by the Politburo of the All-Union Communist Party (Bolsheviks) on 5 March 1940 and by Stalin himself (Sanford 2005).[162] The Polish government had petitioned the Soviet government continuously, following the signing of the Sikorski–Maisky agreement in July 1941, to locate and release these officers. The Soviets stalled and misled the Polish government, in full awareness that these officers were already dead. Following the German declaration of the discovery of the mass graves, the Poles announced, on 17 April, their request for a Red Cross investigation. The Soviets thereupon broke off diplomatic relations on 25 April 1943.

Tensions between the two countries had already been rising steadily through late 1942 and early 1943. In February 1943 information about

124   The Polish Government in Exile in London

two Polish Jewish citizens and leaders of the Bund – Wiktor Alter and Henryk Erlich – reached London from the USSR. Both men were arrested in October 1941 and subjected to lengthy interrogation. Alter was executed by firing squad on 17 April 1943. It is now known that Erlich, with his health failing, hanged himself in his prison cell on 15 May 1942.[163] In 1943 it was thought that the Soviets had executed both Alter and Erlich. After weeks of pressure from the Polish Socialist Party and the Bund, which included a focus on Alter and Erlich in the 15 March edition of the Polish Socialist Party's paper *Robotnik Polski* (published in London), the Polish National Council condemned the Soviet execution on 17 April.

With good reason, the Poles strongly believed that the Soviets were the perpetrators of the Katyń crime, but in the context of wartime alliances, the British sought to limit the propagation of this view, even though Foreign Office officials recognized Soviet culpability. On 6 May 1943, Noel Newsome (the BBC's editor of European news) dined with Anthony Eden and others. Newsome received a specific impression of Eden's views. According to Newsome, Eden thought that the 'Russians probably did kill the Soviet [*sic*] officers'.[164] Later, on 24 May, the British ambassador to the Polish government in London, Owen O'Malley, distributed a report which was circulated within the Foreign Office and the British Cabinet, and which demonstrated Soviet responsibility without much doubt.[165]

On 7 May, Prime Minister Sikorski and Ambassador Raczyński met British Foreign Secretary Anthony Eden. On the British agenda was the control of information about Katyń and inhibiting the publication of anti-Soviet sentiments. Earlier, on 28 April, the directive of the Political Warfare Executive declared that 'it is our job to help to ensure that history will record the Katyn Forest incident as a futile attempt by Germany to postpone defeat by political methods' (Bell 1990: 119). For the British, the priority was to ensure that Anglo-Soviet relations were not jeopardized by Katyń. The interests of Poland, and the truth of the massacre, were of marginal importance. The USSR's contribution to the war effort had to be sustained at all costs.[166]

On 12 May Raczyński sent Eden details of Polish papers and journals published in Britain, summarizing which organizations controlled particular papers. The British aim was to moderate Polish outrage directed at the Soviet Union, by advising Polish editors of British concerns, while at the same time disciplining the anti-Polish, pro-Soviet *Daily Worker*. During May, Brendan Bracken and Home Secretary Herbert Morrison were put under parliamentary pressure robustly to control the Polish press. A debate in the House of Commons on 20 May highlighted

Geopolitics and controlling the Polish press 125

hostility felt towards the Polish government by certain parliamentarians. The pro-Soviet MP William Gallacher asked Morrison, 'Is it not peculiar that the Minister is very careful in his language when dealing with Fascist propaganda and very vicious with his language when it is a question of the "Daily Worker"?' The Labour MP for Wolverhampton East, Geoffrey Mander, in a reference to the Polish press, asked Bracken

whether, in view of the harm that is being done to the Allied war effort by the publication in Allied newspapers published in foreign languages in this country of views hostile to and inconsistent with the policy of the United Nations, he will consider the possibility of withdrawing their licences from the journals concerned?[167]

Bracken replied,

The Ministry of Information is conducting an inquiry into the activities of these foreign language newspapers which are alleged to occupy themselves in attacking the Soviet Government. If this allegation is well founded, we shall be in duty bound to prevent the hospitality of Great Britain being abused by journalists who seem to be more interested in feuds than in news.

He added, 'I do not intend to tolerate these people rushing around the country, publishing in foreign languages the most violent abuse of the Soviet Government, or the Polish Government, or indeed of any Government connected with the United Nations'. Although Bracken had attempted to guide the debate so that due consideration was given to the anti-Polish *Daily Worker*, participating parliamentarians were more concerned with disciplining the Polish press. A subsequent debate on the issue on 2 June followed a similar pattern. Mander queried whether Bracken had 'completed his inquiry into the activities of foreign-language newspapers published in this country hostile to the Soviet Government', and John Leslie, Labour MP for Sedgefield, asked the minister of information 'whether he is aware that certain Polish newspapers in this country are still quoting German stories about the alleged Smolensk massacres; and whether he will consider stopping the publication of these papers in the interest of unity for the prosecution of the war?'[168] Bracken responded by advising that editors had been warned and that, if an appropriate sense of responsibility was not shown, drastic action would be taken.[169]

The final part of the debate took place on 23 June, with Bracken reporting that 'His Majesty's Government have taken measures to ensure that a failure on the part of a foreign publication to observe proper restraint will not be tolerated', though Mander and Gallacher continued to highlight anti-Soviet sentiment in the Polish press. For the British government, these debates, which drew a fairly negative picture of the

Polish press by suggesting that it used 'German stories' or 'Fascist propaganda', were important 'performances' for Soviet observers.[170] It allowed the British to show to its Soviet ally that it was disciplining the Polish press. Churchill had been even more direct. In a letter to Stalin on 10 May 1943, Churchill declared that the 'Polish press will be disciplined in future and all other foreign publications'. He went on to argue that 'the Polish Government is susceptible to improvement, though there would be problems in finding better substitutes. I think, like you, that Sikorski and one or two others should in any event be retained'.[171] Clearly, the Polish desire for transparency regarding Katyń was subservient to Anglo-Soviet relations, and the British were prepared to extensively accommodate Soviet views at the expense of their Polish ally.[172] Less than two months after Churcill had written to Stalin, Sikorski was killed in a plane crash just off Gibraltar. Given that Sikorski was one of the few Polish politicans viewed by both the British and the Soviets as broadly acceptable, his death had an adverse impact on Poland's standing within the Grand Alliance.

By the end of 1943, the new Polish prime minister, Stanisław Mikołajczyk, clearly perceived the trajectory of Allied politics. In a meeting on 30 November with Harold Osborne, an official of the Political Warfare Executive, Mikołajczyk expressed his view that the aim of Soviet propaganda was to prepare world opinion for the execution of Polish Underground leaders on charges of opposing communists in Poland, and advised that he would have liked to have presented the Polish point of view. He was, however, 'resigned to the fact that this is not possible [but he regarded this impossibility as] a serious calamity for his country'.[173] That same month, *Dziennik Żołnierza*, a paper with a rightist hue that was published by the Polish military, was merged with *Dziennik Polski*, in part to bring *Dziennik Żołnierza* under more 'responsible' control. The British Ministry of Information strongly approved of this development.

The Polish government was making strenuous efforts to appease its British ally, but the break in Polish–Soviet relations severely strained the Alliance. It also had an effect on how the Holocaust was reported, since the Soviet characterization of the Polish government as a reactionary clique made the Soviets unreceptive to Polish appeals for Allied declarations against German atrocities, as any such appeal could reflect positively on the Polish government and arouse sympathy for Poland. It therefore became increasingly difficult for the Polish government to highlight German atrocities against Jews or Poles taking place in Poland, as the Soviet government was opposed to any engagement with the Poles, and the US and the UK put up stiff resistance to Polish

Geopolitics and controlling the Polish press

requests for joint declarations for the practical reason that they could stimulate demands for action.[174]

During 1943, Mikołajczyk, as leader of the Peasant Party, privileged the plight of peasants in the Lublin and Zamość regions, both of which had had a significant pre-war Jewish population, but he did not ignore the fate of the Jews.[175] Mikołajczyk saw the Nazi programme as incremental in its targeting of groups – intelligentsia, Jews and, in 1943, peasants. For this reason he pressed for an Allied statement, to which the UK and the US reluctantly agreed in August 1943 after eight months of continuous pressure.[176] The US–UK statement was published on 30 August in *The Times* under the title 'German crimes in Poland – a British warning'. The statement spoke of 'crimes against the population of Poland', highlighted that 'hundreds of thousands of persons have been deported from their homes or exterminated', and promised that the war 'will be prosecuted with utmost vigour until the barbarous Hitlerite tyranny has been finally overthrown'. FO documents make it clear that ethnic Poles were being discussed, but the actual statement was more general and inclusive. By late August 1943, most of Polish Jewry had already been annihilated.

The Polish government's highlighting of deportations and persecutions of people from the Lublin and Zamość region kept the issue of German atrocities in Poland in front of FO officials in a form which mirrored British censorship policy. Ethnic Poles were privileged. But through 1943 the Polish government also supplied Western Allies with a steady stream of information about what was happening to Jews in particular, including information on the fate of the Warsaw ghetto in April and May 1943 and the mass gassing of Jews at Auschwitz. However, in the context of tense Allied relations and the progressive marginalization of the Polish Government in Exile, the story of the Holocaust in 1943 and 1944 never became the focus of sustained attention in the British and American media as it briefly had in July and December 1942.[177] As is shown in Chapters 4 and 5, the stream of news about Auschwitz supplied by the Polish Government in Exile (and others) never received due attention under the constraints of British censorship, despite attempts to give the news wide publicity.

4 Intelligence about Auschwitz: November 1940–February 1943

Information about Auschwitz sent by the Polish Underground and from various other sources arrived in Britain from 1940. This chapter and Chapter 5 trace the various pieces of data about the camp that reached the West, from their origin to their distribution to British and American intelligence, to the Foreign Office, to the pages of newspapers on both sides of the Atlantic, and to the airwaves – that is, to the BBC and Radio Świt.

Reports from the Polish Underground in occupied Poland did not always arrive in chronological order. The journeys of couriers across occupied Europe were fraught with difficulties and not all reports that were sent reached the Polish Government in Exile in London. In the year April 1940 to April 1941, 50 per cent of couriered reports reached London; between 1941 and 1942, the figure was 55 per cent; between 1942 and 1943 only 51 per cent of reports reached their intended destination, but between April 1943 and April 1944 nearly all post (82 per cent) from Warsaw made it across occupied Europe to Britain.[1] Copies of the same report from Warsaw were carried by different couriers along various routes, but the transfer of specific information to the Polish Government in Exile sometimes took several months, depending on the difficulties that couriers encountered on their journeys west.

Communication between intelligence officers in London and Warsaw was made somewhat more complicated as it was not always clear to officers in Warsaw whether their counterparts in London had particular data at a specific moment, despite a system of checks. The delegate in Warsaw would send a radio message indicating the contents of couriered packages prior to their dispatch. Intelligence officers in London would advise that material arrived in London, but since not all radio messages were received, there was room for misunderstandings to arise. Consequently, facts that were well established in Warsaw were not always appreciated in London in a timely fashion because reports that had been sent were delayed or had not reached their destination.

Information transfer flowed both to and from London. The Polish Government in Exile kept the underground state informed of

128

developments in London, of relationships with allies, and sent instructions and requests. Effective communication between London and Warsaw was therefore a crucial aspect of the Polish government's war effort. Communication was often facilitated with the aid of the British. Reports that were couriered out of Poland via Gdynia to Stockholm were transported on a weekly RAF flight from Sweden to Britain. The Polish Underground also operated a courier route to Budapest. Budapest was a key base for Polish intelligence during the war. From there, material was sent on to Bern in neutral Switzerland, or using SOE's facilities, via the diplomatic bag of Hungary, to Istanbul.[2] In Bern, some information from Warsaw could be radioed to London (time and security issues being less pressing than in occupied Warsaw), but most was forwarded via occupied France to Spain and either Gibraltar or Lisbon. The final parts of this journey relied on British co-operation. Facilities for transferring material to the diplomatic bags of neutral countries existed, but the precise details of such practices are unclear. Istanbul was also an important Polish intelligence centre. The contours of the Polish courier network were familiar to SOE and the names of many couriers and intelligence officers were kept on file.[3] Co-operation in ensuring the continual flow of information to and from Poland was well established by the time news of the mass killing of Jews at Auschwitz began to be distributed from Warsaw in August 1942.[4]

The British aided the transfer of material across occupied Europe and trained individuals who would become couriers or SOE agents. Napoleon Segieda, who transported information about Auschwitz in the summer of 1942, was an employee of the Polish Ministry of the Interior, a courier and an SOE agent, for example. Couriers who arrived in Britain, like all entrants to the country during the war, were interrogated either by MI19 at the Royal Patriotic Schools in Wandsworth, London, or debriefed by SOE. The famous Polish courier Jan Karski was questioned for two days in late November 1942 by MI19 before being released to the Polish government. Couriers were also questioned in occupied Europe by British intelligence operatives who aided their passage. The results of many of these interrogations are not known. Not all interrogation or debriefing reports still exist. It is not known what Segieda told his SOE handlers when he arrived in Britain in February 1943, for instance. The British involvement in the complicated Polish courier network highlights the potential for British intelligence to gain information from couriers even if the actual contents of material from Warsaw were not handed over.

The British also had the opportunity to read some material when it was transferred to British custody for delivery to the Polish government in

London – for example on the Stockholm–London route, but there is no hard evidence indicating that they did. The assertion that the Polish government could conceal information that they had about Auschwitz, as implied by some scholarship on Western knowledge of the camp, is weakened by a recognition of how Polish intelligence operations in bringing the news to London actually worked. As is shown later, in Chapter 5, there is a great deal of hard evidence that the Polish government routinely passed on information it had about the mass murder of Jews at the camp from March 1943, and some indication (discussed in this chapter) that information was passed earlier.

In this chapter and the next, the passage of reports about Auschwitz that reached London is traced in order to demonstrate how information was disseminated to various people and institutions. The narrative is broadly chronological, beginning in 1940 and ending with the distribution of the Vrba–Wetzler report in June–July 1944. Three distinct periods of information distribution are identified. In the first period (see 'Early news of the camp' below), roughly from late 1940 to the summer of 1942, knowledge of the camp in Poland (among the Underground leadership), in London (among the Polish Government in Exile) and amongst the wider public in the West was the same: the camp was understood as a very harsh concentration camp, imprisoning, in the main, Poles.

In the second period, from summer 1942 to March 1943 (see 'Disjuncture, delay and suppression' below), there are some discrepancies between what was known in Warsaw and in London. From early August (at the latest) the Polish Underground leadership became aware that Jews were being slaughtered on a massive scale at Auschwitz. This information reached London in November 1942. However, further, confirming information about the camp that was sent from Warsaw in October and November 1942 was delayed due to technical and logistical problems. These include the closure of the Swedish route following the arrest of involved Poles and Swedes in late July and early August; the compromising of a Polish cipher following these arrests, meaning that radio communication with London was adversely affected;[5] the non-functioning of some radio equipment in Warsaw;[6] and the Germans' sealing of both the France–Spain border and the France–Switzerland border in November 1942, which made it far more difficult for couriers to reach Gibraltar or Lisbon in a timely fashion.[7]

Nevertheless, news of the gassing of Jews at Auschwitz did reach London on 12 November 1942 and a courier (Jan Karski) who was in Warsaw in early September, when the Underground had data from the camp, reached the British capital on 26 November. It *was* possible for the information that Auschwitz had become a place where the Nazis were

Early news of the camp   131

gassing Jews to reach the general public in Britain at any point from late November 1942. It did not. The failure of the Polish government and later the British government to publicize this new information is examined.

The third period, which is the subject of Chapter 5 ('British suppression of news of Auschwitz') runs from March 1943 to the distribution of the Vrba–Wetzler report in June–July 1944. But first, attention is turned to early news of the camp to reach the West.

Early news of the camp

The arrival of Witold Pilecki at Auschwitz in September 1940 coincided with the growth of resistance cells within the camp representing the diverse political leanings of the prisoners. These resistance groups eventually agreed to co-operate at an extraordinary meeting on 24 December 1941 in Block 25 (Garliński 1994: 76). Pilecki's specific mission was to sustain morale; to provide extra food and clothing to members of his organization, the Union of Military Organizations; to prepare for taking over the camp should that become possible (i.e. when weapons and/or outside troops became available); and to send out information about the camp to his military superiors.[8]

These messages were sent out in a variety of ways, including through released prisoners and escapees. Often the messages were oral. The first such message, dispatched with Aleksander Wielkopolski in October 1940, reached Warsaw and seems to have formed the basis of a report sent to London.[9] A document entitled 'The camp in Auschwitz' (Obóz w Oświęcimiu), dated November 1940, was prepared by the Polish Underground in Warsaw, and part of it was published in a Polish Ministry of Foreign Affairs booklet entitled *The German Occupation of Poland* in London in May 1941.[10] This publication listed various aspects of the occupation as appendices. Appendix 168A presented, in English translation, parts of the report on Auschwitz prepared in Warsaw, amongst them the following summary:

At the end of November, 1940, 8,000 Poles were at the Oswiecim camps. Theoretically, the prisoners were divided into three groups: 1. Political prisoners; 2. Criminals; 3. Priests and Jews. This last group was persecuted most of all. Scarcely any of them came out alive.

This information was widely circulated amongst British officials. The Polish ambassador to the Vatican handed a French-language version of *The German Occupation of Poland* (*Relation sur la situation en Pologne sous l'occupation allemande*) to the leader of the English Catholics, Cardinal

132   Intelligence about Auschwitz: November 1940–February 1943

Hinsley. In August 1941, Hinsley passed the document to British Intelligence, which forwarded it to Alexander Cadogan, the permanent under-secretary for foreign affairs. Another copy was passed to the British Ministry of Information.[11] The 15 November 1941 edition of the *Polish Fortnightly Review* reported that Jews at Oświęcim were the 'worst treated', that no Jew left 'the camp alive', and noted that 'three crematorium furnaces were insufficient to cope with the bodies being cremated'.[12] The information about the camp was not published in the British press until January 1942. On 8 January 1942, *The Scotsman* noted that priests and Jews were put in special penal units at Oświęcim. No other British media outlet disseminated the information.

Pilecki's report about the camp, prior to the camp's transformation to include a site where European Jews were brought specifically to be killed (from May 1942), is important as it shows that a key Polish intelligence officer was recording how Jews were being treated and was sending this information out of the camp. It also highlights the limited response of the British media to this news. Pilecki's messages from the camp cannot be accurately tracked. However, following his escape in April 1943, Pilecki wrote reports which put the number of Jews killed at the camp at 1.5 million. The first was a short debriefing report written in June 1943 in Nowy Wiśnicz, but a more expansive report, known as Raport W, was written later that year.

This document was for the benefit of Pilecki's military superiors, in the context of ongoing struggle. It charted the activities of Pilecki's resistance organization in the camp, provided details of those it helped to escape, and sketched the contours of life in Auschwitz I. It also mentioned the Jews, who were being killed on an industrial scale in the gas chambers at Birkenau, and indicated that over 1.5 million people had been killed, most of them Jews.[13] Pilecki wrote a further report after the war, which also highlighted the fate of Jews.[14] It is therefore reasonable to assume that the messages that Pilecki sent out of the camp incorporated information about what was happening to Jews, including after April 1942, when the first transports of Jews from Slovakia arrived.[15] A member of Pilecki's organization, Jan Karcz, was imprisoned at Birkenau. Prior to being shot in January 1943, Karcz kept Pilecki informed of what was happening in that part of the camp complex.

Through 1941 and 1942, Oświęcim became increasingly well known in the West as an extremely harsh concentration camp with an exceptionally high mortality rate. Churchill was privy to German radio intercepts and was handed data on deaths in Auschwitz in September 1941. On 1 July 1942, the well-disciplined (i.e. well-vetted) *Polish Fortnightly Review* published details about Oświęcim. It reported that people incarcerated in

Early news of the camp 133

Pawiak prison, Warsaw, were being transported to Oświęcim. The author of the piece attempted to personalize the story of the horrors of Pawiak and Oświęcim by relaying the fate of a lady named Gillewicz. After intense suffering in Pawiak she committed suicide rather than, presumably, endure further torment. At Oświęcim itself, the author highlighted that, in addition to the main camp, a further camp with an even harsher regime existed, noting that the 'prisoners call this supplementary camp "Paradisal" (presumably because there is only one road, leading to Paradise)'. This was a reference to Birkenau.[16] At this camp the crematorium 'is five times as large as the one in the main camp'. Killing people was achieved, it reported, 'through excessive work, torture and medical means'. The article also recorded the murder of Soviet prisoners of war and Poles by gassing in September 1941 and stated, 'It is estimated that the Oświęcim camp can accommodate fifteen thousand prisoners, but as they die on a mass scale there is always room for new arrivals'.[17]

The part of the *Polish Fortnightly Review* carrying the subtitle 'Pawiak prison and Oswiecim concentration camp' also reported, 'It is well known in Poland that last year a party of Jews were taken off to the neighbourhood of Hamburg, where they were all gassed.' The placing of this information in this section of the *Review* does not make editorial sense. Logically, it should have featured under the subtitle 'Destruction of the Jewish population', which began on the following page. The placement of this sentence may just be an editorial error. However, given the structure of this edition of the *Review*, in which a special section was devoted to the destruction of the Jews (with focus on Warsaw), it may be the author's oblique attempt, within the constraints of the censorship regime under which the *Polish Fortnightly Review* operated, to highlight the gassing of Jews.

The following edition of the *Polish Fortnightly Review* again mentioned Oświęcim, but did not specifically refer to Jews. It was listed as one of twenty-three camps incarcerating Poles, others including both Bełżec and 'Tremblinka' (*sic*). In line with general British policy, the particular Jewish plight was subsumed within a narrative of the harsh situation endured by the Polish nation. The same details were republished in *Bestiality . . . Unknown in Any Previous Record of History*, a publication prepared by Brendan Bracken and the Polish Ministry of Information, which was released after the 9 July 1942 conference.

Oświęcim was known in the West as a German concentration camp for Poles, a camp which had claimed the lives of members of the Polish intelligentsia. Until May 1942 this understanding was not far from the truth. Some Jews were known to have been taken to the camp, and the fact that they, along with priests, were positioned by the Germans at

134   Intelligence about Auschwitz: November 1940–February 1943

the bottom of the camp hierarchy had been publicized from May 1941. The transformation of part of the camp complex to include facilities for the systematic murder of Europe's Jews in May 1942 was known to the Polish Underground leadership in Warsaw by the summer of 1942, and to the Polish government and to British and American officials in the autumn and winter of 1942–3. Explaining how this information was handled and why it did not change public perceptions of the camp is discussed below.

Disjuncture, delay and suppression (August 1942–February 1943)

On 20 June 1942, four inmates of Oświęcim escaped. One of them, Stanisław Gustaw Jaster, carried a report about the camp to the Underground leadership. The escape was mentioned in a 26 August internal Home Army document and included in the regular couriered dispatch to London covering the period from 16 July to 25 August 1942.[18] The internal Home Army document ('Informacja Bieżąca 31') reported extensively on the situation in Auschwitz I. It is possible that Jaster carried to Warsaw news of the gassing of Jews at Auschwitz. In addition, the Polish courier and SOE agent, Napoleon Segieda (later known as Jerzy Salski), who gathered material about the camp, was in Warsaw during early August 1942.[19] Segieda was cognizant of the mass killing of Jews at the camp as he spent some time in the town of Oświęcim in the summer of 1942 and he later handed a report describing the full horror of the camp to Ignacy Schwarzbart in April 1943.

The Underground leadership – that is, the Home Army leader (General Stefan Rowecki), the Polish government's delegate in Poland (Cyryl Ratajski), and the head of the Directorate of Civilian Resistance (Kierownictwo Walki Cywilnej) (Stefan Korboński) – became aware of the Nazi systematic murder of Jews at Auschwitz at some point in July 1942, or very early August 1942 at the latest.[20] Given the gaps in the records of radio messages sent to London, it is not possible to state categorically whether this information was sent, but no evidence has been located to indicate that the Polish government in London received any radio message advising of the mass killing of Jews at Oświęcim during the summer or autumn of 1942.

Couriered reports were sent on a regular basis from Warsaw to London. The standard scheduled monthly post which was sent via Budapest was supplemented by couriers travelling different routes. In the summer of 1942, the journeys of two couriers who travelled via Germany and Austria respectively can be documented. One of

Disjuncture, delay and suppression (August 1942–February 1943)   135

these couriers, Napoleon Segieda, as noted, had information about Auschwitz – Segieda wrote two reports which mentioned the killing of Jews at the camp after he arrived in London in February 1943; the other, Jan Karski, almost certainly had knowledge of the camp and it is likely that he carried information about the camp. However, there is no documentary record of Karski speaking of the mass slaughter of Jews at Auschwitz when he reached London (26 November 1942).

On 4 September 1942, the Polish Underground leadership dispatched to London, as far as can be established, the first report about the camp that mentioned the killing of Jews in the gas chambers at Oświęcim via the standard courier route to Budapest.[21] Napoleon Segieda had departed from Warsaw on his journey to London via Vienna on 8 August, but since he encountered severe hold-ups on his journey the news he carried about the camp was seriously delayed. The data from the 4 September material was therefore the first that can be documented as having reached London – on 12 November 1942.[22]

The reference to the gassing of Jews is very brief in the 4 September document and comes at the end of the seventh paragraph (of nine), and forms part of a report describing mortality at Oświęcim from 1 June 1942:

There are different methods of execution. People are shot by firing squads, killed by an 'air hammer' /Hammerluft/, and poisoned by gas in special gas chambers.[23] Prisoners condemned to death by the Gestapo are murdered by the first two methods. The third method, the gas chamber, is employed for those who are ill or incapable of work and those who have been brought in transports especially for the purpose /Soviet prisoners of war, and, recently, Jews/.[24]

The reference to gassing comes third in the list of killing methods and Jews are mentioned last. The harsh regime of Oświęcim was well established by the summer of 1942, but the gassing of Jews was new information and could, therefore, be expected to be emphasized in a report sent to London. Clearly, this data was not highlighted to readers of the document. There are two possible reasons. First, the material sent to London simply reproduced material received from Auschwitz and was not worked on in Warsaw prior to being sent.[25] Second, Segieda was expected to arrive in London before the information dispatched almost a month later on 4 September. In this reading, the 4 September document was designed simply and briefly to record mortality and population statistics at the camp and not to provide a detailed appraisal of the new situation at Oświęcim. Nevertheless, the gassing of Jews was significant and if, as is likely, Segieda advised the Underground leadership of what he saw and heard while staying in the town of Oświęcim in the early summer of 1942, there was scope for more expansive information to be included in material sent to London on 4 September 1942.

Four days after a courier had departed for Budapest carrying the news about Oświęcim, an internal Home Army document (*informacja bieżąca*) on 8 September 1942 reported that there were about 100,000 prisoners in the camp, 70,000 of whom were Jews from the whole of Europe.[26] It recorded that in the last months gas chambers had been installed, and Jews were being killed at the rate of 1,000 people a day. The document also noted that three crematoria were running twenty-four hours a day.[27]

Home Army *informacja bieżąca* was routinely divided into sections and data deemed sensitive was not permitted to be published. The news from Auschwitz, however, was not embargoed and was declared fit for publication. On 10 September, this data was incorporated into a document detailing the most important news from the 1–10 September period alongside news of arrests in Warsaw, the Warsaw ghetto and (Soviet) raids on the city.[28] The information in this document was prepared to be sent via radio to London. No evidence that it was actually transmitted to London has been located.[29] Some documents relating to radio communication between Warsaw and London are missing, but on balance it is likely that it was not transmitted.[30] However, the information was incorporated into a document entitled Aneks 38 and sent via courier to London almost immediately (discussed below).

Between 22 July and 12 September 1942 General Rowecki sent no less than 155 radio messages. Some transcripts of these messages are missing (Puławski 2007: 73), but in the ones that do exist, there is no mention of Jews being systematically killed at the camp. Indeed, in Rowecki's messages there are very few references to Jews at all. One from 19 August 1942 draws attention to the liquidation of the Warsaw ghetto and to Jews being sent to Treblinka and Bełżec. The next message to mention Jews comes six weeks later, on 3 October.[31] The infrequent references to Nazi actions against Jews should *not* automatically be understood as evidence that the Home Army leadership consciously marginalized news about Jews, but as indicating how the underground state organized and managed the vast amount of intelligence which it gathered and sent west.

Rowecki's radio messages to London focused on military and industrial issues, providing the Allies with news of German troop, equipment and ship movements. Rowecki received requests for specific information from Michał Protasewicz of the Polish Bureau VI several times each day. Often these requests originated from British intelligence and generally focused on German military and industrial capabilities.[32] The messages that Rowecki sent west were largely responsive to demands from London

Disjuncture, delay and suppression (August 1942–February 1943)   137

and from the British for particular information. When requests for information about Jews were made, Rowecki radioed information.[33] Such requests originated from the Polish government (the minister of the interior) or from Jewish representatives on the National Council. However, issues to do with civilians were, in the main, the domain of the delegate. While this division of labour was logical, it was not perfect. In the summer of 1942 a number of issues arose that played a role in preventing important news from Auschwitz being radioed to London.

As noted, the loss of the 'Swedish connection', following the arrest of Poles and Swedes couriering information out of Poland, delayed reports reaching London, as the important Warsaw–Gdynia–Stockholm–London route was out of operation during the period when news of the camp reached the Underground leadership in Warsaw during July or early August 1942.[34] These arrests also had implications for radio messages since ciphers were compromised. Given that technical resources had to be allocated to reconfigure radio security (more robust encryption), intelligence actually wanted by the Allies assumed priority over news of another location in the Nazis' genocidal programme. Arguably, this led to a more rigid prioritization of information radioed to London, meaning that news from Oświęcim was squeezed out. It simply was a victim of the technical limits placed on communications to London during a period when communication security had been breached.

Further, between 5 September (Message 115) and 17 September 1942 (Message 116), no radio messages were sent by Cyryl Ratajski (former delegate) or Jan Piekałkiewicz (delegate).[35] In Message 118, from 17 September, Piekałkiewicz informed London that there had been problems in deciphering messages (and, presumably, encrypting messages), that he was waiting for the post (perhaps for equipment) and that he would sign future radio messages 'Wernic' (indicating that the full responsibilities of the post of delegate had been passed to him). The delegate had problems with radio equipment just as significant news from Auschwitz about the mass murder of Jews reached Warsaw (the most important news between 1 and 10 September). Given that the delegate assumed primary responsibility for sending news of civilians (including Jews) to London, it was not possible for him to send this news via radio, exposing the weakness of the underground state's division of labour in radioing information to London. Technical problems with radio equipment continued into October. On 2 October Piekałkiewicz advised Mikołajczyk that his radio was not working and requested that functioning equipment be sent.[36] In addition, the Polish Underground during September came under some physical pressure. Soviet bombing raids on Warsaw in late August and September adversely affected

138   Intelligence about Auschwitz: November 1940–February 1943

intelligence operatives, and German counterintelligence achieved some success.[37] On 18 September, Rowecki reported to London that the important Underground cells of Kot and Bór had been exposed.[38] This had implications for radio communications – both in terms of the potential compromising of codes and in relation to the loss of physical equipment.

Since the news about Oświęcim incorporated in the 8 September 1942 Home Army document had been sent by courier, it seems that by the time radio communication had been restored, the delegate's focus had shifted elsewhere: for example, the few messages between 17 September and the beginning of October refer to the internal politics of the Underground, raids on Warsaw and the progress of couriers, amongst other issues. Nevertheless, it was possible for the delegate (either Ratajski or Piekałkiewicz) to petition the Home Army command to send the news about Auschwitz. It is not known whether this happened, but Rowecki did not send any messages about Auschwitz in either August or September 1942. There are a number of possible reasons for the lack of any radio messages through Rowecki's radio channel to London.

First, the Underground leadership bore witness to the liquidation of the Warsaw ghetto and their proximity to this ongoing process overshadowed news about Jews from elsewhere. News transmitted to London by Piekałkiewicz on 2 October and Rowecki on 3 October reported on the ghetto.[39]

Second, the internal politics of the Polish Underground may have been important. While workers in the Office of Information and Propaganda (Biuro Informacji i Propagandy) (Stanisław Herbst, Henryk Woliński, Ludwik Widerszał) prepared material to be microfilmed and sent via courier, other sections of the Office of Information and those responsible for actually sending radio messages may have been less keen to highlight the slaughter of Jews at Auschwitz as this new development might overshadow Polish suffering at the camp.[40] (This argument, however, needs to be offset by the fact that news of the killing of Jews at Oświęcim appeared regularly and without delay in the reports sent to London that were specifically designed to record the German terror in Poland – *aneks*.)

Third, during the summer of 1942, the delegate, Cyryl Ratajski, was ailing and replaced in that post by Jan Piekałkiewicz on 5 August, though Ratajski did not relinquish all functions of the delegate until mid-September. It is possible that news of the camp was not transmitted to London as technical problems were compounded by administrative confusion during the handover of leadership. In short, insufficient pressure was placed on the Home Army to send information considered important by either Ratajski or Piekałkiewicz.

Disjuncture, delay and suppression (August 1942–February 1943)   139

In addition, the state of the relationship between Polish intelligence officials and Underground leadership in Warsaw, on the one hand, and representatives of the Jewish community in that city, on the other, seems to have been important. Since information from Auschwitz tended to reach Warsaw via Polish couriers travelling north, Jewish leaders are likely to have received news about the mass killing of Jews at the camp after the Underground leadership. So while the flow of intelligence about the Warsaw ghetto generally was from Jewish leaders to the Polish Underground, news of Auschwitz is likely to have flowed in the opposite direction. This had significant consequences. The Polish Underground 'controlled' information about the camp. It is not certain when key Jewish figures in Warsaw were advised. Jewish leaders were very keen for the information that they had – about the Warsaw ghetto, Treblinka, Sobibór and Bełżec – to reach the West, and lobbied the Polish Underground to radio this information to London. News about Auschwitz was not subject to the same pressure. News of the Warsaw ghetto, Treblinka and Bełżec was radioed to London in the summer of 1942.[41] No document indicating that news about the mass killing of Jews at Auschwitz was sent by radio in autumn 1942 has been located.[42] It is likely that a combination of these factors played a role in inhibiting the transmission via radio of the latest news of Auschwitz to London.

In late 1942 and early 1943 it seems that news of Auschwitz as a place where Jews were being systematically murdered was regularly incorporated in reports couriered to London, but not in radio messages. Given the technical problems in Warsaw in September 1942, together with the extended time it took for the post of delegate to be passed from Ratajski to Piekałkiewicz, the failure to send information by radio in September 1942 was not *necessarily* a planned action by the civilian Underground or a deliberate attempt by the military wing (Home Army) to marginalize the news of Jews at Auschwitz. By October 1942, however, there is evidence that news about the mass killing of Jews at Auschwitz was suppressed. In Rowecki's 3 October radio message to Mikołajczyk that reported on the situation in Poland, Auschwitz is mentioned as a place where many Poles had died, but the news received in Warsaw in September about Jews at the camp was not sent. As is discussed below, even without the news from Auschwitz about the mass murder of Jews, Foreign Office officials found Rowecki's report 'hysterical'. The important information that Auschwitz had become a key centre in the destruction of Jews, as noted, did not reach London until November 1942.

Instead of being sent via radio, the information about Auschwitz was immediately incorporated into Aneks 38 that covered the period from 1 to 15 September 1942.[43] The *aneks* was a monthly or fortnightly report

140   Intelligence about Auschwitz: November 1940–February 1943

that was routinely sent to London alongside other regular reports. It focused on the German terror in Poland and was prepared by the Military Historical Bureau of the Information and Press Office of the Home Army central command.[44] In London, the *aneks* was circulated to the Polish military and civilian leadership, and to SOE. The *Aneks* was received in London by Bureau VI of the Polish General Staff, headed by Michał Protasewicz. Protasewicz had regular meetings with his British counterparts at SOE, including Harold Perkins. From July 1942, meetings with representatives from SOE were fortnightly (Bines 2008: 95). The Poles (Protasewicz) would pass on intelligence to the SOE. Intelligence on the British side would often be forwarded to the Joint Intelligence Committee.[45]

Aneks 38 was sent via occupied France along with other materials. It was recorded in Polish intelligence files in London as being amongst Poczta Nr 9. E/X in France on 14 October 1942.[46] Polish intelligence tentatively recorded that 'Ziomek' (the code name of an agent) had the material on 22 October and later that it was in the care of the Americans (a reference to OSS).[47] Like SOE, OSS helped to facilitate the journeys of couriers through occupied Europe. However, this important post did not reach London and its fate was unknown to Polish intelligence.[48] Since the same material was often sent via different routes, and at different times, it is possible that Aneks 38 eventually reached London, but it cannot be traced to the British capital in 1942.

As is evidenced by the reports that reached Warsaw, the resistance movement in the camp was well aware of what was happening to the Jews, and in a report dated 1 July 1942 advised that from June 1941 Soviet prisoners of war were taken straight form trains to the gas chambers.[49] This report also noted that through 1942 around 30,000 Jewish men and 15,000 Jewish women and children had arrived at Oświęcim, most of whom – including all the children – were gassed immediately.[50] The exact date that this information was received in Warsaw is not known, but it was included as an attachment to an internal Home Army report (Informacja Bieżąca Nr 36) on 28 September 1942 and the Underground leadership in Warsaw incorporated this information into the situation report for the period from 26 August to 10 October 1942.[51] This document was compiled by the Department of Information on 24 October and sent to London via courier on 1 November 1942 via Budapest along with twenty-three other reports.[52] These documents, as far as can be established, did not reach London until late winter 1943. The Underground also sent this same information about the gassing of Jews at Oświęcim to London for a second time later in November 1942, but it seems as though it was not received.[53]

Disjuncture, delay and suppression (August 1942–February 1943) 141

The second document sent from Warsaw in November 1942 provided a detailed description of the camp and data about the mass killing of Jews, first revealed by the camp resistance on 1 July 1942. It demanded 'action not just to stimulate protests from Allied or neutral governments, but to move the conscience of millions of people from various countries who have not lost their sense of humanity and who do not want a return to total barbarity'.[54] The document described the camp as a crime against the Polish Nation, and the attachment, comprising twelve thematic paragraphs, used data from the 1 July camp resistance report to identify the groups of people murdered – Poles, Bolsheviks and Jews. Some 35,000 Jews were stated to have been gassed on arrival at the camp in the months of May and June 1942.[55]

Along with the situation report for the period from 26 August to 10 October 1942, 'Pro Memoria' of the situation in the country for the period from 11 October to 15 November 1942 did not reach Britain until late winter 1942–3. It was not until 15 June 1943 that they were distributed to members of the Polish Cabinet and National Council as Sprawozdanie 1-a/43 (Report 1-a/43).[56] The most likely reason for their late arrival was the fact that the courier or couriers who brought them to Britain was or were delayed.[57] It is not possible to establish precisely who couriered these reports, though Colonel Adam Król may have carried the package of material that included the situation report for the period from 26 August to 10 October 1942.[58] The information that they contained, including that 'tens of thousands of people' (mainly Jews and Soviet prisoners of war) had been transported to Auschwitz 'for the sole purpose of their immediate extermination in gas chambers', eventually reached its intended recipients over seven months after they were sent. In addition to delays in transit, the distribution of this specific material was held up in London for at least two months. However, during that time more recent news from Poland about the mass killing of Jews at Auschwitz was distributed to the Allies, to the press and to the BBC.

Despite not radioing information about the killing of Jews at Oświęcim during the autumn of 1942, it does seem that the Polish Underground leadership attempted to ensure that important documents were transferred to London in a reasonable amount of time, given the distance and transit difficulties. On 7 October 1942, the delegate, Jan Piekałkiewicz, sent Mikołajczyk a radio message that provided a list of the contents of the most recent material to be dispatched via courier to London. Piekałkiewicz also indicated that he was listing material that he had sent with the 'last courier' – perhaps Jan Karski (Żbikowski 2011: 272). The list of documents included the situation report for the period from

142   Intelligence about Auschwitz: November 1940–February 1943

16 July to 25 August and a report on the liquidation of the Warsaw ghetto that had six attachments.[59] The contents of these six attachments were not specified, but these attachments were later incorporated into Sprawozdanie Nr 6/42 (Report No 6/42), which was distributed to the Polish Cabinet on 23 December 1942.[60] Five of these attachments were published in the *Polish Fortnightly Review* on 1 December 1942.[61]

The dispatch of 4 September included the situation report from 16 July to 25 August and a document entitled 'Note on the issue of anti-Jewish action in 1942'. It seems that this note incorporated information on the liquidation of the Warsaw ghetto. If this was the case, information about the liquidation of the Warsaw ghetto (and attachments) was sent via courier at different times, not twice, but thrice (4 September, with Karski, and again – on 1 November).[62] Although the precise inventory of material which Jan Karski carried from Warsaw to London is not known with complete certainty and the route he took is contested, scholars generally agree that Karski carried news of the Warsaw ghetto and Bełżec (in reality Izbica).[63] Since news of the gassing of Jews at Oświęcim was included in the documents couriered west via Budapest on 4 September it is probable that Karski also carried this information.[64]

Later, on 13 November 1942, Piekałkiewicz sent a radio message to Mikołajczyk advising him of the contents of the package of material he was about to dispatch.[65] This included an extensive report on Oświęcim that highlighted the gassing of Jews on a mass scale. The general policy of information distribution about the camp followed by the Polish Underground was to forward the news to London via courier.

However, before the crucial reports mentioned above were received, others were discussed in London. On 11 November 1942, Frank Savery wrote to Frank Roberts at the Foreign Office to report on his latest meeting with the Polish minister of the interior, Stanisław Mikołajczyk. Savery indicated 'that fear for the future of the [Polish] race has been for at least a year very vividly before the eyes of the Polish Government and that they still fear it acutely – for very good cause, I am sorry to say'. Savery enclosed two translated reports received from Mikołajczyk, one of which mentioned Oświęcim (the other focused on pro-Soviet communist partisan activity in Poland). This report stated that all Polish political groups demanded reprisals as a means of checking the Germans' terror regime. It proceeded to outline political trends in the Polish Underground before summarizing the intensification of the Germans' policy of oppression. It recorded the 'very numerous deaths at Oświęcim and in other camps, which are regarded as the manifestation of a definite extermination policy directed against Poles'. This report also noted,

Disjuncture, delay and suppression (August 1942–February 1943) 143

'The population in general is beginning to regard the German terrorist policy as the commencement of an action of annihilation similar to that employed against the Jews', remarking that 'there are very few Jews left'.[66] Savery suggested that the report was written by the delegate and that it 'had something hysterical about it', and relayed that the British ambassador to Poland thought it was the 'product of despair'.[67]

In fact this report was radioed by General Rowecki, the man responsible for sending prized military intelligence west, to the Polish government in London on 3 October, and it was de-encrypted on 12 October.[68] Its brief mention of Oświęcim was part of a discussion of the intensification of violence against Poles (and omitted the news about Jews at the camp), which aimed to persuade the Polish government and Western Allies to pursue a policy of retaliation against the German occupiers.[69] However, the initial British response to the information was to criticize its author for having 'his eyes glued on what was happening in Poland and not to have any grasp of possibilities in the suggestions he makes for action by the Polish and Allied governments'.[70] The British response is significant because it highlights how unreceptive Poland's key ally was to news about Oświęcim and atrocities even without any mention of Jews. As argued in Chapter 2 above, the British were less likely to respond to news about Jews.

Strategically, the British position posed a dilemma for the Polish government – specifically for the minister of the interior, Stanisław Mikołajczyk. On the one hand, the Polish government desperately wanted to persuade the British of the merits of a policy of retaliation to stem German actions at Oświęcim. On the other, news of the mass gassing of Jews at the camp was, from November 1942, received, but could not be presented easily in Britain. The argument that Jews were being gassed at the camp held no traction with the British as a rationale for retaliation. Indeed, news of Nazi actions against Jews was not of particular interest to the British, and any action not sanctioned by the British to disseminate sensitive information (i.e. referring to Jews) about Oświęcim risked souring Polish–British relations. The British context was a significant element in the decision taken by Mikołajczyk not to widely disseminate the latest news from Auschwitz during the winter of 1942–3, but other considerations played a role too (discussed below). Nevertheless, Mikołajczyk clearly was concerned about what was happening to Jews. Repeatedly he sent messages to Warsaw requesting information about the situation of Jews and he was responsive to demands for data made by Jewish representatives on the National Council.[71]

The report originally sent on 4 September via Budapest that was received in London on 12 November 1942 briefly noting that Jews were

144   Intelligence about Auschwitz: November 1940–February 1943

now also being gassed at Oświęcim was selected by Mikołajczyk and staff in the Interior Ministry for incorporation into the formal report of news from Poland that was distributed to the Polish Cabinet on 23 December 1942 as Sprawozdanie Nr 6/42. No documentary evidence has been located to suggest that information about the transportations of Jews to be gassed at Oświęcim was formally passed to the Cabinet of the Polish government before Mikołajczyk distributed Sprawozdanie Nr 6/42.[72]

Sprawozdanie Nr 6/42 was a compilation of reports and messages from Poland which the Interior Ministry had received and worked on for distribution to members of the government. The part of the report which mentioned the gassing of Jews at Oświęcim was a small section of a broader text providing data on mortality rates at the camp, which juxtaposed the total number of prisoners registered up to 1 June 1942 with the number still alive on that date.[73] This information was possibly sent again: for example, with Jan Karski at some point in September (the date of his departure from Warsaw is not known with certainty – more on this below). The merit of this particular report was that it provided a succinct overview of the camp at a particular point in time that was not too challenging for presentation into Anglo-American sociopolitical environments.[74]

The camp was portrayed as very harsh and the mention of Jews was brief and not emphasized. Information about the gassing of Jews was, however, included. It also recorded that 250 people were dying daily at the camp, *excluding* those who perished at Brzezinka (Birkenau), thereby indicating that the death rate was even higher. By not mentioning the systematic murder of Jews at Brzezinka specifically, the 4 September data incorporated in Sprawozdanie Nr 6/42 was able to be distributed in Britain and later in the United States. Readers were forced to work hard to understand the full significance of the information, but important audiences, including officials in the British Foreign Office, should have been able to read between the lines and recognize that far more people were dying on a daily basis at the camp, and that in the context of December 1942, when a good deal about the systematic extermination of Jews was published, those being killed at the camp were likely to be Jews. (There is documentary evidence that FO officials received news that Jews were being slaughtered at a mass scale at Auschwitz in early January 1943 – this is discussed below.)

When the 4 September data arrived in London it was already several months old. Engel (1987: 202) argues that the Ministry of the Interior buried the mention of Jews being killed in gas chambers. This was not the

Disjuncture, delay and suppression (August 1942–February 1943)   145

case with this report: distributed to the Polish Cabinet and to members of the Polish National Council, Sprawozdanie Nr 6/42 included a verbatim copy of the source report couriered from Poland, which mentioned the gassing of Jews at Oświęcim. It is likely that the report was written soon after the start of the mass murder of Jews began (May 1942) and therefore speaks to the commitment of the camp resistance to ensure that information about was happening at Oświęcim reached Warsaw. However, Engel (1987) is right in noting that news from Auschwitz was suppressed (but probably not from British intelligence or the FO) – but not in the way he suggests.[75] The British, specifically the PWE and FO, share responsibility with the Polish government for suppressing data that revealed that Jews were being gassed at Auschwitz, since they determined the propaganda and censorship regime in Britain, and shaped the discursive landscape into which news about Jews was to be presented.

It is likely that some senior members of the Polish Cabinet were advised of the contents of the 4 September source report that discussed Oświęcim very soon after it arrived in London on 12 November, since that report was immediately translated into English and dispatched to the Polish Embassy in the United States as part of a 108-page document entitled 'Report on conditions in Poland'.[76] This English-language document carries the handwritten date of 27 November 1942.[77] It is not clear whether this date refers to the date the translation was completed, the date the document was sent to the United States or the date it was received in Washington, DC.[78] But if the intention was to bury the information that Jews were being gassed at Auschwitz, then it made no sense to translate the source report and send it across the Atlantic. Given that no translation was required if the objective was to communicate information to Polish officials, the targeted audiences for 'Report on conditions in Poland' were evidently English-speaking officials and politicians in both the US and Britain. Both British and US censorship also had the capacity to intercept transatlantic post (even that carried in diplomatic bags), but no copy of this report has so far been located in British or American files in the archives.[79]

Engel (1987: 202) notes that the 'Poles in London' were aware that Auschwitz had 'been enlisted in the campaign to annihilate the Jews of Europe' by November 1942, and suggests that the reason the name of the camp was not included in the list of death camps in Raczyński's 10 December memorandum to Allied governments was because 'the Poles wished Auschwitz to continue to serve as a symbol of their own suffering and feared that their distresses might be overshadowed were it to become widely known that Jews were being gassed to death there'. The swift translation and dispatch across the Atlantic of the news from

146 Intelligence about Auschwitz: November 1940–February 1943

the 12 November report brings this contention into question. It is probable that news from Auschwitz was shared with the British during November 1942.

Since the 12 November report was swiftly translated into English, it seems as though the Polish Government was preparing to release the information for wide dissemination. In the context of British (and American) censorship policy, the fact that information about the gassing of Jews at the camp was new and uncorroborated, and hence generally unacceptable to key audiences, would have been well appreciated by senior Polish politicians such as Stanisław Mikołajczyk and Edward Raczyński. The other camps highlighted in November and December 1942 – Treblinka, Sobibór and Bełżec – were recognized and, importantly, accepted by the British as sites where Jews were being systematically killed.[80] Raczyński was well aware that new information about the mass murder of Jews had to take account of British Foreign Office sensibilities. Without a good deal of corroborating evidence (for example, British radio intercepts, eyewitness testimony, several reports from different sources reporting the same news) and, most importantly, Foreign Office approval, *publicly* presenting the news about Oświęcim would have been politically difficult in Britain.

The failure of the Polish Interior Ministry to highlight the new information received about Oświęcim, prior to the 17 December UN declaration, may therefore reflect the Polish desire to ensure that a declaration was actually made. New data could have jeopardized the timely issuance of a declaration by providing the Allies with a reason to delay, as this intelligence would need to be evaluated. For instance, Laqueur (1998: 225) records R.B. Reams, who was responsible for Jewish affairs in the US State Department, expressing 'grave doubts in regard to the desirability or advisability of issuing a statement'. In addition, given that it is highly probable that both British and American officials had access to the 'Report on conditions in Poland' (the report sent to the Polish Embassy in the United States), it is possible that the Polish government (Mikołajczyk or Raczyński) received some informal 'advice' on framing the Polish government's 10 December memorandum from their Western Allies.

It is therefore likely that even the brief mention of Jews at Auschwitz in the 12 November report (sent on 4 September) was deemed too sensitive by the Polish government for *formal* presentation to the British (that is, Polish officials had internalized the British propaganda policy – though there is an argument that some Polish leaders, including Mikołajczyk, were themselves sensitive to 'Jewish' news) or that the British provided the Poles with off-the-record 'advice'. In January 1943, the 12 November

Disjuncture, delay and suppression (August 1942–February 1943)   147

report on Oświęcim was publicised by the Polish government without the mention of Jews being killed by gas, in the context of tightening British censorship. It formed the basis of Raczyński's letter to Eden on 20 January. Later in 1943, however, the reference to Jews and gassing was returned to the text and included in the Ministry of the Interior's typescript English-language publication 'Document appertaining to the German occupation of Poland: Poles in German concentration camps'.[81] Sprawozdanie Nr 6/42, including the complete statistics from Oświęcim with the mention of Jews being sent to the gas chambers, was translated into English by the Polish Ministry of Information at some point in the first half of 1943 (Schwarzbart received an English translation of the report on 29 May 1943) and distributed, presumably, to the British press, government officials and politicians.[82]

The preface to the English-language version requested that if material from the report was reproduced, the Polish Ministry of Information be advised. The information from Oświęcim was also published in the United States in the 5 April 1943 edition of *Poland Fights* – a fortnightly newspaper of the Polish Labour Group, which co-operated with the Polish Information Center in New York (the Polish government's information and propaganda office in the US).[83] This reincorporation of the news about Jews highlights the shift in the Polish government's information distribution policy that occurred in March 1943, which is discussed in Chapter 5 below. By March 1943 a great deal more information about the camp had reached London, including reports sent in autumn 1942 that had been delayed in their transit across occupied Europe.

Before this, in late November and early December 1942, the Polish government and members of the National Council worked hard to bring about a joint Allied declaration on atrocities committed by the Germans on Jews. Jan Karski's eyewitness testimony of Bełżec and the Warsaw ghetto enhanced the prospect of persuading the Allies to make a statement. The situation in Warsaw and at Bełżec had been highlighted the previous July at the conference at the British Ministry of Information. Karski's testimony and the reports he couriered about these places (which arrived in London before he did) provided powerful evidence of German crimes. The information about the Holocaust that was publicized in late November and early December 1942 reiterated, expanded and provided more detail of German actions in places that had been first highlighted at the Ministry of Information conference in July 1942. New information revealing that Auschwitz had become an important location in the destruction of Jews was suppressed.

The fact that the Polish government in London knew that Jews were being gassed at Auschwitz by November 1942 is supported by hard

148   Intelligence about Auschwitz: November 1940–February 1943

documentary evidence. British knowledge is more problematic due to the manner in which files have been managed and weeded, but also due to how information was gathered. For example, MI19 interviewed Jan Karski on 26 and 27 November 1942. The report from the interrogation notes that Karski spoke about the Warsaw ghetto. There is no mention of Bełżec. Since Karski thought he had visited that camp, it is very likely that he would have informed his British interlocutor. Given that Karski's news of Bełżec was tightly controlled by the PWE (it was not broadcast on the BBC until July 1943) and that Karski received the low 'C' rating as an informant by MI19, it is reasonable to suggest that Karski provided British intelligence with more information about the situation of Jews in Poland than is found in the interrogation report. The 'C' rating reflected the fact that Karski provided data that was not of interest to MI19. It is also possible that Karski spoke of Auschwitz – though, like news of Bełżec, there is no mention of the camp in the MI19 interrogation report. Given that Karski was probably advised of the killing of Jews at Auschwitz in August or early September 1942, it is important to assess Karski's role in the dissemination of information about Auschwitz.

Jan Karski: informant about Auschwitz?

The Underground leaders in Poland were aware of the mass killing of Jews at Oświęcim by early August 1942 at the very latest. During 1942 Karski worked in the Underground's Information and Propaganda Office (Biuro Informacji i Propagandy) and it is likely he became aware of the true function of Auschwitz at some point in the summer of 1942. Karski could have been advised of the situation at Oświęcim directly by Polish civilian or military leaders in Warsaw, or through his work in the Information and Propaganda Office. Wood and Jankowski (1994: 130) place Karski at the side of Stefan Korboński in the basement of Warsaw Polytechnic on 1 September 1942. Korboński had probably been informed of the true nature of Oświęcim by that date and could have briefed Karski at the polytechnic.

Information about the gassing of Jews at Oświęcim was sent to London on 4 September. The significant news that 1,000 Jews a day were being killed at the camp was in Warsaw on 8 September and incorporated into a document prepared for a radio dispatch to London on 10 September. The later Karski left Warsaw in September 1942, the more likely it is that this information had reached him.

It is probable that the microfilm that Karski carried from Warsaw contained information about the killing of Jews at Oświęcim. However, defining the exact contents of the microfilm that Karski carried is

Jan Karski: informant about Auschwitz? 149

problematic. The Hoover Institute in Stanford, for example, has a file in the collection of the Polish Ministry of Foreign Affairs entitled 'Nr 6/42, War Terror, delivered by Jan Karski'.[84] This file is Sprawozdanie Nr 6/42 (Report 6/42), which contains the first mention of Jews being gassed at Oświęcim, distributed to the Polish Cabinet on 23 December 1942. However, since Sprawozdanie Nr 6/42 was put together in London, the title of the file is not entirely accurate.[85]

The fact that material carried by Karski reached London before he did is confirmed in a 17 November 1942 cable from Michał Protasewicz of Bureau VI to Stefan Rowecki in Warsaw, which read 'Witold in Lisbon. Post in his headquarters'.[86] Mikołajczyk also sent a message confirming the receipt of Karski's materials on 23 November.[87] 'Witold' was Karski's pseudonym. Protasewicz's message is also important because it problematizes the account which Karski gave describing his journey across occupied Europe. In his book, *Story of a Secret State*, published in 1944, Karski claimed that he left Warsaw in October 1942 and travelled via Berlin, Brussels, Paris, Madrid, Algeciras and Gibraltar, to London. This account has been uncritically accepted, most notably by Wood and Jankowski (1994). Wood and Jankowski (1994: 143) ignored the reference to Lisbon altogether and translated Protasewicz's cable to Rowecki as 'Witold's mail is at headquarters'. As Karski noted in a report to the Polish government that outlined the aims and objectives of *Story of a Secret State*, the book was primarily a propaganda exercise which was 'not written for Poles but for foreigners who do not know Poland and her problems'.[88] Furthermore, in 1944 when the book was released, the war was still in progress and Karski had to be circumspect about any information useful to the enemy. It is therefore essential that Karski's story is juxtaposed with the documentary record of his journey across occupied Europe that can be found in Polish intelligence files.

Piecing together various cables sent by Polish leaders and intelligence officers from Warsaw, Bern, Lisbon and London it is clear that Karski was scheduled to fly from Lisbon to Britain, but that he was taken by British intelligence agents to Gibraltar.[89] Polish intelligence in Lisbon reported to Polish colleagues in London that Karski was in Barcelona on 20 November and in Gibraltar five days later.[90] Protasewicz's message to Warsaw on 17 November was incorrect. It seems that Protasewicz accepted the view, expressed by the head of Polish intelligence in France, Aleksander Kawałkowski (Roland),[91] on 14 October, that Karski would be in Lisbon three to four days after leaving France.[92] Kawałkowski had indicated that Karski's departure date would be between 18 and 20 October. Despite some contradictions in the intelligence record of Karski's journey across Europe, it is clear that as soon as he entered

150   Intelligence about Auschwitz: November 1940–February 1943

Spain, Polish intelligence officers liaised closely with the British, most probably SIS.[93] On 6 November, a Polish intelligence officer sent Mikołajczyk a message stating that he had already been in touch with the English in relation to Karski.[94] The British were involved in facilitating Karski's transit through Spain and clearly had some opportunity to interview him. Karski's journey through Western Europe is significant because it highlights Allied co-operation in facilitating the transit of intelligence and people to Britain. According to Karski (2012: 141), OSS were also involved in supporting his journey.

Despite at least twenty-five separate intelligence messages between early September and late November 1942 referring to Karski's journey across Europe, the documentary record only provides an outline of Karski's route. The date of his departure from Warsaw is not certain. Żbikowski (2011: 272) argues that Karski departed between 12 and 18 or 19 September 1942.[95] On 3 September 1942 Cyryl Ratajski sent a message to Mikołajczyk in which Ratajski described an itinerary that would see Karski in Paris on 15 September, Toulouse on 20 September and Bern on 1 October.[96] On 9 September Protasewicz sent a message to Rowecki asking him to delay Karski's departure by two or three days.[97] That same day Rowecki sent a radio message to London indicating that Karski was scheduled to depart on 11 September.[98] Protasewicz provided an address in Nice, France, for Karski.[99] Ten days later, on 19 September, Rowecki informed Protasewicz that Karski was to be collected from Vichy France.[100] These last two messages indicate the evolving plans for Karski's journey. They were soon made redundant.

On 3 October Kawałkowski, based in Paris, advised Polish colleagues in London that Karski had reported to him.[101] The following day Kawałkowski messaged Mikołajczyk advising that he had sent Karski's report.[102] In the same message Karski reported that he had arrived in Lyon on 30 September and requested that this information be relayed to Warsaw. Karski (2012: 393) claimed that he travelled from Paris to Lyon. Wood and Jankowski (1994: 139) suggest that Karski was in Paris for two weeks. If this is true, then Karski probably arrived at the Gare du Nord around 16 September 1942. Karski then apparently spent around two weeks in Lyon, according to Wood and Jankowski's account (1994: 139).

Meanwhile, Polish intelligence in London on 19 September advised colleagues in Bern that they would organize a British visa for Karski to fly to Britain from Lisbon.[103] On 6 October London informed Aleksander Ladoś, the Polish representative in Bern, that they were in contact with Karski and that Karski wished to go to Bern.[104] That same day, Mikołajczyk advised Kawałkowski that Karski was an important courier whose arrival in London was keenly expected, and called on him to

Jan Karski: informant about Auschwitz?

facilitate Karski's legal transit to Britain. Mikołajczyk also stated that directing Karski to Bern was not advised.[105] Two days later, on 8 October, Rowecki sent a message to London in which he stated that he had an unconfirmed report that Karski was in Bern.[106] It is unlikely that Karski travelled to Bern but the documentary record is not conclusive.[107] Almost a month later, intelligence officials in Lisbon reported to Mikołajczyjk that Karski crossed into Spain around 4 November.[108] This data corresponds roughly with Wood and Jankowski's claim that Karski spent around two weeks in Lyon and a week in Perpignan.

The story in *Story of a Secret State* of a journey via France and Spain did not pose any significant security issues. Discussion of Polish operations in Switzerland could damage Polish intelligence capabilities, both in Switzerland and for the transit of couriers from Poland. Karski therefore omitted his dealings with Polish intelligence in Switzerland from his book. Karski claimed that he handed over the microfilm he carried from Warsaw to Aleksander Kawałkowski in Paris. Wood and Jankowski (1994: 138) argue that it was then delivered to London via the diplomatic bag of an unnamed neutral country. This story can be reconciled with the intelligence record, though it is not known exactly how the microfilm reached London.

The dealings that Polish intelligence in Switzerland, France and Portugal had regarding Karski's transit to London were significant because they had implications for Napoleon Segieda, who also carried information about Oświęcim. Karski was an emissary of the Polish government, not just a regular courier, and his passage to London was prioritized. Karski was valued by the Polish government for his diplomatic experience, his ability to speak in English with a range of audiences and his eyewitness testimony. Karski was therefore the more valuable courier to inform British and American decision makers of conditions in Poland. Segieda also had to cross France and Spain, but in both countries he experienced incarceration in various prisons and a Spanish concentration camp. Karski's journey was less problematic, though the exact route is not known with certainty. Karski did leave via Gibraltar on the night of 25 November and probably, as he stated in *Story of a Secret State*, flew on a military plane (an American bomber).[109]

On arrival in Britain, Karski was driven to the Royal Patriotic Schools in Wandsworth, London, for interrogation by MI19. At first, according to the account given by Wood and Jankowski (1994), Karski was uncooperative. Representations were made by the Polish leadership in London for his release, and a compromise was reached – Polish officials could be present during Karski's interrogation. A recently released file at the British National Archives indicates that Karski discussed the

152 Intelligence about Auschwitz: November 1940–February 1943

persecution of the Jews, noting that in October 1942 only 45,000 ration cards for the Warsaw ghetto were printed. In 1941, the number of Jews in the ghetto had been estimated at 450,000 – some 100,000 were estimated still to be alive; 'the balance had meanwhile died or been killed'.[110]

It is likely that Karski was more expansive about the Nazi extermination programme while held by the British. However, the British intelligence file is summary, reflecting, in part, what British intelligence wanted to know and to share with those agencies and individuals on the distribution list of MI19 (the section of British intelligence conducting the interrogation of civilians that arrived in Britain). This list included the FO, the PWE, Ivone Kirkpatrick and HQ ETOUSA (Headquarters of the European Theater of Operations, United States Army), amongst others. Despite receiving a C rating from MI19, Karski was later granted meetings with senior British intelligence, propaganda and Foreign Office figures, including the Foreign Secretary, Anthony Eden, in February 1943. Karski later met representatives of OSS in the United States and President Roosevelt.

There is no documentary evidence of Karski speaking or writing about the mass murder of Jews at Oświęcim when he arrived in Britain. The Polish government did not actively highlight the information about the camp it had received prior to Karski's arrival (the data sent on 4 September). Assuming Karski knew that the Germans were murdering Jews at Oświęcim (the information was available in Warsaw prior to his departure to London, as noted) there are a number of possible reasons to explain Karski's conduct in relation to the camp.

First, despite the circulation of news from Oświęcim in Warsaw, Karski was not advised. This seems very unlikely given Karski's access to key information gatekeepers in the Polish capital. Second, Karski misinformed Polish intelligence and Polish leaders in London about the camp when asked to confirm the data from Warsaw. Third, Karski was reticent to speak about events to which he was not an eyewitness. He was prepared to talk about the Warsaw ghetto and Bełżec (Izbica) because he had seen German actions in these places. By speaking about other locations of the Holocaust on which he could only provide second-hand reports, Karski, arguably, feared that his credibility as a witness would be undermined. This would be disastrous for the dissemination of news from Poland. It is possible that he remained non-committal about the news from Auschwitz, which influenced how the Polish political leadership responded. Fourth, Karski provided full details which the Polish political leadership chose not to highlight. Fifth, Karski advised both the Poles and the British (i.e. MI19), and the British advised the Poles not to act on the information.

The sparse documentary record can support different interpretations. One interpretation casts Karski as ignorant of the news from Auschwitz, another suggests that he suppressed news of Auschwitz due to his ideological orientation, yet another considers Karski seeking to maintain his credibility by not talking about places he was not familiar with personally, a fourth positions Karski as a loyal adherent to the Polish government's policy line, and a fifth sees Karski as loyal to the Polish government's policy line as set in accordance with British information management. Or, in other words, the news was suppressed because of Karski personally, because of the Polish government or because of the British government, or not at all because the news was not known to Karski.

The most likely scenario, in the absence of solid documentary evidence to establish Karski's knowledge of the camp in September 1942 conclusively, is that Karski was aware of the 4 September report sent to London and would have been advised of the 10 September document prepared to be sent to London if he remained in Warsaw for more than a few days beyond that date. In London, in the absence of supporting documentation (i.e. Aneks 38) it would have been very difficult for the Poles to publicly present the news to the British using only Karski's second-hand testimony and the brief mention of Jews at the camp in the 4 September document. Presenting news derived from Karski on Auschwitz would also be risky, as it could bring into question Karski's credibility as a witness to the Warsaw ghetto and Bełżec. British officials generally accepted the information about the Warsaw ghetto but were less convinced with the material about Bełżec. Frank Savery wrote to Frank Roberts on 3 December and stated that 'the evidence as evidence does not seem to me quite convincing'.[111] This kind of response may have influenced Karski's and the Polish government's policy on publicizing news from Auschwitz.

But there remains the issue of whether Karski would have pressed for news about the camp to be publicized if he knew. In addition to any desire to maintain credibility as a witness, there is an argument that he would not have challenged Polish government policy on news dissemination.

For example, in August 1942, Zofia Kossak-Szczucka of the Front for the Rebirth of Poland (Front Odrodzenia Polski, FOP), a Catholic organization (some members were later involved in the rescue of Jews), published a pamphlet entitled *Protest!* in which she condemned the German atrocities and the silence of the Allies and the Poles. Kossak-Szczucka's Catholic anti-Semitism was also expressed – 'Our feelings towards the Jews have not changed. We still consider them to be political, economic and ideological enemies of Poland'.[112] Scholars agree that this

154   Intelligence about Auschwitz: November 1940–February 1943

protest was one of the documents on the microfilm that Karski carried. It is not known whether Karski was a member of FOP, but as Żbikowski (2011: 227) points out he was close to the organization and to Zofia Kossak-Szczucka, and he seems to have shared some of their outlook. This connection is relevant insofar as it arguably sheds some light on Karski's position regarding Jews. Reading Karski's actions through his relationship with FOP would suggest that he was prepared to speak up for Jews, to highlight their plight at the hands of Nazi Germany, but only up to a point. Oświęcim, from this perspective, may have been for Karski a place of Polish martyrdom.

This view is very weakly supported by the fact that Karski did not discuss Jews at Oświęcim in his meetings with Roosevelt and Frankfurter in the summer of 1943. In the minutes of Karski's meeting with President Roosevelt in July 1943, Karski is recorded as having noted that 80,000 to 100,000 Poles had already lost their lives at Auschwitz, 'the most horrible concentration camp', following a question from Roosevelt regarding the death statistics distributed by the Polish government. This was an opportunity to mention Jews at the camp and it was not taken. However, Karski, in accordance with instructions received from the Polish ambassador to the United States, Jan Ciechanowski, then stated that 'many people are also not aware to what a horrible fate the Jewish population is subject', and highlighted that 1.8 million Jews had already been murdered.[113] Karski highlighted the mass murder of Jews by the Nazis to President Roosevelt, but did not specify that Auschwitz was also a place where European Jewry was being systematically murdered. In June 1943, the American Chiefs of Staff had received Polish government data reporting that 520,000 Jews had been killed at Auschwitz (see Chapter 5). The meeting with Roosevelt was an opportunity for Karski to speak frankly about the camp (assuming he knew, and, in London from March 1943, he would have had the opportunity to learn about the camp from colleagues, including those on Radio Świt), and he did not.

It is likely that *details* of the Holocaust were of secondary importance to ensuring that Roosevelt was advised, in broad terms, of what was happening in Poland. Meetings with US military and intelligence officials in July 1943 were, arguably, the fora where details could be discussed. It is not known what was said at many of these meetings due to a lack of minutes. Similarly, in August 1943, Karski met with representatives of a number of different Jewish organizations.[114] Some of those he spoke with (including Rabbi Stephen Wise) had met Roosevelt in December 1942 and had handed the president a memorandum which mentioned the slaughter of Jews at Oświęcim (see below). Karski's meetings with Jewish

Jan Karski: informant about Auschwitz?

representatives were opportunities for information about the camp to be shared, but it is not clear whether it was.

Earlier, in Britain, in December 1942, Karski was taken by Mikołajczyk to meet Harold Osborne of the Political Warfare Executive. This was a private meeting and no minutes of what was said exist. Since Karski subsequently worked for Radio Świt, some of the meeting would have been taken up with a discussion of aims and objectives of that radio station, and the role Karski was expected to play. It is also possible that Karski was briefed on British propaganda policy in relation to Jews. The extent to which Karski willingly subscribed to this policy cannot be accurately assessed, but in relation to Oświęcim, the British reticence to highlight atrocities against Jews certainly legitimated inaction.

Karski's failure to talk about Auschwitz in 1942 *can* be explained by his adherence to a Polish government policy that was framed in a malign British context. By the time Karski met Roosevelt in June 1943, the Polish government was distributing information about the camp. However, it is not possible to claim definitively that Karski did not mention Auschwitz in meetings with Allied officials. The most that can be asserted is that there is no documentary record of Karski speaking or writing about Auschwitz, and given the attitude of the Western Allies to new news about Jews, this should not be so surprising.

Even if the stronger and, as argued here, unverifiable contention that Karski did not speak about Auschwitz when he knew its true function is made, it is not clear that Engel's thesis regarding the Polish fear that widespread knowledge of the mass murder of Jews at Auschwitz would overshadow Polish suffering has traction in relation to Karski, despite his close relationship with Zofia Kossak-Szczucka. As a young emissary who carefully weighed the questions asked of him, the most that Karski may have been guilty of is excessive caution. Karski therefore remains somewhat enigmatic but is revealed here as a *possible* obstacle to knowledge about the camp reaching a wide public prior to the UN declaration of 17 December 1942. If it is accepted that Karski knew about the mass slaughter of Jews at Oświęcim when he arrived in London in late November 1942, Karski can be depicted as a loyal servant of the Polish government obediently following the government's policy of adhering to the British censorship/propaganda regime or as an actor who suppressed the news that he had carried from Warsaw. It is therefore ironic that the man who, according to Wood and Jankowski (1994), 'tried to stop the Holocaust'[115] through his testimony about the Warsaw ghetto and Bełżec, *may* have been party (willingly or not) in a larger or smaller way to hindering information about Oświęcim reaching a broad audience.

156   Intelligence about Auschwitz: November 1940–February 1943

However, making a full assessment of the decision to suppress the brief news about the mass killing of Jews at Auschwitz that reached London is severely handicapped by gaps in the British and Polish archival records. The fact that no documentary records of this early news reaching the British have been located does not necessarily mean that it was not passed on. Karski spoke with many British officials – intelligence, military, propaganda personnel – but the contents of these conversations are not known. Given that from March 1943 the Polish government released information about the mass killing of Jews at Auschwitz for dissemination to the general public, it is very likely that British officials were advised of the true function of the camp earlier, probably soon after Mikołajczyk was informed. Since the Polish government was very keen for the British to sanction the bombing of the camp and was aware that information about the mass slaughter of Jews had no persuasive force with the British to achieve this goal, through early 1943 the Polish government *publicly* highlighted the harsh regime at the camp (for example, Raczyński's letter to Eden of 20 January 1943 – discussed below) and sought military rationales for bombing that would appeal to the British. On 20 February 1943, Mikołajczyk cabled Warsaw noting that the English had asked whether the Germans were manufacturing 'Hexagon' (RDX – Royal Demolition Explosives) and if they were doing so in Silesia; he proposed to *return* to the question of bombing Oświęcim.[116] The Polish government had learnt over the course of 1942 to frame its demands in relation to British policy. News of the camp was suppressed from the general public in late 1942 and early 1943, in line with British sensitivities about Jews, but in all probability not from British intelligence and the Foreign Office.

However, the effect of the decision not to publicize news of the camp by the Polish government in November 1942 was disastrous for the dissemination of information about the gassing of Jews at Auschwitz for the next year and a half. The length of time between initial receipt of news of the gassing of Jews at Oświęcim (12 November) and the distribution of Sprawozdanie Nr 6/42 to members of the Polish government and the Polish National Council (23 December) was very significant in the context of British censorship and choreography of news about the Holocaust. The brief conjectural window that existed in the week prior to and just after the UN declaration on 17 December 1942, when it was possible for Polish and Jewish representatives to speak relatively freely, and be listened to, about the Jewish tragedy, including the gassing of Jews at death camps, was closing by the time the Polish Cabinet and National Council became aware of the report. If, as argued here, Mikołajczyk and Raczyński concluded that mentioning Jews being gassed at Oświęcim risked jeopardizing the Allied declaration, the lack of pressure from the

From Palestine to the president 157

Cabinet and Jewish representatives on the National Council allowed the caution of the senior Polish politicians to be uncontested.

The expansion of Oświęcim to include giant crematoria at 'Paradisal' (Birkenau) was known in the West by July 1942, but news of the mass gassing of Jews that began in May 1942 was not available in London until November (Polish intelligence, Stanisław Mikołajczyk) and December 1942 (Polish Cabinet) and then, it seems, only through the message sent on 4 September and via any undocumented testimony given by Jan Karski.[117] Aneks 38, which incorporated the significant news from 10 September 1942, recording the murder of 1,000 Jews a day at the camp, as far as can be established, was not received by the Polish Government in Exile in 1942.

Unknown to the Polish government at the time, the window of opportunity to incorporate Oświęcim into the British choreographed narrative of the German atrocities against Jews was missed. The Polish government sought to position itself as a loyal ally subscribing to the British censorship and propaganda regime in an attempt to gain goodwill for its objective of persuading the British to pursue a policy of retaliation. From August 1942 news about the camp was sent regularly via courier to London from Warsaw but did not break into the Western media in 1942 or the first months of 1943. The one report that can be documented as reaching the Polish government in November 1942 was translated into English but not, as far as can be established, disseminated to the press. Consequently, the first reports of the mass slaughter of Jews at Oświęcim to reach the Western press did not come from the Polish Government in Exile, but from Palestinian subjects who returned to Palestine in November 1942.

From Palestine to the president

On 24 November 1942 the Polish Government in Exile released a memorandum that highlighted the German atrocities against Jews. The *New York Times* London correspondent, James MacDonald, submitted a story on this memorandum that was published deep inside the *New York Times* on 25 November 1942, on page 10. It was reported that only 40,000 ration cards had been printed for Warsaw's Jews for the previous October, whereas in March the population in the ghetto was 433,000. It recorded that Jews were loaded onto freight trains, where deaths from suffocation, starvation and thirst were common, and that those surviving were 'sent to special camps at Treblinka, Belzec and Sobibor'. These people were then mass-murdered. Beneath this story, at the bottom of the page, next to a half-page advert for Seagram Whiskies and under the

158   Intelligence about Auschwitz: November 1940–February 1943

subtitle 'Details reaching Palestine', the *New York Times* published a report received from Jerusalem. It read:

> Information received here of methods by which the Germans in Poland are carrying out the slaughter of Jews includes accounts of trainloads of adults and children taken to great crematoriums at Oswiencim [*sic*], near Cracow. Polish Christian workers have confirmed that concrete buildings on the former Russian frontiers are used by the Germans in which thousands of Jews have been put to death.

This report was the first news drawing attention to the mass killing of Jews at Auschwitz to reach a mass audience. The first sentence referred directly to the camp, the second referred to a different camp – most probably Sobibór – on the former Russian frontier, which divided the Soviet and German zones of occupation (Laqueur 1998: 192). On 23 November 1942, the Jewish Agency Executive in Jerusalem released a report on 'murders and massacres carried out against Polish Jews and against Jews from Central and Western Europe who had been deported to Poland'.[118] On 24 November 1942, *The Times* in London reported on the Jewish Agency Executive's communiqué recording that the news of the massacres had been received from 'persons who recently arrived ... from Europe'. The article, entitled 'Nazi war on Jews' and located at the bottom of page 3, noted that a special commission had been set up to direct the destruction of Jewish communities, the depopulation of ghettos, the burning of 1,500 Jews in the synagogue in Białystok, and the transport of able-bodied male Jews to an 'unknown destination'.[119] *The Times* did not name any concentration or death camps.

The Jewish Agency Executive's communiqué followed a volatile meeting that it held on Sunday 22 November 1942. News from Europe was derived from the testimony of 114 Palestinian subjects, sixty-nine of them Jewish, who had arrived on 16 November as part of an exchange deal for German internees in Palestine. Over 18–19 November many of these people spoke to officials from the Jewish Agency's immigration department, including its head, Eliyha Dobkin, Moshe Shapira, and Chaim Barlas, who was responsible within the agency for Turkey.[120] On 20 November, these interviewers released a summary report (the Dobkin report) to colleagues in the Jewish Agency. This report noted that there were three crematoria at Oświęcim, that two more were under construction and that Jews were taken to the camp to be murdered.[121]

According to Gilbert (2001a: 88), 'almost all of the information brought by the returning Palestinians had already been forwarded to London, Washington and Jerusalem in the previous three months, from the Jewish Agency representatives in Geneva, or had been publicized in

From Palestine to the president   159

London by the Polish Government in Exile'. Scholars have long known about this early reference to the mass killing of Jews at Auschwitz, but have not traced the distribution of the information in the Dobkin report. Penkower (2002: 165), for example noted that the arrivals in Palestine 'spoke of methodical massacre, gassing at Chelmno and Treblinka; three crematoria burning Jews at Oswiecim ... with two more under construction'.[122] Laqueur (1998: 23) stated that

a Palestinian citizen, a resident of Sosnowice [sic] who was repatriated in November 1942, reported to the Jewish Agency about the chimneys of nearby Auschwitz – and what they were used for. Her evidence together with that of others ... was distributed by the Information Department of the Jewish Agency on 20 November 1942. She must have heard [about the function of Auschwitz] by August or September 1942 at the latest.

The original source for both the 25 November story in the *New York Times* and a memo passed by Jewish representatives to President Roosevelt on 8 December 1942 was a member of this party of returnees to Palestine: the lady from Sosnowiec whom Gilbert identified as being the bearer of the first news about Jews being killed on a mass scale at the camp and whom Laqueur identifies as a Palestinian citizen. The Jewish leadership in Palestine had been advised and her information was sent to the United States.[123]

On receipt, the *New York Times* editorial team ordered the news from various sources and gave greater prominence to the official release from an Allied government. The news about Auschwitz merited that single sentence only. However, the same information was reused two weeks later. At noon on 8 December 1942, a delegation of representatives from Jewish organizations submitted a memorandum to President Roosevelt at the White House. The organizations represented included the American Jewish Committee, the American Jewish Congress, B'Nai B'rith, the Jewish Labour Committee, the Synagogue Council of America, and the Union of Orthodox Rabbis of the United States.[124] This twenty-page memorandum summarized the German genocidal policy against the Jews in some detail, drawing on a variety of sources. It outlined the fate of Jews from occupied countries, and discussed the deportations and killings. Citing a Polish Underground paper, it reported on the transfer of Jews from around Warsaw and highlighted that those 'unable to keep pace with their German guards, whether they are adults, old people or children, were indiscriminately shot on the spot'.[125] After this extended introduction, the memorandum discussed the death camps in a section entitled 'Extermination centers'. On page 11, the memorandum stated,

160   Intelligence about Auschwitz: November 1940–February 1943

Centers have been established in various parts of Eastern Europe for the scientific and cold blooded mass murder of Jews. Polish Christian workers, eyewitnesses, have confirmed reports that concrete buildings, on the former Russian frontiers, are used by the Germans as gas chambers in which thousands of Jews have been put to death.

The slaughter of trainloads of Jewish adults and children in great crematoriums at Ozwiencim [*sic*] near Cracow is confirmed by eyewitnesses in reports which recently reached Jerusalem.

As is readily seen, the wording from the memo is more or less the same as that in the *New York Times* article, including the spelling of Ozwiencim/Oswiencim, instead of Oświęcim. This indicates that the *New York Times* article was either an intermediary source, or that the report sent to the newspaper was published as received and that the same data was sent to at least one of the Jewish organizations responsible for the memorandum. Barbara Rogers (1999b: 100), who first drew scholarly attention to this memorandum following its public release at the National Archives at Kew in the mid-1990s, argues that '[t]he fact that American Jewish organisations mentioned Auschwitz well into the report (p.11) demonstrates the camp was not considered a secret, and although known to be the largest camp, was probably not perceived as being any more horrific than any other camps at that time'. The camp was certainly not deemed to be a secret, at least amongst those who lent their authority to the memorandum submitted to the president, but the placing of the information in the middle of the text reflects the memo's structure, which moves from a general discussion of facts and summaries of the disappearance of Jews from occupied countries through to more precise details in sections entitled 'Hitler's extermination order', 'Caravans of death', 'Extermination centers', 'Massacres', 'Slow death' and 'Religious persecution'. The document concludes with an appeal, clearly pitched to US policy makers prior to the UN declaration of 17 December: 'the Jews of Europe, whom Hitler has marked out as the first to suffer utter extinction, have no assurance at present that a United Nations victory will come in time to save them from complete annihilation'.[126]

In New York, Sylwin Strakacz of the Polish Consulate reviewed the American press and sent both his analysis and press cuttings to the Polish Ministry of Foreign Affairs in London. In the review of the press for the period 23–8 November 1942, Strakacz devoted considerable attention to the 25 November story in the *New York Times*, providing an extended summary of James MacDonald's article. The Polish representative also noted that a telegram from Jerusalem provided further information. Strakacz had read details about the mass slaughter of Jews at Oświęcim, but it seems that he did not appreciate the significance of this data at this

From Palestine to the president 161

stage.[127] It is not known when Strakacz's review and the accompanying press cuttings reached London.

On 2 December, the Polish prime minister, Władysław Sikorski, arrived in the United States to meet President Roosevelt. On 15 December, the Polish Information Center in New York reported that early in his stay Sikorski had met with Jewish representatives, including Stephen Wise, Maurice Perlzweig, Nahum Goldmann and Arieh Tartakower.[128] At this meeting, the information within the memorandum passed to President Roosevelt on 8 December may have also been handed to Sikorski or to Polish officials. Although no such document has been located in the Polish files, the newspaper *Poland Fights*, which liaised closely with the Polish Information Center, published an article on page 5 entitled 'Innocent blood cries for vengeance', which quoted from the memorandum handed to Roosevelt. It is therefore possible, though not certain, that the Palestine-sourced information about Oświęcim, published in the *New York Times* on 25 November and reprinted in the memorandum to Roosevelt, had reached senior Polish politicians in London by January 1943.

The chairman of the British Section of the World Jewish Congress, Maurice Perlzweig, was in possession of a copy of the memorandum handed to President Roosevelt, which he passed on to the British Embassy in Washington on 30 December 1942. At the embassy Perlzweig spoke at some length with an unnamed official about American Jewry's attitude to Britain. Both the memorandum and a summary of Perlzweig's conversation at the British Embassy were sent by diplomatic bag to London, arriving at the Foreign Office on 7 January 1943. Officials at the Foreign Office did not comment, at least in writing, on the memorandum. Rather, Perlzweig's comments on refugees and Jewish representation on a future war crimes investigation committee attracted written attention.

During late November and December, Foreign Office officials had been preparing for the UN declaration of 17 December, and liaising with Allied governments to that end. The declaration did not mention Oświęcim as a place where Jews were being killed on a mass scale. It is reasonable to expect that the part of the 8 December memorandum referring to the mass murder of Jews at Oświęcim would have elicited a response if it had been new information. The lack of commentary suggests five possibilities – the memorandum was scanned, but not closely read, meaning that the news of Oświęcim was missed; the mention of Oświęcim was seen, but not recognized as something new; the extermination function of Oświęcim was, like that of Sobibór, Treblinka and Bełżec, well understood, and hence required no further commentary;

162   Intelligence about Auschwitz: November 1940–February 1943

the information about Oświęcim was new, but, in the post-UN declaration context, was deemed unsuitable for further discussion as other issues came to the fore; or simply the memorandum was deemed unimportant following the UN declaration, and the Jewish response to that declaration was what concerned British officials. It is the last option which is most persuasive: the Foreign Office folder into which the memorandum was filed highlights officials' concerns. It was entitled, 'Effect of joint declaration on German atrocities against Jews on United States Jewry'.

Despite the lack of interest shown by officials (at least in the documentary record), it is apparent that news of Oświęcim as a camp where 'trainloads' of Jews were being slaughtered had reached the Foreign Office, and that at least three officials – Frank Roberts, Roger Allen and Gregory Wedgwood Harrison – had access to the memorandum, since they all commented on Perlzweig's conversation with the embassy official in Washington. The fact that Roger Allen read the memorandum is particularly noteworthy. Allen was charged with collecting data about atrocities that British agencies received and liaising with British intelligence.[129] The British were storing information about atrocities, including those with non-British victims, with a view to future war crimes prosecutions. Such prosecutions were much discussed amongst the Allies in late 1942 and early 1943.

News of Auschwitz as an extermination centre for Jews had reached important officials in the US by December 1942 and the UK by January 1943[130] (though it is likely that they received such data earlier from the Polish government). In the US, the memorandum was in all likelihood handled by White House staffers, and in neither case is it clear whether senior political decision makers actually read the memorandum. It is unlikely that Roosevelt did, and, from the commentary at the Foreign Office, it seems unlikely that it was forwarded to British Foreign Secretary Anthony Eden. But on both sides of the Atlantic it was possible for political decision makers to know about Auschwitz. Jewish leaders, both in the US and in the UK, also had the same information about the camp. Arguments that these leaders did not really believe this information in late 1942 have to be set against the fact that they submitted an official memorandum to the President of the United States on 8 December. Such a document is not the place for speculation or the inclusion of doubted information, which could, if rejected, scupper credibility and endanger the achievement of objectives. British and American analysts were in a position to note the new function of Auschwitz and to recognize that the process of Nazi extermination of Jews had expanded. But as far as can be established, the new data was merely filed away.

However, in early 1943, the Polish government highlighted the horror of Oświęcim in a letter from Edward Raczyński to Anthony Eden. Such official communication followed certain protocols and the contents of such letters rarely came as a surprise to recipients. Prior informal and often undocumented communication between officials took place to ensure needless embarrassment was not caused to either the sender or the recipient, while allowing a core message to be delivered. The objective of this letter was to emphasize the terrible situation at Oświęcim in a form that would be acceptable to key audiences, and would persuade the British government to initiate retaliatory strikes. The letter reveals more about how the Polish government comprehended British sensibilities than, for example, about the Polish government's marginalization of news of Jews at Auschwitz.

Concentration camps: Raczyński letter to Eden (20 January 1943)

On 20 January 1943, the Polish ambassador, Edward Raczyński, wrote to the British Foreign Secretary. Referring to his 10 December 1942 note, which detailed the mass extermination of Jews, Raczyński drew attention to fresh reports from Poland detailing twenty-five concentration camps in the country and other camps in Germany where Poles were being held. He stated that there were approximately eighty camps in Poland, and that the 'most notorious of these camps is that at Oświęcim'. He proceeded to describe the camp, drawing on the data cited in the document received on 12 November and incorporated in Sprawozdanie Nr 6/42:

Deportation to this camp is tantamount to death by prolonged torture. The camp at Oświęcim situated 30 km west of Cracow, is divided into two sections – one for women, the other for men. According to the camp register, the number of women interned amounted on 1st June, 1942 to 8,260. The number of men at the same date was 38,720 of whom 8,170 were Jews, including about 1,100 French Jews and about 5,000 Czechoslovak Jews.

According to information which has reached the Polish Government, there have passed through the register 54,720 men and 8,620 women, or a total of 63,340 people up to 1st June, 1942. In addition, 22,500 men and women passed through the camp without being registered. Of this total of 85,840 men and women, 23,000 were until still recently alive, while 5,000 had been released or transferred to other camps. It must be presumed that up to 58,000 people have perished in the camp.[131]

Raczyński then appealed for reprisals, in line with the policy formulated by the Polish National Council, and earlier discussed by Stanisław Mikołajczyk with Frank Savery in November 1942. The focus on

164   Intelligence about Auschwitz: November 1940–February 1943

Oświęcim in January 1943 demonstrates that the Polish government wished to keep the pressure on the British for retaliation. Already by this point, as discussed in Chapter 2, the British Foreign Office and Home Office were seeking to limit attention on Jews and further action by the Polish government highlighting the slaughter of Jews is likely to have run up against stiff British resistance. For the Poles, reference to Oświęcim also had the benefit of satisfying a broad constituency within the Polish community in Britain and in Poland, including those on the political Right. The statistics from Oświęcim were sent from Warsaw more than once, encouraging the Polish government to act on this information.

Raczyński's letter is important because it focused British Foreign Office attention on the camp. As noted, there is hard evidence that key figures in that department had received information about the killing of Jews at Auschwitz from the British Embassy in Washington, DC, and probably received confirming data from the Polish government (i.e. the full 4 September (12 November) report). Foreign Office officials therefore were equipped to recognize the significance of Raczyński's letter with regard to the situation of Jews at Oświęcim.

The data in Raczyński's letter was over six months old, and, while noting a Jewish presence at the camp, it did not mention that Jews were now being gassed there. It therefore conformed with British sensitivities while highlighting to the Foreign Office Polish concerns about the camp. Since Raczyński's objective was to persuade the British to act and initiate retaliatory strikes against the Germans, he adopted a cautious approach which would not antagonize the British – or, more bluntly, he self-censored. In this context, highlighting the brief mention of the killing of Jews at the camp did not make political or strategic sense, though there is a strong argument that given the material Raczyński had to hand about Oświęcim, including perhaps the press cuttings from Strakacz and the 8 December memorandum to Roosevelt, he had the duty to Polish Jewish citizens to be bolder, despite the constraints imposed by the British.[132] On some level, senior Polish government politicians recognized this as, two months later, following the arrival of further devastating news from the camp, the Polish government began to push British censorship to the limit and disseminate news about the camp to the press and to a lesser extent in official publications: the full text of the June 1942 report from Oświęcim included in Sprawozdanie Nr 6/42 was retranslated and printed in English by the Ministry of the Interior in 1943.[133] The circulation of this English-language document cannot be accurately traced.[134]

Raczyński's letter was the subject of an extended article in the *Jewish Chronicle* on 12 February 1943, with the title 'The death-camp at Oswiecim – Polish note to UN'. In the post-UN declaration context, in

Concentration camps: Raczyński letter to Eden (20 January 1943)   165

which the death camps of Treblinka, Bełżec and Sobibór had been extensively mentioned in the quality press, the title of this article could reasonably encourage readers to associate Oświęcim with those three camps as a camp of a similar sort.[135] It cannot be ruled out that the editor of the *Jewish Chronicle* had seen the Polish original source report. Both Ignacy Schwarzbart and Shmuel Zygielbojm maintained cordial relations with the staff of the *Chronicle* and may have passed the information on. It is also possible that Perlzweig had forwarded a copy of the memorandum handed to the American president to the newspaper. In short, it was possible for the *Chronicle* to have had an evidentiary base to support the article's title. The *Jewish Chronicle*'s report did not mention any details not included in Raczyński's letter. But the framing of the article certainly pointed its mainly Jewish readership to the view that Oświęcim was the worst of all the camps. It read:

A note on the intensification of the German physical and moral destruction of the Polish nation has been addressed by the Polish Government to the Governments of the UN.

The note, which recalls the previous communication of the Polish Government concerning the mass extermination of Jews, describes conditions in the 24 concentration camps by the Nazis. The camp at Oswiecim is described as the most notorious of these. Deportation to the camp, says the note, means death by prolonged torture. Among the inmates of the camp last summer were 8,170 Jews including 1,100 French Jews and about 5,000 Czechoslovak Jews.

Details from the 12 November report continued to be used into the spring of 1943, as further information about the camp reached London, and increased the pressure on the Polish government to be bolder in its dealing with its Allies' information dissemination strategy. In the United States, the 5 April 1943 edition of *Poland Fights* (published in English and in Polish) reported to its American readership that '[m]any carloads of Russian war prisoners and Jews have suffered death by gas in this notorious camp', referring to Oświęcim.[136] By this point, the Polish government had committed itself routinely to distributing news from Oświęcim following the arrival of Napoleon Segieda in London in February 1943 and the receipt of further news from Warsaw about the situation at Oświęcim in March 1943.

Prior to this, disjuncture in knowledge about Oświęcim between the Polish Underground and the Polish government was the result of how the Underground sent information west and the way in which the Polish Ministry of the Interior handled the information it did receive. The scale of the slaughter at Oświęcim was known in Warsaw from 8 September, but this data was not radioed. The only information to reach the British capital in 1942 from Warsaw mentioning the gassing of Jews at the camp

166   Intelligence about Auschwitz: November 1940–February 1943

was the brief 4 September document and any undocumented information divulged by Jan Karski.[137] The Polish Ministry of the Interior released material regularly to the Cabinet, but Sprawozdanie Nr 6/42 was not distributed until after the UN declaration of 17 December 1942, which meant there was little opportunity for the news about the camp to reach a wider public in a context where Poland's dominant ally was sensitive to news of Jews. There were delays in the transmission of specific data due to the time it took couriered reports to reach London, but from November 1942 the crucial information that Auschwitz had become a location where Jews were being murdered in gas chambers was in London.

Documents at the National Archives in Kew show that the White House and the Foreign Office received data about the mass killing of Jews at the camp (in December 1942 and January 1943 respectively) and did nothing about it. The British probably also received information from the Polish government ('Report on conditions in Poland'). This cannot be confirmed by records at Kew due to the way British SOE and Foreign Office files have been managed, destroyed and weeded.

The ascendency of the Allies in the European theatre of war, marked most dramatically by the Soviet victory at Stalingrad in February 1943, did not encourage the Western Allies to adopt a more liberal approach to the distribution of news about the Nazi persecution and extermination of Jews. In the next chapter it is shown that report after report received from the Polish Underground about the systematic killing of Jews at Auschwitz was routinely distributed by the Polish government. The way this information was handled highlights the strength of the British censorship regime, the inaction of the British and American governments and the weaknesses of the Polish Government in Exile.

5 British suppression of news of Auschwitz: March 1943–June/July 1944

The third period of information management about Auschwitz runs from March 1943 to the distribution of the Vrba–Wetzler report in June and July 1944. During this period, knowledge of the camp in both Warsaw (Polish Underground) and London (Polish Government in Exile) more or less coincides. As will be shown in this chapter, the data that reached London was routinely distributed by the Polish government. There can be absolutely no doubt that many key officials in the British Foreign Office and the Political Warfare Executive had been informed of the true function of Auschwitz by May 1943 at the very latest. News from Polish reports about the camp appeared (with some delay) in English-language newspapers printed in London – the *Polish Jewish Observer* and the *Jewish Chronicle* in 1943 and 1944. News of the killing of Jews at Auschwitz reached London at an average rate of around one report a fortnight between March 1943 and June 1944. However, British government documentation (the FO, the PWE and intelligence files) for this period does not contain a great deal of information about Auschwitz – a fact which, as will be shown, speaks to the issue of how information about the camp was managed and filed rather than to British knowledge. This is very important, as recognizing how the British handled the news from Auschwitz after March 1943 – for which there is documentary evidence – sheds light on the earlier period (autumn 1942–March 1943) where the documentary record is considerably thinner.

In addition to interviewing, in November 1942, Jan Karski, who, as was argued in Chapter 4, almost certainly had knowledge of Auschwitz, the British had access to a further informant with data about the camp in February 1943. The power of eyewitness testimony in relaying news of the Holocaust was important, so long as the credibility of the eyewitness was not in doubt. Jan Karski was held in some esteem in both Polish and British circles and his accounts of the Warsaw ghetto and Bełżec (Izbica) were significant in sustaining press interest in Nazi actions against Jews in the first half of December 1942. On 19 February 1943, the Polish courier and SOE agent Napoleon Segieda, later known as Jerzy Salski

167

168   British suppression of news of Auschwitz: March 1943–June/July 1944

(codename 'Wera'), who was connected with the Polish Ministry of the Interior, arrived in Britain after a six-month trip through occupied Europe.[1] According to Polish documents, Segieda did not arrive until 27 February 1943, which suggests that he was held for debriefing by SOE for several days prior to release to the Poles. Salski's arrival was very important for the dissemination of news about Auschwitz. First, he provided eyewitness testimony about Auschwitz, drawing on his stay in the town of Oświęcim in the late spring–early summer of 1942. Second, he could comment on the veracity of shocking reports about the camp that were sent from Warsaw from late 1942 and early 1943 onwards. Salski therefore played a role in weakening the Polish government's complicity with the Western Allies' policy of burying the news from Auschwitz.

From March 1943, hard documentary evidence exists demonstrating that the Polish government routinely passed on the intelligence reports it received from Warsaw about the mass killing of Jews at the camp to the Western Allies and to the press. Jerzy Salski wrote two reports while in London in April 1943 that recorded the mass murder of Jews at Auschwitz. Before these were written, news about the camp arrived in London via radio from Warsaw.

Reports from Stefan Rowecki and Jan Stanisław Jankowski (4 and 12 March 1943)

As Raczyński was preparing his letter to Eden in January 1943, part of the Polish Underground in Warsaw compiled detailed statistics about mortality at Auschwitz. Although Aneks 44 (covering the period from 16 to 31 December 1942), which reported a daily death rate of between 120 and 180 people, with an underlying 'natural' daily death rate of thirty people (compared with eighty the previous year), had not reached London, a new report compiled by the State Security Corps of the Interior Department of the Delegature revealed even more shocking statistics.[2] According to the State Security Corps report of 1–15 January, 502,000 Jews from France, Belgium and Holland, and 20,000 Polish Jews, had been gassed at Auschwitz.[3] This data was incorporated into the regular internal Home Army report (*informacja bieżąca* – 'current information') of 17 February 1943 and was placed, significantly, in the section of the document covering Jewish affairs.[4] There was no attempt to minimize the murder of Jews at Auschwitz in this report or in subsequent issues of *informacja bieżąca* in which news of Auschwitz was presented. It was then immediately repackaged into Aneks 48 that covered the period from 16 to 28 February and also included in the 'Pro Memoria' of the

Reports from Stefan Rowecki and Jan Stanisław Jankowski

situation in the General Government for the period from 24 January to 24 February, both of which were sent by courier to London.[5]

However, the information was not radioed to London until 4 March 1943 – a delay of around six weeks. On the one hand, some delay should be expected. Data had to be checked and worked over by the underground state's Department of Information, the data had to be forwarded up the command chain, and in the case of this particular information coordination between the military and civilian wings of the Underground had to be arranged – the radio message was sent jointly by General Rowecki and the delegate, Stanisław Jankowski.[6] By sending the message jointly, the evident aim of the Underground leadership was to signal to the Polish government in London that the information was, as far as the Underground was concerned, correct. On the other hand, the delay in transmitting such news seems excessive and although reconstructing the precise manner in which the information was handled in occupied Warsaw is not possible, it is feasible that the data could have been sent some weeks earlier – at some point in mid-February. Thus, in addition to technical, logistical and organizational difficulties, the argument articulated by Adam Puławski (2009) that the Underground delayed news about Jews due to social distance may have played a role. But, as noted, the data was also sent by courier in two different documents, indicating that the Underground was committed to ensuring that this news reached London, and the Home Army repeatedly circulated news of the mass murder of Jews at Auschwitz through 1943 in *informacja bieżąca* which provided regular updates of the situation in the country.[7]

The message sent on 4 March, though necessarily brief, was devastating. It reported that 520,000 Jews had been killed at the camp.[8] The message was de-encrypted on 31 March. It is not clear why it took over three weeks for this message to be deciphered. However, since it did not relate to military matters, it may have been queued behind time-sensitive military intelligence. The time lag could reflect work management difficulties in London: the volume of material requiring de-encryption was great, meaning that delays in processing some data from Warsaw took time; it could also have been incorrectly flagged in Warsaw. Thus it seems possible that, had this information been prioritized in Warsaw and flagged as urgent, the minister of the interior could have been advised a month earlier than was the case.

In his discussion of the Irving trial, Robert Jan van Pelt (2002: 145) argued that this information was not acted on. This is incorrect. Breitman (2004: 194) shows that this message was passed by Polish intelligence to American intelligence in May. It was then handed by the OSS to the American Joint Chiefs of Staff in June 1943.[9]

170   British suppression of news of Auschwitz: March 1943–June/July 1944

The information about the mass murder of Jews at Oświęcim was included in Sprawozdanie Nr 4/43 (Report 4/43), which presented information from Poland received in London during the first half of 1943.[10] This document, prepared by the Polish Ministry of the Interior, was distributed to the Polish Cabinet by Władysław Banaczyk on 20 August 1943. Ignacy Schwarzbart had received a copy by 28 August, though he had been advised of the information by May 1943 as he incorporated it into his English-language summary of the latest news from Poland for that month.[11] On 3 September 1943, the information sent by Rowecki and Jankowski was published with only minor changes in the subscription-only supplement of the *City and East London Observer* – the *Polish Jewish Observer*. The front-page headline of 3 September 1943 read 'Oswiecism [*sic*] camp is grave of 629,000 Jews, Poles and Russians', while the accompanying article reported,

At least 520,000 Jews, 83,000 Poles and 26,000 Russian prisoners of war died or were murdered in Oswiecim concentration camp in Poland up to the end of 1942. This is revealed in a new report from secret sources just received by members of the Polish National Council in London … Among the half million Jewish victims were Jews deported from France, Belgium, Holland and Yugoslavia.

The article also reported on the liquidation of the Kraków ghetto, drawing on cables sent by Stefan Korboński, the head of the Directorate of Civilian Resistance, during March and April 1943 (see below).[12] The news of the murder of 520,000 Jews at Oświęcim was reported in a short article on page 8 in the *Jewish Chronicle* on 10 September 1943, entitled 'The toll of Oswiecim'.

The information about the mass murder of Jews at Oświęcim was also distributed by the Polish Consulate in Istanbul. The consulate issued regular mimeograph publications that provided news from occupied Poland – one in Polish (first issued in Istanbul during the summer of 1942) and another in French. The two bulletins drew on the same source material, but were slightly different – the French-language bulletin was generally shorter and more succinct. The two publications reported on the Holocaust through the war, and were aimed at representatives of the international community in Istanbul and beyond.

The data sent by Rowecki and Jankowski was one of the sources for reports published in the Polish-language bulletin *Polska pod okupacją niemiecką* on 14 May 1943, and in the French-language bulletin *Pologne occupée* on 22 May 1943. *Polska pod okupacją niemiecką* informed readers that 550,000 Jews from Poland, France, Belgium, Holland and other countries had been gassed at Oświęcim. The bulletin also referred to the sterilization of women and a new crematorium at the camp, drawing on other messages sent from Warsaw during March and April 1943 (see below). *Pologne occupée* recorded that 580,000 Jews had been killed at Oświęcim.

It is not clear why the figures of Jews killed at Oświęcim in the Polish- and French-language publications were different – both from each other and from the source data. One possibility is that the official responsible for *Polska pod okupacją niemiecką*, Adam Nowina-Kurcyusz (real name Jerzy Kurcyusz), who also had responsibility for ensuring communication between Warsaw and London via Istanbul, recognized that the source information was some months old and updated the information for the Polish-language bulletin, and later revised his figures upwards for the French-language bulletin the following week. It is almost certain that the information published in Istanbul reached the West.[13] On 13 December 1943, the Jewish Telegraphic Agency (JTA) published an article reporting that 580,000 Jews had perished at Oświęcim. It is probable that the source for the JTA article was the 22 May edition of *Pologne occupée*, though it is not known when the JTA first came into possession of the Polish Consulate's bulletin.[14]

The JTA's article was published several weeks after the English-language supplement to the New York-based Polish Jewish newspaper *Nasza Trybuna* (*Our Tribune*) republished the *Polish Jewish Observer*'s 3 September article on Oświęcim. The editors of *Our Tribune* (Jacob Apenszlak and Arieh Tartakower) printed the story on page 5 on 21 October 1943 with only minor corrections to the original text from the *Polish Jewish Observer*.

It is now known that the data from Rowecki and Jankowski's March 1943 radio message was not accurate. Franciszek Piper (1992) conducted painstaking research on how many people died at Auschwitz. His work informed Laurence Rees's (2005: 179) claim that 200,000 people perished at the camp during 1942. The Polish Underground did not intentionally exaggerate the figures. Rather, this was the best estimate that could be arrived at in the very difficult conditions in Poland during 1942 and early 1943. Most important, however, is the fact that significant data showing that hundreds of thousands of Jews were being systematically killed at Auschwitz reached the West and was distributed to the press, and presented to the public in London, Istanbul and New York.

So far, no sign of the information sent by Rowecki and Jankowski has been found in the British National Archives. But, given that it was advanced to a high level in the US, and that the information was published in London in early September 1943, it can be assumed that the report was also passed to British officials both within the Foreign Office

172   British suppression of news of Auschwitz: March 1943–June/July 1944

and in British intelligence, most probably prior to its dispatch to the United States. The British also had the opportunity to access the information through their routine interception of transatlantic communications. The destruction of some Polish documents after the war, and the Secret Intelligence Service's (SIS) practice of destroying intelligence once they had forwarded it to whoever required it, means that it is not possible to map accurately the circulation of this information amongst British officials (Stirling 2005: 11).

The significant point is that the information reached the Americans soon after it was received by the Polish government in London. News of the mass murder of Jews at Oświęcim was released to the press and to the international community in London and in Istanbul. There is no reason to think that the Polish government would not also have passed the news directly to the British and no convincing argument why they would deliberately not advise British officials at the Foreign Office or within the intelligence community, even in the context of British sensitivities about Jews. Roger Allen of the Foreign Office was collecting data on atrocities, and the news from Auschwitz would have been passed to him. As noted earlier, Allen's atrocity file has not been located.[15]

The information could have been passed through a variety of means: from the Polish General Staff's Bureau II to British counterparts, via Bureau VI to colleagues at SOE during the fortnightly meetings, directly by Mikołajczyk to Savery in their regular meetings. By March 1943, as we saw in Chapter 2, stories about Jews were being marginalized by Foreign Office officials as they sought to contain the fallout from the December 1942 declaration. Any public mention of this information in the mainstream press would have led to overwhelming pressure for a more active and generous refugee policy. This was something the Foreign Office was not prepared to countenance. The delayed publication in an obscure newspaper, and deep within the *Jewish Chronicle*, without comment, meant that its impact on broader British opinion was negligible.[16] Similarly, repeated publication by the Polish Consulate in Istanbul of the news that over half a million Jews had been gassed at Oświęcim during 1943 (in May and again on 9 September 1943) had no impact on British or American opinion.[17]

On 23 March 1943, Polish General Staff Headquarters received another radio message about Auschwitz, sent by Rowecki and Jankowski to Mikołajczyk. It reported that the new crematorium at the camp could burn 3,000 people a day, and added that the sterilization of women was taking place.[18] The message was sent (encrypted) on 12 March and was deciphered on 29 March. The information was also incorporated in a situation report sent from Poland on 12 March and carried by three couriers (one of whom was Jan Nowak-Jeziorański) via three different routes. This situation report arrived in London in the first half of May 1943. The radio message was immediately passed to the British. On 8 April the PWE's Central Directive advised PWE officials that '1000 Jews from Krakow have been evacuated to the notorious camp of Oswiecim in the past week. Here the Germans have constructed with Jewish labour a crematorium said to be capable of burning 3000 corpses a day.'[19] This data was published several months later in an article in the *Polish Jewish Observer* (3 September 1943). On 23 March, Stefan Korboński sent another radio message with more or less the same data dispatched on 12 March by Rowecki and Jankowski. Korboński's message was deciphered in London on 27 March.[20] Given that Korboński provided extremely time-sensitive data for Radio Świt, his messages tended to be swiftly de-encrypted. On 30 March, Stefan Korboński sent yet another radio message to London (once more to Mikołajczyk), advising that the Kraków ghetto had been liquidated and its inhabitants sent to Oświęcim, and that thousands of Jews were also killed in the ghetto.[21] This message formed the basis of a BBC broadcast less than two weeks later.[22] This broadcast is discussed below. It seems that Radio Świt also transmitted the information.[23]

In sum, by the end of March 1943, the Polish government had four significant reports detailing the destruction of Jews at Auschwitz. It set about distributing this information to its US and UK allies, and pressing for wider dissemination.

Broadcast on the BBC (11 April 1943)

On 11 April, the BBC broadcast to Europe the news sent by Korboński.[24] It was not featured on the Home Service, or sanctioned to be published in the mainstream press in Britain. The broadcast was designed, in the main, to advise Polish audiences of Allied knowledge of the continuation of German atrocities, to indicate to the Polish Underground that the information they had supplied had been received by the Allies, and to placate the Polish Government in Exile in a way that did not embarrass the British government in the context of continual anxieties about potential refugees. The 4 March 1943 report, detailing the massive scale of killing at the camp (520,000 Jews murdered), would not even have been broadcast had the Polish Government devoted significant resources to achieve this goal. The data was simply incompatible with British policy. Confining the news of Auschwitz to the European Service ensured that monolingual English-speakers remained unaware of the news about Auschwitz, and this no doubt inhibited knowledge of the

174   British suppression of news of Auschwitz: March 1943–June/July 1944

camp becoming widely known in Britain, and, importantly, ensured that British civil-society organizations (including the Catholic and Anglican churches, refugee aid providers) did not mobilize on behalf of potential Jewish refugees due to news about Auschwitz. The Polish Service informed listeners that:

> On 13th, 14th and 15th March, the Germans took action to liquidate the Cracow Ghetto ... The inhabitants were sent to so-called 'Camps of Death' where they were murdered. During the liquidation Germans killed over one thousand Jews on the spot. The remaining were sent by lorries to the concentration camp of Oswiecim, which as it is known, has special installations for mass murder, that is gas chambers, and iron floors conducting an electric current.[25]

This broadcast is also significant because it demonstrates that the Political Warfare Executive and, specifically, individuals connected with the Foreign Office – such as Ivone Kirkpatrick and Frank Savery – were aware of the function of the camp by April 1943 at the very latest. Savery arguably had knowledge earlier. The same information is likely to have been used on Radio Świt, since the source data from Korboński's 30 March message is also found in Stanisław Mikołajczyk's files dealing with the radio station.[26] People at the PWE such as Harold Osborne, Moray McLaren, Rex Leeper and Ernest Thurtle (responsible for liaison between the Poles and the PWE) would all have had the opportunity to engage with Korboński's intelligence about Oświęcim. Since the 4 March message from Warsaw was passed to the Americans in May, it is likely that both British intelligence and members of the PWE had access to the same data.

The next day (12 April) the Jewish Telegraphic Agency published an article that referred to the information from Korboński's 30 March message. The piece informed readers that 'thousands of Jews in the Cracow ghetto were slaughtered and other thousands were deported to the dread concentration camp at Oswiecim'. Large groups of Jews, it reported, were forced onto cattle trucks decribed as 'death wagons', and taken to Oświęcim, which was 'equipped with special facilities for mass executions'. The precise nature of these facilities was not revealed. The article noted that these Jews were presumed to be dead, and that Polish sources indicated that the ghettos were being used 'merely as assembly points from which the victims are taken for extermination'.[27]

Later that week (Friday, 16 April), the *Jewish Chronicle* published the information sent by Korboński. Though the article featured deep inside the paper on page 7, it reported very significant information. Jews from Kraków were 'transferred to the notorious camp of Oswiecim, which was recently converted into a death camp for Jews and equipped with all the implements necessary for mass execution'.[28] The *Chronicle* had again indicated to its mainly Jewish readership that Oświęcim was a death camp, though it did not specify the Nazi methods of murder.

There was no follow-up on the BBC to the broadcast, both due to the British being unreceptive to news of atrocities against Jews, and because the serious crisis in Polish–Soviet relations dominated the attention of the Polish political class following the revelation of the Katyń graves, which featured heavily in the broadcasts over the BBC in the second half of April. A broadcast on 27 April, reporting on the publication of a pamphlet from the Inter-Allied Information Committee (IAIC) which gave details of atrocities against Jews, was severely cut. All specific details were deleted, including the assertion that the Germans

transformed POLAND into one vast centre for murdering Jews. Not only Polish Jews but Jews from every part of Europe are herded into Polish ghettos and labour camps [*sic*]. Those unfit for work are massacred by shooting, poison gas or electrocution.[29]

The report on the BBC was aimed at a European audience and sought to adhere to the PWE's particular propaganda objectives. The data in the IAIC pamphlet did not entirely accord with those objectives and was therefore cut. The broadcast did, nonetheless, include the warning made by the Allied governments that those responsible would be severely punished, but in March and April 1943 new and specific news about Jews was distinctly unwelcome. However, the repetition of previous warnings and information could be cautiously disseminated through certain – limited – channels.

The Segieda–Salski report (18 April 1943)

The shift in Polish policy in distributing news about Auschwitz that occurred in March 1943 was the result of a great deal of information about the camp reaching London from February 1943 and, it seems, was due to the presence of Napoleon Segieda in the British capital. Later known as Jerzy Salski, codenamed 'Wera', and with a further 'Gustav Molin' alias, Segieda had various loyalties – to the SOE and to the Polish Ministry of the Interior.[30] Relatively little is known about him and he remains an enigmatic figure to scholars. But the reports he wrote in London – one directed to the Polish government and a second to Ignacy Schwarzbart – both discuss the mass killing of Jews at Auschwitz. It is not known exactly what he did in London in late February or March 1943, whom he met or where he stayed. It is likely, however, that he spoke to Mikołajczyk about his journey and divulged the information he had about

176   British suppression of news of Auschwitz: March 1943–June/July 1944

Auschwitz. Confirmation from an eyewitness may have influenced the Polish government's reaction to the news from Rowecki and Jankowski that was sent on 4 March.

Segieda arrived in Britain on 19 February 1943, after a trip of several months through occupied Europe.[31] He left Warsaw on 8 August 1942 and was in Kraków on 9 August, Oświęcim on 10 August, Vienna on 11 August and Bern on 13 August. In Bern, his journey was delayed. On 18 August an order from Stanisław Mikołajczyk instructed Polish representatives in the city to ensure that Segieda had safe and legal passage to London (Frazik 1998: 410), and so to this end Polish representatives in Bern worked to secure visas to France and Spain for Segieda's journey. It is also possible that the British (the SOE) requested this high-level intervention,[32] but the intervention was fruitless. The visa for France did not materialise, and the visa for Spain expired. Segieda was arrested in France in mid-November 1942, and in Barcelona on 24 November. On 6 January Segieda was imprisoned at the camp at Miranda del Ebro, where he staged a hunger strike. He was freed on 24 January. At the beginning of February he travelled to Gibraltar and from there he was transported to Britain. Information about Segieda's progress across Western Europe was sent to the Ministry of the Interior by two different sources in February 1943. On 9 February, a Polish Ministry of Defence official sent a telegram noting Segieda's presence in Gibraltar, and a week later Paweł Siudak of the Social Department of the Ministry of the Interior received a letter from the Jewish Refugee Committee advising that Segieda was in Spain.[33]

From Bern, Segieda did not dispatch an expected report with the diplomatic post to London, on the grounds that he did not have full confidence in the security of the post and anticipated being in London himself shortly (Frazik 1998: 411).[34] The valuable data remained with him until he arrived in London. It included information about experiments with seeds (rubber) that were being conducted at Oświęcim (Segieda did not specify which part of the camp complex these experiments were taking place at). Women at the camp handling these seeds were killed, according to Segieda's report, to maintain secrecy, but through the camp underground, Segieda was able to obtain 100 specimens.[35] He eventually managed to transfer a few tens of these seeds to London. Segieda was very well informed of what was happening at the camp, including the German systematic murder of Jews in the gas chambers.

On arrival in Britain, Segieda's name-change was arranged by Major John O'Reilly of SOE, who had been seconded from Scotland Yard to act as the SOE–police liaison officer. The rationale for the name-change was

The Segieda–Salski report (18 April 1943)

to ensure Segieda's security.[36] From 19 February 1943 Napoleon Segieda used the name Jerzy Salski.[37]

In London, Salski wrote two reports. The first, directed to the Polish Government in Exile, provided an overview of the situation in Poland, the condition of society and the state of the various political groups. Salski discussed press activity, political orientations and the views of the ZWZ, the peasant party, nationalists, socialists and the PPR. The report also included a discussion of Oświęcim, which noted the killing of thousands of Jews.[38] The second report, directed to Ignacy Schwarzbart, was written on 18 April 1943. It repeated some of the data from the much longer first report, but it had a greater focus on the situation of Jews in Poland and on Jews in Oświęcim.[39] Schwarzbart in turn circulated it to Berl Locker, chairman of the Jewish Agency in London, that same day, and to Rabbi Irving Miller, a leading American Zionist. In his covering letter to Locker, Schwarzbart commented, 'How to publish it we shall consider jointly'.[40] As far as can be established, the important information about Oświęcim was not published at all.[41]

On 27 April, Schwarzbart sent further copies to the British Section of the World Jewish Congress, the Jewish Agency's Polish Jewish Department in Tel Aviv, and the World Jewish Congress in New York.[42] Alexander Easterman, the political secretary of the World Jewish Congress, received the report at the end of April.[43] In sum, leading Jewish figures in Britain, the US and Palestine were advised of the Salski report. And, since communications leaving Britain were routinely checked by British censorship, it found its way to British intelligence and to the Foreign Office. Postal and Telegram Censorship intercepted Schwarzbart's letter to the World Jewish Congress in New York, which included Schwarzbart's translation of Salski's 18 April report, on 4 May 1943.[44] The intercept was widely circulated within the British intelligence community and in the Foreign Office. But the fact that this document remains in Foreign Office files is because Salski's report was rather wide-ranging and touched on a number of issues considered relevant by FO officials.[45] The summary page of the intercept states that it includes information on the lack of anti-Semitism in Poland, conditions in the ghettos, the state of various political parties, and loyalty to Sikorski. The summary does not mention Oświęcim.

The Foreign Office's cover sheet to the intercept provides an indication of who read the report and offers an insight into the FO's information-management procedures. Although not all signatures of officials are legible, the following people read the report: Roger Makins, Alice Davids, Mr Williams and Roger Allen, amongst others. It was also passed to the British ambassador to Poland, Owen O'Malley, and to the

178   British suppression of news of Auschwitz: March 1943–June/July 1944

Central Department. Page 3 of the intercept, which referred to Oświęcim, was specifically passed to Roger Allen – the official responsible for collecting data on atrocities. The circulation list of the intercept also included the PID (Political Intelligence Department – i.e. Political Warfare Executive),[46] ISR (Inter-services Research Bureau), DRW (Division of Reports, Washington) and 'CHA'.[47] This last acronym is not listed in Postal Censorship's allocation list which provides details on the acronyms used by that office, or in the official history of the Postal and Telegraph Censorship Department.[48] Speculatively, it could refer to a PWE department based at Woburn Abbey. Woburn Abbey was referred to as the Country House headquarters, or CHQ.[49]

The Inter-services Research Bureau's objective was 'to co-ordinate information useful in impeding the enemy's war effort, both in its political and economic aspects'.[50] The Division of Reports, Washington, was the channel through which material intercepted by British censorship was passed to corresponding offices in the United States and then onwards to particular American government agencies.[51] At the PWE it is likely that the intercept was seen by Robert Bruce Lockhart, Ivone Kirkpatrick and officials dealing specifically with Poland. The intercept was also seen by the naval adviser, air adviser and MI12 (Censorship). Given this expansive distribution it is almost certain that at some point Salski's report was passed to, or discussed with, Anthony Eden, though there is no documentary record of this.

American intelligence also obtained a copy through the interception of transatlantic mail by the censorship office (Breitman 1996: 179).[52] In addition, given that Salski was an SOE agent, he would have been extensively debriefed on arrival in Britain, and almost certainly passed information about Oświęcim directly to the SOE, though no documentary record of this debriefing has been located.[53]

In the report passed to Schwarzbart (and intercepted by both the British and the Americans), Salski advised that he had lived in Oświęcim (the town) for a number of weeks, and received detailed information about the camp from released prisoners. He reported that when he left the town in September 1942 (sic) 'the number of registered prisoners was over 95,000 but there were also such who were not registered', and that 'Jews were exterminated en masse'.[54] Salski then outlined the killing methods employed at the camp:

a. Gas chambers, the victims were undressed and put into those chambers where they suffocated.
b. Electric chambers, those chambers had metal walls, the victims were brought in and then high tension electric current was introduced.

The Segieda–Salski report (18 April 1943)

c. the so called Hammerluft system. This is a hammer of air. Those special chambers where the hammer fell from the ceiling and by means of a special installation the victims found their death under air pressure.

d. Shooting. This is used as a collective form of punishment, in cases of lack of subordination, thus killing every tenth.

The first three methods were used most frequently. The last seldom. Gestapo [*sic*] men stood in a position which enabled them to watch in gas masks the death of masses of their victims.

The Germans loaded the corpses and took them outside Oświęcim, by means of huge shovels they made huge holes where they buried the dead and then they covered the holes with lime. The burning of victims by means of electric ovens was seldom applied. This was because in such ovens only about 250 could be burned within 24 hours.[55]

Parts of the report were factually inaccurate. Neither electric chambers nor the Hammerluft system existed. Gassing and shooting occurred through 1942. Like the Polish Government in Exile, Schwarzbart and his Jewish colleagues faced an unreceptive British Foreign Office and Ministry of Information, though no document indicating that representations were made has been located. But since the Foreign Office had the data from the Salski report from May 1943, any such representation would have simply reiterated information widely known in the FO.

In the report for the Polish Government in Exile, Salski argued that without the delay in Bern caused by the high-level intervention to ensure that he had legal passage across Western Europe, he would have been in England a month after leaving Switzerland – at some point in September 1942.[56] If he had arrived in London in September or indeed at any point prior to late November or early December 1942, the story of the news about the Holocaust, and about Oświęcim in particular, might have been different. Salski's information would have brought more pressure onto Polish politicians and officials to highlight the gassing of Jews at Oświęcim. And though Polish policy was strongly influenced by the British censorship and propaganda regime, the physical presence of Salski in London might have allowed more people to learn about the camp in a timely fashion. Whether sufficient pressure could have been applied to add Salski's information to the Polish government's 10 December note to Allied governments would have depended on how tightly the Polish government could control Salski and the degree to which Salski could alter the Polish government's strategic calculations with regard to its dealings with the British government and the demand for the timely issuance of a UN declaration. Too little is known about the man to make

180   British suppression of news of Auschwitz: March 1943–June/July 1944

an informed judgement on this issue, other than to state that Salski would have had to be extraordinarily vocal about the gassing of Jews at Oświęcim for the Polish government to have acted differently than it did.[57]

Salski's reports about Oświęcim were not the only data about the camp to be received in London in April. At the end of the month, on 29 April, Stefan Korboński sent another radio message highlighting the liquidation of the Kraków and Stanisławów ghettos and the killing of Jews in situ, with others sent to Oświęcim.[58] This report repeated much of the data he sent in the 30 March message, indicating the anxiety felt by some in Warsaw that the news they sent was not being received or acted on.

On 3 May Korboński sent a further message, which both caricatured German propaganda regarding the Katyń massacre and critiqued the Polish government's singular focus on the killing of Polish officers at Katyń over the previous couple of weeks. Korboński seems to have been trying to shift the government's focus from Katyń to Auschwitz, from those already dead to those who faced imminent death at the hands of the Nazis. He stated that the Polish Underground had distributed a poster around Kraków purporting to be a German information notice that contrasted the primitive Bolshevik killing methods with the Germans' methods of murder. The poster, using gallows humour, stated that the Germans were organizing trips to Oświęcim, Majdanek and so on to demonstrate humane mass murder through the use of gas chambers and other means. Three thousand people a day were passing through Oświęcim's crematoria. On arrival in London, Korboński's message was distributed to the press. On 25 May 1943, on page 4, the *Daily Mirror* published an extract from the message. It mentioned Oświęcim, but did not report on the fact that 3,000 people a day were passing through the camp's crematoria or on the use of gas chambers.[59]

Eventually, on 1 June 1943, *The Times* reported that Jews from Kraków were being sent to Oświęcim. On page 4 the newspaper stated that '[t]he Cracow ghetto has been emptied. 1,000 Jews were murdered in the streets and houses and the others were taken off to the Oswiecim concentration camp'. Their likely fate there was not mentioned. The report was filed by the diplomatic correspondent of *The Times*.[60] The data in the story echoes the data in Korboński's 30 March telegram, and it is probable that the publishing of this story was co-ordinated between the Polish Government in Exile and the British Ministry of Information.

During late April and early May, the ghetto rising in Warsaw was entering its final phase as the Germans systematically killed the Jewish insurgents. The liquidation of the ghetto and the murder of his family are rightly understood as underpinning Shmuel Zygielbojm's decision to take his own life on 12 May 1943, in protest at the world's passivity

A report handed to a Foreign Office official (18 May 1943)

towards the destruction of the Jews.[61] In his suicide letter addressed to the president and prime minister of Poland, he wrote,

I cannot continue to live and to be silent while the remnants of Polish Jewry, whose representative I am, are being murdered. My comrades in the Warsaw ghetto fell with arms in their hands in the last heroic battle. I was not permitted to fall like them, together with them, but I belong with them, to their mass grave.

By my death, I wish to give expression to my most profound protest against the inaction in which the world watches and permits the destruction of the Jewish people.[62]

Had he been informed of them, as is probable, the March messages and April reports about Auschwitz could only have exacerbated Zygielbojm's despair. The document sent by Raczyński to Alec Randall at the Foreign Office on 18 May (discussed below) reported an inquest into Zygielbojm's death, stating that 'he committed suicide under the shock of the latest reports on the dreadful tragedy of the Jews in Poland'.[63] Zygielbojm's death was widely publicized in the British press. His criticism of the Allies' passivity was not.

A report handed to a Foreign Office official (18 May 1943)

On 12 March, Stefan Rowecki dispatched the regular situation report for the period from 26 February to 5 March 1943 from Warsaw.[64] This report highlighted the mass killing of Jews at Auschwitz, stating,

On the basis of news that has only just reached Warsaw, conditions in Oświęcim have become considerably harsher. Numerous executions are being carried out, but unfortunately it has not so far been possible to establish [victims'] names.

Attempts to sterilize women are being carried out on a greater scale.

A huge new crematorium activated not long ago can incinerate about 3,000 people a day. Jews constitute the vast majority of those currently being incinerated ...

One of the couriers was Jan Nowak-Jeziorański, who travelled to Gdynia, smuggled himself onto a ship to Stockholm, and handed the report to the Polish intelligence station located in that city on 5 May.[65] The report was dispatched to London on the weekly RAF flight. Nowak-Jeziorański then returned to Poland. The British had the capacity to read this report, but there is no documentary record to prove that they did. However, on 18 May 1943 Edward Raczyński sent through Józef Zarański, counsellor of the Polish Embassy, a document detailing the plight of Jews, which mentioned Oświęcim, to Alec Randall at the Foreign Office.[66] Raczyński may have sent this document at the request of Ignacy Schwarzbart, who called for the data to be *officially* handed to the British.[67] Randall was

182   British suppression of news of Auschwitz: March 1943–June/July 1944

responsible for refugee issues, and the document, the Poles hoped, would inform the debate in the House of Commons on refugees scheduled for the following day. Raczyński also sent a copy of the document to several MPs. Randall suggested what the Foreign Office's response to potential questions in the House about the report should be – in the margin of Zarański's covering letter, which was circulated with the report in the Foreign Office. As noted in Chapter 2, Randall advised,

If this has been sent to MPs some may raise it today. If so, the reply could be that we have been acquainted by the Polish Govt with this fresh evidence of Germany's extermination policy, and that all such information can only stir us to renewed determination to beat down the Hitlerite system and inflict just punishment on those responsible for these crimes.

This general line was followed in the debate on the refugee problem on 19 May 1943, as the government reiterated that there was little that could be done in terms of rescue.[68] There is little sense in the archival record that Foreign Office officials engaged with the report other than to ensure that the information it contained did not derail current British policy on refugees.

The document sent to Randall was entitled 'Extermination of the Jews in Poland', and discussed in detail the death camp (and killing methods) at Treblinka. On page 7 of the document it was noted 'that conditions similar to those prevailing in TREBLINKA prevail in other concentration camps established by the Germans in Poland, both for Poles and Jews, – to name the most notorious, such as OŚWIĘCIM, SOBIBÓR and MAJDANEK'.[69] From the prior discussion of Treblinka, the reader was directed to link Oświęcim with the mass killing of Jews, even though the report did not reprint the detailed statistics which the Polish Government in Exile had received in March 1943.

This report is the fourth reference to Oświęcim received by the Foreign Office in the space of six weeks for which records exist in FO files (including the intercept of the Salski report). The first report was submitted by Ridley Prentice, based in Lisbon, to the Political Intelligence Department at the Foreign Office on 22 March, and related the story told by Count Thierry de Lichtervelde of his chauffeur, who was imprisoned at Oświęcim for eight months.[70] It did not indicate whether the chauffeur escaped or was released. Prentice was informed that there were between 300,000 and 400,000 Jews at the camp, and that 'Jews, Poles and Russians are frequently shot at once if they stop work'. Though the number of (living) Jews at the camp was incorrect, the information is significant insofar as it reiterates a Jewish presence at Oświęcim.

The fact that Jews were mentioned first highlights the fact that Jews were known to be at the bottom of the camp hierarchy and its primary

Information received in the summer of 1943 183

victims. The chauffeur was probably interned at the camp up to early 1942, as the transformation of the camp to include mass-gassing facilities was unknown to him. The chauffeur's story restated the early news of the camp as being especially harsh on Jews – it noted that Jews were pushed into water tanks by guards and allowed to drown, and that the chauffeur was traumatized by seeing so many atrocities. Prentice had apparently sent a report on Oświęcim earlier to the Ministry of Information. However, according to a handwritten annotation on the report about the chauffeur in the FO file, this was not received.

The second reference to Oświęcim was in a letter from the Movement of the Polish Working Masses to the Executive of the British Labour party, passed to Clement Attlee by Jan Kwapiński, the Polish minister for industry, commerce and shipping, on 26 March 1943. This was forwarded to the Foreign Office, where officials composed a response. Frank Roberts initialled the draft reply on 7 April. Anthony Eden also initialled the document, indicating that the Foreign Secretary had read the message handed to Attlee. The letter received by Attlee recorded that

the whole machinery of destruction is working at high speed in the concentration camps of Oswiecim, Treblinka, Radogpsziz [sic], Majdanek where several hundred thousand people have already been murdered. The Germans cynically declare that they must reduce the number of Poles, because so many Germans are being killed on the fronts, and equilibrium must be maintained.[71]

Though no reference to Jews specifically is made in this letter, its significance rests in the fact that Oświęcim is associated with systematic murder (rather than the camp being seen just as having a very harsh incarceration regime), and in the formulaic British response which praised the Polish war effort, extended sympathy for 'the long martyrdom with which the Polish nation has suffered at the hands of the German oppressors', and reiterated the 'all-out effort for the early and complete defeat of the enemy, which alone can deliver our heroic Polish allies from their present martyrdom'. No specific retaliatory actions were promised, no change in British policy regarding the prosecution of the war was considered and, importantly, there was no real engagement with the information about any of the camps. This pattern of non-engagement was repeated through the summer of 1943.

Information received in the summer of 1943

During the summer of 1943 Jewish organizations and the Polish Government in Exile received further information that highlighted the killing of Jews at Oświęcim. News that Jews were being experimented on was also

184 British suppression of news of Auschwitz: March 1943–June/July 1944

received. Gilbert (2001a) notes only a fraction of the information that reached the West.[72] The first message of the summer was sent by Stefan Korboński on 7 June 1943 to the Polish government in London and reported the killing of socialists and communists from Silesia and Zagłębie with phenol injections to the heart. The same message noted that, in Block 10, castrations, sterilization and artificial insemination were conducted by the Waffen SS Institute of Hygiene. Twenty Jews and twenty-five Jewesses had already been experimented on.[73] This final piece of information was published by the Jewish Telegraphic Agency on 13 June and by the *Jewish Chronicle* on 25 June.[74] On Wednesday 16 June, the Jewish Telegraphic Agency published an article entitled 'Polish Government compiles "black-lists" of Nazi scientists gassing Jews', which reported that the names of those German scientists 'conducting experiments in the death chambers of Oswiecim and Treblinka will be made public soon'.[75] News of experiments at Oświęcim was also published in the *Courier-Mail* (Brisbane, Australia) on 17 June, but the article did not mention Jews.[76]

The following week, on 22 June, Cywia Lubetkin and Icchak Cukierman, leaders of the Jewish Fighting Organization (Żydowska Organizacja Bojowa) sent a message via the Polish Underground to London, advising that a 'killing action' was taking place in Będzin, and that a ŻOB member, Frumka Płotnicka, was in the town.[77] This message was not deciphered until 4 August 1943. However, on 27 July 1943, Michał Protasewicz of the Polish Bureau VI in London sent a message to Tadeusz Bór-Komorowski in Warsaw, in which he noted that, following the rising in the Warsaw ghetto, some Jews had resolved to fight. The Będzin region was selected for armed resistance. Protasewicz called on Bór-Komorowski to contact Frumka Płotnicka and Dawid Kozłowski in Będzin. Clearly Płotnicka's presence in the town was known to Polish intelligence operatives in London.

The Polish leadership in London instructed the Home Army commander to provide weapons to ŻOB in Będzin and to share intelligence.[78] It is not absolutely clear whether Bór-Komorowski was able to make contact – Frumka Płotnicka was killed by the Germans on 3 August 1943 in a Będzin bunker aged twenty-nine – but in a report from 5 August 1943 (sent 9 August) Bór-Komorowski indicated that the Underground did not 'shy away' from providing weapons to the fighting Jews and that they had contact with Będzin.[79] Jewish resistance in Będzin was significant. Alexander von Woedtke, the German police president in Sosnowiec responsible for the liquidation of the Będzin ghetto, was forced to extend the liquidation operation from a few days to two weeks. SS personnel from Auschwitz itself were also called up to assist in the 'clearance' of the ghetto (Fulbrook 2012: 294).

Information received in the summer of 1943   185

On 17 July, members of the Jewish Fighting Organization in Będzin sent a letter reporting that Jews from Będzin were 'killed by shooting and burning' at Auschwitz.[80] This letter reached the Jewish Agency in Istanbul (Gilbert 2001a: 151); its route is not known for certain, but it was probably dispatched via Slovakia.[81]

On 4 August, the Polish interior minister, Władysław Banaczyk, sent a message to the Polish government's delegate in Warsaw, Stanisław Jankowski, requesting information about Jews in Będzin and the wider situation of Jews in Poland.[82] Banaczyk's message was in response to requests for information from Jews in Britain, and probably a reaction to Lubetkin's and Cukierman's message, which had just been deciphered. The Jewish circles to which Banaczyk referred in his message to Jankowski included both Polish Jews and representatives of the Jewish Agency. On 21 July 1943 Ignacy Schwarzbart sent a message to the Council of Polish Jews (Rada Żydów Polskich) in Warsaw, reporting the raising of funds to aid Jews in Będzin, and advising that he was in touch, together with Berl Locker of the Jewish Agency, with the Polish government.[83] Some £10,000 had been received from the Polish government, £5,000 from the Jewish Agency.

The answer to Banaczyk's query was sent on 31 August (deciphered 29 September 1943). The delay in the Polish Underground's response can, in part, be explained by the logistics of gathering intelligence and the process of repeated encryption and de-encryption. During August the Jews of Będzin had been sent to their deaths at Oświęcim.[84] Following de-encryption in London, this information was immediately circulated. Ignacy Schwarzbart passed it to the *Polish Jewish Observer*. On 8 October 1943 the *Polish Jewish Observer* reported that Schwarzbart had received two messages from Poland. The first, from 31 August, advised that 7,000 Będzin Jews had been deported to Oświęcim, and the second, sent on 23 September (deciphered on 29 September), stated that there were no Jews left in Będzin.[85] This information was also published by the Jewish Telegraphic Agency on 8 October and in the English-language supplement to *Nasza Trybuna* – a New York-based Polish Jewish newspaper – on 20 November 1943.[86]

In actuality, a small group of 150 Jews remained in Będzin to clear away debris from the German operation to deport and murder the town's Jews. This small group was taken to Auschwitz at the end of 1943 (Fulbrook 2012: 295). On 29 October, the *Polish Jewish Observer* reported again on the ghetto at Będzin, and also carried a front-page article entitled 'New gas tried out at Oswiecim camp'. It reported that experiments with the new kind of poison gas were taking place 'on prisoners, particularly Jews'.

186   British suppression of news of Auschwitz: March 1943–June/July 1944

British intelligence was kept abreast of the latest developments at Oświęcim. The few remaining documents of SOE that deal with atrocities in Poland cover late July and August 1943. These documents are either summaries or copies of *aneks* produced by the Military Historical Bureau of the Information and Press Office of the Home Army Central Command that had the specific objective of documenting the German terror campaign in Poland. An English-language document dated 23 August 1943 entitled 'German policy in Poland in July 1943' stated that the camp population was 37,000 and that '[t]he greater part of the Jews has already been murdered. Mass executions of Gipsies have started. The first transport of about one thousand was gassed'.[87]

The report was passed to SOE by the Polish Bureau VI. It is not clear whether the Polish original and more expansive report, Aneks 57, covering the period from 16 to 31 July 1943, was also handed over, but it is certainly possible since Aneks 58 was passed to SOE complete and untranslated (Aneks 58 is discussed below).[88] The presence of these documents in surviving SOE records suggests that the Polish Bureau VI routinely handed over *aneks* or information from it to the British. It is likely that these reports were passed to Roger Allen at the Foreign Office as he collated reports on atrocities. Aneks 59, which is not in SOE files, for example, would have been of particular interest to Allen since it named SS officers at Auschwitz responsible for a range of serious crimes, including the mass killing of Jews.[89]

Jewish organizations were advised (again) of the function of Auschwitz in the summer of 1943. The second piece of information noted by Gilbert (2001a) was dated 1 September 1943. It recorded, 'Today we know that Sobibor, Malkinia-Treblinka, Belzec and Auschwitz are liquidation camps'. This information was from a report compiled in Bratislava, which was distributed to Jewish organizations in Istanbul, Jerusalem, London and New York (Gilbert 2001a: 155).[90] The provenance of data in this document cannot be conclusively established, but, since ŻOB was involved in smuggling Polish Jews from Silesia into Slovakia, it is possible that a Jewish refugee conveyed news of Auschwitz to Jewish representatives in Bratislava.

On 15 September 1943 Tadeusz Bór-Komorowski reported the killing of Jews and Poles at Oświęcim. Bór-Komorowski had taken over the leadership of the Home Army in Poland following the arrest of Stefan Rowecki, who was subsequently murdered in Sachsenhausen during the Warsaw Rising of 1944. Komorowski's message stated, 'A "week of destruction" of Poles and Jews took place in Oświęcim. Several thousand Polish men and women alone were gassed'.[91] Some of this data was incorporated into a BBC talk given by the Polish minister of the

Information received in the summer of 1943 187

interior, Władysław Banaczyk, broadcast on the Polish Service on 22 October. Banaczyk's script was closely vetted by the British Foreign Office, as the original version mentioned Poland's eastern frontiers and 'debatable areas such as Vilna and Volhynia'.[92] Ambassador Raczyński met with Alexander Cadogan that same day to discuss this issue. In the broadcast Banaczyk focused on 'a new wave of German terror', recording that 'Oswiecim, Majdanek, Belzec, Tremblinka [*sic*] and other factories of sudden death swallow up thousands of Poles and Jews'.[93] The broadcast did not mention the recently arrived information (6 October 1943) that at Brzezinka (i.e. Birkenau) 30,000 people had been gassed in a single day.[94] Rather, Banaczyk's broadcast conformed with British sensibilities – the Jewish fate was not privileged but was presented as an experience shared with other Polish citizens, the scale of the killing was reduced and non-specific, and the methods of murder were not mentioned. Nevertheless, attention was again drawn to Jews at Oświęcim but, like the broadcast on 11 April, this talk was directed to an audience in Poland. Other than officials in the Foreign Office and Polish-speakers, few in Britain would have known about it or its contents. Banaczyk's script, including the reference to Oświęcim, was passed to the Polish Telegraphic Agency and released to the press in London the following day (23 October), but the information about the camps was, as far as can be established, not published by the British press.[95] However, news about Jews at Oświęcim was published in London on 22 October. The *Polish Jewish Observer* carried a front-page story that reported on 200 rabbis at the Oświęcim concentration camp. The Jewish Telegraphic Agency reported on the rabbis two days later on 24 October.[96]

In addition, on 17 September 1943, the Polish Ministry of Information released an article entitled 'Conditions in the Oswiecim camp described by a Polish workman'.[97] This was sent from London to the Polish Information Center in New York, for further circulation as a press release in the United States.[98] The distribution of material about Oświęcim to the Polish Information Center also suggests that the Polish government was exploring ways of pressuring the Anglo-American propaganda and censorship regime, and seeking to engage with an American Jewish audience who would be receptive to news about Jews. Despite the high level of co-ordination on both sides of the Atlantic the Polish government evidently hoped to exploit any differences in the way the censorship and propaganda regime was implemented in the United States compared with Britain. According to this document, the witness was contracted to work at the camp for several months. The report focused on the main camp (Auschwitz I), but also recorded selections and the mass killing of Jews,

188   British suppression of news of Auschwitz: March 1943–June/July 1944

suggesting that it referred to events at the camp through late 1941 and 1942. The key section read:

> The Russian prisoners of war are mown down in masses by machine gun for the slightest infringement of the regulations, whereas Jewish prisoners are slaughtered by electricity. I have not seen the place where this takes place personally, but I have been shown a little wood, in which an eyewitness assures me the massacres are carried out. I did see a group of a thousand Jews arrive, from which the old, infirm and children were separated immediately and driven towards the wood. Near it there is civilian clothing stripped from the murdered people. I have seen it packed into parcels and sent off to Germany. Local people relate that some tens of thousands of Jews have passed through the Oswiecim camp.

The cable to New York repeated this information. Although the testimony contains a number of factual errors (the use of electricity, for example), the document highlights once more that important information about the camp had reached the Polish Government in Exile, which had then made significant moves to distribute this information to the Allies and Western audiences. The information from the Polish workman about Oświęcim was published in New York in October 1943 in the *News Bulletin* of the Representation of Polish Jewry – American Division, an organization affiliated to the World Jewish Congress.[99]

News about Jews was continually sent by Cywia Lubetkin and Icchak Cukierman via the Polish Underground to London and onwards to Jewish representatives.[100] In a message dated 15 November 1943 (it is not known for certain when it was received and de-encrypted, but probably prior to the end of 1943) Lubetkin and Cukierman advised Yitzhak Tabenki (United Kibbutz Movement, Palestine), Meir Jaari (Hashomer Hatzair, Palestine),[101] Eliyha Dobkin (Jewish Agency), the Palestinian Federation of Labour and Ignacy Schwarzbart (who was tasked with forwarding information from Poland to Jewish representatives in Palestine and the United States) of the terrible reality in occupied Poland. 'All centres of Jewish life have been deleted from the surface of the earth. Their inhabitants have found their deaths in the torture camps in Treblinka, Sobibor, Belzec and Oswiecim'.[102] Once more Jewish representatives were provided with information that presented Oświęcim as a kind of camp similar to well-known death camps. Given that Schwarzbart's communications were monitored by British censorship, British intelligence would have had access to this information too.

However, during the summer of 1943, the official line, evidently sanctioned by the British, about the camp was rehearsed. In August the Inter-Allied Information Committee published a booklet entitled *Punishment of War Crimes (2)*. It provided an overview of various war crimes committed by the Germans. In the section about Poland,

Information received in the summer of 1943

Raczyński's letter to Eden from 20 January formed the basis of a discussion about Oświęcim. Though Raczyński's letter was written in a particular context in January 1943, with the aim of persuading Western Allies to pursue a policy of retaliation against the Germans, it was used by the Inter-Allied Information Committee, under British guidance, to manage the reception of news of the camp that reached London. On page 37, *Punishment of War Crimes (2)* stated, 'Authentic statistics show that an average of 62 persons are dying daily at Oświęcim', before citing figures from Raczyński's letter.

It is not entirely clear where the figure of sixty-two persons came from, or who authorized its publication. It is possible that a Polish Ministry of the Interior report on the fate of women at Oświęcim, released on 19 December 1942, which claimed that the overall death rate at the camp was sixty-two people a day, was the source.[103] However, reports from Poland during 1943 cited higher figures. As already noted, Aneks 44 (covering the period from 16 to 31 December 1942) reported a daily death rate of between 120 and 180 people (registered prisoners).[104] The effect was to suggest that the camp remained a very harsh concentration camp, but not a centre for the industrial-scale annihilation of European Jews. The tendentious use of the word 'authentic' indicates that the document sought to delegitimate the statistics that flowed into Britain during the spring and early summer of 1943. This was not entirely successful. On 3 September, in a front-page article ('Nazis indicted afresh'), the *Jewish Chronicle* indicated that *Punishment of War Crimes (2)* 'gave some account of the appalling slaughter in the death camps of Treblinka, Belzec, Sobibor and Oswiecim'. Readers of the paper were invited to understand Oświęcim as the same sort of camp as the three widely recognized death camps, though *Punishment of War Crimes (2)* provided no basis for such an association.

Nevertheless, the Inter-Allied Information Committee's booklet broadly achieved its objective as a propaganda tool in hindering public comprehension of what was happening at Oświęcim. In effect, the public was offered a choice: believe the figures cited in an obscure local paper (the *Polish Jewish Observer*) and a British Jewish paper (the *Jewish Chronicle*) or figures relayed by an official body, published by His Majesty's Stationery Office. For non-subscribers of these two papers, *Punishment of War Crimes (2)* revealed that there were other statistics about the camp in circulation, gave no indication of what those statistics were and pre-empted any independent evaluation of those statistics. *Punishment of War Crimes (2)* was not the only publication which presented a false picture of Auschwitz in the face of overwhelming evidence of its true function.

190   British suppression of news of Auschwitz: March 1943–June/July 1944

Reading between the lines: *The Black Book of Polish Jewry*

The potent cocktail of censorship, self-censorship, and the tendency to use outdated information in official texts was seen not only in Britain, but also in the US, and even in publications put together by those who had access to the full horror of what was going on in the camp. In late 1943, a book entitled *The Black Book of Polish Jewry: An Account of the Martyrdom of Polish Jewry under Nazi Occupation* was published in New York by the American Federation for Polish Jews, in co-operation with the Association of Jewish Refugees and Immigrants.[105] The book was sponsored by a range of leading American, Polish and Jewish personalities: Eleanor Roosevelt; Congressman Emanuel Celler; New York mayor Fiorello LaGuardia; US Secretary of the Interior Harold Ickes; Adolph Sabath, chairman of the Committee on Rules of the House of Representatives; Freda Kirchwey, the editor of *The Nation*; Sol Bloom, chairman of the Foreign Affairs Committee of the House of Representatives; Jos Sharkey, vice-chairman and majority leader of New York City Council; Professor Salo Baron of Colombia University; Professor Chaim Tchernowitz of the Jewish Institute of Religion; Senator Robert Wagner; Henri Torres; Dr Ignacy Schwarzbart; Professor Albert Einstein; and Sylwin Strakacz of the Polish National Council.[106] In addition, the book had a fifteen-member publication committee and three co-editors, as well as its principal editor, Jacob Apenszlak. It was therefore a collective endeavour, in which several different constituencies had a stake. It was also pitched at an American public which was marked by a high level of anti-Semitism.[107] Editorially, it sought to chart a course between, on the one hand, relaying the horrors of the Nazi occupation and the almost complete destruction of Polish Jewry and, on the other, attempting to elicit the empathy of its readership. Like officials in the British PWE, neither the editor of the text, Jacob Apenszlak, nor his collaborators stated the true scale and manner of the liquidation of Polish Jewry.[108]

Apenszlak relied on data from over a year earlier. The book failed to highlight the systematic gassing of Polish Jews in a key section listing the cause of death of 769,000 Jews. Instead, Apenszlak reported that 371,938 were victims of sickness and epidemic, 37,000 were fallen soldiers, 67,000 were the victims of fires and bombardments, 24,000 were tortured to death in concentration camps, 150,000 were murdered at the beginning of the occupation, and 150,000 were victims of deportations (Apenszlak 1943: 201) – though the true meaning of 'deportation' was left unstated.

The Black Book of Polish Jewry illustrates the Nazi campaign against the Jews through the reproduction of photographs.[109] On the back of the

Reading between the lines: *The Black Book of Polish Jewry*

dust jacket, designed by the Polish Jewish graphic artist Arthur Szyk, is a collage of smiling Nazis, terrified Jews and executions. Within the text, photographs of Jews engaged in forced labour (guarded by armed Germans), of German orders prohibiting Jews' use of public transport, of the Warsaw ghetto, of German soldiers shooting defenceless people, of the bodies of those who succumbed to starvation, and of mass graves stacked with the naked corpses of Jewish victims illustrate graphically the incremental anti-Jewish policy that ended with the death and murder of Polish Jews. No photographs illustrating the deportation of Jews were included in the book. These photographs, evidently carefully chosen and vetted, forcefully presented the horror of the German actions against Jews, but highlighted the impact of ghettoization, rather than the systematic killing of Jews at death camps.[110]

The number of those who perished due to ghettoization – i.e. through disease and starvation – was very high (in total over 800,000, according to Hilberg (1985: 1219), a high proportion of whom would have been Polish Jews). Clearly, the editorial policy was to marginalize news of the death camps and focus on the Nazi policies and practices, which had a better chance of resonating with American audiences. Even if the view is taken that statistics about the number of victims at the death camps were questioned at the time, the fact that such camps existed was well appreciated. Figures that had been published in the mainstream press in December 1942 could have been cited.

The back page of the book reproduces a map of Poland, which includes the location of Poland's major cities and the borders of the German Reich at various points in time. It does not locate the death camps, though this information was available, for example, in the 15 July edition of the *Polish Fortnightly Review*, indicating that the use of the powerful medium of cartography to illustrate the final stage of the Nazi extermination programme was rejected.[111]

The book mentions Oświęcim ten times, but there is no systematic attempt to synthesize knowledge of the camp or to present all the facts that members of the book's sponsoring team knew. The details presented to Ignacy Schwarzbart by Jerzy Salski, and forwarded to leading Jewish figures in April 1943, are conspicuous by their absence in this publication, mirroring the high degree of (self-)censorship evidenced throughout the text. Nevertheless, some of the horror of the camp, and the fact that Jews were dying there, was discussed. Page 56 noted a report from the *East London Observer* from 20 March 1942, which stated that 'the ashes of 14 Warsaw rabbis who died in the concentration camp of Oswiecim had already been sent to their families'; on page 59 a story from the 27 February 1942 edition of the same paper was quoted, which

192   British suppression of news of Auschwitz: March 1943–June/July 1944

reported that the ashes of a Varsovian Jewish lady's son who perished in the camp were sent to her.

These stories were not published in the *East London Observer* proper, but in the subscription-only supplement the *Polish Jewish Observer*.[112] The stories pre-date the expansion of the camp to include facilities for mass killing. Though the information reported was dated, and did not reflect the state of knowledge of the camp that readers of the supplement had gained through 1942 and 1943, the reference to the *East London Observer* did inform curious readers of *The Black Book of Polish Jewry* where further information about the fate of Jews in occupied Europe could be found. Had any reader been able to obtain copies of the *Polish Jewish Observer*, s/he would have become quickly acquainted with the scale of the Holocaust and the function of Auschwitz within that program.

Pages 85–7 of *The Black Book of Polish Jewry* included three references to the camp. The first of these noted the statement of Palestinian citizens (who returned to Palestine in October 1942) that '[f]or the slightest offence against the administration, the Germans would ship the offenders to the penal colony in Oswiecim, whence none returned'. The editor chose not to restate the information published in November 1942 in the *New York Times*, and in the memorandum to President Roosevelt in December 1942, that 'trainloads' of Jews were slaughtered at the camp. The second mention of the camp referred to it as 'Oswiecim, seat of the notorious concentration camp to which many Jews were deported'. On page 87, the text speaks of 'Oswiecim, where thousands of Poles and Jews, mostly of the educated classes, were tortured, many of them to death'. This last point would not look out of place in a Polish government broadcast under British censorship policy.

Later in the book, on page 158, the situation in Sosnowiec was discussed. Green cards were given to those to be deported, yellow to those whose fate was to be decided, and blue to those to stay in the ghetto. Some of those given a green card committed suicide rather than be deported to an unknown destination. The book highlighted that there 'also began a wholesale deportation of many Jews guilty of alleged violations of numerous regulations to the dread concentration camp of Oswiecim'. Page 201 gave some statistics from the middle of 1942, indicating that there were 9,390 Polish Jews and 10,000 unregistered Jews at the camp, and noted that the death rate was running at 250 a day. The source of this figure is the 4 September report on Oświęcim that was received in London on 12 November 1942 and incorporated into Sprawozdanie Nr 6/42 that was distributed to the Polish Cabinet on 23 December 1942. However, that figure, as the 4 September report made clear, did not include those systematically killed at Brzezinka (i.e. Jews).

Reading between the lines: *The Black Book of Polish Jewry* 193

Contributors to *The Black Book* were well aware that quoting this figure was misleading, though it did conform to the Anglo-American censorship regime. *The Black Book* also did not mention that Jews were being gassed at Oświęcim despite the fact that the information from Sprawozdanie Nr 6/42 had repeatedly been translated into English and distributed to the press (see Chapter 4 above). The following reference – on page 230 – drew on a Jewish Telegraphic Agency dispatch dated 13 March 1943, which reported that 100 Jewish intellectuals were shot at the camp.

The only theme developed in this text was that Oświęcim was a very harsh concentration camp. There was no indication that it was the location of the systematic murder of European Jewry in gas chambers. This was not, as indicated above, because the information was not available to significant personages involved in the publication of this text. Rather, the information was withheld. Throughout, the book frequently emphasized the small-scale – of the fate of individuals and small groups – in an effort to personalize the horror in a way that potential readers could engage with and respond to. It also repeated information that had been widely circulated in 1942 and 1943, but the scale of the Nazi extermination programme was not clearly articulated. Excluding details about the Warsaw ghetto, new information that emerged after the UN declaration of 17 December 1942 was far less evident in the text. Only a few sections of the book provided a glimpse into the reality of the Nazi extermination policy against the Jews, and these sections did not fit easily with either the tone or the narrative arc of the book.

The contributions that jarred within *The Black Book of Polish Jewry* included the submission by the Polish Government in Exile on Treblinka; the introduction by Schwarzbart in which he stated that 'the Germans have murdered at least one fifth, maybe one quarter, of the population of the Jewish nation' (Schwarzbart in Apenszlak 1943: xv); a chapter on extermination which included Schwarzbart's statement to the Polish National Council on mass extermination given on 15 November 1942; and information derived from Jan Karski on Bełżec.[113] These sections generally repeated information publicly available since 1942, and did not, therefore, pose any challenge to US or British censorship or refugee policy. The murder of Jews in the gas chambers of Bełżec and Treblinka was mentioned, but not highlighted.[114]

Other than the sections noted above, the fate of Polish Jewry was narrated without, in the most part, reference to the death camps.[115] It is difficult to map accurately the line between self-censorship and compromises made in this joint project, and firmer 'advice' given by US censorship and propaganda organs. Regardless, the consequence was that the story of Oświęcim remained an inside story, so that a false

194   British suppression of news of Auschwitz: March 1943–June/July 1944

picture of the camp was drawn, and the American public remained uninformed of its true nature.

However, an observant reader was given strong clues that Oświęcim was something other than what was presented in the book. On 30 January 1944, Walter Bara in the *New York Times* reviewed the book and linked Oświęcim with camps where the presence of gas chambers was well known, noting that Jews from across Europe were taken there to be killed. And while the reviewer did not criticize the book for its omissions, he wrote,

In addition to the local Polish Jewry butchered in medieval ghettos in Poland, tens of thousands were also brought from Germany and German-enslaved countries of Europe to be destroyed in those hells-on-earth, the monstrous concentration camps of Oswiecim, Lublin, Treblinka and nameless others.

The correct links were being drawn, but *The Black Book of Polish Jewry* was not the only book published in English to give an inaccurate picture of Oświęcim.

Camp of Death

In December 1942, Natalia Zarembina's pamphlet *Obóz Śmierci* (*Camp of Death*) was published in Warsaw (in Polish) by the WRN – the conspiratorial wing of the Polish Socialist Party, which was also known as the Movement of the Polish Working Masses (Ruch Mas Pracujących Polski), and was an important part of the Polish Underground. It presented evidence gathered from released prisoners and from Polish intelligence reports on the situation in Oświęcim.

The pamphlet generally reported on the situation at Oświęcim during 1941, noting, for example, the gassing of Soviet POWs (which began in late August 1941). The focus on 1941 and early 1942 explains, in part, the lack of any discussion of the systematic murder of Jews. However, the pamphlet does not highlight that it is referring to a specific period, but gives the impression that it is providing an accurate overview of the camp, through, for example, referring to 'verified information up to July 1942' (Zarembina 1942: 4). Consequently, by suggesting that the situation of the camp in July 1942 was the same as it had been previously, Zarembina gave a false impression of what was happening in Auschwitz. Zarembina claimed that by July 1942 '125,000 persons [had] passed through the camp' (Zarembina 1942: 4). This information was derived from a detailed report on Oświęcim that was prepared in Warsaw and sent to London by the delegate, Jan Piekałkiewicz, in November 1942.[116] That report extensively discussed what was happening to Jews at the camp.

Camp of Death

Zarembina did not use the references to Jews in her text. Her motive was probably to highlight Polish suffering at the camp for a Polish audience. But by failing to mention the mass killing of Jews that was recorded in the source report, Zarembina's text highlights the ambiguity felt by some Poles towards Jews. It is possible that she was concerned that Jewish suffering could overshadow that of Poles or that, like officials in Britain, she was worried that significant mention of Jews could heighten anti-Semitism amongst her target audience.[117]

Zarembina's text was sent to London, and once there its subsequent circulation was heavily influenced by the limits of the British censorship regime. It was republished a further three times during the war. The pamphlet was reprinted in Polish, verbatim, as a booklet in London in August 1943, and translated into English and published in New York in March 1944 by *Poland Fights*.[118] The only mention of Jews is brief: 'Thus in addition to its Polish backbone, Oświęcim has appendages – Czechs, Germans, Jews, Serbs, and now Russians' (Zarembina 1944b: 32). In July 1944, after information about Auschwitz had been circulated in the mainstream press on both sides of the Atlantic, *Camp of Death* was published in English, in London, by Liberty Press.[119]

Even when it was first released in Warsaw, the booklet was dated and inaccurate, as the author probably knew. It contributed to a narrative about the camp which depicted it as primarily a place of immense Polish suffering. Its publication in London in 1943 (in Polish) was eased by the fact that the lack of significant reference to Jews meant that it concurred with the dominant official British discourse about the suffering of the Polish people, i.e. it did not stimulate anxieties about possible refugees, or domestic anti-Semitism. Its later US publication in March 1944 occurred just prior to the release of news in the American media of the mass killing of Jews at the camp (as we shall see).[120] It therefore inadvertently inhibited the American public's comprehension of the news of the camp when this was finally sanctioned for mainstream release on 22 March 1944.

By July 1944, the true function of Auschwitz had become known to publics on both sides of the Atlantic. The version of *Camp of Death* released by Liberty Press in London therefore offered the public a very dated account of Oświęcim. This was understood by the editors. This English text is the only one that does not give a verbatim translation of Zarembina's original. The reference to statistics from July 1942 was cut, reference to Treblinka and Bełżec removed. Instead, Liberty Press editors cited statistics from March 1943 that were reported in Aneks 54 covering the period from 1 to 15 June 1943.[121] As Ważniewski and Marczewska (1968: 106) note, even if only those prisoners who were

196   British suppression of news of Auschwitz: March 1943–June/July 1944

registered were included, the figures in Aneks 54 underrecorded the number of those who perished at the camp. The 94,000 deaths noted in other editions of *Camp of Death* were reduced to 76,000.

Aneks 54 did highlight the Nazi programme against Jews by stating that in the last few weeks 7,000 Jews from Greece had been murdered in the gas chambers, but this information was not given in the revised edition of Zarembina's text. It seems that the statistics from Aneks 54 were used, despite the reports which arrived in London both before and after it recording higher numbers of people perishing at the camp, because Aneks 54's figures were lower than those given in other reports. This suggests that the editors were very well aware of the sensibilities of their British audience and sought to establish credibility. But even if this tactic was successful, the footnote that editors included on the final page of the main text would have seriously confused any reader. The footnote completely undermined the narrative of the main text:

The official camp-roll includes only part of the murdered prisoners. Large transports of people have been directed from the trains immediately to the gas chambers and killed there without registration on the camp-roll. The Polish Underground Labour Movement estimates the number of people, largely Jews, who died at the camp up to December 1943, without formal registration, to amount to 1,000,000.[122]

In addition, unlike the version published in the United States in March 1944, in the appendix that listed over 150 concentration camps, one part of Oświęcim is recorded as being 'used for executions only'. It is very unlikely that this information or the data in the footnote would have been revealed if the text had been published earlier in 1944. But given that *Camp of Death* was recognized by its editors as giving an inaccurate account of the camp, publishing the text at all speaks to the continued power of the British censorship regime which privileged accounts about 'nationals' of particular states and systematically sought to marginalize news of Jews.[123] By July 1944 a different, updated account of the camp was urgently needed. Nevertheless, publishing the footnote did advise readers of important information, though the way the mass killing of Jews was presented would have hindered comprehension. A million people had been killed, and that should have been the main story, not a footnote.[124]

Jan Nowak-Jeziorański

Although late 1943 and early 1944 witnessed texts published in English that gave inaccurate and misleading accounts of Auschwitz, descriptions closer to the truth were also delivered to a wider public in Britain than previously. Jan Nowak (Zdzisław Jezioranski) was one of the Polish government's most trusted couriers, and was responsible for bringing several reports about the situation in Poland to Stockholm and London. He was in Britain between December 1943 and July 1944, and again from January 1945. Whilst in London he was debriefed by British intelligence and he had contact with officials from the Foreign Office. Nowak-Jezioranski was given the highly reliable 'A' rating by British intelligence, and his information was weighed seriously.[125] On 6 January 1944 the chairman of the Joint Intelligence Committee, Victor Cavendish-Bentinck, wrote to Alexander Cadogan at the Foreign Office:

As a rule I do not trouble you with these reports from foreigners in this country from enemy or enemy-occupied territory, but I think that the annexed report is worth a glance. This clerk is not a Jew, but quite an intelligent middle-class Pole.

Cavendish-Bentinck drew attention to German ships in Gdynia, which Nowak-Jezioranski had seen on his way to Stockholm, but during debriefing with British intelligence Nowak-Jezioranski also spoke extensively about Jews. He was familiar with the mass slaughter of Jews at Oświęcim as he had couriered a report that discussed the camp to Stockholm the previous April. In the debriefing summary of Nowak-Jezioranski's interrogation of December 1943 prepared by the British, and forwarded to more or less everywhere within the British intelligence community, War Office and Foreign Office, Nowak-Jezioranski mentioned the camp.[126] The summary was organized on the page in following way:

(a) BELZEC   )
     TREBLINKA   )   all 'death camps'
     SOBIBOR   )   i.e. places of extermination
(b) MAJDANEK, OSWIECIM – largest camp, 50,000 persons.

The list continued to (m). To date, this document, though known to scholars, has not attracted a great deal of attention in relation to the annihilation of Jews at Oświęcim, for the obvious reason that it does not mention it. However, since it is now known that Nowak-Jezioranski knew of the mass killing of Jews at the camp,[127] and spoke extensively about Jews during his debriefing, the failure to highlight that both Majdanek and Oświęcim functioned as both concentration and death camps with gas chambers looks odd. In the context of an intelligence summary this may merely reflect the fact that news of the camps was not a high priority for Nowak-Jezioranski's interrogators, and placing Majdanek and Oświęcim together was an efficient way to summarize, or to indicate that these places were large multifunctional camps without explicitly stating this fact. Given that Nowak-Jeziorański reported the setting up of a gas chamber on the remnants of the Warsaw ghetto, and reported the fate of torture and death that awaited Jews who were discovered in hiding, it is possible that he also spoke of the gas chambers and killing of Jews at Oświęcim. Later in the document Nowak-Jeziorański is recorded as having stated that 3,300,000 Jews had been massacred.[128]

On 21 January 1944 Nowak-Jeziorański met Frank Roberts of the Foreign Office, and was later scheduled to meet Prime Minister Churchill. The Secret Intelligence Service (SIS) had advised Churchill that such a meeting would be 'well worth his while', and Churchill's private secretary had twice made the proposal that Nowak-Jeziorański should be received.[129] Churchill himself decided to reject the meeting after the Foreign Office had initiated preparations in late January, calling on the Foreign Office to 'politely discourage' Nowak-Jeziorański and the Polish government from petitioning for the meeting. The reasons for Churchill's decision are not clear. Officially, reference was made to Churchill's busy schedule. But Churchill maintained an interest in Nowak-Jeziorański and, on 10 February, in the presence of the counsellor of the Polish Embassy, Józef Zarański, Nowak-Jeziorański met with Churchill's adviser on intelligence, Major Desmond Morton.[130] It may well be the case that Churchill's schedule did prevent the meeting with Nowak-Jeziorański from taking place. Alternatively, Churchill may have been advised of the likely topics that Nowak-Jeziorański could raise, and wished to steer clear of any potentially embarrassing requests or revelations. The meeting with Morton did not proceed smoothly and neither man warmed to the other. According to the minutes of the meeting, Morton pressed Nowak-Jeziorański on the military situation in Poland, the strength of the Germans, and the Germans' programme of terror in Poland. No mention of Jews in the meeting is recorded in the minutes.[131]

However, a piece of evidence that lends itself to the conclusion that Nowak-Jeziorański advised British intelligence of what he knew about Oświęcim is contained in a speech on the position of the churches in Poland which Nowak-Jeziorański delivered to the Orthodox Committee of the Church of England Council on Foreign Relations on 29 February 1944. In a section on the Jews, Nowak-Jeziorański repeated some of the data passed to British intelligence the previous December. He stated that 'almost the whole Jewish population has been systematically exterminated', and estimated that of the 3.5 million Jewish population of Poland, only 70,000 remained. He hazarded that no more than 200,000 were in hiding. He then declared, 'Some 3,000,000 Jews have been murdered either in the gas chambers of the concentration camps of Treblinka, Belzec, Chelm [sic], Majdanek and Oswiecin [sic] or by other methods'.[132]

Finally, an influential British audience had been directly, explicitly and publicly informed of Auschwitz's deadly nature, but no evidence has been located to suggest that members of this audience pressed for action specifically with regard to the camp. However, the archbishop of York issued a call to rescue Jews from the Nazis that same day in a conference at Central Hall, London.[133]

Further and more widespread dissemination of this news was more difficult in the context of British censorship. In January and February two reports were published in the *Jewish Chronicle* that referred to the camp, but their full significance may not have been appreciated. On 21 January 1944 a front-page story in the paper, entitled 'Slovak Jewish Martyrdom – young girls' ghastly fate', reported that the 'remaining baptised Jews were deported together with 50,000 Slovakian Jews to Oswiecim, the notorious death camp in Poland. No reports have been received about their ultimate fate'. A month later, on 25 February, a page 9 article in the paper, entitled 'Camps in Upper Silesia', noted that 'Jews from Salonika and Belgium and Holland taken to Birkenau according to information from neutral sources. There are also 7,000 Czechoslovak Jews in the camp. They had been deported to Birkenau last summer'.[134] The newspaper did not link Oświęcim and Birkenau, so the connection between the two camps would not have been appreciated by readers. However, the relationship between Birkenau and Oświęcim would have been appreciated by Jewish representatives who had received Polish intelligence from Ignacy Schwarzbart.

In late March 1944, news about Oświęcim was again distributed to influential people in Britain and to the press. On 24 March, information about Oświęcim was handed to the British deputy prime minister and leader of the Labour Party, Clement Attlee, by Adam Ciołkosz and Jan Kwapiński of the Polish Socialist Party.[135] On 10 January 1944 Zygmunt Zaremba of the PPS in Warsaw had written a letter to the Executive of the Labour Party on behalf of the Polish Socialist Party. The letter, along with other documents, including a report on Oświęcim, was couriered by Jerzy Lerski and arrived in London on 4 March. The letter focused on the problems posed by the advance of Soviet forces into Poland, rejected the Soviet annexation of Poland's eastern lands, and called for the Western Allies to help prevent a Russian occupation of Poland. However, the first page of the document highlighted German atrocities, stating,

In Oświęcim, Bełżec, Majdanek, and Treblinka [the Germans] have built special gas chambers to destroy prisoners wholesale ... Our losses have mounted to 5–6 million dead – of whom 2.5 million are Polish citizens of Jewish faith, who were murdered last year for the simple reason that they were born Jews.[136]

200   British suppression of news of Auschwitz: March 1943–June/July 1944

Although the letter did not directly state that Jews were being murdered by gas at Oświęcim, this fact was implied, given that Oświęcim was linked with Bełżec and Treblinka – camps already noted in the British press as sites where Jews were systematically killed. The document was clear in indicating that Oświęcim was more than a labour camp, and confirmed the presence of gas chambers.

Although the letter was directed via Attlee to the Executive of the Labour Party and was not supposed to be released to the press without the authorization of the recipient, it seems that Jan Kwapiński distributed it to the Polish Telegraphic Agency and it reached a number of journalists, including Isaac Deutscher at *The Observer* and Freddie Kuh – at this point working for the New York journal *PM* (Ciołkosz 1983: 199).[137] At the end of March and beginning of April 1944, several articles appeared in the British press commenting on Zaremba's letter and focusing exclusively on the issue of Polish–Soviet relations.[138] The brief reference to Oświęcim and other camps was ignored. Nevertheless, Zaremba's letter is important as it indicates that information about Oświęcim as a site with gas chambers had once more been advanced to decision makers (Attlee, the Executive of the Labour Party) and to the press. Attlee acknowledged receipt of Zaremba's letter on 5 April 1944, advised that he had forwarded it to the Executive of the Labour Party and expressed his concern that its contents had been leaked to the press.[139]

Thus, in late December 1943 and in January and February 1944, significant information about the true function of Auschwitz was passed to British churchmen, and in all probability to British intelligence (again), and highlighted to the general public in the *Jewish Chronicle*. None of this elicited a response from the British government. Data about the camp was also distributed in March 1944. Zaremba's reference to Oświęcim was ignored by both decision makers and the press. However, further and specific information about the camp was also released. As is discussed below, in Britain this information was heavily censored in the mainstream press.

The distribution of reports written in summer 1943 (December 1943–April 1944)

In January 1944 a Polish intelligence report, written in the summer of 1943, was received at the Polish General Staff headquarters in London. It recorded that up to September 1942, 468,000 non-registered Jews had been gassed at Oświęcim. From September 1942 to June 1943, approximately 60,000 Jews from Greece; 50,000 from the Protectorate and Slovakia; 60,000 from Holland, Belgium and France; and 11,000 from

The distribution of reports written in summer 1943 201

Polish towns had arrived at the camp. Only 2 per cent of those who had arrived were still alive, meaning that just more than 645,000 Jews had been gassed. This document has been discussed by Raul Hilberg (1985: 1127), Richard Breitman (2004: 191) and Laurence Rees (2005: 246).

The report was handed by Major Langenfeld of the Polish General Staff to Captain Paul M. Birkeland (US assistant military attaché, London) on 13 March 1944, and was then circulated to the US's War Department Military Intelligence on 17 March 1944, where it was given the high reliability rating of A-2.[140] Referring to Birkeland's covering note, Hilberg contends that the document was written by a female Polish agent. Breitman (2004: 191) goes further and suggests that the report was written by a Polish agent called Wanda. This was not the case.[141] The story of a female agent told to Birkeland and reported to his superiors, and since cited by Western scholars, was a Polish ploy to conceal the source. The report handed to the Americans included sections dated 10 July and 12 August 1943. In actual fact it was composed of three reports from the same source: the first, dated 10 June 1943, was joined with the second report – of 10 July 1943 – in Warsaw. It was the first of these three component reports that provided the numbers of those killed.

The first report, from 10 June, included the number of prisoners (137,000) and the mortality rate of Poles in the camp from 1940 to 1942 (average 80–130 per day) caused by undernourishment, disease and mistreatment by warders. It provided an extended discussion of German actions against Jews, and stated that 468,000 non-registered Jews had been gassed up to September 1942. It discussed three crematoria at Brzezinka (Birkenau), which had the capacity to burn 10,000 people a day. The report then outlined the women's camp at Birkenau, noting that Jewish girls were used in experiments in artificial insemination and sterilization. The final section of the report described the Gypsy camp and the gassing of Gypsies.

The second report, from 10 July, noted the arrival of people from Nice, Berlin, Salonika, Brandenburg, Sosnowiec and Lublin at the camp, of whom 80 per cent were Jewish and 20 per cent Gypsy. Ninety per cent of these people were gassed. This report also advised that the gassing of non-Jewish Poles was taking place. The escape of sixteen Ukrainians who had been trained as warders was also revealed. These Ukrainians were armed, and engaged Germans in combat. Four were captured and tortured to death. Subsequently, prisoners were escorted by German and Ukrainian warders. The final section of the report described an outbreak of typhus at the women's camp and at the Gypsy camp at Birkenau.

The third report, from 12 August, described a series of mass executions of Polish hostages between 15 July and 8 August, and highlighted

202   British suppression of news of Auschwitz: March 1943–June/July 1944

the German announcement that any escape attempt would result in the execution of 100 Poles. It noted the killing of Poles arriving at the camp; the killing of those who had been at the camp for some time; the arrival at the camp of two convoys of 100 Czechs, half of whom were executed; the arrival of Jews from Germany who were gassed at Birkenau on arrival; and the arrival of Jews from Sosnowiec and Będzin. It highlighted that the record number of people gassed at Birkenau in a single day was 30,000. The report concluded by providing the names of fourteen officers at the camp responsible for the crimes that took place there.

In contrast to scholarship written in the West, Polish-language scholarship has been aware of the origin of the entire tripartite report since at least 1968, but not its final destinations. There has been a significant disconnect between Western and Polish scholarship on this very important document. In 1968, a special edition of the journal *Zeszyty Oświęcimskie* reprinted all three sections of the report, complete with commentary. The report, according to the Polish Underground, was written by an unidentified SS officer in the camp.[142] It was for this reason that its origin was hidden from Poland's Western Allies, and the (unidentified) Polish Underground personnel handling the report specifically called for the source of the information not to be revealed. The editors of the 1968 edition of *Zeszyty Oświęcimskie*, Władysław Ważniewski and Krystyna Marczewska (1968: ix), speculate that the Underground claim may have been a cover story to protect couriers if caught in transit, but since then no convincing alternative source to the data in the documentary record has emerged.

The original report (that is, all three source reports) was in German, and was translated completely into Polish by 22 September 1943.[143] The part of the report giving the number of Jews who had been killed had been translated earlier as a dispatch for the BBC and Radio Świt. On 10 July an extensive report for the BBC was prepared by the Western Section of the Department of Information (part of the underground Polish state), including the most salient information from the 10 June report that recorded the murder of 468, 000 Jews at Auschwitz by the end of 1942.[144] Five days later, this data was compressed into a succinct broadcast proposal for Radio Świt and the BBC. Both the first and second reports (of 10 June and 10 July) were translated from the original German into Polish by the second week of July. The proposed Świt/BBC broadcast written on 15 July read,

From 24 to 27 June the Będzin ghetto was liquidated. About 2,500 Jews were taken to the Oświęcim camp in a heavily armoured convoy. 200–300 Jews were shot in the streets of the Będzin ghetto during the liquidation action.

The distribution of reports written in summer 1943   203

... By the end of 1942 468,000 Jews, not included in the general registration, were gassed in the Oświęcim camp. – From the beginning of the existence of the camp in Oświęcim to the end of 1942, during winter periods, the average number of deaths among Polish prisoners oscillated between 80–130 a day. From September last year to the beginning of June this year, 181,000 Jews from Poland, Greece, France, Belgium and Czechoslovakia were brought to Oświęcim. Of this figure, 177,000 have been gassed to date. Only 2% are still alive. – From 25 June of the current year transports of men have arrived in Oświęcim: 870 from Nice (France), over 500 from Berlin, 900 from Salonika, 1600 from Sosnowiec, 391 from Lublin and two transports from Będzin. 80% were Jews and 20% were Gypsies. About 10% of them are still alive. – Transports of Poles, mostly from around Radom, Lublin, Tarnobrzeg and Sandomierz, have lately also arrived. Most of them were immediately gassed. Recently death by beheading has also been introduced in Oświęcim.[145]

In recent days in Oświęcim and in the women's camp in Brzezinka typhus has been spreading. Female inmates of blocks suspected of having typhus are gassed.[146]

It is not clear where the proposed broadcast stalled as the surviving documentary record is partial. The raw material used by Świt is either lost or destroyed and the broadcast has not been located in the incomplete files of the Polish Government in Exile in London.[147] There is no mention of it in the (incomplete) BBC records of Polish Service broadcasts or meeting minutes.[148] But like the reports from Rowecki and Jankowski received in March 1943, and from Salski in April 1943, there was little chance that the Political Warfare Executive would have permitted these statistics to be broadcast or disseminated at all in 1943. This dispatch also called attention to the situation in Będzin, and would have supported claims made in the letter from Będzin that reached the Jewish Agency in Istanbul in July 1943.

An edited version of the information in the proposed BBC broadcast was radioed by the delegate, Stanisław Jankowski, to London on 18 July alongside news of German pacification actions and a report on a letter from the Polish Episcopate to Hans Frank, governor-general of the General Government, condemning the deportations and round-ups of Poles. In Jankowski's radio message, reference to the 468,000 Jews killed by the end of September was omitted. It referred only to the second report from 10 July 1943 and reported on transports from Nice, Berlin, Salonika and Sosnowiec.[149] The omission may indicate that the delegate was aware of the kind of information that would be useful and *acceptable* in London. The data from the 10 June report was, however, sent west via courier.

The main report (that is, the three reports originally dated 10 June, 10 July and 12 August 1943) was sent by courier to Budapest (an established

204   British suppression of news of Auschwitz: March 1943–June/July 1944

courier route) and then to Istanbul (a key Polish intelligence centre), and dispatched to London on 5 January 1944, where it was received on 24 January.[150] Polish intelligence officer Stanisław Sulma of the Istanbul station indicated in his covering note to his colleague in London, Michał Protasewicz, that Polish intelligence in Poland requested that this report be given publicity. Protasewicz was head of the Polish Bureau VI in London, which assisted in the organization of subversion in occupied Poland and received intelligence reports. The report was widely circulated within the Polish Government in Exile. It was sent by the deputy chief of Bureau II, Colonel Tadeusz Skinder, to the following individuals and offices: the commander in chief of Poland's armed forces, General Kazimierz Sosnkowski; the Ministry of the Interior; the Ministry of Foreign Affairs; the Ministry of Information and Documentation; the head of the military mission in Cairo; and the Polish military attachés in Washington, Ottawa, Mexico City and Ankara.[151]

However, the information about the gassing of 468,000 Jews up to September 1942 at Oświęcim, and the killing of a further 180,000 Jews in the period to June 1943, both items derived from the 10 June 1943 report, was received by the Polish Ministry of the Interior earlier. This information was included in Sprawozdanie Nr 11/43 (Report No 11/43), which provided data from Poland dealing with July and August 1943.[152] The Polish minister of the interior, Władysław Banaczyk, distributed Sprawozdanie Nr 11/43 to the Polish Cabinet on 2 December 1943, but the Polish government received information derived from the first two summer reports during the autumn of 1943. Aneks 58 highlighted the murder of 468,000 Jews up to September 1942 and was forwarded by Michał Protasewicz (Polish Bureau VI) to senior Polish officials – the minister of defence, Marian Kukiel; the minister of the interior, Władysław Banaczyk; the commander in chief, Kazimierz Sosnkowski – *and* Harold Perkins of the SOE on 23 November 1943.[153] The Polish government and, most probably, Polish Jewish representatives on the Polish National Council, had access to this important news from Oświęcim in December 1943. The arrival of the full report in January 1944 was therefore anticipated and had evidently been sanctioned for wide circulation.[154]

In addition to being passed to the US military attaché in London, the full report was forwarded to the United States Office for Strategic Services (OSS). In Washington, it was passed from F. L. Belin to Dr William Langer (chief of the Research and Analysis Branch). Though the report came from the Polish Underground, Belin did not indicate the reliability of the source. A third copy of the report was given to the US member of the United Nations War Crimes Commission, Herbert Pell

The distribution of reports written in summer 1943 205

(Hilberg 1985: 1127; Breitman 2004: 191).[155] The report has so far not been located in the British National Archives. Given that the Polish government distributed the report widely, swiftly and with some energy, this absence is distinctly odd. There are three possible explanations. First, the report was not given to the British as the Poles considered the British (that is, the Foreign Office and the PWE) unreceptive; second, the report was handed over and deliberately destroyed when various files were weeded out over the past several decades; or third, the report is buried in closed files.

The wide circulation of the information from the summer 1943 report among the members of the Polish Government in Exile and the apparent vigour devoted to its distribution would suggest that the report could have followed several routes to significant British officials at the Foreign Office, in British intelligence and at the SOE. The SOE (through Harold Perkins) had already received the most significant information contained in the report from 10 June 1942, with the receipt of Aneks 58 in November. There is further evidence in Polish archives in London that the full summer 1943 report was handed to the British. The third part of the report (from 12 August 1943), which listed German personnel at the camp, was released by the Polish Telegraphic Agency (Ministry of Information) as an English-language press release and widely distributed in Britain in mid-March 1944.[156]

It seems that the Polish government made moves to distribute the important information about the Nazi killing of Jews earlier – in February 1944. On 16 February 1944, the *Palestine Post* (Jerusalem) reported on a Polish Telegraphic Agency (London) press release from the previous day. The article, entitled 'Tale of one death camp', was published on the paper's front page and reported that '500,000 Jews had been murdered in the gas chambers of the Oswiecim concentration camp'.[157] It is likely that the PAT release drew on a number of intelligence reports that had arrived in London over the previous year, not just data from the summer 1943 reports. As far as can be established, the news that the PAT release sought to publicize was not published by the press in Britain or in the United States, indicating that the American and British censorship regimes remained robust, at least on the issue of German atrocities against Jews, throughout February 1944.

The limited release of information from the summer 1943 report (i.e. data about German personnel at Auschwitz) in mid-March looks like an uneasy compromise between the Polish government and the Political Warfare Executive, especially given the way news distributed in February failed to reach a mass audience in Britain and in the United States. Naming German officers allowed some information about Auschwitz to

206 British suppression of news of Auschwitz: March 1943–June/July 1944

be distributed in Britain. It is almost certain that the entire summer 1943 report was shown and discussed with (some) British officials, such as Frank Savery and Ivone Kirkpatrick, most probably no later than February 1944. The British policy of publicizing the names of German war criminals had been sanctioned on 22 October 1942. The BBC's European Service was advised that '[i]ndividual speakers in the various languages are now permitted to give lists of typical German criminals who should, in their opinion, be brought to trial on the day of retribution'.[158] By allowing the dissemination of such information, the British were able to maintain that they were responding to Allied demands that publicity be given to the German crimes, whilst limiting the distribution of information they considered sensitive.

In mid-March, most probably on 15 March (it is not possible to be precise because the records are incomplete), the BBC's German Service broadcast information that the fourteen Germans named in the third report (12 August 1943) were facing punishment. The evidence that such a broadcast took place is testimony from Józef Cyrankiewicz, who was imprisoned at the camp. On 9 May 1944 he advised colleagues in the Polish Underground outside the camp (that is, the Polish Socialist Party in Kraków) of the impact of the broadcast:

a short time ago, the announcement from London about the death sentence against fifteen SS men from Auschwitz had such an effect on those sentenced that some of them suffered breakdowns. This is therefore a highly effective method and you should try to prepare everything in this regard so that any future news travels as quickly as possible – these would be short items, suitable for radio.[159]

On 16 March 1944, Oświęcim appeared on the front page of a British national newspaper.[160] The *Daily Mirror* published a story entitled 'Woman torturer of women condemned to die', which reported,

Sentenced to death by the Polish Underground Movement:- Senior Wardress Mandl of the notorious Oswiecim concentration camp – 'one of the most brutal and sadistic women it is possible to imagine.'
. . . In Oswiecim it was she who selected women victims for the gas chambers.

Here the mention of gas chambers at Oświęcim is casual and written as though there were general awareness of these killing facilities at the camp amongst the British public. This was not the case, though it is likely that many journalists were aware of at least some of the information that had flowed into Britain through 1943 and early 1944, and had been published in the *Polish Jewish Observer* and the *Jewish Chronicle*. Significantly, the *Daily Mirror* did not mention Jews, which evidently eased the story's passage into publication.

The distribution of reports written in summer 1943 — — — 207

The *New York Times* published a brief report derived from Reuters on the same day, noting that 'Poles mark 14 Nazis for death', referring to the Polish Ministry of Information press release. On 17 March *Dziennik Polski*, in a page 4 article entitled '14 German butchers from Oświęcim who must be put to death', reported the names of those the Polish Underground had sentenced to death and detailed the crimes each individual had committed to warrant such a sentence.[161]

Two days earlier, on 15 March 1944, A. N. Kurcyusz (Adam Nowina-Kurcyusz) of the Polish Consulate in Istanbul, drawing on new information from Poland and the summer 1943 report, noted in *Polska pod okupacją niemiecką*, a regular mimeograph publication prepared by the consulate, that some 470,000 Jews had been gassed by September 1942, and that between summer 1942 and the autumn of 1943 60,000 Jews from Greece; 60,000 from France, Belgium and Holland; and 50,000 from Slovakia, Bohemia and Moravia had perished in Oświęcim (Świebocki 2000: 311; Gilbert 2001a: 180).[162] In total, up to mid-August 1943, *Polska pod okupacją niemiecką* recorded that 700,000 Jews had been killed at Oświęcim, and estimated that the total number of people who had died at the camp up to that date was 850,000. This information was published again on 22 March in the consulate's French-language publication *Pologne occupée*.[163]

The Polish Government in Exile co-ordinated the dissemination of the information from the summer 1943 report, and Kurcyusz's publication was not, as has previously been thought, an isolated action by a specific official (Gilbert 1994: 549). Nowina-Kurcyusz was a pseudonym of Jerzy Kurcyusz, who was an important member of Polish intelligence in Istanbul operating under the jurisdiction of the Polish Ministry of the Interior. Kurcyusz was responsible for general and political communications between the Polish government and Poland through Turkey (Ciechanowski and Dubicki 2005: 326). Kurcyusz and his colleagues in Istanbul would have had access to the information in the summer report from, at the latest, the beginning of January 1944, but most likely at some point in the autumn of 1943. It is worth noting that Kurcyusz was well known to British intelligence: SOE kept a file on him in just the same way as they kept tabs on other important Polish intelligence operatives whom they dealt with. SOE documents indicate that Kurcyusz may have been in London in February 1944.[164] Kurcyusz is recorded as visiting Professor Stanisław Kot in London during early April 1944.[165]

It seems that simultaneous press releases were planned in London and Istanbul. The London release of 15 March, however, only included the final section of the complete report. The Polish Consulate in Istanbul, which was not under the direct pressures of the British censorship

208   British suppression of news of Auschwitz: March 1943–June/July 1944

regime, was an important place to publish the data. In that city, representatives of British, American and German intelligence operated. The Jewish Agency also had a presence. All these organizations would have had an interest in the activities of the Polish Consulate and its publications.[166]

It has not been possible to ascertain the extent of the readership of *Polska pod okupacją niemiecką* amongst the personnel of these organizations, but it is reasonable to assume that the publication was read by at least some people associated with them. After all, all these organizations followed what was happening in Poland and how the Polish government understood and responded to these events. The French version of the paper (*Pologne occupée*) was clearly aimed at the international (diplomatic) audience. Gilbert (1994: 549) notes, 'No copy of [the report about Oświęcim in *Polska pod okupacją niemiecką*] appears to have been sent to London, Washington, or Jerusalem', but, given the path of the information it contained and the wide dissemination of the information on which it was based in London (see below), there was no need to. Gilbert's subsequent assertion that the 'facts, at last so fully reported, remained as secret as if they had never been published', is not true.[167] Important details from the summer report (10 June 1943) had already been published in Jerusalem in the bulletin of the Jewish Agency Committee for the Jews of Occupied Europe in February 1944.[168]

Through the first part of 1944, the War Refugee Board in the United States maintained pressure on President Roosevelt to make a statement on German crimes relating to the deportations to Poland. Unlike Eden in Britain, Roosevelt was inclined to make such a declaration. From the American perspective, the summer 1943 tripartite report from Oświęcim, which had reached US intelligence in mid-March 1944, and had possibly earlier been mentioned to American colleagues by the Polish military attaché in Washington, could help provide a receptive discursive context to any presidential statement.

In mid-March 1944, a difference of opinion existed between the British and Americans regarding the merits of making official statements and warnings to the Germans on the issue of deportations of Jews. This cleavage was reflected in their varying censorship of a 21 March 1944 Polish Ministry of Information press release. It was published in English in London and telegrammed to the Government in Exile's Polish Information Center in New York, and was distributed. American papers with representation in London reported the source as the Associated Press, London. Therefore British officials had access to the press release in London directly from the Polish government and through the censors stationed at the Associated Press. Transmission of the message overseas

The distribution of reports written in summer 1943 209

to the United States must have been approved – an indication that the press release was seen by officials in the United States as an important way of preparing the public prior to the scheduled presidential warning to the Germans on deportations. The press release stated,

The notorious concentration camp of Oswiecim has become German [*sic*] largest death factory. Three crematoria capable of handling 10,000 bodies daily were erected within the camp. It is not possible to estimate the exact figure of people put to death in gas chambers attached to crematoria but it certainly exceeds half a million, mostly Jews, both Polish and from other countries. 60,000 Jews from Greece, chiefly from Athens and Salonika were taken to Oswiecim. 50,000 from Bohemia, Moravia and Slovakia, 60,000 from Holland, Belgium and France. Only a small fraction have survived. When a transport arrives men and women are separated, the majority, especially women and children are packed into trucks and without further selection, removed to gas chambers. The execution takes about ten to fifteen minutes after which bodies are thrown into crematoria. As the supply of poison gas is limited some victims are not dead when removed for cremation. Before entering the gas chambers the doomed people are forced to take baths. Three crematoria are working at full steam night and day and local people call them "everlasting fire". The womens [*sic*] section of the camp is the most appalling place one can imagine. There is no water nor even most primitive hygienic arrangements and typhus is spreading. Those infected are gassed at once. Apart from all this, strong Jewish girls are used in men's camps for experiments in artificial insemination and sterilization. In winter prisoners have to work out of doors with a temperature 25 below zero, clad in wooden clogs and their ordinary drill prison garb ...[169]

The following day (22 March), American newspapers ran the story. The *Los Angeles Times* reported on its front page that 'the Polish Ministry of Information said today that more than 500,000 persons, mostly Jews, had been put to death at a concentration camp at Oswiecim' (reprinted in Świebocki 2000: 312). In its 'War sidelights' column on page 2, the *Washington Post* ran the headline 'Poles report Nazis slay 10,000 daily', and the *New York Herald Tribune* had a small column entitled '500,000 executed in Poland'. The *Daily News* (Perth, Australia) also reported on Oświęcim, highlighting that over 500,000 people, mostly Jews, had been killed in the camp's gas chambers.[170] The reports all mentioned the killing of Jews, the use of gas and crematoria, and reproduced text from the Polish Ministry of Information's press release.

On 23 March 1944, four Australian newspapers (three of which were based in Tasmania) reported on the Polish government's press release. Though none of the papers published news that over 500,000 people had been murdered at Oświęcim, all noted that 60,000 Jews from Greece; 50,000 from Bohemia; and 60,000 from Holland, Belgium and France had been taken to the camp and that only a small number of these people

210 British suppression of news of Auschwitz: March 1943–June/July 1944

had survived.[171] That same day, the Jewish Telegraphic Agency reported on the Polish government press release. The second paragraph of the article revealed the scale of the slaughter, recording that more than 500,000 people, mainly Jews, had been killed at the camp.[172] However, as Leff (2005: 274) notes, the American paper of record, the *New York Times*, did not run the story. Similarly in Britain, none of the major quality dailies mentioned the report. In a brief article entitled 'Experiments', which was placed on page 5 under the story 'Service girls will get cash and clothes coupons at demob', the *Daily Mirror* (22 March 1944) reported, 'The healthiest of the Jewish girls in the notorious German concentration camp at Oswiecim, Poland are being used in the men's camp for experiments in artificial insemination and sterilisation, according to the Polish Ministry of Information.' There was no reference to the more than half a million killed, the gas chambers or the crematoria mentioned in the Polish Ministry of Information's release and noted in the American and Australian press, highlighting how information about the camp and Jews in particular was tightly managed by the British press and the British Ministry of Information. However, on 24 March, the *Jewish Chronicle* published a more detailed article on page 8, indicating that the British press had been given access to the Polish government press release of 21 March and the earlier release of 15 March. The article was entitled 'Butchers of Oswiecim to die'. It read:

Death sentences have been passed by the Polish Underground Authorities on fourteen German officials at the notorious Oswiecim concentration camp, reports the Polish Telegraphic Agency in London.

Among those condemned is the Governor of the camp, Obersturmbahnnführer Hoess. Two others are described as having been chiefly concerned with selecting Jews for the gas chambers. Women were chosen for execution in the gas chambers by a senior wardress who is also included in the list of the sentenced criminals.

The report states that Oswiecim is the largest German concentration camp; 150,000 people are named in its records, apart from many thousands of Jews from Czechoslovakia, Holland, Belgium, France and Greece who, taken there to be exterminated, were not even entered in the camp's books.

This report is one of the frankest expressions of what was happening at Oświęcim to appear to that point in the *Jewish Chronicle*. And even though the report mentions 'many thousands of Jews', it was either unable or chose not to publish the full extent of the slaughter at the camp. However, the editor was aware of the contemporary significance of the Polish government's press release in the context of the German invasion of Hungary. The editorial that week was entitled 'And now Hungary?', and spoke of 'grave threats to Jews in that country'. The

The distribution of reports written in summer 1943   211

paper also included an article entitled 'Hungarian Jews' fate – drastic steps feared'.

The *Jewish Chronicle* was not alone in fearing for Hungarian Jewry. That same day, the US president warned of dire penalties for anyone who participated in 'the deportation of the Jews to their death in Poland' (cited in Gilbert 1994: 549). This was the result of prolonged lobbying by the War Refugee Board (Wyman 2007: 312). In London, the PWE released an extensive report entitled 'Special Annex on the persecution of the Jews' to contextualize the president's speech for PWE officials. The report ran to six pages and was split into two parts. The first section was entitled 'The extermination policy' and included subsections on 'Before 1939', 'During the war: the purging of Europe', 'Ghettos and camps', 'Deportations' and 'Massacre'. The second section focused on 'The Jews who remain' and provided a summary of conditions faced by Jews in occupied Europe. In the subsection on 'Massacre', Oświęcim was extensively discussed:

several other ghettos has been [*sic*] liquidated, including the Cracow ghetto, which was cleared in 3 days (March 13th, 14th, 15th 1943). More than 1,000 persons were murdered on the spot, the others were taken to Oswiecim for mass killing by gas and electricity. The majority of other ghettos have since been liquidated. In regard to those at Sosnowice [*sic*], Dabrowa Gornicza and Bendzon [*sic*], the procedure was more than customarily bestial. The ghettos were surrounded by S.S. men, and illuminated by reflectors. Jewish children were removed in sacks, whilst the adults were driven by trucks to Oswiecim for execution.[173] At this camp the slaughter goes on incessantly, and the bodies burnt in the crematorium and on open pyres. Smoke covers the whole district and a Pole who recently reached London stated that the stench was indescribable, causing faintness among those who lived several miles away.[174]

This document, as far as can be determined, is the first text of those available in the British National Archives in which British officials *acknowledge* Oświęcim as a place where Jews were being slaughtered on a mass scale. Although dated 24 March 1944, it is extremely unlikely that it was written on that day in preparation for, or in response to, Roosevelt's speech. The data in the document had been collected through the war, but it is not possible to date precisely when the PWE came into possession of all of the information. However, the first two sentences discussing the Kraków ghetto were with the PWE prior to 11 April 1943, as they were derived from Korboński's cable of 30 March 1943 and broadcast on the BBC.

The rest of the PWE overview of Oświęcim draws on information sent by the Polish Underground, which was incorporated into Sprawozdanie Nr 1/44 (Report No 1/44). Sprawozdanie Nr 1/44 was compiled by the

212   British suppression of news of Auschwitz: March 1943–June/July 1944

Polish Ministry of the Interior using information from Poland covering September and October 1943, and was distributed to the Polish Cabinet on 18 January 1944.[175] The information was also published in London on 4 February 1944, on page 2 of the *Polish Jewish Observer*, and was summarized by Ignacy Schwarzbart for colleagues at the World Jewish Congress in the United States.[176] But given that the documentary record of Oświęcim in the British archives is suspiciously thin, it is not possible to come to rock-solid conclusions on precisely when PWE officials received this information on Oświęcim.

On 27 March, six days after the Polish government press release, and having given the British press the opportunity to publicize the story, *Dziennik Polski* published the news on page 2. Under the headline '137,000 victims of German murderers: the eternal fire never goes out in Oświęcim', the article, like the earlier report in the *Jewish Chronicle*, did not publish the horrific number of 468,000 murdered up to September 1942.[177] Instead, it highlighted the deaths of registered prisoners. However, it referred closely to the summer 1943 tripartite report, noting that Jews above all were murdered in the gas chambers, and cited the summer report by recording that on one day 30,000 people were gassed at Birkenau.

Ten days later, on 7 April, the *Polish Jewish Observer* published on its front page an eyewitness's story entitled 'In the Charnel House of Oswiecim'. This article referred very closely to the summer 1943 report, recording that up to October 468,000 Jews had been killed in gas chambers in Oświęcim and that the three crematoria at Brzeznika (*sic*) could burn 10,000 bodies a day. The information from Oświęcim detailing the mass killing of Jews was published in English, in London, and was available to all subscribers to the supplement to the *East London Observer*.

By the end of March 1944, there can be absolutely no doubt that British decision makers had *acknowledged* that Auschwitz incorporated a death camp for Jews, and knew that well over half a million Jews had already perished there before the end of 1943. British officials were informed of the true function of the camp through 1943 (and probably in late 1942) and the intercept of Schwarzbart's mail (the Salski report) in May 1943 demonstrates how widely this information was disseminated within the Foreign Office, the PWE and the British intelligence community.[178]

In March 1944 the British were very reluctant to make any declaration warning Germany to desist from deporting Jews. On 24 February 1944, the Polish ambassador, Edward Raczyński, sent Anthony Eden an appeal on behalf of Polish Jews, addressed to Prime Minister Churchill. It protested 'against the latest outrages of the German occupants of Poland aiming at the extermination of what remains of the Jewish population of Poland'.[179] Eden advised Churchill on 17 March that the issue of a warning was discussed by the Cabinet Committee on Refugees on 14 March, where it was concluded that 'it would be useless to make further declarations in regard to Germany, but that appeals or warnings to the satellite countries might very well be worthwhile'. Eden continued,

The position is complicated by the determination of the United States Government to go ahead independently, unless we agree promptly, with a warning to Germany as well, and if we cannot shake them in this we shall have to find some way of associating ourselves with the American declaration, however strong our view that this kind of repetition merely debases the currency.[180]

On 30 March, in the House of Commons, in response to an arranged question tabled by Sydney Silverman on the persecution of Jews, the British Foreign Secretary stated, 'Evidence continues to reach His Majesty's Government and Allied Governments, that the Nazi policy of extermination has not been halted.' He continued,

The persecution of the Jews has in particular been of unexampled horror and intensity. On this His Majesty's Government in common with their Allies, now that the hour of Germany's defeat grows ever nearer and more certain, can only repeat their detestation of Germany's crimes and their determination that all those guilty of them shall be brought to justice. But apart from direct guilt there is still indirect participation in crime. Satellite Governments who expel citizens to destinations named by Berlin must know that such actions are tantamount to assisting in inhuman persecution or slaughter. This will not be forgotten when the inevitable defeat of the arch-enemy of Europe comes about.[181]

This statement, though frank in its warning to the Nazis and their collaborators, did not provide any details on the programme of extermination. It was made with reluctance in order to maintain a front of unity with the United States following Roosevelt's declaration on 24 March. This reticence fully to engage with the threat posed to Jews in Europe is illustrated by the Foreign Secretary's advice to Churchill not to reply to the Representation of Polish Jews.

Józef Cyrankiewicz's report (May–June 1944)

As the British Foreign Office was trying to maintain its policy of inaction in the face of the more proactive stance of the United States, as expressed by the War Refugee Board, and the increased pressure from the Polish government (manifested in the two press releases in mid-March), data about Auschwitz was still being collected and forwarded to the Polish Underground leadership in Warsaw, and ultimately to London. On 25 March 1944 a key member of the Kampfgruppe resistance group and the Polish Socialist Party, Józef Cyrankiewicz, wrote the following message,

214   British suppression of news of Auschwitz: March 1943–June/July 1944

which was smuggled out of Auschwitz to Adam Rysiewicz of the Underground Polish Socialist Party in Kraków:

In Bohemia there is the special Jewish city of Theresienstadt, where the Czech Jews have been assembled ... The Germans used promises of work in good conditions to deceive two transports of Czech families, numbering about 6,000, to leave there last year for a special Lager [i.e. camp] near Oświęcim. They are treated in a suspiciously polite way. They were permitted to live in that lager with their families, and not forced to work ... This lasted for several months. Now two further large transports are scheduled to arrive from Theresienstadt. To make room for the new guests, the whole previous transport of 3,800 (1,800 women, 2000 men) that arrived here several months ago was taken on order from Berlin ... and packed into the gas plant. The rest who are still alive, or the second transport (around 2,500) are not to know what happened to the first transport ... In order to delude the rest of the Jews from Theresienstadt and the International Red Cross, use was made of the favourite German trick with letters to their loved ones – in Bohemia – telling them how well they are doing. They were ordered to date the letters 25 March, when in fact the writers of the letters were already asphyxiated with gas on March 15. In the meantime, these letters waited in the Political Department until March 25, when they were sent to lure new victims, and to prove the falsity of the assertion that anyone was gassed here.[182]

This message is the probable source for a dispatch from Stanisław Jankowski to the Polish minister of the interior, sent on 5 April and received in London on 5 June 1944 (Świebocki 2000: 306).[183] Further information was sent by Bór-Komorowski to the Polish government on 27 April 1944 (received 31 May, de-encrypted 1 June 1944), reporting that in February 7,000 Jews had been gassed at Oświęcim – 'mainly men from Italy, Denmark, France, [and on] 15 March 1944, 4,000 Jews from Theresienstadt'.[184] In London, the information was passed to the British Foreign Office, which forwarded it to the British Embassy in the United States to pass it, via the Polish Embassy, to the Polish prime minister (who was in Washington, DC to meet with President Roosevelt).[185] The message received by the Polish Embassy was dated 12 June.[186] The significance of this document is that it demonstrates that Foreign Office officials yet again had access to clear information about Oświęcim as a killing centre prior to the arrival of the Vrba–Wetzler report (the Vrba–Wetzler report is discussed in the next chapter), and that the Polish government handed such information to the British.[187]

The Polish government's official newspaper, *Dziennik Polski*, published the information sent on 5 April by Jankowski in a 9 June article (page 2) entitled '7,000 Czech Jews murdered in Oświęcim'.[188] The article itself was sited left of centre, its headline written in large bold type and prominently placed on the page. It reported that 7,000 Czech Jews from Thereseinstadt had been murdered in the gas chambers at

Józef Cyrankiewicz's report (May–June 1944)

Oświęcim. The article informed readers that the victims were made to write letters to kin prior to being killed, advising them of their good work conditions in Poland, and stated that the International Red Cross had been informed of their fate. The final sentence of the report recorded that the first transports of Hungarian Jews had arrived in Poland and that 'this was the first stage of the liquidation of Hungarian Jewry'. This information was released by the Polish Telegraphic Agency and two days later the *Palestine Post* reported on its front page that 7,000 Czechoslovak Jews had been murdered in the gas chambers at Oświęcim.[189]

Świebocki (1997: 78) notes that the publication of data derived from Cyrankiewicz's report in *Dziennik Polski* pre-dates the forwarding of information from the Vrba–Wetzler report to London by five days. All three reports (Jankowski's of 5 April, Bór-Komorowski's of 27 April and the initial data from the Vrba–Wetzler report) informed a BBC broadcast on the German Service's women's programme at 12 noon on 16 June 1944. The dissemination of the news to this programme suggests that its propaganda value in influencing audiences in Germany was the most important consideration. The aim of the broadcast was certainly not to advise the world, and in particular British audiences, of what was known about Oświęcim. There was no information about the camp on the Home Service. The broadcast on the German Service was frank in its delivery of the news and in its warning to those responsible:

Here is an important announcement. News has reached London that the German authorities in Czechoslovak [*sic*] have ordered the massacre of 3,000 Czechoslovak Jews in gas chambers at Birkenau on or about June 20th. These Jews were transported to Birkenau from the concentration camp at Theresienstadt on the Elbe last December.

4,000 Czechoslovak Jews who were taken from Theresienstadt to Birkenau in September 1943 were massacred in the gas chambers on March 7th.

The German authorities in Czechoslovakia and their subordinates should know that full information is received in London about the massacres in Birkenau. All those responsible for such massacres from top downwards will be called to account.[190]

The BBC news scripts for the Polish, Czechoslovak and German Services for June 1944 are lost or destroyed, so it is not possible to state with complete confidence whether this broadcast was the first to mention the Czech Jews. The European news directive for 16 June 1944 strongly suggests that it was not, since it advised the Service to '[r]eport *again* our warning the Germans about the massacres of Czech Jews' (my italics).[191] Drawing on German press monitoring, Karny (1993: 209) indicates that from 15 June a warning of promised retribution was broadcast on the BBC Czechoslovak Service for several days.

216   British suppression of news of Auschwitz: March 1943–June/July 1944

Cyrankiewicz's (Jankowski's) and Bór-Komorowski's reports provided confirmation that the information from the Vrba–Wetzler report regarding the Jews of Czechoslovakia was correct. The unusually rapid response to broadcast the information was not just because Vrba and Wetzler (or, more precisely, Dr Jaromir Kopecky of the Czechoslovak Legation in Switzerland, who had sent urgent telegrams with the information about Czech Jews) had indicated that Czechoslovak Jews at Auschwitz would shortly be massacred, or the intrinsic 'believability' of that report. Rather, the circulation of the earlier Cyrankiewicz and Bór-Komorowski reports provided a more receptive environment for the Vrba–Wetzler information about Czech Jews amongst officials at the Foreign Office and the PWE.

Data from the Vrba–Wetzler report was corroborated by earlier reports. Furthermore, the fate of Hungarian Jews, which had been a more or less continuous feature of PWE directives since March, was highlighted with some unusual frankness in the week from 9 June to 16 June, the same week that the Foreign Office dispatched Bór-Komorowski's message to Washington.[192] The directive circulated to the BBC's European Service, written on 8 June 1944, noted that 'Hungarian Jews are now being sent to concentration camps in Poland. Every Hungarian should, for the sake of Hungary's reputation, do all he can to succour the Jews and prevent their despatch to Poland'. The version sent to the British Embassy in Washington, written the same day, was even more revealing: 'Report the sending of Hungarian Jews to Polish death camps [*sic*], despite the Government's assurance that it does not wish to exterminate them. Urge Hungarians for their country's credit, to help Jews and prevent their deportation.'[193] The difference – 'concentration camps' in the directive to the European Service, and 'death camps' in the message to the United States – may indicate that the person(s) responsible for composing these instructions felt a greater degree of freedom in messages to the United States. Even though the instructions to the British Embassy in the US were frank, press practices in the US routinely marginalized news of the Holocaust. This ensured that blunt news from the PWE tended not to be highlighted by the press which had access to it despite the increasing divergence in the narration of the Holocaust on the different sides of the Atlantic.

The British retained (habitually) a greater degree of circumspection for European audiences, in part because of the ingrained institutional belief that broadcasting the full and true information would be counterproductive. In the case of people being sent to a death camp, this made no sense. By not broadcasting the truth about the deportations to Auschwitz, the PWE provided space for the Nazis to disseminate their propaganda

Józef Cyrankiewicz's report (May–June 1944)

unchallenged. According to a message sent on behalf of Leon Feiner to Emanuel Scherer on 1 June 1944, Hungarian Jews were sent to Oświęcim under the pretext of a (population) exchange at Calais.[194] The Nazis, according to the delegate, Stanisław Jankowski, indicated to Hungarian Jews that they were being resettled in the east or were part of an exchange deal the Nazis had made with the English.[195] The PWE had the opportunity to dispel these illusions, and it is possible that some Hungarian Jews might have been encouraged to evade capture and deportation if they had been frankly advised by the BBC of the fate that awaited them.

The new information derived from the Vrba–Wetzler report offered the PWE and the BBC the opportunity to achieve propaganda goals (warn Germans that their actions were known), and to satisfy Jewish and Polish demands to publicize the information. On the same day that the BBC broadcast news to Germany (16 June 1944), derived in part from the Vrba–Wetzler report, readers of the *Polish Jewish Observer* in Britain were confronted by a front-page article entitled 'Three years in Oswiecim hell'. The paper reported on the testimony of a certain Jan Wolny, who was presented as an escaped prisoner.[196] Wolny confirmed 'that at least one million Jews – Polish, German, Belgian, Dutch, French and Czechoslovakian – have passed through the death chambers there'.[197] This testimony had been available to journalists in London from at least the beginning of June 1944, as on 5 June the *Milwaukee Journal* published a page 2 article entitled 'Fugitive describes "slave town" built by Nazis in Poland', which gave a limited overview of Wolny's testimony. The fate of Jews at Oświęcim was marginalized; the piece referred only to the fact that in 1942 'trainload after trainload of Jews were shipped to camps for execution', and to 'common gossip' that by the end of 1942 '800,000 persons had been killed or permitted to die in the two camps', named as 'Oswiecim and Brzezinka (Burkenau)' (*sic*). The *Milwaukee Journal* picked up the story from the *New York Times* News Service (London office), but the American paper of record chose not to publish Wolny's story. The *New York Times* had information about Oświęcim and this news did not pass through the paper's own censorship regime.[198]

The arrival of the first pieces of data from the Vrba–Wetzler report did not signal a change in how news of the massacre of Jews at Oświęcim was to be handled in Britain for British audiences. It is clear from the data presented above that the now standard claim – that the Vrba–Wetzler report was accorded wide distribution because it was the first report to be seen as credible – can no longer be sustained. The significance of the Vrba–Wetzler report is discussed in the next chapter and its importance is highlighted, but it did not provide British decision makers with reliable information of the systematic murder of Jews at Auschwitz for the first time.

News of the camp flowed steadily through 1943 and 1944, and there are good reasons to argue that British officials (Foreign Office, SOE) had data in late 1942. The memorandum handed to Roosevelt was in the possession of significant figures in the Foreign Office in January 1943, news of the mass killing of Jews was broadcast on the BBC in April 1943, and in May 1943 the intercept of the Salski report was widely circulated in the Foreign Office, in the PWE, and among British intelligence. It also seems that the Polish Bureau VI routinely passed *aneks* to SOE, and since news of atrocities was being collected by Roger Allen, this data would have reached the Foreign Office.

Data on the mass killing of Jews had been incorporated within the PWE's 'Special annex on the persecution of the Jews' printed on 24 March – a clear sign that policy makers found earlier data credible.[199] Credibility or believability were not the reasons for the suppression of information about the camp through 1943 and 1944. Auschwitz was not obscure to the Foreign Office or to British intelligence, but news of the camp was suppressed by the British in order to limit pressure to provide sanctuary for refugees, to stem calls for retaliatory strikes against Germany, to limit the circulation of news about Jews in Britain due to anxieties about British anti-Semitism, and in order to narrate the war in a particular way to the British people. As is shown in the next chapter, these practices and concerns did not disappear with the arrival of the Vrba–Wetzler report.

6 Reassessing the significance of the Vrba–Wetzler report

From the moment that German forces entered Hungary on 19 March 1944, the Western Allies expressed increasing concern about the fate of Hungarian Jewry. Roosevelt sounded a warning to Germany on 24 March, and Eden on 30 March cautioned satellite countries about the deportation of people (he did not highlight that these were Jews). Officials at the Political Warfare Executive were under no illusion about what the new situation would mean for the Jews. As the 17 December 1942 document 'Special Annexe on the Extermination of the Jews' and the 24 March 1944 document 'Special Annexe on the Persecution of the Jews' make clear (discussed in Chapter 5 above), the PWE understood the incremental measures taken against Jews, which ended with deportation to death camps in occupied Poland.[1] It is not known whether the PWE or any branch of British intelligence undertook research into the likely death camp to which Hungarian Jews would be transported.[2]

Bełżec, Sobibór and Treblinka were no longer in operation in March 1944. Auschwitz's true functions were known to the PWE, to the Foreign Office and to British intelligence, as well as to corresponding offices in the United States. A detailed Polish map of the Oświęcim region from 1937, drawn at the ratio of 1:100,000, included railway routes and the places Oświęcim, Brzezinka and Monowice, and other significant locations such as Rajsko, and had been catalogued by the geographic section of the British General Staff in June 1943.[3] Given its geographic location and its killing capacity, as indicated in the reports which, we have seen in the previous chapter, were received in London, the camp would have featured high on any scenario planner's list of possible places where Hungarian Jews could be deported to. This assertion is based firmly on what was known in March 1944 by the PWE, and it is in the context of the PWE's knowledge that British propaganda policy on the issue of Hungarian Jewry has to be assessed.

The 30 March PWE directive to the BBC's Hungarian Service called for the president's and any Allied statement to be run several times, and for warnings to be given to the Hungarian government and administration

219

220   Reassessing the significance of the Vrba–Wetzler report

that 'racial persecution will be regarded as a war crime'. It also instructed that appeals should be made to the 'Hungarian people to prevent persecution and to help the persecuted'.[4] Three weeks later, in light of 'fresh anti-Jewish measures or evidence of German plans for destroying the Jews in Hungary', the directive sent to Washington asked that reference should be made to the Roosevelt and Eden statements, and to the statements of senior British clergy.[5] The version handed to the BBC's Hungarian Service indicated that it 'may be possible to release information about German plans for the destruction of the Jews in Hungary, which would obviously be an opportunity for recalling these warnings and appeals fully'.[6] Clearly, the PWE and the Foreign Office were aware of both the growing need for greater clarity and the need to respond to increasing public concern about the situation of Hungarian Jewry.

The *Jewish Chronicle* on 7 April had a front-page story entitled 'Zero hour in Hungary'. Given that the editorial staff at the *Jewish Chronicle* had seen the 21 March 1944 Polish government press release about Auschwitz and, like the PWE, were familiar with the incremental process of Nazi anti-Jewish actions, this measured article obliquely alluded to the fate that awaited Hungarian Jewry. Three weeks later, on 28 April, the paper included an article entitled '300,000 Hungarian Jews arrested – the hideous process begins'. However, the PWE release of information about German plans to destroy the Jews was not forthcoming. In a letter dated 2 May 1944 to Alexander Easterman, George Hall (parliamentary under-secretary of state for foreign affairs) explained,

As we agreed in conversation on 13 April it seems superfluous to inform the Jewish population in Hungary in wireless broadcasts from this country what they should do to seek refuge . . . we feel that we have done all that we can in the present circumstances and think it inadvisable to make any reference to Riegner's report which, even if entirely reliable (and this may unfortunately be the case), would surely only cause unnecessary alarm amongst the Jews of Hungary who must in any case be only too well informed of the measures which may be taken against them and against which they will presumably take such measures as they are able.[7]

It is unlikely that Hall was correct in his assertion that the Jews of Hungary were well informed of the measures to be taken against them. As noted in Chapter 5, the Germans used a number of ruses to smooth the deportation to Auschwitz, including advising Jews that they were part of an exchange deal with the British and that they were being sent to work in the General Government.[8] The British could have undermined the German assertions if the European Service of the BBC had been permitted to broadcast details of the Nazi genocidal programme.

However, some information continued to be broadcast. On 4 May the PWE directive to the Hungarian Service noted that 'further brutal anti-Jewish decrees' had been introduced in Hungary; the 19 May directive gave details of property confiscations, including the taking of radio sets and the shifting of Jews to locations near military installations. However, by the end of May the PWE had come to the view that championing the Jews was counterproductive. The 25 May directive to the Hungarian Service noted that the procedures of the latest anti-Jewish decrees were likely to be summary, but argued that 'too warm an advocacy of the Jews' case is liable, in the present temper of Hungary, only to aggravate their lot'. The directive sent to Washington was considerably more blunt: 'Do not champion the Jews, as this may provoke worse treatment'.[9] The first transports from Budapest had arrived in Auschwitz twenty-three days earlier. Some 2,698 Jews were murdered on arrival in the gas chambers (Czech 1992: 650).

Late May had seen the PWE focus on Jewish property confiscations. In June, attention was turned to those Germans seeking to benefit from the removal of Jews from industry. The directive of 3 June also reiterated a call for the churches in Hungary to denounce the persecution of the Jews, and praised nameless priests who were extending aid. The general British policy was to attempt to increase the moral pressure on important institutions to act in support of the persecuted Jews, and thereby stimulate the wider society to resist the Nazi anti-Jewish agenda.[10] However, there remained no mention of deportations and death camps in these important directives until 8 June. There was a seven-week gap between the PWE mooting the release of information about German plans for the destruction of the Jews in Hungary on 20 April, and the first mention of deportations and death camps in the PWE directives on 8 June.

This significant time lag can, in part, be explained by the *decrease* in pressure put on the British (in both the FO and the PWE) to act decisively. These seven weeks witnessed a redirection of the energies of Polish government representatives and Jewish representatives, and the media. It was not the fate of Hungarian Jewry or Polish Jews in Hungary which dominated the thinking of these two important groups, but the issue of anti-Semitism in the Polish Army. Consequently, as the sanctions against the Jews in Hungary became harsher and the deportations to Auschwitz started, the two groups best placed to lobby the British to act and warn Hungarian Jewry of their fate were engaged in prolonged and, at times, acrimonious exchanges.

Anti-Semitism in the Polish Army

The issue of anti-Semitism in the Polish Army had been a continuous problem for the Polish Government in Exile, in terms of both the harm inflicted on Jewish service personnel and the damage done to the government's reputation. Ignacy Schwarzbart had highlighted the issue in a note to the minister of defence, Marian Kukiel, on 8 June 1943, and some moves were made to combat anti-Semitism that year,[11] such as Kukiel's demand that the Polish Army's field bishop, Józef Gawlina, advise chaplains in the Army to participate in the action against anti-Semitism (Gąsowski 2002: 182). The damage done to the Polish government's reputation was exacerbated by pro-Soviet British MPs and publications (such as the *Daily Worker*), which often used charges of anti-Semitism as a strategy to undermine the Polish government.

In April 1944, twenty-one Polish Jewish soldiers based in Scotland were court-martialled for desertion. The number of deserters, in total, reached over 200, and those deserting expressed a wish to be incorporated within the British Army. They were not seeking to escape military service. There is no evidence that the intensity of anti-Semitism in early 1944 increased, but it was becoming apparent to many soldiers that a return to Poland was looking unlikely. Jewish communities in Poland had been annihilated, and the failure to imagine Jewish life in postwar Poland seems to have encouraged some deserters to think seriously about ways to get to Palestine and/or to stay in the West. Service in the British Army broadened possibilities. The first serious wave of desertion occurred on 16 January 1944, when sixty-eight soldiers deserted. This provoked an enquiry, which reported that the lack of emotional ties with Poland, the loss of families in Poland, the uncertainty over the future political situation in Poland, and the possibility that service in the British Army was a route to British citizenship underpinned the desertions. A second wave of desertions in February was similarly understood.[12] An accommodation with the British to quietly accept these soldiers into the British Army was quickly reached (Gąsowski 2002: 188), but desertion from the Polish Army continued, as did allegations of anti-Semitism. Following the transfer of the January and February deserters to the British Army, the Polish Army sought to draw a line under the affair and stem the flow of desertion. Subsequent deserters were court-martialled if they refused to return to the ranks.

The question of anti-Semitism in the Polish forces and the court-martials reached the British parliament and, over the course of April and May 1944, they were debated on no fewer than five occasions (on 5, 6, 26 April and 10, 17 May) in the House of Commons. The repeated discussion and public exposure of the issue in Parliament gave newspaper editors a steady stream of news to publish that did not attract the special attention of British censorship. Given that news from Hungary was not as verifiable as speeches made in Parliament, and that much of

Anti-Semitism in the Polish Army

what news there was was subject to continued control, it is not so surprising that the *Jewish Chronicle* through April and May carried front-page stories on anti-Semitism in the Polish Army virtually every week.

The 14 April edition's front page reported, 'Antisemitism in Polish Army – shocking revelations in parliament'. The Polish government's 'vigorous condemnation' of anti-Semitism was tucked away on page 7. It quoted the declaration of the Polish commander in chief (Kazimierz Sosnkowski) that the 'creation of differences and disharmony on the grounds of faith, nationality or politics, I regard as equally harmful. All such acts injure the interests of Poland and put weapons in the hands of her enemies'. The 21 April edition reported that the issue of anti-Semitism was not to be raised in the House of Lords, while the 28 April edition highlighted the court martial of 21 Polish Jews for desertion. The story again made the paper's front page on 1 May, and was featured in the 19 and 26 May editions also. The tone became somewhat harsher on 2 June 1944, with a story entitled 'Polish Nazism in Palestine'. The issue of Polish anti-Semitism and the courts-martial of Polish Jewish army deserters dominated the paper during the key months of spring 1944. Some Nazi actions against Hungarian Jews were mentioned (not the mass murder in the gas chambers at Auschwitz), but news of Hungarian Jews was a secondary running story.

Similarly, the Polish press in Britain focused on the allegations of anti-Semitism and the courts-martial during these months. Dariusz Stola (1995: 268) rightly observes, 'More was written about the desertion in the Polish London community than about the Holocaust of the Jews or about their future status in Poland.' This was due, in no small part, to British sensitivities over reporting in Britain about Jews' plight and the ready availability and tractability of news from Parliament. The general effect of all this publicity was to increase dissonance between Jewish and Polish communities. Stereotypes of Polish anti-Semitism amongst sections of one side were mirrored by stereotypes of Jewish disloyalty in sections of the other.[13]

Ignacy Schwarzbart and Emanuel Scherer were well aware of the damage being done. In opposition to a sizable body of British Jewish opinion, which sought the transfer of Polish Jewish servicemen to the British Army, both Jewish representatives on the Polish National Council came out against the desertions, and argued that the Polish Army needed to make more vigorous efforts to combat anti-Semitism.[14] Eleanor Rathbone MP (Combined English Universities) made reference to this in the parliamentary debate on 5 April, noting that 'the representatives of Polish Jewry in the Polish National Council did their best to persuade these men to return to, or remain with, their units, without success'.[15]

224   Reassessing the significance of the Vrba–Wetzler report

Schwarzbart's influence on British Jewry was minimal by this stage, so there was little scope for him to moderate or guide the debate on Polish anti-Semitism within British Jewish milieux.

The Polish government was extremely concerned about the desertions. On 4 February 1944 Emanuel Scherer had discussed anti-Semitism in the Army with the commander in chief, Kazimierz Sosnkowski, and minister of war, Marian Kukiel, and on 11 February Ignacy Schwarzbart had focused on the same issue in a meeting with Sosnkowski.

In the House of Commons, the independent MP Tom Driberg initiated the debate on anti-Semitism in the Polish armed forces on 5 April 1944. Driberg had dabbled with communism in his youth and remained on the left of the political spectrum. His initial objective seems to have been to encourage the British government to facilitate the transfer of Polish Jewish soldiers to British units. Though this had earlier taken place, as we have seen, in order to ease tensions within the Polish Army and inhibit damaging publicity, it was considered an exceptional arrangement, not precedent. The British had asked the Polish government to investigate the issue of anti-Semitism in the Army. Foreign Secretary Anthony Eden reported to the Commons that

a full inquiry has, in fact, been made and that the Polish authorities have taken all steps in their power to ensure that their declared policy of suppressing all manifestations of anti-Semitism is brought to the notice of all ranks in the Polish Armed Forces and that appropriate action is taken to carry it into effect.[16]

Aware of the serious damage being done to the reputation of the Polish government, the Polish Embassy approached the Foreign Office on 5 April, requesting that information about the debate be withheld from broadcast. The embassy was advised that the BBC would not withdraw the information 'in view of their duty to report to their listeners the proceedings of the House'. The Polish government contended that 'if this point of view is comprehensible when it applies to the Home Service, it does not seem convincing in connection with the European Service, which has a purely propaganda character'.[17]

The following day, in a full debate at the Commons, Driberg explained that his decision to raise the issue of anti-Semitism in the Polish Army had been provoked by the action of military police raiding a hostel in London where the deserters were staying, and again reiterated his goal of securing the transfer of the Polish Jewish deserters to British Army units. He argued,

I do not believe that you can stamp out anti-Semitism by instructions, by Orders of the Day, or by anything else of that formal kind. I repeat that I know that the Polish Government's intentions in this respect are admirable: there is nothing

Anti-Semitism in the Polish Army

225

whatever to be said against them for the very vigorous way in which they have tried to deal with the matter; but anti-Semitism, being essentially an emotional thing, cannot be dealt with in that way. It can be cured only by the process – a rather slow process, probably – of education.[18]

Driberg attempted to keep the tone of the debate measured. However, Eleanor Rathbone, one of the few MPs to champion the cause of Jewish refugees and to press for a more open refugee policy, queried the merits of holding the debate at all:

I cannot help feeling very deep doubt as to whether – especially after what has happened during the last few months, and especially after this Debate – it is going to be possible for really cordial relations to be established between Polish Jews and the non-Jewish Poles in the Army. The non-Jewish will feel that the Jews have, so to speak, blackened them in the eyes of the British public. I cannot see really good relations being established, whatever the Polish Government does – and I am sure it will do its best – or whatever our own Foreign Office does.[19]

The minister of state, Richard Law, Anthony Eden's deputy at the Foreign Office, also doubted the debate's merit, suggesting that Polish–Jewish relations were unlikely 'to be improved by a Debate of this kind. I have no objection to the spirit in which the Debate has taken place, although I still do regret that it had to take place'. He had earlier maintained that there was nothing more the Polish government could do, mentioning military orders against anti-Semitism, sanctions and education courses, and had suggested that bringing the issue before Parliament altered the cost–benefit calculus that any potential deserter would make:

[if] a man who is a victim of a trivial incident that may develop into something rather more important, is perfectly free not only to desert, not only to come to London but to approach Members of Parliament, and know that his case will be heard on the sounding board that Parliament is, and to know that some Members will bring pressure upon the Government to bring pressure, in their turn, upon the Polish Government to release him from the Army, then you are bound to get a continuance of indiscipline of that kind. I think that that is absolutely certain.[20]

The British sought to uphold a point of principle. Personnel transfers between Allied armed forces would not be approved. The British were concerned about the fighting strength of military units prior to the Allied invasion of France. The Poles were worried not only about the reputational damage being done by the parliamentary attention focused on anti-Semitism and the courts-martial, but about re-establishing military discipline. Members of other minorities in the Polish Army – Ukrainians and Belarusians – had also deserted in April 1944. These desertions had implications for the Polish demand to reconstitute the country's 1939 borders after the war.

On 28 April 1944, the *Polish Jewish Observer* published the Polish government's official statement on the desertion affair. It pointed out that only those who refused to return to the ranks when ordered to on 13 March were court-martialled (twenty-one Polish Jewish servicemen). It noted that 207 Polish Jewish soldiers had previously been allowed to join the British Army, but, the Polish statement made clear, this was an exceptional case. It further recorded that although courts-martial were normally held in camera, dispensation had been made for Jewish members of the Polish National Council to attend. Ignacy Schwarzbart and Emanuel Scherer were present throughout.

Two weeks later, the *Polish Jewish Observer* reported on a meeting of the Polish National Council. The article entitled 'Polish War Minister faces critics in PNC debate on soldiers' sentence' highlighted Schwarzbart's argument that the Army had not been energetic enough in combating anti-Semitism. On page 3 of the same issue, the paper informed readers that Professor Marian Heitzman, the head of the political department of the Polish Ministry of Defence, had initiated an investigation into seventeen anti-Semitic incidents. Legal proceedings had commenced. A week later, on 19 May, the paper reported that '[a]ngry Polish MPs attack military chiefs – in 4-day heated debate demand drastic steps to clear up antisemitism'. Representatives from the Polish Socialist Party, together with Jewish representatives, argued strongly for action to be taken. They met with intransigence from the Polish Right, which did not recognize the issue of anti-Semitism as serious, and instead focused on how the scandal of allegations of anti-Semitism in the Polish Army was damaging the reputation of the Polish government and armed forces.

For those representatives concerned about anti-Semitism, the course of action was clear – punish anti-Semites, outlaw anti-Semitism, and enhance measures to inhibit its development. For rightist representatives, the solution to the scandal was to ignore the substantive issue and to close down the discussion. These diametrically opposed understandings of the problem and solution posed difficulties for the Polish government and Army leadership. Intolerant right-wing sentiment had a constituency within the Polish armed forces, as well as within sections of the Cabinet and National Council, and could not, politically, be seen to be ignored. The solution was for statements against anti-Semitism to be made without the swift implementation of the thorough and rigorous actions demanded by Scherer, Schwarzbart and the Polish Socialist Party, though some measures were taken, including the investigation of cases of anti-Semitism.

The BBC's Polish Service kept its reporting of the desertion issue lowkey, in the main, factual and without commentary. On 22 April it simply reported that sentences of between one and three years had been passed, noting that the soldiers had alleged ill-treatment by non-Jewish Poles and had come to London to join the British Army.[21] The following day it broadcast Sosnkowski's Order of the Day, in which he stated, 'The armed forces must be based on equality of rights and duties without regards to faith or political opinion, always mindful of loyalty to Poland and her interest'.[22] On 24 April, the BBC broadcast a resolution of the Board of Deputies of British Jews, which expressed 'deep concern at the conditions in the Polish Army that have culminated in recent court-martials of Jewish soldiers', and called for ways to be found for these Jews to join the British Army.

The only dissent from the measured reporting of the issue was broadcast in the form of a review of press coverage in Britain. The publications *Time and Tide* and *The Tablet* from 6 May were discussed on the BBC's Polish Service. *Time and Tide* argued that the 'desertions must have been organised, for all the deserters were at the same Jewish hotel in London', and contended that, although there was evidence of conspiracy, the applicable article in the Polish military code was not applied, suggesting that a great deal of leniency was granted, since the conspiracy charge carried a fifteen-year tariff or capital punishment. *The Tablet* lamented the effect that the entire affair was having, and stressed that some non-Jews hid Jews in Poland.[23] This review, which was guided to a Polish audience in Poland, did not reflect the spread of opinion in Britain, but did suggest to its intended audience that the British press were broadly sympathetic to the situation faced by the Polish government.

The PWE made efforts to keep the tensions between Poles and Jews off the BBC's Polish Service and to project a united Polish front to the audience in Poland and elsewhere in Europe. On 19 April the Polish Service broadcast Mikołajczyk's message to the Federation of Polish Jews in Great Britain, commemorating the 'heroic defenders of the Warsaw ghetto'.[24] On 1 May Dr Emanuel Scherer, who became the Bund's representative on the National Council following Shmuel Zygielbojm's suicide a year earlier, delivered a May Day talk on the Polish Service, promising that 'a future without reaction, without anti-semitism and capitalism is approaching', since the 'Jewish people will outlast their Nazi oppressors'.[25] The following day the BBC's Polish Service reported that 'between October 1943 and February 1944, 1,104 Poles [were] executed in Cracow for sheltering Jews'.[26] Eleven days later, on 13 May, Noel Newsome, in the general directives for the European Service, noted that the 'amnesty for Polish Jews who were sentenced for desertion has not received all the coverage it deserves', and advised that such broadcasts could be 'quite short'.[27]

228   Reassessing the significance of the Vrba–Wetzler report

On 26 April Eden informed the House that the Jewish deserters had received prison terms of between one and two years. One year was the minimum sentence allowed in the Polish military code. Leniency had been urged by senior Polish politicians, but some form of disincentive to other potential deserters had to be created. Tom Driberg, however, drew attention in Parliament to the absorption of previous deserters into the British Army and the sentences passed on the more recent group. Ivor Thomas MP (Labour) asked Driberg whether he was 'aware that a state of things highly prejudicial to discipline in the Polish Army would be created, if it got abroad that deserters could secure the protection of the British Parliament?'[28]

Three weeks later, on 17 May, Eden reported to the House that on 12 May the Polish president had amnestied those who had deserted prior to 3 May, and that the soldiers had been sent for reassignment in the Polish Army. Eden continued that he was 'satisfied that the Polish authorities, for their part, have done and are doing all in their power to stamp out any trace of racial or religious discrimination in the Polish Forces'.[29] The net result of sustained press and Parliamentary attention was that Polish Jewish deserters returned to the Polish Army, incentives to desert in the hope of joining the British Army were eventually removed, Polish activities against anti-Semitism were stepped up, Polish–Jewish relations and the reputation of the Polish government were harmed, and – most damagingly of all – the news of Hungarian Jewry was marginalized in the British and Polish press.

Throughout the scandal, there was a distinct difference of opinion between representatives of Polish Jews and representatives of British Jews. The Polish Jewish perspective was that anti-Semitism must be combated everywhere. If Polish Jewish soldiers were permitted to transfer to the British Army, it would not solve the problem of anti-Semitism in the Polish Army; in effect it would mean abandoning the fight against anti-Semitism amongst Poles. Representatives of British Jewry, along with some non-Jewish MPs, on the other hand, saw the issue as protecting Jewish service personnel from the harm of anti-Semitism. But this understanding only makes sense if it was assumed that changes in the behaviour and attitude of the Polish Armed Forces towards Polish Jewish servicemen were not possible. Arguably, Scherer and Schwarzbart were better placed to make such an assessment – and they continued to engage with the Army's leadership to effect the necessary changes. The scandal therefore highlights the limited influence that Polish Jews had on co-religionists in Britain.[30]

On 12 June the Jewish Telegraphic Agency published the information sent by Józef Cyrankiewicz that had first been published in Poland in the

The Vrba–Wetzler report

Polish Socialist Party's organ *Robotnik* on 7 May and in *Dziennik Polski* on 9 June, reporting that the information came from the Jewish Underground Movement in Poland.[31] Four days later (16 June), the *Jewish Chronicle* published a front-page article entitled 'New wave of Nazi terror':

A message which has just been received from the Jewish Underground Movement in Poland, reports that the liquidation of the Terezin (Bohemia) concentration camp, in which there were 70,000 Jews, has begun.

The first 7,000 have already been sent to their doom in Poland. Told that they were going to another labour camp, the victims were transported to the notorious death-camp of Oswiecim, where they were put to death in the lethal chambers.

The BBC also had the same information, but chose not to broadcast it on the Home Service. At noon, the BBC broadcast snippets of information derived from the Vrba–Wetzler report to Germany from a Britain shaken after a night of pounding by V-1 rockets. Across the channel, the Battle of Normandy, which began on 6 June, was in progress.

The Vrba–Wetzler report

According to Ruth Linn (2004: 30),

The Vrba–Wetzler report may be credited with making three major breakthroughs. First, before its arrival the Allies thought Auschwitz was a huge labor concentration camp mainly for Poles. Second, unlike previous Polish reports, it was the first detached and reliable report. Third, it shook Swiss (pro-German) neutrality and jolted the Swiss into undertaking wide publication of the German mass killing at Auschwitz.

Only the third claim is true, but it is very important to understand the impact of the Vrba–Wetzler report. As shown in Chapter 5, the Allies had received a number of reports on the camp through 1943 and 1944, and were well aware that it was not 'just' a concentration camp. In mid-March 1944, the US had sanctioned the press release of the Polish Ministry of Information that summarized the detailed and reliable summer 1943 reports sent by the Polish Underground. Censored parts of it had appeared in the mainstream press in Britain and an article which faithfully reported the first part of the report, highlighting the scale of the Nazi killing of Jews at the camp, was published in the relatively obscure *Polish Jewish Observer* on 7 April 1944.

More information about Auschwitz was able to come into the open in June and July 1944, despite resistance in Britain, for a number of reasons. First, the information from the Vrba–Wetzler report was distributed through different channels, meaning that a range of actors who were not constrained by British censorship policy were informed of

230   Reassessing the significance of the Vrba–Wetzler report

Auschwitz's true function for the first time. Second, the Vrba–Wetzler report itself was very compelling testimony. Third, the account of the camp given in the Vrba–Wetzler report was confirmed by the reports of Mordowicz and Rosin and the Polish major (Jerzy Tabeau), and was supported by information about the camp that had arrived in Britain over the previous year and half.

The path to the West of the Vrba–Wetzler report is now well documented (Baron 2000; Linn 2004; Penkower 1983). It passed through the hands of many different people, most of whom were not privy to the knowledge of the camp held by the Polish Government in Exile; leading Jewish representatives; members of the British PWE and FO and the US State Department, War Office and OSS; and readers of the *Polish Jewish Observer* (see Chapter 4). Rudolf Vrba and Alfred Wetzler escaped from Auschwitz on 11 April 1944 and crossed into Slovakia eleven days later. They came into contact with a Dr Pollack, whom Vrba had met when first imprisoned, and they were directed to Žilina to meet the Slovak Jewish Council. They met the German-speaking lawyer Dr Oskar Neumann, the head of the Slovakian Jewish Working Group. Neumann put the two escapees in different rooms, where each reported his account to Neumann's assistant, Oscar Krasnansky. Over three days Vrba and Wetzler were questioned, convincing Neumann and Krasnansky of the veracity of their experiences. The written reports of the two men were merged into a single report and translated into German. The report gave details of the evolution and geography of the camp, a chronology of transports of Jews and descriptions of the gas chambers, and provided figures for the number of people killed.[32] On 6 June Arnošt Rosin and Czesław Mordowicz, who had escaped from Auschwitz on 27 May, also crossed into Slovakia. Believing the war to be over on hearing news of the Allied landings in Normandy, they bought drinks with dollars pilfered from Auschwitz. They were arrested on currency violation charges and imprisoned for eight days. A fine paid by the Slovak Jewish Council saw their release and, on 17 June, they were questioned by Krasnansky. These two escapees corroborated Vrba and Wetzler's account, adding that between 15 and 27 May more than 100,000 Hungarian Jews had reached the camp, where almost all had been summarily gassed.

In late April, the deputy chairman of the Aid and Rescue Committee in Budapest, Dr Rezső Kasztner, was handed the Vrba–Wetzler report on one of his regular trips to Bratislava. Kasztner was engaged in negotiations with Adolf Eichmann, head of Section IV B4 of the Reich Security Main Office responsible for Jewish affairs and evacuation, during May and June. The stakes of Kasztner's discussions with Eichmann could not be higher. On 25 April, Eichmann had summoned Joel Brand, another

The Vrba–Wetzler report

member of the Aid and Rescue Committee, to a meeting to propose an exchange of Jews for trucks. Eichmann stated,

I have got you here so that we can talk business. I have already made investigations about you and your people and I have verified your ability to make a deal. Now then, I am prepared to sell you one million Jews ... Blood for money – cash for blood. You can take them from any country you like, wherever you can find them – Hungary, Poland, the Ostmark, from Theresienstadt, from Auschwitz, wherever you like.[33]

Brand travelled to Istanbul, leaving Budapest on 17 May, to make contact with the Allies. The British were not interested in the deal and were able to detain Brand when he travelled on to Aleppo to meet Moshe Shertok (also known as Moshe Sharett), head of the Jewish Agency's political department.[34] The British finally ended any hope of the 'blood for goods' deal by publicly leaking details to the press on 19 July. Since the deal was first reported on the BBC it seems that the PWE (and hence the Foreign Office) released the information. The following day *The Times* framed the issue as one in which the Germans sought to 'blackmail, deceive and split the Allies'. However, the possibility of a deal had allowed Kasztner to extract a small concession from Eichmann and save 1,685 Jews.

Kasztner did not disclose the existence of the Vrba–Wetzler report to the Hungarian Jews during the period of his negotiations with Eichmann, and his failure to reveal the truth about Auschwitz has remained controversial. In 1957 he was shot dead as he arrived home in Tel Aviv by Ze'ev Eckstein. Eckstein and his collaborators received a life sentence, but were pardoned after seven years. For Holocaust scholar Yehuda Bauer (1997: 206), Kasztner's rescue efforts made him a 'real-life hero'; that is, a man with faults trying his best in negotiating with a totalitarian regime and succeeding in saving at least some Jews.

The Vrba–Wetzler report is also thought to have been handed to the Czechoslovak Legation in Switzerland, along with Tabeau's report, on 10 June (Linn 2004: 28). Jerzy Tabeau had escaped from Auschwitz in November and travelled west, hoping to get to London. He reached Budapest on 19 March, the day of the German invasion of Hungary, and decided to return to Poland. Prior to departure he handed his report to the Polish Underground in Budapest. The Polish Underground forwarded the report to Switzerland (Świebocki 1997: 22).

In Bern, the Czechoslovak representative, Dr Jaromir Kopecky, understood that Czech Jews were in imminent danger of being gassed after six months of quarantine. That six-month period had started on 20 December. Kopecky contacted the British Legation in Bern, Allen

232   Reassessing the significance of the Vrba–Wetzler report

Dulles (head of US intelligence in Switzerland), and the World Jewish Congress in Geneva. Elizabeth Wiskemann of the British Legation sent Kopecky's message to London on 14 June.[35] It was received the following day (Karny 1994: 558). Dulles passed Kopecky's telegram message on to Roswell McClelland, the representative of the War Refugee Board, who cabled it to Washington on 16 June. The telegram advised that 'the first group of approximately 4,000 Jews that had arrived in Birkenau from Terezin at the beginning of September 1943, was after six months of quarantine, killed with gas on the 7th of March 1944'.[36] Part of Kopecky's telegram of 14 June read,

According [to the] report made by two Slovakian Jews who escaped from Birkenau to Bratislava and whose reliability is assured by Jewish leaders there, 3000 Czechoslovakian Jews who were brought from Terezin to Birkenau on December 20 1943 ... will be gassed after six months' quarantine on about June 20 1944. Appealing most urgently that this news may be broadcast immediately through the BBC and American radio in order to prevent at the last moment this new massacre ... Please issue without delay most impressive warning to German butchers who [are] directing slaughter [in] Upper Silesia. Do not mention Bratislava as source. Further reports following. Please inform immediately also the Czechoslovakian government.[37]

The Vrba–Wetzler report was also sent elsewhere. In the second half of June the Jewish leadership in Hungary began distributing it. Miklos Krausz, secretary of the Budapest branch of the Palestine office, received a copy from József Reisner of the Turkish Legation in Budapest (Baron 2000: 21). Krausz was exempt from anti-Jewish laws and had enjoyed refuge at the Swiss Legation. He forwarded a summary of the report to Florian Manoliu of the Romanian Legation in Bern, who passed it to Georges Mantello, then acting as secretary for the El Salvadorean general consul in Geneva. The report was ultimately passed to Walter Garrett of the British Exchange Press in Zurich. From there it was forwarded to London (Linn 2004: 32). Garrett also showed Dulles the actual report on 22 July. Dulles apparently wired the US Secretary of State on 23 June.

Richard Lichtheim of the Jewish Agency in Geneva secured the report and sent a summary to the Agency's leadership in Jerusalem on 19 June. Copies were also distributed by Reverend József Éliás, who had received it from Geza Soos of the small resistance organization known as the Hungarian Independent Movement. Ultimately the report reached Catholic cardinals, Lutheran bishops, the daughter-in-law of the Hungarian regent Admiral Horthy, and members of the Budapest Jewish Council (Judenrat). The BBC's Hungarian Service had been calling for the Church in Hungary to 'denounce racial persecution as clerics have done elsewhere even in Germany' since late May, and these broadcasts might

The Vrba–Wetzler report

have played a role in framing how the Hungarian clergy responded to the Vrba–Wetzler report in the last third of June.[38]

On 20 June Mario Martilotti, a member of the papal nuncio's office in Bern, interviewed Czesław Mordowicz and Rudolf Vrba. The information gathered by Martilotti may have influenced Pope Pius XII's telegram to Admiral Horthy on 25 June. The telegram read,

> We are being beseeched in various quarters to do everything in our power in order that, in this noble and chivalrous nation, the sufferings, already so heavy, endured by a large number of unfortunate people, because of their nationality or race, may not be extended and aggravated. As our Father's heart cannot remain insensitive to these pressing supplications by virtue of our ministry of charity which embraces all men, we address Your Highness personally, appealing to your noble sentiments in full confidence that you will do everything in your power that so many unfortunate people may be spared other afflictions and other sorrows.[39]

As can be readily seen, the telegram was couched in general terms, but its objective to stop the persecution of people because of 'their nationality or race' was clear and the telegram added to the pressure on Admiral Horthy to stop the deportations. Horthy replied via telegram on 1 July assuring the Pope that he would do all he could to ensure the maintenance of humanitarian Christian principles (Morley 2004: 164).[40] The previous day (30 June), King Gustav of Sweden had sent Horthy a telegram which noted the 'extraordinary harsh methods [his] government has applied against the Jewish population of Hungary' and begged 'in the name of humanity that [he] take measures to save those that remain to be saved of this unfortunate people'.[41] The pressure placed on Horthy by the Church and by neutral states, together with the fear of Allied bombing raids on Hungary, influenced Horthy's decision to order a stop to deportations on 6 July, but this news took several days to filter through to Britain (Gilbert 2001a: 266).[42] The last deportation of Jews from Hungary took place on 25 July, well after Horthy had prohibited further transports (Frojimovics 2011: 257).

Information about Auschwitz that arrived in Switzerland was found convincing by the Swiss press. All three reports – Vrba–Wetzler, Mordowicz–Rosin and Tabeau – were distributed in Switzerland concurrently. The circulation of this news in continental Europe also added pressure on the Hungarian regent. Between 23 June and 11 July at least 383 articles about the camp appeared in the Swiss press (Conway 1997). This figure exceeds the number of articles published about the Holocaust during the entire war in *The Times*, the *Daily Telegraph*, the *Manchester Guardian* and the whole of the British popular press.

It is in this context, i.e. public knowledge of the camp in continental Europe, that British responses have to be situated. The dominant view to

234   Reassessing the significance of the Vrba–Wetzler report

date has been that the British political leadership, specifically Prime Minister Winston Churchill and Foreign Secretary Anthony Eden, first learnt of the camp's extermination function in late June 1944. This view is predicated on the assertion that reliable information about the camp did not reach the West until the Vrba–Wetzler report. As Chapters 4 and 5 demonstrated, this is not true. A second argument could be made that neither Churchill nor Eden were aware of information held lower down the command chain. Such a view relies on the claim that the only acceptable proof of their knowledge is documents describing the camp which they can be shown to have seen. Such documents have not been located (though this does not mean that they do not exist or did not, at some point, exist). But if it is argued that neither Churchill nor Eden knew of the extermination facilities at Auschwitz until late June 1944, then this can only be explained (i) by failures, wilful or not, in information dissemination from and within the Foreign Office, the PWE, the Ministry of Information, British intelligence, and by the shortcomings of Brendan Bracken and Desmond Morton, or (ii) by a top-down policy of 'don't tell'. Such a high degree of inefficiency or organized concealment has not been mentioned in the literature on the Second World War, and such a scenario is not convincing. The 'don't tell' thesis may have some merit if it is understood as 'don't be documented telling'. The most likely explanation is that both Churchill and Eden knew of the true nature of Auschwitz by March 1944 at the very latest (more probably they had knowledge of the camp by April 1943), but maintained their silence on the issue due to concerns about refugees, the Second Front and the belief that there was nothing that could be done practically.[43] On 17 March 1944, Eden had even advised Churchill that there was no point to issuing warnings to Germany (see Chapter 5).[44]

The argument that Churchill and Eden knew that the camp was a location where Jews were being systematically murdered in gas chambers is based on powerful and persuasive circumstantial evidence. It is not unthinkable that a confirming document may someday be located in intelligence files. There were several routes by which information about the camp could reach Churchill without leaving a trace in the documentary record. As minister of information, Churchill's close friend Brendan Bracken had responsibilities over the Political Warfare Executive, which on 24 March 1944 acknowledged the killing function of the camp, and he could and should have known about the camp in spring 1943, following the BBC broadcast about Auschwitz in April 1943 and the circulation of the Salski report in May 1943. At any point between April 1943 and mid-1944 Bracken could have advised Churchill during one of their 'kitchen cabinet' evening discussions. A second way the information about the

The Vrba–Wetzler report   235

camp could have passed to Churchill was through his adviser on intelligence, Major Desmond Morton. Morton interviewed Jan Nowak-Jeziorański, who knew about the camp, in early February 1944. Only a couple of weeks later, Nowak-Jeziorański spoke publicly about the slaughter of Jews at Auschwitz and other camps.

The minutes of the Morton–Nowak-Jeziorański meeting do not mention Auschwitz. Since Churchill received intelligence from radio intercepts about the camp in 1941, we can venture that he had some interest in what was happening there. The Morton–Nowak-Jeziorański meeting, though short, was an opportunity for information to be gathered and ultimately passed to Churchill. It is possible that Morton did not raise the issue of the camp because the killing of Jews at the camp was already well known. The third path was through Anthony Eden. There can be no doubt that Frank Savery and Ivone Kirkpatrick knew about the camp in early April 1943 (the BBC's Polish Service broadcast information from Stefan Korboński's 30 March 1943 message about the camp on 11 April 1943), and given that in May 1943 news from Salski's report to Schwarzbart had been distributed to a broad range of officials in the Foreign Office and the Political Warfare Executive and to various branches of British intelligence and military, it is inconceivable that Eden was not advised.[45] Foreign Office officials were well versed in FO protocol and, in the wake of the December 1942 declaration, were cautious in their writings of new information linking atrocities and Jews. Any discussion of the camp is likely to have been conducted orally rather than in writing.

Churchill's attitude to receiving news about the plight of Jews did not always provoke an active response. Reacting to the representation of Polish Jews protesting at the continuation of the German extermination programme, sent by the Polish ambassador Edward Raczyński on 24 February 1944, Churchill informed Eden on 10 March that he (Churchill) 'ought either to keep out of this thing, or make some vigorous protest. A mere acknowledgement would be rather unsuitable'.[46] Eden recommended silence – a response from the prime minister risked encouraging further demands such as the provision of refuge, rescue and/or retaliation – and no reply was sent to the Polish Jews.

In light of these considerations, the scholarly opinion about Churchill's and Eden's response to the information contained in the Vrba–Wetzler report needs reassessment. Penkower (1983: 192) states that Lichtheim's cable on the Vrba–Wetzler report, prepared for Chaim Weizmann and Moshe Shertok, was received on 27 June at Whitehall (Foreign Office). The cable, as well as giving details about Auschwitz, called for reprisals and the bombing of the railway lines and death camp.

236 Reassessing the significance of the Vrba–Wetzler report

On reading the cable Churchill scribbled a note to Eden: 'What can be done? What can be said?' This has, to date, been understood as Churchill gearing up for a proactive response to revelatory news. In the light of the evidence presented here, it looks more like a genuine query in reaction to a rapidly changing environment in which the policy of severe restraint in acknowledging the camp was becoming unsustainable. The British had lost some control of the news agenda, for the most part because of the wide publicity given to the news of Auschwitz published in neutral Switzerland.[47] Despite this, Eden did not meet Jewish representatives – Weizmann and Shertok – at the end of the month. George Hall met them on 30 June. The focus was the Brand mission – the exchange of vehicles for Jews – which had been rumbling through May and June.[48] The British played along until they effectively jettisoned the plan on 7 July after the world had been fully informed of mass extermination of Jews at Auschwitz, and publicly distanced themselves on 19 July by leaking the plan to the press. There would be no deal that could be seen as providing Nazi Germany with resources as this could severely strain the relationship with the USSR.

From 8 June, when the PWE directives to the Hungarian Service called for attention to be focused on Jews being dispatched to Poland, the propaganda policy was to restrict information about the fate of Hungarian Jews to the Hungarian Service (broadcasts might have been made on other European Services, but the records no longer exist to confirm this). On 15 June, PWE directives to the Hungarian Service highlighted the various strands of argument to provide succour to the Jews:

admit that some Hungarians are trying to help the Jews and protect them. At the same time, warn Hungarians that they must do all that is in their power to continue to help the Jews and, above all, to prevent their deportation to Poland.

It might also be pointed out, by a responsible commentator, that it is the special task of the Church and the schools to counter anti-Semitic propaganda and to prevent this poison from spreading in Hungary.

Otherwise, we should continue to quote the earlier authoritative appeals and warnings from Allied spokesmen and Church leaders, and should not put out unofficial appeals.[49]

The following directive written on 22 June (for the period 23 June to 30 July) does not mention Jews, despite information arriving in London from the Vrba–Wetzler report. This may indicate that a policy response to the new situation had not been completely worked out. On 26 June, Alexander Easterman of the WJC wrote to the news director of the BBC, calling for full publicity of the news about Hungary.[50] The following week the directive, written on 29 June, focused on the war situation. The section on Jews stated, 'Do not use unconfirmed reports of the killing of

The Vrba–Wetzler report

Hungarian Jews, but state generally that we know deportation to Poland continues, and recall yet again authoritative warnings and appeals on the Jewish question issued shortly after the occupation.'[51] 'Unconfirmed reports' referred to reports not sanctioned for dissemination by the Foreign Office. This included the Vrba–Wetzler report. Even at the end of June, the British were still attempting to manage the flow of information, despite the widespread dissemination of news of Auschwitz in the Swiss press, among sections of the Hungarian elite and, importantly, amongst an increasing number of people in London. For example, on 28 June George Hall wrote to Alexander Easterman stating that he had nothing to add to the reasons given by Ernest Thurtle (Ministry of Information/Political Warfare Executive) for refusing to broadcast appeals to Hungary from 'distinguished personalities'.[52] Six days later Thurtle himself wrote to Easterman explaining that the PWE did 'not feel appeals by private persons have any useful effect at present' and that the BBC was doing all it could to inform the Hungarian people about the atrocities.[53]

The news management policy adopted in June 1944 certainly supports the view that the information reported in Kopecky's telegram was only broadcast because it was confirmed by Cyrankiewicz's earlier message, and due to pressure from the Czechoslovak Government in Exile and the continuing efforts of the Polish Government in Exile. It further illustrates that the conventional view that the British promptly and decisively set about ensuring the distribution of the Vrba–Weztler report is wide of the mark. Instead, the British demonstrated considerable lethargy in altering their policy position.[54]

It was only on 6 July that the PWE directive to the BBC's Hungarian Service became more direct, calling attention to the fate awaiting Jews at camps in Poland in its summary of news over the previous week. It also noted that King Gustav of Sweden, in a telegram to Admiral Horthy, the regent of Hungary, made an appeal '"in the name of humanity" to use his influence to save Hungarian Jews from further persecution'. The PWE directive did not specify that Hungarian Jews were being sent to Auschwitz, but instructed the Service,

Use any British press comment on the King of Sweden's statement and on any subsequent statement from authoritative Allied sources. Keep any BBC comment to the bare minimum, suggesting only that the fact that Hungary has allowed many thousands of Jews to be deported to Poland, to almost certain death, is in the public opinion of the United Nations, one of the greatest sins of Hungary's war record.[55]

In late June and early July, stories on the mass killing of Jews reappeared in the inside pages of national newspapers on both sides of the Atlantic.

238   Reassessing the significance of the Vrba–Wetzler report

The Vrba–Wetzler report opened a window for information held by Polish Jewish representatives and the Polish Government in Exile to be disseminated, and stimulated even more strenuous efforts to inform the public. To date, most of the stories published during this period have been read as referring exclusively to the Vrba–Wetzler report. But this is not the case with regard to most of the newspaper articles published in late June and early July, including reports mentioning Oświęcim featured in the *Jewish Chronicle*. One report that was derived, at least in part, from data sourced from the Vrba–Wetzler report was published on page 5 of the *New York Times* on 20 June 1944. Entitled 'Czechs report massacre', it stated that the Czechoslovak State Council had released a report on 19 June advising that 7,000 Czechoslovak Jews from Terezin had been killed and 'that the victims were dragged to gas chambers in the notorious German concentration camps at Birkenau and Oswiecim'.[56] This short twenty-two line article was unusual for the *New York Times* in that it named the camp, noted gas chambers and made reference to Jewish victims. It also advised readers that the existence of the gas chambers had been confirmed by a young Pole recently arrived in London – a reference, in all likelihood, to Jan Wolny.

Earlier, in Britain, on 16 June, in addition to reporting on Cyrankiewicz's March message about Jews from Czechoslovakia, the *Jewish Chronicle* carried a story on page 8 that evidently took British government sensibilities into consideration in its presentation of the news. Entitled 'Bomb death camps', the *Jewish Chronicle* reported on the 11 June demand by Isaac Gruenbaum (Jewish Agency, Jerusalem) that Auschwitz be bombed. Gruenbaum was well informed of Auschwitz's function as a death camp and had seen at least some of the data from the Vrba–Wetzler report.[57] The newspaper indicated that Gruenbaum had 'introduced an unusual idea which might commend itself to the humanitarian democracies when he demanded that the Allied Air Forces should smash up the Nazi death camps in Poland, giving such measures the same priority as the military objectives'.

A week later (23 June 1944), the tone of the *Jewish Chronicle* remained cautious and restrained. A page 6 article entitled 'Peril to Jewish remnant – Archbishop's plea' reported that the chief rabbi contended that the Council of Christians and Jews could assist in stimulating public opinion in the Allied nations to aid Jews in peril.

On 14 June a report sent from Tadeusz Bór-Komorowski in Poland, and de-encrypted by Polish intelligence in London on 19 June, recorded that 100,000 Jews from Hungary had been killed at Oświęcim.[58] This reiterated data de-encrypted on 16 June that was sent by Stanisław Jankowski on behalf of Leon Feiner for Emanuel Scherer.[59] The Jewish

The Vrba–Wetzler report 239

representatives on the Polish National Council continued to play a key role in disseminating news from Auschwitz, as they had in 1943 and in the first half of 1944. The information sent from Warsaw was released by the Polish government. The *New York Times* on 25 June 1944 quoted Emanuel Scherer in a page 5 article entitled 'New mass executions in Poland report – victims come from all groups, Underground says'. The *New York Times* framed the Jewish fate as part of a wider experience of German atrocities 'regardless of race or creed', though it did note that at Oświęcim the Jews were gassed first, followed by war prisoners and then invalids. The report did not specify that the victims of the 'new mass murders' were from Hungary.

The following day, the *Jewish Telegraphic Agency* frankly reported the information sent from Poland, stating that 'one-hundred thousand Hungarian Jews have been deported to Poland and executed in gas chambers in the notorious Oswiecim "death camp"'.[60] The reporting of the data released by the *New York Times* and the JTA may have encouraged the BBC's Home Service to broadcast the information in its 6 p.m. news bulletin on 26 June. The broadcast was unusually frank, but did not name the camp, stating that '100,000 Jews, recently deported from Hungary, have been murdered by mass gassing in the lethal chambers of the notorious German camp in Polish Galicia'.[61] Since directives to the Home Service no longer exist, it is not possible to establish precisely why the 'German camp' was not named. However, the use of the word 'notorious' indicates that the camp was well known. For many journalists, FO and PWE officials it was. But the listening public would not have been able to identify the camp. The BBC's reference to 'the notorious camp' suggested that its audience should have known which camp was being talked about and thereby gave the impression that news had been readily available previously. It had not. By suggesting that it had, the Home Service implied that the audience had not been paying attention if they did not know, rather than, as was the case, that the Home Service had failed to broadcast news about the mass killing of Jews at Auschwitz that had flowed steadily into Britain through 1943 and 1944.

Given that the Polish government routinely handed information about the camp to the British through 1943 and 1944, the argument that the camp's name was withheld because the Poles did not want Jewish suffering to overshadow that of Poles can be rejected. It is more likely that the British were attempting to manage the flow of information about Auschwitz to the general public. The withholding of the name of the camp hindered efforts to leverage public opinion to pressure the British government to sanction the bombing of Auschwitz.

240   Reassessing the significance of the Vrba–Wetzler report

The next day, on 27 June 1944, the *Manchester Guardian* published an article on page 4 entitled 'The massacres of Jews'. It reported that Emanuel Scherer had received a message from the Jewish Underground labour movement in Poland informing him, according to the newspaper, that 'in the Oswiecim concentration camp the Germans are now gassing and slaughtering the remnants of Polish Jews'.[62] The *Manchester Guardian* was clearly referring to the same material reported in the *New York Times* on 25 June and, like the American paper, it discussed the fate of Polish Jews alongside others. It reported 'prisoners of war and Poles being slaughtered in masses'. On page 6, a second article discussing the fate of Jews was published, entitled 'Fate of Jews in Hungary'. This short, three-paragraph piece advised readers, 'Information that the Germans are systematically exterminating Hungarian Jews, has lately become more substantial'. Again, the article drew on material passed by the Polish government.

On 28 June, the *Manchester Guardian* reported on a statement made by the World Jewish Congress which referred directly to the 14 June message from Poland. The newspaper informed readers that '100,000 Jews, recently deported from Hungary to Poland, have been slaughtered by mass gassing in the lethal chambers of the notorious German death-camp in Polish Galicia'. This sentence is more or less the same as that used on the BBC's Home Service broadcast of 26 June. This may signal that the WJC used the BBC's formulation to encourage its British audience to respond to the information. The WJC also declared that the 'Jewish victims of Nazi mass-murder in Europe now number 4,000,000', while its reference to the period from 15 May to 27 May, during which 'the Germans transported from Hungary 62 railway trains laden with Jewish children, aged between two and nine ... [passing] through Plaszow, near Cracow, bound for an unknown destination', was derived from information provided in Bór-Komorowski's 7 June radio message and possibly supported by data from Mordowicz and Rosin.[63] Tellingly, the WJC did not mention Oświęcim by name, despite the 'unknown destination' being cited in the reports from which their material was taken. Bór-Komorowski had been specific, writing that the trains passed via Płaszów en route to Oświęcim. The use of this data indicates that the WJC had access to additional information not incorporated in the WJC statement. The lack of editorial comment on the WJC statement in the *Manchester Guardian* suggests that the British censorship regime continued to impact on the dissemination of news about the camp in the British press.

On its front page for 30 June, the *Jewish Chronicle* related the information released by the Polish government regarding the 100,000 Jews murdered at Oświęcim. This data was supplemented by information

The Vrba–Wetzler report 241

derived from the Vrba–Wetzler report that was publicized by the Czechoslovak State Council on 19 June. The paper noted that 7,000 Czechoslovak Jews from Terezin (Theresienstadt) had been 'dragged to the death camps of Oswiecim and Birkenau and slaughtered there'. The editorial in the *Jewish Chronicle* sought to rationalize the general lack of response in Britain to the mass slaughter happening less than 1,000 miles away. It recorded, 'few cries of indignation are heard in this country, perhaps because the chords of sympathy have been dulled or atrophied by sheer over-use – one of the sinister by-products of the orgy of German official murder'. In reality, the vast majority of British citizens had no idea of what was happening in Auschwitz, since the information had not been widely disseminated in the national press.[64] The *Jewish Chronicle* itself did not publish much of the information which was available.

In contrast, the *Polish Jewish Observer* was, as usual, direct, and gave full prominence to the horrendous news. On 30 June its main front-page story was entitled '100,000 Hungarian Jews put to death at Oswiecim camp, says secret cable'. It repeated the information from the Polish government that had appeared in the *New York Times* and the *Manchester Guardian* during the previous week. The newspaper predicted that 'the extermination of the entire Hungarian Jewish community will be completed within possibly a few weeks unless some precipitous action is taken'. The paper's editorial for that day was entitled 'Bomb Oswiecim' and made reference to Isaac Gruenbaum's demand that the death camps in Poland be bombed. Unlike the *Jewish Chronicle* article from 11 June, the *Polish Jewish Observer* provided the name of the camp – Oświęcim.

Three days later, on 3 July 1944, the *New York Times* published the frankest report to appear in that paper describing Auschwitz. Significantly, the newspaper never explained that Auschwitz and Oświęcim were the same camp, which no doubt inhibited many readers from linking this and subsequent stories referring to Auschwitz with the June stories describing Oświęcim.[65] The article, on page 3, was entitled 'Inquiry confirms Nazi death camps – 1,715,000 Jews said to have been put to death by Germans up to April 15'. Drawing on reports of relief committees with headquarters in Switzerland (International Church Movement Ecumenical Refugee Commission, Geneva, and the Flüchtlingshilfe of Zurich, headed by Paul Voght), the paper named Auschwitz and Birkenau as the location of '"extermination camps" where more than 1,715,000 Jewish refugees were put to death between April 15, 1942 and April 15, 1944'. It listed the number of Jews killed according to their country of origin and made reference to the fate of Hungarian Jewry.[66] The fact that the list of the number of Jews killed corresponded to the Vrba–Wetzler report, and the naming of the camp as Auschwitz and

242   Reassessing the significance of the Vrba–Wetzler report

Birkenau (rather than Oświęcim, as the camp was described in Polish-origin reports), indicate that the Vrba–Wetzler report was the source of the story (Świebocki 1997: 61; Lipstadt 1986: 234). The *New York Times* ran the story after the data from the Vrba–Wetzler report had been repackaged into what became known as the Voght report (Leff 2005: 276). Until this date, reports in the printed press referred, with some exceptions, to material sent by the Polish Underground.

The 'Inquiry confirms Nazi death camps' article constituted the first time that the particularity of the Nazi extermination of Jews at the camp was highlighted in the *New York Times*. Earlier reports either were very brief (20 June article, 'Czechs report massacre') or depicted the Jewish fate as an experience shared by other groups (25 June article, 'New mass executions in Poland report – victims come from all groups, Underground says'). This is significant both in terms of the internal policy of the *New York Times*, and in the context of American propaganda and censorship policy. Clearly, pressure on the War Refugee Board by Jewish representatives (and others), and later by the War Refugee Board on other branches of the American government and on the *New York Times* itself (Arthur Sulzberger was a friend of Henry Morgenthau, War Refugee Board chair), had an effect.

In addition, the repackaging of data from the Vrba–Wetzler report into the report of the churchman Paul Voght was important as it lent additional credibility to the information published by disguising its Jewish origin to audiences encumbered by varying degrees of anti-Semitism. On 6 July, the *New York Times* again published information from the Voght report in an article, on page 6, entitled 'Two death camps – places of horror – German establishment for mass killing of Jews described by Swiss'.[67]

In Britain, information from the Vrba–Wetzler report was not referred to in the national press. The *Daily Telegraph* on 3 July reported a big raid on Budapest and mentioned oil refineries and railway infrastructure as targets. There was no mention of the deportation of Jews. On 4 July 1944 the *Manchester Guardian*'s special correspondent, in an article on page 6 entitled 'Mass slaughter of Hungarian Jews – a notorious camp', wrote, 'No further reports have yet been received about the extermination of Hungarian Jews in the Polish [*sic*] death camp at Oswiecim', and referred to the previous week's statement from the Polish government 'that about 100,000 Hungarian Jews had already been put to death in one of the most notorious German slaughter-houses in Eastern Europe'.[68] It then referred to the Polish Underground paper *Robotnik*, which had published the information from Józef Cyrankiewicz's March report on the camp on 7 May 1944. The article mentioned the killing of Jews in gas chambers at Oświęcim.

The Vrba–Wetzler report

However, in the context of widespread knowledge of the camp amongst key British, Polish and Jewish leaders and officials in Britain, and public knowledge in Switzerland, the strained tone of the article – indicated by reference to the fact that by June 1942 an estimated 50,000 had been killed and 'since then the death-rate has increased almost daily' rather than to the more recent data available – strongly suggests constraints imposed by the British censorship regime. The *Manchester Guardian*'s special correspondent evidently had contact with members of the Polish National Council (material in the article was derived from Polish sources), most probably Emanuel Scherer and Ignacy Schwarzbart, who were well informed of the scale of the slaughter at the camp. The identity of the special correspondent is not known.[69]

David Engel (1993: 287) notes that the Polish government had been sent a message from the Polish Consulate General in Istanbul on 25 June that put the number of Hungarian Jews deported to Poland at 400,000.[70] The date that this message was received and de-encrypted is not known. It is very unlikely that it occurred prior to 28 June, the date the *Manchester Guardian* published the Polish government's earlier figure of 100,000, but on 3 July the Polish Ministry of Foreign Affairs advised Owen O'Malley, the British ambassador to the Polish government, and Rudolf Schoenfeld, the United States' chargé d'affaires, that 400,000 Jews had been deported and 'directed to the concentration camp in Oświęcim and there put to death'.[71] Given that some time was required to process intelligence, to translate the data and to formulate an official letter to representatives of Allied governments, it seems that the Polish government responded to the information as soon as it was received. Schoenfeld acknowledged receipt of the information on 5 July, indicating the he had advised the US government. On 6 July, O'Malley informed Tadeusz Romer, Polish minister of foreign affairs, that he had advised Anthony Eden.[72]

In addition to the information from Polish sources, an appeal made to the Christian world by the Federal Council of Churches of Christ of America, which had received a report from the World Council of Churches in Geneva, was published by the Jewish Telegraphic Agency on 30 June. It claimed that 450,000 Hungarian Jews had already been deported 'to Auschwitz in Upper Silesia'.[73] There does not seem to be any reference in the British press to the appeal or to the article by the JTA, although the information reported was available in London. Isaac Gruenbaum sent the news on 27 June to Moshe Shertok, via the British Foreign Office.[74]

It is not possible to state with certainty whether the information from the Polish Consulate in Istanbul was passed to the British press prior to 4 July. However, the message was circulated beyond the diplomatic corps

244 Reassessing the significance of the Vrba–Wetzler report

in London. Sydney Silverman asked British Foreign Secretary Anthony Eden in the House of Commons on 5 July to 'confirm the figures which have been given in some quarters, namely, that in recent days the number deported amounted to 400,000'. Eden's response was, 'I would really rather not give figures unless one is absolutely sure'.[75] He did not confirm any figures or provide any indication of the true state of knowledge of the camp in the Foreign Office.

The previous day (4 July) the Foreign Office had received an eight-page summary of what was happening at Auschwitz from the Czechoslovak Ministry of Foreign Affairs.[76] This summary was put together using data from the reports of Vrba and Wetzler, Mordowicz and Rosin and Tabeau. The covering note to the summary indicated that the Czechoslovak president, Edvard Beneš, was prepared to 'associate himself with any protest that might be organised'. The Foreign Office therefore faced considerable pressure to act from the Czechoslovak and Polish governments, and from Jewish representatives.

On 6 July, the *Daily Telegraph* devoted three short paragraphs at the bottom of page 2 to the Jewish deportations, and paraphrased Eden's statement in the House of Commons, reporting that there was 'no definite information about the mass deportation of Jews from Hungary to Poland for the purpose of massacre', but that during the process of deportation 'many persons [had] been killed'. Eden's statement was at odds with the information supplied by the Polish government.[77] Eden's refusal to speak clearly about what was happening to Hungarian Jewry was a crucial part of the British strategy to regain control of the news agenda. By withholding confirmation of the news received from the Polish government and from the reports distributed in Switzerland, including those of Vrba and Wetzler and Tabeau, the British Foreign Secretary sought to exercise control over how information about the camp was assessed and reported in Britain, and to limit the extent to which it was reported, and thereby obviate civil-society pressure to act decisively.

The *Polish Jewish Observer* again provided the frankest report on the fate of Hungarian Jewry in Britain. On 7 July it published an article entitled 'Toll of Hungarian Jews now reaches 400,000'. The same day, in contrast to its previous caution, the *Jewish Chronicle* published a page 6 article entitled 'The Hungarian massacres – Mr Eden's tragic confirmation', which reported on the debate in the House of Commons, and a page 7 article entitled '400,000 Hungarian Jews liquidated'. Despite Eden's very cautious statement, the debate had loosened the grip of the voluntary censorship regime. That evening, the BBC's Home Service in its 9 p.m. bulletin mentioned Oświęcim as a place of extermination for the first time (Milland 1998b: 190).

The contents of this broadcast were extraordinary given the tight control exercised over the BBC by the PWE through the war and the general reticence of the Home Service to draw attention to the mass murder of Jews. Unfortunately, it is not possible to reconstruct the decision-making process that led to this broadcast, or the discussions within the Home Service subsequent to the transmission, as the news directives to the Home Service are not available.[78] Although the broadcast took place after some information about Oświęcim had been published in the national press, it provided new information to a mass audience and lent the BBC's credibility and authority to the information about Oświęcim.

However, the story was not prioritized. It was not mentioned in the introductory preamble to the news which alerted the audience to the stories that would be developed later in the programme. Instead, the account about Oświęcim was the last of nine reports on the 9 p.m. news. It was preceded by seven news reports about the progress of the war – in Normandy, in Italy, off the Dutch coast, in the Far East, on the Eastern Front, over Germany and over Upper Silesia – and a report on Roosevelt's and Churchill's message to President Chiang Kai-shek to mark the seventh anniversary of the outbreak of war in China. It was followed by 'War Reports' which broadcast testimony from servicemen on duty engaging the enemy and from BBC correspondents in the field. In short, the Oświęcim story was squeezed between reports describing the progress of the war and the audience was not prepared in advance to receive the important information that was broadcast. Furthermore, there was no substantive follow-up to the broadcast. The *contents* of the Oświęcim story were anomalous in terms of the BBC's and PWE's broader broadcasting policy in relation to Jews, but the way the story was framed, both in the news programme on 7 July and in the subsequent treatment of the story, was very much in line with BBC, Ministry of Information and PWE policy not to stress the mass murder of Jews.

The broadcast noted that the information had been received from the Polish authorities in London. It stated that more than 'four hundred thousand Hungarian Jews [had been] sent to the concentration camp at Oświęcim', most killed in gas chambers.[79] The report then referred to Bór-Komorowski's message of 7 June regarding the transport of Jewish children, and noted that adults had also been deported to Poland. The broadcast added that 'these people had been told that they would be exchanged for prisoners-of-war'. It is not certain when the BBC came into possession of this last piece of information, but it was supplied to the Home Service by the Council for Rescue of the Jews in Poland, which had received such information in early June.[80] It is therefore likely that

246   Reassessing the significance of the Vrba–Wetzler report

the PWE was aware, at least to some degree, of the Nazi ruses to encourage Hungarian Jews to follow the instructions given to them and to board the trains that were to take them to Auschwitz. The final section of the broadcast declared Oświęcim to be 'the biggest concentration camp in Poland' and that in 1942 gas chambers had been installed capable of killing 6,000 people a day.

The following day (8 July) *The Times* reported in a page 3 article entitled 'Hungarian Jews' fate – murder in gas chambers' that the Polish Ministry of Information had received details of the 400,000 Hungarian Jews sent, in the main, 'to the concentration camp in Oswiecim', and proceeded to repeat some of the information published in the *Manchester Guardian*'s report of 28 June and broadcast on the Home Service the previous evening. The index of the paper on page 5 reported that 'most of the Hungarian Jews whom the Germans sent to the concentration camp at Oswiecim in Poland were put to death in gas chambers there'. However, the lack of official British government confirmation of these stories impacted on how they were received by the general public. The report in *The Times* on 8 July and the 9 p.m. Home Service news bulletin from 7 July strongly suggest that there was some relaxation in British censorship policy, most likely as a result of Polish and Czechoslovakian government pressure, as well as due to the lobbying efforts of Jewish representatives in Britain.

The news released in London was also published in Australia over the weekend of 8 and 9 July. Five Australian newspapers revealed that 400,000 Hungarian Jews had been killed at Oświęcim, and all drew on Bór-Komorowski's 7 June radio message recording the transport of Hungarian Jews through Płaszów en route to Oświęcim.[81]

By 14 July, much of the previous circumspection displayed in the *Jewish Chronicle* had disappeared. A front-page story highlighted 'Hungarian Jews doomed – planned extermination', and reported on Brendan Bracken's comment that the slaughter of the Jews was the '[b]iggest scandal in the history of human crime'. It cited data from the Vrba–Wetzler report, stating that the death toll from the death camps (meaning Oświecim and Birkenau) was 1,715,000 Jews, and gave readers of the *Jewish Chronicle* (mainly British Jews) a fuller picture of what had happened at the camp.[82] This data was not published in the British national press, or broadcast on the BBC's Home Service.

The national media in Britain did not report the reliable and significant information published in the *Polish Jewish Observer* in April 1944, or that contained in the 21 March 1944 Polish government press release. Only very limited use was made of the Vrba–Wetzler report. The news of the camp that was disseminated in Britain's national newspapers came

The Vrba–Wetzler report

mainly from Polish sources, and only selective use was made of information from other sources (Vrba–Wetzler, Mordowicz–Rosin and Tabeau). These reports were distributed widely in Switzerland in June 1944, but their data was used very sparingly in Britain. The first significant mention of information from Vrba and Wetzler was the 14 July story on Hungarian Jewry in the *Jewish Chronicle* – that is, after Eden spoke in the Commons and eleven days after the same news had been reported in the *New York Times*.

In the US, the references to the camp that drew on Vrba and Wetzler were camouflaged under the cover of the Voght report. Furthermore, the packaging of the Vrba–Wetzler report with the corroborating data from Mordowicz–Rosin and, importantly, the report of the Polish major (Jerzy Tabeau) was crucial for the publicity that the information about Auschwitz received in Switzerland and in US decision-making circles (War Refugee Board, State Department). This triptych of reports *did* break the US and British censorship regime on the reporting of the mass murder of Jews at Auschwitz in the mainstream press, and news of the camp complex did reach sections of the general public in Britain and in the US. However, as illustrated above, the release of information even then remained partial, limited or marginalized inside mainstream newspapers. These reports did permit those with knowledge of the camp to press for action, and added a renewed sense of urgency to their efforts, but because the general population in Britain and the US remained largely ignorant, those calling for action could not leverage public opinion to their cause.

Tony Kushner (1997: 165) contends that British activists campaigning for aid for, and the rescue of, Europe's Jews 'were exhausted and demoralized by the summer of 1944'. This was in no small part due to the sustained refusal of the British government, in particular the Foreign Office, to alter its policy position on refugees, declarations and warnings. In short, the British state apparatus's negative response to appeals relating to Europe's Jews after the Bermuda conference in April 1943 wore down British, Polish and Jewish campaigners. By mid-1944 any response at all from the British government was appreciated by those seeking to aid and rescue European Jewry. The discourse that nothing more could be done, and that the government was doing everything possible, had been internalized to the extent that 'a sense of indebtedness and an unwillingness to embarrass the state' (Kushner 1997: 167) characterized those British Jewish representatives who were offered an audience at the Foreign Office.

This 'cult of gratitude' can be linked to the way in which representatives of the British state responded to reports about Jews. On 13 December 1943, for example, Ignacy Schwarzbart argued at a meeting of the British

248   Reassessing the significance of the Vrba–Wetzler report

Section of the World Jewish Congress that reports relating to Jews were 'dismissed as propaganda'.[83] Both the Foreign Office and the Home Office did not welcome news about Jews that would demand a response, and Schwarzbart's view was undoubtedly correct. Such dismissals should be seen as a strategy to marginalize news of the Holocaust, which aimed to inhibit demands to engage in actions that did not have purely military or strategic aims as their focus. When information was reluctantly released, as, for example, the BBC's broadcast about gassing at the 'notorious camp' in Polish Galicia, it was framed as though this news was well known to the public, thereby undermining its impact. Even when more complete information about the camp was broadcast on 7 July during the 9 p.m. news bulletin on the Home Service, the lack of subsequent commentary or follow-up weakened its efficacy in informing the public about the camp.

In contrast, in the US, the creation of the War Refugee Board invigorated activists during 1944. State funding for the institution was not particularly significant, but the need to raise money (and in reality this meant fundraising among American Jewish communities) engaged the concerned public.[84] On 14 May 1944, an interview with John Pehle, executive director of the War Refugee Board, was broadcast by the National Broadcasting Company (NBC). In this interview Pehle outlined the need for co-operation with civil-society organizations (United Jewish Appeal, Joint Distribution Committee, the United Palestine Appeal and the National Refugee Service), and expressed the hope that those who supported the work of the WRB would 'respond generously to the campaigns of effective private agencies'.[85] Such publicity bore results. Donations for rescue and relief to the American Jewish Joint Distribution Committee doubled in 1944 to $20 million (Kushner 1997: 198). Donors became stakeholders in the activities of agencies engaged in rescue and relief activities, producing a virtuous circle of activism between the WRB, various civil-society organizations and some publics. Nevertheless, even in the US, what was happening to European Jewry was not widely understood, given the way in which the news was presented in the American press (Lipstadt 1986; Leff 2005). This certainly limited the pressure that could be applied on the British and American governments to sanction bombing raids on Auschwitz.

Calls to bomb the camp

The distribution of the Vrba–Wetzler report led to calls to the British and American governments to bomb the camp.[86] On 16 May 1944 Rabbi Michael Weissmandel and Gisa Fleischmann of the Jewish Underground in Slovakia sent a message west, calling for the railway line from Budapest to Auschwitz to be bombed (Gilbert 2001a: 245; Penkower 1983: 185, 190).[87] This message reached Isaac Sternbuch of the American Orthodox Jewish Rescue committee, Va'ad Ha Hatsala, on 19 May. Sternbuch travelled immediately to the British military attaché in Bern, Switzerland, to press for the tracks to Auschwitz on the Kosice–Presov route to be bombed. Via the Polish Legation, Sternbuch sent cables to Agudas Israel, an important Jewish organization, in London and New York. The Jewish Agency's Isaac Gruenbaum made similar demands, but also asked for the death camps in Poland to be bombed.

In mid-June the Czech government's representative in Switzerland, Jaromir Kopecky, cabled his government in London with the request that the camp be bombed. On 24 June Roswell McClelland of the War Refugee Board cabled John Pehle with the view that the only way to slow or to stop the deportations of Hungarian Jewry was to bomb the railway track on the Csap–Kosice–Presov route. Pehle passed McClelland's telegram to the assistant secretary of war, John McCloy, on 29 June. The War Department had, on 26 June, already rejected such a request made by the president of Agudas Israel, Jacob Rosenheim (Penkower 1983: 192; Wyman 1994: 570). This decision was not the result of analysis of air operations, but of War Department policy (Wyman 1994: 571) not to use armed forces to rescue refugees. The fact that these 'refugees' were targeted by the Nazis for elimination did not alter War Department policy. McCloy rejected the new request on 4 July.

In London, the appeal calling for the camp and railway lines to be bombed that was handed by Richard Lichtheim to the British representative in Switzerland with the request that it be forwarded to Chaim Weizmann and Moshe Shertok was received at the Foreign Office and read by Winston Churchill on 27 June. But no concrete action was forthcoming. Scholars have generally argued that Eden and Churchill were in favour of a bombing raid on the camp (Wyman 1994: 574; Penkower 1983: 192), and these two important figures did make very supportive comments. Churchill wrote to Eden on 7 July, stating, 'You and I are in entire agreement. Get anything out of the Air Force you can, and invoke me if necessary'. Gilbert (1993) rightly notes that such a direct request was unusual – he would normally give verbal instructions to raise the matter at a subsequent War Cabinet. Eden contacted the Secretary of State for Air, Sir Archibald Sinclair, who advised him that bombing the railways was not possible. Though Eden displayed some displeasure with this response, the issue was not followed up. Wyman (1994: 575) suggests that Foreign Office officials were reticent about the entire plan to bomb the tracks and camp, and failed to provide the Air

250 Reassessing the significance of the Vrba–Wetzler report

Ministry with maps that it had requested at the beginning of August. Technical issues were cited as a reason for not pursuing the bombing plan (Gilbert 2001a: 285).[88] However, since the Air Ministry had already reviewed the issue of bombing in 1941 (see below), and, as noted, a map of the Oświęcim region was catalogued by the geographic section of the British General Staff in June 1943, the argument about a lack of maps is not convincing.[89] On 1 September, Eden's deputy (Richard Law) advised both Weizmann and Archibald Sinclair that the bombing proposal was off the agenda.

The view that Churchill and Eden were actually supportive of the bombing plan rather than simply asserting their support can be questioned. First, this support was not extended continuously. As both Churchill and Eden were well aware, changing policy in the way that they allegedly wished – that is, to support a bombing raid with a non-military objective – would require repeated intervention with officials who were supposed to plan and execute the proposal. This did not happen. Second, the underlying assumption behind our previous understanding of Churchill's and Eden's comments has been that June 1944 was the first time that either Eden or Churchill learnt of the camp as a place where Jews were being systematically murdered in vast numbers. This assumption is now, to say the least, highly questionable. Their response to the public knowledge of the camp, and hence the public knowledge of their knowledge of the camp, has to be taken into account.[90]

Both Churchill and (to a lesser extent) Eden harboured concerns about how their actions would be seen in the future. Churchill went so far as to write (with a coterie of able assistants) a history of the Second World War, which helped promote his view of how the war should be understood.[91] To this extent, the actions and comments of these two figures in late June and early July 1944 should not be understood uncritically. Third, a literal understanding of Eden's and Churchill's remarks overestimates the independence of the Foreign Office. Its senior officials usually followed policy. Any substantive change would have been discussed by Eden with officials such as Alexander Cadogan, William Strang and probably Ivone Kirkpatrick, and such figures could and would have carried the department as a whole. If Eden was serious about implementing a plan to bomb Oświęcim, he would have had to liaise closely with senior FO officials, and not just send a request to the Air Ministry. Wasserstein (1999: 287) suggests that Foreign Office officials were able to scupper the bombing proposals.[92]

Churchill's 7 July call to mobilize the RAF was not, as far as the documentary record indicates, followed by subsequent intervention. Churchill wrote to Eden in early July,

Calls to bomb the camp

There is no doubt this is the most horrible crime ever committed in the whole history of the world, and it has been done by scientific machinery by nominally civilised men in the name of a great State and one of the leading races of Europe. It is quite clear that all concerned in this crime who may fall into our hands, including the people who only obeyed orders by carrying out the butcheries, should be put to death after their association with the murders has been proved.[93]

This statement, rather than being read as one of Churchill's initial responses to news about Auschwitz, should be understood as simply a reiteration of long-standing British policy to punish perpetrators of atrocities – a policy that had been broadcast over the BBC's European Service, and a recognition of facts long known.[94] There is no doubt that the new information derived from the triptych of reports about the camp that reached the West in June 1944 had an impact on Churchill (and perhaps even on Eden), but it is no longer credible to suggest that this information was the first data they received about the mass killing of Jews at the camp, or to interpret their subsequent actions on this assumption.

In the United States, in July, calls for a bombing raid increasingly focused on targeting the camp itself. The Emergency Committee to Save the Jewish People of Europe wrote to President Roosevelt on 24 July, requesting that the camp and railway tracks be bombed. On 9 August Aryeh Leon Kubowitzki of the World Jewish Congress forwarded a message to John McCloy from Ernest Frischer of the Czech Government in Exile, requesting the camp and tracks be bombed. McCloy replied on 14 August and followed the well-rehearsed script – forces employed elsewhere, the doubtful efficacy of any raid, the possibility that the raid might do more harm than good by provoking the Germans to greater cruelty.[95]

Regardless of the questionable validity of these reasons, the camp was within the reach of Allied air forces. Industrial targets around Oświęcim were bombed from July 1944. The synthetic fuel factory at Blechhammer (Blachownia) north-east of the camp was bombed ten times between 7 July and 20 November, a mission which required aircraft to fly near or over the camp (Świebocki 2000: 231). On 7 August a plant at Trzebinia twenty kilometres from Oświęcim was bombed, and on 20 August the Buna-Werke synthetic rubber plant at Monowitz (Monowice). It was again targeted on 13 September; on this occasion some bombs fell by mistake on Auschwitz I, killing some SS men and prisoners, and on Birkenau, damaging the railway spur to the camp (Gilbert 2001a: 315; Świebocki 2000: 321).

The appeals to bomb the camp in the summer of 1944 were not the first such requests.[96] The first request had been made by the Polish prime minister, General Władysław Sikorski, on 4 January 1941 (Engel 1993: 205; Westermann 2004: 195) to the British government. It was made in

252 Reassessing the significance of the Vrba–Wetzler report

response to information coming from Poland about the camp. It is likely that Mikołajczyk informally broached the issue of bombing the camp with the British in late 1942 or early 1943. As noted in Chapter 4, Mikołajczyk sent a radio message to Warsaw on 20 February 1943 asking where 'Hexagon' (RDX) was being manufactured. If it was being fabricated in Silesia, he assured the Underground that he would *return* to the question of bombing Oświęcim (with the British).[97]

The British were again approached in August 1943 by the Polish government. The 1941 and August 1943 requests have hitherto been understood within the academic community and beyond as being motivated by the desire to stem the suffering of Poles at the camp. However, the volume of information that had arrived in London about the camp from November 1942, most of which highlighted the systematic mass killing of Jews, suggests that any requests made in late 1942 or early 1943 and in August 1943 were, at least in part, motivated by this devastating news.[98] The first appeal (1941) was directly refused, and the later appeals did not result in any action. Further calls by a range of actors took place from mid-1944 onwards, especially after the distribution of the Vrba–Wetzler report, but none met with success. Neither Auschwitz I nor Birkenau were ever targeted in any bombing raid.

Westermann (2004) has noted that the reasons for refusing to bomb the camp in 1941 have striking similarities with those advanced in 1944. The 1941 request was motivated by news from the camp, received in London in late December 1940. Part of the message read,

The prisoners of the concentration camp in Oswiecim implore for a bombing of the camp in the shortest possible time.
The camp in Oswiecim is at present one of the worst organized and most inhuman concentration camps.
The prisoners number many thousands (the figure is estimated at 20,000).

The request was handed to the Royal Air Force for expert consideration. It was ultimately refused on 15 January 1941 on the ground that such a bombing raid would divert resources from more strategically valuable targets (in this case industrial targets in Germany) and because it was thought that any raid on Oświęcim would not achieve its objectives. These objectives included the destruction of the barbed wire fence and ammunition dump to allow the escape of prisoners. Air Chief Marshal Sir Richard Peirse further advised Sikorski that such a raid 'would need to be extremely accurate if serious casualties were not to be caused amongst the prisoners themselves. Such accuracy cannot be guaranteed'.[99]

In August 1943 the Polish Government in Exile floated the idea to bomb the camp to liberate the prisoners (Breitman 2004: 184), as it had done previously on 4 January 1941. The Polish government recognized that any straight request to attack the camp to free prisoners was unlikely to be approved (as indicated in Mikołajczyk's 20 February message to Warsaw), and incorporated its aim to free the prisoners with a plan to target industrial facilities within the Auschwitz complex and town.

Information about the expansion of industrial capacity at the camp complex had been disseminated by inmates to the Polish Underground in June. Stanisław Kłodziński had sent a message from the camp on 14 June 1943 in which he called for the 'Krupp firm ... [to] ... be destroyed and razed to the ground'.[100] On 24 August Władysław Banaczyk, the Polish minister of the interior, telegrammed the government delegate in Poland, Jan Stanisław Jankowski, advising him,

The British staff has expressed readiness to bomb Oświęcim, and particularly the rubber and gasoline factories and other factories of this sort in Silesia. For our part, we would like to combine this with the mass freeing of prisoners in Auschwitz. Your utmost cooperation is required to release them immediately after the attack and to provide aid to them. Aside from that, you must help us in selecting targets according to their importance and leading the aircraft to their targets in such a way as to avoid Polish casualties. Please indicate what you think of this and what you require in this regard, and whether the prisoners can be prepared in advance. The operation is foreseen during the period of the longest nights.[101]

For the Polish government one of the key aims of the proposals to bomb the camp was to liberate prisoners. The objective to stop or interrupt the slaughter of Jews at the camp was not mentioned in the 1943 Polish documents pertaining to a possible bombing raid on Oświęcim. But this points to the fact that neither liberating prisoners nor stemming the Nazi slaughter of Jews at the camp could be clearly advanced as reasons to bomb the camp in the British context. The British continued to prioritize military and strategic targets. Oświęcim could become such a target not on account of the mass slaughter and suffering at the camp, but due to its industrial importance. The industrial facilities at the Monowitz part of the camp, for British war planners, were far more significant than either Auschwitz I or Birkenau. Any requests to bomb the camp therefore had to be couched in the language of military strategy rather than in terms of ending human suffering or mass killing. In May 1943, as noted in Chapter 5, the Foreign Office had received Salski's account of the mass slaughter of Jews at Oświęcim, and in late August the SOE had received Aneks 57 from the Polish Bureau VI, recording that the greater part of the Jews had already been murdered and that the mass execution of Gypsies had started at the camp.[102]

254   Reassessing the significance of the Vrba–Wetzler report

Bombing was not seen by members of the Polish Underground as the only way to liberate the camp. Following his escape from Auschwitz in April 1943, Witold Pilecki drew up plans to attack Auschwitz and free its prisoners. On 29 October 1943 Pilecki met with Karol Jabłoński of Kedyw, the Directorate for Diversion (Kierownictwo Dywersji) formed in January 1943 from previous units within the Home Army, and 'presented the plan of the Oświęcim attack'.[103] The proposal was passed up the chain of command, and Pilecki received a negative response from the commander of the Home Army, Tadeusz Bór-Komorowski. Bór-Komorowski was of the view that any Home Army attack, given its limited resources, would be able to hold the camp for, at best, half an hour. This would liberate only 200–300 people and the remaining inmates would have to fend for themselves. Such an outcome, it was thought, would result in a massacre.

The area around Auschwitz, and the camp itself, were well resourced in terms of German Army and Police personnel and weapons. As Pilecki became fully aware of the severe limits of Home Army capabilities, he accepted the decision but, according to the Institute of National Remembrance, was given permission to carry out an attack on the camp if the Germans chose to murder all the registered prisoners.[104] This compromise seems to have been taken to reassure Pilecki that his colleagues in the camp were not forgotten and special efforts would be made should the Germans move to liquidate the camp, though such an attack would only offer some inmates a slim chance of survival. The possibility of acting to save the trainloads of Jews arriving at Birkenau to be immediately murdered, like a general assault on the camp, does not seem to have been seen as a realistic option. The lack of documentary evidence prevents a full assessment of any deliberation on this issue by the Polish Underground.

Any attack on Auschwitz I would have implications for the functionality of Birkenau since armed conflict in Auschwitz I or at both Auschwitz I and Birkenau would disrupt the camp's administration and communications. No evidence has been discovered to suggest that the land-attack plan on Auschwitz was forwarded to the Polish Government in Exile in London, but, by October 1943, senior Home Army commanders were well aware that the required additional weapons would not be available and Allied assistance was very unlikely. In June 1943, the Home Army Command had requested that arms be sent to Poland from the West. In September, this request was refused by the Combined Chiefs of Staff.[105] The Soviets had protested against the 'arming of Poles in Poland' (Kersten 1991: 4). Any effort by the Home Army to secure British aid to facilitate an attack on Auschwitz in particular was unlikely to have met with success, as

Calls to bomb the camp

through 1943 and 1944 the British became increasingly sensitive to Soviet sensibilities. In the absence of widespread knowledge of the camp, pressure to explore all options to effect a successful attack was non-existent.

On 12 June 1944, Emanuel Scherer and Anzelm Reiss (a member of the Representation of Polish Jews) wrote to the Polish minister of the interior requesting that the camps, including Oświęcim, be attacked during Polish military operations.[106] Scherer addressed the same request to Mikołajczyk at the end of the month (27 June).[107] When a land attack was again considered, this time in the US by the WRB's John Pehle, in July 1944, it was immediately dismissed, as 'the apparently deep-rooted anti-Semitism' in the Polish Underground would prevent an attack taking place in 'good faith' (Penkower 1983: 197). On 1 July Kubowitzki had written to Pehle explaining that he was against bombing the camp because it would allow the Germans to claim Jews had been killed by the Allies, and that he favoured a land assault on the camp.[108] Pehle decided not to refer the possibility of a ground attack to the US War Department. Pehle's view of the Polish Underground highlights the pervasiveness of the stereotype of Polish anti-Semitism and the malign impact it had on policy formulation.

Western pressure for an attack on the Auschwitz complex, or an operation focused on Birkenau, in late 1943 or early 1944, would have had a receptive audience within sections of the Home Army, especially if weapons and other support could have been supplied. By spring and summer of 1944, it was too late. The Home Army, in line with the Polish government's political strategy, had launched Operation Tempest to soften up the Germans and take over towns and cities prior to the Soviet Army's main assaults. Often Home Army soldiers fought alongside (though not under the command of) the Soviets. On defeating German forces, Home Army soldiers were routinely arrested by the NKVD; some were executed, others deported. By August, the Home Army had no resources with which to attack Auschwitz following the initiation of the Warsaw Rising.

The issue of liberating the camp, of which the debate about bombing Auschwitz is the most significant element, needs to be recalibrated to take into account the fact that British and American officials and Jewish representatives had reliable information about the camp a lot earlier than has been thought.[109] Information about the mass killing of Jews at Auschwitz was routinely passed by the Polish government to the British. The Vrba–Wetzler report played a key role in weakening the British censorship regime about the camp in June and July 1944, but it was not the first reliable report to reveal that Jews were being systematically killed.

Medoff and Zucker (2012: 25) base their essay analysing the demands of representatives of various Jewish organizations to bomb Auschwitz in the summer of 1944 on the assumption that the Vrba–Wetzler report was the first credible report about the camp, and argue that the arrival of the Vrba–Wetzler report was the turning point in encouraging Jewish Agency officials to lobby for the bombing of the camp. At the meeting of the Jewish Executive Agency on 11 June 1944, the same day that the *Palestine Post* reported that 7,000 Czech Jews had been murdered in the gas chambers at Oświęcim on its front page, David Ben-Gurion is minuted as summarizing, 'It is the position of the Executive not to propose to the Allies the bombing of places where Jews are located.'[110] This was a general policy statement. Subsequent to this meeting there is no record in the minutes of the Jewish Agency of a follow-up discussion or vote on the bombing issue, as Medoff and Zucker (2012: 12) note. Making reference to this statement, Levy (1996: 272) argued that 'there is no indication that the JAE ever changed its collective mind and some indication that it did not'. However, Levy does not give due weight to the lobbying efforts of Isaac Gruenbaum and others. For Medoff and Zucker (2012), the actions of Gruenbaum from late June 1944, and the efforts of Nahum Goldmann in Washington and Joseph Linton and Berl Locker in London, amongst others, strongly indicate that the Jewish Agency had changed its position and called for Auschwitz to be bombed, even though there was no official vote on the issue.

However, Medoff and Zucker's (2012) suggestion that Jewish Agency representatives did not know of the true function of the camp prior to the arrival of the Vrba–Wetzler report cannot be sustained. As we saw in Chapters 4 and 5 (see also Appendix I), Jewish Agency representatives received news about the true function of Auschwitz from returnees to Palestine in late 1942, and repeatedly through 1943 and 1944. If David Ben-Gurion (whom Medoff and Zucker discuss) did not know that Jews were being killed on a mass scale at Auschwitz, it was not because information had not reached the Jewish Agency in Palestine.[111] Demands for bombing or other Allied interventions could have been made by Jewish representatives much earlier.[112] However, some consideration has to be given to the way in which Jewish representatives' responses to news about Auschwitz were influenced and guided by the British and American anti-Jewish climate and censorship regime.[113]

In Britain especially, this censorship regime played a key function in limiting the actions that those who knew about the camp could take. The Polish government's press release of 21 March 1944 should have broken the controlled silence about the camp in the British media. It did not.

The scandal of anti-Semitism in the Polish Army diverted the attention of those best placed to lobby the British government, and made it easier for the 'voluntary' censorship of news about Auschwitz to continue. In the next – concluding – chapter the impact and significance of the censorship regime in Britain (and the United States) are discussed.

7   Conclusion

News that Jews were being killed en masse at Auschwitz reached the West in November 1942. This news was published in the *New York Times* on 25 November 1942, and passed to President Roosevelt on 8 December 1942. By early January, the same information had been handed to the British Foreign Office. This data originally came from a Jewish woman returned to Palestine from Poland in November 1942.

The Polish Government in Exile also passed on information about the camp. The Polish government can be documented as continually forwarding reports about the Nazi programme of extermination at the camp, including the use of gas chambers, to the Allies from March 1943. It is likely that such information was handed over earlier – in late 1942. There is powerful circumstantial evidence that information was not concealed from British intelligence, propaganda and FO officials during November and December 1942.

First, the news of the gassing of Jews at Auschwitz that arrived in London on 12 November 1942 was immediately translated into English and incorporated into a document entitled 'Report on conditions in Poland'. Translating the Polish source reports strongly suggests that English-speaking officials were the target audience. Second, in Chapter 4, it was argued that Jan Karski knew about the camp and is likely to have couriered a report noting the gassing of Jews at Auschwitz. It is possible that this information was shared with MI19 during his interrogation at the Royal Patriotic Schools on 26–7 November 1942. Third, the high degree of co-operation between Polish and British intelligence (Bureau VI and SOE especially) including the passing over of *aneks* – the Polish Underground reports that specifically focused on the Nazi terror campaign in Poland and repeatedly reported on the mass murder of Jews at Auschwitz from September 1942 – suggests that information was shared with the British immediately.

Fourth, the passing of information from spring 1943 can be documented. There is evidence in PWE, FO and SOE files, but a great deal of the documentary proof of British knowledge is found elsewhere – in newspapers, occasional BBC transcripts, Radio Świt files and archives in the US and Israel. Given that early news of the gassing of Jews at

258

Auschwitz was tightly controlled (see Chapter 4), it was not published or broadcast by these 'secondary' sources in late 1942. Judgement about whether the British knew about the camp from Polish sources in late 1942 cannot depend on the partial documentary record – one has to assess Polish information-sharing practice. The available evidence indicates that Polish intelligence routinely passed on information, including details about Auschwitz. Fifth, weight has to be given to the Polish government's adherence to the British censorship and propaganda policy. Recognizing that the Polish government sought to play the loyal ally in the run-up to and aftermath of the 17 December 1942 UN declaration helps to explain why there was no *public* statement on the murder of Jews at Auschwitz during this period. But the lack of such a statement should not automatically be understood as implying that data about the camp was concealed from key British officials.

The reports that the Polish government received from the Polish Underground in Poland about the fate of Jews at the camp were routinely forwarded to allies and, through intermediaries, to the press; information about the camp was also conveyed by Ignacy Schwarzbart to Jewish leaders in Britain, the United States and Palestine.

The intelligence that arrived in London about Auschwitz was, in the main, ignored by the mainstream press and 'ghettoized' in the obscure, and largely unknown, supplement to the *City and East London Observer* – the *Polish Jewish Observer*. During the years of its existence (1942–4), the supplement was not even registered in the authoritative *Willings Press Guide*.[1] The *Jewish Chronicle* also published some news about Auschwitz. From the beginning of 1943 to July 1944, the *Chronicle* featured several articles that mentioned the camp, most of them deep within the paper.[2] It repeatedly described the camp as a death camp, and even published data from Jankowski's and Rowecki's message of 4 March 1943, reporting that 520,000 Jews had been killed at the camp, in its 10 September 1943 issue (albeit on page 8). Such frankness was unusual, and information about the camp to which *The Chronicle* had access was frequently either buried in the inside pages or ignored.

The British 'voluntary' censorship regime effectively controlled the flow of information about the camp. Records of the Ministry of Information do not shed light on the informal advice of Brendan Bracken (minister of information) to newspaper proprietors and editors, and, since Bracken had his own papers burnt on his death, it is not possible to define precisely where the line between British state 'advice' and newspapers' own choices to exclude information about the camp should be drawn.

The 1941 Ministry of Information Planning document 'Combating the apathetic outlook of "What have I got to lose even if Germany wins"'

260   Conclusion

is one of the most direct articulations of a policy to exclude Jews from the war narrative.[3] Home Office and Foreign Office concerns regarding 'Jewish stories' provoking anti-Semitism and stimulating demands for refuge and rescue were reflected in the limited amount of news about Jews either transmitted by the BBC's Home Service and European Service or published in the British mainstream press.[4] The widespread anti-Semitism of the period, linked with the widely shared notion that Jews brought anti-Semitism with them, meant that excluding and marginalizing the news of the Holocaust and of Auschwitz in particular was normal practice. The discursive environment – including stereotypes about Jews and frequently unpremeditated self-censorship – helped keep the news of the Holocaust and Auschwitz something of an inside story, literally in the sense of where the news was featured in newspapers, and figuratively by often restricting it to small sections of the governing class and press editors.

There is also evidence that the dissemination of news about Auschwitz prior to early July 1944 was more tightly controlled than other data about the Holocaust. The 21 March 1944 press release from the Polish Government in Exile was seen by the British press, but none of the mainstream national papers published the main piece of information that over half a million Jews had been killed at the camp. Even the *Jewish Chronicle*'s article 'Butchers of Oswiecim to die' of 24 March 1944, which drew on the 21 March press release, did not report the scale of the mass murder at the camp. In the US, on the other hand, in the context of President Roosevelt's 24 March warning speech, the key section of the Polish government's press release was reproduced in several important newspapers.

In Britain, the refusal of the Foreign Office to confirm the validity of information about Auschwitz from Polish intelligence sources played a key role in restricting the circulation of knowledge. British officials were well aware, as Jock Brebner (director of the News Division of the Ministry of Information) had pointed out in March 1941, 'that in war time more news becomes public through the medium of official announcements than in peacetime'.[5] Withholding confirmation on the one hand, and failing to distribute information on the other, were very effective in restricting and controlling the news agenda. Broadcasting policy played a crucial role in limiting stories about Jews and atrocities on the airwaves. News about camps (Treblinka, Sobibór, Bełżec) which had become known through the July 1942 press conference at the Ministry of Information and in the period around the UN declaration of December 1942 could be repeated; news of the true function of Auschwitz was effectively embargoed by British government policy.

Through the manipulation of various tools – stock notions about Jews, advice to proprietors and editors, direct instructions not to highlight 'Jewish stories', formal policy to depict Jews as simply citizens of the

Conclusion   261

country in which they lived, and the refusal to confirm intelligence reports – the British government, via the Foreign Office, the Ministry of Information and the Political Warfare Executive, was able to choreograph news of the Holocaust. The output of the European Service of the BBC was effectively controlled by the PWE, as was that of Radio Świt – the clandestine station that appeared to be broadcasting from Poland, but was in fact based in Britain. And since the weekly PWE directives were passed to the Americans, a great deal of transatlantic coordination in managing the news agenda was possible. It was only with the creation of the War Refugee Board in 1944 that US and British policy towards the distribution of news about Jews in Europe began to diverge.

The tight control the British exercised over information about Auschwitz is reflected in the dearth of Polish-origin reports mentioning the camp in the British National Archives at Kew. At the very least, the archives should hold more intercepts of Schwarzbart's post to the US and Palestine, original copies or translations of documents passed by Stanisław Mikołajczyk and Stanisław Kot to Frank Savery, and copies of Polish intelligence reports passed to the US.[6] As is discussed in detail in Appendix II, the way information about Auschwitz was managed by the Foreign Office helps to explain the limited number of documents at Kew that mention the camp. News of atrocities, including those at Auschwitz, was collected by Roger Allen. It is likely that news of the camp, including Polish intelligence's *aneks* series, was deposited with Allen with a view to postwar war crimes trials. These files have been misfiled or destroyed, or they remain with the Foreign Office or the British Intelligence Services (MI5/6).

The scarcity of documents about the mass slaughter of Jews at Auschwitz in the British National Archives has played an important role in sustaining the contention that Auschwitz was unknown in the West, and the argument that information from 'Polish sources' was seen as unreliable (Bauer 1997, 2001: 240).[7] In the first case, the work of Martin Gilbert has continued to dominate the field, despite important challenges from Richard Breitman and Barbara Rogers. The significance of those few documents that relate to Auschwitz in the National Archives has not been fully appreciated, as the provenance of their information has not, hitherto, been subjected to scrutiny.

Documents released in the 1990s – for example, the memorandum passed by Jewish organizations to President Roosevelt in 1942 – have undermined the idea that the true function of Auschwitz was unknown, but have not completely dismissed it. This is largely because the origin of this data has not, until now, been appraised by or known to scholars. Tracking the trajectory of reports about the camp demonstrates that the argument about reliability is wide of the mark. British intelligence was

262   Conclusion

well aware that information from 'Polish sources' was sent by the Polish Underground via radio messages and couriers to the Polish Government in Exile. British intelligence was drawing on this same source for military and strategic information, and sections of the British intelligence community (SOE) and Polish intelligence (Bureau VI) enjoyed exceptionally close relations.[8] Many Polish couriers were also SOE agents. SOE received *aneks* from Bureau VI and, despite the destruction and weeding of files during and since the Second World War, SOE files at Kew contain a copy of Aneks 58, received in November 1943, recording that 468,000 Jews had been murdered at Auschwitz by the end of 1942, for example.

On 24 March 1944, the PWE made extensive use of 'Polish sources' in its briefing document, 'The persecution of the Jews', which noted the mass killing of Jews at Auschwitz. This document was produced for internal circulation within the PWE and the FO, in response to the strong signals through early 1944 that the US was to make a statement on the persecution of European Jewry with or without British participation. It can therefore be assumed that these British officials found the information reliable. And, given that some of this data was among the latest available from a series of reports from the same Polish sources, it indicates that the reliability theme was nothing more than camouflage to justify inaction. The only surprising fact is that the 'reliability' narrative has been accepted for such a long time by Holocaust scholars. The task is to explain its longevity and tenacity over the last three decades.

The utility of the 'reliability' myth is that it functions to discredit Polish intelligence a priori. If the information at the time was seen as unreliable, then there is no strong reason to trace this information or to rigorously investigate its distribution. However, the subsequent failure to assess critically Polish intelligence on Auschwitz has contributed to the longevity of the myth that knowledge about Auschwitz was 'elusive', and helped to conceal the role played the British censorship regime in suppressing over thirty-five pieces of news about the camp that reached London between November 1942 and June 1944.

In scholarship on the Holocaust, it is rarely specified who exactly found the information unreliable, but it must be assumed that the British and American governments are being referred to. As Chapter 2 demonstrated, these governments' position on matters relating to Jews and atrocities was strongly inflected by concerns about British and American anti-Semitism respectively, and a determination to narrate the war in a particular way in order to inhibit demands for a more generous refugee policy or calls for retaliation or for rescue. Wyman (2007: 324) points out that, late in the war, the American Army magazine *Yank* chose not to

Conclusion 263

use the War Refugee Board's material derived from the Vrba–Wetzler report, as it was 'too semitic' and could stir up 'latent anti-semitism in the Army'. In such a context, British and American government officials' assertions regarding the unreliability of Polish sources when referring to Jews have to be treated with a great deal of scepticism.

The myth also functions to conceal what was known to various Jewish representatives. Sensitivity on this issue is mostly misplaced. The fact that senior Jewish representatives in the US, Britain and Palestine knew about the camp does not change the fact that they could not do much to persuade the US and British governments to intervene through 1943. The War Refugee Board, which changed the dynamics of reporting the Holocaust, was established in early 1944. The formation of the War Refugee Board had its own history, and far more than lobbying by American Jewry would have had to be different for it to have emerged earlier. Consequently, observations of the sort that 'Zionists, including WJC leaders, were so absorbed in planning for after the war's end that they were paying little attention to what was happening in Europe' (Bauer 1981: 192) are mainly relevant insofar as they highlight that American Jewry took time to absorb the full scale of the horror in Europe.[9] But the contention that there was scope for Jewish representatives to press more vigorously for news about the camp to be more widely disseminated and to call for bombing or attacks on the camp earlier cannot be dismissed.

The suggestion that leading representatives of British Jewry could have pressed the British government harder needs to give due weight to the disabling impact of British anti-Semitism, the internalization of anti-Semitic stereotypes, and the manner in which Foreign Office obduracy wore down not only representatives of British Jewry, but also non-Jews concerned about the fate of European Jews. In the US, a range of factors, including Jewish pressure, Polish intelligence reports and briefings, and the American political calendar, eventually led to the creation of the War Refugee Board, which despite its limitations did result in President Roosevelt's declaration on 24 March 1944, which stirred some response from the Foreign Office (Eden's 30 March speech to the House of Commons), and contributed to a discursive environment in which the possibility of rescue became thinkable.[10]

A further function of the myth is to imply that the Polish government was not doing enough to aid Jews in peril. The suggestion is that, if only the government could have provided 'reliable' information, then the news of the mass killing of Jews at Auschwitz would have become public and action would have been taken. This is pure fantasy. The reports that the Polish government received from the Polish Underground were no

264 Conclusion

less reliable than any other pieces of intelligence that, on non-Jewish or non-atrocity issues, were widely accepted within the British military and intelligence establishments. And while the contention that the Polish government could have done more (as could have all Allied governments) is difficult to reject, it is, in the most part, unfair and untrue to contend that the circulation of information about Auschwitz in the West was limited by the Polish government.[11] In this respect, the rejection of the myth of the unreliability of Polish intelligence reports has the possibility to reconstruct Polish–Jewish relations, as the recognition that the Polish government did in fact gather and pass on reliable information about the camp to the British and the Americans could contribute to improving present-day Polish–Jewish communication and reorient current debates over historical memory.

Through 1941 and 1942, Auschwitz was widely known as a particularly harsh camp, predominantly for Poles. However, intelligence sent out of the camp by Witold Pilecki and others (for example, Stanisław Dubois) advised that Jews and priests were at the bottom of the camp hierarchy and was repeatedly published during 1941 and early 1942. When information about the gassing of Poles and Soviet prisoners of war was published in July 1942, it would not have taken a great deal of imagination for anyone to ask what was happening to those groups that until then had been most harshly treated. With the awareness that Jews were being systematically exterminated at Sobibór, Bełżec and Treblinka, news that arrived in London in autumn 1942 and through 1943 that Auschwitz was also a place where Jews were being slaughtered en masse only added a new location to the Nazis' topography of genocide. In this context, claims of unreliability speak more to the way in which news of the Holocaust and the camp was choreographed than to the real views of recipients of the data. Here the issue of believability re-emerges. Even after several decades it remains difficult to fully process the systematic slaughter of a people who were, and are, a fundamental if always ambiguously tolerated part of European society. Processing knowledge of the Holocaust, including that of Auschwitz, was complicated, as Bauer (1978) has noted, but news of Auschwitz's function arrived after the Nazis' extermination policy and practice was well known. News of the mass slaughter of Jews at Auschwitz that arrived in London in 1943 should have been *more* believable than the first stories of mass killing at death camps that had arrived in the West in 1942, not less.

The failure of the Polish Ministry of the Interior to highlight the brief first message (12 November 1942) about the mass killing of Jews at Auschwitz, prior to the UN declaration of 17 December 1942, was disastrous for the dissemination of fuller information in the more tightly

Information about Auschwitz 265

controlled British context of 1943 and 1944.[12] In the absence of an official Allied statement describing the true function of the camp, the over thirty-five pieces of source data that arrived in Britain prior to the Swiss media commentary on the Vrba–Wetzler report (in June and July 1944) had little impact, despite some of the data being broadcast on the BBC, and published in the *Jewish Chronicle* and regularly in the *Polish Jewish Observer*.

The Polish government had a brief opportunity to publicize the first news from Auschwitz, and it was missed. This fact may help explain the entry in Ignacy Schwarzbart's diary on 24 October 1944, where he states that he 'will never forgive Mikołajczyk for the concealment of news on the extermination of the Jews in the period late July to September 1942'.[13] At this point Schwarzbart was fully aware that the mass of Polish Jewry had been murdered by the Nazis. He had received information about Auschwitz through 1943 and 1944, which he forwarded to various Jewish organizations and which was published in the *Polish Jewish Observer*. Schwarzbart worked hard to get another Allied declaration, but was thwarted (ultimately because of British policy). Given that other news on the extermination of Jews was publicized in December 1942, this diary entry can reasonably be understood as a reflection of how the information on Auschwitz did not reach a Western audience when it had the chance to be responded to, though, admittedly, this interpretation is one of several possibilities.

Information about Auschwitz

The seven pieces of information about the slaughter of Jews at Auschwitz that Gilbert (2001a) records as reaching the West – a report from a lady from Sosnowiec of 25 November 1942,[14] a report composed in London by a Polish courier on 18 April 1942 (the Salski report), a report in *The Times* on 26 May 1943, a report in *The Times* on 1 June 1943 (neither *Times* report mentioned the killing of Jews at Auschwitz), a letter from Będzin from 17 July 1943, a report from Bratislava of 1 September 1943, and a report printed by the Polish Consulate General in Istanbul in *Polska pod okupacją niemiecką* on 15 March 1944 – are just a fraction of the information that reached London and was passed on to the Western Allies. These seven pieces of information include both eyewitness testimony and distributed data. They therefore occupy different positions on the information chain along which data passed in order to be disseminated to different audiences.

As Chapters 4 and 5 demonstrate, some of these pieces of information are far more significant than Gilbert (2001a) suggests. The table in

266   Conclusion

Appendix I lists the source, the intermediaries that handled the information, and the final destinations of data about the camp that reached the West following the expansion of the camp to include gas chambers to murder Europe's Jews. Between November 1942 and early July 1944 over forty separate pieces of source data about the camp produced no less than fifty distinct pieces of distributed data about the mass killing of Jews at Auschwitz.[15] This distributed data was published in the *Polish Jewish Observer*, the *Los Angeles Times*, the *Washington Post* and *Our Tribune*, amongst other newspapers; it found its way to the PWE, to the OSS and to Jewish representatives in Britain, Palestine and the United States. The fact that Auschwitz was a place where European Jews were being systematically killed was well known through 1943 to the Polish government in London; to many Jewish representatives in the US, Palestine and Britain; to sections of the US government; to readers of the *Polish Jewish Observer*; and, without doubt, to key sections of the political and military establishment in Britain. The intercept of Schwarzbart's letter to the World Jewish Congress in New York containing Jerzy Salski's account of Auschwitz was very widely distributed in May 1943.

The volume of data distributed by the Polish government in London about Auschwitz *complicates* David Engel's (1987; 1993) thesis on the Polish government's attitude to Jews. Engel maintained that the government was ambivalent towards Jews, that many of its policies which favoured minorities (including Jews) – for example, equal rights – were instrumental policies only made to appease the Western Allies, and that it systematically marginalized news about Jews. First, every piece of intelligence about the camp that Engel (1987; 1993) suggests stalled with the Polish government was, in fact, distributed. Second, the marginalization of news about Jews can best be explained by the British and American censorship context, rather than simply by an anti-Jewish bias of the Polish government, which has been the default explanation hitherto. This issue is likely to be subject to continuing debate, though it is apparent that the significance of British (and American) censorship has not been sufficiently acknowledged.

It is doubtlessly true that right-wing sections of the Polish government needed no encouragement to ignore the plight of Poland's Jews, and to focus exclusively on the difficulties faced by Christian Poles. The British context certainly empowered those keen to narrate the war in such a way, but the Polish government should not be defined exclusively in reference to its nationalist right wing, and, as the story of news of Auschwitz makes clear, the government did distribute information which scholars have previously argued was concealed or ignored.[16] Nevertheless, anti-Semitism amongst Poles (including within the Polish Cabinet) *did* play

Information about Auschwitz 267

a role in the way in which news about the camp was disseminated in Britain, but the exact manner in which its influence was exercised has not hitherto been fully recognized by scholars. To date, the standard argument about the Polish government has been that it concealed or suppressed important data about Auschwitz due to its desire for the camp to remain exclusively known as a site of Polish martyrdom.

This study has demonstrated that data was forwarded to Poland's allies and to the British press. But anti-Semitism within the Polish milieu proved useful for the British policy of suppressing news of Auschwitz in a number of ways. First, it provided the British with an important group of Poles who were sensitive about 'Jewish' stories, and who echoed the British desire to see such stories marginalized or excluded from the news agenda. The alignment of views on this issue between the British and anti-Semites in the Polish Cabinet no doubt strengthened the Polish Right and shaped the way in which the Polish government could distribute news from Auschwitz. The issuance of clear, unambiguous government statements about the camp was inhibited politically (by the strength of the Right) and diplomatically (by the Allied – i.e. British government – policy on Jews and atrocities). When the Polish government did issue a clear statement on 21 March 1944, as a result of a shift in American policy – ultimately expressed in Roosevelt's warning to the Germans on 24 March – it was ignored by the national British media.

Second, anti-Semitic factions in the Cabinet and National Council, together with intelligence from Poland pointing to a decrease in tolerance towards minorities, undermined efforts to highlight the Jewish tragedy made by Jewish and socialist representatives on the National Council. In Britain, in their attempts to publicize news about what was happening to Jews in Poland, people like Schwarzbart, Scherer and Adam Ciołkosz (Polish Socialist Party) had to contend with Polish anti-Semites and, more importantly, with British reticence to disseminate the information that was passed to them.[17]

Third, the widespread stereotype of Polish anti-Semitism, sustained by the well-documented attitudes of significant Polish personalities, adversely affected the comprehension of information about Jews provided by the Polish government – frequently the motives of the messenger (the Polish government) elicited greater attention than the message it delivered.[18] Polish anti-Semitism also provided a believable cover story, one that has lasted until now, to explain the relative dearth of information in the British and American press about Auschwitz – that is, the argument that data was not passed on because of Polish anti-Semitic prejudice. Polish anti-Semitism therefore played a key role in undermining efforts to bring the true functions of Auschwitz to the attention of the general public, and

268   Conclusion

aided the PWE and the FO in concealing their knowledge of the camp. It also severely damaged the image of the Polish Government in Exile by providing fertile ground for pro-Soviet propaganda, describing the government as a reactionary clique, to take root. Given the relative strength of the Polish Right in the Cabinet (as well as concerns about security), the fact that information about Jews was routinely passed to the press was not highlighted by the Polish government. Consequently, information that would problematize the assertions of pro-Soviet MPs and others remained unknown. Polish government announcements about Jews in Poland were therefore seen by many in Britain (including British and Polish Jews) as exceptional and as politically inspired.

The irony here is that those who most vociferously sought to defend Poland through a restricted notion of Polishness (restricted to Catholic, ethnic Poles) were the very people who thus provided tools to hostile parties (USSR, pro-Soviet British parliamentarians and publicists) to marginalize the Polish government. Polish anti-Semitism was harmful to Poland's Jews; it was also detrimental to non-Jewish Poles and the Polish Government in Exile.

This study has shown that the difficulty in distributing news of the Holocaust, and of Auschwitz in particular, was not due to the actions of the Polish government in withholding information. The chief rabbi of British Jewry, Dr Joseph Herman Hertz, spoke at a conference at Central Hall, London, alongside the archbishop of York, calling for action to aid European Jewry, on 29 February 1944. In his speech Dr Hertz implied that censorship was inhibiting the mobilization of the British people to demand that their government act:

Our great foe is the ignorance of the rank and file of the people concerning the heartbreaking and utterly unprecedented horror of the situation. If the press throughout the country would but unveil to them the scientific fiendishness displayed by the Nazis in the foul massacring of an entire people, we should have a large and determined body of public opinion behind us in our representations to Governments. And be it remembered that the Nazis are not confining extermination to one race or people.

As to the difficulties in the way of large-scale human salvage, they are not of such a nature that the might, practical wisdom and humanity of Great Britain and USA could not overcome them. The procrastination shown by Allied Governments in this direction is by many taken as evidence of a terrible cheapening of human life in the democracies; as a virtual endorsement of Hitler's doctrine of the nothingness of the individual human being.[19]

The chief rabbi's complaint, like his criticism of the British censorship regime made at the Albert Hall on 29 October 1942, did not receive a great deal of attention. It was confined yet again, as was so much news about the fate of European Jews, to the pages of the subscription-only supplement to the *City and East London Observer* – the *Polish Jewish Observer*.

At the conference, the archbishop of York had highlighted that nearly 3 million Jews had been killed since the start of the war and demanded that the British government take steps to rescue Jews, arguing, 'The great mass of English people are passionately urging that we take our full share in rescuing the victims'. His demands elicited no response, despite an audience of around a thousand people, including representatives from Allied governments.[20]

Censorship and Polish–Jewish relations

British censorship had a malign impact on the standing of the Polish Government in Exile. The suppression of news of Soviet atrocities against Polish citizens in the 1939–41 period, including the deportation of 320,000 people (Sanford 2005: 29) and the Katyń massacre, together with the British government's refusal to permit the publicization of Polish intelligence detailing Soviet partisan excesses against Polish citizens during the war, meant that the British public was denied the opportunity to assess critically the Polish government's policy towards the Soviet Union. The negative sentiment towards the USSR expressed by many Polish citizens was likewise misunderstood. Instead, Polish hostility to the USSR was comprehended amongst many sections of British society, especially the political Left, as evidence of the reactionary nature of the Poles and the Polish Government in Exile.[21]

As noted, the public standing of the Poles and the Polish government was considerably undermined by anti-Semitism, especially in the ranks of the Polish Army. Polish anti-Semitism was often less sophisticated than its British and American counterparts, and grated with the liberal politics of 1940s Britain. These factors produced a vicious cycle of mistrust and misunderstandings between the different Polish and Jewish publics in Great Britain, which undercut possibilities for co-operation when Hungarian Jewry was faced with extermination after the Germans assumed control of Hungary on 19 March 1944.

No doubt Jewish leaders who were advised of Auschwitz's deadly function were disappointed by the Polish government's failure to persuade the British and Americans to react, to retaliate or to issue declarations. But even in the case of the peasants of the Lublin and Zamość regions, on whose behalf the Polish prime minister (and leader of the Polish Peasant Party) Stanisław Mikołajczyk battled with the FO for an Allied statement, it took the best part of eight months before

270   Conclusion

anything happened (a statement by the American and British governments (but not the Soviet government) condemning crimes against the population of Poland – see Chapter 3), and then only with the greatest of reluctance. The plight of Poland's Jews was even further down the Allies' priority list.

The strategic importance of the Polish government for the British declined steadily after the Soviet Union joined the Allied cause, and precipitously in April 1943 with the breaking of Polish–Soviet diplomatic relations. 'Flings', as Ivone Kirkpatrick described Polish statements and broadcasts that were not fully approved by the British, became fewer, as Britain readjusted her relationship with Poland in response to Soviet interests. Britain became less likely to respond to Polish government requests through 1943 and 1944, and every Polish issue was viewed by FO officials in the light of Soviet sensibilities. In taking this position, the FO was able to inhibit the Polish government speaking to and about the various national minorities that resided in pre-war Poland. Talking to and about Ukrainians, Belarusians and Jews brought up the uncomfortable issue of Poland's eastern border; talking to and about Jews also had the potential to enhance the Polish government's status as it would challenge the view that the government was anti-Semitic. Reference to these minority populations therefore could 'step on Russian toes'.[22]

Because of its strong reticence to allow news of Jews and atrocities against them to be freely disseminated, the FO handicapped the Polish government in combating the malign stereotype of Polish anti-Semitism, and of the government being, in essence, reactionary. Since Britain officially had a 'free' press, the British limits placed on the dissemination of news of Jews and atrocities were not widely recognized. The result was that the propaganda put about by the *Daily Worker* and other pro-Soviet papers, as well as pro-Soviet MPs, was able to construct a jaundiced picture of the Polish government, whilst the circulation of news about Poland's Jews was not published in the mainstream press, despite being forwarded from the Polish Government in Exile. Such an outcome accorded with Soviet objectives of de-legitimating the Polish government. Had the 'free' press published all the information passed on, the pro-Soviet propagandists' objective of depicting the Polish government as hostile to Jews would have been more difficult, and the levels of distrust and acrimony demonstrated in the anti-Semitism scandal that engulfed the Polish Army in 1944 might have been reduced.

The presence of anti-Semites within the broad coalition of the Polish government and National Council certainly inhibited a trusting relationship between the Polish government and various Jewish publics, including the Board of Deputies and the Reprezentacja (the Representation of

Censorship and Polish–Jewish relations

Polish Jewry in Palestine). The National Democrats certainly had a broad constituency. But the British and American suppression of the news that the Polish government passed on about the German extermination of Polish and European Jewry led to the impression (which still resonates today) that the Polish government was dominated by National Democrats. The diversity of opinion within the Polish government has not been sufficiently recognized.

The reactionary views of the Polish Right were accorded a greater weight within Britain, not because they were dominant in the Polish Cabinet and National Council (though they were significant), but because the voice of Polish liberals and leftists in highlighting the Jewish plight was effectively muted by British censorship. The nationalist Right's agenda of marginalizing news about Jews paralleled British censorship policy, but it also reinforced the perception of important groups (pro-Soviet MPs, some British Jews, some officials in the Foreign Office) that the Poles were *essentially* anti-Semitic. The promulgation of this malign stereotype provided discursive resources to the PWE to keep news of Nazi atrocities against Jews off the airwaves and the front pages. This deficit of news further reinforced the notion of Polish anti-Semitism, since British censorship was not recognized. In essence, a vicious circle of misrecognition and growing mistrust was sustained by the undue weight given to the pronouncements of the Polish nationalist Right, which helped the British justify their marginalization of Jewish news. Had British censorship in relation to Jews been less rigorous, due recognition might have been given to Polish Underground operations in gathering and distributing the news of the Holocaust, which could have limited the souring of Polish–Jewish relations both during the war and in its aftermath. As it was, British censorship undermined the attempts of information gatekeepers such as Ignacy Schwarzbart, Joel Cang and others to promulgate the news within Britain. It was very difficult for Polish and Jewish representatives in the Cabinet and National Council respectively to press for intervention on behalf of European Jewry. In the case of Auschwitz, their efforts were thwarted, in the final analysis, by the FO and the PWE.

During the war, the Polish government echoed the Western view that multicultural states were weak, and endorsed liberal assimilationism as a policy for a postwar independent Poland. This opened up the government to legitimate, though in the context of 1940s Britain somewhat hypocritical, criticism. Both the British and the Americans took the view that postwar Europe should be composed of largely homogeneous nation-states. Throughout the war, a range of Polish politicians and officials had voiced the opinion that the size of the Jewish population in Poland was a problem for the stability of the Polish state and that those

272   Conclusion

Jews who remained in Poland should assimilate to mainstream norms. This was not an unusual position to take in the mid-twentieth century, but it was clearly disadvantageous to Poland's surviving Jews. The expression of these views also did not serve the Polish government well. When articulated clearly, the inherent injustice of such a policy became obvious, and Stanisław Kot (who discussed the matter with representatives of British Jewry in May 1940) and Roman Knoll (who wrote a report for Tadeusz Romer, minister of foreign affairs, in the summer of 1943) were criticized by Maurice Perlzweig and Ignacy Schwarzbart respectively.[23] For others, such views were further evidence of Polish anti-Semitism, though they were widely shared in the US and Britain, where Jews were expected to assimilate (Kushner 1994).

Anti-Semitism (of a different order) was a stain marking sections of the Polish armed forces and the Polish Cabinet. David Engel (1993) and Joanna Michlic (2006) rightly highlight anti-Semitic statements and attitudes of some well-positioned Poles. The demands of Ignacy Schwarzbart and Emanuel Scherer, inter alia, that anti-Semitism be combated within Polish milieux with increased vigour, were responded to with too little effort and too late.[24] As well as being a fundamental point of principle that citizens should be treated equally both formally and in substance, it should have been a strategic priority for the Polish government in 1942, 1943 and 1944 to neutralize left-wing British critics and simultaneously discipline right-wing Polish politicians and officials. The fact that it was not prioritized reveals the plethora of problems faced by the government during these years, the ascendancy of nationalist sentiment in Poland itself (in relation to which the government had to position itself if it was to maintain legitimacy and, importantly, authority), and also a lack of strategic thinking and leadership. In the context of pervasive American and British anti-Semitism, the lack of an energetic substantive programme to combat anti-Semitism in Polish milieux should not be seen as an aberration from contemporary Western norms, but, given the hostility faced due to allegations of anti-Semitism from the moment it re-established itself in London in 1940, the government should have recognized the scale of the challenge.

In the case of news dissemination, the Polish government was aware of the importance of distributing information from Poland. But, arguably, it misjudged the balance between playing the role of the loyal ally and working to ensure that the fate of all Polish citizens was reported and ensuring that its reputation was not compromised by British censorship policy. This misjudgement can, in part, be attributed to sections of the Polish Cabinet being 'sensitive' to news about Jews, which limited pressure on the government to vigorously and publicly speak about what was happening to Poland's Jewish citizens. This political compromise had profound implications for the government since the failure of the British press to publish a great deal of information relating to the plight of the Jews blinded many MPs to those efforts undertaken by the Polish Underground and Polish government to publicize this information. However, even if the Polish government had pushed the Western Allies harder to distribute information about what was happening to Poland's Jewish citizens it is unlikely that the British or the Americans would have responded with alacrity. Indeed, this study has demonstrated that the British (and the Americans) maintained significant control over the material that was actually publicly disseminated.

Information about Jews was seen as unhelpful by the Foreign Office. Within the Polish Underground, delays and marginalization of the news occurred (Puławski 2009), but it was nonetheless continuously collected, analysed and sent. Of course, we cannot rule out marginalization as a result of anti-Jewish sentiment in some quarters within the Polish Underground. Given that the Polish government was being discouraged by the British from highlighting the Jewish fate, it is surprising how much, rather than how little, information about Jews actually reached London. This becomes even more striking when we consider the relative inactivity of Allied European governments, whose Jewish citizens were being deported by the Germans to Poland, in pressing for action or seeking information from the Polish Underground via the Polish government.[25]

British censorship of news of the Holocaust, and of Auschwitz in particular, during the Second World War continues to distort the historical record and mar contemporary Polish–Jewish relations. On the one hand, the Polish Underground's activities in forwarding information has not hitherto been properly recognized and, on the other, the very limited scholarly engagement with Polish intelligence operations dealing with Auschwitz has resulted in a slew of specious claims – a result, in part, of the widespread view that Polish information on the camp was not distributed or was unreliable. This is most clearly seen in relation to the summer 1943 report written by an unknown SS man, information from which was distributed in Britain and the US in March 1944 (discussed in Chapter 5).

Over the last decade, unsubstantiated claims have been made that this report was written by Konstanty Piekarski, an Auschwitz inmate and member of the Union of Military Organizations resistance group (Wysocki 2005), or by Witold Pilecki.[26] There is no documentary evidence to endorse this view, and a great deal of material against it. Neither Pilecki nor Piekarski were in the camp during June, July or August 1943, when the report was written; the report was originally

274   Conclusion

written in German; neither man claimed to have written the report; Pilecki cites radically different figures for the number of those murdered in his June debriefing document; and the Polish Underground identified an SS man as the author.

The promotion of Pierkarski or Pilecki in this way works to affirm Polish 'ownership' of the camp, and, given the lack of documentary evidence pointing to their role as authors, should be viewed within the conflicts over memory about the camp which emerged with some force in the early 1990s. Pilecki has been co-opted by sections of the Polish Right in this task, and his story has been used to promote a tendentious narrative of Polish responsiveness to Jews that was met with betrayal in the postwar period.[27] Such narratives are profoundly damaging to Polish–Jewish relations, and, given Pilecki's concern about the fate of Jews at the camp, is a disservice to the Polish captain. Clearly, the excesses of contemporary memory politics cannot be vanquished by historiography, but specific claims can be rebutted and space created for dialogue premised on historical facts rather than unfounded suppositions.[28]

Liberal assimilationism and British anti-Semitism

The information about the extermination of Jews at Auschwitz did not reach a wide audience not because of problems with the information or its sources, but because of the policies pursued by the British and American governments. In Britain, the Home Office was very concerned about news of Jews stimulating anti-Semitism in the country, and Home Intelligence reports do indicate high and fairly persistent levels of anti-Semitism in Britain. The Ministry of Information issued instructions not to publicize news of Jews, and the Political Warfare Executive and the Foreign Office saw Jews as nationals of the states in which they resided and sought to narrate the war in those terms. Thus it was not a question of Jews in occupied Europe, but of Poles, Czechs, the Dutch, the French and so on. Underpinning these policies was a liberal assimilationist view that minorities should accede to the norms of the majority. Jews could be integrated into different societies so long as they adhered to those societies' norms and did not distinguish themselves, or express Jewish identity in any other form than as religious practice – a practice which also had to follow the dominant norms of worship in form, if not content. The situation in the United States was remarkably similar. The State Department inhibited the dissemination of information about the Holocaust, and American propaganda organs occasionally intervened to prevent publication of 'Jewish stories' when the voluntary censorship regime was put under pressure.

The problem with the liberal assimilationist model, as a range of scholars have noted (Kushner 2004; Alderman 1995), is that it is fundamentally oppressive, since it not only coerces minorities to adopt the norms of the majority, but privileges the majority to determine how close or far from majoritarian norms minority actions actually are. Liberal assimilationism perpetuates an unequal power relation, which denies the minority the opportunity to fully express itself, and engenders the perennial threat of exclusion or the accusation of simulation. It is due to this positional power disparity that the claim, prevalent in the 1940s, that Jews bring anti-Semitism with them makes any sense at all. Antipathy to Jews was understood as a result of Jews not conforming to majoritarian demands. Consequently, the organs of the British state worked hard to keep Jews off the political and news agenda through 1943 and 1944, and Wyman's (2007: 307) point that '[t]o the American military Jews represented an extraneous problem and an unwanted burden' also applies to the UK and US governments, though the foundation of the War Refugee Board in January 1944 complicates the position in the US.

Anti-Semitism in both Britain and the US was not limited to the general public. Government policy towards Jews may have had a certain internal rationality: suppressing news of atrocities against Jews freed the FO from potential demands for rescue and refuge. Suppression of such news also conformed with some decision makers' antipathy towards human interventionism in general, an antipathy which Michael Marrus (2013) has argued developed in tandem with the League of Nations' minority rights regime during the interwar period.[29] But officials were also part of their respective cultures, and elite anti-Semitism, though frequently better disguised than that of the general public, certainly played a role in marginalizing news of the Holocaust. For example, the credibility of the Polish courier Jan Nowak-Jeziorański was enhanced by the fact that he was not Jewish: the chairman of the Joint Intelligence Committee, Victor Cavendish-Bentinck, wrote to Sir Alexander Cadogan at the Foreign Office in January 1944 recommending that he read a report detailing information that Nowak-Jeziorański had provided, advising Cadogan that Nowak-Jeziorański was 'not a Jew, but quite an intelligent middle-class Pole'.[30]

In May 1944, Sir Herbert Emerson, director of the Intergovernmental Committee on Refugees, wrote a memorandum for the Foreign Office describing the War Refugee Board. Emerson considered the board a response to the American electoral cycle and the large Jewish vote in New York. He stated that 'Mr Pehle [director of the War Refugee Board] is not a Jew, but many of his officers are'.[31] Clearly, being Jewish or not had a bearing on how individuals were appraised and how their activities

276   Conclusion

were understood, and influenced the weight to be accorded to their views. Such practices are obviously discriminatory, but such clear-cut examples are infrequent. More common is a dismissive tone or the use of euphemism. For example, Alec Randall of the Foreign Office (with responsibility for refugees) described those petitioning for a more generous refugee policy (a group which was not exclusively composed of Jews) as 'refugee enthusiasts', prior to Eden's statement to the House cautioning satellite states of Nazi Germany about deportation on 30 March 1944. Another official (who cannot be identified as his signature is illegible) commented on the same issue, arguing that the 'main purpose of the statement, alas, is to encourage the Jew enthusiasts ...',[32] in order to support his view that Jews should be specifically mentioned in Eden's speech.

Gabriel Milland (1998b: 56) has rightly argued, 'There can be no doubt that anti-Semitism, or at least a deep unwillingness to challenge it, were present at many levels in PWE'. Since the PWE ultimately directed the propaganda pitch to continental Europe, through its control over the BBC's European Service, and had some influence on the BBC's Home Service, anti-Semitism in that institution constituted a significant barrier to news about the Holocaust, and Auschwitz in particular, reaching the general public.

The presence of anti-Semitism within the British (and American) governing classes, together with the blind acceptance of liberal assimilationism, fostered the view that the only way to manage societal anti-Semitism was to marginalize news of the Nazi onslaught on Jews, especially through 1943 and 1944, after the brief success of the Polish government and Jewish organizations in persuading the Allied nations to issue the UN declaration of 17 December 1942. The parliamentary focus on anti-Semitism in the Polish Army in April and May 1944 readily illustrated that British politicians could at least think of other measures to inhibit anti-Semitism, including education and sanctions. However, the British image of Britain as a tolerant and open society inhibited recognition that the measures being recommended to the Poles (on anti-Semitism in the Army) would equally benefit Britain. It was easier to condemn a foreign country which, along with its politicians and officials, was seen as backward than to face up to the malign impact of anti-Semitic sentiment in Britain amongst the general public and the governing class.[33]

Moderating anti-Semitism in Britain by any means other than removing Jews from the news agenda was not seriously considered, and the lack of any alternative policy lends support to the contention that officials' and politicians' references to society's anti-Semitism helped disguise the scale of elite anti-Semitism. This phenomenon did not determine policy, but it provided an extra (if generally unarticulated) level of support for decisions relating to Jews – propaganda, refugees, rescue – in the context of war. It generally took the form of symbolic violence – a guiding 'range of postulates, axioms, which [went] without saying and require[d] no inculcating' (Bourdieu and Wacquant 2004: 273).

The governing class was in a strong position to narrate the story of the war and to guide social sentiment. The decision to marginalize the Holocaust led to considerable misunderstanding between different national groups in the postwar period and contributed to the suppression of Jewish memory of the Holocaust in the first postwar decades.[34] The social and individual cost of denying survivors the opportunity to tell their stories in those years was high. And while many survivors simply *wanted* to move on and forget, they had no alternative. British and American citizens had no real comprehension of the scale of the Nazi slaughter, not because the data was not available to officials and newspaper editors, but because the US and British governments and the 'free' press decided it was not a central story of the fight against Nazi tyranny.

Cartographies of inclusion and exclusion

For over three decades the contention that Jews were outside Poles' 'universe of obligation' (Fein 1979) has guided and informed scholarship on Polish attitudes to Jews during the Holocaust. This view was most fully supported by David Engel in his benchmark studies of the Polish Government in Exile and the Jews (1987; 1993), but it also informed Gunnar Paulsson's (2002: 42) detailed research on Jewish survival in Warsaw:

even the most progressive elements of Polish society regarded the Jews as outside their 'universe of obligation', an alien element whose fate was of little concern to Polish society as whole … [This was not] the result of some Polish policy of apartheid, but had existed by mutual consent for centuries … [This] protected Jews from assimilation. The disadvantage became apparent when they desperately needed their neighbours' help and found them, even when friendly, preoccupied with their own affairs.

At a general level, the notion of 'universe of obligation' has certainly had heuristic traction and, in demarcating the boundary between 'them' and 'us', has provided a productive frame to investigate intercommunity relations. However, the concept offers two mutually preclusive options: inclusion or exclusion. It reifies group identity and cannot accommodate the essentially fluid dynamics of group boundary formation. For example,

278   Conclusion

the perception that harsh and collective punishments awaited not only those who aided Jews, but their families, friends and neighbours as well, played a role in hardening in-group discipline to ignore the Jewish plight, and narrowed the scope of that in-group too. The fact that many Poles who extended help to Jews during the war hid this fact in the postwar period is not so surprising. Expectations of in-group behaviour were breached, bringing, it was thought, the possibility of German reprisals during the war; saving Jews, from this perspective, could be seen as selfish, especially since those hiding Jews were presumed to have been paid. In the context of immediate postwar Poland, the suspicion that Jews had been hidden, linked with the assumption of payment having been made, easily became a rationale for robbers to target anyone who had sheltered Jews.

Social distance, not only between Jews and Poles but between Poles as well, was not stable during the course of the war. German policy played a key role in hardening group boundaries and extending the social distances between some groups of Poles and Jews. Recent detailed studies of Polish responses to the German onslaught on the Jewish population have highlighted that in many locations Poles were frequently incentivized by the occupiers to turn over Jews by a system of rewards and punishments, and that for some (and not just from the ranks of perennial criminals) coveting Jewish property was sufficient motivation to attack and murder Jews (Grabowski 2011; Engelking 2011).

Since Helen Fein's (1979) study, the diversity of Polish responses to the Holocaust has become considerably clearer. The scale of Polish aid to Jews is increasingly recognized. Paulsson (2002: 240) convincingly argues that 'but for the Hotel Polski affair and the Warsaw Uprising, the survival rate among Jews hiding in Warsaw would have been about the same as that in Western Europe, contrary to all expectations and contemporary perceptions'.[35] At the same time, the scope and depth of Polish anti-Semitism amongst certain sections of society has been revealed through the extensive debates about Jedwabne (a town in north-east Poland where several hundred Jews were crowded into a barn and burnt to death by Poles in 1941), and the scope of anti-Jewish sentiment in the country during the war is now increasingly recognized through the work of Jan Gross, Barbara Engelking and Jan Grabowski, amongst others.[36] The Catholic hierarchy, for example, did not make any statement on the fate of the Jews, but the Nazi targeting of converts did stimulate some action, and some Jewish children were hidden on Church property (Polonsky 2004: 68).[37] The Catholic Church, as the pre-eminent moral authority for most Poles, had a duty to offer guidance to the Polish population. The primate, August Hlond, fled to Rome and,

Cartographies of inclusion and exclusion 279

despite pleas from Jewish representatives who were very aware of the potential influence of the Church, no significant statement from the Church hierarchy encouraging Poles to help Jews was issued.[38] So although the Nazis persecuted the clergy, the moral vacuum created by the Church's ambivalence towards Jews and its silence about their plight provided space for Polish anti-Semites to act, often murderously, against Jews.

The myth of impeccable Polish conduct during the war, pushed by nationalist historians, is slowly unravelling under the strain of its own contradictions.[39] In this more complicated context, there is the risk that the notion of 'universe of obligation' may now disguise as much as it reveals and encourage generalization when nuance is required. It therefore should be used with increased caution and sensitivity, as its *analytical* capacity to add understanding to Polish–Jewish relations is diminished. The concept can provide insight both into the form and substance of aid to Jews *and* into hostile, even murderous, attitudes and actions, and functions best as an analogue for social distance between groups. It no longer has the explanatory resonance that it once had. In short, the idea of Jews being outside Poles' 'universe of obligation' works best as one of several possible general, abstract, starting points for more detailed analysis.

The cartography of inclusion and exclusion was more complicated and fluid than much scholarship up to the early 2000s recognized, as it did not always neatly demarcate Poles from Jews, as the history of Żegota indicates.[40] But at the same time, the scale and depth of some Poles' hostility to Jews and the scale of criminal opportunism has become clearer. The murder of Jews by Poles during the war, as Engelking (2011) and Grabowski (2011) have shown, was not a rare occurrence.

It is therefore more useful to consider the notion of universe of obligation in its variety and multiplicity – as unstable universes of obligation – and map how different groups, sections of society and indeed individuals responded over time and in particular places to reproduce a Polish culture that *both* differentially incorporated Jews into the broader nation *and* worked to exclude them. Social distance between groups stretched and shrank, and the boundaries between groups changed over time during the war. The stable binary frame of in-group/out-group does not capture the complications of wartime relationships or the multiple oscillations as individuals and groups moved closer to, and further from, each other.

Through the war, groups and individuals made choices on how to respond to the Nazi onslaught against the Jews. The Poles occupied a superior position in relation to the Jews. As Barbara Engelking (2001: 24) has noted,

280   Conclusion

The Poles did not need the Jews in order to wage their war against the Germans. Meanwhile, the Jews – if they wished to avoid certain death at the hands of the Germans – could not manage without the Poles. They were condemned to suffer the consequences of their neighbours' charity, pity, decency, hatred, indifference or greed.

In this asymmetrical relationship, Poles could choose how to respond to their neighbours' plight. Any action to aid Jews faced both German sanctions (those aiding Jews were punished with death) and, with a varying geography, the disapproval of sections of the wider Polish population. But the choice was there. And, in choosing a response, Poles also chose their own identity from a world of possibilities – as helper, defender, persecutor, bystander, etc. Reports from Poland, and from Auschwitz, gathered by the Polish Underground and sent west, expanded the number of people who were confronted by the same question faced by Poles on a repeated basis during the war.

For the British government and the American government (until the creation of the WRB in January 1944) European Jews were outside their respective universes of obligation. For some British citizens, including broad sections of British Jewry, European Jews were to be assisted. It may be the case that, had more been known to the general public, then more British citizens would have claimed that they too had obligations to European Jews, as Rabbi Hertz suggested. As it was, the British government worked to ensure that Britons' universes of obligation were not expanded to include European Jews. Despite the efforts of the War Refugee Board, which largely tapped into the American Jewish community, the situation in the United States was remarkably similar.

Zygielbojm's protest against the West's passivity in face of the annihilation of European Jewry went unheeded. His accusation of responsibility (echoed by the chief rabbi in February 1944) was ignored:

The responsibility for the crime of murdering all Jewish population in Poland falls, in the first instance, on the perpetrators, but indirectly, also weighs on the whole of humanity, the peoples and Governments of the Allied States, which, so far, have made no effort towards a concrete action for the purpose of curtailing this crime. By the passive observation of this murder of defenceless millions and maltreated children, women and men, *these countries have become accomplices of the criminals.*[41]

In 1942, 1943 and 1944 the machinery of mass murder destroyed hundreds of thousands of Jewish lives at Auschwitz. This process was reported, with some delay, to the West. Churchill and Eden maintained positions of deniability, since no document clearly demonstrating that they knew of the systematic killing at Auschwitz has been found.

Cartographies of inclusion and exclusion

281

However, the sheer volume of data about the camp that reached London, and Churchill's and Eden's awareness that the Nazis were gassing Jews elsewhere, makes the claim that these senior British leaders did not know about the true function of the camp increasingly suspect. Indeed, the full meaning of Frank Roberts's comment in an interview with Barbara Rogers (1999b: 97) in 1995, that the 'FO is never short of would be "do gooders" sending us lots of information. The difficulty of the FO is too much information not too little', is now clear. Many officials in the Foreign Office did not sympathize sufficiently with those seeking to aid European Jews, or with European Jews themselves, to alter policy and take into account the Nazi genocidal programme. Above all, British and American *raison de guerre* triumphed. But the cost was high. In spring and summer of 1944, with the full knowledge of the Allied powers, Hungarian Jewry was sent to its doom by the Nazis.[42] Western governments looked on as European Jews were murdered in the gas chambers at Auschwitz-Birkenau.

Appendix I Information about Auschwitz to reach the West, November 1942–June 1944

Piece of information	Date sent	Data	Source	Archival reference	Intermediary	Date received	Distribution	Date information published/ broadcast/ received	Archival reference
1	4 September 1942 Circa 11 September 1942?	Mortality statistics at Oświęcim: 'the gas chamber is employed for those who are ill or incapable of work and those who have been brought in transports especially for the purpose/Soviet prisoners of war, and, recently Jews'	Polish Underground. Couriered by Jan Karski?	AAN 1325 202/I-31 (213) PUMST A3.16 (158) AAN 1325 202/I/31 (57), Microfilm 2201/9I PISM PRM 76/1 (13) 238–240. (Raport o sytuacji w kraju na podstawie wiadomości nadeszłych do dnia 31.X.1942)	Stanisław Mikołajczyk. Letter from the Polish ambassador (20 January 1942) (no mention of gas chambers)	12 November 1942	Polish Embassy, United States (Report on conditions in Poland) Cabinet of the Polish government (Sprawozdanie Nr 6/1942) British Foreign Secretary, Anthony Eden *Jewish Chronicle* (no mention of gas chambers) *Poland Fights* (New York) – 'Many carloads of Russian war prisoners and Jews have suffered death by gas in this notorious camp.'	27 November 1942 23 December 1942 23 January 1943 12 February 1943 5 April 1943	HIA-US (Embassy of Poland), Box 29, Folder 2 Sprawozdanie Nr 6/1942, PUMST MSW Volume II (1942) FO 371/34549 C856/34/55 Polish Library, London. Also at US.NA. Nazi Black Record, RG 165, Poland 6950

Piece of information	Date sent	Data	Source	Archival reference	Intermediary	Date received	Distribution	Date information published/ broadcast/ received	Archival reference
							'Document appertaining to the German occupation of Poland: Poles in German Concentration Camps', Polish Ministry of the Interior	1943	PUMST A3.16 (158)
							Report 6/42 (English-language version)	May? 1943	IPN BU 2835/25
2	20 November 1942	Slaughter of Jews	Returnee from Poland – a lady from Sosnowiec (Dobkin report)	CZA S26/1203	Jewish Agency		*New York Times*	25 November 1942	
					American Jewish Committee, the American Jewish Congress, B'Nai B'rith, the Jewish Labour Committee, the Synagogue Council of America and the Union of Orthodox Rabbis of the United States		President Roosevelt	8 December 1942	
							Poland Fights (extracts from document handed to Roosevelt – mention of Oświęcim not published)	5 January 1943	
							British Foreign Office	10 January 1943	NA.FO 371/ 34361 (CM255)

3	15 December 1942	Statistics: Oświęcim – 520,000 Jews killed	Polish Underground	Addition to report of the State Security Corps of the Interior Department of the Delegature. AAN 1325 202/ II-35 (84) Aneks 48 (16–28 February 1943). AAN 1325 202/ III-8 (171) 'Pro Memoria' 24 January 1943–24 February 1943 AAN 1325 202/ I-32 (130). Also in *Zeszyty Oświęcimskie* 1 (1968), 89.					
	4 March 1943		Polish Underground (Cable from Jankowski and Rowecki)	AAN 1326 203 I-23 (291) AKD, Volume VI, Document 1751	Stanisław Mikołajczyk, Władysław Sikorski	31 March 1943 (de-encrypted)	US OSS	18 May 1943	US NA RG 218 CC334, Folder 3.0
						May? 1943	US Joint Chiefs Ignacy Schwarzbart	June 1943	IPN BU 2835/43 (185)
							Polska pod okupacją niemiecką, Istanbul (cites a figure of 550,000)	14 May 1943	

(*cont.*)

Piece of information	Date sent	Data	Source	Archival reference	Intermediary	Date received	Distribution	Date information published/ broadcast/ received	Archival reference
				Sprawozdanie Nr 4/43, PUMST MSW, Volume III (1943)	Cabinet of the Polish Government	20 August 1943	*Pologne occupée*, Istanbul (cites a figure of 580,000)	22 May 1943	
							PAT, Polish Information Center, New York (640,000 people perished at Oświęcim)	31 May 1943	National Library, Warsaw, Microfilm 113236
							Polish Jewish Observer	3 September 1943	
							Polska pod okupacją niemiecką, Istanbul	9 September 1943	
							Jewish Chronicle	10 September 1943	
							Our Tribune, New York	21 October 1943	National Library, Warsaw
							JTA (cites a figure of 580,000)	13 December 1943	

4	12 March 1943	New crematorium, with a capacity of killing 3,000 people a day – mostly Jews. Sterilization of women	Polish Underground (Cable from Jankowski and Rowecki)	PUMST 3.16 (9)	Stanisław Mikołajczyk, Władysław Sikorski	23 March 1943	PWE Central Directive *Polish Jewish Observer*	8 April 1943 3 September 1943	FO 371/34383
5	12 March 1943	The mass killing of Jews at Oświęcim	Polish Underground (Rowecki)	AKD, Volume II, Document 401	Polish government	circa 12 May 1943	Informed Polish ambassador's letter to Alec Randall		
6	22 March 1943	Jews at Oświęcim	Former inmate of camp		Ridley Prentice, Political Intelligence Department, Lisbon		Foreign Office	3 September 1943	FO 371/34550 C3694
7	Unknown	Killing at Oświęcim (no mention of Jews)	Movement of the Polish Working Masses		Jan Kwapiński (Polish minister)	26 March 1943	Foreign Office (Frank Roberts), Clement Attlee (Labour Party)	7 April 1943	FO 371/34550
8	23 March 1943	New crematorium, with the capacity to kill 3,000 people a day – mostly Jews. Tests on sterilization of women	Polish Underground (Korboński)	HIA Stanisław Mikołajczyk Papers, Box 38, dispatches from intelligence outposts, Folder 17, General, March 1943–July 1944. Also at Poland's National Digital Archive, 800/22/0/-/38 (jpeg 816)	Polish government	27 March 1943	*Polish Jewish Observer*	3 September 1943	

(cont.)

Piece of information	Date sent	Data	Source	Archival reference	Intermediary	Date received	Distribution	Date information published/ broadcast/ received	Archival reference
9	30 March 1943	Liquidation of the Cracow ghetto. Jews sent to Oświęcim	Polish Underground (Korboński)	HIA Stanisław Mikołajczyk Papers, Box 38, Dispatches from intelligence outposts, Folder 19, March 1943. Also at Poland's National Digital Archive, 800/22/ 0/-/38 (jpeg 885)	Polish government		BBC broadcast (Polish Service) (gas chambers at Oświęcim)	11 April 1943	BBC WAC European news bulletins – Polish 1943
							Radio Świt	April 1943	HIA Stanisław Mikołajczyk Papers, Box 38, Radio Świt, Folder 7. Also at Poland's National Digital Archive, 800/22/0/-/38 (jpeg 152)
							JTA (no mention of gas chambers. Jews deported 'to the dread concentration camp at Oświęcim)	12 April 1943	
							Jewish Chronicle (no specific mention of gas chambers: 'implements . . . for mass execution'	16 April 1943	
							Jewish Chronicle –'the martyrdom of Oswiecim'	30 April 1943	
							The Times (partial)	1 June 1943	
							PWE aide-mémoire – Special Annex on the persecution of the Jews	24 March 1944	NA.FO 371/ 39014 (441)

No.	Date	Subject	Source	Reference	Sent to	Date	Recipient	Date	Archive reference
10	14 April 1943	Food parcels for labour camps in Upper Silesia: Auschwitz, Sosnowitz, Birkenau …	Gerhart Riegner, WJC, Geneva	Cited in Gilbert (2001a: 129) WJC archives, General Secretariat	Stephen Wise, WJC, New York		Rabbi Irving Miller	April 1943	YVA M2. 261 IPN BU 2835/56
11	18 April 1943	Mass killing of Jews; gas chambers	Polish Underground (Salski reports)	PISM A9 III 2A 3	Ignacy Schwarzbart	18 April 1943	Berl Locker	April 1943	
							British Section of World Jewish Congress (Alexander Easterman)	30 April 1943	HL MS 238/2/52 Folder 4
							Jewish Agency, Polish Jewish Department, Tel Aviv	May 1943	
							World Jewish Congress, New York	May 1943	
							Postal and Telegraph Censorship, MI12, Foreign Office, Political Warfare Executive and others	4 May 1943	NA.FO 371/ 34552
							OSS	5 May 1943	US NA RG 226, Entry 191 National Library, Warsaw

(cont.)

Piece of information	Date sent	Data	Source	Archival reference	Intermediary	Date received	Distribution	Date information published/ broadcast/ received	Archival reference
							Our Tribune, New York (no mention of gas chambers or systematic murder of Jews)	21 October 1943	
12		Jews missing in the region of Cracow	Jewish or Polish source in Istanbul?		*The Times* correspondent in Istanbul		*The Times*	26 May 1943	
13	29 April 1943	Liquidation of Cracow and Stanislawow ghettos – Jews killed on the spot – others to Oświęcim	Polish Underground	AKD, Volume VI, 313, Document 1761	Polish government		*The Times*	1 June 1943	
14	3 May 1943	3,000 people per day killed at Oświęcim	Polish Underground (Korboński)	HIA Korboński, Box 1, Reel 2. Cable from N, 3 May 1943 (78)	Stanisław Mikołajczyk	6 May 1943	*Polish Jewish Observer*	3 September 1943	
15	Various dates	Description of mass killing at Treblinka – Oświęcim listed as a similar camp	Polish Underground (various reports)		Letter from Józef Zarański (Polish Embassy, London)	18 May 1943	Alec Randall, Foreign Office		NA.FO 371/ 34550 (65)

16	7 June 1943	Castrations, sterilization and artificial insemination, 20 Jews and 25 Jewesses experimented on	Polish Underground (Korboński)	AKD, Volume VI, Document 1773, p. 341	Polish government	10 June 1943	JTA *Jewish Chronicle*	13 June 1943 25 June 1943	
17	Various dates	Nazi scientists gassing Jews … experiments in the death chambers of Oswiecim and Treblinka	Polish Underground (various reports)		Polish government	15 June 1943	JTA	16 June 1943	
18	17 July 1943	Jews from Będzin 'killed by shooting and burning'	Letter from Będzin				Jewish Agency, Istanbul		YVA O-67
19	Summer 1943	468,000 Jews killed by end of September 1942 at Oświęcim	Unknown SS man/ Polish Underground	AAN 1325 202/ III-7 (169–72)					
	10 June 1943	468,000 Jews killed by end of 1942 at Oświęcim		PUMST A3.1.1.4 (56), p. 4 (Aneks 58 covering period 1–31 August 1943)	Polish Bureau IV/ Stanisław Mikołajczyk/ Władysław Banaczyk	31 August 1943	Harold Perkins SOE	23 November 1943	PUMST A3.1.1.4 (90) NA.HS 4/212
	10 July 1943	Jews from Nice, Berlin, Salonika (and Będzin) to Oświęcim		PUMST A3.1.1.4 (51) (Nr 316)	Polish Bureau IV/ Stanisław Mikołajczyk/	13 August 1943	Władysław Banaczyk, Marian Kukiel (minister of defence)	14 August 1944	PUMST A3.1.1.4 (61)

(*cont.*)

Piece of information	Date sent	Data	Source	Archival reference	Intermediary	Date received	Distribution	Date information published/ broadcast/ received	Archival reference
	Collated reports of 10 June, 10 July and 12 August 1943	468,000 Jews killed by end of September 1942 at Oświęcim Jews from Nice, Berlin, Salonika to Oświęcim Names of SS officers		Sprawozdanie Nr 11/43, PUMST MSW, Volume III (1943)	Polish government	2 December 1943			
				PUMST 3.16		5 January 1944–28 January 1944	Polish military missions in Mexico, Ottawa, Ankara, Stockholm	Uncertain: January/ February 1944	
							Jewish Agency Committee for the Jews of Occupied Europe Bulletin (p. 10, partial)	February 1944	FO 371/42807 (122)
							OSS, US military attaché.	13 March 1944	
							Polska pod okupacją Niemiecka, Istanbul	15 March 1944	

						Polish Ministry of Information Press release	21 March 1944	*New York Times* (partial)	16 March 1944	HIA Polish Information Center – cable from London. Box 3.9
								Daily Mirror (partial – 14 SS criminals)	16 March 1944	
								Pologne occupée, Istanbul	22 March 1944	
								Los Angeles Times	22 March 1944	
								Washington Post	22 March 1944	
								New York Herald Tribune	22 March 1944	
								Daily News (Perth)	22 March 1944	
								*Daily Mirro*r (partial)	22 March 1944	
								JTA	23 March 1944	
								Morning Bulletin (Rockhampton)	23 March 1944	
								The Mercury (Hobart)	23 April 1944	

Piece of information	Date sent	Data	Source	Archival reference	Intermediary	Date received	Distribution	Date information published/ broadcast/ received	Archival reference
							Examiner (Launceston)	23 March 1944	
							Advocate (Burnie)	23 March 1944	
							Jewish Chronicle (partial)	24 March 1944	
							Dziennik Polski (partial)	27 March 1944	
							Polish Jewish Observer	7 April 1944	
20	31 August 1943, 7 September 1943 and others	Slaughter of Jews at Oświęcim goes on incessantly. Also, 7,300 Jews from Greece gassed at Oświęcim	Polish Underground	AAN 1325 202/ III-148 (314/323) and others. See *Zeszyty Oświęcimskie* I (1968), 120, 122, 123	Polish government		*Polish Jewish Observer*	4 February 1944	
							Jewish Chronicle	4 February 1944	
							News Bulletin (Representation of Polish Jewy – American Division)	January– February 1944	

				Sprawozdanie Nr 1/44, PUMST MSW, Volume IV (1944)	Ignacy Schwarzbart	18 January 1944	A. Leon Kubowitzki (WJC)/Benjamin Teller (Independent Jewish Press Service)	8 March 1944	AJA MSS 361 Box G17 Folder 2
							PWE aide-mémoire – Special Annex on the persecution of the Jews	24 March 1944	NA.FO 371/ 39014 (441)
21	Summer 1943	'50,000 Slovakian Jews to Oswiecim, the notorious death camp in Poland'	Jew from Slovakia who arrived in Tel-Aviv				*Jewish Chronicle*	21 January 1944	
			Polish Underground	Sprawozdanie Nr 11/43, PUMST MSW, Volume III (1943)	Polish government/ Ignacy Schwarzbart				
22	August 1943	The greater part of the Jews has already been murdered	Polish Underground	Aneks 57, 16–31 July 1943, AAN 1325/202/III-8, k.211	Bureau VI	23 August 1943	SOE	23 August 1943	HS 4/210
23	31 August 1943	Liquidation of Jews from Będzin. 7,000 to Oświęcim	Polish Underground (Jankowski)	PUMST 3.1.1.13.5 (125)	Władysław Banaczyk/ Ignacy Schwarzbart	29 September 1943	*Polish Jewish Observer* JTA	8 October 1943 8 October 1943	
24	August 1943	'… appalling slaughter in the death camps of Treblinka, Belzec, Sobibor and Oswiecim' (quote from *Jewish Chronicle*)	Various including Raczyński's letter to Eden, 20 January 1943	British Library	Inter-Allied Information Committee		*Jewish Chronicle*	3 September 1943	

Piece of information	Date sent	Data	Source	Archival reference	Intermediary	Date received	Distribution	Date information published/ broadcast/ received	Archival reference
25	1 September 1943	'Today we know that Sobibor, Malkinia-Treblinka, Belzec and Auschwitz are liquidation camps'			Report from Bratislava – Slovak Zionists		Jewish organizations in Istanbul, Jerusalem, London and New York		CZA S26/1520 (formerly CZA S26/1428)
26	15 September 1943	Killing of Jews and Poles at Oświęcim	Polish Underground	PUMST 3.16 (13)	Polish government	30 September 1943 (de-encrypted)	Informed BBC Polish Service broadcast	22 October 1943	NA.FO 371/ 39449 (C869)
27	September 1943?	'Local people relate that some tens of thousands of Jews have passed through the Oswiecim camp'	Polish Underground: 'Conditions in the Oswiecim Camp described by a Polish Workman'	PISM A10 9 5	Polish government	17 September 1943	Polish Information Center, New York	16 September 1943	HIA, Polish Information Center, New York, Box 3.3 Cable from London 16 September 1943
							News Bulletin of the Representation of Polish Jewry – American Division	October 1943	PUMST AALC, Kol. 133/266

#	Date	Details	Source/Informant	Reference	Recipient	Date	Informed	Date	Archive
28	28 September 1943	Record number of people killed in one day at Brzezinka by Oświęcim – 30,000. (Jews not specifically mentioned.) Mass gassing of Poles	Polish Underground (Stefan Korboński)	PUMST MSW 73 (280) Also at PISM PRML/4 (43)	Polish government	6 October 1943	Informed BBC Polish Service broadcast *Dziennik Polski*	22 October 1943 / 27 March 1944	NA.FO 371/ 39449 (C869)
29	5 November 1943	Between 15 July 1943 and 30 September 1943, 6,800 Czech Jews deported from Theresienstadt to Birkenau	Gerhart Riegner, WJC, Geneva	Cited in Gilbert (2001a: 161). WJC Archives, General Secretariat	WJC, London. Czechoslovak Government in Exile, London		*Jewish Chronicle*	25 February 1944	
30	November 1943?	Those incapacitated 'shipped to the Oswiecim "death camp" for execution'	Two Antwerp Jews returned to Belgium		Belgium newspaper *L'independence*		JTA News Bulletin of the Representation of Polish Jewry – American Division	12 November 1943 January–February 1944	PUMST AALC, Kol. 133/266
31	15 November 1943	'All centres of Jewish life have been deleted from the surface of the earth. Their inhabitants have found their deaths in the torture camps in Treblinka, Sobibor, Belzec and Oswiecim'	Cywia Lubetkin and Icchak Cukierman (via Polish Underground)	IPN BU 2835/59 (51)	Polish intelligence (London), Ignacy Schwarzbart	unknown	Yitzhak Tabenki, Eliyha Dobkin, 'Jaari', Palestinian Federation of Labour		

Piece of information	Date sent	Data	Source	Archival reference	Intermediary	Date received	Distribution	Date information published/ broadcast/ received	Archival reference
32	Late 1943?	Around 30,000 Jews killed in the gas chambers at Oświęcim in the last weeks (November 1943)	Polish Underground	Sprawozdanie Nr 1/44, PUMST MSW, Volume IV (1944). Also at British Library SK48/4.	Polish government	18 January 1944	Provided support for *Dziennik Polski* article	27 March 1944	
33	10 January 1944	'In Oświęcim, Bełżec, Majdanek, and Treblinka they have built special gas chambers to destroy prisoners wholesale' 50,000 Poles, around a million Jews and other nationalities killed at Oświęcim (gassed).	Zygmunt Zaremba (PPS), Polish Underground. Couriered by Jerzy Lerski	PUMST AALC Kol. 133/15 PUMST AALC, Kol. 133/15 'Zalacznik 2 do listu Nr.K/70'	Adam Ciołkosz, Jan Kwapiński	4 March 1944	Clement Attlee, Executive of the Labour Party Polish Telegraphic Agency Isaac Deutscher (*The Observer*), Freddie Kuh (PM – New York), *New Statesman* *Camp of Death*, Liberty Press	24 March 1944 July 1994	Lerski (1988: 232); Lerski (1986: 123); Ciołkosz (1983: 199); Friszke (2011: 323) PUMST AALC Kol. 133/297

34	30 January 1944	Jews destroyed in Oświęcim	Various sources					*New York Times* (book review of *The Black book of Polish Jewry*)		
35	Various dates	Mass murder of Jews in gas chambers in 'death camps' at Bełżec, Majdanek, Oświęcim, Treblinka …	Polish Underground	Various				*Polska pod okupacją niemiecką*, Istanbul	27 January 1944	
36	Various dates	500,000 Jews murdered in the gas chambers at Oświęcim	Polish Underground	Various	Polish Telegraphic Agency	15 February 1944		*Palestine Post*	16 February 1944	
37	Various dates	Jews killed at Oświęcim	Polish Underground	Various	Jan Nowak-Jeziorański	Various		Church of England, Foreign Relations Committee	29 February 1944	(FO 371/39451 C9609)
38	Various dates	Liquidation of ghettos: Jews killed in situ or deported to death camps (Bełżec, Treblinka, Oświęcim-Auschwitz, Sobibór, etc.)	Polish Underground	Various				*Pologne occupée*, Istanbul	9 March 1944	
39	25 March 1944	Gassing of several thousand Czech Jews	Polish Underground, Józef Cyrankiewicz, via Stanisław Jankowski (5 April 1944)	ABSM Mat. RO, Volume 2, p. 68a PUMST MSW 17 (27)	Polish government	5 June 1944		*Dziennik Polski Palestine Post* *Jewish Chronicle*	9 June 1944 11 June 1944 16 June 1944	

Piece of information	Date sent	Data	Source	Archival reference	Intermediary	Date received	Distribution	Date information published/ broadcast/ received	Archival reference
							Informed BBC Czechoslovak Service and German Service – News for Women – Noon broadcast	15 June 1944 16 June 1944	Karny (1993: 209), ABSM Mat. RO, Volume 131, p. 3. BBC WAC German Service Files/Lindley Fraser Reports, File C165)
40	19 April 1944	Gassing of 7,000 Jews in February 1944 (on 15 March 4,000 Jews from Theresienstadt killed)	Polish Underground	Informacja Bieżąca Nr 16 (140), AAN 1325 202/III-7, k.95			Foreign Office to British Embassy (Washington, DC)	8 June 1944 12 June 1944	NA.FO 371/ 39451 (C7873), p. 134 HIA Polish Embassy (US), Box 42, Folder 4.
	27 April 1944		Polish Underground. (Tadeusz Bór-Komorowski)	AKD, Volume III, Doc. 611	Polish government	31 May 1944 (de-encrypted 1 June 1944)	British Embassy (Washington, DC) to Polish Embassy (Washington, DC), for Mikołajczyk JTA Informed BBC Czechoslovak Service and German Service – News for Women – Noon broadcast	12 June 1944 15 June 1944 16 June 1944	 Karny (1993: 209) BBC WAC German Service Files/Lindley Fraser Reports. File C165

41	May 1944?	Children pretend to be older to 'escape deportation to the death camp at Oswiecim'	*Le flambeau* – underground newspaper of the Belgian Defence Committee				*Jewish Chronicle*	19 May 1944	
42	May/June 1944?	Gas chambers at Oświęcim and Brzezinka; 'at least one million Jews' killed in 'death chambers' at Oświęcim	Testimony from camp escapee Jan Wolny		The *New York Times* News Service (London office) *Polish Jewish Observer*	16 June 1944	*Milwaukee Journal* *New York Times* War Refugee Board	5 June 1944 20 June 1944	War Refugee Board Collection, FDR Library, Hungary, Volume 1, Folder 2, February–August 1944 – copy of *Polish Jewish Observer*
43	1 June 1944	100,000 Hungarian Jews killed at Oświęcim	Polish Underground (Stanisław Jankowski)	PUMST MSW 17/58 (145)	Polish government/ Emanuel Scherer	16 June 1944	*New York Times*	25 June 1944	
44	7 June 1944	Six transports a day of Hungarian Jews enroute to Oświęcim between 15 May and 27 May	Polish Underground (Tadeusz Bór-Komorowski)	AKD, Volume III, Doc. 632	Polish government	12 June 1944 (de-encrypted)	*Manchester Guardian* *Jewish Chronicle*	28 June 1944 30 June 1944	

Piece of information	Date sent	Data	Source	Archival reference	Intermediary	Date received	Distribution	Date information published/broadcast/received	Archival reference
45	14 June 1944	100,000 Hungarian Jews killed at Oświęcim	Polish Undergound (Tadeusz Bór-Komorowski)	AKD, Volume III, Doc. 638	Polish government	19 June 1944 (de-encrypted)	*New York Times*	25 June 1944	
							BBC Home Service (6 p.m. news bulletin (partial))	26 June 1944	
							JTA	26 June 1944	
							Manchester Guardian	27 June 1944	
					World Jewish Congress		*Manchester Guardian*	28 June 1944	
							Jewish Chronicle	30 June 1944	
46	14 June 1944	Warning to Germans	Vrba–Wetzler report (The report was widely circulated. See chapter 6 for more details)		Telegram from Dr Kopecky, British representative, and Jewish representatives in Switzerland		BBC Czechoslovak Service	15, 16 June 1944	Karny (1993: 209; 1996: 558)
							BBC German Service – News for Women – Noon broadcast	16 June 1944	BBC WAC German Service Files/Lindley Fraser Reports, C165

	19 June 1944	Hungarian Jews 'sent to the death camp of Birkenau near Oswiecim . . . where in the course of last year 1,500,000 Jews from all over Europe have been killed'			Czechoslovak State Council	19 June 1944	*New York Times*	20 June 1944		
					Letter from Miklos Krausz (Palestine Office, Budapest) to Chaim Pozner (Palestine Office, Geneva); Richard Lichtheim (Jewish Agency, Geneva) to Douglas MacKillop (British Legation, Bern); Clifford Norton (British Minister, Bern)	26 June 1944	Foreign Office	27 June 1944	FO 371/42807 (148)
47	27 June 1944	From mid-May thirteen trains a day with forty-five wagons carrying Jews from Hungary arrived at Oświęcim. They were gassed	Polish Underground	PUMST 3.1.1.13.5B (199)	Polish government	30 June 1944	Informed data released to the press in July, i.e. *The Times*	8 July 1944	
							Alexander Easterman	11 July 1944	HL MS 238/2/18
48	29 June 1944?	450,000 Jews from Hungary deported to Auschwitz: 'many die en route . . . others are killed and cremated on arrival'	World Council of Churches (Geneva)		Federal Council of Churches of Christ of America		JTA	30 June 1944	

Appendix II   Archives and historians

The discussion of knowledge about Auschwitz in Chapters 4 and 5 demonstrated that the National Archives in Kew *should* have more documents pertaining to Auschwitz. The logbook of telegrams sent and received by Polish intelligence in London indicates extremely close liaison between Polish Bureau VI and SOE's Polish Section. Bureau VI routinely passed *aneks*, which dealt specifically with the German terror campaign in Poland, to the British. Few of these reports remain in the National Archives.

In addition to the tight relationship between Bureau VI and SOE, communication between the British and the Poles occurred at all levels: Józef Retinger, an adviser to General Sikorski, met frequently with William Strang at the Foreign Office. General Sikorski was often accompanied by the British liaison officer Colonel Victor Cazalet (MP) in Britain (Cazalet was killed alongside Sikorski in a 1943 plane crash). Frank Savery received reports from various Polish politicians and officials including Stanisław Mikołajczyk and Stanisław Kot, two individuals especially well placed to know about the mass slaughter at the camp. Savery's translations of these documents are also conspicuous by their absence.

The British also had access to Polish reports that were sent overseas as the British intercepted outgoing mail through their censorship procedures and had the capacity to access diplomatic bags at their customs posts in the Caribbean. The files of the Foreign Office do include the occasional telegram intercept, including, for example, a telegram in which representatives of the Bund comment on Roman Knoll's 1943 document detailing social sentiment in Poland and the possibility that the return of Jews to postwar Poland would stimulate anti-Semitism.[1] Clearly, the British were monitoring the communications of significant Polish Jewish figures. Schwarzbart in particular regularly informed colleagues in the US and Palestine about the slaughter of Jews at Auschwitz, but only the May 1943 intercept of Schwarzbart's letter to the World Jewish Congress, which provided details of the Salski report, remains to demonstrate FO and PWE knowledge of the camp through this source.

304

Archives and historians

Some absences in the British archives can be accounted for. Intelligence operations tended to destroy documents. The Foreign Office, in 1943, pursued a robust policy which inhibited the Poles from publicly discussing Jews and atrocities, explaining the limited reference to Jews being killed at the camp in official, formal written communications. In 1944, the British Embassy to the Polish Government in Exile was bombed and files, including any documents from the Polish government, were destroyed. However, it is not known for certain if any documentation about Auschwitz was lost as a result of the bombing.

Foreign Office files shed little light on the camp, but the volume of data that reached London indicates that the Foreign Office, and the British government more generally, were not particularly interested in news about the Nazi concentration and death camps in which 'foreigners' were incarcerated and killed. For historians, this is a timely reminder of the limits of archives. Foreign Office files indicate what the Foreign Office wanted to know, but do not always reflect the full extent of what was known by Foreign Office officials. Focus only on singular archive collections, or on archives sharing similar gaps in their records, can lead to erroneous conclusions. This, in part, accounts for the sustained traction of the narrative about Auschwitz being elusive. However, the intercept of the Salski report passed to the Foreign Office and Political Warfare Executive has, according to the file at the National Archives, been available since 1972. Information from newspapers such as the *Jewish Chronicle* and the *Polish Jewish Observer* has always been readily available.

A further significant absence from the British archives is that of the papers of the minister of information, Brendan Bracken. Bracken was well positioned in the British government to be very well informed about Auschwitz. He liaised closely with newspaper proprietors to ensure that the war was narrated in the appropriate way, had some responsibility over the Political Warfare Executive, liaised with the Foreign Office on reporting the war, and was a member of Churchill's 'kitchen cabinet'. His papers would, in theory, have provided further detail on British fighting and narrating of the Second World War. On his death he instructed his servant to burn all his papers. This wish was complied with. The full extent of Bracken's activities remains unknown.

To combat absences in the documentary record, 'echoes' or copies of missing documents can be found often, but not always, in different archival collections or elsewhere. In the case of Western knowledge of the Holocaust, the *Polish Jewish Observer* is an excellent source, which has generally been overlooked by Holocaust scholars. Many of the articles about Auschwitz in that newspaper reproduce to a great extent text from the source Polish intelligence reports. Reports in the *Polish Jewish*

306   Archives and historians

Observer bring into question Walter Laqueur's (1998: 117) contention that July 1942 witnessed a change in the Polish government's 'information policy'. The number of Jewish victims was not lowered all of the time and not in all fora where the information was presented.

The study of the Polish Government in Exile is particularly problematic. Many Polish documents have been destroyed and there are significant gaps in 'Polish files' in British archives. Currently, there are efforts to track Polish government and intelligence documents; many files are thought to have been taken by former officials of the Polish government or intelligence services following the withdrawal of recognition of the Polish Government in Exile in July 1945. The records of Radio Świt, for example, are incomplete. Some documents relating to Świt can be found at the Hoover Institute and references to some Świt broadcasts can be found in Polish Telegraphic Agency documents held at the Polish Institute and Sikorski Museum, London, but there are significant absences. Since Świt sought to give the impression that it operated from Poland, it received a steady stream of up-to-date information via radio. Further details of data received and prepared for broadcast by Świt would have augmented our knowledge of what was known, and when, to PWE officials, and allowed further analysis of the Polish Underground's information policy.

The Polish government (Cabinet) had knowledge of the mass killing of Jews by 23 December 1942, when Sprawozdanie Nr 6/42 was distributed, and more detailed information was disseminated through 1943 and 1944. Once the nature of the camp was known to the Polish Cabinet and Polish National Council it would have been virtually impossible to keep secret. The fact that reports that arrived in London in 1943 and 1944 can be tracked to the BBC, the *Polish Jewish Observer* and the *Jewish Chronicle*, but frequently not to the various offices and agencies of the British government (the FO, the PWE, British intelligence), highlights the degree to which FO, PWE and intelligence files have been weeded.

News of Auschwitz as a site where European Jewry was being murdered was published in London using material from Polish intelligence sources, but a great deal of this material is not found in the National Archives in Kew. This absence speaks to the information-handling policies of the British government. Reports on atrocities, including those against Jews at Auschwitz, were forwarded to Roger Allen at the Foreign Office. The fate of Allen's atrocity file is not known. It may have been misfiled, broken up for postwar war trials, destroyed or withheld. There is a real possibility that either the FO or British intelligence (MI5/6) hold this file. The recent 2012 release of colonial documents from a secret FO archive – documents that legally should have been released in the 1980s – indicates that sections of the British state were prepared to hold on to sensitive material. Given that Allied knowledge of Auschwitz falls into this category, it is certainly possible that material passed to Roger Allen remains under lock and key.

Notes

I INTRODUCTION

1 By 2001, Bauer had shifted his position as a result of Richard Breitman's scholarship, stating, 'I also maintained that Auschwitz was almost unknown until 1944, and I was wrong'. In 2012 Bauer clarified his view, writing 'that while the Allies knew there was a concentration camp at Auschwitz, and some intelligence items mentioned gas chambers, the extent of the horror was not known' (Bauer 2012: 143). Bauer has now come full circle. In October 2013 he contended that 'information about the Auschwitz camp being an extermination camp originated in a report by two escapees from the camp, Rudolf Vrba and Alfred Wetzler'. See 'The Israel Air Force flyover at Auschwitz: a crass, superficial display', *Haaretz*, 8 October 2013, available online at www.haaretz.com/weekend/magazine/.premium-1.551256, last accessed 14 October 2013. In this book, I will show that the extent of the horror was known to British Foreign Office officials by May 1943 at the latest.

2 For a discussion and the texts of these reports see Świebocki (1997).

3 Gilbert notes two further pieces of information about the camp that reached the West. On 14 April 1943 Gerhart Riegner of the World Jewish Congress in Geneva sent a telegram to Stephen Wise (WJC) in New York which depicted Auschwitz and Birkenau as labour camps where deportees were located. In Chapter 4, it is demonstrated that Wise had been advised that Jews were being killed on a mass scale at Auschwitz in late 1942. Later, on 5 November 1943, Riegner telegraphed the WJC in London and the Czechoslovak government, also in London, advising that 6,800 Czech Jews had been taken from Theresienstadt to Birkenau. See Gilbert (2001: 129, 161). These two references are excluded from Gilbert's summary in the epilogue to *Auschwitz and the Allies* of the seven significant pieces of information that reached the West. Those seven pieces of information were connected, according to Gilbert (2001: 340), as they all mentioned 'the killing of Jews at Auschwitz'. In actuality, two of those reports do not. The reports in *The Times* on 26 May 1943 and 1 June 1943 do not record the killing of Jews at Auschwitz. The report from 26 May 1943 does not mention Auschwitz at all.

308

Notes to pages 3–6

4 The source report that Gilbert cites was released on 20 November 1942. It is not clear why Gilbert gives the date as 25 November. See Dobkin et al. report, 20 November, CZA S26/1203 (formerly S26/1159/I).

5 See Chapter 4.

6 There are a number of problems. First, it is not clear precisely which reports about Birkenau Van Pelt is referring to. Second, most reports that reached the West in 1943, which highlighted the murder of Jews at Auschwitz, came from Polish Underground sources, named the camp Oświęcim and did not specify Birkenau. A report sent from Bratislava to Jewish representatives in Istanbul, New York and London on 1 September 1943 noted Auschwitz as a liquidation centre. See Gilbert (1981/2001: 155), CZA S26/1520. Also see Appendix I.

7 See Engel (1993: 231 fn. 122). In Chapter 5, I show that the specific messages that Engel refers to were, in fact, disseminated. One actually formed the basis of a BBC broadcast (11 April 1943) on its Polish Service.

8 The 18 April 1943 report referred to by Breitman is the same report cited by Gilbert. Gilbert (2001: 130) noted that it was not made public, but failed to advise readers that it was given to Ignacy Schwarzbart, a Jewish representative on the Polish National Council, who in turn circulated it to Jewish leaders in London, the US and Palestine. This information was available in the late 1970s. Yad Vashem received Schwarzbart's files in 1962, and a catalogue (in Hebrew) was compiled in 1976. According to Yad Vashem, Schwarzbart's files were made available to scholars for the first time between 1962 and 1976. (Personal correspondence with Yad Vashem, Reference and Information Services, 3 December 2012.) For details of the circulation of the 18 April report to Jewish representatives, see YVA M2. 261.

9 See NA.HW1/929. The deaths of 6,829 men and 1,525 women were reported.

10 Also see Laqueur (1998: 105) and AK w Dokumentach, Volume II, pp. 296–7 (Document 327).

11 Michael Marrus (2013) has made the argument that the peace settlement after the First World War contributed to the eclipse of humanitarian interventionism. In the context of the League of Nations' regime of minority rights, minority champions were seen as troublemakers who threatened the political stability of Europe. Marrus suggests that the framing of minorities by decision makers as troublemakers who sought to exploit the postwar political settlement played a role in militating against an effective response to aid European Jews during the Holocaust. Humanitarian interventionism, Marrus argues, was effectively de-legitimated during the interwar period. If Marrus is correct, the attempts of British and US representatives to limit the scale and scope of reports about atrocities that could stimulate demands for intervention can be seen, at least in part, as a policy response to the ingrained bureaucratic antipathy towards humanitarian intervention in general. It is also worth noting that William Rubinstein (1997) has argued that the significance of anti-Semitism in the West as a factor influencing responses to the Holocaust has been overstated in scholarship on the topic. He also maintains that there was little further that the Western Allies could have done to aid Jews in occupied Europe. In this book, I demonstrate that both these arguments are extremely problematic.

310   Notes to pages 7–12

12 Indicatively, see the message of Michał Protasewicz (head of Bureau VI, Polish intelligence, London) to General Stefan Rowecki (head of the Home Army, Warsaw) of 5 August 1942, in which Protasewicz outlines the British assessment of intelligence gathered from Poland. See AK w dokumentach, Volume II, pp. 293–5, Document 325.

13 There is some change in the American demand for news about Jews following the establishment of the War Refugee Board in the United States by President Roosevelt. The British saw the creation of this institution as an electoral ploy to gain Jewish votes for the Democrats, and were very uneasy about its 'rescue' remit. See FO 371/42727 (W1953), 7 February 1944, Eden to War Cabinet; FO 371/42730, Foreign Office to Washington, 3 February 1943; FO 371/42730 (26), memo by Emerson, 16 May 1944.

14 HIA, Polish Information Center Papers, cable from London, Box 3.9 21 March 1944.

15 To date, the news distributed by the Polish Telegraphic Agency on the Holocaust has not been subject to sustained scholarly attention. In order to assess the Polish government's distribution of information about the Holocaust, PAT's news bulletins, as well as reports in the *Polish Fortnightly Review* and *Dziennik Polski*, have to be considered. Copies of PAT bulletins are available at the Hoover Institute; the New Documents Archive, Warsaw; the Polish Institute and Sikorski Museum, London; and the National Library, Warsaw. For an overview of PAT, see Grabowski (2005).

16 FO 371/26463, 19 February 1941.

17 FO 371/26463, 11 February 1941.

18 This figure excludes the well-known reports of Vrba and Wetzler, Mordowicz and Rosin, and Jerzy Tabeau. It also does not include two derivative reports. These are an article in the *Jewish Chronicle* on 3 September 1943 that discussed the Inter-Allied Information Centre's *Punishment of War Crimes (2)* and the review of *The Black Book of Polish Jewry* published in the *New York Times* on 30 January 1944. See Appendix I.

19 Some Polish Jews were taken to Auschwitz to be gassed in February and March 1942. Deportations of Jews to Auschwitz from Slovakia began in May 1942. News of the systematic, mass gassing of Jews reached the Polish Underground in Warsaw by July, or early August, 1942 at the latest. See Chapter 4.

20 NA.CAB 81/90. It should also be noted that the British Embassy to the Polish Government in Exile was bombed in 1944 and its files incinerated (Bauer 2012: 43). Any Polish documents held at the British Embassy rather than at the Foreign Office were destroyed.

21 NA.FO 371/34552 (C5452). This intercept, according to the file's cover, has been available at the National Archives, Kew, since 1972. See Chapter 5.

22 As Chapters 4 and 5 will make clear, a great deal of information about the camp was available in London during the war. The question why the myth of Auschwitz being 'elusive' has remained so dominant is therefore pertinent to debates on researching history.

23 'Domestic affairs' refers mainly to the internal politics of the Polish underground state. In June 1943, Graham Stewart Menzies, head of SIS, advised an American official that he was aware of the data received by the Poles. US. NA. RG 319, Box 956, Poland 350.09. See Breitman (1985: 371).

Notes to pages 12–22

24 One possibility is that this tranche of Auschwitz documents is at a secret Foreign Office archive, like some colonial files that were finally released in 2012.

25 Appendix II provides a discussion of Auschwitz in the British National Archives.

26 Frankfurter had been advised of the Riegner Telegram by Stephen Wise in September 1942 (Riegner, 2001: 564). The Riegner Telegram reported Nazi plans to exterminate Jews. See below, page 106 (Chapter 3).

27 The term 'United Nations' was first used by US President Roosevelt on 1 January 1942 when representatives of twenty-six nations agreed to continue the fight against the Axis powers. The UN would ultimately supersede the League of Nations (which the US had refused to join). The League of Nations was dissolved in April 1946 and many of its functions passed to the UN.

28 To be clear – unbelievable in the sense of the news not being believable and unbelievable in the sense that the news was simply incredible – hard to believe, but believed.

29 *Żydokomuna* is an anti-Semitic stereotype that links Jews with communism and disloyalty to the country (Poland). Michlic (2006, 2007) discusses how Jews have been represented in Poland.

30 Auschwitz had forty sub-camps, some of them tens of kilometres from the main camp. See Strzelecka and Setkiewicz (2000: 103–35) for details of each sub-camp. Prisoners worked in mines, in a foundry, farmed, and built a power plant under the administrative control of the main camp.

31 Political prisoners included those engaged in illicit economic activities.

32 The site was badly waterlogged in autumn 1941, and extensive drainage ditches had to be dug. For an account of the construction process and the terrible conditions endured by prisoners, see Piper (2002: 152).

33 See Rees (2005: 202–5) for testimony of some of those who made use of the brothel. Piper (2002) suggests that around a dozen women were assigned to work in the brothel and the 'clients' were, in the main, prison functionaries and common criminals. Piper argues that most prisoners boycotted it on political or moral grounds.

34 Those deemed to be economically productive stood a better chance of remaining in the ghetto.

35 Klemperer avoided deportation from Germany to Poland. He was married to a gentile.

36 FO 371/39014 (439–49).

37 'Social murder' refers to the indirect 'murder' of one section of society by another. Poor nutrition, sanitation and housing are well known to stimulate disease and lead to increased death rates. By artificially creating such conditions, the Nazis engineered the death of hundreds of thousands of Jews. The concept of 'social murder' is discussed in Engels (1993: 38) in relation to nineteenth-century England.

38 See Hilberg (1985: 1219). Hilberg states that 50,000 Jews were murdered at Majdanek. More recent research indicates that 60,000 Jews were killed at that camp. See State Museum at Majdanek website, www.majdanek.eu, last accessed 24 December 2012.

39 This is not to say that the death camps were latent (or predictable) within German racial policy. As Fulbrook (2012) notes, as the tensions and problems

312   Notes to pages 22–6

of Nazi racial colonialism mounted, more radical 'solutions' became thinkable and possible. It is a mistake to read the history of Nazi racial policy backwards.

40 Franciszek Piper's research has been instrumental in calculating the number of people killed. He estimates that the number of Jews killed, both those registered and unregistered, is 960,000.

41 PUMST A3.8.3.3 (11).

42 Prior to the war, Perkins had business interests in Poland and he could speak Polish.

43 Adamczyk and Gmitruk (2012: 46) note that the Social Department, under the direction of Paweł Siudak, had its own radio station at Mill Hill near London from March 1942. Siudak was close to both Stanisław Kot and Stanisław Mikołajczyk and was an important official in ensuring news from Poland reached the minister of the interior. The documents of the Social Department, held at the Polish Institute and Sikorski Museum, London, frequently refer to the situation of Jews in Poland.

44 Documents handed to Schwarzbart by the Interior Ministry can be found at Schwarzbart's Archive at the Institute for National Remembrance (IPN), Warsaw, and at Yad Vashem, Jerusalem.

45 The Polish underground state operated a complex and rigorous intelligence-gathering operation. This intelligence was assessed in Warsaw prior to dispatch to the Polish government in London. Periodic reports were sent via courier on microfilm, urgent matters were radioed to London, and some detailed reports were dispatched on very thin paper. Information was also circulated amongst Home Army commanders. Data sent to London were packaged in a variety of ways. Reports entitled 'Pro Memoria', about the situation in Poland, were edited (in the sense of being tidied up, not necessarily cut) by the underground state's department of Information and Press, and sent to the Polish prime minister in London. Situational reports were similarly worked on and sent to London. Annexes and attachments to reports were produced by the Military Historical Bureau of the Bureau of Information and Propaganda of the main command of the Home Army, and passed to the Department of Information and Press of the Government Delegature. Urgent messages sent by radio were normally addressed to Stanisław Mikołajczyk. For full details of the different types of report and an overview of the evaluation and editing procedures see Ważniewski and Marczewska (1968: vi).

46 At the Stockholm base (codenamed 'Anna'), the experienced intelligence officer Edmund Piotrowski, also known as Edward Podgórski, Edmund Pilewski, 'Zeus' and most frequently 'Ren', played a key role in gathering intelligence and assisting couriers from Poland.

47 In Poland and Polonia (that is, amongst the Polish diaspora), there is a hagiographic discourse about Witold Pilecki, claiming both that Pilecki came up with the idea for getting into Auschwitz and that he volunteered for the mission. In actual fact, the circumstances of Pilecki ending up in Auschwitz are somewhat more complicated. In a document hitherto ignored by many scholars writing on Pilecki, entitled 'How I found myself in Auschwitz' ('W jaki sposób znalazłem się w Oświęcimiu'), written almost certainly by Pilecki himself probably in the summer or early autumn of 1945, Pilecki highlights political differences in TAP. Pilecki was keen to bring TAP under

Notes to pages 26–7 313

the wing of the ZWZ, whereas some of his superiors were not. Furthermore, Jan Włodarkiewicz wished to make new recruits take an oath which reflected a particular political ideological position (i.e. rightist), whereas Pilecki wanted to accept anyone who sought the independence of Poland. According to Pilecki, the issue was raised in a meeting in the summer of 1940 and Włodarkiewicz took deep offence that Pilecki did not support him. Amicability was maintained, but pressure was placed on Pilecki to take the Auschwitz mission. In *Witold's Report* of 1945, Pilecki recalls the summer of 1940: 'There flashed in my mind some words of Janek W. [Major Jan Włodarkiewicz], who had told me after the first street round-up (in August 1940) in Warsaw, "So! You see, people caught in the street are not charged with any political case – this is the safest way to get into a/the camp".' On page 15 of 'W jaki sposób znalazłem się w Oświęcimiu', Pilecki adds some further detail: 'Witold was not all that thrilled by the project, but TAP was ending as an independent organization.' Further evidence that Pilecki was pressured into taking the Auschwitz mission can be found in the interrogation notes taken by Eugeniusz Chimczak on 8 May 1947, whilst Pilecki was imprisoned by the communist authorities at Mokotów prison in Warsaw. Also see Cyra (2000: 61, 172).

48 Reports on transports and mortality rates were transmitted, but the reception of these broadcasts is unknown. None of those who monitored the broadcasts survived the war (Garlinski 1994: 101).

49 Scholars writing on Western knowledge of the genocidal function of the camp have routinely argued that information on the mass killing at the camp, which reached the West from Polish sources, 'was ignored as being basically unreliable' (Bauer 1997: 203). Readers are not given examples of this information, who received it or whence it came. Nor is any indication given as to what criteria were used to assess reliability, who was in the privileged position to determine reliability, and how the dissemination of reliable versus unreliable information was policed. These are serious lacunae, since the failure to explain the nature of Polish sources prevents readers from making an informed assessment about the argument. In order to assess the 'reliability' thesis, it is necessary to establish what is meant by 'Polish source material' and to come to an understanding of the credibility of this information. Though rarely specified, reference to 'Polish material' describes Polish intelligence radio messages, couriered messages and eyewitness testimony of Polish arrivals in Britain, including couriers. As noted above, Polish intelligence reports were the outcome of a complex gathering, evaluation and dissemination operation. The information sent from Poland by the leader of the Home Army and the government's Delegate was generally highly rated by the British. The British gave feedback to the Poles, and liaison between SOE and the Polish Bureau VI was very close. British intelligence also rated informants. One Polish informant, who was well informed of the mass slaughter of Jews at Auschwitz, was given the top A reliability rating from British intelligence. This informant (Jan Nowak-Jeziorański) was so highly rated that Churchill himself was advised to take a meeting with him. It is apparent, then, that the claim concerning Polish sources' reliability relates specifically to the mass killing of Jews. This obviously raises the question why information about the systematic murder of Jews at Auschwitz from an otherwise reliable source would be seen as

314   Notes to pages 30–9

unreliable. As I will show, the reception of information about the systematic murder of Jews at Auschwitz had nothing to do with the reliability of Polish source material, but the reliability thesis has had a profound impact on how Holocaust scholarship on knowledge of the camp has been conducted.

50 See www.archive.jta.org, last accessed 22 December 2012.

2 CENSORSHIP, SELF-CENSORSHIP AND THE DISCURSIVE ENVIRONMENT

1 For example, Jo Moore, a 'spin doctor' for the British Ministry of Transport, noted in an email that 11 September 2001 was a 'good day to bury bad news'. Her point was that while the media's attention was diverted by the terrorist attacks on the United States, the ministry could afford to release potentially damaging information without coming under media or public scrutiny. See 'Moore and Sixsmith fall on their swords', *The Guardian*, 15 February 2002, at www.guardian.co.uk/media/2002/feb/15/marketingandpr.byers1? INTCMP=SRCH, last accessed 29 July 2012.

2 Editors' judgement of 'newsworthiness' often takes into account the guidelines of the particular censorship regime in operation. Such judgements may be the result of 'common sense' rather than critical appraisal. 'Common sense' draws on stock notions that circulate in society at a particular moment and is usually not subject to conscious reflection.

3 In this, Britain, in the first half of the twentieth century, was far from alone. Recent work by Daniele Conversi (2010: 720) has highlighted the ubiquity of processes of cultural homogenization, and Ugur Ümit Üngör (2011: 7) has reiterated the connection between the rise of the modern nation-state and homogenizing processes in his study of the development of modern Turkey.

4 Quoted by David Feldman (2003) in 'Excluding immigrants, including minorities: Britain 1880–1910 and 1948–1970', working paper presented at the workshop Paths of Integration: Similarities and Differences in the Settlement Process of Immigrants in Europe, 1880–2000, University of Osnabrück, IMIS, 20–1 June 2003.

5 Hansard, House of Commons Debates, 29 January 1902, Volume 101, cols. 1273–4.

6 Hansard, House of Commons Debates, 29 January 1902, Volume 101, cols. 1279–80.

7 Marrus's (2013) argument that minority champions were seen as troublemakers threatening the stability of the post-First World War settlement helps to explain the way in which anti-Jewish actions in Germany were understood and framed by decision makers in Britain (see above, Chapter 1, note 11). It is also worth noting that the voices of those opposing the British government policy of appeasement were generally excluded from the airwaves as a result of government pressure. Listen to Nick Robinson, *Battle for the Airwaves*, Episode 2 (produced by Rob Shepherd), first broadcast 26 February 2013 at 13.45, BBC Radio 4, available at www.bbc.co.uk/iplayer/episode/b01qx0jp/ Battle_for_the_Airwaves_Episode_2, last accessed 27 February 2013.

8 1905 Aliens Act, available at www.uniset.ca/naty/aliensact1905.pdf, last accessed 4 February 2012.

Notes to pages 39–42

9   The riots targeted non-white minority groups, not Jews. Competition for jobs and housing shortages saw white working-class violence unleashed on black communities. See Jenkinson (2008).

10 1919 Aliens Act, available at www.legislation.gov.uk/ukpga/1919/92/pdfs/ukpga_19190092_en.pdf, last accessed 4 February 2012.

11 Hansard, House of Commons Debates, 22 March 1938, Volume 333, cols. 1003–12 (Austrian refugees and naturalization), also available at http://hansard.millbanksystems.com/commons/1938/mar/22/austrian-refugees-immigration-and#S5CV0333P0_19380322_HOC_268.

12 The Nazi genocide of Jews in occupied Europe, and the way it was reported in Britain, do not seem to have been discussed at the meetings between Bracken and Jewish representatives (including the chairman of the Board of Deputies, Professor Brodetsky). Instead, these meetings focused on ways to tackle domestic anti-Semitism. See WL 1658/10/27 for the summaries of the meetings that took place on 17 March 1942, 18 May 1943 and 16 December 1943.

13 On 7 April 1933, the Jewish community (represented by Neville Laski, president of the London Committee of Deputies of British Jews; Lionel Cohen, the Law and Parliamentary Committee of the Board of Deputies; L.G. Montefiore, president of the Anglo-Jewish Association; Otto M. Schiff, chairman of the Jewish Refugee Committee) pledged that no Jewish refugee admitted to Britain would be a charge on the public purse, and undertook to cover refugees' expenses. The Jewish representatives anticipated helping 3,000–4,000 refugees from Germany. CAB 96/33, 'Proposals of the Jewish Committee as regards Jewish refugees from Germany', Appendix I to memorandum by Home Secretary. See Sherman (1973: 33). This undertaking, as Sherman notes, had unforeseen consequences in the year before the war, as the Home Office was very reluctant to issue visas (and, more often than not, did not) to those 'for whom private guarantee of maintenance could not be found'. Entry to Britain was desperately sought by an unanticipated number of people in the late 1930s. Without guarantees of maintenance entry was generally denied.

14 The Board of Deputies was well aware of the damage being done by the anti-Semitic attempt to link Jews with black markets and was energetic in using its influence to bring home to those few Jews engaged in black market activities 'the enormity of the crime they were committing against the war effort'. See WL 1658/10/27, 'Note of interview with the Minister of Information' (17 March 1942).

15 See, for example, the edition of 31 July 1942: 'Stepney mayor and Jewish trades' (page 1) and 'Board of Deputies deny synagogue stored black market goods' (page 4).

16 In the period between 1933 and 1939, 50,000 Jews from the Reich and 6,000 from Czechoslovakia were granted entry to Britain. In the same period the US granted entry to 136,000 Jews from Spain and the Reich. Sherman (1973: 265) argues that '[a]lthough the US admitted more refugees from the Reich than any other single country, its record in relation to capacity was far less generous than that of many, including Great Britain'.

17 The response of the British Jewish community to the Holocaust remains a controversial subject. Geoffrey Alderman (2001), for example, has argued

316   Notes to page 43

that the community's leaders could have taken a more proactive position to aid those confronting Nazi tyranny. For a discussion of British Jewry during the Holocaust, see Bolchover (1993).

18 Wedgwood identified that anti-Semitism in 'certain exalted circles' played a role in Belisha's exit from the War Office (See Hansard, House of Commons, Volume 356, cols. 60–2). Prime Minister Neville Chamberlain encouraged Hore-Belisha to resign from the War Office on 4 January 1940, noting that there was prejudice against him. Chamberlain had considered Belisha for the Ministry of Information but Alexander Cadogan of the Foreign Office was of the view that moving Belisha to that ministry would be disastrous because Belisha was Jewish, a view echoed by Lord Halifax (see Grimwood, 2006: 165; Dilks, 1971: 242; also see Wasserstein, 1999: 84). In his diary for 1 January 1940, Cadogan wrote that he had come 'to the conclusion that Jew control of our propaganda would be a major disaster'. Belisha was offered the presidency of the Board of Trade (an effective demotion), which he refused. Cadogan was of the view that Chamberlain should have just got 'rid of H-B [Hore Belisha] altogether' (diary entry, 4 January 1940; see Dilks, 1971: 242). Wilkinson (1997), who places some stress on Belisha's alleged character flaws, conduct and class background (middle-class) grating with upper-class soldiers, also acknowledges that prejudice played a role in the removal of Belisha from office. The 12 January 1940 edition of the weekly journal *Truth*, which was taken by some MPs into the chamber prior to Belisha's resignation speech, included anti-Semitic copy (Minney 1991: 287). The forced resignation of Belisha highlighted to Jewish leaders in Britain the malign force of anti-Semitism. On 29 October 1954, the new editor of *Truth* acknowledged that some articles attacking Belisha were unfair, baseless and motivated by racial prejudice (Minney, 1991: 288).

19 NA.INF 292, Home Intelligence Report 115.

20 NA.INF 292, Home Intelligence Report 116. William Rubinstein (1997) has argued that the significance of anti-Semitism in Britain in framing responses to the Holocaust has been overstated. In a recent contribution to a book examining anti-Semitism, Rubinstein (2010) considers anti-Semitism in the English-speaking world. In his discussion of Britain during the twentieth century, Rubinstein does not mention the dismissal of Hore-Belisha, the evidence of anti-Semitism documented in Home Intelligence Reports or the concerns about anti-Semitism expressed by British Jews, British government officials and others. Consequently, Rubinstein's account is partial.

21 Christopher Browning (2010: 50) records the hanging of Poles in the town square of Wierzbnik in August 1941 by a Jewish execution squad coerced by the Nazis. One of the hangmen rationalized his conduct over fifty years later by stating that he knew he had hanged the right people because they were members of the Home Army. This rationalization depends on the view that the Home Army was particularly hostile to Jews. It is not clear that this was the case in 1941. The Poles were executed for resisting the Germans, not for any action against Jews. Today, blaming the victim continues to influence discussions about rape, for example. The clothing choices, social habits and alcohol consumption of victims are frequently seen to be relevant by judges and juries in rape cases.

Notes to pages 43–5 317

22 NA.INF 1/251, 25 July 1941, p. 2. The document is cited later in this chapter.
23 NA.INF 292, Home Intelligence Report 117.
24 NA.INF 292, Home Intelligence Report 118.
25 See McLaine (1979: 168). The Defence Committee of the Board of Deputies also noted that Jews were being blamed. Of the 173 who died, five were Jews. According to a Defence Committee report entitled 'Memorandum on anti-Semitism' (p. 5), Jews tended to avoid using the shelter at Bethnal Green since the area had been a stronghold of the British Union of Fascists. See WL 1658/10/27.
26 CAB 65/34/21, War Cabinet, 10 May 1943. In June 1943, the rise in anti-Semitism was noted by the director-general of the Political Warfare Executive (discussed below), Robert Bruce Lockhart, as part of 'growing xenophobia which is doubtless provoked by the large number of foreigners in our midst'. See Young (1980: 241).
27 It is likely that Raczyński sent this letter at the suggestion of Ignacy Schwarzbart. Schwarzbart wrote to Raczyński on 17 May 1943. See IPN BU 2835/9 (77).
28 FO 371/34550/C5628 (see Chapter 4).
29 NA.INF 292, Home Intelligence Report 191.
30 The *Jewish Chronicle* reported the estimates of Mr A.P. Michaelis, vice-chairman of the Association of Jewish Refugees, of the number of Jewish refugees in Britain, in its 21 January 1944 edition (p. 6). According to Michaelis, there were 50,000 Jewish refugees from Austria and Germany, 10,000 from Czechoslovakia and 5,000 from Poland.
31 In May 1945 Morrison came under pressure from Tory MPs, who asked when the refugees would be repatriated. See Cesarani (1994: 182).
32 NA.CAB 95/15, 16 May 1945, Meeting of War Cabinet Committee on the reception and accommodation of refugees. So in effect Morrison was calling for anti-Semitic measures (discriminating against people on the basis of their Jewish identity, in this case challenging their right to stay in Britain) to hinder the growth of anti-Semitism.
33 In relation to (German) Jews interned by the British government during the early years of the war, Shepherd (1984: 174) argues that some gentile MPs were encouraged to put the internees' case as the Jewish leadership in Britain was afraid of being seen as disloyal to Britain. Thousands of German Jews were able to gain access to Britain due to the efforts of Frank Foley, the passport control officer at the British Embassy in Berlin (and SIS officer) and Wilfrid Israel, a British/German Jewish businessman heavily involved in helping Jews escape Nazi Germany. See Smith (2004) and Shepherd (1984).
34 BBC WAC, C165, Document on Anti-Semitism. Also see WL 1658/10/7/1/1 (note of interview with controller of programmes at the BBC, 28 April 1942), which confirms that Brodetsky considered that 'it would not be politic for the BBC to make any pronouncement on the subject [anti-Semitism]' but argued that there were indirect ways to 'stem this phenomenon'. The meeting was not with the Home Service controller, A.P. Ryan (Patrick Ryan), but with his deputy A.E. Barker.
35 BBC WAC, R34/277, Policy, Censorship of Programmes, Anti-Semitism, 1941–1948 & 1957. Harris (2004: 303) cites the same quote, but provides a

318   Notes to pages 47–54

reference to a file that does not exist (R33/277, Policy File), provides an inaccurate date (April 1943) and suggests that Locker-Lampson spoke with 'Director-General' Frederick Ogilvie (Ogilvie was not director-general in April 1943). These errors, however, do not undermine Harris's main argument regarding the BBC's coverage of the Holocaust.

36 NA.INF 1/770, Memo 314, Document 20 (p. 7), Publicity Division, Planning Section meeting, 10 July 1939. This policy seems to have been articulated in anticipation of conflict in Europe. European Jews, in line with British liberal assimilationism, were to be discussed as nationals of the countries in which they lived. The Ministry of Information operated as a shadow ministry prior to being officially established on 4 September 1939. See Taylor (1999).

37 From autumn 1938, British policy in Palestine was increasingly governed by strategic considerations in the event of war and the need to maintain friendly relations with the various governments in the Middle East. See Wasserstein (1999: 14–18).

38 Between October 1939 and April 1940 censorship responsibilities passed to the Press and Censorship Bureau. They then reverted to the Ministry of Information. Propaganda to enemy and enemy-occupied countries was passed to the Political Warfare Executive, where the Ministry of Information was represented alongside the Foreign Office and the Ministry of Economic Warfare (McLaine 1979: 3).

39 See Crozier's correspondence with Bracken, Rylands Library, Manchester Guardian Archive, B/B261/1–22.

40 Gorny (2012) provides a useful discussion of the Jewish press and the Holocaust during the war. He examines a sample of papers and journals published in Palestine, Britain, the United States and the Soviet Union. Gorny (2012: 17) contends that the *Jewish Chronicle* was the leading Jewish paper to which other Jewish newspapers responded. However, Gorny's analysis does not include a number of important newspapers. The *Polish Jewish Observer* (Britain), *Nasza Trybuna/Our Tribune* (US) and the *Palestine Post* – papers which published news of the genocide taking place at Auschwitz – are not discussed. Gorny does not examine the reporting of Auschwitz in the Jewish press.

41 CAB 65/18/41 21 (WP (41) 269), 12 November 1941.

42 CAB 65/18/41 21 (WP (41) 269), 12 November 1941, p. 2.

43 INF 1/64, 7 March 1941.

44 Messages sent by the Jewish Underground in Poland (including from the Jewish Fighting Organisation) were frequently transmitted via the Polish Underground to the Polish Government in Exile for distribution to the two Jewish members of the Polish National Council. See Chapters 3 and 4.

45 The PWE enjoyed close relations with the Foreign Office. Lockhart was able to set himself up in the Locarno room at the Foreign Office, Whitehall.

46 NA.FO 898/10 (129). For the organizational structure of the PWE see NA. FO 898/10 (30).

47 NA.FO 898/421.

48 NA.FO 898/57 (275). For a discussion of Radio Świt see Laskowski (1966), Korboński (1968: 200–214), Mazur (1987: 66–8).

49 Lockhart, the director-general of the PWE, records in his diary that the PWE moved to Bush House on Friday 27 February 1942 and started work the

Notes to pages 54–60   319

following Monday. His offices were on the floor above the rooms occupied by members of the BBC's European Service (Briggs, 1995: 380). Lockhart also notes that Foreign Secretary Anthony Eden visited Bush House on 29 April 1942, but it is not clear whether Eden visited the PWE offices only, or also spent time with the BBC's European Service. See Young (1980: 147 and 160).

50 FO 954 23A, 6 June 1944.
51 Kirkpatrick's duties were spelled out in a PWE document entitled 'Mr Kirkpatrick's functions' dated 23 September 1941. NA.FO 898/10.
52 In a document dated 3 May 1943, discussing the relationship between the BBC, the Political Warfare Executive and the Foreign Office, Noel Newsome, director of European broadcasts, wrote that the representatives of the PWE and the FO had agreed that 'the relationship between them and the BBC depends on the physical presence of Mr Kirkpatrick, who alone has the right (it was intimated) to direct the broadcasts to Europe and to direct policy decisions, etc.' CAC NERI 3/13A.
53 FO 954 23A, 6 June 1944.
54 For a discussion of the deportations from the Lublin and Zamość regions, see Kubica (2006) and Piper and Strzelecka (2009). Poles were sent to various camps, including Auschwitz.
55 FO 371/34549, J.K. Roberts, 26 January 1943 (FO commentary).
56 This issue is elaborated on in Chapter 3.
57 BBC WAC, E1/1148/3, File 1c, January–December 1943.
58 FO 371/26723, Kennard to Eden, 17 February 1941.
59 Arrivals in Britain were interrogated at the Royal Patriotic Schools at Wandsworth by MI19. Arrivals were routinely asked about their BBC listening habits, reception issues and the general response to and standing of BBC broadcasts in their milieu. There are very few references to Jews in any of the summaries, indicating that the fate of Jews was not of particular interest to British intelligence. These reports were circulated to the British and American intelligence communities, to the Foreign Office, to the PWE and to Ivone Kirkpatrick. See NA.WO 208/3688–NA.WO 208/3736 for MI19 interrogation reports from October 1942 to August 1944.
60 FO 371/39449.
61 CAC NERI 6/8. Nowak-Jeziorański also mentioned the murder of over three million Jews, stating that most had been gassed. See page 8, 'Mr Nowak's talk delivered on January 18th 1944'.
62 'BBC surveys of European audiences: enemy-occupied countries (other than France)' (10 March 1943). NA.FO 371/34383 (C3345) page 11.
63 BBC WAC, European News, April 1943 (Polish Service).
64 NA.INF 1/251, 25 July 1941, p. 2.
65 See www.bbc.co.uk/archive/holocaust/5138.shtml?page=txt, last accessed 21 January 2012.
66 CAC NERI 3/1.
67 CAC NERI 3/13B, 'Presentation of European news bulletins', 12 February 1940.
68 CAC NERI 3/1, 'Propaganda to Europe: January/February/March 1942'.
69 The precise number is not known as not all broadcast scripts exist. A collection of Lindley Fraser's scripts, including those highlighting Nazi actions against Jews, can be found at BBC WAC, C165, Lindley Fraser.

320　Notes to pages 60–5

70 HIA Stanisław Mikołajczyk Papers, Box 38, Folder 1 (Radio Świt). Also at Poland's National Digital Archive, 800/22/0/-/38 (jpeg 33).
71 HIA Stanisław Mikołajczyk Papers, Box 38, Folder 1 (Radio Świt). Also at Poland's National Digital Archive, 800/22/0/-/38 (jpeg 35). Underlining in original.
72 'Sprawozdanie z pobytu u Anglików'. HIA Stanisław Mikołajczyk Papers, Box 38, Folder 1 (Radio Świt). Also at Poland's National Digital Archive, 800/22/0/-/38 (jpeg 28).
73 Other significant British figures include Moray McLaren, responsible for the Polish section of the PWE, and Rex Leeper (PWE, Foreign Office).
74 Former Świt employee Tadeusz Kochanowicz made this clear with reference to Foreign Office censorship in his discussion of the radio station. See Kochanowicz (1975: 64).
75 A further insight into the broadcasts of Radio Świt can be gained from the radio monitoring reports of the Polish Ministry of Information and Documentation. See AZHRL, Archiwum Stanisława Kota, File 249. This collection covers broadcasts from March, April and some of May 1944.
76 BBC WAC, File R34/277, Policy: Censorship of Programmes, Antisemitism, 1941–1948.
77 Libionka and Weinbaum (2006) draw attention to the role of the Jewish Military Union (Żydowski Związek Wojskowy – ŻZW) in contradistinction to the well-known activities of the Jewish Fighting Organisation (ŻOB).
78 BBC WAC, File R34/277, Policy: Censorship of Programmes, Antisemitism, 1941–1948.
79 FO 371/36648 (W122, p. 3). Also at NA.CAB 95/15. War Cabinet Committee on the Reception and Accommodation of Jewish Refugees, first meeting, 31 December 1942.
80 IPN BU 2835/15 (12), 28 July 1943. This is Schwarzbart's translation. ('Wynik konferencji na Bermudach był mniej niż znikomy').
81 The documentary record is unrevealing. The records of the PWE (NA.FO 898), the BBC and the Ministry of Information do not shed light on the decision-making process that resulted in the highlighting of the information from the Bund report. Bracken had his papers destroyed on his death.
82 BBC WAC E2 131 5, New Directives, June 1942.
83 WL 1658/10/7/1/1, *Man in the Street*, 26 June 1942. A selection of the *Man in the Street* talks were published in 1945, including the 26 June broadcast. See Newsome (1945: 62).
84 See Chapter 3 for further elaboration.
85 In the US, the State Department's confirmation of the veracity of the Riegner telegram in November 1942 allowed news of the mass killing of Jews to be widely disseminated.
86 Hansard, House of Commons Debates, May 1943, Volume 389, cols. 148–50. Also at http://hansard.millbanksystems.com/commons/1943/may/05/refugees-bermuda-conference.
87 News about Auschwitz that arrived in London was neither 'hearsay' nor 'rumour', but, for the most part, the product of underground intelligence operations in Poland. See Chapters 4 and 5 of this volume.

Notes to pages 65–9   321

88 FO 371/39014 (439–44), 24 March 1944, 'Special Annex on the persecution of the Jews'. The PWE had produced an earlier file on the persecution of Jews, on 17 December 1942, which concluded with a page entitled 'The final stage: from ghetto to execution camp'. BBC WAC, C165, PWE Central Directive: 'Special annex on the extermination of the Jews'.

89 The talk was broadcast during the 15.45 news bulletin on the Polish Service. Subsequent news bulletins on 2 July mentioned the mass extermination of Jews. See BBC WAC, European News, July 1943 (p. 29). Karski later accepted that the camp he saw was not Bełżec. See Wierzyński and Karski (2012: 102).

90 BBC WAC, European News, July 1943. Scholars think that Karski was mistaken in identifying Bełżec as the camp he saw. This view is undoubtedly correct. This broadcast was the first on the BBC that mentioned the Reinhard camps. See Milland (1998: 68).

91 BBC WAC, Home Service, Talks, Frederick Allen, 5 December 1943 'Report of atrocities against Jews'. The misidentification of Nazi camps as Polish camps continues, with several prominent newspapers apologizing for such harmful mistakes in recent years. US president Barack Obama made a similar mistake in June 2012 during a ceremony honouring Jan Karski.

92 As noted in Chapter 1, Soviet prisoners of war were gassed at Auschwitz I in late August 1941 and 250 Polish political prisoners were gassed in early September 1941. Jews from the Zagłębie Dąbrowskie region were gassed in the gas chamber at Auschwitz I in February 1942 and from 20 March 1942 Jews were murdered in the gas chambers installed in a farmhouse at Birkenau. In May 1942 transports of Jews from Slovakia arrived and were subjected to 'selections' for the gas chambers at Birkenau.

93 These intercepts allowed the number of people killed at Auschwitz to be calculated, and Churchill to be advised on 27 September 1942. These mortality figures referred only to registered prisoners, and included 6,829 men and 1,525 women. HW 1/929, 27 September 1942.

94 NA.FO 371/34551, 27 August 1943.

95 The Quebec conference of 17 August 1943–24 August 1943 brought together British, American and Canadian leaders (Churchill, Roosevelt and William Lyon MacKenzie King (the Canadian prime minister)) to discuss war strategy. Planning for the invasion of France, allied actions in the Balkans and bombing raids on Germany were all discussed. The USSR and China (Chiang Kai-shek) were advised of proceedings. The conference also discussed a British–American statement on Palestine, as well as the statement on German atrocities in Poland. See FRUS, 'Conferences at Washington and Quebec, 1943'.

96 HS4/144, 20 August 1943, S.W. Harman to Owen O'Malley.

97 FO 371/34551. Also cited in Van Pelt (2002: 127).

98 As part of Generalplan Ost – the Nazis' colonial plan of settlement and ethnic cleansing – the Zamość region was selected for German colonization. From late 1942 Poles were evicted from their homes. These people were, from 28 November 1942, concentrated at a transit camp in Zamość. Appalling conditions and lack of food led to a high death rate. Some 1,301 people can be

322   Notes to pages 69–71

documented as being deported to Auschwitz from the Zamość transit camp. Of these, only 230 are known to have survived (Kubica 2006: 25, 38).

99 FO 371/34551.

100 It is now known that some of these peasants were murdered in the gas chambers; others were killed by phenol injections to the heart. Most, however, succumbed to the horrendous conditions in the camp. See Kubica (2006: 36).

101 FO 371/34555, 29 December 1942.

102 NA.FO 371/34381 (75), Annexe III, 'The German Terror in Poland: An Illustration of the Growth of Persecution'.

103 The PWE collated German newspaper reports regarding German policy against Poles. One report cited Arthur Greiser, the *Gauleiter* of the Warthegau, from 26 October 1942: 'After the extermination of the destructive elements of the Polish population, it was possible to grant satisfactory working conditions to submissive Poles.' See NA.FO 371/34381 (41). The PWE had some evidence of an incremental and expanding policy of mass murder and were able to conflate Polish and Jewish persecution.

104 The third and last deportation of Poles from the Zamość region left for Auschwitz on 3 February 1943. Of the 1,000 people on board, 417 were Jews – all of whom were immediately taken to the gas chambers on arrival at Auschwitz. Most of the 583 Poles from this transport died at the camp. Of the 301 women, 231 perished, mainly between February and March 1943. Of the 282 men, records for only 146 exist. 124 are known to have died. Of the boys, 24 were murdered on arrival with phenol injections. See Kubica (2006: 38).

105 The Secret Intelligence Service reported on the significance of Polish intelligence handed to them. Though most of these documents no longer exist, a few such reports remain. An appraisal report covering the period from 1 January to 30 June 1944 noted that information on rockets was 'of great and increasing value' and that reports from Poland were of 'very great value' (Bennett 2005: 439). See Stirling, Nałęcz and Dubicki (eds.) (2005) for details of Polish–British intelligence co-operation during the Second World War.

106 On 9 December 1942, Karski, accompanied by Stanisław Mikołajczyk, met representatives of the Political Warfare Executive at the home of Harold Osborne. See letters from Osborne to Mikołajczyk, 7 December 1942 and 21 December 1942. HIA Stanisław Mikołajczyk Papers, Box 38, Folder 4 (Radio Świt). Also at Poland's National Digital Archive, 800/22/0/-/38 (jpegs 70 and 103 respectively). It is not known what was discussed at this meeting.

107 See Ciechanowski (2005: 538, 543). Also see NA.FO 371/34550, Memo: Eden to War Cabinet, 17 February 1943.

108 Cited in Ciechanowski (2005: 543).

109 Frank Roberts, the official in charge of C Section – the office dealing with Germany in the Foreign Office – maintained a sceptical stance towards reports detailing the annihilation of the Jews. He outlines his views in a BBC radio documentary, *The Unspeakable Atrocity* (produced by Nigel Acheson), available at www.kcrw.com/etc/programs/pc/pc050426the_unspeakable_atro, last accessed 15 June 2011.

Notes to pages 71–4 323

110 The *City and East London Observer* is usually referred to as the *East London Observer*.

111 Though there is some indication that its readership broadened over time, the paper never became well known or widely read. The paper published a letter from a reader in Africa in 1943, and its 16 June 1944 story about Jan Wolny, an escapee from Auschwitz, reached the US's War Refugee Board.

112 NA.KV2/3429 (28a). The cuttings collected by British Intelligence include a report on staff changes in the Polish Ministry of Information, an article on Jerzy Szapiro joining the British and American Section of the Ministry of Information and a piece entitled 'Prof Kot on cultural affinity of nations'.

113 Surprisingly, the *Polish Jewish Observer* has not attracted attention, despite the fact that a good proportion of messages received by the Polish Government in Exile about the situation of Jews in Poland were the source for many articles in this paper. Oświęcim as a camp where Jews were being incarcerated and killed on a mass scale is referred to repeatedly through 1943 and 1944. This includes an article from September 1943 reporting that 520,000 Jews had been killed up to the end of 1942. This data was derived from a report sent from Warsaw on 4 March 1943 by Stefan Rowecki and Jan Stanisław Jankowski (See Chapter 5).

114 Cang wrote periodically to William Crozier, editor of the *Manchester Guardian* during the war, to propose stories and to seek references and stable employment. He also wrote articles. See RL Manchester Guardian Archive, B/C23.

115 In 1947 Cang became a British citizen. See NA.HO 334/230/2481; 'Released by Danzig, Cang Returns to Warsaw', *Jewish Telegraphic Agency*, 11 April 1935; Hansard, House of Commons, 4 December 1946, available at http://hansard.millbanksystems.com/commons/1946/dec/04/poland-british-press-representatives; HL IJA MS 241/7/30 IJA 07.

116 The *Jewish Chronicle* also received information about Jews from the Polish Government in Exile. For example, on 23 December 1942, Professor Olgierd Górka, head of the Polish government minorities department, wrote to Ivan Greenberg, editor of the *Jewish Chronicle*, advising that 'in the future news about Jewish matters received by our department' would be communicated to him (Greenberg). Górka enclosed three detailed documents about the situation of Jews in Poland – a copy of the Polish government's note to Allied governments, Raczyński's radio broadcasts and an article by Frank Savery (of the British Foreign Office) on the persecution of Jews in Poland. See PUMST 3.1.1.13.4 (8).

117 *East London Observer*, 14 May 1943, 4.

118 The list of material of interest to the US was fairly exhaustive – including information on food, black markets, transport, propaganda, the armed forces, communication, social and economic conditions, security and so on. NA.DEFE 1/136/9.

119 NA.DEFE 1/136/9, 1943 Postal Censorship Allocation List (3rd edn), p. 36.

120 See Chapter 5. It is very likely that Schwarzbart was on a Postal and Telegraph Censorship Department 'watch list'. For an outline of the Censorship Department's methods see NA.DEFE 1/333 (Herbert and Graz 1952: 16).

324   Notes to pages 74–9

121 NA.CAB 93/7 SE (SNP), 1st and 2nd meeting, 23 December 1941.
122 NA.WO 193/329 (1 October 1941).
123 Herbert and Graz's (1952) official history of the Postal and Telegraph Censorship Department highlights the breadth and depth of British–US co-operation. By the summer of 1944, the Postal and Telegraph Censorship Department had thirty-eight members of staff working in the US. American censorship teams also worked in Britain. See NA.DEFE 1/333 (Herbert and Graz 1952: 132).
124 Executive Order 9182 Establishing the Office of War Information, 13 June 1942, available at www.presidency.ucsb.edu/ws/index.php?pid=16273#axzz 1lhnnbiwM, last accessed 7 February 2012.
125 CAC NERI 3/1 'Visit to the United States: A Report Concerning Anglo-American Co-operation in Broadcasting', 25 September 1942.
126 NA.FO 371/30863 (173), 10 October 1942.
127 Lockhart (PWE) met with OWI officials in London during the war. However, relations between the PWE and OWI deteriorated as the invasion of France approached, due, in part, to staff changes at OWI in London. See Young (1980: 29).
128 Amongst others, see 'Youth in USA: American anti-Semitism "like a fog"', 28 January 1944; 'Anti-Semitism in USA. To be outlawed in New York', 3 March 1944 (p. 1).

3 THE POLISH GOVERNMENT IN EXILE IN LONDON

1 The evacuation of the Polish government from France is described in NA.FO 371/24481. The Polish president left France on 17 June 1940 and arrived in Britain on 21 June on HMS *Arethusa*. See NA.FO 371/24481 (304).
2 See Stola (1995: 22) for a discussion of the significance of the name of this political body. The 'national' was seen as privileging the ethnic Polish majority vis-à-vis Poland's minorities. An awkward compromise was reached and it became the Rada Narodowa Rzeczypospolitej Polskiej (National Council of the Polish Republic).
3 Szapiro enjoyed good contacts with the Polish Government in Exile. In London, he co-edited *Dziennik Polski* for a month during the summer of 1940 and later carried out freelance work for the government (Leff 2005: 393, fn. 38). He was involved in the work of the Foreign Section of the Polish Socialist Party along with Adam Ciołkosz and Adam Pragier (Lewandowska, 1993: 50). In April 1941 he became the director of the Polish Social Information Bureau (Polskie Biuro Informacji Społecznej – PIS). PIS functioned as an agency of the Polish Ministry of Information and Documentation, with the objective of liaising with the British Labour Movement (see PUMST AALC, Kol 133/108, letter from Jerzy Szapiro to Adam Ciołkosz 12 April 1941). It is highly probable that Szapiro was provided with information about the destruction of Polish Jewry throughout the war – from Shmuel Zygielbojm and Ignacy Schwarzbart, amongst others. Szapiro's obituary in the *New York Times* (2 June 1962, 19) suggested that Szapiro 'headed the press service of the exiled Polish Government'. In reality, he headed PIS, not the entire press service.

Notes to pages 79–83

4 Estreicher contended that 'Słonimski's Jewish origin disqualifies him as a good Pole and as a Polish poet' (Michlic 2006: 146). The British clearly recognized, as illustrated by the memorandum prepared by Bracken, Eden and Morrison in 1941, that having control over media outlets also opened up governments to criticism regarding the content published. The editing of the official publications *Dziennik Polski* and the *Polish Fortnightly Review* was therefore extremely important.

5 See Rojek and Suchcitz (1995: Volume 2, 112), Minutes of the Council of Ministers 26 and 28 August 1940.

6 Kevin Morgan, 'Pritt, Denis Nowell (1887–1972)', *Oxford Dictionary of National Biography*, Oxford University Press, online edition, May 2009, article 31570.

7 The generally accepted number of Polish citizens deported from their homes to the East is 320,000 (Sanford 2005: 29). In a report written by the Lithuanian expert on the Polish General Staff, Lieutenant Commander Lutyv, and handed to the British Foreign Office (circulated 7 September 1942), the names of two Jews are given as examples of Jews being deported to NKVD camps in the Soviet Union. See NA.FO 371/31903 (27).

8 NA.FO 371/24481 (89/92/104/109/110).

9 David Low's cartoons in the *Evening Standard* were particularly damaging to the Polish government. On 6 March 1943, Edward Raczyński complained to Brendan Bracken about Low's cartoon in the 4 March edition of the paper which sought to portray the Poles as 'irresponsible'. Raczyński contended that the cartoon 'printed in Lord Beaverbrook's paper is profoundly misleading'. Bracken replied on 10 March and agreed that the cartoon was 'a deplorable piece of work'. Bracken indicated that he had issued guidance to the press on Polish–Soviet relations and had asked the chief press censor to take up the matter with the editor of the *Evening Standard*. See Raczyński (1997: 131). It was also possible for Bracken to speak to Beaverbrook about the presentation of the Polish government in the papers that he owned. It is not known whether he did. Reproductions of Low's cartoons can be found in Davies (2003: 655). Kochanski (2012: 461) notes that David Low was a friend of the Soviet ambassador, Ivan Maisky.

10 The editor of *Wiadomości Polskie*, M. Nowakowski, was warned by the (British) Ministry of Information to exercise restraint in discussing Polish–Soviet relations – in the summer of 1943, and again in early 1944. The British took the initiative in suspending the publication of the paper. See NA.FO 371/39437 (C1480/74/55).

11 On 26 October 1940 St Clement's Press, the printers of *Dziennik Polski*, was severely bomb-damaged, and the editorial staff were rehoused as guests of the *Daily Telegraph* (Chwastyk-Kowalczyk 2005: 32). This new arrangement, in bringing Polish and British journalists into closer proximity, opened the possibility for informal contacts and information exchange to occur.

12 See Kochanski (2012: 168, 327). Three government ministers resigned over the Sikorski–Maisky agreement – August Zaleski (foreign minister), Marian Seyda (justice minister) and General Kazimierz Sosnkowski (minister for military affairs).

13 *Polish Fortnightly Review*, 1 September 1941, 6.

326   Notes to pages 83–7

14 *Polish Fortnightly Review*, 1 September 1941, 7.
15 This resolution was broadcast to Poland on 12 June 1941, on the 8.45 a.m. BBC news bulletin. See BBC WAC, European News Bulletin (Polish), June 1941.
16 *Polish Fortnightly Review*, 1 September 1941, 7.
17 Joanna Michlic (2006: 145) draws attention to Stanisław Stroński's speech made on 15 January 1942 during a session of the National Council as evidence of the Polish government's instrumental use of the 'Jewish card'. Stroński considered that the proportion of Jews in Anders's army was 'an excellent argument' that could be referred to by the Polish government in discussions over the eastern borders.
18 NA.FO 371/24470/358: 11.
19 NA.FO 371/30917 (C7839) (13 August 1942). Gilbert (2001: 74) incorrectly assigns authorship of this statement to Roger Allen. Roger Allen, along with Sir William Malkin (legal advisor to the Foreign Office), endorsed William Denis Allen's view.
20 Reports indicating little or no anti-Semitism also arrived in London. For example, the Polish courier and SOE agent Jerzy Salski, in a report given to Ignacy Schwarzbart in mid-April 1943, wrote that 'with regard to the Jews the whole Country is of one opinion. There is no antisemitism.' YVA M.2–261, p. 2 and p. 7. This was clearly a very optimistic assessment. Work by Barbara Engelking (2011) has highlighted that Polish peasants regularly murdered Jews in the countryside during the war.
21 For a discussion of Kot's operations and relationship with the British, see Bines (2008: 20). For an analysis of Kot's wartime activities see Rutkowski (2012).
22 On 12 December 1937, at the Conservative Party conference in Warsaw, Radziwiłł supported efforts to fight 'against Jewish influence in the economic and moral spheres' and saw no solution to the 'Jewish problem' other than a 'forcible emigration of Jews'. See Cang (1939: 246). In his analysis of Polish political parties' attitudes towards Jews, the journalist Joel Cang (1939: 247) pointedly noted that 'Prince Radziwiłł, whose family has for centuries dealt with Jews, suddenly discovered that the "Jews smell of garlick", and he joined the anti-Jewish fascist front'. Through his letter to London, Radziwiłł sought to show that his solution to the 'Jewish problem' was correct, and promises of political equality between Poles and Jews in a post-war Poland were redundant. His letter was a clear *political* intervention.
23 Cited in Michlic (2006: 147). The *Jewish Chronicle* published a page 11 article entitled 'Poles support Jewish rights – the die-hard residue – National Council declarations' on 4 April 1941, which reported on the Polish National Council's 'strong support for the Polish Government's policy of equality of rights for the Jews in Poland after the war'. The article also noted some sections of the Council as being anti-Jewish (General Żeligowski).
24 NA.FO 371/26723 (C278). The original Polish letter is found at HIA Stanisław Mikołajczyk Papers, Box 25, Folder 11, Correspondence for October 1940, 'List z Kraju'. Since Radziwiłł speaks of Stańczyk's November broadcast, his undated letter has been misfiled. Also see Engel (1987: 80, 245, fn. 147). Anti-Semitic sentiment was also recorded in other occupied countries. In Czechoslovakia, the resistance movement advised the Czechoslovak Government in Exile in London of a rise in anti-Semitism and the efficacy of Nazi

Notes to pages 87–90

anti-Jewish propaganda in March 1942. See Láníček (2010: 127); Reports from Prague, 24–31 March 1942, NA.FO 371/30837.

25 Kot framed the postwar movement of Jews out of Poland by referring to the concentration of Jews in certain economic activities and the economic problems in pre-war Poland. Kot noted that following the economic crisis of 1929, anti-Semitism in Poland took a real (rather than theoretical) form. The discussion also mentioned possible Jewish settlement of Palestine. Kot suggested that the war offered various options for Jewish emigration from Poland, including to southern Russia along the Black Sea. Kot did not completely alienate the British Jews he spoke to (Selig Brodetsky, Leonard Stein and Adolph Brotman), as Brodetsky wrote to Kot on 16 July 1940 wishing 'to renew the friendly discussions which we had the pleasure of having with you at Angers' and invited him to lunch or dinner. See AZHRL, Archiwum Stanisława Kota, 350, 15; 350, 21.

26 Perlzweig was born in Poland, but was educated in Britain (Cambridge).

27 British propaganda in the United States prior to American entry into the war was frequently managed through the Inter-Allied Information Centre (IAIC), which was created in September 1940. Based at the Rockefeller Center in New York, the IAIC included at its first meeting representatives from most occupied countries of Europe. The Poles joined at the second meeting. Cull (1995: 117) argues that '[t]he IAIC promised to be the perfect puppet propaganda machine, not least because the puppets themselves were eager to participate'. The Polish government was later to set up its own Polish Information Center in New York.

28 NA.FO 371/26723 (C278).

29 NA.FO 371/24481/109.

30 NA.FO 371/39524 (C9465).

31 Scholarship over the last twenty years has explored Jewish responses to the Soviet occupation in 1939–41. It is clear that, other than a minority of Jewish youth, the Jewish population as a whole did not welcome the Soviet occupation, but that the stereotype of pro-communist, anti-Polish Jew was common amongst Christian Poles (Michlic 2007: 145). Also see Polonsky and Davies (1991), Jasiewicz (2002), Żbikowski (2000).

32 See Michlic (2006: 146) and PISM 138/237 (30 November 1941), Memo of Anders (Wincenty Bąkiewicz collection).

33 NA.FO 371/30917, Roberts to Lias (21 August 1942).

34 NA.FO 371/30917, Roberts to Lias (21 August 1942).

35 NA.FO 954/19B, 19 January 1942. During 1941 the Polish government was criticized for proposals of mass Jewish emigration from Poland. In 1940 Kazimierz Głuchowski of the Polish Information Center, New York, printed a pamphlet (*Na marginesie Polski jutra*) which advocated mass Jewish emigration. In 1941, Józef Retinger (Sikorski's *homme de confiance*) published a book which also endorsed such emigration. The World Jewish Congress wrote to the British Foreign Office highlighting that the Polish government had not criticized either author, leading Schwarzbart to believe that the government demonstrated 'at least a certain tolerance of and indifference to the activities of the Endek Party, as well as the ONR'. See Engel (1987: 85); Silverman to Eden, 'Memorandum on Polish Jewish Relations Submitted by the World

328   Notes to pages 90–1

Jewish Congress ...', NA.FO 371/26769 (C4878) (1 May 1941); Schwarz-bart Diary, 10 April 1941, YVA M2/761. By early 1942, senior Polish government officials, if discussing Jewish emigration, tended to do so in private. Nevertheless, damage had been done to the reputation of the Polish government. The Representation of Polish Jewry in Palestine (Reprezentacja Żydowstwa Polskiego), for example, was critical of the government from autumn 1941 and mistrustful of the government's attempts to ensure Polish Jews as well as non-Jewish Poles were able to leave the Soviet Union following the signing of the Sikorski–Maisky agreement. See Engel (1987: 130–1).

36 NA.FO 371/31901. Also see Hoover and Gibson (1942: 315) for Herbert Hoover's endorsement of population transfer as a legitimate policy to eradicate European irredentas.

37 PUMST A1.1.2 (1).

38 Significant effort continued to be expended by Jewish representatives and activists to focus Allied attention on German actions against Jews, though there were significant tensions within the American Jewish community. On 9 March 1943, 40,000 people witnessed the 'We Will Never Die Pageant' at Madison Square Gardens in New York, which highlighted the murder of Jews in Europe. However, the organizers were unable to persuade the White House to send a message to the event. The Polish ambassador, Jan Ciechanowski, did send a message which was read out. Rabbi Stephen Wise thanked Ciechanowski and stated that '[t]hroughout these tragic months it has been a source of strength to us to know that we see eye to eye with the Polish Government on the need for immediate action'. See Wierzyński and Karski (2012: 150). The Western Allies did not share that view. It is important to note that some of Stephen Wise's actions have been heavily criticized. Wise's attempts to block the activities of the Bergson group – officially constituted as the Emergency Committee to Save the Jewish People in Europe in July 1943 – have been described by the Holocaust scholar Yehuda Bauer as 'deplorable' (Bauer 2012: 137). The Bergson group sought to raise awareness amongst Americans of what was happening to Jews in Europe. The group took its name from Peter Bergson – a pseudonym used by Hillel Kook, a revisionist Zionist (Irgun). The group organized the 'March of the Rabbis' on 6 October 1943. Marching in Washington, DC, it sought to draw attention to the Germans' policy against Europe's Jews, and to persuade the US government to aid Europe's Jews. Roosevelt failed to meet the rabbis, it is thought, due to advice given to him by Stephen Wise.

39 On 28 April 1944, the Polish government issued a declaration welcoming the creation of the War Refugee Board and supporting Roosevelt's 24 March declaration. The text speaks of Polish citizens, and states that '[i]n no country in number of persons – both Christians and Jews – who are tortured to death so great, nowhere [is] the persecution so terrible as in Poland'. It is possible that the Polish government could have done more and lobbied harder on behalf of Polish Jewish citizens, but it is extremely doubtful whether any further declaration from Poland's allies highlighting the Jewish plight would have been forthcoming. FO 371/42730 (40).

40 As noted, the editions from 1942 cannot be comprehensively assessed as there are only seven of them available. The *Polish Jewish Observer* was first

Notes to pages 92–3

published in late February 1942. The only edition available for 1942 at the British Library is from 27 February. The Polish Library in Hammersmith has copies of editions from 24 April, 8 May, 15 May, 27 May, 13 November and 4 December 1942. The editions published through 1943 and 1944 provide extraordinary details of the Holocaust as it unfolded. Many articles draw on intelligence reports from the Polish government, which scholars have hitherto considered either to have languished with the Polish government, or to have had only restricted circulation amongst the Allied intelligence communities. Locating copies of the newspaper published in 1942 is therefore an urgent task as it is likely that the reports published in that year would contribute to deepening scholarly understanding of how and when information about the Holocaust was disseminated. The editions from 1943 and 1944 provide the most detailed news of the fate of Jews in Poland available in Britain through the war, including repeated mention of the mass killing of Jews at Oświęcim.

41 NA.INF 1/884, 14 February 1941. This letter was also sent to Anthony Eden and Desmond Morton, Churchill's adviser on intelligence. Laqueur (1998: 116), for instance, notes that the British controlled Radio Świt, and he describes it as 'a British station'.

42 DEFE 53/4, Ministry of Information Defence Notices, Revised Edition (and private and confidential press censorship communications) (1942), p. 4.

43 NA.INF 1/521, 10 May 1943, Powell to Eckersley.

44 The key mechanisms of control were informal, rather than formal; that is, Allied governments were offered 'advice'. In autumn 1942, the Polish government wished to publish *The Story of Wilno*, which the British thought would offend Soviet sensibilities. Officials at the Foreign Office recognized that the publication would not have to pass through the censorship office – unless sent overseas, and thus worked on the Poles stressing the inadvisability of distributing the pamphlet (NA.FO 371/31903 (C9502), Comments of P. Hutton, 5 October 1942). *The Story of Wilno* was published by the Polish Research Centre, which, from April 1940, was based at the Royal Institute of International Affairs. The Poles had earlier obtained paper from a non-official private source. The significance of this example is that it shows how vigorous British intervention could be if their policy (here respecting Soviet sensibilities) was questioned. It also demonstrates the sustained determination required to undertake actions which contravened British advice. The issue of *The Story of Wilno* had been running since spring 1942.

45 Cited in Laqueur (1998: 113). Later, a courier, parachuted into Poland, explained that the telegrams sent by Korboński were not believed by the Polish or British governments, speculating that the British only acted when they received confirming information from their own sources. These British sources could well be German railway radio intercepts. If that was the case, the information that Korboński sent would have allowed analysts privy to the radio decrypts to make sense of train movements and support the intelligence sent from Poland. Information about the deportation of Jews from Warsaw was initially met with incredulity across the Polish government and Polish National Council. The receipt and processing of the Bund report (discussed below) changed this in late May 1942.

330   Notes to pages 93–6

46 Other governments in exile based in London also demonstrated 'sensitivity' in relation to Jews and Jewish stories. See Láníček (2010) for a discussion of the Czechoslovak Government in Exile.

47 There are several reasons why the Polish government would not wish to antagonize the British. The British were an important source of funding for the government and its intelligence operations in Poland. The British also controlled access to the airwaves and to paper supply, which severely limited the Polish government's scope for manoeuvre in the area of information dissemination. When the Polish government did come into conflict with the British – over Katyń and the truthful claim of Soviet responsibility in 1943, and over the restoration of Poland's 1939 borders in 1944 – the British government was uncompromising. See below.

48 Cited in Engel (1987: 201). The original document can be found at the Hoover Institute Archives, Polish Government, Box 700, File 851/e, 'Ratowanie Żydów'.

49 NA.FO 371/26727 (C9226), 15 August 1941 (Savery to Eden).

50 NA.FO 371/26727 (C9226/189/55), 15 August 1941 (Savery to Roberts).

51 'Leaking' information to the British was one way to bypass intransigent elements in the Polish Cabinet.

52 Unfortunately Laqueur does not give any examples of this change in information policy.

53 The figures Mikołajczyk used at the conference at the Ministry of Information on 9 July 1942 are an obvious example – but the figures received from Poland were also cited at that conference.

54 The way in which officials from the Foreign Office pressured Sydney Silverman not to act on the Riegner report is an example of efforts to contain and marginalize news of Jews from occupied Europe.

55 A British propaganda leaflet dropped over Germany, including Berlin, in the first quarter of 1943, reduced the figure for the number of Jews killed. Some 600,000 Jews were said to have died unnaturally in Poland. In December 1942 the British press had cited a figure of 2 million (the *Daily Telegraph*, the *Jewish Chronicle*). Reducing the scale of the Nazi killing was a standard part of British propaganda strategy, aiming to engage various audiences. See NA.FO 371/34550 (C2431). This drop was initiated after the British were approached by the Polish government. The leaflets were prepared in advance of the Polish government's formal approach.

56 Cited in Stola (1997: 10). Original document is at HIA.

57 The possibility of a quisling emerging was discussed with the PWE. Harold Osborne wrote to Moray McLaren on 8 August 1943 noting that recent Polish intelligence reports suggested that the Germans might succeed in establishing a quisling regime. See NA.FO 898/57 (291).

58 NA.FO 371/30917 (82) and HL MS 238/2/10. Also see Sompolinsky (1999: 65).

59 NA.FO 371/30917 (81).

60 At the 90th BBC meeting to discuss Polish Service broadcasts, on 1 December 1943, the call for a specific Jewish bulletin was rejected. Deputy European Service editor Douglas Ritchie 'stressed that the BBC was anxious not to support Nazi racial discrimination', and that a Jewish bulletin 'would in itself

Notes to pages 96–100

imply a different standpoint from that always taken up by the British Government'. Frank Savery (Foreign Office) 'expressed agreement'. BBC WAC, E1 1149 1, Polish Service Minutes, 90th meeting, 1 December 1943.

61 NA.FO 371/30917 (79).

62 NA.FO 371/30917 (77/78).

63 The Bund report can be found at the Hoover Institute Archive, Box 12, File 'Jews in occupied Poland' –'Raport Bundu w sprawie prześladowań Żydów'; and at PUMST MSW 16 (26).

64 See Nowak (1982: 274). Nevertheless, Engel is right to highlight that Polish leaders did not always draw attention to the destruction of Poland's Jews when they had opportunities to do so. Puławski (2009) also argues that reports about Jews compiled in Poland were often delayed, not sent to London, or marginalized within larger dispatches about crimes committed against Poles. However, in the reports specifically dealing with atrocities (the 'Aneks' series) information possessed by the Polish Underground about German actions against Jews was routinely incorporated – including news from Auschwitz.

65 Also see NA.FO 371/31097 (67). The translation circulated to FO officials read, 'The Jewish population in Poland is doomed to die out in accordance with the slogan "all the Jews should have their throats cut, no matter what the outcome of this war may be"'.

66 Within the controlled context of the BBC's European Service, mention of gas vans was omitted and the large number of victims reduced, but the Nazi genocidal agenda was highlighted. Sikorski's speech made (necessary) compromises, but it did not seek to marginalize news of what was happening to Jews in Poland.

67 The placing of the news in the *Daily Telegraph* specifically may be related to the interrelations between staff at that paper and *Dziennik Polski*, which developed during *Dziennik*'s sojourn at the *Telegraph*.

68 On his death, Bracken instructed that all his papers be burnt. His servant dutifully carried out this request. Consequently it is not possible to examine in detail many of Bracken's activities.

69 BBC WAC, E1 1149 1, Polish Service Minutes, 19th meeting, 19 June 1942.

70 BBC WAC, E2 151 5, News Directives, June 1942.

71 The June–July 1942 loosening of censorship policy both highlights the varied agendas of different ministries at a particular point in time during the war and points to the possibilities of key individuals to act against policy guidelines (that is, Bracken and probably Churchill). It is possible that Bracken and Churchill spoke about German atrocities against Jews during one of Churchill's kitchen cabinet meetings.

72 BBC WAC, E2 131 5, News Directives, June 1942.

73 BBC WAC, E1 1149 1, Polish Service Minutes, 20th meeting, 26 June 1942.

74 BBC WAC, C165, Lindley Fraser, 27 June 1942.

75 See Puławski (2009: 502). Some of the news was published in twenty-three papers in Britain. This news was not prominently featured.

76 According to Milland (1998b: 42), the BBC's French Service used the phrase 'Hitler chamber' on 1 July 1942. This would not have been the first time that Newsome's output had been questioned by his superiors. In May 1942

332   Notes to pages 101–3

Newsome was chastised by Bruce Lockhart and Ivone Kirkpatrick for a memo ranking the merits of Allies. See NA.FO 898/41, Kirkpatrick to Lockhart, 13 May 1942.

77 The political secretary of the WJC, Alexander Easterman, attempted to keep colleagues in the United States updated. However, on 30 June 1942, he sent a cable to Stephen Wise, Maurice Perlzweig and Irving Miller, writing that he was 'astonished at your silence'. Again in September he expressed frustration with the silence of his colleagues in the US, in a cable dated 11 September 1942. Whether the lack of communication was due to technical difficulties or something else is not known. But in both these periods, important news about the Holocaust was being disseminated. See HL MS 238/2/10 and MS 238/2/11.

78 Schwarzbart also worked hard to ensure that the British political class was well informed of what was happening to Polish Jews. On 29 June he wrote to Victor Cazalet MP calling on him to make reference to 'the terrible sufferings and atrocities committed by the Germans against Polish Jews'. IPN BU 2835/39 (30). Schwarzbart distributed his 'Statement on German Crimes Committed against the Jewish Population in Poland' to British politicians, bishops and representatives of civil society. He released 768 copies. The statement declared that 'only immediate reprisals could deter Hitler from carrying out his criminal acts. That is the only language he understands'. See IPN BU 2835/42 (26). Interestingly, in the copy of the statement sent to Churchill on 30 June 1942, Schwarzbart's demands were somewhat more muted. He stated that 'only immediate appropriate steps could deter Hitler from carrying on his criminal actions'. See NA.FO 371/31097 (C7107) (final page of document). Schwarzbart was well aware of British sensitivities and moderated his language accordingly. In the covering letter Schwarzbart stressed that the crimes he discussed were 'part of the atrocities committed against the entire population of Poland'.

79 IPN BU 2835/39 (34). Schwarzbart, on the other hand, considered that there had been a 'good response' from the press. Schwarzbart sent his statement at the WJC to members of the Foreign Press Association. IPN BU 2835/39 (35).

80 BBC WAC, C165, 9 July 1942.

81 See Milland (1998b: 48–50).

82 See 'Nazi Atrocities: Mr Churchill's message', *Manchester Guardian*, 22 July 1942, 5.

83 Liberty Press/Publications was the publishing arm of the Polish Social Information Bureau (Polskie Biuro Informacji Społecznej – PIS). It was subsidised by the Polish Ministry of Information and Documentation. *Stop Them Now!* had an initial print run of 25,000 (2 September 1942) and a second print run of 25,000 (25 September 1942). A further 10,000 copies were printed in December 1942. See PUMST AALC, Kol 133/95. It is also worth noting that *Stop Them Now!* was included in material couriered to the Polish Underground from London by Jerzy Lerski in February 1943. Information transfer between Poland and Britain was two-way. See Lerski (1989: 177). The inventory of material Lerski couriered to Poland can be found at PISM MSW, Depesze do Kraju, Poczta Nr. XIII (11 February 1943). See Lerski (1988: 80 and 255, fn. 22).

Notes to pages 103–7

84 However, the recognition of Nazi atrocities against Jews did not stimulate a change in refugee policy. On 23 September, in a Cabinet meeting, Herbert Morrison restated British policy 'not to admit during the war additional refugees to the United Kingdom unless in some quite rare and exceptional cases it can be shown that the admission of the refugee will be directly advantageous to our war effort'. See NA.CAB 66/29 WP (42) 427, 23 September 1942, Morrison memorandum, 'Admission to the United Kingdom of a Limited Number of Jewish Refugees from Occupied France'. Also see London (2000: 200).

85 The news of the rally was buried deep within newspapers. *The Times* carried an article entitled 'Pledge of retribution: Mr Morrison on Nazi atrocities' on 3 September on page 8, and the *Manchester Guardian* had a piece entitled 'Nazi atrocities: British denunciation' on page 6 the same day. Neither mentioned that the Nazi programme against Jews was discussed at Caxton Hall. The popular press did not cover the rally. Liberty Publications published the speeches from the rally in a booklet entitled *German Atrocities in Poland and Czechoslovakia: Labour's Protest* later that month.

86 Hansard, House of Commons Debates, 8 September 1942, Volume 383, cols. 82–110, available at http://hansard.millbanksystems.com/commons/1942/sep/08/war-situation.

87 NA.INF 1/292.

88 Reports of anti-Semitism in Britain allowed British politicians to rationalize the suppression of stories from occupied Europe that highlighted what was happening to Jews.

89 NA.INF 1/292, Home Intelligence Report 98, released 19 August 1942.

90 On 15 October 1942 a protest against the Vichy regime handing Jews to the Germans was broadcast.

91 Also see Raczyński (1997: 151). Raczyński was critical that Vansittart's contribution was broadcast at 6 p.m. rather than during the peak 9 p.m. slot. Vansittart faced repeated criticism from within the BBC (and PWE) for highlighting atrocities. See Seaton (1987: 171). Robert Bruce Lockhart, the director-general of the PWE, questioned the wisdom of what he termed 'Vansittartism' – a frank, honest approach to information distribution. Lockhart considered that it played into 'Goebbels' hands' (Young 1980: 201). Joesph Goebbels was the Reich propaganda minister.

92 The telegram was sent by Mr Norton in Bern to the Foreign Office on 10 August. See FO 371/30917 (92), Cypher 2831.

93 This concern was to prove justified. Leland Harrison, the US representative in Bern, was advised by the State Department on 17 August that Riegner's telegram was not passed on to Wise (Gilbert 2001: 58).

94 NA.FO 371/30917 (101).

95 HL MS 238/2/11, Law to Silverman, 17 August 1942. Also see NA.FO 371/30917 (101).

96 NA.FO 371/30917 (96). The FO wished to maintain the secrecy of sources of information in Germany.

97 HL MS 238/2/11, Easterman to Silverman, 24 September 1942.

98 In the internal Foreign Office discussion following Richard Law's meeting with Sydney Silverman and Alexander Easterman on 26 November 1942, FO

334   Notes to pages 108–11

official William Denis Allen, on 27 November 1942, noted that 'Rabbi Perlzweig has pronounced against publicity or reprisals. That was on 1st October. He may have changed his views since'. See NA.FO 371/30923 (C11923) (65).

99 HL MS 238/2/12, Perlzweig/Miller to Easterman, 1 October 1942. Also see HL MS 238/2/14, Perlzweig/Miller to Easterman, 20 December 1942 – 'Our gravely responsible decisions must be constantly reviewed in light [of] official advice from quarters which have been extremely helpful'.

100 HL MS 238/2/12, Wise/Goldmann/Perlzweig to Easterman, 9 October 1942.

101 AK w dokumentach, Volume II (document 342, p. 345).

102 The original document is at AAN 1325 202/I-2, Depesza 'Stem' Nr 91 do Delegata, 15 October 1942, received 20 October 1942. Mikołajczyk sent several messages through 1942 and 1943, requesting information about Jews. See PUMST 3.1.1.13.5a. It is worth noting that the Czechoslovak foreign minister received news of the Riegner telegram from Alexander Easterman of the WJC in early September 1942. See Láníček (2013: 82).

103 PISM PRM 88/20.

104 The Board of Deputies liaised with the BBC to publicize the protest meeting at the Albert Hall on 29 October 1942. See WL 1658/10/7/1/2.

105 Wood and Jankowski (1994: 228) suggest that Raczyński was 'stalling for time in the hope of obtaining more details from Karski [Jan Karski, the courier] when he arrived'. They refer to Gilbert (1981: 93), who received a letter from Raczyński on 18 September 1980 in which Raczyński stated, 'There is no doubt that his visit prompted us to act'. This is not the case. Karski arrived in London on 26 November 1942 and was not released by the British until 28 November. Prior to his discharge from British custody, the Polish government had issued a press release and held a session of the National Council that discussed German atrocities against Jews. One possible interpretation of Raczyński's letter to Gilbert is that Raczyński was referring to the information which Karski carried from Poland to Paris (according to Wood and Jankowski), and which apparently arrived in London via diplomatic bag at some point before 17 November. The precise details of Karski's autumn 1942 journey to London from Warsaw and the exact inventory of material he carried are subject to continuing debate. See Chapter 4.

106 The Polish government's note can be found at NA.FO 371/30923 (76 and 77).

107 IPN BU 2835/39 (61). Schwarzbart also forwarded information to the Polish government. For example, he passed the 10 December 1942 edition of *Nasza Trybuna*, which described Nazi atrocities against Jews, to Władysław Sikorski. See annotation on the 10 December 1942 edition of *Nasza Trybuna* held at the Polish Library, POSK, London.

108 Original source: Joseph Diary, 26 November 1942, 525/1510, Central Zionist Archive.

109 NA.FO 371/30923 (C11923).

110 NA.FO 371/34361 (CM 255) (26). Also see the weekly PWE directive to the BBC's European Service, 17–23 December 1942: 'It is particularly important, however to continue telling the Poles that we know about the suffering of their Jews. We do not necessarily need to inform them of the details of

Notes to pages 111–12

those sufferings. What we need to impress on them is our knowledge'. NA.FO 371/31903 (184).

111 Instrumental in the sense that by speaking about what was happening to Jews in Poland the Polish government primarily sought to curry favour with Jewish audiences in Britain and the United States, and to demonstrate the government's adherence to liberal values.

112 Handing information to Jewish organizations was important, but it also allowed the Polish government through 1943 to balance the demands of Polish Jewish citizens to do something against not alienating the Polish right wing that was sensitive to news of Jews. The Polish government information strategy was characterized by forwarding a great deal of data to the Allies out of the public gaze (for example, via Bureau VI to SOE). The weakness of this strategy was that Jewish organizations had even less influence than exiled governments in encouraging the national press to publish the news and giving it due weight.

113 The Polish government evidently saw Jewish organizations as having a key role to play in disseminating news of the Holocaust. This view was shared by the Jewish National Committee in Poland (Żydowski Komitet Narodowy), which sent messages via Stanisław Jankowski to be forwarded to various Jewish organizations in the West. Indicatively see AAN 1325 202/I-7, Messages 15 (13 January 1943), 67 (13 April 1943), 81 (28 April 1943), Microfilm 2201/2. Message 92 from 15 May 1943 had an accusatory tone. The Jewish National Committee could not understand the silence of Schwarzbart, and advised that thousands of Jews were being killed and that they had not received desperately needed funds from the Joint (American Jewish Joint Distribution) Committee.

114 Jewish Telegraphic Agency, 27 November 1942, 'Anti-Jewish action of Polish officials provokes stormy debate in National Council'.

115 'Odparcie zarzutu p. Schwarzbarta', *Dziennik Polski*, 3 December 1942, 3.

116 At a meeting of the BBC governors in October 1942, Lady Violet Bonham Carter had called for the BBC to adequately cover the Albert Hall meeting of 29 October on Jewish persecution. Her request was passed to Sir Cecil Graves (joint director-general of the BBC) to see whether this was possible. See BBC WAC, C165.

117 'Trzecia część Żydów polskich wyginęła w czasie okupacji', *Dziennik Polski*, 11 December 1942, 1.

118 The British were fully cognizant of the Nazi extermination programme. A five-page document compiled by the PWE, dated 17 December 1942, gave a brief summary of the Nazi treatment of Jews in Poland up to that point. The Polish Government in Exile was the source of some of the information. Entitled 'Special Annex on Extermination of Jews – Evidence of Nazi Policy and Practice', the document discussed food rationing; forced labour; judicial murder; conditions in the ghettos; and transport to execution camps at Bełżec, Sobibór and Treblinka (BBC WAC, C165). Through the first three weeks of December 1942, the PWE directives to the Polish Service sought to highlight British anger at the German persecution of Jews. See NA.FO 371/31903 (182–6).

119 NA.FO 371/30863, 8 December 1942, pilot to ambassador, Washington.

336 Notes to pages 113–17

120 BBC WAC, E1 131 8, News Directives, December 1942.
121 NA.FO 371/30924, Document 104.
122 NA.FO 371/30923 (723).
123 BBC WAC, R28 67 (37), 2 December 1942. The circular specifically highlights the claim that Hitler had ordered the total extermination of Jews in occupied Europe before the end of the year. Fulbrook (2012: 281) notes that on 19 July 1942 Himmler had called for all Polish Jews to be 'resettled' – that is, either killed or put in a collection camp prior to being killed, by December 1942. This objective was not achieved in 1942, but Himmler restated the goal in 1943.
124 Sydney Silverman was persuaded by the Foreign Office to withdraw a parliamentary question scheduled for 6 December 1942, which stated that '2,000,000 Jews have already died; that 4,000,000 more are in dire and immediate peril', and to wait until 17 December. Silverman's 17 December question was tempered – the number of victims was not mentioned – and used by the Foreign Office as a way for Anthony Eden to announce the UN declaration. See NA.FO 371/30925 (27 and 34). By delaying Silverman's question, the Foreign Office was better able to co-ordinate allies in the lead-up to the declaration, and manage the news agenda prior to the declaration.
125 NA.FO 371/30923 (723).
126 NA.FO 371/30925 (34). Earlier, Frank Roberts worried that highlighting the German treatment of Jews would provoke a negative German reaction that would be felt by French politicians and others interned by the Vichy regime. From 11 November 1942 the Germans occupied the whole of France (Fox 1977: 100).
127 This memorandum also includes a reference to the mass slaughter of Jews at Auschwitz. See Chapter 4.
128 NA.FO 371/30863 (206), 15 December 1942.
129 Hansard, House of Lords, Debates, 15 December 1942, Volume 125, cols. 555–64, available at http://hansard.millbanksystems.com/lords/1942/dec/15/german-atrocities-in-poland, last accessed 13 March 2012.
130 See Newsome (1945: 223). The notion that the actions were a disgrace to the German nation was, according to Hilberg (1985: 1139), expressed by Churchill in his letter to Eden on 11 July 1944, following the dissemination of information from the Vrba–Wetzler report. See NA.FO 371/42809, 11 July 1944, and Chapter 6.
131 NA.FO 371/31097 (C12895).
132 PISM A10 9 7, PAT, 15 December 1942. For an analysis of PAT's operations during the war, see Grabowski (2005).
133 NA.FO 371/30863 (210).
134 Hansard, House of Commons Debates, 17 December 1942, Volume 385, cols. 2082–7, available at http://hansard.millbanksystems.com/commons/1942/dec/17/united-nations-declaration#S5CV0385-P0_19421217_HOC_280, last accessed 13 March 2012.
135 WAC, E2 131 8, General Directive, 17 December 1942.
136 BBC WAC, E2 131 8, News Directives, December 1942, 18 December 1942. See Savery's text on the Warsaw ghetto. NA.FO 371/31097 (C12575) (210),

Notes to pages 117–21

version from 8 December 1942, and C12685 (225), revised version from 16 December 1942.

137 For a discussion of Rathbone's activities in relation to refugees, see Cohen (2010).

138 Hansard, House of Commons Debates, 17 December 1942, Volume 385, cols. 2082–7, available at http://hansard.millbanksystems.com/commons/1942/dec/17/united-nations-declaration#S5CV0385-P0_19421217_HOC_280, last accessed 13 March 2012.

139 See Milland (1998b: 139).

140 IPN BU 2835/15 (12–13).

141 See Chapter 5 for discussion of the 19 May 1943 debate on refugees in the House of Commons.

142 NA.FO 954/19, 7 April 1944, Halifax to Eden. This perspective was clearly shared by officials in the Foreign Office, as censorship in relation to reporting news about Jews, especially Hungarian Jews, was cautiously loosened. From mid-April 1944 onwards, an increasing amount of intelligence received from the Polish Government in Exile and elsewhere was passed for distribution.

143 Richard Breitman (1999: 171) has made the same point, arguing that 'British officials feared the Nazis or the satellites might release large numbers of Jews', and cites the comment of Richard Law (Eden's deputy) that 'we cannot take the risk of the Germans calling our bluff'. See NA.FO 371/36648, Memorandum of Conversation with Alexander Easterman, 7 January 1943.

144 NA.FO 371/34549, 26 January 1943.

145 NA.FO 371/34549, 26 January 1943.

146 Roberts's condescension towards the Poles was not unusual. After the war, the chief press censor, recalling the new powers granted to his office in March 1942 to censor news that was likely to cause disharmony amongst the Allies, wrote about Polish hostility to the USSR. He stated, 'Much as I personally disliked these new censorship powers, they certainly helped us to help the Poles *who so often refused to help themselves*' (Thomson 1947: 161, my italics). The censor was able to inhibit the sending of information about Polish papers to the USSR by pro-Soviet sympathizers.

147 The British ambassador to Moscow, Sir William Seeds, telegrammed the Foreign Office on 30 September 1939 suggesting that the Kremlin could be advised that British war aims were not incompatible with the Soviet Union's 'reasonable settlement on ethnographic and cultural lines' of eastern Poland. See NA.FO 371/23103/237–8. Ivone Kirkpatrick (at the Foreign Office) echoed this view, maintaining that it was 'possible for [the British] to stand for an ethnographical and cultural Poland without standing on Russian toes'. See NA.FO 371/23097/203–209.

148 NA.FO 371/26725 (C7040), 24 June 1941.

149 For example, in April 1943 the British press was very critical of the Polish government's view that the Soviet Union was responsible for the murder of Polish officers at Katyń. On 28 April, the *Daily Mirror* accused the Polish press of an anti-Soviet campaign. The *Daily Mirror* claimed that the Poles quoted German news on Katyń, viewed the Polish claim that Russia was

338   Notes to pages 121–4

responsible for atrocities against Poles and Jews as anti-Soviet propaganda and queried why the British paper control office was supplying the Polish press in Britain with paper. See 'What the Polish papers in England say', *Daily Mirror*, 28 April 1943, 3.

150 NA.FO 371/31903 (26) (104–5).
151 NA.FO 371/31092 (74).
152 NA.FO 371/31903 (152) (146).
153 NA.FO 371/34555 (75).
154 NA.FO 371/34555 (73).
155 NA.FO 371/34555 (C334), Kirkpatrick commentary, 13 January 1943.
156 NA.FO 371/34549 (12).
157 Hansard, House of Commons Debates, 19 January 1943, Volume 386, cols. 53–102 (war situtation), http://hansard.millbanksystems.com/commons/1943/jan/19/war-situation#S5CV0386P0_19430119_HOC_359, last accessed 3 August 2012.
158 BBC WAC, E1/1149/2, Polish Service, 1b 2 1943–1953, Raczyński to Kirkpatrick, 19 January 1943.
159 NA.FO 371/34555 (84).
160 NA.FO 371/34555 (113).
161 BBC WAC, E1/1149/2, Polish Service, 1b 2 1943–1953, 'Extract from output report'.
162 The rank-and-file soldiers were dispersed across the USSR. Following the Sikorski–Maisky agreement of 30 July 1941 a Polish Army under General Anders was formed which left the USSR via Persia. The Polish II Corps later played a key role in Italy (Monte Cassino).
163 See Pickhan (1997).
164 CAC NERI 6/9, 7 May 1943. The reference to 'Soviet officers' instead of Polish officers is clearly a mistake.
165 NA.FO 371/34577 (C166). See Sanford (2005) and Bell (1990) for discussion of the O'Malley report, Foreign Office responses and the British and American suppression of news of Katyń. O'Malley was the British ambassador to the Polish Government in Exile. His report made use of Polish sources. This is significant because it demonstrates that Foreign Office officials privately accepted intelligence from Polish sources but rejected it publicly because it contradicted the FO's policy position. On 29 May 1944, a Polish civilian, Stanisław Wójcik, arrived in Britain. Wójcik was interviewed by British Intelligence (MI19). In 1943 Wójcik had worked for a German firm in Smolensk. The workers of the firm were invited to visit the Katyń graves in July 1943. Wójcik and his co-workers visited Katyń and they left with the view that 'a terrible crime had been committed by the Russians'. Unlike other MI19 interview intelligence reports which were very widely circulated amongst the British (and American) intelligence community, the report derived from Wójcik was restricted to MI19, MI3c (Military Intelligence (Germany)), MI14 (Military Intelligence assessing German strategy), MI6 and the Foreign Office. This limited circulation list highlights how information about Katyń was controlled by the British. See NA.WO 208/3733.
166 Kochanski (2012: 341) rightly observes that 'stark military facts governed the response of the British and American governments to the Katyń

Notes to pages 125–6

revelations and the break in diplomatic relations between the Polish Government and the Soviet Union'.

167 Hansard, House of Commons Debates, 20 May 1943, Volume 389, cols. 1216–20, available at http://hansard.millbanksystems.com/commons/1943/may/20/allied-governments-newspaper-attacks, last accessed 13 March 2012.

168 Hansard, House of Commons Debates, 2 June 1943, Volume 390, cols. 194–5, available at http://hansard.millbanksystems.com/commons/1943/jun/02/foreign-language-newspapers-great-britain, last accessed 13 March 2012.

169 The debate was reported on page 3 of the 4 June 1943 edition of the *Jewish Chronicle*.

170 The British government had the potential to moderate the anti-Polish tone of the debate by liaising with those asking questions in Parliament. William Gallacher was an exception, but Geoffrey Mander had, in the past, been amenable to postponing a parliamentary question so as not to embarrass the government. Had either the Foreign Office or the Ministry of Information wished to, Mander could have been requested to temper his questions further, or even advised of Foreign Office musing on Katyń off-record. (Mander had, in April 1941, postponed a question on a joint Allied Council. See NA.FO 371/26451, 16 April 1941.)

171 NA.CAB 65 34 21. Also see CAC NERI 6/9, 7 May 1943. This view was shared by Anthony Eden. According to Noel Newsome, who dined with Eden on 6 May 1943, Eden thought that the USSR was not seeking to set up a rival Soviet-backed government in exile in Moscow, but wished to see Sikorski change his government, throw out the 'fascists', ban the State Council and control the Polish press. Eden indicated that the British government was using its influence to achieve these goals, suggesting to Sikorski that he decrease the number of people in the Polish Cabinet, and that the British government would control the Polish press.

172 O'Malley's report on Katyń clearly articulated the ethical cost of British political pragmatism. 'In handling the publicity side of the Katyn affair we have been constrained by the urgent need for cordial relations with the Soviet Government to appear to appraise the evidence with more hesitation and lenience than we should do in forming a common-sense judgement on events occurring in normal times or in the ordinary course of our private lives; we have been obliged to appear to distort the normal and healthy operation of our intellectual and moral judgements; we have been obliged to give undue prominence to the tactlessness or impulsiveness of Poles, to restrain the Poles from putting their case clearly before the public, to discourage any attempt by the public and the press to probe the ugly story to the bottom ... We have in fact perforce used the good name of England like the murderers used the conifers to cover up a massacre'. See NA.FO 371/34577. Details of British documents in Katyń can be located using the National Archives record guide at http://yourarchives.nationalarchives.gov.uk/index.php?title=The_Katyn_Massacre, last accessed 1 April 2012.

173 NA.FO 371 34557, 30 November 1943. In December the PWE clearly explained the complicated Polish–Soviet situation, and outlined PWE

340   Notes to pages 127–9

propaganda policy. The document recognized that, to date, propaganda had 'conveyed an impression that we are more timid in defence of our friends and that the USSR are more aggressive in attack'. NA.FO 371 34557 (C14557), 10 December 1943.

174 In discussions about the proposed Allied declaration in August 1943, Mr Harrison of the Foreign Office's Northern Department adjudged that it was necessary to estimate 'whether such a statement now would do greater harm to Anglo-Russian relations or good in Poland'. NA.FO 371 34551, 23 August 1943. In December 1943, Jankowski complained to Mikołajczyk that the terror unleashed in Poland in late 1943 was not being reflected in news broadcast by the BBC. See AAN 1325 202/III/23 (51), Microfilm 2266/4, Jankowski to Mikołajczyk, 10 December 1943, Message 45/43.

175 In an aide-mémoire handed to the Foreign Office on 5 August 1943, the Polish government again demanded reprisals in the context of German actions in the Lublin and Zamość regions: 'When the Polish Government discussed the problem of reprisals with His Majesty's Government in connection with the extermination of the Jewish population they met with certain objections on the part of His Majesty's Government', and called for the matter to be reconsidered in light of the worsening situation in Poland. NA.FO 371/34550 (C8965).

176 Secretary of State Cordell Hull 'felt that any such declaration was not likely to give much help to the Polish population'. NA.FO 371 34551, Cypher telegram, 20 August 1943.

177 On 15 January 1943, codebreakers at Bletchley Park deciphered a telegram from Herman Höfle to Adolf Eichmann (head of Section IV B4 of the Reich Security Main Office responsible for Jewish affairs and evacuation) that provided the number of arrivals at Bełżec, Sobibór, Treblinka and Lublin (Majdanek) up to the end of December 1942. The telegram did not provide the full name of each camp, only the initial letter. Since news of the German extermination programme had been given attention in the press and in Parliament in December 1942, it is possible that the significance of this data was recognized by analysts. However, the information was not acted on. See NA.HW 16/23.

4 INTELLIGENCE ABOUT AUSCHWITZ: NOVEMBER 1940–FEBRUARY 1943

1 See PUMST A.3.8.3.3 (53). Accidents also prevented mail reaching London. According to the list of couriers' post held at the Polish Underground Movement Study Trust, London, a courier, 'Pagkowski', was killed in a plane catastrophe on 4 July 1943. This is probably a reference to the plane crash off Gibraltar in which General Sikorski perished. See PUMST A3.8.3.3 (10) p.46.

2 NA.HS 7/277 (58). The senior Polish intelligence figure at the Polish government's Istanbul station, Jerzy Kurcyusz (who is discussed in more detail in Chapter 5), made use of Hungary's diplomatic bag independently of SOE. The Poles also used the Swiss diplomatic bag to transfer material from Bucharest to Istanbul.

3 The very close co-operation between Bureau VI and SOE extended to the mechanics of securing couriers' passage across borders. On 29 June 1942,

Notes to pages 129–32

Protasewicz advised his opposite number at SOE, Harold Perkins, 'that the Polish organisation in Switzerland had obtained the tacit agreement of the Brazilian Legation in Bern for the issue in very urgent and exceptional cases of Brazilian entrance visas, provided that the British Legation in Lisbon had previously signalled their agreement'. NA.HS 7 277 (p.19).

4 At the British National Archives at Kew there are several files listing the names of several dozen Polish agents. See, for example, NA.HS 4/274.

5 The issue of compromised ciphers is discussed in NA.HS 4/135. A telegram sent by the British Legation in Stockholm to the Foreign Office on 17 August 1942 indicated that the Poles considered that only one cipher was involved and had earlier requested British assistance in identifying messages read by the Swedes. (Telegram from Foreign Office to Stockholm, 15 August 1942.) According to the British, both the Germans and the Swedes had cracked a Polish code.

6 See AAN 1325 202/I-6, Microfilm 2201/2, Messages 118 and 123.

7 On 18 November 1942 Michał Protasewicz advised Rowecki that the Swiss–French border was sealed. The passage of people and post was uncertain and even diplomats had problems (strip searches). The sealing of the French borders had significant implications for the timely passage of news about Auschwitz to London. See AAN 1326 203/1-27, Message 851.

8 See *Raport Witolda* in Cyra (2000).

9 Many reports Pilecki sent from Auschwitz cannot be clearly identified (as distinct from intelligence from other sources), so it not possible to trace with accuracy their circulation or their impact on the picture of the camp being created by key information gatekeepers for wider dissemination. These gatekeepers include intelligence recipients such as Karol Jabłoński, who collated reports about the camp; senior Home Army (Armia Krajowa) commanders, such as Stefan Rowecki and later Tadeusz Bór-Komorowski; the government delegate in Poland – a post held consecutively by Cyryl Ratajski, Jan Piekałkiewicz and Stanisław Jankowski; and the officers in Bureau II (for example, Tadeusz Skinder) and Bureau VI in London. Adam Cyra (2000: 15) notes that it is difficult to ascertain what proportion of Pilecki's reports reached beyond the camp, reached Warsaw, or were transmitted to senior figures in the Polish Government in Exile and thence to Allied governments.

10 See Zaleski (1941). The Polish text can be found at PISM PRM K 86/A3 (Sprawozdania z kraju 1940–1941).

11 NA.FO 371/26726.

12 *Polish Fortnightly Review*, 15 November 1941, 4, 6, 8.

13 Pilecki's co-escapees Jan Redzej and Edward Ciesielski also wrote reports in the summer of 1943. They estimated the number of Jews killed at 1.8 million and 2 million people respectively. These figures were similar to the estimates of other escapees. Jerzy Tabeau estimated 1.5 million; Stanisław Chybiński, writing in the summer of 1943 in Międzybrodzie, suggested 2 million. See Świebocki (2000: 295–297) and Tabeau in Świebocki (1997: 145). Tabeau's report reached the West. It was appended to the Vrba–Wetzler report and is commonly known as 'the report of a Polish major'.

14 *Raport Witolda* (1945) is a detailed account of Pilecki's time in Auschwitz. It charts the changing conditions and sadism of particular guards in the camp,

342   Notes to pages 132–6

and records the fate of Jews. Pilecki highlights Auschwitz as the Nazi killing ground for European Jewry and notes that Treblinka and Majdanek were where Polish Jews were murdered. He also records the building of crematoria in Birkenau and the labour Jews undertook before being killed. See Pilecki (2012) (translated by Jarek Garliński).

15 Jews on this transport were given numbers (they were registered). But by August most had died. See Czech (1992: 160). The *Jewish Chronicle* on 24 July 1942 (page 7) reported that Slovak Jews had been sent to Polish towns and 'to the notorious concentration camp in Oswiecim, where they are employed as forced labourers under horrifying conditions'. The source of this information is not known for certain, but the *Chronicle*'s article indicated that the 'deportees are allowed to communicate with their relatives in Slovakia only once a month'. The source may well have been a letter from a deportee to relatives in Slovakia. The first selections for the gas chambers at Birkenau took place on 4 May 1942.

16 *Polish Fortnightly Review*, 1 July 1942, 2.

17 *Polish Fortnightly Review*, 1 July 1942, 3. The news about Oświęcim in the 1 July 1942 edition of the *Polish Fortnightly Review* was later published in the *Gippsland Times* (Victoria, Australia) on 12 October 1942 (page 2) under the heading 'Savage treatment of Poles'.

18 Informacja Bieżąca Nr 31 (56) reprinted in *Zeszyty Oświęcimskie* 1 (1968), 39.

19 PISM A9 III 2A 3 (1), Salski report for Polish government.

20 Segieda would have briefed the Underground leadership prior to his departure from Warsaw.

21 AAN 1325 202/I-31 (213), Microfilm 2201/9I. Also see *Zeszyty Oświęcimskie*, 1 (1968), 33–4.

22 The date that the report was received in London (by the Ministry of the Interior) is found in 'Document appertaining to the German occupation of Poland: Poles in German concentration camps', Polish Ministry of the Interior, London (1943), PUMST A3.16 (158), and in Raport o sytuacji w kraju na podstawie wiadomości nadeszłych do dnia 31.X.1942, PISM PRM 76/1 (13) 138–40. It is not known when the Polish interior minister, Stanisław Mikołajczyk, first read the report.

23 No evidence has been found to confirm that an 'air hammer' system existed at Auschwitz.

24 This is the English-language translation given in 'Document appertaining to the German occupation of Poland: Poles in German concentration camps', Polish Ministry of the Interior, London (1943), PUMST A3.16 (158).

25 The original source document has not been located to check this.

26 According to documents at the Polish Underground Movement Study Trust, post left Warsaw on 7 September, rather than 4 September. See PUMST A3.8.3.3 (2).

27 Informacja Bieżąca Nr 33 (58), reprinted in *Zeszyty Oświęcimskie* 1 (1968), 44. The original document is at AAN 1325 202/III-7 t.1, Microfilm 2266/2 (146).

28 AAN 1325 202/I-41 (p. 1 and p. 2), Microfilm 2201/11.

29 Radio messages from Warsaw were consecutively numbered, allowing Polish intelligence in London to advise colleagues in Warsaw if a particular message

Notes to pages 136–40

was not received (and vice versa). Today, this practice allows messages sent and received to be cross-checked.

30 For example Message 702 sent by General Rowecki in early September 1942 is missing. See AAN 1326, 203/I-22.

31 See Messages 636 and 803 in AAN 1326 203/I-22. The message about the Warsaw ghetto, Treblinka and Bełżec was received in London on 25 August. See PUMST A 3.1.1.2 (28), Message 728.

32 See AAN 1326 203/1-27 (p. 24), Message 738, from late September 1942 (no specific date is given), for example, included a request from the British Intelligence Service for data on the Germans' production of synthetic benzene.

33 It is important to note that many of Protasewicz's messages to Rowecki are missing or lost. In the messages that survive, it is clear that the British demand for military, industrial and strategic intelligence played a very important role in determining what data Rowecki radioed to London. The British provided regular feedback on Polish intelligence and this was forwarded to Rowecki. See PUMST A3.7.5.2 A and B, 'Brytyjskie oceny meldunków z kraju', for British assessments of Polish intelligence.

34 Deliveries of food parcels from Stockholm were stopped earlier, on 1 June 1942. This is relevant insofar as it highlights that links with the outside world were being constrained. See AAN 1325 202/I-6 Nr 108.

35 See AAN 1325 202/I-6, Microfilm 2201/2.

36 See AAN 1325 202/I-6, Microfilm 2201/2, Message 123.

37 On 12 September 1942, Sikorski sent a radio message to Rowecki advising that the Polish government had issued a protest to the Soviet government demanding that no bombing of Polish areas take place without the prior agreement of the Polish government. See AAN 1326 203/I-27, Message 657. These bombing raids caused approximately 800 fatalities and injuries to Warsaw's civilian population. See AAN 1326 203/I-22, Message 671, 20 August 1942.

38 AAN 1326 203/I-22, Message 749, 18 September 1942 – 'Placówki Kot i Bór spalone'. 'Kot' may refer to a cell connected with operations set up by Stanisław Kot; Bór may refer to a cell organized by Tadeusz Bór-Komorowski.

39 See AAN 1325 202/I-6, Microfilm 2201/2, Messages 124 and 125 (2 October 1942). Also see AAN 1326 203/1-22, Message 803.

40 Stanisław Herbst and Henryk Woliński headed the section within BIP dealing with Jewish affairs.

41 See AAN 1326 203/I-22, Message 636; and PUMST A 3.1.1.2 (28), Message 728.

42 The Polish leadership in London also depended to a degree on how Polish Jews narrated the Holocaust. On 10 November 1942, Mikołajczyk sent a radio message via the Polish Underground addressed to 'Berezowski' – that is, Leon Feiner – requesting information about the situation of Jews and asking for statistics. AAN 1325 202/1-3 (9), Message 23.

43 AAN 1325 202/III-8.

44 See Ważniewski and Marczewska (1968: xii) for a discussion of 'Aneks' and other types of report.

45 Perkins's family had owned a factory in Silesia, and he spoke Polish. It is likely that he was familiar with Polish geography in Silesia. From June 1943

344　Notes to pages 140–2

Protasewicz filed reports with Perkins between the 15th and the 17th days of each month. In addition to formal reports and meetings, contact between Polish and British intelligence, including Bureau VI and SOE, was maintained by intense cable traffic. See PUMST A2.3.4.3.1.3. Document 135.

46 PUMST A3.8.3.3 (2), p. 9 (4). Poczta Nr 9 E/X.

47 Rowecki, in a message to London dated 31 October 1942, mentions his courier 'Jan' as having handed over 'Poczta Nr 9. E/X' in Paris. See AAN 1326 203/I-22, Message 927 (31 October 1942).

48 AAN 203/I-25 (p. 8), Message 1531 (September 1943), Bór-Komorowski to London.

49 These first gassings actually took place in late August and early September 1941.

50 Copy of document 'Oświęcim – Obóz śmierci' reprinted in *Zeszyty Oświęcimskie* 1 (1968), 47.

51 AAN 1325 202/III/7 t.1 (153A), Microfilm 2266/2.

52 AAN 1325 202/I-31 (64), Microfilm 2201/9I. Also see the report entitled 'Sprawy Narodowościowe' (15 July–15 September 1942) that was included in the same package of material sent to London – AAN 1325 202/I-31 (76).

53 *Zeszyty Oświęcimskie* 1 (1968), 58–72, 'Do Centrali'. No evidence that this report was received has been located.

54 *Zeszyty Oświęcimskie* 1 (1968), 58.

55 The document records that 10,000 Jews (3,000 men and 7,000 women) were given numbers (that is, they were not immediately gassed).

56 See PUMST MSW (1943), 'Sprawozdanie Krajowe', Volume III, p. 101. Mikołajczyk advised Cabinet colleagues that these reports arrived late.

57 During the last quarter of 1942 a number of couriers encountered delays reaching London, including Jerzy Salski and Tadeusz Chciuk-Celt.

58 An SOE report reveals that Colonel Adam Król left Poland on 10 November 1942 but was stalled in Switzerland due to the German occupation of Vichy France. The report noted that he was only en route to Spain on 3 January 1943. See NA.HS 7 277 (p. 22).

59 AAN 1325 202/I/31 (p. 57), Microfilm 2201/9I.

60 The attachments included a report on Bełżec, reports of escapees, a declaration of the Jewish Council in Warsaw, a report from a police officer, the Protest of the Front for the Rebirth of Poland and 'Fragment' – an account of the Warsaw ghetto.

61 *Polish Fortnightly Review*, 1 December 1942.

62 The contention that Karski carried the 4 September 1942 dispatch to the West via Budapest can be rejected for the following reasons: Karski claimed (in *Story of a Secret State*) that he travelled via Germany, not Budapest; he did not leave Warsaw until after 11 September; Polish intelligence in London documented post sent West via Budapest and these records suggest that couriers returned to Poland. See PUMST A3.8.3.3 (2) p8, Poczta Nr 6 B/IX. Polish intelligence in London dates some post as leaving Warsaw on 7 September. However, given that the Underground frequently sent identical material via different routes, it is very likely that Karski carried some of the same information that was sent to Budapest.

Notes to pages 142–4   345

63 Wood and Jankowski (1994: 283) refer to a 'ledger' at the Polish Underground Movement Study Trust that allegedly provides details of the material that Karski carried. As discussed below in more detail, there is no such 'ledger'.

64 To be clear, according to the records at AAN (1325 202/I-31, Microfilm 2201/9I (Biuro Prezydialne – Poczta do Rządu 1942 r.), two separate packages were sent from Warsaw on 1 November 1942. The first, mentioned in a radio message from Piekałkiewicz to Mikołajczyk on 7 October, included material on the liquidation of the Warsaw ghetto, and six attachments. The second package sent from Warsaw on 1 November 1942 was prepared by 24 October. It included documents providing further information on the murder of Jews at Oświęcim. When material from the second package (prepared by 24 October in Warsaw) was distributed to the Polish Cabinet on 15 June 1943 (in the form of Sprawozdanie Nr 1-a/43), Mikołajczyk advised colleagues that the material arrived late. If any documents that discussed the mass killing of Jews at Oświęcim sent from Warsaw in the autumn of 1942, in addition to the statistics originally dispatched on 4 September (arriving in London on 12 November), can be shown to have reached London during 1942, it would mean that the Polish government's suppression of news of the mass killing of Jews at Oświęcim was more extensive than argued here.

65 AAN 1325 202/1/31 (107), Microfilm 2201/9I.

66 NA.HS 4/144, Savery to Roberts, 11 November 1942.

67 NA.HS 4/144, Savery to Roberts, 11 November 1942.

68 AK w dokumentach, Volume VI, Document 1717, p. 261 (Rowecki Message 803, 3 October 1943).

69 Rowecki sent a further radio message about Oświęcim in November 1942 (de-encrypted in London on 26 November) that reported the death of a member of the camp resistance, Stanisław Dubois. See PUMST A3 1 1 2, Document 44, radio message from Rowecki No 133; and AAN 1325 202/I t1–57 (62), Microfilm 2201/1. Dubois may have been responsible for the statistics about the camp sent to London on 4 September 1942. His death was significant for Rowecki, and hence Mikołajczyk, as it potentially had implications for the flow of information from the camp. Korboński (1968: 193–9) provides some details of Dubois's incarceration and contribution to Underground activities.

70 NA.HS 4/144, Savery to Roberts, 11 November 1942.

71 See AAN 1325 202/I-2, radio message No 91 (15 October 1942), Microfilm 2201/1; AAN 1325 202/I-3, radio message No 44 (19 March 1943, sent on behalf of Zygielbojm), Microfilm 2201/1.

72 See Ministerstwo Spraw Wewnętrznych, 'Sprawozdanie Nr 6/42', in HIA-MSW, Box 1. The same document can be found at PUMST MSW 1942, 'Sprawozdanie Krajowe', Volume II, London.

73 As previously noted, the first selections for gassing at Birkenau occurred on 4 May 1942. Reference to the arrival of Jews to be immediately murdered in this report speaks to the efficiency of the camp resistance (Czech 1992: 163). See *Zeszyty Oświęcimskie* 1 (1968), 34. The original document is at AAN 1325 202/I-31.

346   Notes to pages 144–5

74 See AAN 1325 202/I-31 (199), Microfilm 2201/9I.
75 Engel refers to a 27 November 1942 report entitled 'Report on conditions in Poland'. HIA Polish Embassy in the United States (Reports 1920–47), Box 29, File 2, 'Report on conditions in Poland', 27 November 1942. This English-language document draws its data about Oświęcim from the information originally sent from Warsaw on 4 September. It is largely a translation of 'Raport o sytuacji w kraju na podstawie wiadomości nadeszłych do dnia 31.X.1942', PISM PRM 76/1 (13). Engel does not explore the significance that this document is in English (that is, it had been translated from Polish).
76 The English translation of the information about Oświęcim in 'Report on conditions in Poland' follows the Polish original more literally than the version published as 'Document appertaining to the German occupation of Poland: Poles in German concentration camps' in 1943, indicating that the information about Oświęcim was given repeated attention, and that consideration was given to how best to communicate the information to English-speaking audiences.
77 David Engel (1987: 202 and 304 fn. 195) suggests that the Polish government may have been advised of the mass killing of Jews at the camp earlier, referring to the escape of two prisoners, the first in May 1942 and the second in June. The prisoners Engel seems to have in mind are Stefan Bielecki and Stanisław Gustaw Jaster. Stefan Bielecki and Wincenty Gawron escaped on 16 May 1942, and Eugeniusz Bendera, Stanisław Gustaw Jaster, Józef Lempart and Kazimierz Piechowski escaped the following month, on 20 June 1942. Both Bielecki and Jaster reported to the Home Army Command in Warsaw with information about the camp collated by Witold Pilecki. Bielecki escaped not long after the first Slovak Jews arrived at the camp. It is possible that he was able to report on the start of selections and gassing at Birkenau. It is likely that Jaster delivered some information about the mass killing of Jews at the camp. Engel also mentions a document in French entitled 'Situation dans les pays occupés par l'ennemi' from July 1942, which was handed to the Vatican, reporting that 'Poles and Russian officers had been killed by poison gas'. This simply repeated information contained in the *Polish Fortnightly Review* of 1 July 1942 – a date only ten days after Jaster escaped from the camp. The gassing of Poles and Russians reported in the *Polish Fortnightly Review* had occurred almost ten months earlier, in September 1941. Even if Jaster did have information about the mass killing of Jews (which is highly probable given his connection with Witold Pilecki; Jaster is certainly a strong candidate for having delivered the data about mortality rates recorded on 1 June 1942), it is extremely unlikely that this could have been transported to Warsaw, evaluated, encrypted and de-encrypted, selected for publication and published in London/sent to the Vatican within such a short space of time. It took varying lengths of time for information that reached Warsaw to get to London. For a discussion of the escapes from Auschwitz, see Garliński (1994: 101–2).
78 HIA Polish Embassy in the United States (Reports 1920–47), Box 29, File 2, 'Report on conditions in Poland', 27 November 1942. The document is also

Notes to pages 145–9

available online at Poland's National Digital Archive, http://szukajwarchi-wach.pl/800/36/0/-/29/str/1/18#tab2, jpeg190, last accessed 5 July 2012. Engel (1993: 209) suggests that the report was couriered by Jerzy Salski. This was not the case. Salski did not arrive in Britain until February 1943.

79 Since 'Report on conditions in Poland' also included criticisms of the Soviet Union, it is possible that circulation of the document was restricted by the Western Allies for political reasons.

80 See BBC WAC C165 (183), PWE Central Directive (17 December 1942), 'Extermination of the Jews', 5.

81 Raczyński's letter to Eden excluded the brief mention of Jews being sent to the gas chambers at Oświęcim. Possible reasons for this are discussed below.

82 IPN BU 2835/25. For the statistics from Oświęcim see p. 39 (47). These statistics, including the mention of Jews being sent to the gas chambers, were translated on three separate occasions – for the 27 November text 'Report on conditions in Poland', for 'Document appertaining to the German occupation of Poland: Poles in German concentration camps' and for Sprawozdanie Nr 6/42. Each translation of paragraph 7 that mentions Jews is slightly different.

83 By 1943, 10,000 copies of each edition of *Poland Fights* were printed (Friszke, 2011: 289).

84 HIA, MSZ Box 74, Folder 27.

85 Wood and Jankowski (1994: 283) claim that a ledger at the Polish Underground Movement Study Trust entitled 'Materiały otrzymane od delegata z kraju' lists the material which Karski carried from Warsaw. In fact there is no such 'ledger'. There is a Ministry of the Interior file entitled 'Materiały otrzymane od delegata z kraju' (MSW 16) which, on pages 4 (the same cited by Wood and Jankowski) and 5, lists the same reports that Wood and Jankowski claim were carried by Karski. This file seems to be the source to which Wood and Jankowski refer, but it contains no reference to Karski (or his pseudonym, 'Witold'). It seems that Wood and Jankowski drew their conclusions regarding the material which Karski carried on the basis of the dates of reports and the contents of reports in this file, the reports Karski wrote in London and Karski's testimony. The contents list of Ministry of the Interior files contains an undated report entitled 'Terror niemiecki w Polsce: Oświęcim' (German terror in Poland: Oświęcim) (position 93). Unfortunately this report is missing from the MSW file, but given that it was filed alongside material that later appeared in Sprawozdanie Nr 6/42 and is identified by Wood and Jankowski as being delivered by Karski, it is possible it was one of the reports that drew attention to the mass murder of Jews at the camp.

86 See PUMST A.3.8.1.1 (50).

87 AAN 1325 202/I-2 (36), radio message No 105.

88 HIA, Stanisław Mikołajczyk Papers, Box 12, Folder 13, p. 3 of 'Sprawozdanie z książki Jana Karskiego "Story of a Secret State"'.

89 PISM A9.III.4/8, Message 122 from Lisbon to London, 25 November 1942.

90 PISM A9.III.4/8, Message 118 from Lisbon to London, 20 November 1942; Message 122 from Lisbon to London, 25 November 1942.

348   Notes to pages 149–51

91 See Frazik (1998: 411). More precisely, Roland was head of Continental Action in France (Akcja Kontynentalna).

92 PISM A9.VI.9.19, Message 113F (14 October 1942). Wood and Jankowski (1994: 189) note that Karski met with OSS officials in Washington, DC, on 9 July 1943, where he advised James Rogers, chairman of the OSS planning group, that the Poles operated 'an escape route across Germany, France to Lisbon'. Also see Rogers and Troy (1987: 118). It is likely that Karski anticipated leaving continental Europe via Lisbon.

93 SIS was involved in assisting the journeys of escapees (POWs) and others through Spain to Lisbon. The escapees who made it to Lisbon were frequently flown back to Britain on the regular BOAC flight to Whitchurch (Bristol) or Poole. This service was also used to fly intelligence officers to and from Portugal. See Lochery (2011: 150 and 162). During late 1942 and 1943, these flights were occasionally targeted by the Luftwaffe. BOAC flight 777-A of 1 June 1943 was attacked and all seventeen people on board perished. One of the most notable victims was Wilfrid Israel, a prominent British/German-Jewish businessman who had worked to help Jews escape Germany and organized a number of kindertransports. After fleeing Germany in 1939, Israel assumed a research post at Balliol College, Oxford, with the Foreign Research and Press Service. As early as March 1942 he had argued that 'Nazi rule is aiming at the extermination of the Jews' (cited in Shepherd, 1984: 216). It took three months for this view to be echoed by an Allied statesman (General Sikorski in a BBC radio address in early June 1942).

94 PISM A9.III.4/8, Message 112 (6 November 1942).

95 The date that Karski left Poland is subject to scholarly debate. Karski in *Story of a Secret State* (2012: 440) claims he left on 1 October. Drawing on cable messages between London and Warsaw, the Polish historian Andrzej Żbikowski (2011: 272) convincingly argues he left earlier. The correspondence between Polish Intelligence in London and Bern also points to the fact that Karski left at some point in early to mid-September 1942. Karski arrived in Britain on 25 November.

96 See AAN 1325 202/I-6, quoted in Żbikowski (2011: 272).

97 AAN 1326 203/I-27, Message 675.

98 AAN 1326 203/1-22 (p. 54), Message 714.

99 AAN 1326 203/1-22, Message 618 (11 September 1942).

100 PUMST A3.8.3.1.1 (50). Also at AAN 1326 203/I-22, Message 754 (Witolda podejmijcie z Klary).

101 PISM A9.VI.9.19, Message 99F.

102 PISM A9.VI.9.19, Message 103F.

103 PISM A9 III 4/5 (40).

104 PISM A.9.III.4/5 (44).

105 PISM A9.VI.9.19, Message 54.

106 '[M]am niesprawdzone wiadomości że emis Witold wasz Jan Karski dobił Wery' (PUMST A3.8.3.1.1 (55)). 'Wera' was code for the communications base at Bern; 'Witold' was Karski's pseudonym. See Przewoźnik 2005: 346.

107 Protasewicz advised Rowecki on 27 October 1942 that Karski was not in Bern. See PUMST A3.8.3.1.1 (58).

Notes to pages 151–8 349

108 PISM A9.IIII.4/8, Message 112 (6 November 1942).
109 See Karski (2012: 409). It is worth noting that scheduled flights from Gibraltar via Lisbon to Whitchurch started in October 1942. Commercial BOAC flights from Lisbon were used to transport couriers to Britain. See NA.AVIA 2/2377 (219A). For a discussion of the significance of the Lisbon escape route see Weber (2011). Also see Lochery (2012).
110 NA.WO 208/3692.
111 NA.FO 371/31097 (191), Savery to Roberts, 3 December 1942.
112 See Rejak and Frister (2012: 34) for the full text of the 'Protest'. The 'Protest' was published in *Dziennik Polski* on 30 November 1942 (p. 2), with three consecutive paragraphs deleted. The criticism of the silence of the US and England, and of 'international Jewry', over the slaughter of millions of innocents was omitted. Kossak-Szczucka's jarring anti-Semitic statement was also removed. Clearly, *Dziennik Polski* took into account how the information from Poland would be responded to in Britain, and censored the 'Protest'.
113 See Engel (1993: 244 fn. 69). Also see PUMST A3.1.2.1.3.3 '"Karski:" Sprawozdanie z rozmowy z Prez. Rooseveltem. VII. 1943'. Ambassador Ciechanowski sent details of Karski's meetings in the US and Karski's account of his conversation with Roosevelt to the Polish foreign minister, Tadeusz Romer, on 5 August 1943. In the preamble to the record of his conversation with Roosevelt, Karski stated that the Polish ambassador asked him to mention the extermination of the Jews. The number of Polish victims at Oświęcim in this document was recorded as being between 60,000 and 100,000. See PIASA, Polish Embassy to USA, Box 12/2. I am grateful to Marek Kornat for providing me with a copy of this document.
114 Karski's initial schedule can be found at PUMST 3.1.2.1.3.3.
115 Karski was well aware of the limits of what one man could achieve. See Wierzyński and Karski (2012).
116 AAN 1325 202/I-3 (31) (20 February 1943), Microfilm 2201/1.
117 However, this history could quite easily have been different. The Polish courier Napoleon Segieda (Jerzy Salski) left Warsaw on 8 August with information about the camp, and should have arrived in London by October. Compared to Karski, Segieda seems to have been a somewhat less diplomatic character and it is possible that he would have been less willing to be party to the Polish (and British) policy of suppressing news about Oświęcim. Instead, Segieda endured arrest and imprisonment on his journey across Europe and only arrived in London in February 1943. Had Segieda been able to deliver his report in a timely fashion, he might have been able to provide additional weight to arguments in favour of revealing more news from the camp.
118 'Himmler's decree of deportation and murder of all Polish Jews' in *Haaretz*, 23 November 1942, www.jewishvirtuallibrary.org/jsource/Holocaust/Haaretz 112342.html, last accessed 7 July 2012.
119 The information on a special commission was incorrect.
120 Dobkin et al. report, 20 November 1942, CZA S26/1203 (formerly S26/1159/I).
121 Dobkin et al. report, 20 November 1942, CZA S26/1203 p2 (formerly S26/1159/I).

350   Notes to pages 159–64

122 Dina Porat (1990) also refers to these returnees. On p. 214, Porat writes, 'In November 1942, refugees who reached Palestine did mention Auschwitz as one of the camps in which extermination was taking place'. However, earlier in the book Porat seemingly contradicts this statement, writing, 'Auschwitz was mentioned too, but as a hard labor camp' (p. 36). This contradiction cannot be readily resolved and may simply be an error. Alternatively, it could point to some of the contemporary difficulties in acknowledging that the function of the camp was known to some Jewish leaders as early as late 1942. See Chapter 6 below.

123 See Barlas report, 17 November 1942; Dobkin et al. report, 20 November 1942, CZA S26/1203 (formerly S26/1159/I). Also see Shertok to Linton, 20 November 1942, CZA S25/1681. Some testimony from returnees to Palestine was published in *Nasza Trybuna* on 16 February 1943.

124 NA.FO 371/34361 (CM 255). A version of the memorandum is available online on the Jewish Virtual Library's website. The provenance of the online version is not known with certainty, but it seems that the memorandum was reprinted (and slightly edited) by the Institute for Jewish Research, New York (YIVO). See www.jewishvirtuallibrary.org/jsource/ww2/RooseveltMemo 1942.html (last accessed 12 November 2013).

125 NA.FO 371/34361 (CM 255) p. 8.

126 NA.FO 371/34361 (CM 255) p. 20.

127 HIA Poland MSZ, Box 165, Folder 5. Also at Poland Digital Archives, Ministerstwo Spraw Zagranicznych http://szukajwarchiwach.pl/800/42/0/-/165 (jpeg 305), last accessed 12 July 2012.

128 HIA Poland Ministry of Information and Documentation, Box 74, Folder 4. Also at Poland's Digital Archive, Ministerstwo Informacji i Dokumentacji, http://szukajwarchiwach.pl/800/41/0/-/74 (jpeg 319), last accessed 12 July 2012.

129 On 22 December 1942 Roger Allen presented a report on atrocities to the Joint Intelligence Committee chaired by Victor Cavendish-Bentinck. NA.CAB 81.

130 British officials may have received the information as early as November 1942 from the Polish Government or via Jan Karski, though, as already noted, there is no hard documentary evidence that they did so.

131 NA.FO 371/34549/C856/34/55. The information sent from Warsaw was also published by the Polish Consulate in Istanbul in *Polska pod okupacją niemiecką*. Though the bulletin did not mention the use of gas chambers, it did note that, of the 22,500 unregistered prisoners received at the camp, 10,000 were Jews, and highlighted that it was referring to data from 1 June 1942. See *Polska pod okupacją niemiecką*, 18 January 1943, 5.

132 No documentary evidence that Raczyński was aware of either the *New York Times* sentence or the memo has been located. As noted, it was possible that information reached him. However, given that British Foreign Office officials had seen the memorandum to the United States president, Raczyński's letter to Eden should have alerted them at least to the possibility that the mass slaughter of Jews at the camp was taking place. Given the Polish government's focus on Oświęcim in January 1943, conversations between Foreign Office officials such as Frank Savery and Polish representatives during this

Notes to pages 164–9 351

period are likely to have considered the camp. The possibility for British officials to gain a fuller picture of the camp certainly existed.

133 To be clear, the information arrived on 12 November and was immediately translated and incorporated in a document entitled 'Report on conditions in Poland' bearing the date 27 November. This was sent to the Polish Embassy in the US. The information was later retranslated and incorporated into a second document entitled 'Document appertaining to the German occupation of Poland: Poles in German concentration camps' that was printed in 1943. It was translated a third time as the English-language version of Sprawozdanie Nr 6/42 that was distributed prior to 28 May 1943.

134 'Document appertaining to the German occupation of Poland: Poles in German concentration camps', Polish Ministry of the Interior, London (1943). PUMST A3.16 (158).

135 It is not known whether the *Jewish Chronicle*'s editorial team was aware of the earlier reports of the camp featured in the *New York Times* or in the memorandum to President Roosevelt. However, Rabbi Maurice Perlzweig had read the memorandum and he probably shared some information from it with others in Britain.

136 'Nazi Black Record', in *Poland Fights*, 5 April 1943, 4, available at the Polish Library, London, and at US.NA.Nazi Black Record, RG 165, Poland 6950. The 5 April 1943 English-language edition of *Poland Fights* had a print run of 13,500; the Polish-language edition had a print run of 1,200. PUMST AALC, Kol. 133/95.

137 Other material, as noted, was prepared and sent from Warsaw, but I have not located evidence that it was received in London during 1942.

5 BRITISH SUPPRESSION OF NEWS OF AUSCHWITZ: MARCH 1943–JUNE/JULY 1944

1 NA.HS 9/1337/7, letter from Major John Dermot O'Reilly (SOE's police liaison officer) to Chief Inspector Robinson, Aliens Registration Office, 26 February 1943.

2 AAN 1325 202/III-8 t2 (152), Microfilm 2266/3.

3 AAN 1325 202/II-35 (84), Microfilm 2225/6.

4 Informacja Bieżąca Nr 7 (Current Information), AAN 1325 202/III/7 t.2 (217). This report notes that the data about Auschwitz was from 15 December 1942. It is not known exactly when this information reached Warsaw.

5 AAN 1325 202/III-8 t.2 (271), Microfilm 2266/3. Aneks 48 was received by Bureau VI in London on 5 June 1943. It was transported from Warsaw via Stockholm. See PUMST A3.1.2.1.4 (15). Reports entitled 'Pro Memoria' were sent specifically to the Polish prime minister in London. See Ważniewski and Marczewska (1968: x).

6 In 1943 joint messages from Rowecki and the delegate are more frequent than in previous years, indicating closer co-operation between the military and civilian wings and perhaps recognition that a rigid division of labour had disadvantages (i.e. important information risked not being sent by radio).

352 Notes to pages 169–73

7 See Informacja Bieżąca Nr 12 (26 March 1943), 16 (20 April 1943), 29 (26 July 1943), 32 (18 August 1943), 37 (22 September 1943), 44 (10 November 1943). AAN 1325 202/III/7 t.2 (238, 260, 310, 339, 364, 424).

8 AK w dokumentach 1939–1945, Volume VI, Document 1751, p. 303. Also see PUMST 3.1.1.3, Document 28. This document is a summary of reports compiled by Michał Protasewicz on 1 April 1943.

9 The dispatch can be found at the United States National Archives, RG 218, Joint Chiefs of Staff CCS 334, Polish Liaison, Washington, Folder 3.0, 18 May 1943.

10 PUMST MSW 1943, 'Sprawozdanie Krajowe', Volume III, London (Sprawozdanie Nr 4/43, p. 7).

11 See IPN BU2835/31 for Schwarzbart's copy of Sprawozdanie Nr 4/43. The distribution of Schwarzbart's summary of latest news from Poland is not documented. See IPN BU 2835/43 (185) and IPN BU 2835/44 (33).

12 Korboński was later to become the last delegate in Poland.

13 It is worth noting that *Polska pod okupacją niemiecką* encouraged the reproduction of the material that it published. On its front page the paper advised readers that reproduction was permitted and that the source – 'Polska pod okupacją' – should be cited.

14 Jewish Telegraphic Agency, 13 December 1943: '580,000 Jews perish in a camp; Nazis use Jewish women for sterilization experiments'. The article reported that 580,000 Jews had perished at Oświęcim since the camp opened until the middle of 1943, and claimed there were still 80,000 Jews at the camp. It also reported on experimental sterilization and 'artificial breeding'. The JTA stated that the information originated from a Polish underground report that reached London. The only Polish report citing a figure of 580,000 that I have located is the 22 May 1943 edition of *Pologne occupée*.

15 See Appendix II for further details about the gaps in the British National Archives.

16 There is no mention of the *Polish Jewish Observer* article in the literature on allied knowledge of Auschwitz as far as I can ascertain. Reference to the *Polish Jewish Observer* in Holocaust scholarship is extremely limited, despite the sustained engagement that the paper had with the plight of Polish Jews through the war. Tony Kushner (1997: 177) makes a brief reference to articles appearing in the paper in the summer of 1944 that discuss Auschwitz, Treblinka, Majdanek and the other death camps.

17 See *Polska pod okupacją niemiecką*, 9 September 1943, 2.

18 PUMST 3.16 (9).

19 NA.FO 371/34383.

20 HIA Stanisław Mikołajczyk Papers, Box 38, dispatches from intelligence outposts, Folder 17, General, March 1943–July 1944. Also at Poland's National Digital Archive, 800/22/0/-/38 (jpeg 816).

21 HIA Stanisław Mikołajczyk Papers, Box 38, dispatches from intelligence outposts, Folder 19, March 1943. Also at Poland's National Digital Archive, 800/22/0/-/38 (jpeg 885).

22 The FO also received news about the murder of Jews from Elizabeth Wiskemann, the FO's representative in Bern, Switzerland, on 12 March 1943. Wiskemann cabled the FO stating that 'a usually reliable source reports an

Notes to pages 173–7 353

S.S. official in S.W. Germany stated the end of February [*sic*] in casual conversation that during the second half of 1942 about 30,000 Polish Jews had been killed by gas. He confirmed that this is the usual fate of Jews who cannot work'. See FO 371/34382 (63). The figure cited was far too low, as FO officials would have recognized given the intelligence that was publicized in December 1942. Wiskemann's data would have been useful to counter any demands to publicize the Jewish death toll at Auschwitz as reported by Rowecki and Jankowski.

23 HIA Stanisław Mikołajczyk Papers, Box 38, Radio Świt, Folder 7. Also at Poland's National Digital Archive, 800/22/0/-/38 (jpeg 152).

24 Harris (2004) suggests that the report was broadcast on all European Services. On inspection it seems that it was confined to the Polish Service.

25 BBC WAC, European News Bulletins – Polish 1943. Killing via electrified floors did not occur at the camp. The inclusion of this information points to some confusion amongst intelligence operatives at the camp.

26 HIA Stanisław Mikołajczyk Papers, Box 38, Folder 7 (Radio Świt). Also at Poland's National Digital Archive, 800/22/0/-/38 (jpeg 152).

27 Jewish Telegraphic Agency, 12 April 1943, 'Cracow ghetto liquidated in "worst pogrom of Nazi annihilation campaign" Poles say'.

28 *Jewish Chonicle*, 7 April 1943, 7. 'Pogrom in Cracow – Ghetto liquidated'.

29 BBC WAC, European News Bulletins – Polish 1943. The internal politics of the IAIC warrant further investigation in order to reveal how certain political positions were arrived at, who exactly was responsible for specific publications at particular points in time, the way in which different governments engaged with the IAIC and the extent to which various governments approved of data published by the IAIC.

30 NA.HS 9/1337/7, O'Reilly to Robertson, 26 February 1943.

31 NA.HS 9/1337/7.

32 Such a request could have been made by Harold Perkins (who ran the Polish section of SOE) to his counterpart Michał Protasewicz of the Polish Bureau VI during their regular meetings. No documentary record has been located.

33 Segieda was not the only courier to encounter serious problems in reaching Britain in the autumn of 1942. Tadeusz Chciuk-Celt did so also. He was in Budapest from June to November 1942 and did not reach Britain until 16 June 1943 after enduring incarceration in Spain. According to Celt's personal communication with Walter Laqueur in 1979, Celt sent a report from Budapest describing the expansion of Auschwitz. Given that Celt was in Hungary prior to information about the mass gassing of Jews being processed in Warsaw, it is unlikely that he knew of the systematic murder of Jews at the camp when he arrived in Budapest. See Laqueur (1998: 238).

34 Also see PISM A9 III.4, Message 38, 11 September 1942.

35 PISM A9 111 2A 3, page entitled 'Nasionka'.

36 NA.HS 9/1337/7, Message of 26 February 1943.

37 The date of Segieda's arrival in Britain is different in the British and Polish documents. British documents note that he arrived at the 'Clyde ports' on 19 February. Polish documents indicate that he arrived on 27 February. The discrepancy is probably due to Segieda being debriefed by British intelligence/ SOE prior to being released to the Poles.

354   Notes to pages 177–8

38 PISM A9 111 2A 3. See Section 12 entitled 'Oświęcim'.
39 YVA M2. 261.
40 IPN BU 2835/56 (110). Schwarzbart's folder containing the report gives Salski the pseudonym 'Krzysztof'. According to Schwarzbart, Salski visited him on his own initiative.
41 *Our Tribune* published extracts from Salski's report on 21 October 1943 on page 6, but did not mention Oświęcim. Instead it printed Salski's assertion that there was no anti-Semitism in Poland. The same article also drew on the first report sent from Warsaw that mentioned the gassing of Jews at Oświęcim (sent on 4 September from Warsaw and received in London on 12 November), but did not report that Jews were being killed. The merging of different reports in the article was particularly awkward and all significant information about Oświęcim was omitted. Given that the same edition of *Our Tribune* reported that 520,000 Jews had perished in the Oświęcim camp, the omission of Salski's information about the camp is odd. It is likely that Salski's description of killing methods at the camp fell foul of US censorship and possibly of *Our Tribune*'s internal censorship policy. A full assessment of *Our Tribune*'s and *Nasza Trybuna*'s reporting of the Holocaust, and of Auschwitz in particular, has not been possible as not many issues of these newspapers have been located (at the Polish Library, London, and at the National Library, Warsaw). It is not known exactly when the editors of the papers, Jacob Apenszlak and Arieh Tartakower, received Salski's report, nor is it known whether the Polish-language main paper, *Nasza Trybuna*, made reference to it.
42 YVA M2. 261, p. 13.
43 See HL MS 238/2/52, Folder 4 (one of the last documents in the folder is Easterman's copy of the Salski report). Also see HL MS 238/2/52, Folder 5, for Schwarzbart note to Easterman on the report.
44 NA.FO 371/34552 (C5452), pp. 160–6.
45 According to the folder in which the intercept is found (NA 371/34522) this file has been available since 1972. There is no indication that parts of the file were held back.
46 PID did exist as a real department early in the war and was later absorbed into a new Foreign Office Research Department. It was later used to provide cover for the PWE. See Balfour (1979: 89–101), and Stenton (2000: 6).
47 NA.FO 371/34552 (C5452), p. 160.
48 See NA.DEFE 1/136/9, 'Postal Censorship Allocation List (1943) 3rd Revised edition'; and NA.DEFE 1/333 (Herbert and des Graz 1952). Archivists at the National Archives, Kew, have been unable to shed light on who/ what this acronym refers to.
49 See Stenton (2000).
50 See NA.DEFE 1/136/9, 'Postal Censorship Allocation List (1943) 3rd Revised edition', 67, for details of the material of interest to the ISR.
51 See NA.DEFE 1/136/9, 'Postal Censorship Allocation List (1943) 3rd Revised edition', 36, for details of the material of interest to the DRW.
52 US National Archives, Censorship Report, 5 May 1943, RG 226, Entry 191.
53 Files at the British National Archives indicate that a Pole named Salski brought news of Polish–Soviet relations 'recently', referring to early 1944.

Notes to pages 178–80 355

This was passed by Eden to Churchill on 9 February 1944. See NA.FO 371/ 39422 (C18), p. 131. It is possible that this Salski was Napoleon Segieda. However, given that there is a dearth of material on Segieda's activities after April 1943, it cannot proved. It is also possible that the mention of Salski referred to Tadeusz Salski. Tadeusz Salski was a key member of the Rampart Group (Szaniec) (a right-wing faction, hostile to Jews) which did not recognize the Polish underground state. He arrived in Britain on 21 December 1943 and was interviewed by MI19. Comparing the data in the MI19 report and in the Foreign Office files does not help in confidently identifying the particular Salski mentioned in the Foreign Office documents. See NA.WO 208/3720.

54 In the report written for Schwarzbart, Salski states that he left Poland in October 1942. In the report handed to the Ministry of the Interior, he notes that he left in August 1942. Intelligence cables through September 1942 place Salski in Switzerland. Couriers were regularly encouraged by the Polish government to change the dates of their journey and arrival in Britain in order to maintain the security of courier routes, to make the data that they divulged to various audiences seem fresher than it actually was and to accentuate the success of Polish intelligence in traversing occupied Europe. Jan Karski, when in the US in the early summer of 1943, stated that he arrived in Britain in February 1943, whereas he arrived in November 1942. Compare YVA M2.261, p. 1 (the report handed to Schwarzbart); and PISM A9 111 2A, p. 1 (the report handed to the Polish Ministry of the Interior).

55 YVA M2. 261, p. 8. The reference to the Hammerluft system has been seized on by Holocaust deniers as evidence of a broader pattern of misinformation. The Hammerluft appears thrice in the documentary record – in the 4 September 1942 dispatch to London and in Salski's 1943 reports. It is possible that Salski provided the data about the Hammerluft system that was included in the 4 September 1942 dispatch. Salski was wrong about the Hammerluft and the electric chambers, but absolutely right in reporting the use of gas chambers and the systematic murder of Jews.

56 PISM A9 111 2A 3.

57 Segieda/Salski has been an enigmatic figure for scholars. It is not known what role he played in London after March 1943 other than the fact that he was in the employ of the Ministry of the Interior and that he was decorated. Even some colleagues and fellow couriers such as Tadeusz Chciuk-Celt did not know he was in London (see Frazik 1998). Files in the British National Archives, including his security service file (released in 2005), shed some light on his activities. He probably commenced six months of training at SOE's Audley End House around 16 June 1941 under the cover of an official role as a clerk in the Polish Ministry of the Interior. Following training he was sent to occupied Europe and spent several months in Poland, returning via Bern, France, Spain and Gibraltar to the 'Clyde ports'. He was debriefed by SOE and later wrote the two reports (for the Polish government and Ignacy Schwarzbart). There are some further references to 'Salski' in the British Foreign Office files. However the mention of 'Salski' as a representative of the National Armed Forces (NSZ) refers to Tadesuz Salski. The NSZ was responsible for the murder of a number of Jews and had a tense relationship with the Polish underground state and the Home Army. It was finally merged

356   Notes to pages 180–4

with the Home Army on 7 March 1944, but relations between the two organizations were not harmonious. See Korboński 1978: 104. Also see FO 371/39423, Memorandum, 29 February 1944; NA.FO 371/39422 (C2061); NA.HS 9/1337/7. Napoleon Segieda's postwar life is also somewhat mysterious. He died aged eighty-two in 1991 in Kent.

58 AKD Volume VI. P313, Document 1761.
59 HIA Korboński, Box 1, Reel 2. Cable from N, 3 May 1943 (Nr 78). Also see 'Poles spoof Huns', *Daily Mirror*, 25 May 1943, 4.
60 This report in *The Times* is one of the seven pieces of information about Auschwitz that Gilbert records as reaching the West. See Gilbert (2001a: 145). Gilbert also notes an article in *The Times* from 26 May entitled 'Jews deported from Salonika'. The newspaper stated that some 55,000 Jews were deported and that 'the survivors were sent to Cracow, where all trace of them has been lost'. The story was filed by *The Times*'s correspondent in Istanbul, which may indicate that the information was derived from either a Jewish or a Polish source in that city.
61 In a radio message to Warsaw addressed to Leon Feiner (Berezowski) on 16 April 1943, Mikołajczyk, on behalf of Zygielbojm, asked about the fate of Zygielbojm's family. By this point, most had been murdered, including his wife and son. AAN 1325 202/1-3 (63), Microfilm 2201/1.
62 NA.FO 371/34550 (90). The full letter is available at http://yad-vashem.org.il/about_holocaust/documents/part2/doc154.html, last accessed 16 March 2012.
63 NA.FO 371/34550 (73).
64 See Armia Krajowa w Dokumentach 1939–1945, Volume II, p. 478, Document 401. Also see Nowak (1982).
65 Rowecki radioed London on 5 April 1943 reporting that Nowak-Jeziorański had been sent to Stockholm. On 20 April he advised London that Nowak-Jeziorański had returned safely. See AAN 1326 203/I-25, Messages 531 and 620 respectively.
66 NA.FO 371/34550 (65).
67 Schwarzbart wrote to Raczyński on 17 May 1943. See IPN BU 2835/9 (77).
68 Hansard, House of Commons Debates, 389, cols. 1117–1204, 19 May 1943, 'The refugee problem', available at www.theyworkforyou.com/debates/?id=1943-05-19a.1117.7, last accessed 14 March 2012.
69 NA.FO 371/34550 (C5628).
70 NA.FO 371/34550 (C3694).
71 NA.FO 371/34550. 'Radogpsziz' is probably a misspelling of Radogoszcz – a prison in Łódź.
72 See Appendix I for a list of the information received during the summer of 1943. Gilbert notes just two reports. Between June and September 1943 at least nine reports were received in the West.
73 See Armia Krajowa w Dokumentach 1939–1945, Volume VI, Document 1773, p. 341.
74 Jewish Telegraphic Agency, 13 June 1943, 'Nazis use Polish Jews for experiments on new methods of artificial impregnation'. This article stated that experiments had commenced on 200 Jewish men. The source report referred to twenty. The figure in the JTA article seems to be a typographic error.

Notes to page 184 357

75 Jewish Telegraphic Agency, 16 June 1943, 'Polish government compiles "blacklist" of Nazi scientists gassing Jews'.
76 'Horror of Nazi Camps', *Courier-Mail*, 17 June 1943, 2.
77 PUMST 3.1.1.13.5 (92). The message was sent via 'Lena' (probably denoting Wanda Kraszewska-Ancerewicz, who was responsible for sending some intelligence during this period). The final 'clearance' of the Będzin ghetto began on 22 June 1943. It is unlikely that Lubetkin's and Cukierman's message referred to this particular action as the information would have taken some time to reach Warsaw. Their message to London reported on the situation of the Jewish Fighting Organisation; called for assistance and finance; and recorded that Jews from Belgium, Holland and France were transported to Poland to be killed. The first deportations from Będzin took place over a year earlier, on 12 May 1942. Some 1,500 Jews (men, women and children) were gassed in bunker number 1 at Birkenau. In August 1942 a further mass deportation of Jews from Będzin to Auschwitz took place. See Fulbrook (2012: 223, 237 and 291).
78 PUMST 3.1.1.13.4 (23).
79 See AAN 1326 203/I-24, Message 1321, also at AAN 1326 203/I-13 (39), Microfilm 2106II, Message 1321, 7 August 1943. These two documents give different dates for the sending of the message – 9 and 7 August respectively. This report is important as it sheds light on the tensions within the Home Army in relation to Jews. Bór-Komorowski distinguished between three groups of Jews – the fighting Jews of Warsaw (and elsewhere, i.e. Będzin), for whom he evidently had respect and to whom he sought to extend aid; a group of Jews that he saw as either bandits or communists that 'plagued' the country and who exhibited cruelty against Poles; and, implicitly, the great mass of Jews who were slaughtered by the Germans. Bór-Komorowski was critical of the image of the fighting Jew promoted, saying it was only in Warsaw that Jews fought valiantly – in the face of the indifference of the mass of Jewry. While aid was extended to the fighting Jews, Bór-Komorowski was cautious about providing further aid – of 'going too far' with the provision of help. He cited three reasons, including the actions of Jews during the Soviet occupation (of 1939–41), the actions of Jewish bandits and communists, and social opinion amongst the Underground that understood the provision of aid as diminishing the Underground's limited resources, which was against the immediate interests of Poland. The first point was based on a widespread stereotype (shared by officials in the Foreign Office); the second gave no weight to the level of anti-Jewish violence of Poles (recently discussed in work by Engelking (2011) and Grabowski (2011)), which framed the hostility of some Jews to Poles; and the third point highlights the fact that Jews were often conceived by some as not being part of the Polish nation, and therefore less valuable. In addition, Bór-Komorowski's final point can be read as indicating that part of the Underground felt its very limited military resources should only be used for specific Polish military objectives, not for 'humanitarian' objectives like saving Jews. This position would not look out of place amongst British decision makers in London. Both place the evident needs of Jews below other objectives. Bór-Komorowski's message was passed to the Polish military leadership in London on 10 September 1943 by Michał Protasewicz. See PUMST 3.1.1.13.4 (25).

358   Notes to pages 185–8

80 The signatories of the letter were Frumka Płotnicka, Hersch Springer, Zwi Brandys, Israel Kosch and 'Klama' L – probably Szlama Lerner. In the letter, these young fighters anticipated their imminent death at the hands of the Nazis.

81 Jewish Agency, Istanbul, YVA O-67.

82 PUMST 3.1.1.13.5 (114).

83 PUMST 3.1.1.13.5 (107). The reference to *Rada Żydów Polskich* here probably signals *Rada Pomocy Żydom* (Żegota).

84 PUMST 3.1.1.13.5 (125).

85 PUMST MSW 73 (277). The message was sent by Stefan Korboński.

86 Jewish Telegraphic Agency, 8 October 1943, '15,000 Jewish force laborers brought to Arsap after liquidation of ghetto [*sic*]'. 'The last news from Poland', *Our Tribune*, 20 November 1943, 4.

87 NA.HS 4/210.

88 Aneks 57 and Aneks 58 can be found at AAN 1325 202/III/8 t.2, Microfilm 2266/3. Aneks 58 can also be found at NA.HS 4/212.

89 Aneks 59 is at 1325 AAN 202/III/8 t.2, Microfilm 2266/3. It provides the names of SS officers cited in an important intelligence report from the summer of 1943 that was widely circulated in early 1944.

90 CZA S26/1520 (former reference S26/1428).

91 This message was sent via radio station Wanda 2, situated in Warsaw, by 'Lawina' – a pseudonym used by Tadeusz Bór-Komorowski. It was de-encrypted on 30 September 1943. See PUMST 3.16 (13). Also see AAN 1326 203/I-25, Message 1575.

92 NA.FO 371/34551 (C12448) (signed by Roberts).

93 NA.FO 371/34551 (page 2 of broadcast script).

94 PUMST MSW 73 (280). Message sent by Korboński on 28 September 1943. The message does not mention Jews. It relates news of the mass gassing of Poles, before moving on to report that the highest number of people killed in one day at Brzezinka was 30,000. This figure seems too high. The capacity of the crematoria was around 10,000 a day. Recipients in Polish intelligence would have been well aware that Jews were also being referred to.

95 PISM A10 9 7, PAT, 23 October 1943.

96 Jewish Telegraphic Agency, 24 October 1944, 'Gestapo tortures 200 rabbis in Polish concentration camp' (*sic*).

97 PISM A10 9 5.

98 The document from the Polish Information Center is dated 16 September. This may reflect time differences between London and New York, or may be a typographic error. See HIA, Polish Information Center, New York, Box 3.3, cable from London, 16 September 1943.

99 News Bulletin No 4, page 10, available at PUMST AALC, Kol. 133/266.

100 In February 1944, Jewish leaders in Warsaw reported to Schwarzbart that they had 'cordial relations with the representatives of the fighting Underground Poland' (Schwarzbart's translation). IPN BU 2835/60 (21).

101 Meir Jaari (Yaari) was a founder member of Mapam (United Workers Party) in 1948, and later served in several Israeli Knessets. Hashomer Hatzair is a socialist Zionist organization.

102 IPN BU 2835/59 (51), Polish text (64). The translation is Schwarzbart's.

Notes to pages 194–6

103 A10 9 17 (part 2), MSW, 'Znowu kobiety polskie padają ofiarą niemieckiego terroru', 19 December 1942.
104 Aneks 44 was part of a package of material sent out of Poland via Gdansk to Stockholm. The courier was arrested, but according to a radio message from Bór-Komorowski in September 1943, the post was not discovered – suggesting that Aneks 44 was forwarded on. See AAN 203/I-25, Message 1531.
105 This book had been announced as being in preparation – in *Nasza Trybuna* on 16 February 1943, 4, and in the *Polish Jewish Observer* on 9 April 1943, 4. There was therefore plenty of scope to include the information about Oświęcim that was received in the West through spring and summer 1943.
106 On 15 December 1943, the Polish Telegraphic Agency reported that Sylwin Strakacz had described the book as a shocking document that demanded the world's attention. See PISM A10 9 19 (part 1), PAT, 15 December 1943. On 29 January 1944, an article in *Nasza Trybuna* (on page 6) commented on the reviews the book received. *The Black Book of Polish Jewry* was formally presented to Eleanor Roosevelt on 6 June 1944. See *Nasza Trybuna*, 27 June 1944, 3.
107 See the discussion of anti-Semitism in the US in Chapter 2.
108 Apenszlak was amongst those scheduled to meet Jan Karski in August 1943. See PUMST 3.1.2.1.3.3. Apenszlak was a co-editor (along with Arieh Tartakower) of the Polish Jewish newspaper *Nasza Trybuna* (New York) during the war years.
109 Many of the photographs were supplied to the editors by the Polish Information Center, New York. See *Nasza Trybuna*, 10 December 1942.
110 The pictures of mass graves may show the Jewish victims who succumbed to the Nazi rationing policy or to mass shooting, but the text encouraged the reader to associate the images with the process of ghettoization rather than with systematic murder.
111 An amended reproduction of the map published in the *Polish Fortnightly Review* on 15 July 1942, 5, could have been used. That map showed the location of Bełżec, Treblinka and Oświęcim. The locations of Majdanek, Chełmno and Sobibór could easily have been added.
112 See Chapter 3 for details of the *Polish Jewish Observer*.
113 See pages 135–8 of the 1943 edition of *The Black Book of Polish Jewry*.
114 For example, the murder of Jews in the gas chambers at Bełżec is framed in *The Black Book* as a consequence of people surviving the process of deportation. 'Because there are not enough cars to kill the Jews in this relatively inexpensive manner many of them are taken to nearby Bełżec where they are murdered by poison gas' (Apenszlak 1943: 137).
115 The *Polish Jewish Observer* discussed *The Black Book of Polish Jewry* positively in an editorial on 7 April 1944. Given that staff at this paper were very well informed about the Holocaust, this positive appraisal probably indicates relief that some news of the fate of Polish Jews in Poland was reaching an American audience.
116 AAN 1325 202/I/31, pp. 194–206, Microfilm 2201/9I. As noted in Chapter 4 above, this report was earlier circulated in an internal Home Army report on 28 September 1942 (Informacja Bieżąca Nr 36). See AAN 1325 202/III/7 t.1 (153A).
117 Since it is not possible to be categorical about Zarembina's motivations, an alternative account of the first edition of *Camp of Death* can be suggested. It

360   Notes to pages 195–7

is not known when Zarembina completed her text or when she passed it on to the publisher. It is possible that the reference to the report about Oświęcim was added later to give a statistical grounding to Zarembina's discussion of the camp in 1941 and early 1942 – that is, the text was completed prior to the information about the mass killing of Jews reaching Warsaw in July–August 1942. But by using the statistics that were sent to London in November 1942, it is clear that at some stage in the pamphlet production process – writing or editing – information about Jews at Oświęcim *was* ignored. Publishing was not straightforward for the Polish Underground. Materials had to be sourced, and publishing a pamphlet had to be organized around regular publishing commitments (newspapers). Zarembina was married to a leading Polish socialist, Zygmunt Zaremba, and was active in Żegota – the Council for the Aid of Jews.

118 Some 37,000 copies were printed (Friszke 2011: 357).

119 Adam Ciołkosz (PPS) wished to make reference to *Camp of Death* in his 24 June 1944 broadcast to Poland on the BBC (Polish Free Time). However, the brief mention of the publication was censored and not broadcast. See PUMST AALC, Kol. 133/22.

120 The March 1944 version published in the United States featured a map of major concentration camps in Poland which included Bełżec, Sobibór, Oświęcim and Majdanek.

121 AAN 1325 202/III/8 (297), Microfilm 2266/3.

122 This is a reference to the report on Oświęcim sent by Zygmunt Zaremba alongside his 10 January 1944 letter to the Executive of the Labour Party that was received in London on 4 March. Zaremba's letter was passed to Clement Attlee on 24 March 1944. See PUMST AALC, Kol. 133/15, 'Załacznik 2 do listu Nr.K/70 – Korespondencja z obozu Oświęcim/październik, listopad, grudzień 1943 r./'. It is not known whether this report about Oświęcim was circulated in London in spring 1944.

123 Some 25,000 copies of *Camp of Death* were printed. However, demand for the threepenny publication was weak compared with some other Liberty publications, such as the 1942 booklet *Stop Them Now!*. By the end of 1944, Liberty Press still had 10,000 copies of *Camp of Death* in stock. PUMST AALC, Kol. 133/95. Through 1945 Liberty Press advertised the booklet, for example in the *Times Literary Supplement* (12 May 1945). It was discussed on the front page of the *London Typographic Journal* in December 1944 (edition number 138) and requested by the university libraries at Oxford, Cambridge, Edinburgh and Dublin (Trinity College) (legal deposit libraries) in October 1944. See PUMST AALC, Kol. 133/98.

124 Liberty Press secured some British political endorsement of the text. Janet Laurel Adamson, a permanent private secretary to the minister of pensions (and a champion of women's rights), wrote the Foreword.

125 NA.FO 371/39449 (C869), p. 12.

126 The address list for the summary includes MI5, MI6, the Foreign Office, Ivone Kirkpatrick, the War Department and Washington, amongst many others. The extent of the distribution of the summary is testament to the importance of the data Nowak-Jeziorański provided and the trust in which he was held.

Notes to pages 197–203

127 The fact that Nowak-Jeziorański couriered a report that mentioned Oświęcim to Stockholm is revealed in Armia Krajowa w Dokumentach 1939–1945, Volume II, p. 478, Document 401. Also see Nowak (1982).

128 NA.FO 371/39449 (C869).

129 NA.FO 371/39422, p. 116.

130 Nowak-Jeziorański also met Brigadier Harvey Watt, the parliamentary private secretary to Churchill; Moray McLaren; and various officials from MI9, amongst others. See Laqueur (1998: 238).

131 NA.FO 371/34550. Also see PUMST A10.1 (229).

132 NA.FO 371/39451.

133 See Chapter 7 below. For a summary of the archbishop's speech see the *Polish Jewish Observer*, 3 March 1944, 1.

134 The information about Czech Jews at Birkenau had been sent by Gerhart Riegner on 5 November 1943 to the WJC and to the Czechoslovak government, both in London (Gilbert 2001a: 161).

135 For a discussion of this letter, see Lerski (1986), Ciołkosz (1983: 199) and Friszke (2011: 323).

136 Cited in Lerski (1988: 232). The original letter from Zaremba is at PUMST AALC, Kol 133/296.

137 Extracts of Kuh's *PM* article can be found at PISM A10 9 8. Kuh accused the Polish leaders of 'intense nationalism' and argued that in nine-tenths of the letter to the British Labour Party, the Poles denounced the Soviets.

138 Stories were run in the *New Statesman and Nation*, and in the *Sunday Times* and *The Observer* on 2 April 1944 (Ciołkosz, 1983: 199). The *Manchester Guardian* published related stories on 3 April ('Poles and Russia – underground army: note to Britain and US' (page 5)) and on 5 April ('Polish underground movement . . .' (page 5)).

139 Attlee to Ciołkosz, 5 April 1944. PUMST AALC, Kol 133/297.

140 US National Archives: Record Group 226, OSS 66059; Record Group 165 (War Department General and Special Staffs), Box 3138, Poland 6950. The Polish report is at PUMST A3.16 (17).

141 There is no mention of the courier in the Polish records. It is true that an important courier on the route Warsaw to Budapest was Wanda Modlibowska (aka 'Marta', 'Halszka'), but in this case 'Wanda' relates to a radio station – Polish radio stations were code-named 'Wanda', followed by a number indicating its location. 'Wanda 27', for example, was sited near London; 'Wanda 1' was near Mińsk Mazowiecki.

142 See AAN 1325 202/III/7 t.2 (364), Informacja Bieżaca Nr 37, Ważniewski and Marczewska (1968: 124–32).

143 The original German-language report is at AAN 1325 202/III/139 (238–48).

144 AAN 1325 202/III-148 (269), Microfilm 2270/3.

145 No corroborating evidence of executions by beheading at the camp has been located. This assertion seems to be false.

146 AAN 1325 202/III-148 (393), Microfilm 2270/3. Also see *Zeszyty Oświęcimskie* 1 (1968), 107. The page given for the archival document in *Zeszyty Oświęcimskie* is incorrect.

362   Notes to pages 203–5

147 The dearth of documentary records noting the data that Świt received from Poland and its broadcasts to Poland means detailed, critical examination of Świt's activities is not possible.

148 Radio Świt ceased broadcasting for two weeks in late July 1943 as, according to Harold Osborne (PWE), its successful transmissions were 'beginning to impose too great a strain on credulity' since no 'genuine secret station could last so long uninterruptedly'. HIA Stanisław Mikołajczyk Papers, Box 38, Folder 10 (Radio Świt), Osborne to Mikołajczyk 22 July 1944. Also at Poland's National Digital Archive, 800/22/0/-/38 (jpeg 279), last accessed 12 July 2001.

149 AAN 1326 203 I-24, Message 1254.

150 PUMST A3.16.17. This covering note to the report indicates its origin. It is addressed to Rawa – the code name for Michał Protasewicz, from Selim – the code name for Stanisław Sulma, at the Bey base in Istanbul, Turkey. Also see PUMST A.4.1.3 (69–72) – a file that includes summaries about Oświęcim registered in London on 24 May 1944. The report originated from Poland and was sent to 'Barbara 214' – code for Budapest – and then to Istanbul, and ultimately to London.

151 PUMST A3.16.18. The distribution list reads: A.W. Washington, A.W. Ottawa etc. 'A.W.' is the abbreviation for *attaché wojskowy* ('military attaché'). The final addressee is 'doss. "Rena"'. This suggests that the report was also to be put in 'Ren's' file. Ren is Edward Podgórski, also known as Edmund Pilewski and Edmund Piotrowski, a key intelligence officer, commander of base 'Anna' in Stockholm.

152 PUMST MSW 1943, 'Sprawozdanie Krajowe', Volume III, London (Sprawozdanie Nr 11/43, p. 11).

153 PUMST A3.1.1.4 (56), Aneks 58 (1–31 August 1943). There are some typographic errors in this document. It refers to the end of 1943 rather than 1942, and only reports 60,000 deaths after that date. These errors and omissions were corrected for the report distributed to the Polish Cabinet as Sprawozdanie Nr 11/43 on 2 December 1943, suggesting that a report with the correct information was sent from Warsaw prior to 2 December 1942. I have not located any documents with the correct data from the SS man's 10 June and 10 July reports other than the broadcast proposal prepared for the BBC and Radio Świt in July 1943. The discrepancy between Aneks 58 and Sprawozdanie Nr 11/43 is the best evidence that the information prepared by the Western Section in July 1943 was actually sent and received. However, it is unknown when the material was either sent or received. For the distribution list for 'Aneks 58' see PUMST A3.1.1.4 (90).

154 The lack of urgency displayed in December 1943 in disseminating the news could well be connected with the Polish government's desire to release the information in a more conducive discursive environment, or with continued concerns about British sensitivities in relation to Jews and atrocities. The documentary record is unrevealing. The creation of the War Refugee Board in the United States in January 1944 changed the dynamics of reporting the Holocaust.

155 The report can be found at the US National Archives: Record Group 226, OSS 66059; Record Group 165 (War Department General and Special

Notes to pages 205–8 363

Staffs), Box 3138, Poland 6950. The same document is at PUMST A3.16.17, the original German document is at AAN 1325 202/III-139, k. 238–48.

156 See PISM A10 9 20 (part 1), PAT, 15 March 1944. The names of the SS officers at Auschwitz were also included in Aneks 59, which covered September 1943. See AAN 1325 202/III/8 t.2, Microfilm 2266/3.

157 I have not located the original Polish Telegraphic Agency press release from Tuesday 15 February 1944. The *Palestine Post* published four stories mentioning Oświęcim prior to the distribution of the Vrba–Wetzler report in June 1944. A front-page story on 18 November 1943 reported that Jews from Bochnia, Tarnow and Kraków were taken by cattle wagons to the 'death camp at Oswiecim'. Five days later (23 November), a page 3 article reported that fifty Jews from the Sosnowiec ghetto were deported on a daily basis to the 'Oswiecim death camp'. On 11 June 1944, the newspaper published a front-page story revealing that 7,000 Czech Jews had been gassed at Oświęcim. By 1944, the *Palestine Post* had a distribution of 50,000. In 1950, the newspaper changed its name to the *Jerusalem Post*.

158 NA.FO 371/30863.

159 Cited in Świebocki (2000: 327). The original document is at the Auschwitz-Birkenau State Museum, Mat. RO, Volume 2, p. 75. Also see Garliński (1994: 230). Pery Broad, an SS functionary at the camp, makes a similar observation of the effect of the broadcast. See Höss, Broad and Kremer (1998: 146).

160 This seems to be the only time Oświęcim appeared on the front page of a British national newspaper.

161 See '14 niemieckich katów z Oświęcimia którzy muszą ponieść śmierć', *Dziennik Polski*, 17 March 1944, 4.

162 A copy of *Polska pod okupacją niemiecką* can be found at the British Library, reference SK1/7.

163 See *Pologne occupée*, 22 March 1944, 5. *Pologne occupée* also described Oświęcim as a death camp in its 9 March edition.

164 NA.HS4/274.

165 NA.KV2/3429 (29b), SOE note dated 12 April 1944. It was passed to SIS on 14 April 1944. Kurcyusz is likely to have been spoken to by British intelligence, though there is no record of any such conversation.

166 Polish operations in Istanbul attracted attention in early 1944, as the British sought greater control over the Polish government's communication with Poland, with a view to placating Soviet concerns. The British were aware that even if they were able to secure access to Polish cipher codes, used to send and receive encrypted messages to and from Poland, and were able to censor messages sent by the Polish government to government and Home Army representatives in Poland, they still could not guarantee the Soviets that they saw (and thereby sanctioned) all communications to Poland. Courier routes via Stockholm and Istanbul remained available to the Polish government to send information to Poland. NA.HS 4 144 (673), 22 January 1944.

167 *Polska pod okupacją niemiecką*/*Pologne occupée* repeatedly reported that Jews were being murdered in gas chambers at Oświęcim during 1943 and 1944.

364   Notes to pages 208–12

See editions of *Polska pod okupacją niemiecką* from 14 May 1943, 9 September 1943, 27 January 1944, 15 March 1944; and *Pologne occupée* from 22 May 1943, 9 March 1944, 22 March 1944. It seems likely that Gilbert did not have access to all these editions while writing *Auschwitz and the Allies*. Copies of *Polska pod okupacją niemiecką* and *Pologne occupée* are available at the Polish Library at POSK, London.

168 NA.FO 371/42807 (122) (page 10 of the bulletin). The bulletin reported the deportation and gassing of Jews from Greece, the Protectorate, Slovakia and France at 'Oswiencim'. It also reported 'three new crematoriums in the village of Bizezinka, near Oswiencim' where on 'one day the Nazis burned 39,000 Jews, Poles, Czechs and gypsies'. This report was sent to the Foreign Office by the Jewish Agency. It was filed at the Foreign Office on 5 July 1944. The figure of 39,000 was a typographic error. The source data gave a figure of 30,000. 'Bizezinka' was a misspelling of Brzezinka (Birkenau). Likewise, Oswiencim was a misspelling of Oświęcim. It is not known for certain when the Jewish Agency first received this information about the camp.

169 HIA, Polish Information Center Papers, Box 3.9, cable from London, 21 March 1944.

170 'Prison camp is largest death factory', *Daily News*, 22 March 1944, 6.

171 See 'Nazi "death factory" in Poland', *Morning Bulletin* (Rockhampton, Queensland), 23 March 1944, 3; New "death factory"', *The Mercury* (Hobart, Tasmania), 23 March 1944, 3; 'Death factory in Poland', *Examiner* (Launceston, Tasmania), 23 April 1944, 1; '"Death factory" in Poland', *Advocate* (Burnie, Tasmania), 23 March 1944, 1, available at http://trove. nla.gov.au/newspaper/result?q=oswiecim&s=20, last accessed 26 March 2013.

172 Jewish Telegraphic Agency, 23 March 1944, '60,000 Greek Jews murdered in Oswiecim "death camp", Polish report discloses'.

173 Putting children in sacks in Upper Silesia during the deportation process seems to have been a common practice. Fulbrook (2012: 288) quotes from the diary of Rutka Laskier, a fourteen-year-old Jewish child who, on 5 February 1943, queried God's existence: 'If God existed, he would have certainly not permitted that human beings be thrown alive into furnaces, and the heads of little toddlers be smashed with the butt of guns or be shoved into sacks and gassed to death'. Also see Fulbrook (2012: 355).

174 NA.FO 371/39014 (441). The identity of the Pole who reached London is not known with certainty, but this could be a reference to Jerzy Salski. Salski's activities after his arrival in Britain in February 1943 are not known with certainty, but it is possible that the Salski who left Poland in October 1943 and arrived in Britain in the first week of 1944, mentioned in British files, is Jerzy Salski, the Polish courier. Salski and Schwarzbart enjoyed cordial relations, and Schwarzbart may have received the information about the plight of Jews in Poland directly from Salski, as he had in April 1943. See NA.FO 371/39422 (C18). In addition, given that all arrivals to the United Kingdom were interviewed by British intelligence, the information about Oświęcim could easily have been shared with the British.

175 PUMST MSW 1944, 'Sprawozdanie Krajowe', Volume IV, London (Sprawozdanie Nr 1/44, p. 85). The part of the text recording the SS surrounding

Notes to pages 212–14 365

the ghettos and the use of reflectors was composed around 10 September 1943 as it featured in the report of the Western Section of the Delagature's Department of Information of that date. For the filed report see AAN 1325 202/III/43 (96); for the original handwritten report see AAN 1325 202/III/147 (114), Microfilm 2270/2.

176 On 8 March 1944 Aryeh Leon Kubowitzki of the World Jewish Congress forwarded 'two reports on the extermination of the remaining Jewish centers in Poland' to Benjamin Teller of the Independent Jewish Press Service in New York. For these reports to reach New York in the first place, they would have had to pass through British and American censorship stations. The first report was derived from the Polish Underground information bulletin. It reported on the Germans' mass murder of Jews at Majdanek (13,000) and at Trawniki (10,000) on 5 November 1943, and 15,000 Jews at the camp at Poniatowa on 8 November. The second report was derived from information received by the Polish government and incorporated in Sprawozdanie Nr 1/44, which Ignacy Schwarzbart summarized and forwarded to the World Jewish Congress. I would like to thank Laurel Leff for forwarding me a copy of these documents. The originals are located at the American Jewish Archives MS 361, Box G17, Folder 2. See Leff (2005: 274).

177 See '137,000 ofiar niemieckich morderców "Wieczny ogień nie gaśnie w Oświęcimiu"', *Dziennik Polski*, 27 March 1944, 2.

178 It is worth noting that on 4 April 1944 a South African plane undertook a reconnaissance mission over Oświęcim (Monowitz) to gather intelligence on the I.G. Farben plant. The aerial photographic data gathered was supplemented with material from 'available ground sources' (i.e. Polish intelligence reports) to produce a fairly detailed map of the Monowitz complex. This material was ready for distribution on 9 June 1944 with the approval of the Ministry of Economic Warfare. See NA.AIR 29/332. The decision-making process that ultimately authorized this reconnaissance mission is not known, but it is likely that Polish pressure played a role. Any pilot flying (at 26,000 feet) over Monowitz would have had sight of Birkenau and Auschwitz I only a couple of miles away. The Air Ministry report on Monowitz does not mention other parts of the camp complex, but Auschwitz I was photographed and a subsequent reconnaissance mission photographed Birkenau on 31 May 1944.

179 NA.FO 371/42790 (W4299).

180 NA.FO 371/42790 (PM 44/164).

181 Hansard, House of Commons Debates, 30 March 1944, Volume 398, cols. 1561–4, available at http://hansard.millbanksystems.com/commons/1944/mar/30/persecution-of-jews-germany-and#S5CV0398P0_19440330_HOC_274, last accessed 20 March 2012.

182 Cited in Świebocki (2000: 306). The original document is located at the Auschwitz-Birkenau State Museum Archives – Mat. RO, Volume 2, p. 68a. The Jews whom Cyrankiewicz mentioned arrived in the family camp at Birkenau on 8 September and most were murdered on 8 or 9 March. Further transports of Czech Jews from Theresienstadt arrived on 16 and 20 December 1943. Few of those who arrived in September 1943 survived. One person who did was Otto Dov Kulka. Kulka has recently written about his experiences at the camp. See Kulka (2013).

366   Notes to pages 214–17

183 The passage of this message to Warsaw is not certain, but it did reach Jewish leaders in the Polish capital. The news of the murder of Czech Jews was sent via radio on behalf of Leon Feiner for the attention of Emanuel Scherer and Ignacy Schwarzbart on 6 April 1944. See AAN 1325 202/1–8, Microfilm 2201/2.

184 Some of this information was inaccurate – there were no transports of Jews from Denmark to Oświęcim. See AK w dokumentach, Volume III, p. 437 (Document 611/Lawina 750/6).

185 NA.FO 371/39451 (C7973), p. 134, 8 June 1944.

186 HIA Polish Embassy (US), Box 42, Folder 4. Also at Poland's Digital Archives: 800/36/0/-/42 (jpeg 583), last accessed 12 July 2012.

187 Barbara Rogers first drew attention to the fact that the Foreign Office sent a telegram to Washington about Jewish men from Italy, Denmark and France being gassed in Oświęcim. However, Rogers incorrectly dated the dispatch of the telegram (Bór-Komorowski did not send the message until April; Mikołajczyk did not arrive in the US until June 1944). The archival reference cited is also incorrect. See Rogers (1999b: 102).

188 See '7,000 Żydów czeskich zamordowano w Oświęcimiu', Dziennik Polski, 9 June 1944, 2.

189 '7,000 Czech Jews Murdered in Gas Chambers', Palestine Post, 11 June 1944, 1.

190 BBC WAC, C165, 16 June 1944.

191 BBC WAC, E2/131/17, 16 June 1944.

192 The directives of the PWE during this period are discussed in more detail in Chapter 6.

193 NA.FO 371/39272.

194 AAN 1325 202/1-8, Message 55, Microfilm 2201/2.

195 AAN 1324 202/111/25 (28), Microfilm 2266/4, Jankowski to Mikołajczyk, 8 June 1944, Message 23/44.

196 The Auschwitz-Birkenau State Museum appears not to have a record of a Jan Wolny who escaped from the camp. The museum has records of four people named Jan Wolny – two survived and two perished at the camp. None escaped. One Jan Wolny was an orderly in the surgical block of the main camp and a member of the camp Underground (Garliński 1975: 254). He was ordered to carry the corpses of the victims of the first gassing at Auschwitz in the summer of 1941 out of the cellar of Block 11. The British National Archive does not have any record of a Jan Wolny arriving in Britain. There are three possible explanations for the reports in the Polish Jewish Observer and earlier in the Milwaukee Journal. First, an individual named Jan Wolny did escape from the camp, but left no trace in the archival record; second, an individual escaped from the camp and used the pseudonym Jan Wolny (which can be translated as John Free) when giving interviews in Britain; third, Polish officials and/or Polish Jewish representatives, recognizing the significance of information received from Poland and the difficulty of getting this information into the mainstream press, created a 'witness' to relay the data to the press. The second possibility is the most resonant, given that the publisher of the Polish Jewish Observer (Joel Cang) had good contacts with Ignacy Schwarzbart of the Polish National Council. As discussed in this chapter, Schwarzbart received a continuous stream of information about

Notes to pages 217–19 367

the situation of Jews in Poland, including from couriers. However, the actual identity of the individual passing as Jan Wolny is not known. Enquiries at the Auschwitz-Birkenau State Museum and at the International Tracing Service, Bad Arolsen, have not to date revealed further details about the Jan Wolny reported in newspapers in June 1944. Regardless of these problems, the testimony of 'Wolny' is important because it restated the function of Oświęcim to English-speaking audiences on both sides of the Atlantic.

197 The War Refugee Board Collection at the Franklin D. Roosevelt Library, Hungary, Volume 1, Folder 2, February–August 1944, holds a copy of the Jan Wolny article published in the *Polish Jewish Observer*. It was forwarded to John Pehle by Aryeh Kubowitzki on 1 July 1944. See IPN BU 2835/52 (18).

198 However, on 20 June the newspaper referred to a 'young Pole', recently arrived in London, who had been imprisoned in both camps. The Pole confirmed the existence of gas chambers at 'Birkenau and Oswieciem'. It is likely that this individual was Jan Wolny. 'Czechs report massacre', *New York Times*, 20 June 1944, 5.

199 On 24 May 1944, Bureau VI in London registered a series of documents sent from Warsaw by the Council of National Unity (Rada Jedności Narodowej). These documents include the full 1943 summer report written by an unknown SS man and several summaries of the situation in Oświęcim. One entitled 'Relacja z Oświęcimia' ('Account from Auschwitz') bore the date 15 March 1944 (the date of compilation in Warsaw) and maintained that 1.5 million Jews had been killed at Oświęcim. This figure, along with other data in the document, suggests that it drew on information provided by Jerzy Tabeau and/or Witold Pilecki. It is likely that Polish officials in London understood that such a statistic had little chance of breaking into the British media. Other information about the camp which arrived in London in late May and early June, and revealed a lower number of victims, such as the murder of 7,000 Czech Jews, was published in a timely fashion. See PUMST A4.1.3 (76–77).

6 REASSESSING THE SIGNIFICANCE OF THE VRBA–WETZLER REPORT

1 See BBC WAC C165 and NA.FO 371/39014 (439–44).

2 In light of Roosevelt's and Eden's messages, and the repeated mention of Hungarian Jews in PWE directives, it is not unreasonable to suggest that consideration would have been given to Nazi plans for Hungarian Jewry and the camp that they would be deported to. Any documents pertaining to this question either have been destroyed (in Britain) or remain sealed (if they exist). It is possible that such documents were never produced, raising the question why no scenario planning was completed on an issue that merited presidential (US) and ministerial (UK) intervention.

3 The map originates from the Polish Military Geographical Institute. In June 1943 detailed maps of Poland, ranging from 1:25,000 scale (including a map featuring Treblinka and surrounding area) to 1:100,000, were filed by the Geographic Section of the General Staff. These maps can be found at the British Library (MOD GSGS 4177).

368   Notes to pages 220–5

4 NA.FO 371/39272, PWE directive, 30 March 1944. For an overview of how the BBC's Hungarian Service generally ignored Hungarian Jews during the war, listen to Thomson (2012). Thomson argues that Carlile Aylmer Macartney was responsible for the policy to marginalize news of Jews on the Hungarian Service. As we have seen in Chapter 2, the policy to marginalize Jews was a general policy adopted by the British government. On the airwaves, Foreign Office sensitivities with regard to Jews were communicated to broadcasters via the PWE.
   As well as working for the BBC's Hungarian Service, Macartney was employed by the Foreign Research and Press Service, which was accountable to the Foreign Office. As Britain's foremost authority on Hungary, his views had weight, but they did not determine policy. Also see Beretzky (2004).
5 NA.FO 371/39272, PWE directive, 20 April 1944 (Washington).
6 NA.FO 371/39272, PWE directive, 20 April 1944 (Hungarian Service).
7 HL MS 238 2/17, Hall letter to Easterman, 2 May 1944 (Foreign Office document WS 806/15/48).
8 AAN 1325 202/1-8, Message 55, Microfilm 2201/2.
9 NA.FO 371/39272, PWE directive, 25 May 1944 (Washington).
10 This strategy was problematic. As Bauer (1997: 195) notes, 'the attitude towards the Jews of the overwhelming part of the Catholic hierarchy, and to a lesser extent of the Calvinists and Lutherans, was one of radical theological anti-Semitism. The Catholic Primate, Justinian Szeredi, supported by most of the hierarchy, persevered in his anti-Semitic stance even against the interventions of the Apostolic Nuncio, the Italian Angelo Rotta'.
11 PISM A.XII3/40a (cited in Gąsowski 2002: 178).
12 The report on the desertions compiled by General Mieczysław Boruta-Spiechowicz can be found at PISM PRM K-36-4.
13 To be more precise, the Polish Right and portions of the Polish armed forces focused on Polish Jewish disloyalty and the damage being done to Poland's reputation, while sections of the British Left and British Jewry focused on anti-Semitism, often framed by the stereotype of the Polish anti-Semite. Polish Jews in Britain were also very concerned about anti-Semitism amongst non-Jewish Poles, but generally disagreed with the solution to the problem proposed by British left-leaning MPs and representatives of British Jewry.
14 See the *Polish Jewish Observer*, 28 April 1944, 1.
15 Hansard, House of Commons Debates, 5 April 1944, Volume 398, cols. 2010–14, available at http://hansard.millbanksystems.com/commons/1944/apr/05/polish-forces-great-britain-anti-semitism#S5CV0398-P0_19440405_HOC_247, last accessed 19 March 2012.
16 Hansard, House of Commons Debates, 5 April 1944, Volume 398, cols. 2010–14, available at http://hansard.millbanksystems.com/commons/1944/apr/05/polish-forces-great-britain-anti-semitism#S5CV0398-P0_19440405_HOC_247, last accessed 19 March 2012.
17 PISM PRM 132A (27).
18 Hansard, House of Commons Debates, 6 April 1944, Volume 398, cols. 2260–303, available at http://hansard.millbanksystems.com/commons/1944/apr/06/polish-forces-great-britain-anti-semitism.

Notes to pages 225–33

19 Hansard, House of Commons Debates, 6 April 1944, Volume 398, cols. 2260–303, available at http://hansard.millbanksystems.com/commons/1944/apr/06/polish-forces-great-britain-anti-semitism.

20 Hansard, House of Commons Debates, 6 April 1944, Volume 398. cols. 2260–303, available at http://hansard.millbanksystems.com/commons/1944/apr/06/polish-forces-great-britain-anti-semitism.

21 BBC WAC, European News Bulletins, April–May 1944.

22 BBC WAC, European News Bulletins, April–May 1944.

23 BBC WAC, European News Bulletins, April–May 1944.

24 BBC WAC, European News Bulletins, April–May 1944.

25 BBC WAC, European News Bulletins, April–May 1944.

26 BBC WAC, European News Bulletins, April–May 1944.

27 BBC WAC, E2/131/17.

28 Hansard, House of Commons Debates, 26 April 1944, Volume 399, cols. 747–52, available at http://hansard.millbanksystems.com/commons/1944/apr/26/polish-forces-great-britain#S5CV0399P0_19440426_HOC_59, last accessed 19 March 2012.

29 Hansard, House of Commons Debates, 17 May 1944, Volume 400, cols. 162–3, available at http://hansard.millbanksystems.com/commons/1944/may/17/polish-forces-great-britain-jewish#S5CV0400P0_19440517_HOC_79, last accessed 19 March 2012.

30 On 6 August the *Jewish Chronicle* published a letter by Dr Solomon Schonfeld that discussed tensions in the Jewish community in Britain. Two weeks later, on 20 August 1943, an article in the *Polish Jewish Observer* rejected Schonfeld's assertions, which, according to the *Observer*, had 'in effect [stated] that continental Jewry is to blame for the very keen and condemnatory party rivalry, or what he calls a "partisan plague", among Jews in Britain'.

31 Jewish Telegraphic Agency, 12 June: 'First transport of Hungarian Jews brought to Poland: 7,000 Czech Jews "liquidated"'. On 5 April 1944 Jankowski (delegate) had sent a message on behalf of Leon Feiner to Banaczyk (minister of the interior) with the request that he forward it to Scherer and Schwarzbart. It was de-encrypted on 5 June. The message repeated news that 7,000 Jews from Theresienstadt had been gassed. It also advised that these Jews were told by the Nazis that they were being sent for work in the General Government. See PUMST MSW 17/27 (98).

32 The report, with commentary, can be found in Świebocki (1997: 169–274).

33 Brand and Weissberg (1958: 15).

34 The British feared that the 'blood for goods' deal was some kind of deception that sought to sow discord in the Allied camp and provoke domestic criticism, as Jews rather than Allied prisoners would be released. See Hilberg (1985: 1137).

35 Wiskemann sent regular intelligence reports from Bern to the Foreign Office through the war. No evidence has been located to suggest that Polish intelligence about Auschwitz that passed through Bern on its way to Britain was shared with Wiskemann. This may be due to the fact that the Poles worked closely with SOE, which often had strained relations with other British agencies.

36 Cited in Karny (1994: 558).

37 Cited in Linn (2004: 30).

38 NA.FO 371/39272.

370   Notes to pages 233–8

39 Cited in Pawlikowski (2004: 59).
40 Also see Blet (1999: 250).
41 Cited in Rozett (1998: 139).
42 Also see Conway (1989: 53) for an account of Horthy's decision to stop the deportations.
43 The issue of opening a Second Front was prominent in discussions between Stalin and Churchill from 1942. Stalin was impatient for the Western Allies to engage the enemy along a Second Front and take some of the pressure off the USSR.
44 NA.FO 371/42790 PM/44/165.
45 See above, Chapter 4, 'The Segieda–Salski report (18 April 1943)', for full details.
46 NA.FO 371/42790, Churchill to Eden, 10 March 1944.
47 A great deal of news about Auschwitz passed through Switzerland in 1942, 1943 and 1944. It is possible that, had the news of the camp been publicized in Switzerland earlier, the censorship regime inhibiting the publishing of information about the mass slaughter of Jews at Auschwitz in the British mainstream press could have been compromised. However, it is not clear how much data Polish and Jewish representatives passed on to Swiss officials and journalists. This is an area in need of further research. Similarly, it is not known, precisely, how much information about the Holocaust was passed on by Jewish or Polish officials to Western diplomatic representatives in Switzerland, though there was some contact. On 19 November 1941, for example, David Kelly of the British Legation in Switzerland sent a message to Frank Roberts advising that 1.5 million Jews in Eastern Poland had disappeared. The source of this information was Aleksander Ładoś, the Polish representative in Bern. See Laqueur (1980: 16).
48 See NA.FO 371/42807 (95).
49 NA.FO 371/39272, PWE 'Weekly directive for BBC Hungarian Service, 16 to 23 June 1944'.
50 HL MS 238/2/17 (26 June 1944), Easterman to news director.
51 NA.FO 371/39272, PWE, 29 June, 'Weekly directive for BBC Hungarian Service, 30 June to 7 July 1944'.
52 HL MS 238/2/17, Hall to Easterman, 28 June 1944 (Foreign Office document W9946/15/48).
53 HL MS 238/2/18, Thurtle to Easterman (6 July 1944).
54 Alexander Easterman also had complaints about the written media. In a robust letter to Easterman, Arthur Cummings, the political editor of a mass-circulation liberal newspaper (the *News Chronicle*), defended the coverage given to the Jewish tragedy in the paper. Cummings was no doubt sincere in his assertions about the *News Chronicle*'s publishing record. Cummings's letter therefore helps historians to calibrate how journalists in the 1940s judged the volume and placement of stories about Nazi actions against Jews. See HL MS 238/2/18, Cummings to Easterman (5 July 44).
55 NA.FO 371/39272, PWE 6 July 'Weekly directive for BBC Hungarian Service, 7 July to 14 July 1944'.
56 As noted, this information had been published in *Dziennik Polski* on 9 June (page 2) and by the *Jewish Telegraphic Agency* on 12 June. The original source of that story was Józef Cyrankiewicz. The mixing of the German and Polish

Notes to pages 238–41   371

names for the different parts of the camp (Oswiecim and Birkenau, rather than Auschwitz and Birkenau or Oświęcim and Brzezinka) suggests that the *New York Times* drew on material from both the Polish Government in Exile and the Vrba–Wetzler report.

57 Gruenbaum was born in Warsaw in 1879 and became leader of the Zionist Federation in Poland in 1918. In 1919 he was elected to the Sejm and helped to establish the Minorities Bloc in 1922, which saw different national minorities in Poland run for office on the same list. Following election to the Zionist executive at the 18th Zionist Congress, Gruenbaum moved to Palestine. During the war he headed the Jewish Agency's Rescue Committee and was consequently well informed of the Holocaust as it was taking place.

58 'AK w dokumentach', Volume III, Document 638, p. 482 (Lawina 1150/5). This same information had been sent by Jankowski on 8 June, but there is no record of it being received. Jankowski's message also indicated that thirteen trains a day from Hungary arrived at Oświęcim, and that 1.2 million Hungarian Jews were to be murdered by the Nazis. See AAN 1325 202/III/25 (28), Microfilm 2266/4 (Message 23/44). News of thirteen trains a day arriving at Oświęcim was sent again on 27 June (de-encrypted 30 June). See PUMST MSW 13/86 (359) or A3.1.1.13.5 (199). Bór-Komorowski on 7 June had reported that between 15 and 27 May six transports of Hungarian Jews a day had passed via Płaszów en route to Oświęcim. He estimated the total number of people at 150,000. He also highlighted the transportation of sixty-two wagons of Jewish children aged between two and eight. See 'AK w dokumentach', Volume III, Document 632, p. 474 (Lawina 1090/3). This message was received on 11 June and de-encrypted on 12 June 1944. The information in Bór-Komorowski's second message of 14 June was not unexpected and was acted on. Through early June, the Western Section of the underground state's Department of Information and Press provided a constant stream of reports detailing the arrival and murder of Hungarian Jews at Auschwitz. Both the civilian and military wings of the underground state radioed this information West. See AAN 1325 202/III/25 (14, 19, 20, 21, 28), Microfilm 2266/4.

59 PUMST MSW 17/58 (145), Message 55. It was sent on 1 June 1944.

60 Jewish Telegraphic Agency, 26 June 1944, '100,000 Hungarian Jews have been executed in Polish [*sic*] death camp, underground reports'.

61 See Milland (1998b: 187); and BBC WAC, News, 26 June 1944 (Home Service, 6 p.m. bulletin (Box 114). The reference to 'Polish Galicia' would not have been helpful to listeners and may have been understood by some as a reference to Bełżec.

62 Messages from Jewish representatives in Poland were sent through the government delegate to the Polish Government in Exile and passed on to Ignacy Schwarzbart and/or Emanuel Scherer.

63 'AK w dokumentach, Volume III, Document 632, p. 474 (Lawina 1090/3).

64 The knowledge of the American public of the Holocaust was also poor due to the way in which the information was disseminated. Also see Lipstadt (1986) and Leff (2005). Chapter 2 above showed that the release of news about the Holocaust in Britain was ultimately controlled and choreographed by the Ministry of Information and the PWE.

65 However, readers with access to a well-resourced library that held any of several gazetteers could find out that Auschwitz was Oświęcim. See, for

372   Notes to pages 241–3

example, Raffelsperger (1845) and Chisholm (1895), amongst others. In London, gazetteers providing both the Polish and German names were available at the British Library.

66 Also see Jewish Telegraphic Agency, 5 July 1944, 'Swiss relief organizations report Nazi killing of 1,715,00 Jews in two camps'.

67 The paper also published Anthony Eden's statement on the deportation of Hungarian Jews, delivered at the House of Commons the previous day, on the same page.

68 The phrase 'Polish death camp' here simply referred to the death camp in occupied Poland. However, semantically, it denotes that the death camp had been set up and was being run by the Poles. The loose grammar fostered misunderstandings and perhaps, inadvertently, contributed to the growing mistrust between some groups of Poles and Jews. The special correspondent should have written 'the German death camp in occupied Poland'. This semantic error has been repeated over the last seventy years by major newspapers and important politicians. There were no Polish death camps.

69 The *Manchester Guardian* maintained good contact with Joel Cang, publisher of the *Polish Jewish Observer*, the one newspaper that published detailed information about Oświęcim through 1943 and 1944. It is possible that the *Manchester Guardian* consulted with Cang, or, more speculatively, that Cang was the special correspondent. The archives of the *Manchester* Guardian held at the Rylands Library, Manchester, do not shed any light on the identity of the special correspondent. According to his son Stephen Cang, Joel Cang tended not to keep records and there is no archive of his activities and correspondence (telephone conversation with Stephen Cang, 3 August 2012).

70 The implication of Engel's (1993: 287 fn. 121) statement that 'the [Polish] government had recently been notified that 400,000 rather than 100,000 Jews had already been deported from Hungary to Poland' is that the Polish government withheld the higher figure. The documentary record does not support this view. The 100,000 figure is from reports sent from Poland that were de-encrypted on 16 and 19 June. The information from these reports was distributed to the press and published first in New York (25 June) and then in Manchester (28 June). The 400,000 figure was only sent on 25 June. The information in both the *New York Times* and, most probably, the *Manchester Guardian* was published prior to the data from Istanbul being de-encrypted. The message from Istanbul can be found at HIA Polish Government, MSZ, Series 851/e, Box 615, Folder 4. Available at Poland's Digital Archive: http:// szukajwarchiwach.pl/800/42/0/615MinisterstwoSprawZagranicznych800/42/0/ 615, Folder 6 (jpeg 53), last accessed 10 July 2012. The data sent from Istanbul came from the Polish intelligence centre in Budapest. The dispatch requested that the information be passed to Berl Locker and Nahum Goldmann. A handwritten annotation dated 1 July indicates that the data was forwarded.

71 HIA Polish Government, MSZ, Series 851/e, Box 615, Folder 6. Available at Poland's Digital Archive: http://szukajwarchiwach.pl/800/42/0/615Ministerst-woSprawZagranicznych800/42/0/-/615, Folder 6 (jpeg72), last accessed 10 July 2012.

72 HIA Polish Government, MSZ, Series 851/e, Box 615, Folder 6. Available at Poland's Digital Archive: http://szukajwarchiwach.pl/800/42/0/615Ministers

Notes to pages 243–50 373

twoSprawZagranicznych800/42/0/?/615, Folder 6 (jpeg84), last accessed 10 July 2012.

73 Jewish Telegraphic Agency, 30 June 1944, '450,000 Hungarian Jews already deported; Federal Council of Churches issues appeal'.

74 NA.FO 371/42807 (97), copy of cable from Jerusalem (received 30 June 1944).

75 Hansard, House of Commons Debates, 5 July 1944, Volume 401, cols. 1160–2, available at http://hansard.millbanksystems.com/commons/1944/jul/05/hungary-mass-deportations-of-jews#S5CV0401P0_19440705_HOC_251, last accessed 5 April 2012. On 4 July, Silverman was discouraged by the Foreign Office from asking a Parliamentary question on the issue of the deportations from Hungary. He was advised that 'ventilation of this question could not do any good and might do harm'. NA.FO 371/42807 (193).

76 NA.FO 371/42809 (WR 218). The document is also cited in Gilbert (2001a: 262–4).

77 It may be contended that Eden chose to characterize the data that the Foreign Office received as uncorroborated. The result was the same: the British government failed to confirm the reports about the deportations from Hungary that reached London, despite being in possession of a great deal of information.

78 The PWE weekly directive to the Hungarian Service for the week 7–14 July, dated 6 July 1944, noted that Hungary had allowed many thousands of Jews to be deported to Poland to 'almost certain death'. NA.FO 371/39272.

79 BBC WAC, Home Service, News Bulletin, 9 p.m., 7 July (page 12 of transcript).

80 AAN 1325 202/1–8, Message 55, Microfilm 2201/2, Leon Feiner to Emanuel Scherer, 1 June 1944.

81 'Jews die in gas chambers', *Daily News* (Perth, Western Australia), 8 July 1944, 8; 'Mass murder of Jews in Poland', *The Mail* (Adelaide), 8 July 1944, 12; 'Gas chamber for 400,000 Jews', *Sunday Times* (Perth), 9 July 1944, 1; 'Wholesale slaughter of Jews', *The Mercury* (Hobart, Tasmania), 10 July 1944, 6; 'Over 2,000,000 Jews sent to death camps', *Examiner* (Launceston, Tasmania), 10 July 1944, 6, available at http://trove.nla.gov.au/newspaper/result?q=oswiecim&s=20, last accessed 26 March 2013.

82 The *Polish Jewish Observer* reported the same information in its 14 July 1944 edition.

83 Cited in Kushner (1997: 162). The archival reference is CZA C2/279, National Council Minutes of the World Jewish Congress, British Section.

84 Arguably, the work of the WRB helped to create this public.

85 NA.FO 371/42730 (97).

86 For an overview of the bombing issue debate see Berenbaum and Neufeld (2000). From December 1943, the US 15th Air Force operated from southern Italy – within bombing range of Auschwitz. It reached full strength in May 1944 and began bombing targets in East and Central Europe.

87 Rubinstein (1997: 160) refers to a document dated 22 May 1944 that incorporates the request which is located in the files of the War Refugee Board at the FDR Presidential Library.

88 By August resources that *could* have been used to bomb the camp were directed to the insurgents in the Polish capital (Gilbert 2001a: 285). The Uprising was initiated on 1 August 1944. However, it is very unlikely that in the absence of the crisis in Warsaw during August and September 1944, Allied military resources would have been employed to bomb Auschwitz or

374   Notes to pages 250–1

the railway lines to the camp. The battle for Warsaw had significant implications for inter-Allied relations; Auschwitz did not. For a brief discussion of how a request to bomb the rail line to Auschwitz was handled by the Americans see Mahoney (2011).

89 The Air Ministry received information from a 4 April 1944 reconnaissance mission over Oświęcim. The report in the Air Ministry file deals exclusively with Monowitz, but it is possible that the Air Ministry received the aerial photographs of Auschwitz I from that mission and of Birkenau from a mission undertaken on 31 May 1944. See NA.AIR 29/332.

90 Public knowledge here does not refer to the general public in Britain, but to representatives of civil society who gained knowledge of the camp via the triptych of reports that stimulated so many articles in Swiss newspapers.

91 See Reynolds (2004: 38).

92 A minute prepared for Eden by an FO official on 25 August referred to the halting of the deportation of Hungarian Jews and the technical difficulties of the bombing mission in order to encourage the minister to contact the Air Ministry and to shelve the bombing plan. NA.FO 371/42814/196, 25 August 1944.

93 NA.FO 371/42809, 11 July 1944.

94 Hilberg (1985: 1139) suggests that 'in these instructions Churchill was not particularly concerned with the safety of the Jews; he was worried about the reputation of the German nation. The culprits had disgraced their race'.

95 IPN BU 2835/52 (12). In 1986, McCloy was interviewed by Henry Morgenthau's son (also named Henry) and stated that he had discussed bombing Auschwitz with President Roosevelt. According to the ninety-one-year-old McCloy, Roosevelt considered that bombing the camp would not do any good and that any bombing of the camp would open the US to accusations of killing innocent people. It cannot be confirmed by the documentary record whether this McCloy–Roosevelt conversation actually took place, and, if it did, precisely when it occurred. Assuming that McCloy remembered correctly, Roosevelt's opinion on the bombing question conformed with the general war policy of targeting military and industrial installations. In order to alter the widely held view that bombing Auschwitz was counterproductive, pressure would have had to have been brought to bear earlier to legitimate the selection of targets according to specific humanitarian objectives. As noted in Chapter 4, Roosevelt had been handed information about the slaughter of Jews at Auschwitz by Jewish organizations in December 1942, and information reached both US government agencies and Jewish organizations in the US through 1943 and 1944. It was certainly possible for civil-society activists to demand that Auschwitz be bombed and for the Roosevelt administration to consider possible military action to stem the killing at the camp earlier than June 1944. See Beschloss (2003: 66). The Polish government made a request to the British government to bomb the camp in 1941.

96 Churchill had received a request for the death camps at Treblinka and Majdanek to be bombed, and for immediate retaliation, from Miss Lucyna Tomaszewska (it is not clear who this lady was, but it seems she was a member of the public) on 20 July 1943. The Foreign Office considered that no response other than an acknowledgement of the receipt of Miss Tomaszewska's letter was required. Such acknowledgement was sent on 31 July 1943. NA.FO 371/34550 (C8857/34/55).

Notes to pages 252–6 375

97 AAN 1325 202/I-3 Number 31, 20 February 1943, Microfilm 2201/1.
98 See Chapter 4. On 31 March 1942, a message from Jankowski and Rowecki that reported that 520,000 Jews had been murdered at Auschwitz was de-encrypted by Polish intelligence in London.
99 Cited in Westerman (2004: 205) and Świebocki (2000: 322).
100 Cited in Świebocki (2000: 326). The original document is at the Auschwitz-Birkenau State Museum: Mat. RO, Volume 1, p. 32.
101 Cited in Świebocki (2000: 326). The Polish document can be found at PUMST MSW 12 (219). I have not located documents discussing bombing the camp in August 1943 in the British National Archives.
102 NA.FO 371/34552 and HS 4/210.
103 Quote from *Witold's Report* (1945). See Cyra (2000: 136).
104 The entry posted online by the Institute of National Remembrance on this issue is not clear. The English translation speaks of genocide of the camp population, the Polish-language version refers to mass murder. See http://en.pilecki.ipn.gov.pl/portal/rpe/1025/8193/?poz=3&update=1, accessed 21 November 2011.
105 NA.FO 371/34557 (C11634), letter to Colonel Leon Mitkiewicz from H. Redman and J.R. Deane on behalf of the Combined Chiefs of Staff, 24 September 1943.
106 IPN BU 2835/12 (124). No record of Banaczyk's response has been located.
107 IPN BU 2835/15 (84) and (104).
108 IPN BU 2835/52 (18).
109 Levy's article on the bombing issue is framed by the view that 'Auschwitz was the only destination of the deportees ... not known until the end of June' (Levy 1996: 271).
110 Cited in Medoff and Zucker (2012: 10), Minutes of the Jewish Agency Executive, 11 June 1944, 4–7, CZA.
111 In an earlier paper, Medoff (2011) maintained that the sixty-nine Jews who returned to Palestine in 1942 'presented the Yishuv leadership with detailed, eyewitness reports about Nazi atrocities, including some of the earliest solid information about the death camps of Treblinka and Sobibor (but not Auschwitz, which was still known to the outside world as a forced labor camp)'. As discussed in Chapter 4, the fact that Auschwitz was a place where Jews were taken to be murdered *was* also revealed by one of these Jewish returnees. Even the source that Medoff cites – Dina Porat's book – later states, 'In November 1942, refugees who reached Palestine did mention Auschwitz as one of the camps in which extermination was taking place' (Porat 1990: 214). Medoff therefore ignores the Dobkin et al. report of 20 November 1942 (CZA S26/1203), the work of Penkower (2002: 165), Laqueur (1998: 23), Gilbert (2001a) and has only selectively read Porat (1990). The contention that news of Auschwitz did not reach the Jewish Agency is an important plank in Medoff and Zucker's (2012) argument that Jewish Agency leadership did not know about the true nature of Auschwitz before the Vrba–Wetzler report. It is, however, false.
112 Medoff and Zucker (2012: 11) argue that A. Leon Kubowitzki was convinced that Birkenau was only a labour camp prior to the dissemination of the Vrba–Wetzler report, citing a cable from Kubowitzki

376 Notes to pages 256–64

to Pehle at the War Refugee Board on 5 July 1944. However, since Kubowitzki regularly received information from Ignacy Schwarzbart about the camp and had even passed information about Auschwitz to Benjamin Teller of the Independent Jewish Press Service on 8 March 1944, this is very unlikely. Instead, it points to Kubowitzki either attempting to rationalize past inaction, or to state the urgency of the current situation. See Kubowitzki to Pehle, 5 July 1944, WRB WJC: I, Box 22 (Franklin D. Roosevelt Library, New York) (cited by Medoff and Zucker 2012); and AJA MSS 361, Box G17, Folder 2 – see Leff (2005: 274).

113 For representatives based in Palestine such considerations were less important, but there remained the demand to maintain decent relations with the Western Allies.

7 CONCLUSION

1 *Willings Press Guide* lists all newspapers published in Great Britain, together with their addresses.

2 See issues from 12 February 1943, 26 March 1943, 16 April 1943, 30 April 1943, 3 September 1943, 10 September 1943, 26 November 1943, 21 January 1944, 4 February 1944, 24 March 1944, 19 May 1944, 30 June 1944.

3 NA.INF 1/251, 25 July 1941, p. 2.

4 Bluntly, the British government sought to limit anti-Semitism, but did not want to help Jews (provide sanctuary, initiate retaliatory strikes). There was tension between these two aims.

5 INF 1/64, 7 March 1941.

6 See Appendix II for a fuller discussion of the gaps in the British archival record.

7 While Bauer accepted in 2001 that information about Auschwitz was available in the West, he insisted that 'the information had not jelled into knowledge, and it was rejected by many – the government officials, the military, and the general public, Jews and non-Jews alike – as preposterous'. This assertion is far too general and gives no weight to the actions of important information gatekeepers in regulating the flow of data about the camp and its presentation, and guiding reception of the news. As Lipstadt (1986) and Leff (2005) demonstrate, burying news of the Holocaust in the inside pages of newspapers had a strong influence on how that news was received.

8 The head of Bureau VI, Michał Protasewicz, was awarded an OBE (Order of the British Empire) in December 1943. NA.HS 7/277 (107).

9 Bauer (1981: 192) contrasts the inactivity in the US with the demands of colleagues in Istanbul for action to 'save the remnants of European Jewry'.

10 For example, the *first* meeting of the Council for Rescue of the Jews in Poland took place on 25 May 1944 in London. It was attended by senior Polish politicians and Jewish representatives, including Władysław Banaczyk and Emanuel Scherer. See IPN BU 2835/13 (101).

11 However, the argument that the Polish government could have pressed British officials harder to ensure that the information was widely distributed has a great deal of merit. Passing information about the camp to British officials was necessary, but insufficient if the objective was to elicit an Allied response to the mass slaughter of Jews at Auschwitz.

Notes to pages 265–9

12 The US could also have drawn attention to the systematic killing of Jews at the camp by referring to the memorandum handed to Roosevelt in December 1942, the 25 November article in the *New York Times* and perhaps even the Polish government's document of 27 November, 'Report on conditions in Poland' (though it is not known for certain to whom this document was circulated, nor when).

13 Cited in Stola (1997: 16).

14 As noted in Chapter 1, it is not clear why Gilbert cites 25 November 1942. The Dobkin report containing this information was released on 20 November. 25 November 1942 is the date news of the slaughter of Jews at Oświęcim was published in the *New York Times*. Gilbert makes no reference to the sentence in the *New York Times* about Oświęcim.

15 I refrain from making categorical statements on the number of reports about the camp that reached the West, as it is possible that further reports may be located. The claim of over forty reports about the camp includes the reports of Vrba and Wetzler, Mordowicz and Rosin, and Jerzy Tabeau.

16 Stola (1995) provides a discussion of the Polish government and National Council. The political make-up of the National Council is outlined. See Stola (1995: 22–40).

17 Friszke (2011) provides a discussion of Ciołkosz's activities during the war, including his contribution to the debate on deserters from the Polish Army in 1944.

18 Láníček (2013: 99) notes that in internal correspondence the Czechoslovak Foreign Ministry understood Polish efforts to secure a UN declaration in December 1942 as an 'attempt to win support from western Jewish groups'.

19 *Polish Jewish Observer*, 3 March 1944, 1. Lord Vansittart, in his reply to Edward Raczyński's letter praising his 1 September 1942 BBC broadcast that highlighted atrocities against Jews, declared that the public response was 'heartening' and that he was 'sure that the people of this country can be deeply moved if only the truth is given to them and with sincerity'. Clarity on the Holocaust was especially lacking during 1943 and the first half of 1944. See Raczyński (1997: 152).

20 *Polish Jewish Observer*, 3 March 1944, 1.

21 Even had details of Soviet crimes been readily available, in all likelihood many on the Left would have dismissed the information as propaganda. In an important article in *Tribune* from 1 September 1944 entitled 'As I please', George Orwell accused the British intelligentsia, with some exceptions, of having 'developed a nationalistic loyalty towards the USSR' and of being 'dishonestly uncritical of its policies', and warned them not to 'imagine that for years on end you can make yourself the boot-licking propagandist of the Soviet regime, or any other regime, and then return to mental decency. Once a whore, always a whore'. The article highlighted the British press's critical attitude towards the Warsaw Rising, then still in progress, and the unswerving loyalty of many in the press to Soviet policy. Orwell characterized the British Left's attitude to the USSR thus: 'This is Russian policy: how can we make it appear right?' See Davies (2003: 672). Orwell was certainly right about the jaundiced view that many on the British Left had about the Poles and the Left's adherence to the USSR. However, other sections of British society may

378   Notes to pages 270–3

have been more accepting of the news of Soviet crimes. At the very least, the Polish government could have publicly justified its policy in relation to the Soviet Union. For a discussion of the British Left's relationship with the USSR, and Stalin in particular, see Amis (2003). Also see the exchanges between Edward Thompson and Leszek Kołakowski in the *Socialist Register* (1973–4). It is worth noting that the British Left was not alone in criticizing the Warsaw Rising. General Władysław Anders of the Polish II Corps saw it as 'madness', a 'flagrant crime' which had not a 'half-chance' of success. See Ciechanowski (2002: 262) and PISM Kol. G.A./46, Anders to Col. 'Hancza', 31 August 1944. Debate about the merits of the Warsaw Rising continues, and the uprising is celebrated at the Warsaw Uprising Museum. The stories of the hundreds of thousands of Varsovians who paid the ultimate price at the hands of the Nazis during the uprising, including at the hands of the infamous soldiers led by Oskar Dirlewanger, are less in evidence at that museum.

22 Ivone Kirkpatrick wrote a document entitled 'The German peace offensive' in autumn 1939, which was circulated in the Foreign Office and endorsed the view that Britain could support an ethnographic and cultural Poland without 'standing on Russian toes'. NA.FO 371/23097/203–9.

23 Roman Knoll was the director of the Commission for Foreign Affairs of the Government Delegation in Poland. Knoll's document can be found at AAN 1325 202/XIV-9, 135: 'Uwagi o naszej polityce zagranicznej', No 1 (1943). The document can also be found at PISM A.9, Ie/15. Also see Stola (1995: 229–33).

24 Schwarzbart had discussed relations in the Polish Army with Marian Kukiel in late 1942, for example.

25 This is an issue which is in urgent need of further research. Given that news of the mass killing of Jews at Auschwitz was available in London through 1943 and published regularly in the *Polish Jewish Observer* it was possible for exiled Allied governments based in London to become aware of what was happening to their Jewish citizens and of where they were being sent. Data about the camp could have been passed to Allies (Dutch, French, Greek, Czechoslovak representatives) in a number of different ways. It could have been passed directly by the Polish government, via reports in the *Polish Jewish Observer*, via British intelligence to counterparts from Allied governments (i.e. from SOE), or by the British government. Ignacy Schwarzbart regularly passed information of German crimes to Allied governments (see, for example, IPN BU 2835/41 (47)). Furthermore, since there were plenty of reports that mentioned deportation to the east, and the killing centres in Poland were known by June 1942, Allied governments could have pressed the Polish government for information. The Netherlands Information Bureau was based in the same building as the Polish Ministry of Information (and the Polish Telegraphic Agency) – Stratton House in Piccadilly, London. It seems that the Dutch government asked the Polish government for information about its Jewish citizens in February 1944, as on 28 February the Polish minister of the interior sent a radio message to Warsaw asking whether any aid could be provided for Dutch Jews. See AAN 1325 202/1-4, Message 45, Microfilm 2201/1.

26 Claims asserting Pilecki's authorship are common online. See, for example, the Wikipedia entry for the Vrba–Wetzler report, http://en.wikipedia.org/wiki/

Notes to pages 274–8

Vrba-Wetzler_report, last accessed 26 February 2012. The loose reference given is Hilberg 1985, but Hilberg (incorrectly) assigns authorship to a female Polish agent.

27 There is a rich literature on the memory politics at Auschwitz. See Charlesworth (1994), Huener (2003), Zubrzycki (2006), for example.

28 This, of course, leaves plenty of scope for determining the significance of particular historical events and how they should be interpreted and understood.

29 As noted in Chapter 1 (note 11), Marrus (2013) argues that minority champions were seen by some decision makers as troublemakers threatening to destabilize Europe during the interwar period. By 1940, antipathy to humanitarian intervention had become ingrained amongst key decision makers and this, according to Marrus, played a role inhibiting an effective response to the Holocaust by Western governments. However, the significance of elite anti-Semitism should be recognized.

30 NA.FO 371/39449.

31 NA.FO 371/42730 (17), 16 May 1944.

32 NA.FO 371/42728 (W4549), 27 March 1944.

33 Broadly 'orientalist' discourses framing Eastern Europe (including Poland) as Other and backward, common in the mid-twentieth century, continue to exert influence. Merje Kuus (2004) has examined this issue in relation to EU and NATO expansion, for example.

34 However, even if relations between Jews and the Poles in the West, and with the Polish Government in Exile, had been more cordial, the rise in nationalistic sentiment in postwar Poland, fanned by the policies of the Polish Workers' Party and the ethno-religious ambitions of the Roman Catholic Church, would have sorely tested relationships. Pogroms in Kraków (1945) and in Kielce (1946) were accompanied by murderous violence against Jews throughout the country. David Engel (2005: 425) suggests that between 1944 and 1946 some 500–600 Jews were murdered by Poles.

35 During the summer of 1943, the Germans set up a scheme to concentrate the remaining Jews in Warsaw. Under the auspices of a prisoner exchange scheme, Jews with the papers of neutral countries would be exchanged for Germans interned abroad. Until transfer was arranged, Jews were allowed to live legally at Hotel Polski on 29 Długa Street. Three hundred Jews were taken to the Vittel camp and between 2,000 and 2,500 people were sent to Bergen Belsen. The final group of 420 Jews scheduled to be sent to Bergen Belsen were taken to Pawiak prison in Warsaw and shot. Some 2,500 Jews with South American papers which were not recognized by South American governments were deported to Auschwitz, where they were murdered. Around 300 people avoided being killed (they had Palestinan papers). See Paulsson (2002: 139) and Haszka (2006).

36 Reports of anti-Semitism in Poland reached the Polish Government in Exile in London from Jan Karski in February 1940, Prince Radziwiłł in January 1941, General Rowecki in the summer of 1941 (see Polonsky 2004: 51), and Roman Knoll in mid-1943.

37 Bogner (1999) puts the number of Jewish children saved in convents in the hundreds rather than thousands. It is not possible to give a precise figure of the number of children saved due to the relative lack of documentary evidence.

380   Notes to pages 279–304

38 Leon Feiner (Berezowski) and Maurycy Orzech (Janczyn) sent a message via Mikołajczyk to Zygielbojm calling for an official intervention from the Pope on 7 February 1943. The Bund leaders in Poland were very conscious of the positive impact that an intervention by the Catholic Church could have. See AAN 1325 202/I/7, Message 39, Microfilm 2201/2. Also see Blatman (2004: 312). The Polish government was also aware of the significance of the Church. The Polish president wrote to the Pope in January 1943 asking him to condemn the German terror. See Chapter 3 above. For President Raczkiewicz's telegram to the Pope see PUMST A1.1.2 (1).
39 See Michlic (2007) for a discussion of the stereotypes and myths that under-pin the thinking of nationalist historians. Michlic focuses on the debate about Jedwabne. She highlights that nationalist historians downplay the Polish role in the massacre and frequently draw on the stereotype of Jewish communist in order to explain or justify Polish actions.
40 Żegota was a council of aid to the Jews organized under the auspices of the delegate of the Polish Government in Exile. It operated between 1942 and 1945. See Friszke and Kunert (2002).
41 NA.FO 371/34550 (90), my italics. A different translation of the letter is available at http://yad-vashem.org.il/about_holocaust/documents/part2/doc154.html, last accessed 16 March 2012 (Yad Vashem O-55). There the translation reads, 'The responsibility for the crime of the murder of the whole Jewish nationality in Poland rests first of all on those who are carrying it out, but indirectly it falls also upon the whole of humanity, on the peoples of the Allied nations and on their governments, who up to this day have not taken any real steps to halt this crime. By looking on passively upon this murder of defenceless millions of tortured children, women and men they have become partners to the responsibility'.
42 Jews from the Łódź ghetto were also gassed at Auschwitz during the summer of 1944.

APPENDIX II

 1 NA.FO 371/39524 (C7711–intercept LON/ULD134824/44).

Bibliography

Adamczyk, M. and Gmitruk, J. 2012. *Polskie Państwo w Depeszach do Rządu RP Stanisława Mikołajczyka w Londynie 1943–1944*, Warsaw: Muzeum Historii Polskiego Ruchu Ludowego

Addison, P. 2005. *Churchill: The Unexpected Hero*, Oxford: Oxford University Press

Alderman, G. 1995. 'English Jews or Jews of the English persuasion', in P. Birnbaum and I. Katzenelson (eds.), *Paths of Emancipation: Jews, States and Citizenship*, Princeton: Princeton University Press, 128–56

2001. *The Holocaust: Why Did Anglo-Jewry Stand Idly by?*, New York: Graduate School of Jewish Studies, Touro College

Allen, M.D. 2002. *The Business of Genocide: The SS, Slave Labor and the Concentration Camps*, Chapel Hill: University of North Carolina Press

Amis, M. 2003. *Koba the Dread: Laughter and the 20 million*, London: Jonathan Cape

Apenszlak, J. (ed.) 1943. *The Black Book of Polish Jewry: An Account of the Martyrdom of Polish Jewry under Nazi Occupation*, New York: American Federation for Polish Jews

Aronson, S. 2004. *Hitler, the Allies and the Jews*, Cambridge: Cambridge University Press

Aynat, E. 1991. 'Auschwitz and the Exile Government of Poland according to the "Polish Fortnightly Review" 1940–1945', *Journal of Historical Review*, 11, 3: 281–319, available www.ihr.org/jhr/v11/v11p282_Aynat.html, last accessed 20 January 2012

Balfour, M. 1979. *Propaganda in War 1939–1945: Organisations, Policies and Publics in Britain and Germany*, London: Routledge and Kegan Paul

Bankier, D. 2008. *Secret Intelligence and the Holocaust*, New York: Enigma Books

Baron, F. 2000. 'The "myth" and reality of rescue from the Holocaust: the Karski–Koestler and Vrba–Wetzler reports', *Yearbook of the Research Centre for German and Austrian Exile Studies*, 2: 171–208, also available at http://kuscholarworks.ku.edu, 1–33

Bauer, Y. 1978. *The Holocaust in Historical Perspective*, Seattle: University of Washington Press

1981. *American Jewry and the Holocaust: The American Joint Distribution Committee 1939–1945*, Detroit: Wayne State University Press

1997. 'Conclusion: the Holocaust in Hungary: was rescue possible?', in D. Cesarani (ed.), *Genocide and Rescue: The Holocaust in Hungary 1944*, Oxford: Berg, 193–209

382   Bibliography

2001. *Rethinking the Holocaust*, New Haven: Yale University Press
2012. 'How to misinterpret history: on "The Holocaust, America, and American Jewry," Revisited', *Israel Journal of Foreign Affairs*, 6, 3: 137–50

Bell, P. 1989. 'Censorship, propaganda and public opinion: The case of the Katyn Graves, 1943', *Transactions of the Royal Historical Society*, 39: 63–83
1990. *John Bull and the Bear: British Public Opinion, Foreign Policy and the Soviet Union 1941–1945*, London: Edward Arnold

Bennett, G. 2005. 'The achievements of the Polish Intelligence Service', in T. Stirling, D. Nałęcz and T. Dubicki (eds.), *Intelligence Co-operation between Poland and Great Britain during World War* II, Volume 1, *The Report of the Anglo-Polish Historical Committee*, London: Vallentine Mitchell, 433–42

Bennett, J. 1966. *British Broadcasting and the Danish Resistance Movement 1940–1945: A Study of the Wartime Broadcasts of the BBC Danish Service*, Cambridge: Cambridge University Press

Berenbaum, M. and Neufeld, M.J. (eds.), 2000. *The Bombing of Auschwitz: Should the Allies Have Attempted It?*, New York: St Martin's Press

Beretzky, A. 2004. 'C.A. Macartney: a devoted and frustrated friend of Hungary (1939–1945): service in the Foreign Office and the BBC', paper presented at British–Hungarian Relations since 1848 conference, 16–17 April 2004, UCL-SSEES, London, available at www.ssees.ucl.ac.uk/confhung/beretzky.pdf

Beschloss, M. 2003. *The Conquerors: Roosevelt, Truman and the Destruction of Hitler's Germany 1941–1945*, New York: Simon & Schuster

Bines, J. 2008. 'The Polish Country Section of the Special Operations Executive 1940–1946: a British perspective', unpublished PhD thesis, University of Stirling

Blatman, D. 2004. 'On a mission against all odds: Samuel Zygelbojm in London, April 1942–May 1943', in D. Cesarani (ed.), *Holocaust: Critical Concepts in Historical Studies*, Volume 4, London: Routledge: 293–320

Blet, P. 1999. *Pius XII and the Second World War: According to the Archives of the Vatican*, Mahwah, NJ: Paulist Press

Bloxham, D. and Kushner, J. 2005. *The Holocaust: Critical Historical Approaches*, Manchester: Manchester University Press

Bogner, N. 1999. 'The convent children: the rescue of Jewish children in Polish convents during the Holocaust', *Yad Vashem Studies*, 27: 235–85

Bolchover, R. 1993. *British Jewry and the Holocaust*, Cambridge: Cambridge University Press

Bór-Komorowski, T. 1984. *The Secret Army*, Nashville: Battery Press

Bourdieu, P. 2000. *Masculine Domination*, London: Polity Press

Bourdieu, P. and Wacquant, L. 2004. 'Symbolic violence', in P. Bourgois and N. Scheper-Hughes (eds.), *Violence in War and Peace*, Oxford: Wiley-Blackwell, 272–4

Bracken, B. 1942. *Bestiality . . . Unknown in Any Previous Record of History . . .*, London: Polish Ministry of Information

Brand, J. and Weissberg, A. 1958. *Advocate for the Dead: The Story of Joel Brand*, London: André Deutsch

Bibliography 383

Breitman, R. (undated) 'What Chilean diplomats learned about the Holocaust', available at www.archives.gov/iwg/research-papers/breitman-chilean-diplomats.html

1985. 'Auschwitz and the Archives', *Central European History*, 18, 3–4: 365–83

1996. 'Allied knowledge of Auschwitz-Birkenau in 1943–1944', in V. Newton (ed.), *FDR and the Holocaust*, New York: Franklin and Eleanor Roosevelt Institute, 175–82

1999. *Official Secrets: What the Nazis Planned, What the British and Americans Knew*, London: Allen Lane

2004. 'Auschwitz partially decoded', in D. Cesarani (ed.), *Holocaust: Critical Concepts in Historical Studies*, Volume 5, London: Routledge, 185–94

Breitman, R. and Goda, N. 2005. 'OSS knowledge of the Holocaust', in R. Breitman, N. Goda, T. Naftali and R. Wolfe (eds.), *U.S. Intelligence and the Nazis*, Cambridge: Cambridge University Press, 11–44

Briggs, A. 1995. *The History of Broadcasting in the UK: The War of Words*, Oxford: Oxford University Press

Browning, C. 1992. *Ordinary Men: Reserve Police Battalion 101 and the Final Solution in Poland*, New York: Harper Collins

2010. *Remembering Survival: Inside a Nazi Slave-Labor Camp*, New York: Norton

Cang, J. 1939. 'The opposition parties in Poland and their attitude towards the Jews and the Jewish problem', *Jewish Social Studies*, 1, 2: 241–56

Cesarani, D. (ed.) 1989. *The Making of Modern Anglo-Jewry*, Oxford: Blackwell

1994. *The Jewish Chronicle and Anglo-Jewry, 1841–1991*, Cambridge: Cambridge University Press

1995. 'Secret Churchill papers released', *Journal of Holocaust Education*, 4, 2: 225–8

(ed.) 1997. *Genocide and Rescue: The Holocaust in Hungary 1944*, Oxford: Berg

1998. *Britain and the Holocaust*, London: Holocaust Education Trust

2003. 'The London Jewish Chronicle and the Holocaust', in R.M. Shapiro (ed.), *Why Didn't the Press Shout? American and International Journalism during the Holocaust*, Jersey City: Yeshiva University and KTAV

(ed.) 2004. *Holocaust: Critical Concepts in Historical Studies*, 6 volumes, London: Routledge

Charlesworth, A. 1994. 'Contesting places of memory: the case of Auschwitz', *Environment and Planning D: Society and Space*, 12, 5: 579–93

Chisholm, G. 1895. *Longman's Gazetteer of the World*, London: Longman

Chmielewski, J. 2012. 'Izbica jako przykład getta tranzytowego (1942–1943)', *Kwartalnik Historii Żydów*, 2, 242: 190–206

Chwastyk-Kowalczyk, J. 2004. 'Kwestia żydowska na łamach londyńskiego "Dziennika Polskiego" w latach 1940–1943', *Rocznik Historii Prasy Polskiej*, 7, 1, 13: 39–59

2005. *Londyński Dziennik Polski 1940–1943*, Kielce: Wydawnictwo Akademii Świętokrzyskiej

Ciechanowski, J. 2002. *The Warsaw Rising of 1944*, Cambridge: Cambridge University Press

2005. 'Reports on the Holocaust', in T. Stirling, D. Nałęcz and T. Dubicki (eds.), *Intelligence Co-operation between Poland and Great Britain during World*

384   Bibliography

War II, Volume 1, *The Report of the Anglo-Polish Historical Committee*, London: Vallentine Mitchell, 535–46

Ciechanowski, J.S. and Dubicki, T. 2005. 'Turkey', in T. Stirling, D. Nałęcz and T. Dubicki (eds.), *Intelligence Co-operation between Poland and Great Britain during World War II*, Volume 1, *The Report of the Anglo-Polish Historical Committee*, London: Vallentine Mitchell, 321–31

Ciołkosz, A. 1983. *Walka o prawdę: wybór artykułow 1940–1978*, London: Polonia

Cohen, M. 2001. 'British policy', in J.T. Baumel and W. Laqueur (eds.), *The Holocaust Encyclopedia*, New Haven: Yale University Press, 90–7

Cohen, S. 2003. *No One Is Illegal: Asylum and Immigration Control, Past and Present*, Stoke-on-Trent: Trentham Books

  2010. *Rescue the Perishing: Eleanor Rathbone and the Refugees*, London: Vallentine Mitchell

Conversi, D. 2010. 'Cultural homogenization, ethnic cleansing and genocide', in R.A. Denmark (ed.), *The International Studies Encyclopedia*, Volume 2, Oxford and Boston, MA: Wiley-Blackwell/ISA, 719–42

Conway, J. 1989. 'Between apprehension and indifference: Allied attitudes to the destruction of Hungarian Jewry', in M. Marrus (ed.), *The Nazi Holocaust: The End of the Holocaust*, Volume 9, Westport: Meckler, 41–64

  1997. 'The first report about Auschwitz', available at http://motlc.wiesenthal.com/site/pp.asp?c=gvKVLcMVIuG&b=394983

Crockett, R. (ed.) 1990. *My Dear Max: The Letters of Brendan Bracken to Lord Beaverbrook, 1925–1958*, London: The Historians' Press

Cruickshank, C. 1981. *The Fourth Arm: Psychological Warfare 1938–1945*, Oxford: Oxford University Press

Cull, J.N. 1995. *Selling War: The British Propaganda Campaign against American 'Neutrality' in World War II*, Oxford: Oxford University Press

Cyra, A. 2000. *Ochotnik do Auschwitz: Witold Pilecki 1901–1948*, Oświęcim: Chrześcijańskie Stowarzyszenie Rodzin Oświęcimskich

  2008. 'Józef Cyrankiewicz nie kolaborował z Gestapo', available at www.bankier.pl/forum/temat_jozef-cyrankiewicz-nie-kolaborowal-z-gestapo,5377047.html

Czech, D. 1992. *Kalendarz wydarzeń w KL Auschwitz*, Oświęcim: Wydawnictwo Państwowego Muzeum w Oświęcimiu-Brzezince

  2000. 'A calendar of the most important events in the history of the Auschwitz concentration camp', in W. Długoborski and F. Piper (eds.), *Auschwitz 1940–1945: Central Issues in the History of the Camp*, Volume 5 (translated by William Brand), Oświęcim: Auschwitz-Birkenau State Museum , 119–232

Dale Jones, P. 2004. 'British policy towards German crimes against German Jews', in D. Cesarani (ed.), *Holocaust: Critical Concepts in Historical Studies*, Volume 6, London: Routledge, 95–129

Davies, N. 2003. *Rising '44: The Battle for Warsaw*, London: Macmillan

Dilks, D. (ed.) 1971. *The Diaries of Sir Alexander Cadogan 1938–1945*, London: Cassell

Długoborski, W. and Piper, F. (eds.) 2000. *Auschwitz 1940–1945: Central Issues in the History of the Camp* (translated by William Brand), 5 volumes, Oświęcim: Auschwitz-Birkenau State Museum

Bibliography

Dobbs, A. et al. 1942. *German Atrocities in Poland and Czechoslovakia: Labour's Protest*, London: Liberty Publications

Engel, D. 1983. 'An early account of Polish Jewry under Nazi and Soviet occupation presented to the Polish Government-in-Exile, February 1940', *Jewish Social Studies*, 45, 1: 1–16

1987. *In the Shadow of Auschwitz*, Chapel Hill: University of North Carolina Press

1993. *Facing a Holocaust: The Polish Government-in-Exile and the Jews, 1943–1945*, Chapel Hill: University of North Carolina Press

2005 'Marek Jan Chodakiewicz, *After the Holocaust: Polish–Jewish Conflict in the Wake of World War II*', in C. Freeze, P. Hyman and A. Polonsky (eds.), *Polin: Studies in Polish Jewry*, 18, 424–29

Engelking, B. 2001. *Holocaust and Memory: The Experience of the Holocaust and Its Consequences: An Investigation Based on Personal Narratives*, London: Leicester University Press in association with the European Jewish Publication Society

2011. *Jest taki piękny słoneczny dzień: Losy Żydów szukających ratunku na wsi polskiej 1942–1945*, Warsaw: Stowarzyszenie Centrum Badań nad Zagładą Żydów

Engelking, B. and Grabowski, J. (eds.) 2011. *Zarys krajobrazu. Wieś Polska wobec zagłady Żydów 1942–1945*, Warsaw: Stowarzyszenie Centrum Badań nad Zagładą Żydów

Engels, F. 1993. *The Condition of the Working Class in England*, Oxford: Oxford University Press

Executive Office of the US War Refugee Board 1944. *German Extermination Camps: Auschwitz and Birkenau*, Washington, DC

Fein, H. 1979. *Accounting for Genocide: National Responses and Jewish Victimisation during the Holocaust*, London: Macmillan

Foot, M.R.D. 1999. *SOE: An Outline History of the Special Operations Executive 1940–1946*, London: Pimlico

2003. *Six Faces of Courage: Secret Agents against Nazi Tyranny*, Barnsley: Leo Cooper

Fox, J.P. 1977. 'The Jewish factor in British war crimes policy in 1942', *English Historical Review*, 92, 362: 82–106

Frazik, W. 1998. 'Wojenne losy Napoleona Segiedy, kuriera rządu RP do kraju', *Studia Historyczne*, 41, 3: 405–15

Friszke, A. 2011. *Adam Ciołkosz: Portret polskiego socjalisty*, Warsaw: Wydawnictwo Krytyki Politycznej

Friszke, A., and Kunert, A.K. (eds.) 2002. *"Żegota" Rada Pomocy Żydom 1942–1945*, Warsaw: Rytm

Frojimovics, K. 2011. 'The special characteristics of the Holocaust in Hungary', in J.C. Friedman (ed.), *The Routledge History of the Holocaust*, London: Routledge, 248–63

Fulbrook, M. 2011. *Dissonant Lives: Generations and Violence through the German Dictatorships*, Oxford: Oxford University Press

2012. *A Small Town Near Auschwitz: Ordinary Nazis and the Holocaust*, Oxford: Oxford University Press

386   Bibliography

Garlinski, J. 1969. *Poland, SOE and the Allies*, London: Allen and Unwin
    1994. *Fighting Auschwitz: The Resistance Movement in the Concentration Camp*,
        London: Orbis Books
Garliński, J. 2012. 'Historical horizon', in W. Pilecki, *The Auschwitz Volunteer:
    Beyond Bravery* (translated by Jarek Garliński), Los Angeles: Aquila
    Polonica, xxxv–liv
Gąsowski, T. 2002. *Pod Sztandarami Orła Białego: Kwestia żydowska w Polskich
    Siłach Zbrojnych w Czasie II Wojny Światowej*, Kraków: Księgarnia
    Akademicka
Gilbert, M. 1993. 'Churchill and the Holocaust: the possible and impossible',
    ICS 25th Anniversary International Conference, US Holocaust Memorial
    Museum, Washington, available at www.winstonchurchill.org/support/
    the-churchill-centre/publications/churchill-proceedings/596-churchill-and-
    the-holocaust-the-possible-and-impossible
    1994. 'What was known and when', in M Berenbaum and Y. Gutman (eds.),
        Anatomy of the Auschwitz Death Camp, Washington, DC: United States
        Holocaust Memorial Museum, 539–52
    2001a. *Auschwitz and the Allies*, London: Pimlico (first published London:
        Michael Joseph Ltd and George Rainbird Ltd, 1981)
    2001b. 'Holocaust writing and research since 1945', Joseph and Rebecca
        Meyerhoff Annual Lecture, 26 September 2000, Washington, DC, United
        States Holocaust Museum, available at www.ushmm.org/research/center/
        publications/occasional/2001–04/paper.pdf
Gmitruk, J. 2007. *Rola Dziejowa Stanisława Mikołajczyka*, Warsaw: Muzeum
    Historii Polskiego Ruchu Ludowego
Gmitruk, J., Hemmerling, Z. and Sałkowski, J. (eds.) 1996. *Z ziemi sowieckiej – z
    domu niewoli: Relacje, raporty, sprawozdania z londyńskiego archiwum prof.
    Stanisława Kota*, Warsaw: Muzeum Historii Polskiego Ruchu Ludowego
Gmitruk, J. and Mazurek, J. (eds.) 1999. *Działalność władz okupacyjnych na
    terytorium Rzeczypospolitej w okresie 1 IX 1939–1 XI 1940: Raport z archiwum
    prof. Stanisława Kota*, Warsaw: Muzeum Historii Polskiego Ruchu
    Ludowego
Gorny, Y. 2012. *The Jewish Press and the Holocaust, 1939–1945: Palestine, Britain,
    the United States, and the Soviet Union*, Cambridge: Cambridge University
    Press
Grabowski, J. 2011. *Judenjagd: Polowanie na Żydów 1942–1945. Studium dziejów
    pewnego powiatu*, Warsaw: Stowarzyszenie Centrum Badań nad Zagładą
    Żydów
Grabowski, W. 2005. *Polska Agencja Telegraficzna 1918–1991*, Warsaw: Polska
    Agencja Prasowa
Grimwood, I.R. 2006. *A Little Chit of a Fellow: A Biography of the Right Hon. Leslie
    Hore-Belisha*, Lewes: Book Guild Publishing
Gutman, Y. 1994. 'Auschwitz: an overview', in Y. Gutman and M. Berenbaum
    (eds.), *Anatomy of the Auschwitz Death Camp*, Bloomington: Indiana
    University Press, 5–33
Gutman, Y. and Berenbaum, M. (eds.) 1994. *Anatomy of the Auschwitz Death
    Camp*, Bloomington: Indiana University Press

Bibliography 387

Harris, J.D. 2004. 'Broadcasting the massacres: an analysis of the BBC's contemporary coverage of the Holocaust', in D. Cesarani (ed.), *Holocaust: Critical Concepts in Historical Studies*, Volume 5, London: Routledge, 298–323

Haszka, A. 2006. *Jestem Żydem, chcę wejść: Hotel Polski w Warszawie, 1943*, Warsaw: Centrum Badań nad Zagładą Żydów/Wydawnictwo IFiS PAN

Herbert, E.S. and des Graz, C.G. 1952. *History of the Postal and Telegraph Censorship Department, 1938–1946*, Volume 1, London: Home Office

Hilberg, R. 1985. *The Destruction of the European Jews*, New York: Holmes and Meier

Hinsley, F.H. and Simkins, C. 1990. *British Intelligence in the Second World War*, Volume 4, London: HMSO

Hirszowicz, L. 1973. 'The Soviet Union and the Jews during World War II: British Foreign Office documents', *Soviet Jewish Affairs*, 3, 1: 104–6

Hoess, R. 2001. *Commandant of Auschwitz: The Autobiography of Rudolf Hoess* (translated by Constantine FitzGibbon), London: Phoenix Press

Hoover, H. and Gibson, H. 1942. *The Problems of Lasting Peace*, New York: Doubleday, Doran and Company

Höss, R., Broad, P. and Kremer, J.P. 1998. *KL Auschwitz Seen by the SS*, Oświęcim: The Auschwitz-Birkenau State Museum

Howarth, P. 1980. *Undercover: The Men and Women of the Special Operations Executive*, London: Routledge

Huener, J. 2003. *Auschwitz, Poland, and the Politics of Commemoration, 1945–1979*, Athens: Ohio University Press

Iwaszko, T. 1963. 'Ucieczki Więźniów z obozu koncentracyjnego Oświęcim', *Zeszyty Oświęcimskie*, 7: 3–54

Jankowski, S.M. 2009. *Karski: Raporty Tajnego Emisariusza*, Poznań: Rebis

Jasiewicz, K. 2002. *Pierwsi po diable. Elity sowieckie w okupowanej Polsce 1939–1941*, Warsaw: Oficyna Wydawnicza Rytm

Jenkinson, J. 2008. *Black 1919: Riots, Racism and Resistance in Imperial Britain*, Liverpool: Liverpool University Press

Kalb, M. 2003. 'Introduction: journalism and the Holocaust 1939–45', in R.M. Shapiro (ed.), *Why Didn't the Press Shout? American and International Journalism during the Holocaust*, Jersey City: Yeshiva University and KTAV, 1–13

Kania, D. 2007. Józef Cyrankiewicz kolaborował z Gestapo?, *Wprost*, 26 December 2007, available at www.wprost.pl/ar/120380/Jozef-Cyrankiewicz-kolaborowal-z-Gestapo

Karny, M. 1993. 'Obóz familijny w Brzezince (BIIb) dla Żydów z getta Theresienstadt', *Zeszyty Oświęcimskie*, 20: 123–215

1994. 'The Vrba and Wetzler report', in Y. Gutman and M. Berenbaum (eds.), *Anatomy of the Auschwitz Death Camp*, Bloomington: Indiana University Press, 553–68

Karski, J. 1986. *Tajna dyplomacja Churchilla i Roosevelta w sprawie Polski 1940–1945*, London and Lublin: Uniwersytet Marii Curie-Skłodowskiej (talk given at POSK, 17 July 1986)

2012. *Story of a Secret State*, London: Penguin

388   Bibliography

Kersten, K. 1991. *The Establishment of Communist Rule in Poland 1943–1948*, Berkeley: University of California Press
Kirkpatrick, I. 1959. *The Inner Circle*, London: Macmillan
Klemperer, V. 1998. *I Shall Bear Witness: The Diaries of Victor Klemperer 1933–41*, London: Weidenfeld and Nicolson
  1999. *To the Bitter End: The Diaries of Victor Klemperer 1942–45*, London: Weidenfeld and Nicolson
Kłodziński, S. 1990. 'Józef Cyrankiewicz w obozie oświęcimskim', *Przegląd Lekarski*, 47, 1: 107–12
Knightley, P. 2001. 'World War II', in D. Jones (ed.), *Censorship: A World Encyclopedia*, London: Routledge, 2650–2
Kochanski, H. 2012. *The Eagle Unbowed: Poland and the Poles in the Second World War*, London: Allen Lane
Kochonowicz, T. 1975. *Na Wojennej Emigracji: Wspomnienia z lat 1942–1944*, Warsaw: Książka i Wiedza
Kołakowski, L. 1974. 'My correct views on everything: a rejoinder to Edward Thompson's "Open letter to Leszek Kołakowski"', *Socialist Register*, 11, available at http://socialistregister.com/index.php/srv/article/view/5323
Korboński, S. 1968. *Fighting Warsaw: The Story of the Polish Underground State, 1939–1945*, New York: Funk and Wagnalls
  1978. *The Polish Underground State: A Guide to the Underground*, New York: Hippocrene
  1984. *Z dziejów łączności radiotelegraficznej Warszawa-Londyn w latach 1939–1945*, Kraków: Promieniści
  1991. *W imieniu Rzeczypospolitej*, Warsaw: Bellona
Kubica, H. 2006. *The Extermination at KL Auschwitz of Poles Evicted from the Zamość Region in the Years 1942–1943*, Oświęcim: Auschwitz-Birkenau State Museum
Kulka, O.D. 2013. *Landscapes of the Metropolis of Death: Reflections on Memory and Imagination* (translated by Ralph Mandel), London: Allen Lane
Kurcyusz, A.N. 1944. *Polska pod okupacją niemiecką*, 5, 5 (15 March 1944), Istanbul: Polish Consulate
Kushner, T. 1994. *The Holocaust and the Liberal Imagination: A Social and Cultural History*, Oxford: Wiley-Blackwell
  1997. 'The meaning of Auschwitz: Anglo-American responses to the Hungarian Jewish tragedy', in D. Cesarani (ed.), *Genocide and Rescue: The Holocaust in Hungary 1944*, Oxford: Berg, 159–78
  2004. 'Britain, the United States and the Holocaust: in search of a historiography', in D. Stone (ed.), *The Historiography of the Holocaust*, London: Palgrave Macmillan, 253–75
  2005. 'The bystanders: towards a more sophisticated historiography', in D. Bloxham and J. Kushner, *The Holocaust: Critical Historical Approaches*, Manchester: Manchester University Press, 176–211
  2013. 'Britain, America and the Holocaust: past, present and future historiographies', in J. Láníček and J. Jordan (eds.), *Governments in Exile and the Jews during World War II*, London: Vallentine Mitchell & Co., 33–46

Bibliography

Kuus, M. 2004. 'Europe's eastern expansion and the reinscription of otherness in East-Central Europe', *Progress in Human Geography*, 28, 4: 472–89

Langbein, H. 1994. 'The Auschwitz Underground', in Y. Gutman and M. Berenbaum (eds.), *Anatomy of the Auschwitz Death Camp*, Bloomington: Indiana University Press, 485–502

1994. *Ludzie w Auschwitz*, Oświęcim: Wydanictwo Państwowego Muzeum Oświęcim-Brzezinka

Láníček, J. 2010. 'The Czechoslovak Service of the BBC and the Jews during World War II', *Yad Vashem Studies*, 38: 123–53

2012. 'Czechoslovakia and the Allied declaration of 17 December 1942', unpublished paper delivered at The End of 1942: A Turning Point in World War II and in the Comprehension of the Final Solution? conference, Yad Vashem, Jerusalem, 17 December 2012

2013. *Czechs, Slovaks and the Jews, 1938–1948: Beyond Idealisation and Condemnation*, Basingstoke: Palgrave

Láníček, J. and Jordan, J. (eds.) 2013. *Governments in Exile and the Jews during World War II*, London: Vallentine Mitchell & Co.

Laqueur, W. 1980. 'Hitler's Holocaust: Who Knew What? When? And How?', *Encounter*, July 1980: 6–25

1998. *The Terrible Secret: The Suppression of the Final Truth about Hitler's 'Final Solution'*, New York: Henry Holt (first published 1980)

Laskowski, J. 1966. 'Radiostacja "Świt"', *Zeszyty Historyczne*, 9: 101–30 and 10: 203–23

Leff, L. 2003. 'When the facts didn't speak for themselves: the Holocaust in the New York Times, 1939–1945', in R.M. Shapiro (ed.), *Why Didn't the Press Shout? American and International Journalism during the Holocaust*, Jersey City: Yeshiva University and KTAV, 31–78

2005. *Buried by the Times: The Holocaust and America's most Important Newspaper*, Cambridge: Cambridge University Press

Lerski, J. 1986. 'Socjaliści polscy do brytyjskich', *Zeszyty Historyczne (Paris)*, 75: 122–39

1988. *Poland's Secret Envoy: George 'Jur' Lerski*, New York: Bicentennial Publishing Corp

1989. *Emisariusz Jur*, Warsaw: Interim

Levy, R.H. 1996. 'The bombing of Auschwitz: a critical analysis', *Holocaust and Genocide Studies*, 10, 3: 267–96

Lewandowska, S. 1993. *Prasa polskiej emigracji wojennej 1939–1945*, Warsaw: IHPAN

Lewandowski, J. 2001. 'A fish breaks through the net: Sven Norrman and the Holocaust', in A. Polonsky (ed.), *Polin: Studies in Polish Jewry*, 14: 295–305

Libionka, D. and Weinbaum, L. 2006. 'Deconstructing memory and history: the Jewish Military Union (ŻZW) and the Warsaw ghetto uprising', *Jewish Political Studies Review*, 18, 1–2, 1–14

Linn, R. 2003. 'Genocide and the politics of remembering: the nameless, the celebrated, and the would-be Holocaust heroes', *Journal of Genocide Research*, 5, 4: 565–86

390 Bibliography

2004. *Escaping Auschwitz: Culture of Forgetting*, New York: Cornell University Press

Lipstadt, D. 1983. 'Witness to the persecution: the Allies and the Holocaust', *Modern Judaism*, 3: 323–9

1986. *Beyond Belief: The American Press and the Coming of the Holocaust 1933–1945*, New York: The Free Press

Lochery, N. 2011. *Lisbon: War in the Shadow of the City of Light, 1939–45*, New York: Public Affairs

London, L. 2000. *Whitehall and the Jews, 1933–1948: British Immigration Policy, Jewish Refugees and the Holocaust*, Cambridge: Cambridge University Press

Lysaght, C.E. 1979. *Brendan Bracken*, London: Allen Lane

McLaine, I. 1979. *Ministry of Morale: Home Front Morale and the Ministry of Information in World War II*, London: Allen and Unwin

Mahoney, K.A. 2011. 'An American operational response to a request to bomb rail lines to Auschwitz', *Holocaust and Genocide Studies*, 25, 3: 438–46

Maresch, E. 2004. 'The Secret Army (AK) intelligence operations during the Second World War', available at http://spp-pumst.org/articles_by_pumst/ 004_Symp_Post_Maresh.pdf

Marrus, M. 2013. 'International witnesses to the Holocaust in historical perspective', unpublished paper given at the Being Witness to the Holocaust: 70th Anniversary of the Warsaw Ghetto Uprising international conference, Warsaw: IPN, 22 April 2013

Mazur, G. 1987. *Biuro Informacji i Propagandy SZP-ZWZ-AK 1939–1945*, Warsaw: Pax

Medoff, R. 2011. 'Golda Meir and the Campaign for an Allied Bombing of Auschwitz', the David S. Wyman Institute for Holocaust Studies, available at www.wymaninstitute.org/special-reports/GoldaReport.pdf

Medoff, R. and Zucker, B.-A. 2012. 'America's failure to bomb Auschwitz: a new consensus among historians', the David S. Wyman Institute for Holocaust Studies, available at wymaninstitute.org/special-reports/ WymanAuschwitzReport2012.pdf

Michlic, J. 2006. *Poland's Threatening Other: The Image of the Jew from 1880 to the Present*, Lincoln: University of Nebraska Press

2007. 'The Soviet occupation of Poland 1939–1941, and the stereotype of the anti-Polish and pro-Soviet Jew', *Jewish Social Studies: History, Culture, Society*, 13, 3: 135–76

Milland, G. 1998a. 'The BBC Hungarian Service and the Final Solution in Hungary', *Historical Journal of Film, Radio and Television*, 18, 3: 353–73

1998b. 'Some faint hope and courage: the BBC and the Final Solution, 1942–1945', unpublished PhD thesis, University of Leicester

2001. 'The Holocaust as it occurred: censorship in Britain, the US, the USSR, Sweden, Germany, and Nazi-occupied Europe', in D. Jones (ed.), *Censorship: A World Encyclopedia*, London: Routledge

Milne, M. 1995. 'The Holocaust: why auntie stayed mum', *The Independent*, 9 May 1995, available at www.independent.co.uk/news...why-auntie-stayed-mum-1618801.html

Bibliography 391

Minney, R.J. 1991. *The Private Papers of Hore-Belisha*, London: Gregg Revivals/ Department of War Studies, King's College London

Modood, T. 2007. 'Multiculturalism: not a minority problem', *The Guardian*, 7 February 2007, available at www.guardian.co.uk/commentisfree/2011/feb/ 07/multiculturalism-not-minority-problem

Morley, J.F. 2004. 'Pius XII, Roman Catholic policy, and the Holocaust in Hungary: an analysis of *Le Saint Siège et les victimes de la guerre, janvier 1944–juillet 1945*', in C. Rittner and J.K. Roth (eds.), *Pope Pius XII and the Holocaust*, London: Continuum, 154–74

Mosley, O. 1936. *Fascism: 100 Questions Asked and Answered*, London: British Union of Fascists

Newsome, N. 1945. *The 'Man in the Street' (of the BBC) Talks to Europe*, Westminster: P.S. King and Staples

Novick, P. 1999. *The Holocaust in American Life*, New York: Houghton Mifflin Company

Nowak, J. 1982. *Courier from Warsaw*, Detroit: Wayne State University

Paulsson, G.S. 2002. *Secret City: The Hidden Jews of Warsaw, 1940–1945*, New Haven and London: Yale University Press

Pawlikowski, J.T. 2004. 'The papacy of Pius XII: the known and unknown', in C. Rittner and J.K. Roth (eds.), *Pope Pius XII and the Holocaust*, London: Continuum, 56–69

Pawłowicz, J. 2008. *Rotmistrz Witold Pilecki 1901–1948*, Warsaw: IPN

Penkower, N.M. 1983. *The Jews Were Expendable: Free World Diplomacy and the Holocaust*, Detroit: Wayne State University Press

2002. *Decision on Palestine Deferred: America, Britain and Wartime Diplomacy, 1939–1945*, London: Routledge

Peszke, M.A. 2005. *The Polish Underground Army, the Western Allies, and the Failure of Strategic Unity in World War II*, Jefferson: McFarland

Pickhan, G. 1997. '"That Incredible History of the Polish Bund Written in a Soviet Prison": the NKVD files on Henryk Erlich and Wiktor Alter', in G.H. Hundert (ed.), *Polin: Studies in Polish Jewry*, 10: 247–72

Pilecki, W. 2012. *The Auschwitz Volunteer: Beyond Bravery* (translated by Jarek Garliński), Los Angeles: Aquila Polonica

Piper, F. 1992. *Ilu ludzi zginęło w KL Auschwitz: Liczba ofiar w świetle źródeł i badań 1945–1990*, Oświęcim: Wydawnictwo Państwowego Muzeum w Oświęcimiu

1994a. 'The number of victims', in Y. Gutman and M. Berenbaum (eds.), *Anatomy of the Auschwitz Death Camp*, Bloomington: Indiana University Press, 61–80

1994b. 'The system of prisoner exploitation', in Y. Gutman and M. Berenbaum (eds.), *Anatomy of the Auschwitz Death Camp*, Bloomington: Indiana University Press, 34–49

2000. 'The origins of the camp', in W. Długoborski and F. Piper (eds.), *Auschwitz 1940–1945: Central Issues in the History of the Camp* (translated by William Brand), Volume 1, Oświęcim: Auschwitz-Birkenau State Museum, 39–62

2002. *Auschwitz Prisoner Labor: The Organization and Exploitation of Auschwitz Concentration Camp Prisoners*, Oświęcim: Auschwitz-Birkenau State Museum

392 Bibliography

2006. 'The Nazi policy to Germanize Polish lands in the years 1939–1945', in H. Kubica, *The Extermination at KL Auschwitz of Poles Evicted from the Zamość Region in the Years 1942–1943*, Oświęcim: Auschwitz-Birkenau State Museum, 7–12

Piper, F. and Strzelecka, I. 2009. *Księga Pamięci: Transporty Polaków do KL Auschwitz z Lublina i innych miejscowości lubelszczyzny 1940–1944*, Oświęcim: Państwowe Muzeum Auschwitz-Birkenau

Piper, F. and Świebocka, T. (eds.) 1996. *Auschwitz: Nazi Death Camp*, Oświęcim: Auschwitz-Birkenau State Museum

Polonsky, A. 2004. 'Beyond condemnation, apologetics and apologies: on the complexity of Polish behaviour towards the Jews during the Second World War', in D. Cesarani (ed.), *Holocaust: Critical Concepts in Historical Studies*, Volume 2, London: Routledge, 29–72

2013. 'Introduction', in J. Láníček and J. Jordan (eds.), *Governments in Exile and the Jews during World War II*, London: Vallentine Mitchell & Co., 1–32

Polonsky, A. and Davies, N. (eds.) 1991. *Jews in Eastern Europe and the USSR, 1939–1946*, New York: St Martin's Press

Porat, D. 1990. *The Blue and Yellow Star of David: The Zionist Leadership in Palestine and the Holocaust, 1939–45*, Cambridge: Cambridge University Press

Puławski, A. 2007. 'Nie ujawniać czynnikom nieoficjalnym: Depesze AK o Zagładzie', *Więź*, July 2007: 69–80

2009. *W obliczu Zagłady. Rząd RP na Uchodźstwie, Delegatura Rządu RP na Kraj, ZWZ-AK wobec deportacji Żydów do obozów zagłady (1941–1942)*, Lublin: Instytut Pamięci Narodowej

2013. 'The Polish Government-in-exile in London, the Delegatura, the Union of Armed Struggle–Home Army and the extermination of the Jews', in J. Láníček and J. Jordan (eds.), *Governments in Exile and the Jews during World War II*, London: Vallentine Mitchell & Co., 111–34

Raczyński, E. 1962. *In Allied London*, London: Weidenfeld and Nicolson

1997. *W sojuszniczym Londynie. Dziennik Ambasadora Edwarda Raczyńskiego 1939–1945*, London: Polska Fundacja Kulturalna

Raffelsperger, F. 1845. *Allgemeines Geographisch-Statistisches Lexikon aller Österreichischen Staaten*, Vienna: K.K.A.P

Rees, L. 2005. *Auschwitz, the Nazis and the Final Solution*, London: BBC Books

Rejak, S. and Frister, E. 2012. *Inferno of Choices: Poles and the Holocaust*, Warsaw: Rytm

Retinger, J. 1941. *All about Poland*, London: Minerva

Reynolds, D. 2004. *In Command of History: Churchill Fighting and Writing the Second World War*, London: Allen Lane

Riegner, G.M. 2001. 'The Riegner Telegram', in J.T. Baumel and W. Laqueur (eds.), *The Holocaust Encyclopedia*, New Haven: Yale University Press, 562–7

Rogers, B. 1999a. 'Auschwitz and the British', *History Today*, 49, 10 (October): 9–10

1999b. 'British intelligence and the Holocaust: Auschwitz and the Allies re-examined', *Journal of Holocaust Education*, 8, 1: 89–106

Bibliography

Rogers, J.G., and Troy, T.F. 1987. *Wartime Washington: The Secret OSS Journal of James Grafton Rogers 1942–1943*, Frederick: University Publications of America

Rojek, W., Suchcitz, A. and Zgórniak, M. (eds.) 1994–2008. *Protokoły Posiedzeń Rady Ministrów Rzeczypospolitej Polskiej*, 8 volumes, Kraków: Secesja

Rozett, R. 1998. 'International intervention: the role of diplomats in attempts to rescue Jews in Hungary', in R. Braham and S. Miller (eds.), *The Nazis' Last Victims: The Holocaust in Hungary*, Detroit: Wayne State University Press, 137–52

Rubinstein, W. 1997. *The Myth of Rescue: Why the Democracies Could Not Have Saved More Jews from the Nazis*, London: Routledge

2010. 'Antisemitism in the English-Speaking World', in A.S. Lindemann and R.S. Levy (eds.), *Antisemitism: A History*, Oxford: Oxford University Press, 150–65

Rutkowski, T.P. 2012. *Stanisław Kot 1885–1975: Między nauką a polityką*, Warsaw: Muzeum Historii Polskiego Ruchu Ludowego

Sanford, G. 2005. *Katyn and the Soviet Massacre of 1940: Truth, Justice and Memory*, London: Routledge

Seaton, J. 1987. 'Reporting Atrocities: the BBC and the Holocaust', in J. Seaton and B. Pimlott (eds.), *The Media in British Politics*, Aldershot: Avebury, 154–82

Shapiro, R.M. (ed.) 2003. *Why Didn't the Press Shout? American and International Journalism during the Holocaust*, Jersey City: Yeshiva University and KTAV

Sharf, A. 1964. *The British Press and Jews under Nazi Rule*, Oxford: Oxford University Press

Shepherd, N. 1984. *A Refuge from the Darkness: Wilfrid Israel: German Jewry's Secret Ambassador*, London: Weidenfeld and Nicolson

Sherman, A.J. 1973. *Island Refuge: Britain and Refugees from the Third Reich 1933–1939*, London: Elek Books

Smith, M. 2004. 'Bletchley Park and the Holocaust', in L.V. Scott and P.D. Jackson (eds.), *Understanding Intelligence in the Twentieth Century: Journeys in Shadows*, London: Routledge, 111–21

Sompolinsky, M. 1999. *The British Government and the Holocaust: The Failure of Anglo-Jewish Leadership?*, Brighton: Sussex Academic Press

Stankowski, W. (ed.) 2010. *Wolni i zniewoleni. Rtm. Witold Pilecki i inni więźniowie KL Auschwitz wobec nowej rzeczywistości powojennej*, Oświęcim: Państwowa Wyższa Szkoła Zawodowa w Oświęcimiu

Stember, C.H. 1966. *Jews in the Mind of America*, New York: Basic Books

Stenton, M. 2000. *Radio London and Resistance in Occupied Europe: British Political Warfare 1939–1943*, Oxford: Oxford University Press

Stillman, S. 2007. 'Missing white girl syndrome: disappeared women and media activism', *Gender and Development*, 15, 3: 491–502

Stirling, T. 2005. 'Polish II Bureau documents passed to the British Government after 1945', in T. Stirling, D. Nałęcz and T. Dubicki (eds.), *Intelligence Co-operation between Poland and Great Britain during World War II*, Volume 1, *The Report of the Anglo-Polish Historical Committee*, London: Vallentine Mitchell, 11–12

394   Bibliography

Stirling, T., Nałęcz, D. and Dubicki, T. (eds.) 2005. *Intelligence Co-operation between Poland and Great Britain during World War II*, Volume 1, *The Report of the Anglo-Polish Historical Committee*, London: Vallentine Mitchell

Stola, D. 1995. *Nadzieja i Zagłada: Ignacy Schwarzbart – żydowski przedstawiciel w Radzie Narodowej RP (1940–1945)*, Warsaw: Biblioteka Polonijna

    1997. 'Early news of the Holocaust from Poland', *Holocaust and Genocide Studies*, 11: 1–27

    2013. 'The Polish Government-in-exile: national unity and weakness', in J. Láníček and J. Jordan (eds.), *Governments in Exile and the Jews during World War II*, London: Vallentine Mitchell & Co., 89–110

Strzelecka, I. and Setkiewicz, P. 2000. 'The construction, expansion and development of the camp and its branches', in W. Długoborski and F. Piper (eds.), *Auschwitz 1940–1945: Central Issues in the History of the Camp* (translated by William Brand), Volume 1, Oświęcim: Auschwitz-Birkenau State Museum, 63–138

Strzelecki, A. 2000. 'The liquidation of the camp', in W. Długoborski and F. Piper (eds.), *Auschwitz 1940–1945: Central Issues in the History of the Camp* (translated by William Brand), Oświęcim: Auschwitz-Birkenau State Museum, Volume 5, 9–76

Suchcitz, A., and Ciechanowski, J. 2005. 'The history of the Polish Intelligence Archives after 1945', in T. Stirling, D. Nałęcz and T. Dubicki (eds.), *Intelligence Co-operation between Poland and Great Britain during World War II*, Volume 1, *The Report of the Anglo-Polish Historical Committee*, London: Vallentine Mitchell, 13–28

Sweeney, M.S. 2001. *Secrets of Victory: The Office of Censorship*, Chapel Hill: University of North Carolina Press

Świebocki, H. 1996. 'Escapes from the camp', in F. Piper and T. Świebocka (eds.), *Auschwitz: Nazi Death Camp*, Oświęcim: Auschwitz-Birkenau State Museum, 235–48

    1997. *London Has Been Informed . . . Reports by Auschwitz Escapees*, Oświęcim: Auschwitz-Birkenau State Museum

    2000. 'The resistance movement', in W. Długoborski and F. Piper (eds.), *Auschwitz 1940–1945: Central Issues in the History of the Camp* (translated by William Brand), Volume 4, Oświęcim: Auschwitz-Birkenau State Museum

Tangye, D. 1990. *The Evening Gull*, London: Michael Joseph

Taylor, A.J.P. 1972. *Beaverbrook*, London: Hamish Hamilton

Taylor, P.M. 1999. *British Propaganda in the Twentieth Century: Selling Democracy*, Edinburgh: Edinburgh Press

Thompson, E.P. 1973. 'An open letter to Leszek Kołakowski', *Socialist Register*, 10, available at http://socialistregister.com/node/15

Thomson, G.P. 1947. *Blue Pencil Admiral: The Inside Story of Press Censorship*, London: Sampson Low, Marston and Company

Thomson, M. 2012. 'The BBC and the Hungarian Holocaust', *Document*, BBC Radio 4 (first broadcast on 12 November 2012), available at www.bbc.co.uk/programmes/b01nt3yd, last accessed 11 January 2013

Üngör, U. 2011. *The Making of Modern Turkey: Nation and State in Eastern Anatolia, 1913–1950*, Oxford: Oxford University Press

Bibliography

United States Department of State 1943. *Foreign Relations of the United States: Conferences at Washington and Quebec, 1943*, Washington, DC: US Government Printing Office, available at http://digital.library.wisc.edu/1711. dl/FRUS.FRUS1943

Van Pelt, R.J. 2002. *The Case for Auschwitz: Evidence from the Irving Trial*, Bloomington: Indiana University Press

Walker, J. 2010. *Poland Alone: Britain, SOE and the Collapse of the Polish Resistance, 1944*, Stroud: The History Press

Wasserstein, B. 1999. *Britain and the Jews of Europe*, Leicester: Leicester University Press

Ważniewski, W. and Marczewska, K. 1968. 'W świetle akt delegatury rządu RP na Kraj', in *Zeszyty Oświęcimskie Numer specjalny (I)*, Oświęcim: Wydawnictwo Państwowego Muzeum w Oświęcimiu, v–xvi

Weber, R. 2011. *The Lisbon Route: Entry and Escape in Nazi Europe*, Plymouth: Ivan R Dee

Westermann, E. 2004. 'The Royal Air Force and the bombing of Auschwitz: first deliberations, January 1941', in D. Cesarani (ed.), *Holocaust: Critical Concepts in Historical Studies*, London: Routledge, 195–211.

Wierzyński, M. and Karski, J. 2012. *Emisariusz własnymi słowami. Zapis rozmów przeprowadzonych w latach 1995–1997 w Waszyngtonie emitowanych w Głosie Ameryki*, Warsaw: PWN

Wilkinson, R. 1997. 'Hore-Belisha: Britain's Dreyfus?', *History Today*, 47, 12: 17–23

Winker, A. 1978. *The Politics of Propaganda: The Office of War Information 1942–1945*, New Haven: Yale University Press

Wood, E.T. and Jankowski, S.M. 1994. *Karski: How One Man Tried to Stop the Holocaust*, New York: John Wiley and Sons

Wróbel, P. 2003. '*Dziennik Polski*: the official daily organ of the Polish Government-in-Exile, and the Holocaust, 1940–1945', in R.M. Shapiro (ed.), *Why Didn't the Press Shout? American and International Journalism during the Holocaust*, Jersey City: Yeshiva University and KTAV, 507–34

Wyman, D. 1994. 'Why Auschwitz wasn't bombed', in Y. Gutman and M. Berenbaum (eds.), *Anatomy of the Auschwitz Death Camp*, Bloomington: Indiana University Press, 569–87

    2007. *The Abandonment of the Jews: America and the Holocaust, 1941–1945*, New York: New Press

Wysocki, J. 2005. 'Wprowadzenie do wydania polskiego', in K. Piekarski, *Umykając piekłu: Wspomnienia polskiego oficera z Auschwitz i Buchenwaldu*, Warsaw: Wydawnictwo Antyk, 7–21, available at http://zory.lpr.pl/download/wstep.pdf

Wysocki, W.J. 2009. *Rotmistrz Witold Pilecki 1901–1948*, Warsaw: Gryf

Young, K. (ed.) 1980. *The Diaries of Sir Robert Bruce Lockhart 1939–1965*, Volume 2, London: Macmillan

Zaleski, A. 1941. *The German Occupation of Poland: Extract of Note Addressed to the Governments of the Allied and Neutral Powers on May 3, 1941*, London: Polish Ministry of Foreign Affairs

Zarembina, N. 1942. *Obóz śmierci*, Warsaw: WRN

396 Bibliography

1943. *Obóz śmierci: zbiór relacji z obozu w Oświęcimiu opublikowanych w kraju przez ruch mas pracujących Polski*, London: Nowa Polska

1944a. *The Camp of death*, London: Liberty Press

1944b. *Oswiecim Camp of Death*, New York: Poland Fights

Zubrzycki, G. 2006. *The Crosses of Auschwitz: Nationalism and Religion in Post-Communist Poland*, Chicago: University of Chicago Press

Zygielbojm, A. and Wedgwood, J. 1942. *Stop Them Now!*, London, Liberty Press

Żbikowski, A. 2000. 'Jewish reaction to the Soviet arrival in the Kresy in September 1939', in A. Polonsky (ed.), *Polin: Studies in Polish Jewry*, 13: 62–72

2011. *Karski*, Warsaw: Świat Książki

Index

Adamson, Janet Laurel, 361
Alderman, Geoffrey, 35, 275
Allen, Frederick, 66, 321
Allen, Roger, 11, 69, 162, 172, 177, 186, 218, 261, 326
Allen, William Denis, 85, 119, 326
American Federation for Polish Jews, 190
American Jewish Committee, 159
American Jewish Congress, 87, 159
Anders, Władysław, 82, 88, 326–7, 338, 377
anti-alienism, 6, 42
anti-Semitism
  in Britain, 36, 38, 80, 104, 118, 195, 218, 260, 263, 274–5
  'causes', 6, 35
  in Czechoslovakia, 326
  elite, 42, 275–6
  in Poland, 85–6, 177, 195, 255, 278, 304
  amongst Poles, 6, 79, 153, 266–7, 270, 272
  in Polish Armed Forces, 80, 82, 221–8, 257, 269, 272
  in United States, 76, 107, 190, 263, 275
Apenszlak, Jacob, 171, 190, 193, 354, 359
archbishop of York, 118
Astor, Lord, 50
Attlee, Clement, 69, 123, 183, 360
Auschwitz
  aerial photography, 365, 374
  bombing, 14–15, 156, 235, 239, 248–53, 256
  broadcasts on the BBC, 173, 186, 244
  censorship issues, 67–8
  development of the camp, 16–21
  early news, 131–4
  elusiveness narrative, 1–5, 10, 256, 262, 305
  escapes, 134
  liberation, 23
  map of region, 219

memorandum passed to Foreign Office, 161
memorandum passed to US president, 159
message from Rowecki and Jankowski (4 March 1943), 169
Napoleon Segieda, 129, 134–5, 151, 165, 168, 175–7
New York Times report (November 1942), 158
news from Jan Karski, 141, 144, 148–56
Polish Cabinet (December 1942), 144
PWE acknowledge camp function (24 March 1944), 262
report of gassing of Jews reaches London, 130
report of the gassing of Jews reaches Warsaw, 135
report translated into English (November 1942), 145
reported in Australian press, 184, 209, 246
Schwarzbart's post intercepted, 11, 74, 177

B'Nai B'rith, 159
Babi Yar, 21
Baliński-Jundziłł, Jan, 56–7, 121
Banaczyk, Władysław, 170, 185, 187, 204, 253, 369, 375–6
Bara, Walter, 194
Barker, A.E., 317
Barlas, Chaim, 158, 350
Baron, Salo, 190
Bauer, Yehuda, 2, 12–14, 98, 231, 261, 263–4, 308, 313, 328, 368, 376
BBC
  broadcasts on Auschwitz, 173, 186, 244
  censors under FO control, 57
  European Service, 29, 54–8, 61, 63, 66, 92, 97, 99, 103, 113, 115–16, 173, 206, 216, 220, 224, 227, 236, 251, 261, 276

397

398　Index

BBC (cont.)
　Home Service, 14, 53, 56, 61, 63, 66,
　　100, 105, 113, 117, 121, 215, 224,
　　229, 239–40, 244, 246, 260
　policy on anti-Semitism, 45, 59, 317
　PWE influence, 54–7
Beauchamp, Brograve, 106
Beaverbrook, Lord, 31, 49–50, 81, 325
Belin, F.L., 204
Bełżec, 3, 5, 13, 19, 21–2, 66, 103–4,
　111–12, 133, 136, 139, 142, 146–8,
　152–3, 155, 161, 165, 167, 193, 195,
　219, 260, 264, 321, 335, 344, 359–60
Bendera, Eugeniusz, 26, 346
Beneš, Edvard, 244
Ben-Gurion, David, 256
Bergson, Peter (Hillel Kook), 328
Bermuda conference, 43, 62, 64–5, 117,
　247
Będzin, 3, 86, 184–5, 202–3, 265, 357
Biddle, Francis, 74
Bielecki, Tadeusz, 79–80, 346
Biessgen, Fritz, 17
Birkeland, Paul, 201
Birkenau. See also Auschwitz
　Bunker I, 19
　confusion over, 3
　construction, 18
　Czechoslovak State Council, 241
　Kopecky's telegram, 232
　'Paradisal', 133, 157
　record rate of murder, 187
　report from September 1942, 144
　report, summer 1943, 201
　reported in Jewish Chronicle (January
　　1944), 199
　reported on BBC (16 June 1944), 215
　Voght report, 241
　Witold Pilecki's reports, 132
　WRB publication (November 1944), 76
Birkett, Norman, 59
Birkland, Paul, 9
Bletchley Park, 4, 14, 67
Bloom, Sol, 190
Bloxham, Donald, 44
Board of Deputies of British Jews, 45, 96,
　109, 117–18, 227, 270, 315, 317, 334
Bolchover, Richard, 41–2, 45, 98, 109
Bór-Komorowski, Tadeusz, 184, 186,
　214–16, 238, 254, 341, 357, 366, 371
Boruta-Spiechowicz, Mieczysław, 368
Bourdieu, Pierre, 34
Bracken, Brendan, 50, 315, 318, 320, 325,
　331
　Allied press, 92, 124–5

Auschwitz, 234, 246
BBC services, 53
conference (9 July 1942), 13, 63, 102,
　133
friendship with Churchill, 49, 234
importance of BBC, 58
influence on BBC, 56, 61
loosening of censorship, 98
PWE, 53–5
relationship with the press, 49–51
Brand, Joel, 230, 236
Brandys, Zwi, 358
Brebner, Jock, 52, 260
Breitman, Richard, vi, 4, 9, 27, 74, 95, 169,
　178, 201, 205, 252, 261, 308–9, 337
Briggs, Asa, 54–8, 61
British Brothers League, 36
British Union of Fascists, 37–8, 317
Brodetsky, Selig, 45, 118, 315, 317, 327
Broszat, Martin, 16
Brotman, Adolph, 327
Browning, Christopher, 21
Brzezinka. See Birkenau
Bund report (1942), 26, 63, 97–102, 109,
　320, 329, 331
Bureau II, 25, 27–8, 172, 204, 341
Bureau VI, 25, 136, 140, 149, 172, 184,
　204, 218, 253, 258, 262, 304, 310,
　313, 335, 340–1, 344, 352–3, 376
Bush House, 54–6, 318
Butler, Richard Austen, 80

Cadogan, Alexander, 8, 11, 132, 187, 197,
　250, 275, 316
Camrose, Lord, 50
Cang, Joel, 29, 72, 271, 323, 326, 367, 372
Cavendish-Bentinck, Victor, 11, 68–70,
　197, 275, 350
Cazalet, Victor, 304, 332
Celler, Emanuel, 190
Cesarani, David, 35, 50–1, 62–3, 67, 317
Chamberlain, Neville, 316
Chciuk-Celt, Tadeusz, 344, 353, 355
Chełmno, 5, 19, 21, 97, 99, 104, 359
Cherwell, Lord, 49
Chimczak, Eugeniusz, 313
Churchill, Winston
　appeal from Polish Jews, 212–13, 235
　approval of PWE, 53
　attitude to bombing Auschwitz, 249, 251
　BBC broadcast (22 July 1942), 103
　early news of Auschwitz, 14
　friendship with Bracken, 49
　'kitchen cabinet', 49, 234, 305, 331
　letter to Sikorski (January 1943), 122

Index

399

letter to Stalin (May 1943), 126
news of Jews (1941), 67
probability of knowledge of Auschwitz, 235, 280
Quebec conference, 69
receives request to bomb death camps, 374
refusal to meet Nowak, 198
statement from Schwarzbart, 332
Zygielbojm's telegram, 115
Chybiński, Stanisław, 341
Ciechanowski, Jan, 13, 328, 349
Ciechanowski, Jan (Professor), 13, 27–8, 207, 322, 377
Ciołkosz, Adam, 267, 360, 377
City and East London Observer, 28, 71, 170, 259, 269, 323
Conway, John, 2, 233, 370
Coughlin, Charles, 75
Council for Rescue of the Jews in Poland, 245, 376
courier routes, 24, 355
Crossman, Richard, 101
Crozier, William Percival, 50, 318, 323
Cukierman, Icchak, 184–5, 188, 357
Cummings, Arthur, 370
Cyra, Adam, vi, 313, 341, 375
Cyrankiewicz, Józef, 15, 206, 213, 215–16, 228, 237–8, 242, 365
Czech, Danuta, 18–19, 23, 221
Czech Jews, 214–16, 231, 308, 361, 366, 369
Czechoslovak State Council, 241

Daily Express, 40, 46, 50
Daily Mail, 38, 50
Daily Mirror, 46, 50, 206, 210, 337
Daily Sketch, 50
Daily Telegraph, 28, 46, 50, 98–101, 111, 113, 116–17, 233, 242, 244, 325, 330–1
Daily Worker, 75, 81, 124–5, 222, 270
Dalton, Hugh, 53–4
Davids, Alice, 177
Davis, Elmer, 75
Defence Regulations, 48
de Grey, Nigel, 67
de Lichtervelde, Count Thierry, 182
Deutscher, Isaac, 200
Division of Reports, Washington, viii, 73, 178
Dobkin, Eliyha, 158, 188, 309, 350, 375, 377
Doboszyński, Adam, 80
Driberg, Tom, 224, 228

Dubois, Stanisław, 264, 345
Dulles, Allen, 231–2
Dziennik Polski, 7, 9, 28, 72, 79, 81, 101, 108, 111–12, 116, 126, 207, 212, 214–15, 229, 324–5, 331, 335, 349, 363, 365–6, 371

Easterman, Alexander, 29, 107–8, 110, 177, 220, 236, 332–3, 337, 354, 368, 370–1
Eckersley, Roger, 92, 329
Eckstein, Ze'ev, 231
Economist, The, 49
Eden, Anthony
  anti-Semitism in Polish Army, 224, 228
  attitude on bombing Auschwitz, 249–51
  committee on refugees, 62
  creation of PWE, 53
  intercept of Schwarzbart's post, 178
  issues warning (30 March 1944), 219
  knowledge of Auschwitz, 234
  meeting with Karski, 71
  meeting with Sikorski (January 1943), 90
  memorandum on press control, 52
  mention of Oświęcim, 183
  on the Polish government, 339
  Polish government memorandum (10 December 1942), 113
  Raczyński's letter (20 January 1943), 147, 163
  reluctance to make statement (March 1944), 208, 213
  significance of BBC broadcasts, 57
  statement to House of Commons (5 July 1944), 244
  UN declaration (17 December 1942), 115
  Warsaw ghetto (August 1941), 94
Eichmann, Adolf, 230–1, 340
Einsatzgruppen, 21–2
Einstein, Albert, 190
Éliás, József, 232
Emergency Committee to Save the Jewish People of Europe, 251
Emerson, Herbert, 275, 310
Engel, David, 4–5, 84–5, 92, 94–7, 109, 144–5, 155, 243, 251, 266, 272, 277, 309, 326–8, 330–1, 346–7, 349, 372, 379
Engelking, Barbara, 278–9, 326, 357
Estreicher, Karol, 79
Evening Standard, 50, 81, 325

Fein, Helen, 277–8
Feiner, Leon, 217, 238, 343, 356, 366, 369, 373, 380

400 Index

Foley, Frank, 317
Foot, Robert, 61
Foreign Office
  anti-Semitism in Polish Army, 80, 225
  attitude to Allied governments, 8
  Auschwitz, 5, 11, 144, 161, 166–7,
    181–2, 197, 214
  Bermuda conference, 117
  bombing Auschwitz, 249
  control of information, 13, 44, 49, 53, 57,
    68, 92, 114
  data on atrocities, 11, 172
  Foreign Research and Press Service, 84
  influence on BBC, 38, 59, 113, 121
  Katyń, 124
  'missing' documents, 12, 305
  narrating the war, 29, 38, 44, 55
  policy/attitude to Jews, 63–4, 66–7, 71,
    85, 88–9, 96–7, 260
  on Polish frontiers, 123
  PWE, 53–4
  reaction to news of atrocities, 139
  refugees, 114, 172, 182
  response to UN declaration (17
    December 1942), 62
  Riegner telegram, 106
Frank, Hans, 203
Frankfurter, Felix, 13, 154, 311
Fraser, Lindley, 60, 100, 319, 331
Front for the Rebirth of Poland, 153
Fulbrook, Mary, 3, 19, 21, 86, 184–5, 311,
  336, 357, 364

Gallacher, William, 81–2, 125, 339
Garliński, Józef, 131
Garrett, Walter, 232
Gawlina, Józef, 222
Generalplan Ost, 321
German Order Police, 14, 21, 67–8
ghettos, 20, 22, 158, 174–5, 177, 194, 211,
  335, 365
Gilbert, Martin, 1–4, 7, 9, 22, 158–9,
  184–6, 207–8, 211, 233, 249, 251,
  261, 265, 308, 326, 333–4, 356–7,
  361, 373, 375, 377
Głuchowski, Kazimierz, 327
Glücks, Richard, 16
Goldmann, Nahum, 108, 161, 256, 334
Gollancz, Victor, 66
Gordon, William Evans, 36–8, 41
Górka, Olgierd, 323
Grabowski, Jan, 278–9, 357
Greenberg, Ivan, 323
Gross, Jan, 278
Guardian, The, 33

Gubbins, Colin, 25
Gustav, king of Sweden, 175, 233, 237
Gutman, Yisrael, 16–18

Halifax, Lord, 54, 119, 316, 337
Hall, George, 220, 237
Harrison, Gregory Wedgwood, 162
Hartford Times, 76
Hashomer Hatzair, 188, 359
Herbst, Stanisław, 138, 343
Hertz, Joseph, 41, 108, 268, 280
Hilberg, Raul, 9, 20–2, 191, 201, 205, 311,
  336, 369, 374, 378
Himmler, Heinrich, 16–17, 111, 336, 350
Hinsley, Cardinal, 63, 101, 132
Hitler, Adolf, 1, 20, 64–5, 100, 102,
  115–17, 119, 160, 268, 331, 336
Hlond, August, 278
Hoare, Samuel, 42
Hoess, Rudolf, 16–17, 210
Höfle, Herman, 340
Home Army, 5, 17, 23–4, 26–7, 31, 134,
  136, 138–40, 168–9, 184, 186, 254–5,
  310, 312–13, 316, 341, 346, 357, 360,
  363
Home Intelligence Reports, 43, 333
Hore-Belisha, Leslie, 42, 316
Horthy, Miklós, 232–3, 237, 370
Hungarian Jews, 22, 65, 211, 215–17,
  219–20, 223, 230–1, 236–7, 239–46,
  337, 367–9, 371–4

Ickes, Harold, 190
Inter-Allied Information Centre, 327
Inter-Allied Information Committee, 175,
  188–9
Israel, Wilfrid, 317

Jaari, Meir, 188
Jabłoński, Karol, 254, 341
Jankowski, Jan Stanisław, 24, 168–73,
  176, 185, 203, 214–17, 238, 253,
  259, 335, 340–1, 353, 366, 369,
  371, 375
Jaster, Stanisław Gustaw, 26, 134, 346–7
Jestem Polakiem, 79, 81
Jewish Agency, 3, 30, 89, 108–10, 158, 177,
  185, 188, 203, 208, 231–2, 238, 249,
  256, 358, 371, 375
Jewish Chronicle, 9, 28, 42, 50–1, 63, 71–2,
  76, 111, 114, 116, 164, 167, 170, 172,
  174, 184, 189, 199–200, 206, 210,
  212, 220, 223, 229, 238, 240–1, 244,
  246, 259–60, 265, 305–6, 317, 323,
  326, 330, 339, 342, 351, 369

Index

401

Jewish Fighting Organization, ix, 184–5, 320, 357
Jewish Labour Committee, 159
Jewish Telegraphic Agency, viii, 30, 171, 174, 184–5, 187, 193, 209, 228, 239, 243, 310, 323, 335, 352–3, 357–8, 364, 369–73
Joint Intelligence Committee, viii, 11, 68, 140, 197, 275, 350

Kalb, Marvin, 1, 2
Karaszewicz-Tokarzewski, Michał, 23
Karcz, Jan, 132
Karski, Jan
  autumn 1942 material to Easterman, 110
  BBC reception, 58
  interrogated by MI19, 129, 148, 151
  journey across Europe 1942, 150
  knowledge of Auschwitz, 135, 141, 148, 152
  Koestler's broadcast, 66
  meeting with Eden, 71
  meeting with Frankfurter, 13
  meeting with Osborne, 155
  meeting with Roosevelt, 118
  meetings with journalists, 66
  Radio Świt, 155
  report, 1940, 85
  Selborne's advice, 66
  Warsaw ghetto, 21
Kasztner, Reszö, 231
Katyń, 123–4, 126, 175, 180, 269, 330, 337–9
Kawałkowski, Roland, 149–50
Kemsley, Lord, 50
Kennard, Howard, 57, 319
Kersten, Krystyna, 254
King, Cecil, 50
King, William Lyon MacKenzie, 321
King-Hall, Stephen, 53
Kirchwey, Freda, 190
Kirkpatrick, Ivone, 29, 31, 54–8, 99, 112, 122–3, 152, 174, 178, 206, 235, 250, 270, 319, 332, 337–8, 361, 378
Klausa, Udo, 86
Kłodziński, Stanisław, 253
Knight, John, 75
Knoll, Roman, 272, 304, 378–9
Kochanowicz, Tadeusz, 320
Koestler, Arthur, 66
Kopecky, Jaromir, 231
Koppelmann, Isidor, 105
Korboński, Stefan, 24, 93, 134, 148, 170, 173–4, 180, 184, 211, 235, 329, 352, 356, 358

Kosch, Israel, 358
Kossak-Szczucka, Zofia, 153–5
Kot, Stanisław, 30, 72, 86–7, 90, 94, 138, 207, 261, 272, 304, 312, 323, 326–7, 343
Kozłowski, Dawid, 184
Krasnansky, Oscar, 230
Kraszewska-Ancerewicz, Wanda, 357
Krausz, Miklos, 232
Król, Adam, 141
Kubowitzki, Aryeh Leon, 251, 255, 365, 367, 375
Kuh, Freddie, 66, 200
Kukiel, Marian, 204, 222, 224, 378
Kulmhof. *See* Chełmno
Kurcyusz, Jerzy (A.N. Kurcyusz), 207, 340, 363
Küsel, Otto, 17
Kushner, Tony, 5, 22, 35, 44, 247–8, 272, 275, 352, 373
Kwapiński, Jan, 183, 200

Labour Party, 103
LaGuardia, Fiorello, 190
Langenfeld, Major, 201
Langer, William, 204
Laqueur, Walter, 1–2, 9, 25, 61, 95, 106, 112, 146, 158–9, 306, 309, 329–30, 354, 361, 375
Laski, Neville, 315
Law, Richard, 106, 110, 225, 236, 250, 333, 337
League of Nations, 275, 309, 311
Leeper, Rex, 174
Leff, Laurel, vi, 13–14, 32, 46–7, 79, 210, 242, 248, 324, 365, 371, 376
Lempart, Józef, 26
Lerner, Szlama, 358
Lerski, Jerzy, 199, 332
Levenberg, Schneier, 101
Lias, Godfrey, 89, 96, 327
Liberty Press, 103, 195, 361
Libionka, Dariusz, 320
Lichtheim, Richard, 108, 232, 235, 249
Linn, Ruth, 2, 229–32, 369
Linton, Joseph, 256, 350
Lipstadt, Deborah, 14, 32, 76, 242, 248, 371, 376
Locker, Berl, 45, 177, 185, 256
Locker-Lampson, Oliver, 49
Lockhart, Robert Bruce, 31, 53–4, 98, 178, 317–18, 324, 332–3
London, Louise, 40
Los Angeles Times, 9, 209, 266
Low, David, 325

402   Index

Lublin, 56–7, 70, 99, 127, 194, 201, 203, 269, 319, 340, 392
Lubetkin, Cywia, 184, 188, 357
Ładoś, Aleksander, 150, 370
Łódź, 19–21, 357, 380

Macartney, Carlile Aylmer, 368
McClelland, Roswell, 232, 249
McCloy, John, 249, 251, 374
McLaren, Moray, 174, 361
Maconachie, Richard, 45, 59, 61, 64
Majdanek, 19, 21, 69, 104, 180, 183, 187, 197–8, 311, 342, 353, 359–60, 365, 374
Makins, Roger, 80, 88, 177
Malkin, William, 326
Manchester Guardian, 28–9, 46, 50–1, 72, 233, 240–3, 246, 318, 323, 372
Mander, Geoffrey, 125, 339
Manoliu, Florian, 232
Mantello, Georges, 232
Marczewska, Krystyna, 195, 202, 312, 352, 361, 395
Maresch, Eugenia, 27
Marrus, Michael, 275, 309
Martilotti, Mario, 233
Maurer, Gerhard, 19
Medoff, Rafael, 2, 256, 375
Michlic, Joanna, 78–9, 82, 84, 87, 92, 272, 311, 325–7, 380
Middleton, James, 101
Mikołajczyk, Stanisław
    Auschwitz, 143, 146, 156
    bomb Auschwitz, 156, 252
    conference (9 July 1942), 102
    distributes reports, 25
    impact of British censorship, 126
    on Jewish emigration, 84
    meeting with Osborne, 155, 322
    meeting with Savery, 142
    radio messages from Poland (autumn 1942), 142
    Radio Świt, 61, 174
    receipt of Karski's material, 149
    requests information, 108
    response to Bund report (1942), 97
    Schwarzbart's anger (diary entry), 265
    Schwarzbart's request, 118
    Zamość deportations, 70, 127, 269
Milland, Gabriel, 38, 45, 76–7, 97, 101, 114, 117, 244, 276, 321, 331–2, 337, 371
Miller, Irving, 107, 177, 332, 334
Milwaukee Journal, 217
Ministry of Information
    Allied governments, 92, 96

Allied press, 125
Board of Deputies, 45
Brendan Bracken, 49
censorship, 7, 13, 49–50, 52, 66, 73, 111, 261
conference (9 July 1942), 64, 102
co-operation with US agencies, 75
Home Intelligence Reports (anti-Semitism), 43
Maurice Perlzweig, 87
planning document (25 July 1941), 58, 259
policy towards Jews, 47, 274
PWE, 53
Mitkiewicz, Leon, 375
Modelski, Izydor, 6, 95
Modlibowska, Wanda, 361
Modood, Tariq, 34
Monowitz (Monowice), 18, 31, 251, 253, 365, 374. *See* Auschwitz
Montefiore, Leonard Goldsmid, 315
Moore, Jo, 314
Mordowicz, Czesław, 2, 230, 233, 242
Morgenthau, Henry, 242, 374
Morrison, Herbert, 44, 48, 52, 62, 73, 124, 317, 325
Morton, Desmond, 49, 198, 234–5, 329
Mosley, Oswald, 37

Nasza Trybuna, 29–30, 171, 185, 334, 350, 359
Neumann, Oskar, 230
New York Herald Tribune, 209
New York Times, 9, 28, 32, 45–7, 75–6, 79, 109, 157, 159–61, 192, 194, 207, 210, 217, 239–42, 247, 258, 301, 324, 351, 372, 377
News Bulletin (Representation of Polish Jewry – American Division), 188, 221
News Chronicle, 371
News of the World, 33
Newsome, Noel, 29, 55, 63, 66, 75, 99–100, 115–16, 124, 227, 319–20, 331, 336, 339
Norrman, Sven, 26, 97
Nowak, Jan, 58, 71, 97, 173, 181, 196–8, 235, 275, 313, 319, 331, 356, 361
Nowakowski, M., 325

Obama, Barack, 321
Office of Censorship, 74
Office of Strategic Services, 4, 30
Office of War Information, 75, 115, 324
Ogilvie, Frederick, 45, 318

Index

403

O'Malley, Owen, 69, 124, 177, 243, 321, 338–9
Orwell, George, 80, 377
Orzech, Maurycy, 380
Osborne, Harold, 61, 126, 155, 174, 322, 330, 362
Oświęcim. *See* Auschwitz
Our Tribune. See Nasza Trybuna

Palestine, 47, 66, 84, 89, 109, 114, 157–9, 161, 177, 188, 192, 222–3, 232, 248, 256, 258–9, 261, 263, 266, 271, 304, 309, 318, 321, 327–8, 350, 371, 375–6
Palestine Post, 205, 215, 256, 310, 363
Palestinian Federation of Labour, 188
Paulsson, Gunnar, 277
Pawiak prison, 133, 379
Pehle, John, 248–9, 255, 275, 367, 375
Peirse, Richard, 252
Pell, Herbert, 204
Penkower, Monty Noam, 110, 159, 230, 235, 249, 255, 375
Perkins, Harold, 25, 140, 204–5, 312, 341, 343, 353
Perlzweig, Maurice, 5, 87–8, 107–8, 161–2, 165, 272, 327, 332, 334, 351
Piechowski, Kazimierz, 26, 346
Piekałkiewicz, Jan, 24, 137–9, 141–2, 194, 341
Piekarski, Konstanty, 273
Pilecki, Witold, 15, 26, 131–2, 254, 264, 273–4, 312–13, 341, 346–7, 378
Piotrowski, Edmund (Ren), 312
Piper, Franciszek, 16, 18–20, 22, 171, 311–12, 319
Pius XII, 91, 233
Płaszów, 240, 371
Płotnicka, Frumka, 184, 358
Poland Fights, 29, 147, 161, 165, 195, 351
Polish Fortnightly Review, 7, 28, 82–3, 102, 112, 132–3, 142, 191, 325, 344, 347, 359
Polish Information Center (New York), 28, 30, 147, 161, 187, 208, 310, 327, 358, 364
Polish Jewish Observer, 9, 28–9, 71–3, 91, 93, 167, 170, 173, 185, 187, 189, 192, 206, 212, 217, 226, 229–30, 241, 244, 246, 259, 265–6, 269, 305–6, 323, 328, 352, 359, 361, 366–9, 372–3, 377–8
Polish National Council, 4, 11, 25, 63, 72, 109–10, 112–14, 123–4, 145, 156, 163, 170, 190, 193, 204, 223, 226, 238, 243, 306, 309, 318, 326, 329, 367

Polish Social Information Bureau, 324, 332
Polish Socialist Party, ix, 26, 87, 97, 124, 194, 206, 213, 226, 229, 267
Polish Telegraphic Agency, 8, 30, 115, 187, 200, 205, 210, 215, 306, 310, 359, 363
Political Warfare Executive
    Allied governments, 92
    Auschwitz, 11, 167, 174, 178, 234
    control of, 54
    established, 53
    Hungary, 237
    influence over BBC, 55–6
    influence over Radio Świt, 60
    Jan Karski, 155
    Katyń, 124
    narrating the war, 29, 53, 203, 261
    Office of War Information, 75
    reports on Jews, 219, 234
Pologne occupée, 29, 170, 207–8, 286, 352, 363
Polonsky, Antony, vi, 278, 327, 379
Polska pod okupacją niemiecką, 3, 170, 207, 265, 363
Ponsonby, Colonel, 106
Postal and Telegram Censorship, 177
Potulicki, Michał, 96
Pragier, Adam, 97
Prentice, Ridley, 182
Press Association, 52, 332
Price, Byron, 74
Pritt, Noel, 80, 82–3, 88, 325
Protasewicz, Michał, 25, 136, 140, 149–50, 184, 204, 310, 341, 343–4, 349, 352–3, 358, 362, 376
Puławski, Adam, vi, 5, 136, 169, 273, 331

Quebec conference, 69, 321

Raczkiewicz, Władysław, 91, 380
Raczyński, Edward, 334
    appeal (Polish Jews), 212, 235
    Auschwitz, 44, 146, 156, 181
    calls for reprisals, 163
    complaint about *Evening Standard*, 325
    Katyń and the Polish press, 124
    letter to Eden, 20 January 1943, 147, 163
    memorandum, 10 December, 113
    protests against censorship, 123
    responds to the *Reprezentacja*, 109
    responsive to British context, 95
    thanks Vansittart (September 1942), 105
Radcliffe, Cyril, 52
Radio Świt, 54, 58, 60–2, 128, 154–5, 173–4, 202–3, 258, 261, 306, 318, 320, 329, 353, 362

404 Index

Radziwiłł, Janusz, 86–7, 326, 379
Rajsko, 17, 219
Randall, Alec, 181–2, 276, 310
Ratajski, Cyryl, 24, 134, 137–9, 150, 341
Rathbone, Eleanor, 117–18, 223, 225, 337
Reams, R.B., 146
Rees, Laurence, 17–18, 22, 171, 201, 311
refugees, 40, 43–4, 46, 62, 66, 114, 117,
    119, 161, 173–4, 182, 190, 195, 218,
    225, 234, 241, 247, 249, 276–7, 315,
    317, 320, 337, 350, 375
Reisman, David, 76
Reisner, József, 232
Reiss, Anzelm, 255
Retinger, Józef, 304, 327
Reuters, 52, 207
Riegner, Gerhart, 105, 107
Riegner telegram, 105, 114, 311, 320, 392
Ritchie, Douglas, 29, 55, 330
Roberts, Frank, 64, 89, 94, 96–7, 106, 111,
    114, 120–1, 142, 153, 162, 183, 198,
    281, 319, 322, 327, 330, 337, 345,
    349, 358
Robertson, David, 62
Robotnik, 124, 229, 242
Rogers, Barbara, vi, 4, 7, 63, 160, 261, 281,
    366
Rogers, James, 348
Romer, Tadeusz, 243, 272, 349
Roosevelt, Eleanor, 190
Roosevelt, Franklin
    Auschwitz, 5, 114, 159, 258
    bombing Auschwitz, 251, 374
    Jan Karski, 13, 154
    Quebec conference, 69
    warning to Nazis (24 March 1944), 65,
        91
    WRB, 68
Roper, Elmo, 76
Rosenheim, Jacob, 249
Rosin, Arnošt, 2, 230, 242
Rothermere, Lord, 38, 50
Rotta, Angelo, 368
Rowecki, Stefan, 23–4, 26, 108, 134, 136,
    138–9, 143, 149–51, 168–73, 176,
    181, 186, 203, 259, 310, 323, 341,
    343–5, 349, 352–3, 356, 375, 379
Royal Patriotic Schools, 129, 151, 258, 319
Rubinstein, William, 309, 316, 373
Ryan, Patrick, 317
Rysiewicz, Adam, 214

Sabath, Adolph, 190
Sachsenhausen, 17, 186
Sagalowitz, Benjamin, 105

Salski, Jerzy, 74, 134, 167–8, 175, 177–9,
    182, 191, 203, 212, 218, 234–5, 253,
    265–6, 304–5, 326, 342, 344, 347,
    349, 354–5, 370
Savery, Frank, 56, 84, 86–8, 90, 94, 99,
    117, 120, 142, 153, 163, 172, 174,
    206, 235, 261, 304, 323, 330–1, 336,
    345, 349, 351
Scherer, Emanuel, 217, 223–4, 226–8, 238,
    240, 243, 255, 267, 272, 369, 371,
    373, 376
Schiff, Otto, 315
Schoenfeld, Rudolf, 243
Schulte, Eduard, 105
Schwarzbart, Ignacy
    allegation against Polish government
        (November 1942), 112
    anger (Mikołajczyk), 265
    anti-Semitism in Polish Army, 222, 224
    Auschwitz, 4, 11, 134, 147, 170, 177,
        179, 185, 188, 212, 266
    Bermuda conference, 62
    Black Book of Polish Jewry, 190
    calls for retaliation, 101
    conference (9 July 1942), 102
    desertions from Polish Army, 223, 226
    forwards information, 177, 212, 259,
        332, 378
    influence on British Jews, 224
    meeting with Mikołajczyk (February
        1941), 84
    message to Warsaw, 185
    National Council, 25, 78
    reduces reported number of victims, 97
    reports dismissed, 247
    Warsaw ghetto, 109
    Washington problem, 117–18
Scotsman, The, 132
Secret Intelligence Service, ix, 27, 172, 198,
    322
Seeds, William, 337
Segieda, Napoleon. See Salski, Jerzy
Selborne, Lord, 54, 66, 115
Shapira, Moshe, 158
Sharkey, Jos, 190
Shertok, Moshe, 231, 235, 249, 350
Sikorski, Władysław
    anti-Semitism in Polish Army, 81
    approved by Churchill, 126
    BBC broadcast (June 1942), 63, 97
    BBC broadcast (October 1942), 108
    censorship, 123
    death, 84, 126
    embarrassing the British, 89
    equality of Polish citizens, 83

Katyń, 124
letters to Jewish organizations (1942), 96
meeting with Eden (19 January 1943), 90
postwar population transfers, 90
rejection of the Sanacja, 78
request to bomb Auschwitz, 251
Sikorski–Maisky agreement (July 1941), 82
St James's Palace Conference, 96
US visit (1942), 161
Silverman, Sydney, 101, 106, 110, 113, 213, 244, 327, 330, 333, 336
Sinclair, Archibald, 249
Siudak, Paweł, 176, 312
Sixsmith, Martin, 314
Skinder, Tadeusz, 204, 341
Slovakia, 19, 22, 132, 185–6, 200, 207, 209, 230, 249, 310, 321, 342
Smoleń, Kazimierz, 18
Sobibór, 3, 5, 13, 19, 21, 104, 111, 139, 146, 158, 161, 165, 219, 260, 264, 335, 359–60
Sonderkommando, 22
Soos, Geza, 232
Sosnkowski, Kazimierz, 23, 204, 223–4, 227
Sosnowice, 159, 184, 211
Soviet prisoners of war, 18, 133, 135, 140–1, 264, 321
Special Operations Executive, 11–12, 25, 54, 129, 134, 140, 166–7, 172, 175–6, 178, 186, 204–5, 207, 218, 253, 258, 262, 304, 306, 313, 326, 335, 340, 344, 353, 356, 363, 369, 378
Springer, Hersch, 358
Stalin, Joseph, 2, 123, 126, 370, 378
Stanley, Oliver, 62
State Department, 108, 146
Stein, Leonard, 327
Sternbuch, Isaac, 249
Stillman, Sarah, 33
Stola, Dariusz, vi, 6, 13, 25, 78, 87, 95, 97, 223, 324, 330, 377–8
Strakacz, Sylwin, 160, 164, 190
Strang, William, 123, 250, 304
Stroński, Stansław, 103, 112
Suchcitz, Andrzej, 27
Sulma, Stanisław, 204, 362
Sulzberger, Arthur, 45–7, 75, 242
Sunday Pictorial, 50
Swedish connection, 25, 95, 110, 137
Świebocki, Henryk, 26–7, 207, 209, 214–15, 231, 242, 251, 308, 341, 363, 365, 369, 375
Synagogue Council of America, 159

Szapiro, Jerzy, 79, 323–4
Szeredi, Justinian, 368

Tabeau, Jerzy, 2, 76, 230–1, 233, 244, 247, 310, 341, 377
Tabenki, Yitzhak, 188
Tablet, The, 227
Tangye, Derek, 66
Tarnów, 17, 26
Tartakower, Arieh, 161, 171, 354, 359
Tchernowitz, Chaim, 190
Teller, Benjamin, 295, 365, 376
Theresienstadt, 214–15, 231, 241, 308, 366, 369
Thomson, George Pirie, 32, 75, 92, 337, 368
Thurtle, Ernest, 61, 174, 237, 370
Time and Tide, 227
Times, The, 3, 28, 41, 46, 50–1, 72, 100–1, 113, 127, 158, 180, 231, 233, 246, 265, 308, 356
Tomaszewska, Lucyna, 374
Torres, Henri, 190
Trades Union Congress, 103
Treblinka, 3, 5, 13, 19, 21–2, 44, 103–4, 111, 136, 139, 146, 157, 159, 161, 165, 182–4, 186, 188–9, 193–5, 197–8, 219, 260, 264, 335, 342, 353, 359, 367, 374–5
Truth, 316

UN declaration (17 December 1942), 13, 43, 62, 67, 91, 104, 111, 114–19, 146, 155–6, 160–2, 164, 166, 179, 259–60, 264, 336
Union for Armed Struggle, 23
Union of Orthodox Rabbis of the United States, 159
United Kibbutz Movement, 188
Universe of obligation, 5, 34, 82, 91, 277, 279
USSR, 13, 21, 23, 73, 75, 80, 82, 110, 115, 120–2, 124, 236, 268–9, 321, 337–40, 370, 377

van Pelt, Jan Robert, 2, 4, 69, 309, 321
Vansittart, Robert, 105, 333, 377
Voght, Paul, 242, 247
von Woedtke, Alexander, 184
Vrba, Rudolf, 2, 230, 233
Vrba–Wetzler report, 2, 4–5, 10, 14, 65, 76, 130, 214–18, 229–36, 238, 241–2, 246–8, 252, 255–6, 263, 265, 336, 341, 375, 378

406　　Index

Wagner, Robert, 190
War Refugee Board, 30, 68, 76, 91, 208,
　211, 213, 232, 242, 247–9, 261, 263,
　275, 280, 310, 323, 328, 363, 367,
　373, 375
Warsaw ghetto, 57, 111–12, 117, 127, 136,
　138–9, 142, 147–8, 152–3, 155, 191,
　198, 336, 344
Washington Post, 9, 209, 266
Watt, Harvey, 361
Ważniewski, Władysław, 195, 202, 312,
　343, 352, 395
Wedgwood, Josiah, 45, 81
Weizmann, Chaim, 235, 249–50
Welles, Sumner, 106, 108, 110
Wetzler, Alfred, 2, 230
Wiadomości Polskie, 81, 325
Widerszał, Ludwik, 138
Wielkopolski, Aleksander, 26, 131
Wigand, Arpad, 16
Wise, Stephen, 87, 106, 108, 110, 154, 161,
　308, 311, 328, 332–3
Wiskemann, Elizabeth, 232
Włodarkiewicz, Jan, 26, 313
Woliński, Henryk, 138, 343

Wolny, Jan, 217, 323, 366–7
World Jewish Congress, ix, 4, 11, 29–30,
　87, 96, 100, 105–6, 110, 161, 177,
　212, 232, 240, 248, 251, 266, 304,
　308, 327, 365, 373
Wójcik, Stanisław, 338

Zamość, 56, 69–70, 127, 269, 319, 321–2,
　340
Zarański, Józef, 44, 181, 198
Zaremba, Zygmunt, 200, 360
Zarembina, Natalia, 194–5, 360
Zeszyty Oświęcimskie, 31, 202, 342, 344,
　346, 362
Zucker, Ben-Ami, 256
Zygielbojm, Shmuel, 346, 356, 380
　calls for reprisals, 114
　forwards information, 97–8
　National Council, 25, 78
　response to Bund report, 100, 102
　Stop Them Now!, 103
　suicide, 180–1, 280
　telegram to Churchill, 115
Żbikowski, Andzej, 141, 150, 154, 327, 348
Żegota, 279

Printed in the United States
by Baker & Taylor Publisher Services